BALKAN BABEL

THIRD EDITION

BALKAN BABEL

◆

The Disintegration of Yugoslavia from
the Death of Tito to the War for Kosovo

Sabrina P. Ramet

with a foreword by
Ivo Banac

Westview Press
A Member of the Perseus Books Group

Copyright © 1999 by Westview Press, A Member of the Perseus Books Group

Published in 1999 in the United States of America by Westview Press, 5500 Central Avenue, Boulder, Colorado 80301-2877, and in the United Kingdom by Westview Press, 12 Hid's Copse Road, Cumnor Hill, Oxford OX2 9JJ

Find us on the World Wide Web at www.westviewpress.com

Library of Congress Cataloging-in-Publication Data
Ramet, Sabrina P., 1949–
  Balkan babel : the disintegration of Yugoslavia from the death of
Tito to insurrection in Kosovë / Sabrina P. Ramet. — 3rd ed.
    p.   cm.
  Includes bibliographical references and index.
  ISBN 0-8133-9034-6 (pbk)
    1. Yugoslavia—History—1980–1992.   2. Yugoslavia—History—1992–
3. Yugoslavia—Ethnic relations.   4. Nationalism—Yugoslavia—
History—20th century.   I. Title.
DR1307.R36   1999
949.703—dc21
                                                                                    99-28670
                                                                                    CIP

The paper used in this publication meets the requirements of the American National Standard for Permanence of Paper for Printed Library Materials Z39.48-1984.

10   9   8   7   6   5   4   3   2   1

To Susan McEachern,
my friend

Contents

Tables

List of Abbreviations

AVNO	Antifašisticko Vijeće Narodnog Oslobodjenja Jugoslavije (Antifascist Council of the People's Liberation of Yugoslavia)
CC	Central Committee
CIA	Central Intelligence Agency
CPY	Communist Party of Yugoslavia
CSCE	Conference on Security and Cooperation in Europe
EC	European Community
EU	European Union
EFTA	European Free Trade Association
FBIS	Foreign Broadcast Information Service
FRY	Federal Republic of Yugoslavia (Serbia and Montenegro)
GATT	General Agreement on Tariffs and Trade
HDZ	Hrvatska Demokratska Zajednica (Croatian Democratic Community)
HVO	Hrvatsko Vijeće Obrane (Croatian Defense Council)
IFOR	Implementation Force
IMF	International Monetary Fund
IMRO–DPMNU	Internal Macedonian Revolutionary Party–Democratic Party of Macedonian National Unity
JNA	Jugoslovenska Narodna Armija (Yugoslav People's Army)
KLA	Kosovo Liberation Army
LCY	League of Communists of Yugoslavia
NATO	North Atlantic Treaty Organization
NDH	Nezavisna Država Hrvatska (Independent State of Croatia, 1941–1945)
OSCE	Organization for Security and Cooperation in Europe
PDP	Party for Democratic Prosperity
RFE	Radio Free Europe
RL	Radio Liberty
SANU	Serbian Academy of Sciences and Art
SAWPY	Socialist Alliance of Working People of Yugoslavia
SDA	Stranka Demokratske Akcije (Party of Democratic Action)

SDS   Srpska Demokratska Stranka (Serbian Democratic Party)
SFOR   Stabilization Force
SFRY   Socialist Federated Republic of Yugoslavia
UDBa   Uprava Državne Bezbednosti (State Security Administration, i.e.,
                   secret police)
UNPROFOR   United Nations Protection Force

Credits

Permission has been generously given to reprint material in this book that has been adapted from the following articles:

Sabrina Petra Ramet, "The Role of the Press in Yugoslavia," *Yugoslavia in Transition—Choices and Constraints: Essays in Honour of Fred Singleton,* eds. John B. Allcock, John J. Horton, and Marko Milivojevib (Oxford: Berg Publishers, 1992), pp. 414–441.

Pedro Ramet, "The Catholic Church in Yugoslavia, 1945–1989," *Catholicism and Politics in Communist Societies,* ed. Pedro Ramet (Durham, N.C.: Duke University Press, 1990).

Pedro Ramet, "The Serbian Orthodox Church," *Eastern Christianity and Politics in the Twentieth Century,* ed. Pedro Ramet (Durham, N.C.: Duke University Press, 1988).

Sabrina Petra Ramet, "Islam in Yugoslavia Today," *Religion in Communist Lands* (published by the Keston Institute and now called *Religion, State, and Society),* Vol. 18, No. 3 (autumn 1990).

Sabrina Petra Ramet, "The Bosnian War and the Diplomacy of Accommodation," *Current History,* Vol. 93, No. 586 (November 1994).

Permission was also kindly given for reprinting parts of the following items:

From *The Dictionary of the Khazars,* by Milorad Pavib, trans., C. Pribibevib-Zorib. Copyright © 1988 by Alfred A. Knopf, Inc. Reprinted by permission of the publisher.

Excerpt from *South to Destiny* by Dobrica Bosib, copyright © 1982 by Harcourt Brace & Company, reprinted by permission of Harcourt Brace & Company.

Excerpt from *Garden, Ashes* by Danilo Kis, trans. William J. Hannaker, English translation copyright © 1975 by Harcourt Brace & Company, reprinted by permission of the publisher.

Foreword:
The Politics of Cultural Diversity
in Former Yugoslavia

The collapse of Soviet and East European communism has upset all the political and ideological conventions in the countries concerned. One noticeable consequence has been the revival of nationalism—that much misunderstood mutant ideology whose many faces have tested a legion of analysts. The nationalisms of Eastern Europe, in particular, have long been a stumbling block for U.S. observers. The example of a stable civil society like the United States, where an assimilationist political culture mitigated the effects of ancestry, really cannot inform the "ethnic" relations of East European multinational states. The latter—and Yugoslavia was a prime example— are really conglomerates of historical nations, each with its own internal subna-tional—or, if you prefer, ethnic—problems. Yugoslavia has not survived the pres-sures of its component parts and no longer exists as a state. For insight into why this has happened, it might be wise to look at the political implications of cultural diver-sity in what used to be Yugoslavia and its successor states. It is to Sabrina Ramet's great credit that she understood the cultural context of South Slavic nationality rela-tions at a time when most of her colleagues promoted entirely unrealistic readings of the subject.

The cultural diversity *among* the nationalities of Yugoslavia has frequently been so acute that there is a tendency to underestimate the elements of diversity *within* each single nationality. Take the Serbs, for example. Vuk Karadžić (1787–1864), the fore-most Serb cultural reformer, was probably not the first Serb scholar to recognize the vast cultural—not just linguistic—differences between the Serbs of the Habsburg Monarchy and those of the Ottoman Empire. Jovan Cvijić (1865–1927), a noted Serbian geographer, developed a whole system for the classification of Serb "cultural belts," having personally identified three Serb "psychological types" (really, cultural types). And, indeed, there are vast differences between the disciplined "imperial sons" from the former Habsburg Military Frontier, the exponents of urban Byzan-tine Orthodoxy from southern Serbia, the patriarchal and natural Orthodox high-landers of Herzegovina and Montenegro, the latitudinarian clergy and burghers

from the Vojvodina, and their no less latitudinarian kinsmen from the harbors of the
Montenegrin littoral, not to forget the Serbs who live in areas of predominantly
Muslim influence. One could go on like this and demonstrate to what extent the
perennial calls for Serb unity (including cultural unity) address the real fears of cultural fragmentation in reputedly one of the most homogeneous of South Slavic nationalities. Slobodan Milošević, currently the paramount Serbian leader, is therefore
as keen as any of his non-Communist predecessors to foster the homogenization of
Serbs throughout the Western Balkans, that is, beyond Serbia itself.

The extreme cultural diversity of the South Slavs stems from the fact that they are
situated at the cultural crossroads of the Old World. The continental crusts of Rome
and Byzantium have been colliding here for a millennium. The subcontinent of Islam dashed at the emerging landmass half a millennium ago. There is a Central European belt (Slovenia, northern Croatia, the Vojvodina) and a Mediterranean belt
(the littorals of Slovenia, Croatia, and Montenegro). There is a Muslim belt and an
Eastern Orthodox belt. And they used to come together. In Mostar, Herzegovina,
before the warlords destroyed it, one was able not too long ago to sip Viennese coffee
and read newspapers mounted on wooden frames, listening all along to a muezzin's
call in the shadow of a Franciscan church (where the chant was Latinate), and then
wander into a fig grove that surrounds a Byzantine-style church (where the chant
was Slavonic). None of this was imported for the tourists. It raised no native eye-
brows. And it did not prompt intolerance.

Because South Slavic cultural diversity is really religiously based, there have been
numerous attempts to link the country's divisions to religious intolerance. In fact,
South Slavic interconfessional relations never occassioned religious wars on the scale
of those fought in Western Europe after the Reformation or along the banks of the
Tigris for the length of the Islamic era. The tragic events of World War II and of the
current conflict, when some of the massacres committed by the contending sides became religiously based, occurred in the context of occupation, not of religious or
even civil war (a much misused term). The hold of religious culture is strong, but
not stronger than the practicality of the usually practical South Slavs. An epic Croat
folk song tells of how the war party of the Uskoks of Senj, a sixteenth-century martial community that lived on piracy and plunder, was faced with an unexpected spell
of cold weather. Instead of permitting his men to freeze, the Uskok leader offered the
following solution:

> I do not know of a stone cave [where they presumably could hide];
> But I know of Saint George's church.
> We shall break the door of the holy church,
> We shall burn fire in it,
> So that God will send us his luck,
> So that we shall warm our flesh,
> And safely return to Senj.
> We shall then build a better church,

And secure it with a new door,
Made of silver and purest gold.

I mention the question of cultural diversity and its misapplications because diversity, as such, is not the fuel of current national hostilities. I personally have been a strong exponent of the idea that the nationality question in Yugoslavia and other East European countries does not derive from religious differences, cultural diversity, or even from the problems of unequal economic development. Rather, I have argued that the nationality question was shaped by the dissimilar structure and goals of various national ideologies that have emerged within the political culture of each of Eastern Europe's national groups. Quite obviously, these national ideologies are historically determined, which is to say that each one of them also contains elements of historically determined cultural diversity. From that point of view, it might be useful to trace the postwar Communist experience in order to discover how Communist ideology operated within the context of Yugoslav cultural diversity, thereby reshaping the national ideologies of Yugoslavia's prinicipal national groups.

The Yugoslav Communists promoted the interests of their respective national groups a great deal more than is usually imagined, and not just since the death of Tito in 1980. The Communists have debated the Yugoslav nationality question from the beginning of their party in 1919 and "solved" it in turns as revolutionary centrists and unitarists, separatists, federalists, and, increasingly in the 1980s, as confederalists. They emerged from World War II with the program of "new Yugoslav socialist culture," which was intended to eliminate the nationality question by eradicating its historical sources. This proved impossible from the beginning. The permitted, mainly traditional, cultural cults could not easily be harmonized and frequently expressed fundamentally irreconcilable cultural and national aspirations. Worse yet, the Communist cults of "new Yugoslav socialist culture" were no more harmonious.

Two of the foremost literary figures of socialist Yugoslavia, Nobel laureate Ivo Andrić and Miroslav Krleža, were the living embodiment of Communist cultural diversity. They were not just stylistic antipodes; their communism itself covered the diapason of Yugoslav Marxist patterns. Like most intellectuals, Krleža came to Leninism from the shipwreck and carnage of Central European civilization, which collapsed on the fields of Galicia in World War I. His prinicipal literary motif was his profound skepticism about the historical mission of the Central European bourgeoisie. The fog that enveloped Croatia (and Eastern Europe) could only be lifted "when whole flotillas of nations and classes start sailing" toward the Leninist beacon. But that beacon, too, was fundamentally chimerical. Krleža's Lenin-types, for example his Christoper Columbus, are crucified by the mindless masses. Nevertheless, Krleža's pessimistic revolutionism brought the intelligentsia to the Communist Party. In terms of nationality programs, it was an expression of a steadfast federalist project, built on the premise, which Krleža shared with many of his non-Communist fellow Croats, that Yugoslavia's cultural diversity (the Rome-Byzantine cleavage) could not easily be filled. In Andrić we have a veteran of the nationalist and mythopoeic Bosnian Youth—the movement that cast forth the Sarajevo assassins—a Yugoslav integralist of profoundly authoritarian bent, a prewar diplomat, and an associate of right-wing cultural journals, who missed the Chetnik train by a very small margin. His postwar membership in the Communist Party was typical of the premium paid to the unitarist intelligentsia by the cultural architects of the new state.

The building of the "new Yugoslav socialist culture" also ended as a failure among the generation of literary partisans—the veterans of Tito's wartime insurgency. Members of the partisan generation failed to integrate Yugoslavia culturally. Moreover, prominent partisan writers became the ideologists of Yugoslavia's new national divisions and contributed to the collapse of Yugoslav cultural unitarism that can be dated from the mid-1960s. The changing nature of official Yugoslav ideology and statecraft, the growing delegitimation of the Communist movement (with the accompanying need to seek national underpinnings of legitimacy), and real national grievances (but also the attempts to explain and cure them) are among the other factors that contributed to the failure of cultural unitarism.

Tito's answer to this failure was a more consistent federalism that substituted democracy with formal axiomatic constructions (the rotation system of leadership, parity in leaderships, constitutional reforms, the refederation of Serbia's two autonomous provinces, and an indirect system of elections). These constructions and changes necessarily prompted resistance, which exploded after Tito's death and reached its culmination in the current war between Serbia and the two other successor states of Yugoslavia—Croatia and Bosnia-Herzegovina. It is important to note here that the content of Communist thinking in all of Yugoslavia's six territorial parties came to resemble, indeed duplicate, the national ideologies that have evolved and prevailed in the given party-state before the war. In other words, when he still espoused Communist doctrine, Serbia's leading figure, Slobodan Milošević, had more in common with the prewar Radical Party, the party of Serbian supremacy, than with Slovene or Croat Communists. Yugoslav communism, national since 1948, had become further nationalized along internal national division before it collapsed. A similar process has occurred in the Soviet Union, where, for example, the pre-August 1991 discourse between Lithuanian and Russian Communists resembled the old contention between the Lithuanian national movement and the imperial Russian state.

The South Slavs have never been more divided than today. Never before in their histories have they shared such deep resentment for one another. As bitter as this assessment certainly is, it is also entirely true. The Yugoslav project is finished, root and branches. At this late date, after Serbia unleashed a war of conquest against its western neighbors, after the destruction of Bosnia, after ethnic cleansing and strategic rape, there is little prospect of peace, let alone reconciliation. In the future, after a semblance of stability returns, after the project of national homogenization is recognized as criminal utopism, the successor states of Yugoslavia will be judged by their fidelity to human rights, especially the protection of minorities. The equality and teritoriality of each of ex-Yugoslavia's nationalities must be protected, as must the legitimacy of the links between the minority nationalities and their matrix-states. For example, the Serbs should be able to enjoy their independent statehood without obstructing the national institutions and the democratic rights of Serbia's minorities. The protection of minorities, especially their cultural unity, could in time be extended to the whole of Eastern Europe, thereby lessening the importance of some of the region's more irrational borders, and perhaps even contributing to their change. Moreover, the full legitimation of the national cultures would necessarily legitimate diversity, which must prevail if peace is to return to the South Slavs.

Ivo Banac

Preface

I have made extensive revisions to this third edition, discarding two earlier chapters as well as the earlier epilogue and composing two new chapters (Chapters 12 and 13) and a fresh epilogue. I have also made significant additions to Chapters 1–3 and 9–11 based on interviews conducted since the publication of the second edition as well as on literature that has become available in the interim. The present Chapters 4–8 appeared in the second edition and remain the same here.

I have been studying Yugoslavia—and now, the Yugoslav successor states—for more than twenty years, and in the old days I was always struck by the perennial sense of crisis in that country. That perennial crisis was a factor of system illegitimacy and, among the successor states, has faded or become magnified in correlation with the increase or decrease of system legitimacy.

In the years since taking up the study of the South Slavs, I have spent time in Belgrade, Zagreb, Ljubljana, Skopje, and Sarajevo as well as in smaller towns and villages. My impressions of Yugoslavia, as of its successor states, have been formed by the people I have met and interviewed in that part of the world and through their writings. I have tried, in my own writings, to convey something of the "spirit" of Yugoslavia—what makes its people tick, what issues concern them, and how they think. That spirit is, for me, the lifeblood of political history. In this book I have aspired not only to convey that spirit but also to suggest a vital interconnection and interaction among the political, cultural, and religious spheres and to show how changes in one sphere are accompanied by parallel changes in the other spheres.

I am grateful to the International Research Exchanges Board (IREX) for funding research trips to Ljubljana (in March 1992), Skopje (in March 1995), and Zagreb (in July–August 1997), during which I was able to interview appropriate persons.

An earlier incarnation of Chapter 1 was published in *Crossroads*, No. 23 (1987). An earlier incarnation of Chapter 2 was published in *Global Affairs*, Vol. 5, No. 1 (Winter 1990). An earlier incarnation of Chapter 4 was previously published in Pedro Ramet (ed.), *Catholicism and Politics in Communist Societies* (Durham, N.C.: Duke University Press, 1990). An earlier incarnation of Chapter 5 was previously published in Pedro Ramet (ed.), *Eastern Christianity and Politics in the Twentieth Century* (Durham, N.C.: Duke University Press, 1988). An earlier incarnation of Chapter 6 was published in *Religion in communist lands*, Vol. 18, No. 3 (Autumn

1990). An earlier incarnation of Chapter 10 was published in *Current History*, Vol. 93, No. 586 (November 1994). I am grateful to the editors of these publications and to the respective presses for permission to reuse this material.

I wish to thank Susan McEachern, my Westview editor for the first and second editions, for her encouragement at those stages and Rob Williams, my editor at Westview for the third edition, for his encouragement and support; I am indebted to both of these editors for their wise counsel on many matters relating to this book. I also wish to thank Professor Nicholas R. Lardy, former director of the Henry M. Jackson School of International Studies, for arranging a pause quarter for me in autumn 1994, during which I was able to carry out revisions for the second edition, and Professor Jere Bacharach, current Director of the Henry M. Jackson School of International Studies, for allowing me to participate in a faculty exchange program with Ritsumeikan University, Kyoto, during the 1998 calendar year, during which time I was able to carry out the revisions for the third edition. I am very much indebted to Viktor Meier for his detailed comments on Chapters 1–3. I am grateful to Professors Ivo Banac, Robin Alison Remington, and Dennison Rusinow for their advice and feedback in connection with the preparation of this edition, to Atsushi Saito for his helpful comments on an earlier draft of Chapter 9, and to Professor Rudi Rizman for comments throughout. I would also like to thank Ljubiša Adamovich, Obrad Kesić, Branka Magaš, and Ognjen Pribićević for sharing their insights into Milošević's character, and Duncan Perry, Larisa Flint, and Ognjen Pribićević for assisting with certain information and research materials. I am also grateful to Elez Biberaj for sharing with me some of his wisdom about Kosovo.

Finally, I owe a special debt to my spouse, Christine Hassenstab, for her enthusiasm about my work as a whole, for her feedback on earlier chapters and new material in both the second and third editions, and for her lively interest in matters relating to the South Slavs.

Sabrina P. Ramet
Seattle, Washington

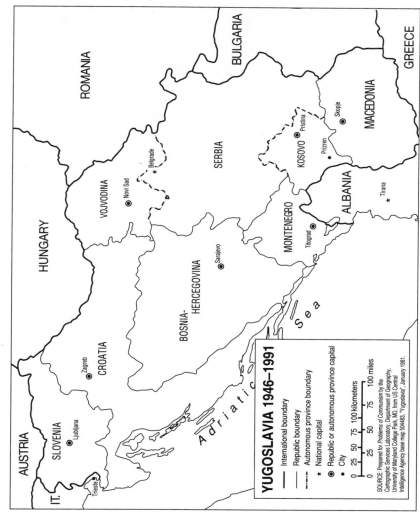

YUGOSLAVIA 1946–1991

——	International boundary
----	Republic boundary
-·-·-	Autonomous province boundary
★	National capital
◉	Republic or autonomous province capital
•	City

SOURCE: Prepared for *Problems of Communism* by the
Cartographic Services Laboratory, Department of Geography,
University of Maryland College Park, MD, from US Central
Intelligence Agency base map 504483, "Yugoslavia", January 1981.

0   25   50   75   100 kilometers
0   25   50   75   100 miles

AUSTRIA

IT.

SLOVENIA
Ljubljana ◉

Trieste •

CROATIA
Zagreb ◉

HUNGARY

VOJVODINA
Novi Sad ◉

Belgrade ★

SERBIA

ROMANIA

BULGARIA

**BOSNIA-
HERCEGOVINA**
Sarajevo ◉

A d r i a t i c   Sea

MONTENEGRO
Titograd ◉

KOSOVO
Pristina ◉
Prizren •

ALBANIA
Tirana ★

MACEDONIA
Skopje ◉

GREECE

Map of Yugoslavia, 1946–1991

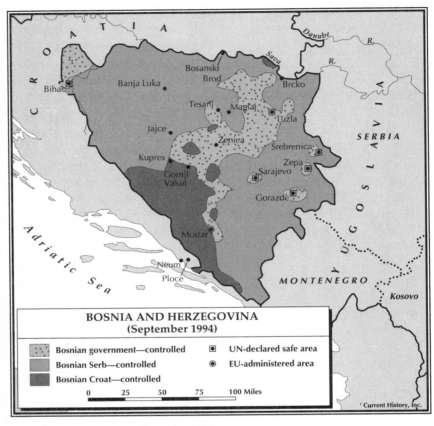

BOSNIA AND HERZEGOVINA
(September 1994)

- ░ Bosnian government—controlled
- ▨ Bosnian Serb—controlled
- ▓ Bosnian Croat—controlled

- ◉ UN-declared safe area
- ◎ EU-administered area

0   25   50   75   100 Miles

¹ Current History, Inc.

Map of Bosnia-Herzegovina, September 1994.
Reprinted from Current History, *by permission of the editor.*

Map of Bosnia-Herzegovina, February 1998.
Reprinted from Current History, by permission of the editor.

PART ONE

Disintegration, 1980–1991

CHAPTER ONE

◆

Political Debate,
1980–1986

Josip Broz Tito ruled Yugoslavia for some thirty-seven years, guiding the country through a major crisis in relations with the Soviet Union, steering it through four constitutions, and creating a political formula centered on self-management (in the economy), brotherhood and unity (in nationalities policy), and nonalignment (in foreign policy). Despite the internal crises which shook the country in 1948–1949, 1961–1965, and 1970–1971, Tito created a network of institutions which many hoped would prove stable and resistant to disintegrative change. Yet, for reasons quite different from and independent of those affecting other countries in Eastern Europe, Yugoslavia's political institutions ultimately proved vulnerable to pressures for change. Such pressures built up gradually and steadily from the grass roots, from the intellectuals, feminists, environmentalists, pacifists, and liberals. Political change was adumbrated first in the cultural sector and borne along by small independent grassroots organizations.

Yugoslavia had been beset with problems from the time of its establishment in 1918, of course, and one may quite accurately say that no sooner was the multiethnic state constituted than it started to fall apart. Over the course of its seventy-year history, Yugoslavia lurched from crisis to crisis, abandoning one unstable formula for another. Finally, in the course of 1989–1991, the unifying infrastructure of the country largely dissolved. In its first incarnation as the interwar Kingdom of Serbs, Croats, and Slovenes, 1918–1941 (renamed the Kingdom of Yugoslavia in 1929), the country experimented with pseudodemocratic Serbian hegemony, royal dictatorship, and Serb-Croat codominion.[1] The system failed to ground itself on legitimating principles and left a legacy of bitterness which fed directly into the internecine conflicts of World War II (1941–1945 in the Yugoslav lands). That war saw the occupation of parts of Yugoslavia by German, Italian, Bulgarian, and Hungarian troops and the erection of quisling regimes in Croatia (under Ante Pavelić) and Serbia (under Milan Nedić).[2] More than a million persons died in the course of the war, and

3

additional seeds of bitterness were sown. Although Tito and his Communist comrades talked endlessly about the need to create "brotherhood and unity" and recognized quite clearly the dangers inherent in national and religious chauvinism, they lacked a clear vision of social tolerance, without which their efforts ultimately foundered.

Tito's Partisans, winning accolades in engagements against occupation and quisling forces, emerged as the only strong force in Yugoslavia at war's end. Communist rule made its debut with brutality when between 20,000 and 30,000 Serb Chetniks and Slovene Home Guards (who had tried to surrender to British forces only to be turned over to the Partisans) were massacred by Partisan forces, along with some 36,000 Croats and 5,000 Muslims.[3] The Communists lost no time in suppressing reemergent political parties after World War II[4] and set about introducing a Soviet-style system. Indeed, Yugoslavia's Communists started out as run-of-the-mill Stalinists. The early years followed the standard formula of arrests, show trials, forced collectivization, attacks on the Churches, and erection of a strict central planning system. But their expulsion from the Soviet bloc by Stalin in June 1948 forced them to find their own formula and, in the process, gave them a new image. Tito became the new David to Stalin's Goliath and came to be seen as a hero in the West. With American and British assistance, Tito's Yugoslavia weathered severe food crises in 1946–1947 and 1950[5] and, under the pressure of the change in the diplomatic environment as well as internal developments, including the peasant rebellion against agricultural collectivization in Cazin region in 1950,[6] began to demarcate an independent path.

In 1950, the Communist Party of Yugoslavia (CPY) introduced the principle of self-management on an experimental basis, promulgating it generally two years later; in the meantime, on 24 November 1951, the CPY Central Committee issued a directive to scrap the collective farm system, blaming the Soviets for providing an example which had proven "completely wrong and harmful in our practice"[7] and authorizing the return of farmlands to private ownership. Stalin was so enraged by Tito's behavior that, in autumn 1952, he had Lavrenti Beria, the head of the KGB, develop a plan to assassinate the Yugoslav leader; the plan foundered as a result of uncertainties associated with Stalin's death in March 1953.[8] Although Tito's example undoubtedly had given some encouragement to Hungarian Prime Minister Imre Nagy and his fellow revolutionaries in Hungary in 1956, Nagy's rapid gravitation toward political pluralism unnerved Tito, who, as recently opened archives reveal, told Khrushchev he felt military intervention was necessary and may even have developed contingency plans of his own to employ Yugoslav military force to restore "socialism" in Hungary.[9] Meanwhile, Yugoslav reformism continued. By 1958, at its Seventh Congress (in Ljubljana), the by now renamed League of Communists of Yugoslavia (LCY) was boasting, much to Soviet annoyance, of its uniquely progressive model and offering it for general emulation.[10]

In the 1960s and 1970s, it appeared that Yugoslavia had finally found the key to solving its most important problems. Aleksandar Ranković, chief of the secret police, had resisted reform, but was stripped of his power in July 1966.[11] Decentralization, which had quietly begun as early as 1952, but which had picked up momentum as a result of the constitution of 1963, gathered steam after Ranković's fall. This formula, which established a network of quasi-feudal national oligarchies and entrenched their power in the constituent republics of the Socialist Federated Republic of Yugoslavia (SFRY), created the institutional fissures along which Yugoslavia would break up; indeed, without the quasi-confederal system of republics, it is unlikely that the SFRY would have fallen apart as soon or as relatively easily as it did. So concerned were the Yugoslav reformers of the late 1960s to build up the infrastructure of the republics that they saw to it that the Federal Assembly adopted a new law on national defense on 11 February 1969, granting the republics the authority to form local territorial militias.[12] Coming partly as a response to the Soviet invasion of Czechoslovakia, the new law also reflected the decentralist convictions of Titoist reformism; the militias created by this law would prove critically important in the case of Slovenia in 1990–1991.

The constitution of 1974 seemed to provide political stability (using cautiously crafted practices of ethnic quotas, strict rotation of cadres, and the universal enjoyment by constituent republics of the right to veto federal legislation). The economy was enjoying a boom. And then there was Tito, who played a crucial role as arbiter in the system, pulling it back from deadlock when all else failed. Even the nationality question seemed—in the years 1971–1981—to have been laid to rest. The late Tito era was an era of optimism, a kind of "golden age," in which regime ideologues could dream of plans "to build a new socialist society, rid of all forms of exploitation, to construct a society in which the economic and political sovereignty of the working class remains the cornerstone both of internal development and [of] foreign policy."[13]

Between 1979 and 1982, however, several things changed, causing Yugoslavia's leaders to reach the point, by 1983, of openly admitting, for the first time since the 1948 expulsion, that the country was in crisis. First, the economy had begun to deteriorate—largely as a result of internal dynamics; the process was sharpened and quickened by the steep increase in oil prices after 1973. Second, the deaths of Vice President Edvard Kardelj in 1979 and President Tito in 1980 deprived the country not only of unifying symbols but, more important, of strong leaders capable of imposing unity. A third factor contributing to the disintegration of the old order was the outbreak, in April 1981, of widespread anti-Serbian rioting among the Albanian population of the then autonomous province of Kosovo. These riots proved to be the clarion call of a new phase, in which Belgrade authorities returned to the repressive style associated with Ranković, resulting in escalating Serb-Albanian tensions in the province. The problems in Kosovo contributed to a sense of crisis in which the basic illegitimacy of the Communist system was ever more clearly laid bare. And fourth, there was the disastrous prime-ministership of Branko Mikulić, whose mismanagement contributed to a general plummeting of public confidence in government officials and whose term of office was blemished, in particular, by the damaging Agrokomerc financial scandal in the summer of 1987.

Yet, for all that, it required an "enabler" to take economically troubled Yugoslavia from "mere" crisis down the slippery path of interethnic war and "ethnic cleansing." That "enabler" was, in the first place, Slobodan Milošević, a soft-spoken banker with a working facility in English who bore the psychological scars of the suicides of both of his parents, although in the years 1988–1991 the army leadership was a key ally, making its own contribution to the crisis, and Milošević had allies and supporters in key positions in the party—among them, Lazar Mojsov, Borisav Jović, Raif Dizdarević, and, in spite of himself, Stipe Šuvar. It was Milošević who, backed by his allies and supporters, exploited the weak points in the Titoist system in order to drive the system in a non-Titoist direction. It was Milošević and the Serbian parliament who declared the abolition of the autonomous provinces, but not of their representatives, claiming instead that the Serbian parliament had "inherited" the right to appoint three representatives to the state presidency, to which, under the constitution, each republic's parliament was authorized to send one representative.[14] It was Milošević who stockpiled heavy weaponry in 1990–1991 in anticipation of a showdown. It was Milošević who advised the Croatian Serbs to refuse Tudjman's olive branches in summer 1990 and to adopt a posture of noncooperation.[15] And it was Milošević personally who took the hatreds, resentments, and accusations generated in sundry quarters and created, on the basis of these diverse sources and with the collaboration of Jović Šolević, and others, a program for massive violence against Croats, Muslims (Bosniaks), and Albanians.

Although I would agree that "Milošević did not engineer the break-up of Yugoslavia single-handed[ly],"[16] requiring, on the contrary, the active complicity and passive docility of certain key players (above all, those mentioned above), some of them frightened by Milošević's behavior as early as 1987 but uncertain about what to do to counter his actions, and may not even be credited with having concocted the breakup on his own, he was nonetheless the key player. Without Milošević, the pace and course of the Yugoslav crisis might have been different. Relativists are fond of spreading the blame and of suggesting that Croatian President Franjo Tudjman was equally culpable for the crisis, even though this position requires that they argue that there was no crisis until Tudjman was elected to office in April 1990—an absurd contention easily refuted by the facts.

The King Is Dead, Long Live the Collective Leadership

Tito lay on his deathbed for four months. He bequeathed to his country a system without a king, without even a president; it was a system without a center, a ship without a captain. In his vision (and Kardelj's handiwork), the country was to be guided by a network of collective bodies in which the republics and autonomous provinces were represented and among whose representatives the chairmanship would rotate (annually in the case of the state presidency, every two years in the case of the LCY Presidium). The uneasiness in the air was, at the time, palpable, and many Yugoslavs confessed a certain amazement when the system of collective leadership did not immediately implode. But as the 1980s progressed, the collective leadership proved unable to reach a consensus on fundamental economic and political is-sues and incapable of enforcing such decisions as it was able to make.[17]

After Tito's death in May 1980, critical voices began to be heard in a way not pos-sible in Tito's time. Gradually, in the course of the 1980s, Yugoslavia saw the aban-donment of the party's claim to have devised an exportable model, abandonment of the central concept of the withering away of the state, abandonment of the idea that self-management was the font of the system and the key to the solution of all policy issues, redefinition of nonalignment in terms of *Realpolitik*, abandonment of the idea that the LCY had a historic or superordinate claim to rule, and rejustification on the grounds that any alternative model would lead to civil war (though increasing numbers of people rejected even this rejustification in order to argue for the estab-lishment of a two-party or multiparty system in Yugoslavia). This post-Tito disinte-gration of ideology in Yugoslavia followed on the heels of a devolution of powers to the constituent republics and provinces which revived, on a nationwide basis, the au-tonomist logic of the Cvetković-Maček *Sporazum* of 1939.[18]

Political Decay

In the course of the years 1980–1986, leading Yugoslav party functionaries and news organs charged almost every major social institution with malfunctioning. Only the army was exempted from criticism at that time. Other organizations were variably charged with unconstitutional practices, corruption, rampant inefficiency, unre-sponsiveness to people's needs, and so forth.

Problems in the functioning of the party remained central to these concerns, of course. Here the pivotal concern was the manifest inability of the eight regional party organizations of Yugoslavia's eight federal units (six republics and two au-tonomous provinces) to coordinate their policies or agree on strategies. This, in turn, gave birth to the realization that the LCY had already ceased to exist as an organiza-tionally unified and politically meaningful unit: the LCY had become merely the in-stitutional arena in which the real powers in the system—the regional party organi-zations—met and discussed their common concerns.

Within the party itself, the real channels of authority often diverged considerably from the formal channels: the removal of the provincial party organizations of Kosovo and Vojvodina from the effective jurisdiction of the Serbian Republic party organization on the authority of the federal constitution was only one example of this. Moreover, the 1974 federal constitution, unlike previous postwar Yugoslav con-stitutions, defined the SFRY (in Part I, Article 2) as consisting of eight constituent units, that is, the six republics and two autonomous provinces, thereby granting the provinces a legal status founded not merely on Serbian law, but also on federal law.[19] Although the party as a whole was weak and disunified, local branches sometimes showed a resilient capacity for intrusion into domains lying outside their jurisdic-tion. Local party members often joined out of sheer opportunism and used their po-sitions for private gain, often, evidently, in disregard of the law.[20] Even *Socijalizam*, the party theoretical organ, admitted in summer 1984 that the LCY was having difficulties with members who ignored party directives and behaved in an irresponsible fashion.[21]

But although the federal party organization had become totally divorced from governmental functions—to the extent that it experienced considerable difficulty in making any headway in applying the 1982 recommendations of the Kraigher Commission for the Reform of the Economic System—the regional party organizations retained a firm grasp on power, thus provoking complaints of "republican etatism." A striking illustration of the balance of power came in the second half of 1984, when the Fourteenth Central Committee (CC) Plenum was held. Under party statutes, the eight regional party organizations (of the six republics and two autonomous provinces) were obliged to meet to compare their own policies with the latest CC resolution (which dealt specifically with the economy and the failure to implement the Kraigher Commission's recommendations). In actual fact, not a single regional party organization bothered to meet in this connection[22]—a sure sign of the flimsiness of central party discipline.

The self-managing interest communities likewise spun out of control. Created in late 1974 with the idea of involving ordinary citizens in monitoring public services in education, health, social welfare, child care, employment, sports, information, and so forth,[23] the communities (known collectively as "SIZ," from the Serbo-Croatian *Samoupravne interesne zajednice*) quickly mushroomed in number and scope. The resulting system, in which two parallel structures exercised jurisdiction in the same area, was mocked as "SIZ-ophrenia" (a pointed pun on "schizophrenia"). Though under the constitution the self-managing communities were supposed to be created by local bodies of citizens and not by republic or provincial legislation, in practice all such communities owed their existence to republic or provincial legislation. Moreover, instead of functioning as consumer advocates—their supposed portfolio—the new institutions quickly adopted the behavior of government agencies.

Finally—where political institutions are concerned—the Socialist Alliance of Working People of Yugoslavia (SAWPY), a front organization designed to involve nonparty people in supportive activity, had long been little more than a marionette of party barons.

The malfunctioning of political organizations might not have acquired quite the salience in the public mind, at least not so quickly, had it not been for repeated revelations and charges to that effect, which resulted in an attendant shrinkage of public confidence in the system. Moreover, the baneful effect of the malfunctioning of public institutions and of the shrinkage of public confidence in the system was reinforced by the economic mire. Precipitated by a combination of uncoordinated investments, unbridled trade imbalances, and overborrowing throughout the 1970s and sharpened by the impact of oil-price hikes after 1973, economic problems by 1985 included spiraling inflation in excess of 100 percent annually and a growing gap between the cost of living and real wages. The latter gap was compensated for by the growth of a barter economy and by smuggling and black-marketeering.

As early as 1979, the deficit in the balance of payments amounted to $3.6 billion, and the foreign debt, which had been a relatively modest $5.7 billion in 1975, had swollen to $15 billion by early 1980, reaching the dangerous level of $19.2 billion the following year. In 1980, the government required 15 percent of all foreign currency earnings just to service the foreign debt.[24] As of 1983, outlays to service the national debt amounted to more than $5 billion, against $10–15 billion brought in by exports.[25] In early 1982, Milka Planinc, a party conservative who had presided over the "normalization" of post-1971 Croatia, succeeded Montenegrin Veselin Djuranović as Prime Minister of the SFRY, promising to make a "new beginning" for the country. But for the first two years of her term, she and her associates continued to rely on "administrative measures" to tackle economic problems, rather than take the "bitter pill" of marketization. Only in 1985 did Planinc slowly begin to undertake some vital reforms, but Branko Mikulić, at that time Bosnia's representative in the state presidency, supported by Deputy Prime Minister Janez Zemljarić (from Slovenia), marshaled political forces to scuttle this incipient reformism. In frustration, Planinc tried to resign in October 1985, but her resignation was declined. Planinc's term came to an end in March 1986, and the more doggedly conservative Mikulić succeeded her in office.[26] What the conservative mind wanted was to correct the economic problems without tampering with the fundamental political institutions of the system. Since at least some of these problems were rooted in those very institutions, the conservative project was doomed from the start.

Crisis and Polarization

That post-Tito developments in the economic and political spheres were pushing Yugoslavia into a very real crisis was at first denied by party spokespersons. Only in 1983—four years after the economic situation began to deteriorate, two years after the province-wide riots by Albanians in Kosovo, and a year after the controversial Twelfth Party Congress—did party elders finally concede that there was a "crisis" in Yugoslavia and even that a "Polish" situation could develop in the country.[27]

This hesitation in turn constricted party participation in the political debate that started in Yugoslavia soon after Tito's death. At first, the chief participants were scholars and journalists. The Twelfth Party Congress, insofar as it opened the floodgates to debate within the party itself, was a turning point.

In the initial phase of the debate (1980–1981), the economic difficulties were not yet far advanced, and discussion therefore centered on press policy, supervision of the universities, and general political democratization, with lesser attention being paid to economic policy. Within this context, there were two broad positions, one partial to liberalization and one opposed, though the "liberals" of the early 1980s were not nearly as liberal as the "liberals" of the late 1980s would be. In the course of that troubled decade, as economic deterioration forced Yugoslavs to confront the sources of strain, four clear factional groupings emerged as constituted by the dual issues of liberalization versus retrenchment and recentralization versus preservation

of the decentralized system. Although almost every constituent regional party organization was factionalized to some extent and although a particular grouping might
be more or less "liberal" on certain issues and more or less "conservative" on others
(as the cases of Vojvodina and Slovenia amply illustrate), one may nonetheless make
certain thumbnail sketches of the dominant political coloration of the respective regional parties. Accordingly, one may say that liberal recentralizers were dominant in
the Serbian party, conservative recentralizers in the Bosnian and Vojvodinan parties,
liberal decentralists in the Vojvodinan party, and conservative decentralists dominant
in the Croatian, Macedonian, and Kosovar parties.[28] In Slovenia, the government of
France Popit was "conservative" on political issues, but "liberal" on certain social issues, such as religion, and more "liberal" in press policy than most of the other regional elites; Popit and his team were committed to safeguarding Slovenia's autonomy and should be counted among the "decentralists" or "autonomists."

To this double polarization one might add that important differences between the
more economically developed republics of Slovenia and Croatia and the rest of the
country also complicated the process the Yugoslavs called "the harmonization of
viewpoints" (*usaglašavanje stavova*). The result of all of this was that it was exceed-
ingly difficult to build an effective coalition and utterly impossible, in the conditions
of the early 1980s, to fashion a *stable* coalition. In consequence, although the disintegration of the center allowed the burgeoning of political debate and the generation
of sundry prescriptions, it simultaneously prevented, under conditions of effectively
triple polarization, the imposition of a new solution on the system, even though
there was widespread consensus that *something* needed to be done. Ultimately, of
course, this irresolution would contribute to breaking the Communist Party's hold
in four republics (Slovenia, Croatia, Macedonia, and Bosnia) in 1989–1990, which
in turn resulted in opening up new strategies for dealing with the crisis.

The weakening of the center after Tito's death allowed the Serbian and Vojvodinan parties, together with the Slovenian party, still under the relatively conservative
leadership of France Popit, to liberalize policies in the spheres of culture, media, and
religion. Controversial plays such as Jovan Radulović's *Pigeonhole* and Dušan Jovanović's *The Karamazovs*—which touched on politically delicate subjects—were
staged in these republics and province, though the former play was eventually suppressed under pressure from the more conservative Croatian party organization. Serbia's most popular weekly magazine, *NIN*, actively encouraged the awakening of
popular interest in Goli Otok,[29] the prison in which the Communist Party had incarcerated and tortured its political enemies in the late 1940s. The media in these
federal units, and to a certain extent also in Croatia, launched a new era of investigative journalism in Yugoslavia—sometimes even to the point of muckraking.[30] Where
religious policy was concerned, Slovenia and Vojvodina achieved a rare tranquillity
in Church–state relations, while in Serbia, the Serbian Orthodox Church was allowed (in 1984) to found a new theological faculty in Belgrade and continued its
lively publication activity with the first *official* Orthodox Church translation of the
New Testament into Serbo-Croatian. That same year, authorities of the Serbian Re-

public also gave a green light to the patriarchate to resume construction of the gargantuan Church of St. Sava (which had been started in 1935 but suspended in 1941).[31] Since liberalization was dependent upon the slackening of authority at the center, it was understandable that few liberals could be found among recentralizers at that stage.

In Croatia and Bosnia, as already mentioned, conservative forces remained dominant. One expression of this more conservative political climate came in the shape of a series of petty harassments of clergymen in these two republics (above all of Catholic clergymen and Muslim ulema and officials). But although Bosnian and Montenegrin conservatives were also recentralizers—with the Montenegrin Central Committee suggesting in November 1981 that regional party organizations should be shorn of their power to elect their own representatives to the LCY Central Committee[32]—the internally divided Croatian party moved from a position partial to system standardization in 1982[33] to a position of jealously safeguarding Croatian autonomy (by 1984).

In Kosovo, finally, local provincial party barons tried, in the years 1974–1981, to maximize their autonomy not merely from the federal administration, but also from Serbian Republic authorities, to which both autonomous provinces were formally, though for a while largely nominally, subordinate. They sought to accomplish these objectives above all by restricting the publication of Serbo-Croatian accounts of party meetings and by constricting the flow of information to Belgrade. The result was that Belgrade was not well informed about the activities of Albanian irredentist organizations in Kosovo at this time, even though the provincial government in Priština was monitoring them. The unconstitutionally broad extent of Kosovar autonomy could only be safeguarded by repressing open discussion of issues; hence, in Kosovo, devolutionary policy was wedded to cultural and political conservatism.

The Search for Solutions

That the political debate had, by the mid-1980s, revived certain themes first bandied about in the late 1960s suggested that the underlying problems were anything but new. As early as 1967, for instance, M. Čaldarević had urged that the principle of democratic centralism was outmoded in conditions of self-management.[34] These same sentiments were voiced by journalist Antun Žvan in 1981, when he urged that since democratic centralism only applied to party members, its effect was to make party members "less free" than nonmembers. Again, the idea of pumping life into SAWPY and transforming it into a second party had a long history.[35] The revival of this idea in the mid-1980s was a measure of the discontent with the political status quo.

By the time party elders convened the Twelfth Party Congress in summer 1982— the first congress since Tito's passing—there were strong expectations that the occasion would prove a breakthrough for the political direction of the system. But all radical proposals for organizational "reform" (most of them inspired by hopes of reconstituting the center) were blocked, including Rade Končar's rather dramatic proposal on the floor of the congress that the republic-based federal organization of the party be scrapped and replaced with organization on the basis of lines of production.[36] The upshot was that although decentralists and liberals alike could gloat over their defeat of the sundry centralizing proposals presented at the congress, the rivalry between the recentralizers and the decentralists in the party had not been resolved and, hence, the pressure for change had not been removed.

Although the Twelfth Party Congress thus accomplished little or nothing, it did signal the impotence of the center, which naturally further encouraged republican and provincial elites to ignore exhortations emanating from the center. A subsequent CC resolution (in April 1983) urging its own members not to misconstrue themselves as representatives of their respective republics or provinces was, for instance, ignored by all concerned. In early summer 1984, the party leadership made another attempt to restore resilience to the central organs. The CC Presidium drew up a report on relations between the central and regional party organizations. The report found that "decisions adopted unanimously at the national level are being carried out only half-heartedly [at the republican and provincial levels], and execution is largely limited to those aspects which suit the particular region at the moment."[37] This report was submitted to the Thirteenth Session of the Central Committee for action. But, despite the urgings of those who warned of the creeping "federalization" of the party itself,[38] the committee demurred and decided to pass the text on to the 70,000 basic organizations of the party for discussion and to delay final action until the Thirteenth Party Congress, in June 1986.

By then, recentralization was no longer rationalized in terms of the vanguard role of the party as the political instrument of the working class. Recentralization was presented, on the contrary, as a pragmatic consideration.[39] Ideologically deflated, the Yugoslavs quietly abandoned their earlier claims to greater fidelity to Lenin.[40] Former Partisan general Peko Dapčević, for instance, told the Twelfth Party Congress that Leninism was outdated—a conclusion presumed by Žvan's earlier effort to scuttle democratic centralism and seconded in 1983 by Svetozar Stojanović[41] and in 1985 by sociologist Vladimir Arzešnek and party theorist Vladimir Goati.[42] Indeed, Arzenšek charged that Leninist ideas remained a serious impediment to necessary change throughout Eastern Europe. Likewise, whereas the Yugoslavs were once fond of claiming that their system was neither a one-party system nor a "bourgeois" multiparty system, but rather something unique,[43] *Socijalizam* now openly conceded that Yugoslavia had been set up as, and hence still was (or should be), a one-party system.[44]

The realization that the system had dead-ended gave birth to an astonishingly wide range of reform proposals. Famed economist Branko Horvat, for example, suggested in 1984 that "all political parties" (i.e., the Communist Party in its sundry regional organizations) be abolished and that Yugoslavia be reorganized as a "partyless" socialist system operated through citizens' associations.[45] Two political scientists from Belgrade suggested in 1983 that a multiparty system be restored[46]—an alternative specifically repudiated at the June 1984 session of the 163-member LCY Central Committee. In reflecting upon the evident support for this remedy, Radoslav Ratković drew a distinction between "the pluralism of self-managing interests" and political pluralism, calling it erroneous to think that the legitimacy of the former could carry over to the latter.[47]

Despite the party's obvious reluctance to share power with noncommunists, sociologist Miroslav Živković did not hesitate, in spring 1985, to call for the establishment of a full-fledged "social democracy" in Yugoslavia.[48] Still others (such as Čedo Grbić) called for a more liberal attitude toward private enterprise, or for the restoration of strong-arm (*čvrsta ruka*) rule, or—more tamely—for the complete rewriting of LCY statutes.[49] Multicandidate elections were also a popular idea, especially as a device to defuse support for multiparty elections.[50]

Within the context of this debate, then, SAWPY appeared as both temptation and, ostensibly, opportunity. Its advocates were able to argue, plausibly, that the organization was entitled under the constitution to a greater role in public life and that the LCY control of SAWPY was an "unnatural partnership."[51] Perhaps drawing lessons from the Polish crisis of 1980–1981, Radoš Smiljković told the Zagreb weekly magazine *Danas* in 1984 that the "marginalization" of SAWPY deprived noncommunist citizens of legitimate political channels and risked pushing them into the illicit "politicization of nonpolitical organizations and associations." Indeed, for Smiljković, "new political groups appear, and they will keep appearing" until legal structures are offered, because "if people are not satisfied with the existing organizations, they create new ones, or [lapse into] a catastrophic political apathy."[52]

The difficulty, according to high-ranking party official Čedo Grbić, was that SAWPY had been controlled by "semi-legal coordinating groups and commissions" which had excluded the public from any voice in personnel questions and which continued to perpetuate the organization's docile subordination to party hierarchies.[53] Seconding this assessment, Aleksandar Grličkov noted that noncommunists had only slight chances of being promoted to republic-level leadership posts in SAWPY. His remedy was to allow 30–50 percent of responsible posts in SAWPY to be filled by noncommunists and to expand its jurisdiction. Going one step further, Serbian political scientist Mihailo Popović told a party symposium in spring 1984 that SAWPY should be allowed to reorganize itself as an independent party in order to provide an independent, critical voice in the role of permanent opposition. Finally, Svetozar Stojanović outlined a program in which SAWPY would gain organizational independence from the LCY, have a separate membership, and share power with a still dominant LCY.[54]

The radical tenor of some of these proposals was a measure of the seriousness with which the participants in the Yugoslav debate viewed the political situation. But any structural or systemic reorganization as well as any far-reaching revisions of the statutes of the LCY, the regional parties, or SAWPY could only be achieved on the basis of a broad consensus among the leaderships of the eight regional party organizations (or nine, if the army's party organization was included). Such consensus was lacking. In early 1984, for example, the Slovenian leadership took the small step of suggesting that it might propose three candidates for its single seat on the collective state presidency and allow a popular vote to determine the outcome. The other republic leaderships objected, and Slovenia withdrew its proposal and simply named Stane Dolanc to the post.

The Serbian Solution

The most comprehensive "reform" package to be proposed by a regional party organization in the first five years after Tito's death came in October 1984, when the Serbian party organization issued a four-part draft reform program calling for the strengthening of the role and autonomy of economic enterprises, the strengthening of the federal government, the democratization of the electoral system, and a roll-back of the prerogatives and overall autonomy of the two autonomous provinces. The last of these points was assured of popularity among Serbia's Serbs, who were becoming disgruntled over the provinces' power to veto legislation. Serbs complained that their republic had unique difficulties in passing important legislation and blamed obstructionism on the part of the autonomous provinces. As part of the package, the Serbs also resurrected the 1981 proposal to divest republican parties of the power to select their representatives on the Central Committee. Earlier, in March 1984, as the Serbian party had been engaged in developing its ideas concerning its vision for reform, Dragoslav Marković, then president of the LCY Presidium and Serbian representative on that body, had told a meeting of top federal, republic, and provincial officials in Belgrade that "sufficient unity is lacking in the LC itself and, if I may say so, in the Central Committee itself."[55]

The regional party organizations of Kosovo, Vojvodina, Slovenia, and Croatia were alarmed by the Serbian "package." But on 23 November 1984, at the opening of a plenary session of the CC of the LC-Serbia, CC member Dušan Čkrebić lashed out against the autonomous provinces without restraint, charging that

> the Provinces did not care about the fact that in the last ten years their Republic had not passed a law on social planning which emphasized the serious claim that the internal link within the republic was only of a formal nature. Čkrebić also noted that the constructive proposal concerning Serbia's direct participation in the more rapid development of Kosovo was interpreted in probably the worst possible manner, implying that it called for the fund to be abolished and Serbia's contribution to it ended. All this had, perhaps unintentionally, given rise to anti-Serbian feelings among [members of] the Albanian nationality.[56]

Two days later, as the plenary session drew to a close, Serbian party president Petar Stambolić told the delegates assembled there that the country's eight regional units were becoming "self-sufficient entities," provoking a "stormy" response from the delegates from the two provinces, who in turn characterized the Serbian proposals as "rash and insufficiently studied."[57]

Kosovo and Vojvodina had been fighting, since the April 1981 Albanian riots in Kosovo,[58] to stay the Serbian backlash. But Slovenia and Croatia were likewise concerned about the threatened erosion of their own hard-won autonomy. Slovenian-Serbian differences came into full view at the Fourteenth CC Plenum in October 1984, when Dragoslav Marković attacked the Slovenian deputies for their opposition to the Serbian package. Marković also called into question the propriety of requiring unanimity among the eight regional organizations before a decision could be made. This challenge in turn impelled Slovene Andrej Marinc to take the podium, observing among other things that the principle of unanimity was a long-standing procedure in the LCY and that Marković's view had been specifically repudiated at a previous session. Marinc added that continued public discussion about changing the system could lead to "a political crisis, to a crisis of society."[59] Slobodan Milošević, then-president of the Belgrade party organization and son-in-law of Draža Marković, replied to Marinc the following month:

> We have been threatened with a political crisis if we continue to discuss these problems. All right, let us enter that political crisis. This crisis is going to produce a great uproar about the question of unity or separatism. In such a crisis, separatism will not prevail, because the people have accepted unity. Those leaders incapable of seeing this will lose the people's confidence. If separatism is not opposed, our country will have no prospects for the future. It can only disintegrate.[60]

The equation of advocacy of the federal status quo with "separatism" was a polemical punch which had some clout in Yugoslavia at the time. But with four other regional parties antagonistic in varying degrees to the Serbian draft and a fifth (the Bosnian) at best "restrained" in its support, the prospects for adoption of this package seemed, and indeed proved to be, slight.

In the wake of this exchange, a new term crept into Yugoslav polemical vocabulary: *autonomism.* Used by Serbian recentralizers as a pejorative term for the Vojvodinan party's desire to maintain the political status quo, the term was incorporated into a draft resolution of the Serbian CC in April 1985, where it was placed in the same category with "Serb nationalism" and "Albanian nationalism."[61] When Vojvodina's press responded to criticism with countercriticism of its own, some Serbian politicians grumbled that Vojvodina's newspapers were launching "an attack on the reputation of the Serbian Assembly"—a charge which suggested a desire to curb the independence of the provincial press.[62]

End of an Era

In October 1984, *Borba,* the Belgrade daily, carried a series of articles by University of Zagreb Professor Jovan Mirić which argued that the 1974 constitution was the source of *all* of Yugoslavia's problems and that the exaggerated decentralization had destroyed the unified market and even interfered with the market mechanism.[63] Mitja Ribičič (a Slovene), Aleksandar Grličkov (a Macedonian), and Hamdija

Pozderac (a Bosnian Muslim) applauded Mirić's series. Others, including partial conservative France Popit (from Slovenia) and archconservatives Jure Bilić (from Croatia) and Dušan Popović (a Serb from Vojvodina), were antagonistic. Jovan Djordjević, a coauthor of the 1974 constitution, himself admitted that the confederal coloration assumed by the system had not been the intention of the constitution's drafters.

Eventually, the party decided to set up a commission to review the political system and prepare recommendations for change and reform. Modeled on the Kraigher Commission for the Reform of the Economic System, this new commission was entrusted to the chairship of Tihomir Vlaškalić, a ranking Serbian party official. The Vlaškalić Commission was asked to prepare a report for submission to the Thirteenth Party Congress.

As the Thirteenth Party Congress approached, sundry party officials broached diverse proposals aimed at reestablishing central authority. The reasoning, according to Tanjug, the official news agency, was that "the orientation of the Twelfth Congress went in the wrong direction."[64] In a strikingly pointed phrase, CC member Dušan Dragosavac told the Twenty-Second Session of the CC in November 1985 that Yugoslavia could "more easily endure a multiparty system along[side] a united League of Communists than a coalition of a number of [regional] party organizations within the League of Communists."[65] Strange solutions started to be proposed, such as eliminating separate status for the regional party organizations, dropping the presidents of republican central committees from ex officio membership in the LCY Presidium, suppressing local autonomy in scientific institutes, and—perhaps most surprising of all—selectively dropping the "ethnic keys," which assigned fixed quotas to specific nationality groups in sundry party and governmental bodies. In the last instance, it was argued specifically that if the LCY CC was ever going to function efficiently, it would have to be reduced in size—a measure which would have required some compromise with the network of ethnic, social, and age keys applied in selecting that body's membership.[66] Ultimately, the CC's membership was reduced slightly to 129.

In a related move, which simultaneously reflected the strains produced by Serb-Albanian frictions in Kosovo, the Constitutional Court of Serbia handed down a decision (in October 1985) annulling a number of decrees relating to cadres policy in Kosovo—decrees which had guaranteed ethnic representation in the leadership in proportion to the given group's presence in the province. These decrees had been the instrument whereby the numerically dominant Albanians had taken over the provincial party apparatus in the course of the 1970s. According to the court, however, "the application of proportional national representation ... facilitates the suppression of the numerically smaller nations and nationalities, which is contrary to the principles of equality laid down in the constitution. Also, this principle endangers the guaranteed rights of citizens to have equal access to every job and function."[67]

On the eve of the Thirteenth Party Congress, regional differences on the subject remained sharp. The Slovenian Party Congress (held in April 1986), for instance, emphasized the "unacceptability" of approaches which used the economic crisis "to put forward centralist-unitarist solutions."[68] By contrast, the Montenegrin Party Congress—held a few days later—underlined the importance of "unity" in finding solutions, to the extent of seconding the earlier call for bringing scientific institutes throughout the country under central direction.[69]

Following established procedure, the federal congress was preceded by congresses held by each of the eight constituent regional party organizations. In Slovenia and Croatia, the congresses of 1986 marked the end of an era, as younger, more liberal Communists took the reins from the more conservative "old guard." In Slovenia, the Tenth Congress of the LC-Slovenia (in mid-April) saw the election of forty-five-year-old Milan Kučan as Slovenian party secretary and the removal of France Popit to a largely honorific post. Important changes were also effected at the Tenth Congress of the LC-Croatia the following month. The retirement of Croatian party president Mika Špiljak was only the beginning; conservatives Milutin Baltić, Dušan Dragosavac, and Jure Bilić were simply removed from office. Stanko Stojčević, a Serb then fifty-seven years of age, became the new party president, while Drago Dimitrović, a young Croat, was elected secretary of the party presidium.[70] It was also at this time, namely, at the Serbian party congress held in May 1986, that Milošević advanced to the post of Serbian party chief, though the significance of this promotion was suspected by few, if any, persons at the time.

In spite of these gains for more liberal orientations, the cause of maintaining the decentralized system was, at least temporarily, thrown on the defensive when centralizers put together a working consensus for a partial reconstitution of central authority. Although they were unable to realize their ambitions in the long run, in the short run the centralists seemed to be setting the agenda for discussion. The Thirteenth Party Congress, thus, held 25–28 June 1986, was replete with calls for party unity and warnings about the effects of the conversion of local party organizations by technocratic interests into agents for purely local interests. The new party statute, adopted at the congress, transferred the right to elect members of the CC from the republics to the LCY Congress, entrusted the CC with the authority to oversee the work of republic and provincial organizations and, if necessary, to convoke extraordinary republic and provincial party congresses to halt local deviations, and—should that fail—to convoke an Extraordinary LCY Congress to rein in a headstrong republic party organization.[71] In addition, the new statute provided a more explicit affirmation of the controversial principle of democratic centralism and strengthened the ability of the party organs to discipline wayward party members.[72] In sum, as Josip Vrhovec put it, the changes were designed to reverse the processes through which the party "was beginning to lose its vanguard role."[73]

There were those who wanted to carry recentralization further yet, and a more general pressure for political change emerged, tending in one direction or in another. But as long as the party maintained its political monopoly there were some serious constraints on political change in Yugoslavia. The first and most important factor, which I have taken pains to document, was the division of the party into eight autonomous regional organizations gravitating toward four distinct and conflictual policy positions. A second factor—which strongly suggested that the decentralization of the 1970s could not be reversed easily, if at all—was the ethnic dimension. The sundry nationality groups had grown accustomed to governing their own republics, and—as would become clearer at the end of the decade—any serious effort at recentralization could, in such circumstances, only carry grave risk.

Third, apart from the regional elites themselves, the decentralized system generated other vested interests, either in the political-administrative hierarchy or in economic decisionmaking, interests which could be expected to fear the consequences of change in the system.

Fourth, where the "national question" was concerned, there was a more specific—if often unspoken—fear of the repercussions that curtailment of autonomy or the introduction of a "new course" would have in Croatia (the scene of a powerful nationalist movement, 1967–1971) and in Kosovo (a province shaken by widespread Albanian riots in 1968 and again in 1981). A curious symptom of party caution in this area was the omission of any reference to Albanian nationalist disorders in Kosovo from the draft platform for the Thirteenth Party Congress—an omission promptly criticized by the Zagreb daily *Vjesnik*.[74]

Fifth, there was the fact that the intelligentsia up to then had by and large accepted the premise that even the most thoroughgoing overhaul of the system should be undertaken in partnership with actors in the regime rather than in opposition to the regime and the system. At that time, thus, declarations that the system had failed tended to be translated into political debate rather than into political opposition. Yet one must register a caveat, for below the surface the process of the defection of the intellectuals had already begun, and by 1987 various intellectuals in Belgrade, Zagreb, and Ljubljana were quietly working to overhaul, and perhaps overthrow, the system.[75] Their voices, inaudible in 1985, became more and more audible, culminating in the formation of alternative political parties by some of these same intellectuals in the course of 1988–1989.

Pandora's Box

Among the intellectuals, it was the Serbian historians who were to make their presence felt first. Among these were several unrehabilitated nationalists, such as novelist Dobrica Ćosić, who had been reprimanded by the weekly newspaper *Komunist* in 1977 for having allegedly claimed that Serbs were being "exploited and denigrated by other Yugoslav nationalities."[76] In the early 1980s, historical revisionism became the dominant discourse among Serbian historians. Where Branko Petranović's *Revolucija i kontrarevolucija u Jugoslaviji, 1941–1945* (1983) went a long way toward effecting the ideological vindication of the wartime Chetnik movement, Djordje Stanković's *Nikola Pašić i jugoslovensko pitanje* (1985) recast its subject as a "selfless" altruist promoting simultaneously the interests of Serbs as such and those of all South Slavs.[77] The year 1985 also saw the publication of a book by Serbian historian

Veselin Djuretić which followed the lines of Petranović's reappraisal, but took the argument further; the book provoked furious controversy but, significantly, the Serbian Academy of Sciences and Art (SANU) rallied behind Djuretić. In May 1985, members of the SANU, gathered for their annual convention, decided to appoint a commission to draft a "memorandum" on the problems of the day. The commission included historians Radovan Samardžić and Vasilije Krestić, economist Kosta Mihailović, novelists Dobrica Ćosić and Antonije Isaković, philosopher Ljubomir Tadić, and former *Praxis* collaborator Mihailo Marković. A copy of the draft-in-progress was eventually leaked to the Belgrade daily newspaper *Večernje novosti*, which published extracts of the document on 24 and 25 September 1986. As Tim Judah notes, the effect was electrifying: "The whole of Yugoslavia was shaken by a political earthquake."[78]

The Memorandum portrayed the Serbs as the great victims of Tito and Communist rule and accused Croats and Albanians, in particular, of alleged "genocidal" policies and actions against ethnic Serbs. Wading in collective self-pity and basking in the certainty that the Serbs were uniquely victimized in the SFRY, their cultural heritage being allegedly "alienated, usurped, invalidated, neglected, or wasted,"[79] the Memorandum was nothing less than an ideological program for revenge and for establishing Serb hegemony over Yugoslavia's non-Serbs. At the time it was first published in the press, it was roundly condemned by most prominent Serbian Communists. But it was, to use a phrase coined by Egyptian President Nasser, a role awaiting a leader, a program awaiting an executor; almost exactly a year later, Milošević would step forward to carry out the program spelled out in the Memorandum.

The year 1986 also saw Andrija Artuković, the Minister of Interior, Justice, and Religious Affairs in the fascist Independent State of Croatia (NDH) during World War II (1941–1945), finally brought to trial on charges of mass persecution and mass murder. Artuković had fled Croatia at war's end and entered the United States with false papers on 16 July 1948, settling eventually in Seal Beach, California. After a delay, the Yugoslav government made its initial request for his extradition on 31 March 1951. The U.S. government denied the request on the grounds that the charges against him were political.[80] After persistent pressure from Belgrade, the U.S. Supreme Court ordered a new hearing on the case for his extradition on 20 January 1958 (by a vote of seven to two).[81] But once again Artuković was able to defend himself against the Yugoslav government's demand for his extradition. Belgrade federal authorities renewed their request to the United States on 21 August 1985, and this time Washington agreed to cooperate.

Artuković was taken into custody and extradited to Yugoslavia on 12 February 1986. Blind and suffering from brain disease at the time of his arrest, the eighty-six-year-old Nazi war criminal arrived in Zagreb on a stretcher. His trial opened on 14 April 1986 in Zagreb, and he was charged with "consciously and deliberately order[ing] and caus[ing] the death of about 231,000 men, women and children—Serbs, Croats, Gypsies, Jews, and other Yugoslav citizens."[82] On 14 May, the court handed down a verdict of guilty and ordered Artuković executed.[83] Appeals for clemency or for a reversal of the verdict were turned down, but in May 1987 his execution was postponed indefinitely—nominally because of his failing health, but in reality more likely because of fear of the repercussions that his execution might have on Serb-Croat relations.[84] Among Croats, the trial excited little interest, but among Croatian Serbs, as Milorad Pupovac, a leading figure among moderates in the Croatian Serb community, told me in 1997, the trial provoked a mixed reaction. Those Serbs who had never heard of Artuković before—and there were some—were given a "crash" history lesson in the atrocities of the Croatian fascists. For other Serbs, who remembered the pain of World War II all too well, the trial opened old wounds, rekindled old memories, and stirred old hatreds. For some, indeed, as Pupovac told me, it was a turning point.[85] Many Croats agreed with Artuković's defense attorney, Silvije Degen, that Serbs needed the Artuković trial "to prove the genocidal nature of the Croatian people."[86]

The Memorandum of the SANU and the trial of Andrija Artuković, both coming in 1986, opened the Pandora's box of nationalism. Often in the past Titoists such as Dragosavac had solemnly intoned, "Every nationalism is dangerous," often spelling out the corollary that complaints against other nations were best left unspoken, unregistered. Now, with these two developments, Yugoslavia had taken a step closer to coming face to face with the legacy of Pandora's open box—in this case, the mephitic vapors of chauvinistic nationalism.

Notes

1. Among a growing number of works devoted to the interwar period, five impress me as particularly outstanding. These are: Ivo Banac, *The National Question in Yugoslavia: Origin, History, Politics* (Ithaca, N.Y.: Cornell University Press, 1984); Branislav Gligorijević, *Parlament i političke stranke u Jugoslaviji 1919–1929* (Belgrade: Institut za savremenu istoriju and Narodna knjiga, 1979); Ivan Mužić, *Stjepan Radić u Kraljevini Srba, Hrvata i Slovenaca*, 4th ed. (Zagreb: Nakladni Zavod Matice Hrvatske, 1990); Svetozar Pribićević, *Diktatura Kralja Aleksandra*, trans. from French (Belgrade: Prosveta, 1952); and Fikreta Jelić-Butić, *Hrvatska Seljačka Stranka* (Zagreb: Globus, 1983). Among the memoirs written by personages of that era, of special interest is Milan M. Stojadinović, *Ni rat, ni pakt: Jugoslavija izmedju dva rata* (Buenos Aires: El Economista, 1963).

2. See Fikreta Jelić-Butić, *Ustaše i Nezavisna Država Hrvatska 1941–1945* (Zagreb: S. N. Liber and Školska knjiga, 1977); Philip J. Cohen, *Serbia's Secret War: Propaganda and the Deceit of History* (College Station, Tex.: Texas A & M University Press, 1996); Jonathan Steinberg, *All or Nothing: The Axis and the Holocaust 1941–43* (London: Routledge, 1990); Branko Petranović, *Srbija u drugom svetskom ratu 1939–1945* (Belgrade: Vojna štamparija, 1992); Bogdan Krizman, *Ante Pavelić i Ustaše* (Zagreb: Globus, 1978); Bogdan Krizman, *Ustaše i Treči Reich* (Zagreb: Globus, 1983); and Jozo Tomašević, *War and Revolution in Yugoslavia, 1941–1945: The Chetniks* (Stanford, Calif.: Stanford University Press, 1975). Regarding Nedić, see also Milan Borković, *Milan Nedić* (Zagreb: Centar za informacije i publicitet, 1985). Regarding the Bulgarian occupation, see Dimitrij Kulić, *Bugarska okupacija 1941–1944*, Vol. 1 (Niš: Prosveta, 1970).

3. Nikolai Tolstoy, "The Klagenfurt Conspiracy: War Crimes and Diplomatic Secrets," in *Encounter*, Vol. 60, No. 5 (May 1983), p. 27; Vladimir Žerjavić, *Opsesije i megalomanije oko Jasenovca i Bleiburga* (Zagreb: Globus, 1992), p. 77.

4. See Vojislav Koštunica and Kosta Čavoški, *Party Pluralism or Monism: Social Movements and the Political System in Yugoslavia, 1944–1949* (Boulder: East European Monographs, 1985), esp. pp. 29–125.

5. *The Times* (London) (21 March 1947), p. 3; (28 March 1947), p. 3; (20 June 1947), p. 3; (10 October 1950), p. 5; (12 October 1950), p. 4; (1 November 1950), p. 5; (18 November 1950), p. 5; (20 November 1950), p. 6; (25 November 1950), p. 6; (7 December 1950), p. 4; (30 December 1950), p. 5; U. S. Department of State, *Records Relating to the Internal Affairs of Yugoslavia 1945–1949*, Decimal file 860h—files 00/4–346 to 00/10–1046, reprinting articles from the *Milwaukee Journal* (12 May 1946) and *New York Post* (17 May 1946).

6. Regarding changes in the diplomatic environment, see Ann Lane, *Britain, The Cold War and Yugoslav Unity, 1941–1949* (Sussex: Sussex Academic Press, 1996), pp. 125–149. Regarding the peasant rebellion in Cazin, see Vera Kržisnik-Bukić, *Cazinska buna 1950* (Sarajevo: Svjetlost, 1991); and Melissa K. Bokovoy, *Peasants and Communists: Politics and Ideology in the Yugoslav Countryside, 1941–1953* (Pittsburgh: University of Pittsburgh Press, 1998), pp. 136–138.

7. *Borba* (Belgrade) (25 November 1951), quoted in *The Times* (27 November 1951), p. 3.

8. Article by Dmitry Volkgonov in *Izvestiia* (Moscow) (10 June 1993), summarized in UPI (10 June 1993), on *Nexis*.

9. Johanna Granville, "Hungary, 1956: The Yugoslav Connection," in *Europe-Asia Studies*, Vol. 50, No. 3 (1998), pp. 497–498.

10. See *Yugoslavia's Way: The Program of the League of the Communists of Yugoslavia*, trans. Stoyan Pribechevich (New York: All Nations Press, 1958); and "Criticism of the Yugoslav Communists' Draft Program," in *Kommunist*, No. 6 (April 1958), trans. in *The Current Digest of the Soviet Press*, Vol. 10, No. 18 (11 June 1958), pp. 3–13.

11. See Zoran Sekulić, *Pad i ćutnja Aleksandra Rankovića* (Belgrade: Dositej, 1989).

12. Ilija Jukić, "Tito's Legacy," in *Survey*, No. 77 (Autumn 1970), p. 102. Among the major works dealing with the Tito era, one may mention: Dennison I. Rusinow, *The Yugoslav Experiment, 1948–1974* (Berkeley and Los Angeles: University of California Press, 1977); April Carter, *Democratic Reform in Yugoslavia: The Changing Role of the Party* (Princeton: Princeton University Press, 1982); Dušan Bilandžić, *Historija Socijalističke Federativne Republike Jugoslavije: Glavni procesi* (Zagreb: Školska knjiga, 1978); Branko Petranović, *Istorija Jugoslavije 1918–1988, Vol. 3: Socijalistička Jugoslavija 1945–1988* (Belgrade: Nolit, 1989); and Duncan Wilson, *Tito's Yugoslavia* (Cambridge: Cambridge University Press, 1979).

13. Džemal Bijedić, "Self-Management as a Necessity and Practice," in *Socialist Thought and Practice*, Vol. 17, No. 2 (February 1977), p. 4.

14. Stipe Mesić, *Kako je srušena Jugoslavija—Politički memoari*, 2nd ed. (Zagreb: Mislav Press, 1994), pp. 11–14.

15. Christopher Bennett, *Yugoslavia's Bloody Collapse: Causes, Course, and Consequences* (New York: New York University Press, 1995), pp. 129–130.

16. Anika Inder Singh, Review of Christopher Bennett's *Yugoslavia's Bloody Collapse* (1995), in *Nations and Nationalism*, Vol. 2, No. 2 (July 1996), p. 342.

17. Jasminka Udovički and Ivan Torov, "The Interlude: 1980–1990," in Jasminka Udovički and James Ridgeway (eds.), *Burn This House: The Making and Unmaking of Yugoslavia* (Durham, N.C.: Duke University Press, 1997), p. 80.

18. The *Sporazum* established an autonomous banovina (federal unit administered by a governor) of Croatia, comprising roughly 30 percent of the territory and population of Yugoslavia and enjoying budgetary and administrative independence and independent authority in most spheres of domestic policy. The monarchy was in fact the sole remaining constitutional link between Croatia and the rest of Yugoslavia.

19. Sami Repishti, "The Evolution of Kosova's Autonomy within the Yugoslav Constitutional Framework," in Arshi Pipa and Sami Repishti (eds.), *Studies on Kosova* (Boulder: East European Monographs, 1984), p. 202. See also Dragoljub S. Petrović, *Konstituisanje federalne Srbije* (Belgrade: Nova knjiga, 1988).

20. *Start* (Zagreb) (26 March 1983), trans. in Joint Publications Research Service (JPRS), *East Europe Report*, No. 83734 (22 June 1983), p. 54; *Vjesnik* (Zagreb), (6 April 1985).

21. Miroslav Stojanović, "Opštepartijska debata o ulozi Saveza komunista," in *Socijalizam*, Vol. 27, Nos. 7/8 (July–August 1984), p. 996.

22. *Borba* (Belgrade) (20 November 1984).

23. Milan Dimitrijević, "Samoupravne interesne zajednice," in *Opština*, Vol. 29, No. 5/6 (1976), pp. 116–118.

24. Viktor Meier, *Wie Jugoslawien verspielt wurde*, 2nd ed. (Munich: C. H. Beck, 1996), pp. 26–27.

25. Ibid., p. 34.

26. Ibid., pp. 32–37.

27. For particulars, see Pedro Ramet, "Yugoslavia and the Threat of Internal and External Discontents." in *Orbis*, Vol. 28, No. 1 (Spring 1984), pp. 104–105.

28. Evidence for these characterizations will be provided in the text.

29. Interview with the editor of *NIN* , Belgrade, July 1982.

30. For details, see Pedro Ramet, "The Yugoslav Press in Flux," in Pedro Ramet (ed.), *Yugoslavia in the 1980s* (Boulder: Westview Press, 1985).

31. See Sabrina P. Ramet, *Nihil Obstat: Religion, Politics, and Social Change in East-Central Europe and Russia* (Durham, N.C.: Duke University Press, 1998), pp. 165–166.

32. *NIN*, no. 1601 (15 November 1981), p. 9.

33. *NIN*, no. 1645 (11 July 1982), p. 10.

34. M. Čaldarević, *Komunisti i samoupravljanje* (Zagreb: FPN, 1967), p. 486, as cited in Simo S. Nenezić, "Divergentne koncepcije u SKJ o demokratskom centralizmu," in *Socijalizam*, Vol. 18, No. 1 (January 1975), p. 53.

35. See, for instance, "Jugoslawischer Theoretiker für Zweiparteiensystem," in *Osteuropäische Rundschau*, Vol. 13, No. 12 (December 1967), pp. 19–21.

36. Rade Končar, a Serb, was at the time chair of the Novi Beograd (city) party organization and a member of the party committee of the city of Belgrade. He was forced to resign these posts after the Congress.

37. CK SKJ Predsedništvo, *Ostvarivanje vodeće uloge SKJ u društvu i jačanje njegovog idejnog i akcionog jedinstva* (Belgrade: Komunist, 1984), pp. v–vii, as quoted in Wolfgang Höpken, "Party Monopoly and Political Change: The League of Communists since Tito's Death," in Ramet (ed.), *Yugoslavia in the 1980s*, p. 37.

38. See Vjekoslav Koprivnjak, "Protiv tendencije federalizacije Saveza komunista," in *Socijalizam*, Vol. 28, No. 1 (January 1985).

39. See, for instance, *Politika* (Belgrade) (17 January 1985).

40. For details, see Pedro Ramet, "Self-Management, Titoism, and the Apotheosis of Praxis," in Wayne S. Vucinich (ed.), *At the Brink of War and Peace: The Tito-Stalin Split in a*

Historic Perspective (New York: Brooklyn College Press, 1982), pp. 169–170, 174–177, 192–193.

41. Svetozar Stojanović, "Marks i ideologizacija marksizma—kritika jedne predrasudne moći" (based on a talk given in Novi Sad in December 1983), in *Gledišta*, Vol. 25, No. 1/2 (January-February 1984), pp. 28–33.

42. *Radio Free Europe Research* (24 July 1985), pp. 19–22.

43. Edvard Kardelj, *Democracy and Socialism*, trans. Margot and Boško Milosavljević (London: Summerfield Press, 1978), p. 69.

44. Stipe Šuvar, "Sloboda misli—da, ideološki i politički pluralizam—ne," in *Socijalizam*, Vol. 27, No. 7/8 (July-August 1984), p. 1129.

45. Miladin Korac, "Branko Horvat: 'Politička ekonomija socijalizma'—kritička analiza trećeg dela knjige," in *Socijalizam*, Vol. 27, No. 10 (October 1984), pp. 1518–1519, 1526–1530.

46. Koštunica and Čavoški, *Party Pluralism or Monism* (note 4). The book was originally published in Belgrade in summer 1983.

47. Radoslav Ratković, "Interes nije bazična kategorija," in *Socijalizam*, Vol. 27, No. 7/8 (July-August 1984), p. 1057.

48. *Večernje novosti* (Belgrade) (16 April 1985).

49. On the last of these points, see *Vjesnik* (Zagreb) (19 March 1985).

50. See, for instance, *Politika* (8 January 1985).

51. *Borba* (7/8 April 1984); *Duga* (Belgrade) (10 March 1984).

52. *Danas* (9 April 1984), trans. in JPRS, *East Europe Report*, No. EPS–84–076 (18 June 1984), p. 91.

53. *Borba* (7/8 April 1984).

54. For more details on these two proposals, see Pedro Ramet, "Apocalypse Culture and Social Change in Yugoslavia," in Ramet (ed.), *Yugoslavia in the 1980s*, pp. 19–20.

55. Belgrade home service (22 March 1984), trans. in *BBC Summary of World Broadcasts* (26 March 1984).

56. Tanjug (23 November 1984), trans. in *BBC Summary of World Broadcasts* (28 November 1984).

57. *Reuters* (25 November 1984), on *Nexis*.

58. Regarding Kosovo, see Slavko Gaber and Tonči Kuzmanič (eds.), *Zbornik: Kosovo—Srbija—Jugoslavija* (Ljubljana: Knjižna zbirka Krt, 1989); and Miloš Mišović, *Ko je tražio republiku: Kosovo 1945–1985* (Belgrade: Narodna knjiga, 1987).

59. Quoted in Höpken, "Party Monopoly," p. 41.

60. *Politika* (24 November 1984).

61. *Dnevnik* (Novi Sad) (21 April 1985), p. 3, trans. in Foreign Broadcast Information Service (FBIS), *Daily Report* (Eastern Europe), 2 May 1985, p. 17.

62. *Politika* (20 December 1984), p. 5, trans. in JPRS, *East Europe Report*, No. EPS-85-012 (23 January 1985), p. 29.

63. *Borba* (12–15 October 1984). See also the Editorial Report in JPRS, *East Europe Report*, No. EPS-84-135 (1 November 1984), 120.

64. Tanjug (14 November 1985), trans. in FBIS, *Daily Report* (Eastern Europe), 15 November 1985, p. 16.

65. Tanjug (18 November 1985), trans. in FBIS, *Daily Report* (Eastern Europe), 20 November 1985, p. 16.

66. Ibid., p. 17; and Tanjug (18 November 1985), trans. in FBIS, *Daily Report* (Eastern Europe), 26 November 1985, pp. 16–18.

67. Tanjug (24 October 1985), trans. in FBIS, *Daily Report* (Eastern Europe), 1 November 1985, p. 19.

68. *Politika* (20 April 1986).

69. *Politika* (24 April 1986).

70. Meier, *Wie Jugoslawien*, pp. 67–69.

71. *Vjesnik* (30 June 1986); also Tanjug (16 February 1986), trans. in FBIS, *Daily Report* (Eastern Europe), 20 February 1986, p. 13; and *Vjesnik* (29 June 1986).

72. *Vjesnik* (30 June 1986).

73. *Vjesnik* (27 June 1986).

74. *Vjesnik* (24 August 1985).

75. For details and discussion, see Pedro Ramet, "Yugoslavia: Stirrings from Below," in *South Slav Journal*, Vol. 10, No. 3 (Autumn 1987).

76. Quoted in Tim Judah, *The Serbs: History, Myth and the Destruction of Yugoslavia* (New Haven: Yale University Press, 1997), p. 157.

77. Ivo Banac, "The Dissolution of Yugoslav Historiography," in Sabrina Petra Ramet and Ljubiša S. Adamovich (eds.), *Beyond Yugoslavia: Politics, Economics, and Culture in a Shattered Community* (Boulder: Westview Press, 1995), pp. 49–50, 52–53.

78. Judah, *The Serbs*, p. 158.

79. *Memorandum of the Serbian Academy of Science and Arts* (1986), trans. Dennison Rusinow with Aleksandar and Sarah Nikolić, reprinted in Dennison Rusinow, "The Yugoslav Peoples," in Peter F. Sugar (ed.), *Eastern European Nationalism in the Twentieth Century* (Washington, D.C.: American University Press, 1995), p. 342.

80. EE/8183 Part 2, in *BBC Summary of World Broadcasts* (14 February 1986).

81. "U.S. Supreme Court Supports Yugoslavia on Extradition of Artuković," in *Yugoslav Review*, Vol. 7, No. 10, (1958), pp. 14–15.

82. Tanjug (15 February 1986), quoted in *Reuters* (15 February 1986), on *Nexis*. See also *Reuters* (20 March 1986), on *Nexis*; and EE/8233 Part 2, in *BBC Summary of World Broadcasts* (15 April 1986).

83. Željko Olujić, *Kako nisam obranio Andriju Artukovića* (Zagreb: Revije Vjesnik, 1991), pp. 217–250.

84. UPI (5 May 1987), on *Nexis*.

85. Milorad Pupovac, in interview with the author, Zagreb, 29 July 1997.

86. Silvije Degen, recalling his views at the time of the trial, in *Croatia Weekly* (Zagreb) (15 May 1998), p. 1.

CHAPTER TWO

◆

The Gathering Storm, 1987–1989

As the 1980s wore on, it became increasingly clear that the deepening economic crisis and the political inertia which characterized the system were profoundly incompatible. Rising ethnic frictions in Kosovo and, just below the surface, in Bosnia were straining the political fabric at another level too. Increasingly, voices were calling for a "return" to some imagined pristine centralism—calls originating largely among Serbs.

In 1987, the entire political picture changed virtually overnight. A forty-six-year-old banker-turned-politician named Slobodan Milošević, who had made his name in the early 1980s as Secretary of the Belgrade City Committee of the LCY and who had risen to the post of President of the Serbian Communist Party in May 1986, on the recommendation of his friend and mentor Ivan Stambolić, used his control of patronage to assume de facto control of Serbia. Turning against his erstwhile friend, Stambolić, who had served as best man at his wedding, Milošević first orchestrated the firing of Dragiša Pavlović, a key Stambolić supporter, as Belgrade party chief (in which position he had succeeded Milošević the year before); this took place at the Eighth Conference of the CC of the LC-Serbia on 28 September 1987. Pavlović was only the proverbial tip of the iceberg; his exit was accompanied by a wholesale firing of Stambolić supporters in the Serbian party apparatus. The conference did not merely put Stambolić on the defensive; it neutralized him. He remained in office for another ten weeks, increasingly unable to make any imprint on policy, and finally, on 14 December 1987, Stambolić too was fired.[1]

Now in control, Milošević quickly abandoned the long-standing strategies of the LCY and the Serbian party organization and set out to suppress the autonomous provinces (placing them fully under Serbian administration), to recentralize the system (at the expense of the autonomy of the other republics), and to rehabilitate the Serbian Church, coopting it to serve as the vehicle of a revived Serbian nationalism. His policies destroyed what remained of any consensus in the system, and by late

1989, for all practical purposes (legislative, economic, cultural), Yugoslavia had already ceased to exist. In its place were four emerging national environments which claimed the primary loyalty of their citizens: Slovenia, Croatia, Serbia (including the autonomous provinces of Kosovo and Vojvodina, as well as the republic of Montenegro), and Macedonia. These four regions were increasingly self-contained and even isolated from one another, and cultural contact between them, at one time actively stimulated by the party, had become, by then, largely superficial. Serbian and Slovenian nationalism was in full blaze, while in Croatia, despite a certain passivity which could be dated to the suppression of the "Croatian Spring" in December 1971, there was a marked hostility toward everything Serbian, and the traditional Western orientation was reasserting itself. Only in Macedonia did one still find a real sense of "Yugoslavism," although even there increasing signs of grumbling about Macedonia's alleged second-rate status in the federation were apparent. Finally, multiethnic Bosnia-Herzegovina—43.77 percent "ethnic Muslim," 31.46 percent Serbian, and 17.34 percent Croatian (in 1991)—was internally divided and its political infrastructure shattered along ethnic lines. Bosnian officials openly described the political situation in the republic as "difficult"; some observers called Greater Serbian nationalism the greatest problem at this point, and others charged that fundamentalist Islam was driving Bosnian Serbs to take flight.[2]

The Serb-Croat conflict was always at the center of political strife in the country, at least potentially, and, in the fragile conditions associated with the rise of Slobodan Milošević in Serbia, reemerged as the pivotal conflict in Yugoslavia. Serbian politicians spread stories of a "Vatican-Comintern conspiracy" (supposedly designed in part to benefit Croatia) and accused Croatian politicians of genocidal tendencies. Radio Mileva in Belgrade accused Croat Ante Marković, the chair of the Federal Executive Council, of being a CIA agent, and Serbian poet Gojko Djogo's description of the Croatian Communist authorities as "pro-*Ustaša*" was given publicity.[3] At the same time, Serbs talked of the Orthodox (hence "Serbian") ancestry of Croatia's Dalmatian population, revived demands for autonomy for Serbs living in Croatia, and even talked of the political rehabilitation of wartime Chetnik leader Draža Mihailović.[4]

Croatian politicians in turn accused Serbian leader Slobodan Milošević of "Stalinist" and "unitarist" tendencies and charged that Serbian politicians were trying to destabilize and neutralize Croatia.[5] Hence, when economist Jovo Opačić attempted to organize a Serbian cultural society in Croatia in July 1989, Croatia's Communist leaders had him arrested and tried.

In quasi-confederal Yugoslavia, the six constituent republics already enjoyed vast autonomy and operated, to a considerable extent, as independent mini-states. This system had been developed in the course of the late 1960s and early 1970s in order to satisfy the desires of the distinct nationality groups for a measure of political self-determination, while at the same time preserving the Communist power monopoly. The alternate route—maintaining a unified political system but opening it up to other parties—had been rejected. Conscious of the relationship between pluralization and self-determination, the Communists in effect substituted regional pluralization (administrative decentralization and the creation of a plurality of autonomous Communist organizations) for political pluralization (multiparty democracy) and justified the substitution by arguing that a multiparty system would only lead to fratricidal war in Yugoslav conditions. To maintain this fiction, Yugoslav politicians stoked the fires of interethnic distrust by constant commentaries on the ethnic genocides of World War II. Indeed, for many, the conflict of 1991–1995 seemed to figure as a return to and a continuation of that earlier war.

Regional pluralization quickly became a powerful force for liberalization—both because some of the leading advocates of decentralization were also liberals and because the division of power created alternatives within the system: for example, people who were unable to publish a text in one republic might turn around and publish it in another republic.

This system could function reasonably smoothly as long as two conditions were present. First, it was necessary to have a final arbiter who could resolve interrepublican differences if need be. President Josip Broz Tito functioned as this arbiter until his death in May 1980; but the system he bequeathed to Yugoslavia, based on collective decisionmaking at all levels and the right of veto by any republic in many areas of decisionmaking, lacked such an arbiter. The principle of consensus was mandated for all state bodies, with a partial exception only for the state presidency. But even this body was expected to observe the rule of consensus where important decisions, such as the deployment of the army, were concerned.

Second, the system presumed a degree of prosperity such as existed in the later 1970s. When the economy eroded, however, the political seams were exposed to full view and the "quasi-legitimacy" of the system disintegrated. Now, with inflation roaring at more than 1,000 percent annually and incomes sagging below minimal levels, people were becoming desperate. In some cities, people decided to live without electricity, since they could not pay the bills.[6] Crime also soared, and the authorities linked the increase with economic crisis.[7] In Montenegro, 30,000 desperate citizens took to the streets in August 1989 to protest against hunger and poverty and to demand effective action.[8] Increasingly, there was talk of the need to revitalize the economy.

The Second Coup

Milošević's overthrow of Stambolić, Pavlović, and their adherents was only the first of two coups Milošević carried out. The second coup was a more complex operation, in which Milošević used a combination of pressure from organized street demonstrations and redrafting of constitutional and legal documents to take effective control in Kosovo, Vojvodina, and Montenegro. Unlike his lethargic and often hesitant cohorts in the LCY, Milošević moved with dazzling celerity and certainty of purpose. As early as 11 January 1988, the Serbian Assembly began work on revising Serbia's constitution with the express purpose of whittling down the autonomy of the two provinces. As resistance to these changes was voiced in the two provinces, Milošević moved to eliminate the voices of dissent. In May 1988, Azem Vllasi was removed from the post of chairman of the party leadership in Kosovo; his immediate replacement, Kaqusha Jashari, was no protégé of Milošević, but Vllasi's removal had sent a strong signal to the Kosovar party that it could not ignore Milošević's programmatic preferences. In fact, Jashari continued to argue for preservation of the status quo, and, in a report to a conference of the LC-Kosovo at the end of June 1988, shortly after the publication of a new draft of the Serbian constitution that proposed to recentralize the Republic of Serbia, she noted that the Serbian constitutional revisions then in progress would have a negative impact on Kosovo's autonomous status. She also pointed out that in discussions at the republic level, there was mention only of the rights and jurisdiction of the Republic of Serbia, while nothing was conceded to either Kosovo or Vojvodina.[9] Meanwhile, resistance also emerged in Vojvodina, where politicians such as Boško Krunić, Djordje Stojšic, Milovan Šogorov, and others were quite frank about their distaste for Milošević's so-called bureaucratic revolution.

Milošević now mobilized several hundred Serbs from Kosovo, who were brought to Novi Sad, where they organized two days of antigovernment protests beginning on 7 July. Local leaders were shaken, but refused to buckle to pressure from the streets. At this point, the LCY Presidium was chaired by Croat Stipe Šuvar, a chain-smoking old-style socialist whom Branka Magaš once described as "a dangerous man"[10] and who, when I talked with him in August 1997, spoke in a dry monotone. To the surprise of some observers, the LCY Presidium, instead of endorsing the leadership of Vojvodina, issued a declaration on 30 July endorsing Milošević's position, which was that Krunić and the other politicians in Vojvodina were guilty of "factionalism." The declaration went further and held that, however illegal the demonstrations may have been, the Vojvodina leadership should have felt obliged to receive a delegation from the demonstrators and, further, to meet with the demonstrators en masse![11] Moreover, in taking this position, the LCY Presidium was going against the clear sentiment predominating in the CC, which understandably felt that a group of street demonstrators did not possess the right to demand the resignation of an elected leadership. Indeed, at a CC meeting in late July, Vidoje Žarković, a delegate from Montenegro, "compared the style of the Serbian leader with that of the Chinese Cultural Revolution."[12] The battle for Vojvodina had barely begun, but even before that battle was resolved—indeed, immediately after the CC session of late July—Serbs of Kosovo established a committee to organize street demonstrations, or "meetings" as they were euphemistically called. Such "meetings" were, strictly speaking, illegal under the 1974 constitution, but at the end of September, the army leadership, which was bound by oath to uphold the federal constitution, expressly endorsed the holding of illegal "meetings," provided only that their participants described their purpose as involving the securing of their "rights," broadly defined.[13]

On 5 October, about 100,000 Serbs, once again mostly from Kosovo and adjacent areas in southern Serbia, assembled in Novi Sad. The next day, these supporters of Milošević's line staged a massive demonstration to demand the resignation of the elected leadership of the province. Ordinarily, one would not expect the leaders of one province to be at all troubled by angry protests from permanent residents of another province, but tensions in Yugoslavia were running so high and the sense of crisis was so intense, that oddities such as this became almost routine. Their confidence shaken, the leaders of Vojvodina tendered their resignations, which were subsequently ratified by the CC of the Vojvodinan party organization in a vote of eighty-seven to ten.[14] Milošević now placed his supporters in key positions in that province, thereby obtaining de facto control over the judiciary, the police, social and financial planning, and other key sectors in the provincial administration.

On 7 October, equally large crowds of pro-Milošević agitators descended on government buildings in Titograd in hopes of toppling the Montenegrin leadership in the same way. Instead of crumbling, however, the Montenegrin leadership brought out the police to disperse the demonstrators. Two days later, almost as if nothing of consequence had happened in Montenegro, Raif Dizdarević, chair of the state presidency, made a televised address expostulating the Serbian line; addressing himself to all Yugoslavs, Dizdarević said that it was time for "real reforms" and demanded that a package of constitutional amendments prepared by the Serbian party and made public two months earlier be adopted in toto. Waking briefly, as it were, from its slumber, the LCY Presidium managed, at its Seventeenth Session on 17 October, to eject Milošević's close ally, Dušan Čkrebić, as a sign of its fundamental opposition to Milošević's methods. Thereupon, Milošević announced that he did not accept the vote against Čkrebić.[15]

But the Milošević juggernaut hardly paused. On 17 November 1988, the leadership of the Kosovar party was forced to resign, and Rahman Morina, who had been named provincial police chief under Vllasi, was put in charge of the provincial party apparatus. With the two provinces at least tamed, Milošević turned his attention once more to Montenegro, where the tactic of "meetings" again proved its worth. In early January 1989, Milošević's followers staged massive demonstrations in Titograd. This time the demonstrations produced the desired effect, and on 11 January 1989 the top figures in Montenegro's leadership stepped down, among them former Yugoslav Prime Minister Djuranović. The young Milošević-loyalist Momir Bulatović was installed as party chief in Montenegro; the mustachioed Bulatović, with his ample shock of hair, cut a dashing figure, but he revealed few, if any, ideas of his own at the time. Milošević had justified the pacification of the provinces by appealing to the principle of the supposed sanctity of a unified republic apparatus within Serbia, but the conquest of Montenegro could not be justified in this way. As Milošević put his supporters into office in that republic, shock waves rippled through the rest of the country. Indeed, the second coup was virtually complete.

Milošević now controlled four of the eight federal units de facto, and the Serbian constitutional amendments in preparation, once adopted, promised to assure Milošević also of de jure authority in the two provinces. For the time being, the Kosovar delegate to the state presidency remained an appointee of the previous (independent) leadership, but the pressure now generated by Milošević assured that this delegate, like the other three in what came to be called "the Serbian bloc," generally voted in accord with the Serbian line. Later, the Serbian Assembly would even see fit to name "the delegate of the Kosovo Assembly," even though such an action could not be grounded on any constitutional provision or legal act.[16] Moreover, several of Macedonia's leaders, including Lazar Koliševski, Lazar Mojsov, and Milan Pančevski, were broadly sympathetic to Milošević's aspirations to bring the provinces under control—perhaps in part because Macedonia's own Albanians remained restive, staging protest demonstrations in Kumanovo in August 1988 and Gostivar in October 1988.[17] The result was that Macedonia often voted with the "Serbian bloc" in the state presidency, until Milošević alienated Skopje with his foolhardy draft law which proposed to allow Serb settlers from the interwar era who had been barred from Macedonia after World War II to "reclaim" land in Macedonia.[18]

The final act in the second coup involved downgrading the subsequent abolition of the two hitherto autonomous provinces. On 22 February 1989, the constitutional commission of the Serbian Assembly unanimously accepted the controversial amendments that had been presented by the Serbian leadership. Two days later, the Serbian Assembly itself unanimously approved these same amendments. The tale surrounding these events will be told in somewhat more detail in Chapter 13. Suffice it here to note that on 27 February the state presidency declared the introduction of "special measures" in Kosovo. There were two elements of procedural irregularity here. The first is that the state presidency specifically met when the Slovenian representative (Stane Dolanc), whose government was opposed to this approach, was out of the country; the second is that Yugoslav law did not provide for anything called "special measures." On 2 March Azem Vllasi and two other Albanians were arrested, and Serbian police held private meetings with members of the provincial Assembly to "persuade" them to vote yes on the proposed amendments. Serbian police "persuasion" was effective, and on 24 March, of the 187 deputies in the three houses of the provincial parliament, only 10 voted against the constitutional amendments.[19]

Tomislav Sekulić (a Serb) became the new provincial party chief; as an "old settler," he wanted to keep the lines of communication with Albanians open. He lasted about a year before being pushed to the margins. At that point, the fiction of Kosovar provincial status was barely being honored at all, and instead of a provincial party chief, Kosovo was assigned a governor of sorts, Momčilo Trajković, who was granted unrestricted powers of administration.[20] Less than a week after his appointment, Serbian authorities sealed the chambers of the provincial assembly (on 2 July 1990). Three days later, the Serbian government declared the dissolution of the provincial parliament and threatened its (114) deputies with prosecution, because of their belated resistance to Serbian actions. Most of them went underground, hiding or fleeing to Slovenia or Croatia. The second coup was complete.

The Mobilization of Slovenia

In the meantime, there were stirrings in Slovenia. Already in February 1987, the Slovenian journal *Nova Revija* published a set of articles advancing a "Slovenian national program" which included political independence. The weekly magazine of the

Slovenian Youth Organization, *Mladina*, was even more wayward and was rapidly establishing itself as a major forum of dissident opinion. *Mladina* seemed to be especially critical of the army, publishing a negative article about the sales of Yugoslav weaponry to Ethiopia and about the use of Yugoslavia People's Army (JNA) conscripts to build an elegant Adriatic villa for then–Defense Minister Admiral Branko Mamula. The generals convened a meeting of its Military Council to discuss the evolving situation in Slovenia. The council found that *Mladina* was pursuing a "counter-revolutionary" line. Comparing *Mladina* to the Polish independent trade union "Solidarity," General Veljko Kadijević, a Croatian Serb who had served as a political commissar during the Partisan resistance and who had just recently taken over as Minister of Defense, declared that developments in Slovenia constituted an attack on the army.[21]

Less than a month later, *Mladina* came into possession of a secret document from the Ljubljana Military District 5044-3 of 8 January 1988, which outlined steps to be taken in introducing martial law in the country. Franci Zavrl, the magazine's editor, passed the document along to Janez Janša, a firebrand known for his vocal demands that the military budget (which absorbed about 70 percent of the federal budget in 1988)[22] be drastically slashed, asking him to prepare a story. Janša now obtained a transcript of the CC's 25 March 1988 session, and on 13 May *Mladina* prepared a story alleging that the army had drawn up a list of Slovenes it planned to arrest in order to abort Slovenia's liberal evolution; the Slovenian leadership intervened to block its publication, however. The military now arrested Janša, Zavrl, army sergeant Ivan Borštner, who had stolen the incriminating document, and David Tasić, the *Mladina* journalist to whom the document was first given. The army put the four on trial, creating a sensation throughout Slovenia. It was bad enough that the army had planned a coup; now the army was compounding its transgression by putting Slovenia's advocates on trial. Moreover, waiving aside Slovene law, the army conducted the trial in Ljubljana, but in Serbo-Croatian. The Slovene public was outraged three times over and amassed for huge demonstrations in downtown Ljubljana. A Committee for the Defense of Human Rights was hurriedly formed, under the chairmanship of Igor Bavčar, and it began issuing periodical bulletins in English. It also circulated petitions on behalf of "the Slovene Four."[23] More than 100,000 persons signed protest petitions drawn up by this committee; protests were also registered by more than 1,000 collective organizations, including the local trade union and the Slovenian Bishops' Conference of the Roman Catholic Church. On 22 June 1988, at least 40,000 persons from all over Slovenia flocked to Ljubljana's Liberation Square for a demonstration in protest of the trial; it was the largest public gathering of Slovenes since World War II.[24]

It was out of this milieu—*Nova Revija*, *Mladina*, human rights activists, and active supporters of "the Slovene Four"—that an active "opposition" now emerged in Slovenia. As already mentioned, there was a new generation in control in the Slovenian party organization, and as time wore on, the leading figures in this new generation cooperated increasingly with leading figures in the "opposition;" both groups were concerned to defend Slovenia against the encroachment of either army or Milošević. Indeed, it became steadily more and more difficult to refer to "government and opposition" in Slovenia; the truth was that both Communists and noncommunists in Slovenia were highly critical of Milošević and dedicated to a vision of a reformed, democratic Slovenia. In this context, several embryonic political parties were launched in the course of the next few months, including the Social Democratic Alliance, the Slovenian Democratic Union, the Slovenian Christian Socialist Movement, and a "Green" Party. Meanwhile, a previously existing Slovenian Peasant Union experienced rapid growth and by September 1989 claimed some 25,000 members from all parts of Slovenia.[25]

This pluralization was tolerated by the Slovenian authorities, and this tolerance in turn encouraged both the vibrant Slovenian Youth Organization and the long stagnant Socialist Alliance—both nominally transmission belts for party policy—to begin plans to transform themselves into independent political parties and to field their own candidates in Slovenia's spring 1990 elections.[26]

It was in the early stages of this process that Ciril Ribičič and Zdravko Tomac—the former a member of the CC of the LC-Slovenia and the latter a member of the political science faculty of the University of Zagreb—coauthored a book in which they argued for the "de-etatization" of the economy and the strengthening of certain features of the federation in order to assure optimal conditions for the development of a modern market economy. As they argued, "A new economic system requires a new political system, a new economic system cannot be built within the framework of the old political system."[27]

By 1989, there was a growing consensus in Yugoslavia that the status quo could not endure much longer. In such conditions, solutions which only a year or two earlier would have sounded extreme were now openly discussed. In late summer 1989, for example, Vladimir Rabzelj, a Slovenian writer, proposed the secession of Slovenia and Croatia and their association in a new confederal state.[28] Along parallel lines, Serbian writer Antonije Isaković, famous for his novels *Tren 1* and *Tren 2*, argued for the redrawing of republic boundaries and the confederalization of the system.[29] Milošević would publicly embrace this concept that republic boundaries be redrawn somewhat later, in June 1990.

Rabzelj's proposal did not come out of the blue. As early as 8 May 1989, Slovenian opposition groups had issued a "May Declaration" registering their demand for state independence within a confederal union. The Slovenian political establishment responded the following month with the issuance of a "Fundamental Charter of Slovenia," which spelled out the Slovenian political elite's commitment to assuring the protection of human rights, democracy, and the sovereignty of the Slovenian people. A constitutional commission was appointed under the chairmanship of Miran Potrč and entrusted with the task of preparing a series of amendments to realize the objectives stated in the charter. By August these amendments were ready and at the end of September, defying bitter criticism from the Serbian party, the army leadership, and the federal leadership, the Slovenian Assembly adopted the amendments.

These amendments claimed for Slovenia the right of secession as well as the inalienable right to approve or disapprove the proclamation by federal authorities of extraordinary measures in their republic and the exclusive right to make determinations concerning the movement of military personnel in the territory of the republic. This highly controversial move, which excited protest meetings in Montenegro and which was immediately taken to the Federal Constitutional Court for resolution, was thus only symptomatic of the breakdown of the sense of community, of consensus on the rules of the game.[30]

In spite of the proactive orientation of the LC-Slovenia, its membership declined steadily during the second half of the 1980s. Party organizations at many factories and enterprises completely disintegrated, as Ciril Ribičič admitted to me in 1989.[31] To the extent that the party still commanded some prestige, it was in part attributable to the party's popular leader, Milan Kučan, who was easily the most popular politician in that republic (as demonstrated by his subsequent election as Slovenia's president in the free elections of spring 1990).

The Slovenes claimed that their republic, the richest and most efficient in the country, was being milked by the less efficient republics. Partly for that reason, they jealously guarded their autonomy and, at a minimum, hoped to preserve the quasi-confederal character of the system. In the wake of the trial of "the Four," the Slovenes increasingly talked about the virtues of "asymmetric federation"—an idea that originated with a graduate student named Mitja Žagar.[32] Under this concept, the Slovenes would enjoy certain special prerogatives not enjoyed by other republics. A key demand associated with this concept was for a special Slovenian military district, with all Slovenian recruits serving in Slovenian regiments and Slovenian as the local language of command. Secession was described by essentially all Slovenes in September 1989 as a "last resort," if all else should fail. Furthermore, Ribičič, in a speech to the Slovenian CC on 26 September, described the new amendment sanctioning secession as consistent with the existing federal constitution.[33]

The party leaderships of Serbia, Montenegro, and Bosnia looked with dismay at Slovenian developments. The Yugoslav collective presidency at first demanded that the proposed Slovenian amendments be discussed at one of its sessions—but the Slovenian presidency categorically rejected the suggestion.[34] Arguments were heard in Belgrade that whatever the Slovenes might say, their amendments, including the amendment concerning secession, were in fact contrary to the federal constitution. When the Slovenes remained undaunted, others talked of summoning an urgent, extraordinary session of the Federal Assembly.[35] The fact that the Slovenes proceeded with adoption of their amendments showed that they did not intend to allow themselves to be intimidated in this way. Serbian political elites now called on Serbian enterprises to boycott the Slovenian market; responding to this call, Serbian enterprises canceled orders for Slovenian goods and services, refused to fulfill Slovenian orders for Serbian goods and services, and terminated all forms of economic cooperation. The unity of the country had been sundered with this declaration of economic war.

The Serbian National Revival and Its Effects

The Serbian party championed a very different solution. As early as September 1981, sounding a call that Milošević would echo later, Ivan Stambolić had argued that a "unified and strong Serbia" was a prerequisite for a strong Yugoslavia.[36] The extension of vast autonomy to the autonomous provinces of Kosovo and Vojvodina, he argued, had resulted not merely in the federalization of Serbia, but in its effective disintegration.[37] By 1984, Serbia was actively pressing for the reduction of the autonomy of the provinces as well as for an expansion of the decisionmaking powers of the federal organs vis-à-vis the republics. The Serbs thus were once more championing a strong center—a position often tainted with the pejorative term "unitarism" in Yugoslav parlance. Slobodan Milošević, at the time a member of the Serbian CC, struck a defiant note. "We must free ourselves of the complex of unitarism," he said in November 1984. "Serbian Communists have never been champions of unitarism. On the contrary, we have throttled every attempt at such a policy. The Serbian Communists have long been saddled with a complex about unitarism, and unjustly so, and made to feel guilty for a relationship with the Serbian bourgeoisie."[38]

Despite the clarity of the Serbian position, there seemed to be little progress toward realizing the objectives of the Serbian party. Stambolić, who had served as president of the Serbian CC since April 1984, was seen by many as a careerist whose commitment to the Serbian program was largely formal. Milošević, in particular, wanted a new strategy. By summer 1987, the waxing conflict between Milošević and Stambolić was in the open, and, as already noted, by the end of the year Stambolić had been forced to resign.

In the months after this coup, Milošević consolidated more power than any Yugoslav leader had enjoyed since Tito—although with the important reservation that Milošević's power was limited to the republics of Serbia and Montenegro. Milošević removed a large number of party functionaries and replaced many of the journalists at the "Politika" publishing house. Risto Lazarov, a veteran Macedonian journalist, served as Director-General of Tanjug 1990–1992, just as Milošević was turning up the heat. Lazarov told me in 1995, "Every day we had to fight with Milošević; he was trying to penetrate Tanjug with his people but it was not possible for him to achieve his aims overnight."[39] But the pressure continued and Lazarov eventually gave up in disgust and returned to Skopje, where he established *Balkan Forum*, an independent quarterly journal. Meanwhile, Milošević appealed to Serbian pride and Serbian nationalism—for example, by introducing more Cyrillic in a republic which had, for years, been shifting more and more to the Latin alphabet. He granted the Serbian Orthodox Church permission to build new churches and to restore old ones and contributed to creating a mood intolerant of Serbs who were non-Orthodox, as several people told me in Belgrade in 1989. By summer 1989, the Serbian Assembly was weighing which of two traditional hymns to adopt as the official anthem of Serbia: the popular but militant song "March to the Drina," composed by Stanislav Binički after a Serbian military victory in 1914, or "Tamo daleko" ("There, afar"), composed in 1916 by an unknown hand while the Serbian army was in exile on the Greek island of Corfu.[40] In Tito's time, part of the text of "Tamo daleko" had been banned.

All of these measures, but especially the measures to erode the autonomy of the provinces, described earlier, were enormously popular among Serbs broadly, and Milošević was genuinely loved by many (though not all) Serbs as no other leader had been since Chetnik leader Draža Mihailović. But the very reasons which endeared him to nationalist and traditionalist elements among the Serbs made him hated and feared in Croatia and Slovenia. Milošević was a unifying force among Serbs, but a divisive force in Yugoslavia as a whole.

In the course of 1989, Milošević tried to create a base of support among non-Serbs by talking about a program of "anti-bureaucratic revolution." This campaign was widely viewed with a combination of distrust and cynicism outside Serbia, however, and Croats in particular were mindful of the fact that Serbian nationalists were raising awkward issues, among them:

- Serbs began to talk about the large-scale transfer of industry from Serbia to Croatia and Bosnia in the years 1945–1951, a transfer which had been part of an effort to move factories away from areas that might fall rapidly to Soviet control in the event of a Soviet bloc invasion, but that Serbs now said had been intended to weaken Serbia;
- Serbs now talked of the "Orthodox" origin of Dalmatian Croats;
- Serbs revived a long latent claim that Montenegrins were actually Serbs, and many Montenegrins responded warmly (though such a claim had been taboo as long as Tito was in power);
- Serbs, stoked by the Serbian Academy's incendiary Memorandum, attacked the entire legacy of Tito, arguing that it had been above all anti-Serbian in thrust, and suggested that it was time to weed out the confederal elements introduced by Tito (such as the veto system).[41]

Slovenia, Croatia, and Macedonia responded by trying to defend Tito's legacy, and Tito personally, against Serbian attacks. In the process, Tito received support in unlikely quarters. For example, Miko Tripalo, the Croatian party secretary purged by Tito in December 1971 for "liberalism," told me in September 1989, "Croatia can, at this point, be satisfied with its position in the federation. But it is gravely threatened by Milošević, who is trying to bring about a totalitarian revolution and achieve Greater Serbian hegemony. This threatens not only Croatia, but the other republics as well. It is critical, in these circumstances, to defend Tito. He is the symbol of everything that has been achieved."[42]

Milošević's strategy was both populist and nationalist. In endeavoring to undermine the autonomy of the autonomous provinces (successfully) and to restore the primacy of the federal government (unsuccessfully), he restored to grace many Serbian and Montenegrin dissidents, including Milovan Djilas and the controversial poet Gojko Djogo. He restored the *Praxis* philosophers to positions of eminence (and some of them returned the compliment by joining Milošević's crusade). He allowed rumors to circulate already in the late 1980s about an eventual rehabilitation of Draža Mihailović, whom Tito had executed in 1946 (fulfilling the promise implied in these rumors in 1992, when he arranged for a monument to be erected in Mihailović's honor).[43] By the end of 1989, it was essentially impossible to speak of an opposition in Serbia: most of the opposition had gone over to Milošević. For example, rock singer Bora Djordjević, elected in 1989 to the Serbian Writers' Association in recognition of his prolific poetry, wrote nationalist poems about Kosovo[44] and praised Milošević for what he had done in the provinces. Throughout Serbia, Kosovo was in the air. Serbs gloated over their "reconquest" of the province. The shelves of Serbian bookstores filled with books about Kosovo. Musical artists dedicated songs to Kosovo.[45] There was even a new perfume, "Miss 1389"—an allusion to the Battle of Kosovo of that year, when an invading Turkish army had decimated the Serbian army, leaving the Kingdom of Serbia helpless and preparing the way for the Ottoman conquest of Serbia seventy years later. The Orthodox Church likewise waxed enthusiastic and in June 1989 published an interesting St. Vitus' Day message in its newspaper, *Glas crkve*, that said, among other things: "The recent proclamation of the Republic Constitution restored to Serbia the sovereignty of the state over the whole of its territory, while retaining the existence of the two autonomies in its composition—*which can be accepted only as a temporary solution.*"[46]

The response of the Serbian opposition to Milošević's rise had parallels in the other republics as well. It would be too much to speak of an "alliance" between regional elites and their "oppositions," but it was obvious to all concerned that there was a partial symbiosis of purpose between the Serbian political elite and the Serbian opposition and between the Slovenian political elite and the Slovenian opposition, and the beginnings of an awareness in at least some sectors of the Croatian public that there were interests shared between the Croatian Communist establishment and estranged noncommunist elites who were about to organize themselves; the suppression of the Serbian "Zora" society and imprisonment of its principal organizer by the Croatian Communist regime in summer 1989—to be discussed more fully in the next chapter—was one reflection of this emerging, partial symbiosis in Croatia. This had consequences both for the internal politics of each republic and for the wider political climate in the country as a whole. (On the other hand, the Serbian Writers' Association, infused by nationalism as it might be, boldly issued a seven-point appeal for political pluralism on 10 May, accusing Serbia's leadership of obstructing democracy.)[47]

Directly related to this was the form assumed by the emergent national revival in Yugoslavia. Throughout the country there was a renewed interest in the past, especially in the national literature and national history. But in every case, this revival focused on the local nationality; in no instance did this revival assume an all-Yugoslav dimension. For example, in Serbia the revival of interest in earlier Serbian writers Njegoš, Ivo Andrić, and Miloš Crnjanski, which had begun at least a decade earlier, deepened and became politicized; there was increased interest as well in contemporary Serbian writers Dobrica Ćosić, Matija Becković, and Vuk Drašković. In Slovenia, the literary revival focused on the earlier Slovenian writers Primož Trubar, France Prešeren, and Ivan Cankar, with strong interest in such contemporary Slovenian writers as Andrija Hieng, Rudi Šeligo, Tomas Salamun, and Drago Jančar. In both cases, the interest in the literary past was growing in direct proportion to the rise in national consciousness and, in the Slovenian case, to the growth of interest in Slovenian sovereignty.[48]

The national revival was also reflected, in part, in the growth of underground cultural groups. The cultural underground saw, in particular, the sprouting of multimedia "new art" groups in several cities: Neue Slowenische Kunst (New Slovenian Art) in Ljubljana, Novi Evropski Poredak (New European Order) in Zagreb, Autopsija in Ruma (near Belgrade), Aporea (Apokrifalna Realnost, or Apocryphal Reality) in Skopje, and Metropolie Trans in Osijek. These groups infused their art with political meanings, in multimedia "happenings" that featured avant-garde music. Neue Slowenische Kunst (with its rock group, Laibach) is the best-known group in the West, because of its strident coquetting with totalitarianism and expert marketing; the group also distributed, at one point, a map showing Slovenian settlements at their greatest extent (in the seventeenth century)—which, given the quasi-Nazi effect of their music, suggested a kind of "Slowenien über Alles." Aporea, by contrast, looked to the more distant past—to the Byzantine Empire—for inspiration. The result was innovative music with strong liturgical sources and overtones. But in much the same way that Neue Slowenische Kunst came across as "foreign" to most Yugoslavs outside Slovenia, Aporea appealed even more strictly to a Macedonian audience, for only in Macedonia does Byzantium stir the soul. Nor is it merely a question of historical imagery; it is a question of differing national values.

At the most fundamental level, the peoples of Yugoslavia lost the ability to understand each other—because they ceased to understand each other's values and concerns or each other's perceptions. The president of the Serbian Writers' Association told me, for instance, that "the Albanians in Yugoslavia have more rights than minorities in any other country. They have their academy of sciences, their university, their institutes for language and culture, all the perquisites of cultural autonomy. The only thing they lack is their own national state on the territory of Serbia. The Serbs in Croatia do not enjoy as many rights as the Albanians in Kosovo."[49] To a Serb, this statement was perfectly clear and rational (never mind that all the institutions mentioned here were shut down or Serbanized within the next three to four years). To a Croat or a Slovene or a Macedonian, however, this statement was essentially unintelligible and came across, at best, as the emotionally charged lament of a Serbian nationalist.

Political and cultural ethnocentrism was reinforced by the tendency of Yugoslavia's nationality groups to read "their own" newspapers, as will be documented in the next section. As Goran Bregović, the leader of the White Button rock group, told me in 1989, "The Yugoslav idea is starting to become unpopular in Yugoslavia.

Nobody wants to be Yugoslav anymore. People want to be Serbian or Croatian or Slovenian. Yugoslavia doesn't mean anything anymore."[50]

Accompanying these developments was a revived interest in monarchy. Almost no one was seriously thinking of restoring the monarchy (although a Yugoslav opinion poll conducted in late 1988 showed that 5 percent of Slovenes would ideally have preferred a monarchical government), but in Serbia, Croatia, and Montenegro, there were signs of a "pop" nostalgia for kings and queens. In Serbia, for example, Princess Jelena Karadjordjević (who was nominally living in Paris and Peru) was invited by the Serbian patriarchate to attend the six-hundredth-anniversary celebrations of the Battle of Kosovo and received permission from Milošević to do so. The Orthodox Church's nostalgia for the monarchy was also shown in its periodical *Crkveni život*, which in 1989 featured a portrait of King Aleksandar on its front page.[51] Also in Serbia, on 10 September 1989, the remains of King Lazar were ceremoniously reinterred at the monastery of Ravanica, while local citizens hoisted a huge banner displaying the fourteenth-century king's likeness,[52] and there was talk of transporting the last remains of King Petar II back to Yugoslavia for burial in Oplenac.[53] Meanwhile, in Montenegro, the republic presidency agreed to receive back the remains of Montenegrin King Nikola I and his family, and arrangements were made for transporting them back from San Remo.[54] And in Croatia, the decision was made to restore the equestrian statue of Ban Josip Jelačić, the nineteenth-century governor of Croatia, to the Square of the Republic (from which it had been removed in July 1947).[55] Jelačić, a loyal retainer of the Habsburgs, had been condemned by Marx for his role in suppressing the short-lived Hungarian republic (1848–1849) and accordingly became an important symbol for anticommunist sentiment in Croatia.

As Yugoslav unity disintegrated and nostalgia for monarchy waxed, Crown Prince Alexander, heir to the throne of the Kingdom of Serbs, Croats, and Slovenes, offered himself as a potential king in a revived kingdom. He argued that he could provide an important symbol of unity and that no other symbol could do the same. Despite his Serbian blood, Alexander had lived basically his entire life in England and was, for all practical purposes, a refined English gentleman first and foremost. He had not been entangled in the politics of Communist and postcommunist Yugoslavia—a fact which encouraged some Yugoslavs to consider him a viable candidate. So removed from Yugoslavia was Alexander, in fact, that as of 1991, he was trying to learn Serbo-Croatian from a tutor. But English or not, Alexander had no power base of his own, and political discussions in the country made no reference to him. With some qualifications where Alexander is concerned (in that his popularity seemed to be greater among émigré Yugoslavs than among Yugoslavs in the country), the revival of interest in the monarchy, thus, was always nationally specific (Serbian, Croatian, Montenegrin) and thus likewise reflected the fragmentation of the country into four environments.

The Media and the Dissolution of the SFRY

The growing fragmentation of the country was also reflected in the republicanization of the press and was one of a number of factors pushing the country toward disintegration.[56] People in Bosnia commonly said that local Muslims read the Bosnian Republic press (*Oslobodjenje, AS*), local Croats read the Croatian Republic press (chiefly *Vjesnik* and *Večernji list*), and Bosnian Serbs read the Serbian Republic press (chiefly *Politika*, but also *Politika ekspres*). In October 1989, Belgrade's *Borba* published the results of a public opinion poll in which 120 persons (20 per republic) were asked which papers they considered the most influential in the country, which they most respected, which they least respected, and which they read most frequently. Although the results for Slovenia and Macedonia were clearly affected by the fact that the people of these republics speak different languages, it was clear that for all republics there was a close correlation between republic of residence and preferences for newspapers and periodicals.

Only Macedonians (8 percent), for example, cited the Skopje daily, *Nova Makedonija*, as one of the most influential papers in the country, and only Slovenes cited Slovenian periodicals (*Delo*, 18 percent; *Mladina*, 11 percent; and *Večer*, 7 percent) among the most influential. Fifty-four percent of Serbs mentioned *Politika*, but only 8 percent of Croats did so. Only residents of Croatia and Bosnia cited the Croatian press.[57]

Asked which periodicals they most respected, 54 percent of Serbs cited a Serbian periodical, though 14 percent mentioned the Croatian weekly magazine *Start*. Fifty-eight percent of Croats cited a Croatian periodical (*Slobodna Dalmacija* was the most often mentioned, with 19 percent of Croats citing this paper). Fifty-eight percent of Montenegrins cited either a Montenegrin or a Serbian periodical. The results in the other republics were more mixed.

In terms of readership, 56 percent of Macedonians relied chiefly on Macedonian periodicals, 42 percent of Serbs relied chiefly on Serbian or Vojvodinan periodicals (in Vojvodina, the Novi Sad daily, *Dnevnik*), 79 percent of Croats relied chiefly on Croatian periodicals, 72 percent of Slovenes on Slovenian periodicals, 68 percent of Montenegrins on Montenegrin or Serbian periodicals, but only 26 percent of residents of Bosnia-Herzegovina relied chiefly on Bosnian publications for their information. Some 9 percent of Bosnian residents cited the Serbian daily *Politika* as their main source of print information, while 9 percent of Bosnian residents cited the Croatian daily *Večernji list*. Only in Bosnia did a large number of respondents (17 percent) cite women's magazines as their major source of news and information.

Naturally, the influence any newspaper enjoyed fluctuated over time. *Borba* and *Slobodna Dalmacija* were marginal papers in the 1970s; by 1989, they were, together with *Delo*, arguably the most widely respected papers in the country. But neither *Slobodna Dalmacija* nor *Delo* could claim a wide readership outside its respective republic. Leaving aside ethnically mixed Bosnia, only the Serbian periodicals *Politika* and *NIN*, the Croatian weekly *Danas* and fortnightly *Start*, and the Belgrade publications *Borba* and *Večernje novosti* could claim wide readerships extending beyond the boundaries of the republics in which they were published.[58]

The highest circulations were enjoyed by the evening tabloids (*Večernji list*, *Večernje novosti*, and *Politika ekspres*), although *Politika* and *Slobodna Dalmacija* also had circulations over 100,000 (see Table 2.1). Among Church publications, only the Catholic papers *Druzina* and *Glas koncila* had circulations in excess of 100,000.

The role played by the Serbian media, and most especially by the magazines *Duga* and *Intervju* and the newspapers *Politika* and *Politika ekspres*, in creating resentments against Croatia and Slovenia for an alleged "theft" of Serbian factories and for alleged complicity in the "theft" of land from Serbia in the creation of the autonomous provinces, in stirring up anger against Kosovo's Albanians for alleged acts of rape and arson against local Serbs, and in debunking Tito and Titoism, including even Tito's dream of "brotherhood and unity," cannot be underestimated. Without the active participation of the press, the Serbian national movement could never have created the anger and resentment which, in time, would drive the Serbs into battle against their erstwhile fellow Yugoslavs—anger and resentment which had been muted or, in certain cases, even nonexistent prior to the period 1986–1987.

The media thus contributed to both the breakup of the SFRY and the outbreak of interethnic warfare. In this connection, one cannot overemphasize the importance of the national fragmentation of the readership in Bosnia in stimulating growing tensions in the late 1980s and early 1990s. With Bosnian Croats reading *Vjesnik* and *Večernji list*, Bosnian Serbs reading *Politika* and *Politika ekspres*, and Bosnian Muslims reading *Oslobodjenje*, the growing divergences in the points of view among the respective media were very quickly reflected in growing divergences in the perspectives of the three largest nationality groups of Bosnia-Herzegovina. Moreover, the same proclivities manifested themselves in the choice of which television news to watch. The conversion of *Borba* to a progressive, critical line (between 1988 and 1989) and the establishment of the nonnationalist independent TV studio "Yutel" (in 1991) as a voice for tolerance and liberalism came too late to block the accelerating slide toward armed confrontation.[59]

Political Fragmentation

Yugoslavia was not only becoming fragmented culturally and economically; its fragmentation, as has been already indicated, was also political, to the extent that it was necessary to speak of the emergence of different political systems in the separate republics. On the *formal* level, the political systems of the republics were still, as of autumn 1989, interchangeable; each republic had the same governmental and party structures and—the Slovenian constitutional amendments aside—the same underlying legal-constitutional framework. On the *informal* level, however, there was a widening gap between the republics, not just in the matter of what was permitted, but also where basic procedures and operational strategies were concerned.

Serbia, for example, had reverted to a traditional patrimonial system and saw a revival of ethnic chauvinism and male chauvinism to underpin this reversion. Slobodan Milošević was clearly the dominant figure in Serbia, and people in key positions were either admirers and advocates of his or afraid to speak out. Montenegro, run at that time by supporters of Milošević, was for all practical purposes a colony of Serbia

TABLE 2.1   Yugoslav Newspapers with Circulations Larger than 10,000, in Rank Order (1990, compared with 1983)

	1990 Sales (no. of copies)	1983 Sales (no. of copies)
Večernje novosti (Belgrade)	222,282	339,859
Večernji list (Zagreb)	221,942	309,839
Politika ekspres (Belgrade)	198,790	249,758
Politika (Belgrade)	184,551	243,826
Slobodna Dalmacija (Split)	107,483	71,571
Druž ina (Ljubljana, Catholic)	100,000[a]	n/a
Glas koncila (Zagreb, Catholic)	100,000[a]	n/a
Delo (Ljubljana)	94,280	99,840
Ognjišće (Koper, Catholic)	n/a	80,000[b]
Vjesnik (Zagreb)	74,563	73,030
Sportske novosti (Zagreb)	70,597	141,247
Večernje novine (Sarajevo)	66,911	35,049
Novi list—Glas Istre (Rijeka)	56,586	71,274
Večer (Maribor)	54,561	55,476
Mali koncil (Zagreb, Catholic)	n/a	50,000[d]
Oslobodjenje (Sarajevo)	47,690	71,557
Sport (Belgrade)	45,670	106,781
Sportski žurnal	42,142	n/a
Dnevnik (Novi Sad)	39,677	34,158
Borba (Belgrade)	31,408	30,976
Preporod (Sarajevo, Islamic)	n/a	30,000[d]
Nova Makedonija (Skopje)	23,404	25,089
Večer (Skopje)	22,948	31,959
Pravoslavlje (Belgrade, Orthodox)	n/a	22,000[c]
Magyar Szö (Novi Sad)	20,708	26,485
Pobjeda (Titograd)	19,570	20,073
Glas Slavonije	12,349	26,485

[a] 1987.
[b] 1973.
[c] 1982.
[d] Number printed.
SOURCES: Naša štampa (July-August 1983), pp. 9–10; Naša štampa (February 1984), p. 9; AKSA (May 20, 1983); NIN (May 22,1983), trans. in Foreign Broadcast Information Service, Daily Report (Eastern Europe), June 1, 1983; interviews, Belgrade and Zagreb, July 1982; and interviews, Zagreb and Ljubljana, June-July 1987; and Slobodna Dalmacija (Split), March 21, 1991, p. 23, trans. in FBIS, Daily Report (Eastern Europe), April 9, 1991, p. 42.

(though this situation later changed). Bosnia, divided into three competing ethnic groups, was riven by intra-elite conflict and distrust and mired in corruption. A local quip had it that Bosnia combined Austrian bureaucracy with Ottoman slowness and inefficiency—a deadly combination. Slovenia had allowed opposition parties to organize, meet, and sell their newspapers on the street and subsequently allowed them to field candidates in the spring 1990 parliamentary elections. As in Serbia, there was a waxing rapport between the party and certain sections of the opposition, but in Slovenia it was the opposition which was taking the initiative, not the other way around.

In Croatia and Macedonia, loyalty to Tito was combined with incipient liberalism—in the former taking the form of efforts to democratize the party—while in Macedonia there were strong currents within the party in favor of moving toward a multiparty system. For example, in October 1989, Vasil Tupurkovski, the Macedonian member of the Yugoslav collective presidency, called pluralization the "top priority" on the agenda.[60] More conservative elements within the Croatian party spoke of advocating a *Jugoslavenska sinteza* ("Yugoslav synthesis")—a formulation championed in the first place by Stipe Šuvar—by which it meant essentially preservation of the federal system in something approximating its Titoist form; but at the same time, more liberal elements within the Croatian party clearly favored a transition to a market economy and the establishment of a "semi-multiparty" system (in which nationalist parties would be proscribed).[61] At times, Croatian politicians seemed willing to go even further. For example, Marin Buble, a member of the Croatian CC, told *Slobodna Dalmacija* in late 1989, "a multi-party system has become a necessity, indeed only a matter of time, because the development of a modern society presumes above all a modern economic market, as well as a developed democratic system. You can't have one without the other. They are two sides of the same system."[62]

Ironically, the political fragmentation of the system was aggravated by Milošević's attempt to consolidate a strong center. In the case of Macedonia, for example, which in 1988 was gravitating toward Milošević's camp, the Serbian government alienated the Macedonian leadership and people alike, as already mentioned, by drafting a measure which would have allowed Serbs who had land titles from the interwar period to reclaim their land. Although aimed primarily at Kosovo, the measure would have had consequences in Macedonia too. As a result, the two republic leaderships fell out. Later, in October 1989, the Serbian leadership compounded this error by insensitively backing a proposal to declare 1 December—the day on which Yugoslavia was first united in 1918—a national holiday. This move again inflamed the Macedonians, who recalled that, in its first incarnation, Yugoslavia had been known as the "Kingdom of the Serbs, Croats, and Slovenes"—the Macedonians, then called "south Serbs," were excluded.[63] Almost at the same time, evidence surfaced that the Serbian security service had been operating in Bosnia without the knowledge or approval of Bosnian authorities; Ivan Cvitković, secretary of the Bosnian party presidency, denounced Serbia's actions as "an attack on the sovereignty of Bosnia-Herzegovina."[64]

Milošević's championing of "an effective, modern state" also won him enemies. The reaction to Milošević recapitulated, in some ways, the reaction sparked by eighteenth-century Habsburg emperor Josef II, who sought to consolidate a strong center, spoke of political "modernization," championed a certain kind of liberalism, and ultimately inflamed insecurity among the non-German peoples of his empire by promoting German as the single language of administration. A central demand in Milošević's program was for a reform of the Federal Assembly. Under the system bequeathed by Tito, both houses of the bicameral legislature apportioned equal numbers of delegates to each constituent republic. Milošević argued that this was inconsistent with the democratic principle of "one citizen, one vote." He demanded that *one* of the two chambers—specifically, the Federal Chamber—be reorganized so that the delegates to that chamber would represent equal numbers of citizens. In formal terms, his proposal would have closely followed the American model. The Slovenes, however, angrily rejected this proposal as a device to undermine their sovereignty, and both Slovenes and Croats worried that the proposal might be designed to give the Serbs political hegemony within the system. The fact that Serbs were enthusiastic about the proposal only seemed to confirm Slovenian and Croatian fears.

Issues on the Agenda

There were four pivotal issues on the Yugoslav political agenda in the late 1980s: the federal question, the economy, pluralization, and the breakdown of the sense of community.

The Federal Question.   Four alternate scenarios attempted to preserve the Yugoslav state: confederalization (not yet endorsed by the Slovenian government at this stage, but championed by a few Slovenian intellectuals, along with Serbian novelist Antonije Isaković and others), asymmetric federation (championed by the Slovenian party for a few months in late 1989), consolidation of a strong center (championed by the Serbian party and most Serbian intellectuals), and continuation of the status quo (not really championed by anyone, although Macedonia was clearly wary of any of the alternatives being proposed). Beginning in 1988, both Communists and non-communists tended on the whole to discuss the first two scenarios within the framework of the continuation of the post-Titoist system of regional state monopolies, that is to say, with local republic elites making the key decisions affecting economic development and political life within their republics. Taken in isolation, thus, the federal question accentuated the nationalities question, even as it distorted it. Indeed, the federal question dominated discussion and marginalized all other questions—which was dangerous because all four issues were serious.

The Economy.   There was a broad consensus among both economists and the general public in Yugoslavia that radical economic reform was needed. In the more developed republics, the tendency was to talk of reprivatization and the establishment of a true market economy. In the less developed republics, chiefly Macedonia and Bosnia, there were those who feared that such a change would only benefit the more developed regions and that they would be net losers. More fundamentally, reprivatizing the economy was a political question. Dismantling nationalized enterprises meant that republic elites, state-appointed directors, and the self-managing interest communities would all lose power. Inevitably, there were those who resisted reprivatization.

Pluralization. There were about a dozen independent political parties in Yugoslavia as of late 1989—some legally registered, some awaiting registration, and some denied registration and thus technically illegal. Most of these were based in Ljubljana or Zagreb. There were also between one and two dozen independent social- and political-interest groups, devoted variously to feminist, ecological, gay rights, pacifist, cultural, or other concerns. Most of these were based in Belgrade, Ljubljana, and Zagreb, although some were to be found in other cities. Many of them were issuing bulletins or other periodicals; some of them (particularly in Slovenia) were protected through registration as activities of the local youth organization (a legal fiction).

Political pluralization in Yugoslavia was a symptom of societal mobilization and reflected, at the same time, the breakdown of the old political order. Also, the question of pluralization was organically tied to the federal question, since it lay within the jurisdiction of republic, not federal, authorities to grant it or withhold the registration of political associations.

Breakdown of the Sense of Community. The foregoing issues were well understood in Yugoslavia and were being intelligently, albeit often polemically, debated. Surprisingly, the breakdown of the sense of community, which was intuitively clear, received almost no explicit attention in the press, and there were no serious proposals to deal with this issue—that is, unless secession of one or another republic was counted as a "solution."

Yet this fourth dilemma threatened the stability of the Yugoslav political order. The breakdown of communication across republic borders and nationality groups is the key to the disintegration of interethnic relations in Yugoslavia in the late 1980s—a process which can be traced, on one level, to the Kosovo riots of April 1981[65] and, on another level, to the very foundation of the state. So far advanced was this process by 1989 that people spoke openly of impending civil war and compared Yugoslavia to Lebanon.

Reprivatization and political pluralization might have defused the crisis had they been carried out at the end of the 1970s, or even by 1984 or 1985. But the longer the delay, the more economic deterioration aggravated the entire political climate and contributed, in particular, to the worsening of interethnic relations.

Some Yugoslavs took to citing the Helsinki Accords, which barred any change in European borders, as an impediment to Slovenian secession or to the breakup of Yugoslavia. The citation was folly. Western powers were, to be sure, ready to provide Yugoslavia with much needed credits, at least until Milošević's unconstitutional moves in spring 1991, but it was scarcely to be believed that the signatories of the Helsinki Act would use armed force to hold Yugoslavia together against the will of a large portion of its own people.

Notes

1. Reneo Lukić and Allen Lynch, *Europe from the Balkans to the Urals: The Disintegration of Yugoslavia and the Soviet Union* (Oxford and New York: Oxford University Press, 1996), pp. 148–150; Laura Silber and Allan Little, *The Death of Yugoslavia* (London: Penguin Books & BBC Books, 1995), p. 47. For details of Milošević's career and political activities, see Slavoljub Djukić, *Kako se dogodio vodja: Borbe za vlastu Srbiji posle Josipa Broza Tita* (Belgrade: Filip Višnjić, 1992); and Slavoljub Djukić, *Izmedju slave i anateme: Politička biografija Slobodana Miloševića* (Belgrade: Filip Višnjić, 1994).

2. *Večernji list* (Zagreb) (15 September 1989), p. 2; and *Politika* (Belgrade) (8 September 1989), p. 9. Last SFRY census figures, as reported in Tanjug (30 April 1991), trans. in Foreign Broadcast Information Service (FBIS), *Daily Report* (Eastern Europe), 1 May 1991, p. 53.

3. *Večernji list* (6 September 1989), p. 5; (11 September 1989), p. 2; *Nedjeljna Dalmacija* (Split) (19 September 1989), p. 6; *Večernji list* (19 September 1989), p. 6.

4. On the last point, see *Večernji list* (21 September 1989), p. 10.

5. *Večernji list* (11 September 1989), p. 2; (15 September 1989); p. 5; (24 September 1989), p. 4.

6. *Danas* (Zagreb), no. 394 (5 September 1989), p. 11.

7. *Vjesnik* (Zagreb) (28 August 1989), p. 5.

8. *Intervju* (Belgrade), no. 215 (1 September 1989), p. 19.

9. Viktor Meier, *Wie Jugoslawien verspielt wurde*, 2nd ed. (Munich: C. H. Beck, 1996), pp. 136–137.

10. Branka Magaš, *The Destruction of Yugoslavia: Tracking the Break-up 1980–92* (London: Verso, 1993), p. 135.

11. Meier, *Wie Jugoslawien*, p. 138.

12. Ibid., p. 139.

13. Ibid., p. 144.

14. Lukić and Lynch, *Europe from the Balkans to the Urals*, p. 152.

15. Silber and Little, *Death of Yugoslavia*, p. 64; Magaš, *Destruction of Yugoslavia*, p. 208.

16. Stipe Mesić, *Kako je srušena Jugoslavija*, 2nd ed. (Zagreb: Mislav Press, 1994), pp. 11–12.

17. Hugh Poulton, *Who are the Macedonians?* (Bloomington: Indiana University Press, 1995), p. 130; Meier, *Wie Jugoslawien*, pp. 343–344.

18. The conflict between Macedonia and Serbia came into the open in April 1989. See Meier, *Wie Jugoslawien*, pp. 199–200.

19. Ibid., p. 169.

20. Ibid., p. 177.

21. Veljko Kadijević, *Moje vidjenje raspada* (Belgrade: Politika, 1993), pp. 99–105.

22. Meier, *Wie Jugoslawien*, p. 131.

23. Interview with Igor Bavčar, Ljubljana, 4 September 1989.

24. Gregor Tomc, "The Active Society," in *Independent Voices from Slovenia, Yugoslavia*, Vol. 4, No. 3 (July 1988), p. 6.

25. Interview with a leading member of the Peasant Union, Ljubljana, 1 September 1989.

26. For further discussion, see Sabrina P. Ramet, "Democratization in Slovenia—The Second Stage," in Karen Dawisha and Bruce Parrott (eds.), *Politics, Power, and the Struggle for Democracy in South-East Europe* (Cambridge: Cambridge University Press, 1997), pp. 189–225.

27. Ciril Ribičič and Zlatko Tomac, *Federalizam po mjeri budučnosti* (Zagreb: Globus, 1989), p. 183.

28. *Mladina* (Ljubljana) (1 September 1989), p. 4.

29. *Intervju*, no. 215 (1 September 1989), p. 32.

30. See *Politika ekspres* (Belgrade) (24 September 1989), p. 2.

31. Interview with Ciril Ribičič, Ljubljana, 5 September 1989.

32. Interview with Mitja Žagar, Seattle, 24 November 1997.

33. *Večernje novosti* (Belgrade) (27 September 1989), p. 4.

34. *Večernji list* (12 September 1989), p. 6.

35. *Večernje novosti* (27 September 1989), p. 2.

36. Ivan Stambolić, *Rasprave o SR Srbiji, 1979–1987* (Zagreb: Globus, 1988), p. 49.

37. Ibid., p. 62.

38. Quoted in Wolfgang Höpken, "Party Monopoly and Political Change: The League of Communists since Tito's Death," in Pedro Ramet (ed.), *Yugoslavia in the 1980s* (Boulder: Westview Press, 1985), p. 41.

39. Risto Lazarov, in interview with the author, Skopje, 21 March 1995.

40. *Intervju*, no. 213 (4 August 1989), pp. 23–25.

41. Regarding transfers of industry, interview, Belgrade, 23 September 1989; *Duga*, no. 406 (16 September 1989), pp. 82–83. For an example of an attack on the "confederal" aspects of the system, accompanied by a demand for a "modern efficacious system," see Radoslav Stojanović, *Jugoslavija, nacije i politika* (Belgrade: Nova knjiga, 1988), p. 213.

42. Miko Tripalo, in interview with the author, Zagreb, 8 September 1989.

43. *Politika* (15 May 1992), p. 9.

44. Bora Djordjević, in interview with the author, Belgrade, 18 July 1988. In 1989, I accompanied Bora to a nightclub in Novi Sad where he was the featured entertainment. Bora was not scheduled to perform his music that night, but to read some of his poetry, which he did, interspersing his usually nationalistic and often anti-Albanian poetry with disparaging comments about the Albanian people of Kosovo. See Bora Djordjević, *Nećču* (Belgrade: Književna zadruga, 1989), pp. 11, 18–19.

45. E.g., Vanja Brkić's album, *Kosovo je moja domovina (Kosovo Is My Homeland)*, released by ZKP RTV, Ljubljana.

46. *Glas crkve* (Šabac), quoted in *Borba* (Belgrade) (25 July 1989), p. 3, trans. in Foreign Broadcast Information Service (FBIS), *Daily Report* (Eastern Europe), 4 August 1989, p. 43, my emphasis.

47. Yugoslav Situation Report, *Radio Free Europe Research* (26 May 1989), pp. 33–34.

48. Interview with Matija Bečković and several other members of the Serbian Writers' Association, Belgrade, 21 September 1989; and interview with Rudi Šeligo, President of the Slovenian Writers' Association, Ljubljana, 4 September 1989.

49. Matija Bečković, in interview with the author, Belgrade, 21 September 1989.

50. Goran Bregović, leader of Bjelo dugme, in interview with the author, Sarajevo, 14 September 1989.

51. Interview, Ljubljana, 1 September 1989.

52. *NIN*, no. 2020 (17 September 1989), pp. 42–43.

53. *Slobodna Dalmacija* (Split) (22 September 1989), p. 16.

54. *Večernje novosti* (18 September 1989), p. 3; *Večernji list* (23 September 1989), p. 12; and *Frankfurter Allgemeine* (2 October 1989), p. 1.

55. *Vjesnik* (10 September 1989), p. 5; *Slobodna Dalmacija* (22 September 1989), p. 16; and *Politika* (25 October 1989), p. 7.

56. This section is based on and draws liberally from a section of my essay "The Yugoslav Press," first published in John B. Allcock, John J. Horton, and Marko Milivojevic (eds.), *Yugoslavia in Transition: Choices and Constraints—Essays in Honour of Fred Singleton* (Oxford and Hamburg: Berg Publishers, 1991).

57. *Borba* (2 October 1989), p. 7, trans. in FBIS, *Daily Report* (Eastern Europe), 23 October 1989, pp. 58–60.

58. According to the data reported in ibid.

59. See Milan Milošević, "The Media Wars: 1987–1997," in Jasminka Udovički and James Ridgeway (eds.), *Burn This House: The Making and Unmaking of Yugoslavia* (Durham, N.C.: Duke University Press, 1997), pp. 114–115.

60. *Slobodna Dalmacija* (10 September 1989), p. 13.

61. Zlatko Tomac, in interview with the author, 8 September 1989.

62. *Slobodna Dalmacija* (10 September 1989), p. 10.

63. *Politika* (20 October 1989), p. 7.

64. *Danas*, no. 401 (24 October 1989), p. 15.

65. See Sabrina P. Ramet, *Nationalism and Federalism in Yugoslavia, 1962–1991*, 2nd ed. (Bloomington: Indiana University Press, 1992).

CHAPTER THREE

◆

Brotherhood and Disunity, 1989–1991

Sustained economic deterioration always contains within itself the potential for revolutionary or transformative repercussions, as Ted Robert Gurr argued in a 1970 work.[1] Gurr describes the effects of "decremental deprivation," in which economic production and strength decline while expectations remain constant; the result, not surprisingly, is intense frustration and a rise in the proclivity to violence. Gurr notes, in this connection, that people "are likely to be more intensely angered when they lose what they have than when they lose hope of attaining what they do not yet have."[2] Needless to say, if declining economic capacity can be successfully connected, by elite propaganda, with some designated out-group(s), popular anger will tend to be focus on the designated out-group(s). Discontent can also generate value fluidity and open the gates to thunderous change. When people are economically satisfied, few will see the need for radical ideological shifts or for the embrace of new ideological doctrines. By contrast, as Gurr points out, "intensely discontented people are most susceptible to new doctrines when they are uncertain about the origins of their discontent, and more generally are anxious about the lack of certainty in their social environment."[3]

In the Yugoslav context, the declining economic performance of the system, measured in absolute declines in national income and agricultural output, steadily climbing foreign indebtedness and rates of unemployment and inflation, and, beginning in 1982, recurrent problems in the rate of growth in industrial output (see Table 3.1) had massive and tangible repercussions for the population, as already briefly noted. An illegitimate government lacks certain resources available to legitimate governments which enable them to weather economic storms more successfully. That the Yugoslav Communist system never succeeded in solving its "legitimacy problem" is shown in the fact that its leading figures continued, down to the final days of the system, to speak of the importance of "democratizing" the system; a democratic system does not need to be "democratized," a legitimate system does not stand in need of supplemental or more intense legitimation.

TABLE 3.1   Annual Economic Growth Rates, 1981–1988 (in percentages)

	National income	Gross industrial output	Gross agricultural output
1981	−0.4	4.0	1.0
1982	−0.2	−1.0	7.0
1983	−1.5	1.9	−1.0
1984	0.0	5.7	2.0
1985	−0.5	2.7	−7.0
1986	3.5	3.9	11.0
1987	−1.0	1.0	−5.0
1988	−2.0	−1.0	−5.0

SOURCE: Sabrina P. Ramet, *Social Currents in Eastern Europe: The Sources and Consequences of the Great Transformation,* 2nd ed. (Durham, N.C.: Duke University Press, 1995), pp. 33–35.

But when an illegitimate system confronts economic crisis, its ability to make a unified response is highly dependent upon the structure that system has assumed. In the case of federalized Yugoslavia, the regional elites of the six republics (leaving aside, for the time being, the question of whether the Montenegrin elite should be counted as an independent actor as of 1989–1991) enjoyed far-reaching autonomy, independent structures, and the capacity for independent policy formulation. As hate speech became steadily more commonplace in the late 1980s, the regional elites in Slovenia and Croatia, and later Macedonia and Bosnia, increasingly felt the need to defend themselves against Serbian pretensions, whether ideological, political, or territorial. As the presuppositions of system stability ceased to function, the Yugoslav system ceased to function.

The Disintegration of the Economy

The Yugoslav economy was, by 1988, in extreme crisis. In that year, national income declined 2.0 percent, industrial output declined by 1.0 percent, agricultural output declined by 5.0 percent, unemployment stood at 16.8 percent, the inflation rate had reached 160 percent, and the foreign debt had reached an all-time high of $20 billion.[4] By 1990, by which time the foreign debt had risen to $22 billion and a trade deficit of $2.7 billion was recorded, the economic infrastructure itself was becoming unraveled, holding the promise of continued deterioration. All six republics experienced economic decline in 1990. Worst off was Montenegro, where industrial production fell 15.8 percent in the first nine months of 1990. During the same period, industrial production declined 13.5 percent in Serbia, 10.8 percent in Croatia, 10.6 percent in Slovenia and Macedonia, and 6.2 percent in Bosnia-Herzegovina.[5] During 1985–1986, IMF pressure resulted in the passage of eighteen laws which dismantled key elements in the self-management system, abolished the Kardeljian basic organizations of associated labor, and opened the economy to foreign ownership of domestic firms.[6] But the federal government later backed away from the IMF program, accusing the creditor of "interference" in Yugoslav domestic affairs. Prime Minister Ante Marković's widely touted program of economic reform, which was introduced at the beginning of 1990 and which represented an attempt to bring Yugoslavia back into harmony with the IMF program, froze wages and prices and brought inflation down from a rate of 2,000 percent annually to about 4 percent, virtually overnight. But soon inflation once again crept upward. Marković's reform itself included pegging the dinar to the German mark, thus making the Yugoslav currency convertible. Unfortunately, the fixed exchange rate gave the dinar artificial strength, and the immediate result was a surge in imports and the bankruptcy of many once wealthy exporters.[7] Foreign-currency reserves plunged from $6.5 to $3.6 billion within a year,[8] forcing the Marković government to abandon convertibility and devalue the dinar.

Reprivatization came too late to avert economic catastrophe. Although the private sector had been measurably more efficient than the social sector, Yugoslavia's 16,490 private firms (as of February 1991) accounted for only 2.4 percent of the overall income of the Yugoslav economy—too little to make a difference.[9] Meanwhile, foreign investors were once again scared off. Political instability and talk of civil war and military coups were bad enough. But add to that the severe difficulties in doing business across republic lines and the fact that local courts no longer recognized the validity of other republican laws, and potential investors could only view Yugoslavia as an especially undesirable investment prospect. Nationalism played a role in this too, as the republics took actions injurious to the economic interests of companies based in other republics. In Serbia, for example, the Croatian-based INA petrochemical company was forced to pay a 150 percent surcharge on all gasoline sales, even though Serbian petrochemical companies paid no such tax; as a result, INA decided, early in 1991, to curtail its operations in Serbia.

The Yugoslav government approached the West, hat in hand, with a request for yet another economic bailout, this time to the tune of $4 billion. Meanwhile, the Swiss newspaper *Neue Zürcher Zeitung* questioned whether it was realistic to pin any hopes on yet another infusion of money into this economically inefficient country, underlining the fact that for all practical purposes the productive sector in Yugoslavia had collapsed.[10] Even in relatively more prosperous Slovenia, before the JNA wreaked severe damage on the republic's economic infrastructure in June–July 1991, local authorities expected the economy to decline for at least another two years before any revival could begin.

The Spread of Civil Turmoil

The past was never laid to rest in the Socialist Federated Republic of Yugoslavia. By contrast with the United States, where historical memory is quite short, peoples in the Balkans have long talked about events in 1389, 1459, 1921, 1941, 1948, 1966, and 1970–1971 as if they were fresh. The wounds of the past have never healed—in part, as Philip Cohen has argued, because the past has not been confronted honestly.[11] In a striking illustration of the way in which the past haunts future generations, tens of thousands of anticommunist demonstrators assembled on 27 March 1991 to mark the fiftieth anniversary of the military coup which overthrew the government of Prince Paul after the regent signed a pact with Nazi Germany and to draw a parallel to the Milošević regime, which many accused of "fascism." Or again, the Party of Democratic Action (SDA) in Kosovo included in its program a demand for autonomy for the Sandžak of Novi Pazar, on the argument that the Sandžak was a constituent part of the Bosnian Pashaluk until the 1878 Congress of Berlin.[12]

The past also figured actively in the lively polemics between the pro-Milošević and anti-Milošević camps during 1989–1991, most especially in the arsenal of anti-Croatian rhetoric spewed out by Serbia's controlled press. For Yugoslavs, World War II seemed never to have ended. Even today, Serbs assail the Catholic Church for alleged complicity in wartime atrocities—provoking the Church, at one point, into publishing a wartime Vatican decree in which the Holy See had explicitly forbidden its clergy to collaborate in any way with the Croatian fascist authorities (the *Ustaše*). Croatian historian and political activist Franjo Tudjman, who would be elected Croatian president in April 1990, devoted his 1989 *Absurdities of Historical Reality*, in Viktor Meier's words, "to no less than highlighting the evil of genocide in general and freeing Croats from the polemical reproach which has been pressed by the Serbian side, that Croats are, by nature, inclined to genocide."[13]

Of course, different nationalities remember the past in different ways, and these perceptions themselves may change over time. The Serbs now remember the Tito era as an anti-Serbian era and, in the late 1980s, regularly cited Tito's transfer of large numbers of industrial plants from Serbia to Croatia and Slovenia at a time when Stalin was threatening to invade the country, claiming that Tito's "real" motivation was the desire to weaken and despoil Serbia. But Serbs forget that although Tito restored the old Ottoman-Habsburg boundary between Serbia and Bosnia without alteration, he aggrandized Serbia in the north by transferring to its jurisdiction a slice of eastern Croatia, Srem, which had never before belonged to Serbia.[14] Serbs also complained that the creation of the republics of Montenegro and Bosnia was artificial and that those territories, along with the territories established as autonomous provinces, should have been placed under direct Serbian control.

Croats and Albanians, by contrast, are apt to remember Tito's many concessions to the Serbs, in particular in the first twenty years of communism. To begin with, Tito had accepted into Partisan ranks converts from the Chetnik movement who may or may not have abandoned all their Chetnik proclivities,[15] and this infusion of Serb nationalist ex-collaborators colored the perspectives at the center of power. Serbs were granted disproportionate influence in the regional party organizations in Croatia, Bosnia, and Kosovo and were especially overrepresented in the military, the police, the media, trade unions, and sports organizations. The 1946 trial of Zagreb Archbishop Alojzije Stepinac on trumped-up charges of collaboration with the *Ustaše* was, in Croatian eyes, a concession to Serbian hatred (especially among Orthodox clergy and believers) of Catholics and Croats alike. Likewise, Croats, Macedonians, Albanians, and ethnic Muslims alike remember that, until July 1966, Tito worked closely with Aleksandar Ranković, head of the secret police, in pursuing a centralist policy injurious to the interests of non-Serbs. These different memories, set atop unhealed wounds, provided the seedbed for deep bitterness, resentments, and recurrent desires for revenge.

Of all the memories, shared and disputed, the most dangerous was the memory of World War II. Probably in no other country of Europe in the 1980s did World War II so often figure as a topic of café conversation. In the late 1980s, historians and polemicists raked at the open wounds by engaging in one-sided and largely undocumented revisions of the figures of war dead. In the SFRY, the official number of war dead had been set at 1.7 million, though later computations showed that the actual figure was closer to 1.027 million.[16] But, riveting on the *Ustaše*-run camp at Jasenovac, Serbian historians began to offer strangely inflated figures. Already in his *Prilozi za biografiju Josipa Broza Tita*, Vladimir Dedijer asserted, without documentation, that some 700,000 persons had died at Jasenovac during the war. In another work of that period, Serbian historian Velimir Terzić revised this already high figure upward, claiming that "more than a million" persons had died at Jasenovac, mostly Serbs, while D. Živojinović claimed in the pages of the weekly magazine *Intervju* in January 1986 that more than a million Orthodox (i.e., Serbs) had died in wartime Croatia.[17]

Those making these extraordinary claims never betrayed how many people they thought had died in Yugoslavia overall during World War II; nor did Serb revisionists spend much time worrying about how many members of other nationalities died in the war or at one or another camp. Possibly the highest figure to appear within the context of a longer historical treatment was that offered by Radomir Bulatović in his 1990 book about Jasenovac; he claimed there that 1,110,929 people had died at Jasenovac alone![18] But the Serbs were not allowed to enjoy a monopoly on historical revisionism, and their claims about Jasenovac were matched by equally extravagant claims, registered by Croats, about the number of Croats who lost their lives at Bleiburg. I already cited (in Chapter 1) a figure of 36,000 Croats who lost their lives at Bleiburg, but figures offered by émigré Croats went as high as 300,000 dead, mostly Croats.[19]

There were several problems with these revisions. First, these extraordinary claims were registered without proper documentation, indeed, often without any documentation at all. This in turn betrayed a deep-seated disrespect for historical truth and a willingness to reconstruct the truth to suit one's own fancies. But this can only be accomplished by repudiating moral universalism altogether and repudiating the notion that others have equal rights (in this case, of factual claim and factual verification) and that only an honest search for the truth may adjudicate historical disputation.[20] Second, the revisions of casualties at Jasenovac and Bleiburg were, essentially without exception, politically motivated, driven by the desire to paint one's own nation as "the Great Victim." And third, the failure to set claims about Jasenovac specifically against the number of overall war dead verged on lunacy. After all, even if the admittedly too-high figure of 1.7 million war dead is accepted, for the sake of argument, how likely is it that two-thirds of these (as Bulatović would have us believe) lost their lives at one solitary camp? Moreover, if Žerjavić's better-documented figures for overall dead are accepted, then we would be left with the absurd claim that of the 1.027 million who died in the Yugoslav lands during World War II, 1.111 million (as per Bulatović) lost their lives at Jasenovac! Mathematical nonsense is also historical nonsense—but, of course, dangerous nonsense.

The Tito era did not need to have ended as it did. In the late 1960s and early 1970s, Tito allowed liberals in Slovenia, Croatia, Macedonia, and Serbia to chart a new course. The result was the growth among people of a sense of control over their own destiny and the beginnings, indeed perhaps just a hint, of the possibility of an eventual legitimation of the system. Comparisons of the "Croatian Spring" with the "Czechoslovak Spring" of 1968 were not misplaced. Croats vested great hope in their republic's leaders at that time—Miko Tripalo and Savka Dabčević-Kučar— who came to be seen as legitimate leaders. Tripalo told me in 1989 that as a result of the loosening up of the power structure, "There developed a rather broad democratic popular movement, which started to publish a large number of its own newspapers and magazines, thus creating forums in which people could speak freely. And the whole political life, which had been closed to the public, now opened up, and people started to speak their minds, both about the way things were then and about how things had been in the past."[21]

In December 1971, Tito removed Tripalo and Dabčević-Kučar from power. He subsequently also fired liberals in the other republics. As a result, these liberals were mythologized in the public consciousness and even gained in stature as late Titoism cracked and crumbled. By late 1990, Tripalo and Dabčević-Kučar had emerged from a kind of internal exile and were once again taking part in political discourse, albeit without the prospect of a return to office. In Macedonia, Kiro Gligorov, one of the liberals of the 1970–1971 era, returned to politics as president of Macedonia. In Slovenia, the memoirs of the late Stane Kavčič, the leading liberal of the early 1970s, were published and widely read. In Slovenia, Croatia, Bosnia, and Macedonia, it was the dissidents of yesteryear who took hold of the reins of power in 1990. In fact the current presidents of Croatia and Bosnia, Franjo Tudjman and Alija Izetbegović, both spent time in prison in the early 1980s after being tried on charges, respectively, of Croatian nationalism and Islamic fundamentalism.

Political Transformation

Until summer 1989, there were some who continued to believe that the Communist state system could be preserved in Yugoslavia in some variant or other. But about that time, transformations of the political landscape accelerated, as if the country had been hit by a political earthquake. The Serbian coups in Novi Sad, Titograd, and Priština and the passage of the controversial constitutional amendments in Slovenia were mentioned in the previous chapter, as was the Serbian proclamation of an economic boycott of Slovenian goods and markets. Further developments in subsequent months only deepened the ideological fissures in the country. In mid-December 1989, at the Eleventh Congress of the LC-Croatia, Ivica Račan (an avowed liberal) was elected chair of the LC-Croatia, replacing the bland Stanko Stojčević, who was stepping down. Račan was the choice of party liberals and outpolled the "centrist" candidate, Ivo Družić, and the conservative choice, Admiral Branko Mamula (who was also favored by Stojčević). Račan, with his commitment to a multiparty system and a free-market economy, and Milošević, with his commitment to a nationalist hegemony and state capitalism, were natural enemies, and Račan's election set the stage for the demise of the LCY at the Fourteenth Extraordinary Congress of the LCY, which had been set, under pressure from Milošević, for the following month.

When the congress convened, the Slovenian delegation introduced motions to transform the LCY into a confederative association of independent parties, to end all prosecution of "counter-revolution" and all political trials anywhere in Yugoslavia, to ban the use of torture (which would have affected Serbia's treatment of incarcerated Albanians, for example), and to provide a clearer guarantee of the right of disassociation on a constitutional basis; the Slovenes also asked the congress to condemn the Serbian economic blockade of their republic which had been imposed the previous month. All the Slovene motions were rejected by the Serbian bloc, without their even having been dignified with serious discussion. At this point, the Slovenian and Croatian delegates walked out of the Fourteenth Extraordinary Congress and the Macedonian and Bosnian delegations refused to continue the congress in their absence.[22]

Meanwhile, multiparty elections had been set for 8 April in Slovenia and for 22 April in Croatia. In Slovenia, an anticommunist alliance (DEMOS) defeated the reform Communists (with a solid 55 percent of the vote) and took control of the government, installing Christian Democrat Lojze Peterle as prime minister; Milan Kučan was swept into office as president by a near landslide. In Croatia, the Croatian Democratic Community (HDZ), led by retired General Franjo Tudjman, won 41.4 percent of the vote for the lower house and 44 percent of the vote for the Council of Communities; under the electoral rules which had been adopted, this result gave the HDZ more than 60 percent of the seats in the two houses. Elections in November in Macedonia and Bosnia brought coalitions into power; in the former case, the reform Communists were in the leading position, but in the case of Bosnia, the coalition brought together nationalist representatives of the republic's three "constituent peoples"—Muslims, Serbs, and Croats—in what proved to be an unstable formula. As for Serbia, on 16 July 1990, Milošević staged the founding congress of the Socialist Party of Serbia, refashioning the LC-Serbia for a new era. Elections were scheduled in Serbia for 9 December. It was on this occasion that Milošević unilaterally arranged for an unsecured "loan" of 28 billion dinars (about $1.8 billion) from the National Bank of Yugoslavia to the Republic of Serbia, which was used to liquidate the debts of certain Serb enterprises as well as for cash. Despite the colossal scale of this loan, it was arranged behind closed doors, without the knowledge of officials of the other republics.[23] The "loan" broke the back of the Yugoslav economy and

dealt a deathblow to Prime Minister Marković's hopes of engineering tͱ
resuscitation of Yugoslavia. But in the short term, the sudden inflow oͬ ͼ͞
Serbia's suffering economy may have helped to sway some voters. Be that as it may,
Milošević's Socialist Party handily won the elections, while Milošević himself col-
lected 64 percent of the votes in the presidential race.

The Federal Budget

In November 1990, Slovenia, Serbia, and Vojvodina had already announced that
they would make no further tax payments to the federation.[24] After the Serbian
bank theft of $1.8 billion in December, the Slovenian and Croatian governments an-
nounced that they would recognize no further debts incurred by the federal government. As a result of these pressures, in December, the federal government was operating at a level 15 percent below its basic budgetary needs and had had to lay off
some 2,700 federal officials, thus reducing the ability of the central government to
function.[25] The federal government was unable, in turn, to meet its commitments to
the republics (in the form of subsidies to the three less developed republics, funds for
stimulating exports, war veterans' pension supplements, and other funds), and in
March the government of Bosnia-Herzegovina announced that unless the federal
government settled its debts with Bosnia "within a week," Bosnia would cease all
payments to the federal budget.[26] The governments of Montenegro and Macedonia
also complained about the federal government's failure to honor financial commitments.[27] The republics, most especially Serbia, Croatia, and Slovenia, also slowed
their contributions to the military budget. More particularly, the Slovenian government declared that it would not pay off its obligations to the army as long as there
was a threat of the introduction of emergency measures, and that it was unilaterally
reducing its contribution to the 1991 military budget from 15 billion dinars to
about 3 billion dinars.[28] As a result, the army was not able to pay its bills, and some
food suppliers refused to send any more provisions to the army because they had not
been paid in two months. To address this situation, the Federal Executive Council
redirected some funds earmarked for other purposes to the army and in February
took out a loan with the National Bank of Yugoslavia in order to permit the army to
continue to function.[29]

The Spread of Civil Turmoil

During the years 1989–1991, civil turmoil, which had overtly afflicted Kosovo since
1981, spread through much of the country, giving rise to serious fears of impending
civil war. Civil turmoil often figures as a preliminary phase ultimately giving rise to
civil war. Yugoslavia was clearly in a state of civil turmoil by summer 1989. Moreover, Serbian leader Milošević even told an enthusiastic crowd of one million Serbs
at Kosovo Polje on 28 June 1989, at the six hundredth anniversary of the battle
which had led to medieval Serbia's precipitous decline and ultimate conquest by Ot-

toman Turkey, that Serbia was engaged in a new battle and that armed conflict might not be far off.

Neither the suppression of human rights in Kosovo nor the alienation of Slovenia was sufficient to push the Yugoslav state over the brink into open conflict. The heart of the Yugoslav national question was always the Serb-Croat relationship, since these two long-standing rivals together constituted, in the last days of the SFRY, about 56 percent of the country's population. Accordingly, the turning point came in the form of an uprising by Croatia's small Serbian minority (12.2 percent).[30] This uprising was adumbrated in summer 1989, when Dr. Jovo Opačić, a forty-five-year-old Serbian economist, attempted to establish a cultural society for Croatia's Serbs (for the purpose of building up special theaters, newspapers, radio stations, and other cultural and media infrastructure in the Serbian variant of the language). What Opačić demanded on behalf of Croatia's Serbs was "cultural autonomy." Croatia's then-Communist authorities, headed by Croatian Serb Stojčević, argued that such an alternative infrastructure would remove Croatia's Serbs from the cultural mainstream of the republic and lead to their cultural ghettoization; they therefore balked and put Opačić in prison. He was released at year's end, and, at the encouragement of Dobrica Ćosić, made contact with Jovan Rašković, a Šibenik psychiatrist with whom Ćosić had maintained steady contact since the early 1970s and, more particularly, an articulate Croatian Serb.

In February 1990, Rašković and Opačić agreed to create a political party; against the urgings of Rašković, who wanted to leave out any national marker in the party's name, the organization took flight on 17 February as the Serbian Democratic Party (SDS).[31] Among the more prominent members of this party was Milan Babić, a young dentist from the provincial town of Knin. Significantly, when Croatia's elections were held two months later, Rašković's Serbian Democratic Party garnered only about a third of the Serbian votes; most Croatian Serbs voted for Račan's reformed Communists.

The victorious Tudjman, despite his preelection nationalist rhetoric, was not blind to the need to win the Serbs to his banner. Although he moved with insensitive haste to fire Serbs from positions in the administration and in the police in order to correct the disproportional overrepresentation of Serbs in these sectors of the Croatian republic apparatus, Tudjman was also prepared to make concessions. Tudjman met with Rašković in May, offered him the post of vice president, and indicated his readiness to negotiate the grant of cultural autonomy, thereby offering to meet Opačić's demand of the year before. Rašković did not consider this adequate and pressed Tudjman for more broadly defined autonomy and for retaining mention of the Serbs as a "constituent nation" of Croatia, together with the Croats, in the new constitution—demands which Tudjman was not prepared to grant. But Rašković consulted with Belgrade before replying to President Tudjman; on Belgrade's advice, Rašković declined the initial offer and called for a boycott by members of his party of the Croatian parliament.[32] The publication of the supposedly private Tudjman-Rašković talks in the pages of *Danas* in August succeeded in discrediting Rašković among his own supporters, but instead of encouraging a more moderate line in the Serbian Democratic Party, it had the opposite result. In September 1990, Rašković went abroad to try to raise funds for his young party, and while he was out of the country, Milošević orchestrated his ouster as head of the SDS; the more militant Babić now took the helm.[33]

In the meantime, Croatian Serbs had set up the Serbian National Council in July 1990 in defiance of the Croatian authorities with the explicit purpose of working for Serbian territorial autonomy within Croatia or, in the event that the SFRY should dissolve, the secession of Serb-inhabited regions from Croatia. The council was, in fact, a revolutionary body and its creation, at the prompting of Milošević's agents, signaled the formal beginning of the Serbian revolt against Croatia, eleven months before Croatia declared its independence. During August and September 1990, the council conducted an illegal referendum among Croatia's 567,317 Serbs; some 567,127 Serbs voted for Serbian autonomy.[34] Serbs living outside Croatia were also invited to vote in the referendum—reflecting a curious understanding of democratic procedure—and Tanjug admitted that the number of "yes" votes cast by this group (189,422) was larger than the number of voters from outside the republic (183,464), suggesting that some of the voters voted twice (or were counted twice). But the Serbian uprising only turned violent in October, when local Serbs raided gun shops and police stations to arm themselves, set up barricades (often felling trees across roads), and mined sections of railway lines leading into the districts of greatest Serbian concentration. Soon, arms shipments supposedly earmarked for the Yugoslav People's Army were "inexplicably" routed through the Croatian town of Knin (center of the Serbian rebellion) with the doors left unlocked; local Serbs were informed in advance of the shipments and unloaded the arms under cover of night.[35]

Thus armed, Croatian Serbs proclaimed "autonomy" in September 1990. In declaring their autonomy, the Krajina Serbs made use of the institutional vehicle of communal associations which had arisen as part of the SFRY constitutional framework; the Croatian Constitutional Court now ruled that the communal associations were themselves, within the context of the new constitutional-legal conditions, illegal.

Already in May, the JNA undertook to confiscate weapons of the Slovenian Territorial Defense (STD) forces; the Slovenian collective presidency reacted belatedly and authorized that further confiscations be prevented. But by that point, the army had already confiscated about 70 percent of STD armaments.[36] Parallel operations were carried out in Croatia and Bosnia-Herzegovina about the same time, except in Serb-inhabited districts, where local Territorial Defense arms were used to provide the basis for the future Serb militias.[37] The army now became involved in the formation of the Chetnik militias in Croatia, dispatching JNA officers to train the new militias for combat.[38] Meanwhile, the JNA retired Slovenian and Croatian officers, promoting Serbs to take their places.[39] The Serb-controlled JNA made similar preparations in Bosnia. In an operation code-named RAM, Serbian authorities began arming newly established Bosnian Serb militias in eastern Herzegovina, the Bosnian "Krajina," and in the mountainous Romanija region near Sarajevo as early as 1990.[40] On 9 April 1991, according to Donia and Fine, "Bosnian police stopped three trucks containing over 1,000 (automatic) rifles near Mostar. . . . A similar incident in May 1991 involved trucks bringing arms into Bosnia from Montenegro."[41] Bosnian President Izetbegović knew what these developments portended and, in 1991, he came out in favor of Bosnia's joining in a tight federation with Serbia and Montenegro; the opposition this proposal kindled among his own supporters was so strong that he was compelled to withdraw it.[42]

With Slovenia already threatening secession, Croatia promised to secede if Slovenia did so, and Bosnian President Izetbegović, having been chastised for his offer to federate with Serbia and Montenegro, underlined on several occasions that Bosnia would not remain associated with a truncated Yugoslavia ruled by Milošević and that if Croatia seceded, so too would Bosnia.[43] Serbian President Milošević, in turn, declared that if the federation broke up, Serbia would seek to annex Serb-inhabited portions of Croatia and Bosnia—which was geopolitical nonsense, since the populations in Bosnia were dispersed in such a way that it was utterly impossible to draw a clear border dividing ethnic groups, unless population exchanges, voluntary or involuntary, were employed. On 28 September 1990, Serbia adopted a new constitution which went far beyond the Slovenian constitution in placing defense and security *entirely* in the hands of authorities of the Republic of Serbia. Ironically, perhaps, the army leadership, which had fulminated against the more modest assertions of the Slovenian constitutional amendments, had nothing critical to say about the more radical claims asserted by the Serbian constitution. In March 1991, Serbia organized Serbian defense units not under federal command,[44] following similar moves by Slovenia and Croatia.

The Serbian-dominated army, meanwhile, grew apprehensive of Slovenian and Croatian moves to slash their contributions to the military budget and, in November 1990, had formed a revived Communist Party, with Slobodan Milošević's wife, Mirjana Marković, among the leading figures of the party. In December 1990, General Veljko Kadijević, federal Minister of Defense, told a *Danas* reporter that the army would not permit Yugoslavia to become another "Lebanon,"[45] and the following month the army came close to invading Croatia. An eleventh-hour interrepublic agreement averted immediate danger, but the threat prompted Slovenia and Croatia to conclude an agreement to coordinate in the spheres of security and defense. A subsequent "assurance" from the army (in March) that it would not interfere in the political negotiations going on among the heads of the six republics was not particularly assuring, in that the generals' communiqué clearly left open the possibility of military intervention to suppress any Slovenian escape from the waxing tyranny in Yugoslavia and to quash the conflict between Serbs and Croats in Croatia[46]—moves which could only contribute to intensifying interethnic hatreds and igniting a war between the republics. Rumors circulated in early 1991 to the effect that Admiral Branko Mamula, the former defense minister, supposedly intended to launch a coup, declare military rule, and set himself up as dictator.[47] But neither Kadijević nor Mamula was in a position, in this multiethnic country, to play Jaruzelski. And even Jaruzelski, it will be recalled, ultimately failed and was forced to scuttle his own regime.

The Republics Awaken

Enough has been said already to make it clear that the will to remain in union had, by 1989, seriously atrophied. As of late 1990, some 88 percent of Slovenes considered secession their best option. In May 1991, 94.3 percent of Croats likewise voted for independence. A sizable majority of Albanians (in Kosovo) and a growing number of Macedonians were also coming to favor this solution for their own regions.[48] The figures for Slovenes and Croats were close to 100 percent by mid-1991. Prosecessionist movements emerged among the Muslims of Novi Pazar, the Albanians of Kosovo, and the Macedonians, alongside Serbian secessionist groups operating in parts of Croatia and Bosnia who were seeking the annexation of parts of Croatia and all or parts of Bosnia to Serbia.[49] By the beginning of 1991, thus, Milošević's earlier disavowal of any aspiration to redraw any interrepublican borders[50] was starting to seem to have been cruelly prophetic of the Serbian leader's real intentions.

After the confiscations of much of their Territorial Defense weaponry, Slovenia and Croatia were in desperate need of armaments and turned to foreign sources. Already in autumn 1990 these two republics began to receive arms deliveries across the Hungarian border. Jović writes, in his memoirs, that between November 1990 and early January 1991 Croatia received ten barges of arms and ammunition from Hungary, including tens of thousands of new Kalashnikov automatic rifles as well as several million rounds of live ammunition.[51] Kadijević, Jović, and Milošević watched this process with concern. As early as November 1990, Kadijević and Jović were discussing preparations for the arrest of General Martin Špegelj, Croatia's defense minister, who had arranged for the deliveries to Croatia and who was doing his best to prepare Croatian defenses.[52]

On 9 January, the state presidency adopted an order requiring that all militias which were not part of the JNA command or associated with organs of the Ministry of Internal Affairs be disbanded and that all weapons held by such units be surrendered to the JNA. The order was interpreted as applying to armed formations under the authority of the Slovenian and Croatian governments, but not to armed formations of Serbs that had been organized completely illegally in Croatia and Bosnia. On 21 January, Stipe Mesić, Croatia's representative on the SFRY collective presidency, informed Jović, then serving as president of the SFRY presidency, that Croatia would not surrender its weapons and that it was prepared to secede if Belgrade pressed the point.[53] Four days later, JNA criminal prosecutors arrested two active JNA officers and two civilians in the territory of Croatia on suspicion of involvement in arms trafficking. That same night, the army was placed on full alert. Troop movements in Croatia raised the level of tension and gave rise to rumors that a coup d'etat was imminent. The federal Ministry of Defense circulated a secret document at that time to all JNA commanders called "A Report Concerning the Actual Situation in the World and Yugoslavia and the Immediate Tasks of the Yugoslav People's Army."[54]

The limiting factor was that Kadijević insisted on a legal cover for any military action against Croatia or Slovenia, and this could only come from the presidency. The

Serbian bloc tried to push through authorization for armed intervention by the JNA in Croatia, but the Bosnian delegate was not prepared to support the Serbian bloc on this, and there was no other possible ally available. Frustrated at this level, Kadijević then determined that he would have Špegelj arrested. Thereupon, Špegelj went into hiding.

A Last Chance?

One of the great "what-ifs" in South Slav history is associated with the date 9 March 1991, when some 40,000 Serbian protesters, mostly supporters of Vuk Drašković's opposition Serbian Renaissance Party, took to the streets of Belgrade to demand that Milošević step down. What if they had succeeded? What if their protest had rallied leaders in other republics? What if Milošević had been toppled? Could war have been averted? Or were the hatreds already at too high a pitch and other figures (such as Jović, Babić, and Bosnian Serb leader Karadžić) too committed to a Greater Serbian concept for even Milošević's eleventh-hour removal to have made any difference? But Milošević had no intention of falling victim to street protests, even though he had used precisely such tactics to bring down nonnationalists in Novi Sad, Titograd, and Priština. The question was how to obtain the approval of the state presidency in a hurry, so that troops might be sent against the protesters without delay. Jović saved the day for Milošević, employing the constitutionally dubious tack of obtaining votes from fellow presidency members by phone rather than calling an emergency meeting; by midday, Jović had secured six votes in support of the use of armed force against the protesters, with only the Slovenian and Croatian representatives not giving their assent.[55] Tanks rolled onto the streets of Belgrade in the afternoon, police raided and shut down the liberal B-92 radio station, and police were sent against the protesting Serbs. Although the police and army won the day, tens of thousands of anti-Milošević protesters continued to gather on Belgrade's streets over the subsequent week, singing "Give Peace a Chance" and making clear their opposition to ethnic intolerance, jingoism, and war mania.[56]

But the protests ultimately scarcely made a dent. At the end of the same month, Serb insurgents seized control of a police station at Plitvice National Park in Croatia. Conflict broke out between the insurgents and Croatian police, resulting in the first casualties of the war. The JNA moved in "to separate the sides."

In October 1990, Slovenia and Croatia had issued a formal joint proposal for transforming the Yugoslav state into a confederation.[57] Although this proposal held the best prospects for saving what could still be saved, it was immediately rejected by the Serbian and Montenegrin governments. Indeed, Jović, who as president of the state presidency was supposed to pass along that proposal to the Federal Assembly for discussion, did not do so, passing along only a subsequently drafted Serbian proposal. Even so, the confederal idea did not die immediately. During the early months of 1991, Slovenia, Croatia, and Macedonia continued to argue for confederalization, Bosnia was willing to go along with confederalization, and Serbia and Montenegro remained opposed, insisting instead on a recentralized scheme. Of the six republics, four viewed their borders as state borders not subject to administrative change or negotiation; only Serbia and Montenegro held to the view that the borders separating the republics were administrative in character and hence subject to revision. Slovenia, Croatia, and Bosnia wanted to depoliticize the army—a move opposed by Serbia and Montenegro—while Macedonia had not yet worked out a clear policy in this area.[58]

It was in this context that, throughout the early months of 1991, the six republics conducted a series of summit talks to avert civil war and find a path to interrepublican agreement, but none of these meetings were productive. And it was unclear, as long as Milošević was in power in Serbia, how any progress might be made. By April 1991, Bosnia and Macedonia had been more or less converted to the confederalist cause being advocated by Slovenia and Croatia.[59] Slovenia and Croatia and Bosnia had already declared their sovereignty, and Slovenia and Croatia were, by then, making preparations for independence, though the Slovenes were much farther along with such preparations than the Croats. On 7 April, the Internal Macedonian Revolutionary Organization–Democratic Party for Macedonian National Unity (IMRO-DPMNU) embraced the same concept and approved a statute advocating the "comprehensive political, economic, and spiritual independence of the Macedonian state."[60] Slovenian President Kučan had already admitted, in an address to the Slovenian Assembly on 20 February, "We [have] proceeded from the fact Yugoslavia, as a joint federal state, has politically and economically disintegrated."[61]

The interrepublican summit meetings remained deadlocked, inasmuch as Serbia and Montenegro were unwilling to turn back from their hegemonist course. Meanwhile, the country continued to unravel. Slavonian Serbs—including many who had come to the region from Serbia and other parts in the 1970s in search of jobs[62]—declared their intention to secede from Croatia and join Vojvodina, thus coming under Milošević's rule.[63] The self-proclaimed Krajina, declared by Croatia's Serbs, announced its plan to seek annexation to Serbia—which, in the prevailing conditions, was tantamount to a declaration of war. In response, Croats living in the Krajina region took steps to register their opposition to this move and to proclaim their intention to remain part of Croatia.[64]

In spite of the growing tensions between Croatia and Serbia, manifested, for example, in Serb-instigated disturbances in Pakrac in early March, the Croatian government was, nonetheless, receiving some mixed signals from Belgrade. When I talked with Stipe Mesić in 1997, he recounted how he approached Jović, who was then finishing his term as president of the SFRY state presidency, and told him that the Croatian government had evidence that the JNA was arming Serb inhabitants of villages in Croatia; Mesić wanted to resolve this through negotiations. To his surprise, Jović replied that Serbia had no interest in any Croatian territory and that the question of the armed Serbian militias was "a Croatian internal affair." He underlined that Serbia had no interest in the Croatian Serbs and no pretensions to any Croatian territory.[65] When Mesić probed a little further, Jović said that what interested Serbia was Bosnia and that Serbia wanted to annex two-thirds of Bosnian territory. Thereupon, Mesić proposed a meeting of Milošević, Tudjman, Jović, and himself. Jović responded positively and said he would talk with Milošević about the proposal. An hour later, Jović called Mesić back and said that Milošević had agreed to have such a meeting. Croatian President Tudjman could be expected to warm to the idea, as he had argued in print for many years that portions of Bosnia should be "restored" to Croatia; it was generally thought that Tudjman was thinking along the lines of a reversion to boundaries approximating those of the Croatian Banovina established in 1939. Tudjman, however, preferred to exclude Jović and Mesić, in the belief that Milošević would talk more frankly if only the two of them were present.[66] On 30 March, therefore, Tudjman went to Karadjordjevo for secret talks with Milošević about the partition of Bosnia.[67] Tudjman came back giddy with the illusion of success, pleased with a guarantee from General Kadijević that the JNA would not attack Croatia and gratified by Milošević's agreement that Croatia could annex up to one-third of Bosnia-Herzegovina.[68] Some months later, after the war's "official" inception on the Slovenian front, Tudjman and Milošević dispatched groups of academic experts presumably to work out the details of the partition of Bosnia. The substance of their talks was classified "top secret."

In Montenegro—long divided between pro-Serbian and anti-Serbian Montenegrins—the biggest change in the months between September 1990 and June 1991 was an increase in pressure on Montenegro by Milošević's supporters to submit to annexation by Serbia. A Movement for the Unification of Serbia and Montenegro was organized and on 6 November it submitted an appeal, signed by 10,000 citizens of Montenegro and Serbia, to the Serbian and Montenegrin assemblies for a referendum on the unification of the two republics.[69] The Montenegrin government resisted such pressures, even as pro-Serbian and anti-Serbian groups proliferated in the republic.

Even Macedonia saw a sudden rise in national consciousness among all the nationality groups living there: Macedonians, Albanians, Serbs, Gypsies/Roma, and others. There were at least two active nationalist organizations in Macedonia, both of which demanded the immediate secession of the republic from Yugoslavia: the Movement for All-Macedonian Action, and the IMRO–DPMNU.[70] The latter urged that the Yugoslav People's Army be withdrawn from Macedonia. In that organization's view, "only the Territorial Defense [Forces] can stand as the legitimate defender of Macedonia."[71] Not surprisingly, the Bulgarian government expressed its opinion about Macedonian statehood, but, in an ostensible reversal of the policy of the Zhivkov era, the Bulgarian Foreign Ministry declared its full support for an independent Macedonian state and affirmed that it no longer nurtured any territorial pretensions vis-à-vis Macedonia.[72] This Bulgarian declaration was probably designed to further weaken Milošević's position in the south.

There was even new wind filling the sails of regional autonomist movements. Aside from the aforementioned movements of Muslims in the Sandžak of Novi Pazar, of Albanians in Kosovo and western Macedonia, and of Serbs in Croatia and

Bosnia-Herzegovina, there were also signs in 1990–1991 of waxing autonomism in Istria, Dalmatia, and Vojvodina, as well as a sharp anti-Hungarian backlash among some of Vojvodina's Serbs (generally among more recent settlers to the province).

In mid-May, Borisav Jović (a Serb) was supposed to step down as president of the state presidency. He was supposed to be succeeded in office by Stipe Mesić, the non-communist representative from Croatia. But Mesić had already shown that he was not inclined to support centralist proposals and "emergency measures" proposed by the Serbian bloc, as his predecessor from Croatia, Stipe Šuvar, had repeatedly done. Moreover, Mesić was already on a collision course with the army chief of staff.[73] Thus, when it came time for the supposedly routine installation of Mesić in office— which was supposed to occur on 15 May 1991—a street meeting of Serbs took place in front of the federal *Skupština* to protest against Mesić's succession. Those present shouted "Death to Mesić!"[74]

Back in March, the Assembly of the Republic of Serbia had removed Riza Sapunxhiu as Kosovo's representative on the state presidency in contravention of the constitution; in his place, Milošević and Jović installed their protégé, Sejdo Bajramović, who was duly ratified by the Serbian Assembly in the "absence" of the Kosovar provincial Assembly, which had been dissolved.[75] Bajramović, thus, was in theory supposed to represent a body which did not exist, but which had been granted representation on the grounds that it did exist and, indeed, exist as an autonomous decisionmaking body! Sapunxhiu, who had been elected by the Provincial Assembly of Kosovo before its suppression on orders from Milošević, had already displayed an independent spirit,[76] and Milošević and Jović would not have been able to count on his support for their flagrantly unconstitutional actions to block Mesić's succession. When Slovenia and Croatia raised objections to this procedure in the federal *Skupština*, the resolution was delayed,[77] but in the meantime, Jović and Milošević saw to it that Mesić was denied sufficient votes to endorse his succession. It would not be until 1 July that Mesić would finally be installed as president, as part of a compromise brokered by the European Union (EU).

The army clashed with Croatian workers in Slavonski Brod, when the latter tried to prevent the army from removing 100 new tanks from an arms factory.[78] Army tanks and troops were also deployed against Croats in Listica (a Croatian town in Bosnia). In several instances, there were reports that Serbian forces were making use of former members of Romania's secret police, the *Securitate*, who had fled Romania after the ouster of Romanian President Nicolae Ceauşescu in December 1989. Croatian police, in fact, intercepted some radio transmissions among Serbian forces: they were in Romanian.[79] In Borovo Selo, a Croatian town whose largely Serbian inhabitants were among those who had entered Slavonia in the 1970s in search of work, shooting erupted in early May, resulting in sixteen deaths and an unspecified number of wounded. When Croatian authorities dispatched police to the region, the Serbs agreed to give the police safe passage under a white flag. But when the Croatian police entered the village, white flags in hand, the Serbs opened fire on them, killing thirteen police and wounding twenty-one. Some Croatian police were mutilated by Serbs; their eyes were gouged out, their throats slit, and their genitals cut off.[80] Once again, the army sent in troops, as it had done in previous weeks in Plitvice National Park, as well as in Kijevo, Šibenik, and other towns in Croatia.

In mid-May, the chiefs of staff of the Yugoslav army, navy, and air force met in Belgrade, behind closed doors, to plan the disposition of forces in the coming action. "Duties were determined for the army commands, units and institutions of the Yugoslav People's Army," said a Defense Ministry statement after the meeting.[81] The army amassed large concentrations of forces in the northern part of Bosnia-Herzegovina,[82] sent troops to Maribor the night of 26 May to arrest Colonel Vladimir Milošević (no relation to Slobodan), the commander of Slovenia's eastern Territorial Defense district,[83] and drew up plans for seizing control of Slovenia's borders and the airport at Ljubljana.[84] Meanwhile, the JNA continued to demand the complete disarmament and disbanding of the Slovenian and Croatian defense militias—moves which would have left those republics defenseless and which were accordingly resisted. Meanwhile, as already noted, Slovenia and Croatia turned to private arms merchants in Western Europe and the United States in search of heavy artillery and other weaponry.[85]

War

On 27 May, Stipe Mesić, whose accession to the Yugoslav presidency was still in limbo, delivered a confident speech in Krasić, at a ceremony to mark Croatian statehood. Debunking pessimistic forecasts, Mesić reviewed the failed efforts to topple the Marković government and said that any recourse to the army had "no chance." He concluded that it was "quite unlikely" that the army would take any steps to block the secession of either Slovenia or Croatia.[86] Two days later, the Serbian parliament refused to take up Croatian Serbs' appeal for annexation to Serbia—thus giving some encouragement to Croatia.[87]

But Slovenia and Croatia faced a serious obstacle. In spite of early expressions of sympathy from the German and Austrian governments, the states of Western Europe held back from offering diplomatic recognition or support to these two republics. On the contrary, the United States, the Soviet Union, China, France, and other countries issued statements supportive of Yugoslav unity and hostile to Slovenian and Croatian secession. Where the United States was concerned, this policy was the fruit of the Bush administration's concern not to do anything to aggravate Moscow or to send the "wrong message" to the Soviet Union. In fact, the Bush administration applied pressure on the European Community (EC) to ostracize Slovenia and Croatia, made IMF loans contingent upon the preservation of Yugoslav unity, and sent Secretary of State James Baker to Yugoslavia in June 1991 to declare publicly that the republics should "negotiate." The only form of "negotiation" compatible with the preservation of Yugoslav unity, as Bush and Baker should have known, would have been the complete surrender of the Slovenian and Croatian governments to Serbian *diktat*, resulting in the removal of the local democratically elected governments and their replacement by quasi-socialist quislings. It is ironic, in this context, to note that Jović, Šuvar, and Lazar Mojsov—and no doubt other Yugoslav leaders as well—unable or unwilling to admit their own culpability, were becoming increasingly obsessed with the notion that the United States and Western Europe were actively plotting the dismemberment of the SFRY. Indeed, Šuvar told me in 1997 that, in his view, Milošević's suppression of the autonomous provinces, conquest of Montenegro, dispatch of Serbian secret police into Bosnia, economic embargo against Slovenia, and repeated violations of the federal constitution had, in his view, essentially nothing to do with the breakup of Yugoslavia![88]

The Slovenian government had previously announced that it would secede from Yugoslavia by 26 June if no progress had been made by then toward resolving the crisis. The Croatian government had promised to follow any Slovenian exit. True to their word, Slovenia and Croatia unilaterally declared their independence on 25 June 1991. Two days later, the Serb-controlled Yugoslav People's Army (JNA) sent tanks and helicopters crashing across the Croatian-Slovenian border into Slovenia, though without proper authorization.[89] The JNA strafed civilian trucks, bombed private homes and farms, and shot and killed civilians sitting at cafés, working in their fields, and engaging in other peaceful pursuits. The army also wrought considerable damage to Slovenia's economic infrastructure, including roads and bridges. After two days of fighting, the JNA controlled the Ljubljana airport and all major access roads to Italy, Austria, and Hungary. According to Nicole Janigro, casualties totaled 17 deaths and 149 wounded on the Slovenian side and 37 dead and 163 wounded on the part of the JNA.[90] The European Community signaled its refusal to recognize Slovenian or Croatian independence and sent a delegation to pressure the combatants to find a peaceful solution.

As of June 1991, the JNA had 138,000 troops on active duty and 400,000 troops in the reserves. It had 1,850 battle tanks (mostly old Soviet T-54 and T-55 tanks, but also some Yugoslav T-72s). It had some 2,000 towed artillery pieces, 500 armored personnel carriers, and other Soviet-made weaponry. The navy commanded 10,000 troops, with 4 frigates, 59 patrol and coastal craft, and 5 small submarines at its disposal. The 32,000-strong air force had 455 combat aircraft, including MiG-29s and 198 helicopters.[91] Slovenia had a small militia comprising about 20,000 troops as of June 1991, but both Slovenia and Croatia claimed to be able to mobilize about 200,000 troops on short notice.[92] Slovenia and Croatia also possessed an unspecified number of tanks, antitank weapons, and other weaponry, most of it allegedly imported from Germany or Hungary.

Of the two breakaway republics, Croatia was, in military terms, the more desperate, in spite of the valiant efforts of General Špegelj. So short of arms were the Croats that, as Christopher Bennett reports, when the war came to Croatia, the Croatian armed forces ransacked museums and film studios for old weaponry from World War II. Some of the weapons obtained in this way had originally been parachuted to Tito's Partisans fifty years earlier.[93]

Slovenia had, to some extent, relied on a defense agreement concluded with Croatia to present a solid front against Serbia. But in May 1991, Croatian President

Tudjman had allowed himself to be persuaded to abandon his Slovenian ally in exchange for Serbian promises of goodwill. Hence, when JNA tanks were sent rolling out of Croatia into Slovenia, Tudjman made no move to hinder their advance. Tudjman did not believe that these same tanks might be used against Croatia once the battle in Slovenia had ended.

The chances of reviving Yugoslavia had died long before the JNA's brutal assault on Slovenia in late June 1991. But the assault, launched in the name of "unity," was a logical capstone to the program pursued by Milošević since 1987 and a fulfillment of long-standing fears among Yugoslavs that this multiethnic country was heading toward civil war.[94] The delayed confirmation of Stipe Mesić as president of the state presidency on 30 June could not dispel tensions created by the resort to arms and came too late to constitute a reason for especial hope. Meanwhile, by the beginning of July, mediation by the EC had obtained JNA agreement to take its troops out of Slovenia,[95] though the process was only completed in October.

But no sooner did things calm down in Slovenia than tensions flared in Croatia, where the local secessionist Serbian council was said to enjoy the confidence and support of all Serbs living in the "Krajina."[96] Between July and August, Serbian militias loyal to Milan Martić and Milan Babić brought an ever expanding area under their direct control, in what Silber and Little have accurately described as an "undeclared war."[97] Croatian villagers fled before the Serbian militias, while the Croatian National Guard attempted to maintain some shred of order, scurrying around the frontlines in commandeered grocery vans and adapted tourist buses. Ratko Mladić, then a Lieutenant Colonel in the Croatian Serb forces, took charge of the assault on Kijevo, a Croatian-populated village surrounded by Serb-held territory. On 18 August, Mladić delivered a forty-eight-hour ultimatum to the residents of Kijevo, demanding that they abandon their homes and lands. When the residents of Kijevo refused to leave peacefully, Mladić ordered his troops to destroy the town. On 26 August, in the course of a twelve-hour bombardment, Kijevo was completely leveled.[98] By the end of October, Serbian insurgents controlled about a third of Croatia and continued to press forward. About that time, a Serbian spokesperson from Croatia declared, "The Serbs of Croatia [12.2 percent of the republic's population in 1991] are not a minority and the [European Conference] on Yugoslavia has understood that."[99] Of course, if 12.2 percent is not to be understood as a "minority," then it follows that it construes itself as a "majority"—meaning, at the same time, that the remaining 87.8 percent is the "real minority." One is reminded that Lenin's Bolsheviks acquired their name in a claim to represent the majority of the Social Democratic Party, although, in fact, they were, at the time the claim was made, a distinct minority.

Croatia's situation was complicated by the fact that the JNA was ensconced in barracks in various locations across Croatia. There were two theories about how to deal with this. General Špegelj's preferred approach, which Mesić also supported, would have entailed a combination of siege and denial of electricity and water to compel the JNA troops to surrender, leave their arsenals behind, and leave Croatia empty-handed.[100] The risk here, as Slavko Goldstein underlined when we talked in 1997, was that the JNA had every reason to want to fight its way out of such situations and that could have risked armed conflict breaking out in the middle of some of Croatia's largest cities, including in downtown Zagreb.[101] Indeed, precisely such a situation developed in Gospić in southern Croatia, where the Croatian National Guard surrounded the JNA barracks and ordered the JNA to surrender. Instead of surrendering, the JNA garrison decided to force its way out; reinforcements were drawn up at the outskirts of town and added mortar and artillery firepower. After three days of mutual bombardment, the barracks fell, but in the meantime, most of Gospić had been severely damaged, most of the town having been rendered uninhabitable.[102] On the other hand, Norman Cigar believes that Špegelj and Mesić, and not Tudjman, were urging the more sensible approach. Cigar argues that

> The garrisons were surrounded and vulnerable, and it is unlikely that they could have disengaged themselves. . . . The JNA, in fact, could not even have removed all its equipment or personnel without Croatian cooperation. . . . The JNA garrisons were seriously undermanned even after their readiness levels had been raised in 1991 and were beset by low morale. . . . The besieged garrisons would have had little choice but to surrender.[103]

Even today there is no agreement as to which policy would have been best.

Aside from Vukovar (prewar population of about 50,000), which by October 1991 had been reduced to rubble, Serbian militias, backed by the JNA, also laid siege to Osijek (population 200,000, including 30,000 Serbs),[104] Dubrovnik (population 60,000, including fewer than 6,000 Serbs),[105] Petrinja (which fell to Serbs after a struggle), Glina (which *Danas* reporter Jasmina Kuzmanović dubbed the "Croatian Alamo,"),[106] Okučani (14 kilometers from the Bosnian border), Vinkovci (a city near Vukovar in eastern Slavonia), Borovo, and other Croatian towns and villages. Zagreb, Karlovac, Osijek, Vukovar, Borovo, and other towns were subjected to aerial bombardment.[107] In early October, air strikes were even carried out against the presidential palace in Zagreb, nearly killing Croatian President Tudjman. In the midst of the fighting, Serbian President Milošević accused Croatia of trying to pursue a "policy of genocide."[108]

By the end of December 1991, more than half a million persons had been driven from their homes, many of them fleeing abroad (chiefly to Germany and Hungary). At least 3,000 persons had been killed in the war, and thousands more wounded. Up to 40 percent of Croatia's factories had been destroyed, and the cost of rebuilding was estimated at some $18.7 billion.[109]

Between July and mid-November, some twelve cease-fires collapsed. Peace plans presented by the EC proved to be unacceptable to Serbia, and peace plans presented by Serbia proved to be unacceptable to other republics.[110]

In early August, Milošević called for a meeting of the representatives of three of the four republics that, as of then, had not seceded from what was, by then, at most a legal concept—the SFRY—namely, Serbia, Montenegro, and Bosnia. The purpose of the meeting was to discuss the restructuring of the Yugoslav state.[111] The meeting took place on 12 August and was attended by: Milošević, the president of Serbia; Aleksandar Bakočević, president of the National Assembly of Serbia; Momir Bulatović, the president of Montenegro; Risto Bukčević, the president of the Assembly of Montenegro; and Momčilo Krajišnik, the president of the Assembly of Bosnia-Herzegovina. Alija Izetbegović, president of Bosnia-Herzegovina, had of course been invited to attend, but he had declined. Krajišnik's participation, thus, reflected intra-elite discord at the highest level of the Bosnian state apparatus.[112] The meeting issued a call for a new constitution, enumerating a number of bland principles.[113] Krajišnik, hailed in Belgrade, faced severe criticism back in Bosnia for having attended the Belgrade meeting at all.[114]

Macedonia and Bosnia-Herzegovina at first held back from issuing any declarations, but under the pressure of events, first Macedonia, then Bosnia, declared its intention to establish an independent state. Moreover, in October 1991, the Albanian opposition in Kosovo conducted a referendum among that province's Albanian population: an overwhelming majority of those taking part voted for secession and annexation to Albania. For them, the Yugoslav option was likewise dead.

At the same time, demands were being heard in Serbia that historic Dubrovnik be taken away from Croatia. The Belgrade magazine *Intervju* published an interview with academician Miroslav Pantić, who demanded that the Dubrovnik area be set up as an "independent" republic separate from Croatia. Pantić blamed Austria and the Catholic Church for having Croatized Dubrovnik and claimed that a group of Dubrovnik citizens—how many he did not say—had framed a demand in 1945 that the city be set up as an autonomous province, if not as a republic.[115] Despite international protests, the Serb-dominated army kept a stranglehold on historic Dubrovnik, reinforcing its siege force in late October. The army informed the city's defenders that "only surrender can save Dubrovnik."[116] That there could have been a class dimension to the siege of Dubrovnik was suggested by "the systematic destruction, by wire-guided missile, of every last yacht in the harbour of the old town" in November 1991.[117] But in May 1992, the Croatian authorities reached an agreement with the JNA, which agreed to withdraw from Dubrovnik's hinterland.

In July 1991, the federal government issued a statement that it was slashing the military budget from $34 to just under $15 billion.[118] This decision was quickly countermanded and Belgrade began printing money, without backing, to pay the army.[119] As a result, instead of shrinking, the military budget increased as a proportion of the total federal budget from 40 to 65 percent by October.[120] A Western diplomat assigned to Belgrade commented, "Only 25 percent of the budget is covered [by reserves]. They are printing the rest."[121] At the same time, Serbia was losing hard-currency income on sales of electric power to Italy and Austria, because the grid that ran through Croatia was closed down by the war. Croatia also shut down the oil pipeline to Serbia.[122] Industrial production slumped everywhere as a result of the war, including in Serbia, and Western credits dried up.[123]

By late September, there were confirmed reports that the JNA was experiencing growing problems recruiting soldiers. Jović, in his memoirs, admitted that, as of October 1991, Serbian and Vojvodinan reservists were resisting mobilization and that desertion from the front was a problem.[124] On 7 November 1991, the Serbian government renamed the army and abandoned any pretense that that force represented any republics other than Serbia and Montenegro (and perhaps Bosnia-Herzegovina).[125]

Meanwhile, within Serbia itself, critical voices could still be heard.[126] Some domestic critics expressed the conviction that Milošević would ultimately fall. "Milošević is not a man of vision," said Miloš Vasić, editor of the privately owned Belgrade magazine *Vreme* and one of Milošević's more deadly critics. "The Greater Serbia that he is trying to create will be undefendable and unsustainable."[127] Dragan Veselinov, head of the opposition Serbian Peasant Party, linked Milošević's fortunes to the war: "The moment Milošević stops his territorial campaign, he will face social unrest in Serbia."[128] And Zoran Djindjić, leader of the opposition Democratic Party in Serbia, seconding this point of view, told an American correspondent in 1991, "It's impossible to defeat Milošević in Serbia. All our internal problems have been dissolved in the war. Milošević, like Napoleon, will be defeated on the battlefield. The army in Croatia will come back to Serbia and they will overthrow Milošević. . . . The only question is how long it will take to defeat him."[129]

Such views were commonly expressed in 1991 and even in the early months of 1992, when there was still some degree of attachment to "the old Yugoslavia" in Serbia and before the heady nationalism of the battlefield totally effaced those old attachments. In spite of opposition confidence, Milošević, a consummate politician, has confounded his opposition time and time again, even weathering the opposition protests of November–December 1996.[130] Moreover, with steady economic and materiel support from Russia, Greece, Romania, and China and de facto diplomatic support from Britain and France, Milošević appeared to have a chance even to ride out his economic woes.

Conclusion: The Pied Piper of Belgrade

Milošević and his cohorts (Jović, Kadijević, Miroslav Šolević, Babić, Martić, Momir Bulatović, and others) repeatedly and flagrantly violated both the valid constitution and the valid laws of the land as well as established procedural guidelines for governmental bodies and openly discriminated against Croats and Albanians and in favor of Serbs. The threat of military action against Slovenia in early spring 1988 was patently unconstitutional, as was the abolition of the autonomous provinces. The mobilization of antigovernment protesters to topple the legal governments in Novi Sad, Titograd, and Priština was obviously illegal, but the Serbian authorities took action against Albanian protesters who *supported* their legally elected leaders and arrested Albanians who signed a petition of support for the constitution![131] The installation of Momir Bulatović as party chief in Montenegro and of Rahman Morina as party chief in Kosovo violated established procedures, which called for the appointments to be made locally, not in Belgrade. The amendments to the Serbian constitution adopted in February 1989 stood in contradiction to the federal constitution, while the tactics of police intimidation applied against members of the Kosovo provincial Assembly prior to the 24 March vote could not be justified under Yugoslav law. Both the Serbian suppression of the provincial Assembly in Priština and the Serbian pocketing of Kosovo's and Vojvodina's votes on the state presidency were contrary to the constitution. Belgrade's suppression of the Albanian-language newspaper *Rilindja* and of Radio-TV Priština's Albanian service in 1990 was illegal. Then there were the sundry violations of the basic human rights of Albanians in Kosovo, ranging from job dismissals to the use of house searches as a form of harassment to beatings of local intellectuals (to be discussed more fully in Chapter 13).

The use of official channels (such as SAWPY) to call for a boycott of Slovenian goods was illegal. So too were the Serbian bank swindle of December 1990, the holding of Serbian referenda in Croatia in summer 1990, the unilateral proclamation of Serb autonomous regions in Croatia and Bosnia between August 1990 and April 1991, the establishment and arming of Serbian militias not subordinate to the republics in which they were operating (which began in summer 1990), and the failure of the military to report its budget to the *Skupština* in December 1990. The purchase of Soviet weaponry without the foreknowledge of Prime Minister Marković (in early 1991) violated established procedures, as did the state presidency's adoption of "special measures" in the absence of one of its members (Dolanc from Slovenia). Borisav Jović's refusal to pass along to the Yugoslav *Skupština* the Slovenian-Croatian proposal to convert the Yugoslav federation into a confederation also represented a procedural irregularity, which was only magnified by his simultaneous decision to pass along a subsequently drafted Serbian proposal for recentralization. Serbian disturbances in Pakrac (Croatia) in early March 1991 were strictly illegal; so too was the use of force against anti-Milošević demonstrators on 9 March 1991 (in turn adopted through the highly irregular procedure of a telephone "meeting"). Jović himself resigned his post as president of the collective presidency in mid-March 1991 in a bid, by his own admission, to give the military a free hand in Croatia and Slovenia.[132] Nor was there any legal basis for Milošević's demand that, if the SFRY were to break up, interrepublican borders would have to be revised. Even Milošević's comporting himself during 1991 as if he were the legitimate Yugoslav leader—as manifested, for example, in his arrogation to himself of the authority to allow (on 3 July 1991) that he had no objections to Slovenia's "disassociation"[133]—was, at a minimum, not in keeping with the spirit of the law.

But in spite of the Serbian side's flagrant violation of the constitution, laws, and procedural guidelines, Milošević was able to retain the support of the international community down to the bitter end. This was accompanied on the part of the Western diplomatic community in Belgrade by "an arrogant rejection and even open hostility toward the two Western republics," in Viktor Meier's words.[134] In this way, Milošević, enjoying the confidence and complicity of the army leadership, displayed some of the talents of the fabled Pied Piper of Hamlin, who led the children of Hamlin to their doom. Milošević's talent for beguilement is considerable, but it is not unique. Shakespeare has King Richard III, in his play of the same name, confess,

I do the wrong, and first begin to brawl.
The secret mischiefs that I set abroach
I lay unto the grievous charge of others.
Clarence, who I indeed have cast in darkness,
I do beweep to many simple gulls ...
And tell them 'tis the Queen and her allies
That stir the King against the Duke my brother.
Now they believe it, and withal whet me
To be revenged on Rivers, Dorset, Grey.
But then I sigh, and with a piece of Scripture
Tell them that God bids us do good for evil;
And thus I clothe my naked villainy
With odd old ends stol'n forth of holy writ,
And seem a saint when most I play the devil.[135]

The result was a confused policy on the part of the West, which continued also during the war years 1991–1995 and which was fueled by illusions about Yugoslavia and Milošević, inadequate use of the expertise available to the West's policy-makers, outright disinformation (as, for example, British Prime Minister John Major's conviction that the problems in Yugoslavia were of ancient vintage), a Germanophobia which predated any hint of advocacy on behalf of either Slovenia or Croatia on Bonn's part, insensitivity to human rights violations in the region, and a misunderstanding of the West's own interests in the Yugoslav area.[136]

Notes

1. Ted Robert Gurr, *Why Men Rebel* (Princeton: Princeton University Press, 1970), especially chaps. 2 and 4.

2. Ibid., p. 50.

3. Ibid., pp. 197–198.

4. Figures for national income, industrial output, and agricultural output are taken from Table 3.1. Figures for inflation and foreign debt are derived from Viktor Meier, *Wie Jugoslawien verspielt wurde*, 2nd ed. (Munich: C. H. Beck, 1996), pp. 183, 185.

5. *Danas* (Zagreb), no. 459 (4 December 1990), p. 18.

6. Susan L. Woodward, *Socialist Unemployment: The Political Economy of Yugoslavia, 1945–1990* (Princeton: Princeton University Press, 1995), p. 256.

7. *Wall Street Journal* (18 March 1991).

8. *Neue Zürcher Zeitung* (29/30 March 1991), p. 18.

9. Tanjug (28 February 1991), in Foreign Broadcast Information Service (FBIS), *Daily Report* (Eastern Europe), 1 March 1991, p. 39.

10. See *Neue Zürcher Zeitung* (8 February 1991), p. 16, and (29/30 March 1991), p. 18.

11. See Philip J. Cohen, *Serbia's Secret War: Propaganda and the Deceit of History* (College Station, Tex.: Texas A & M University Press, 1996).

12. *Borba* (Belgrade) (6 March 1991), p. 3.

13. Meier, *Wie Jugoslawien*, p. 241. See also Franjo Tudjman, *Bespuća povijesne zbiljnosti: Rasprava o povijesti i filozofii zlosilja* (Zagreb: Nakladni zavod Matice Hrvatske, 1989).

14. Noel Malcolm, *Bosnia: A Short History* (New York: New York University Press, 1994), p. 205.

15. See Jozo Tomasevich, *The Chetniks: War and Revolution in Yugoslavia, 1941–1945* (Stanford, Calif.: Stanford University Press, 1975), pp. 347, 414.

16. Vladimir Žerjavić, *Gubici stanovništva Jugoslavije u drugom svjetskom ratu* (Zagreb: Jugoslavensko Viktimološko Društvo, 1989), pp. 61–66.

17. These figures, as cited critically in Vladimir Žerjavić, *Opsesije i megalomanije oko Jasenovca i Bleiburga* (Zagreb: Globus, 1992), pp. 20–21.

18. Radomir Bulatović, *Koncentracioni logor Jasenovac, s posebnim osvrtom na Donju Gradinu* (Sarajevo: Svjetlost, 1990), as cited critically in Žerjavić, *Opsesije*, p. 53.

19. Žerjavić, *Opsesije*, p. 75.

20. On this point, see Immanuel Kant, *The Metaphysics of Morals*, trans. Mary Gregor (Cambridge: Cambridge University Press, 1991), pp. 225–226.

21. Miko Tripalo, in interview with the author, Zagreb, 8 September 1989. The full text of the interview is published in *South Slav Journal*, Vol. 12, Nos. 3/4 (Autumn/Winter 1989), pp. 87–93.

22. Details in Meier, *Wie Jugoslawien*, chap. 5; Laura Silber and Allan Little, *The Death of Yugoslavia* (London: Penguin Books and BBC Books, 1995), pp. 84–86; and Reneo Lukić and Allen Lynch, *Europe from the Balkans to the Urals: The Disintegration of Yugoslavia and the Soviet Union* (Oxford: Oxford University Press, 1996), chap. 8.

23. Meier, *Wie Jugoslawien*, p. 288.

24. *Oslobodjenje* (12 November 1990), p. 1, trans. in FBIS, *Daily Report* (Eastern Europe), 29 November 1990, p. 74.

25. Regarding the 15 percent shortfall, see *Borba* (26 December 1990), p. 3. Regarding the layoff of 2,700 employees, see Tanjug (3 March 1991), trans. in FBIS, *Daily Report* (Eastern Europe), 4 March 1991, p. 41.

26. Tanjug (4 March 1991), trans. in FBIS, *Daily Report* (Eastern Europe), 5 March 1991, p. 56.

27. Tanjug (5 February 1991), in FBIS, *Daily Report* (Eastern Europe), 6 February 1991, p. 57. See also *Borba* (7 September 1990), p. 3.

28. Tanjug (11 January 1991), trans. in FBIS, *Daily Report* (Eastern Europe), 12 January 1991, p. 57; and Tanjug (15 March 1991), in FBIS, *Daily Report* (Eastern Europe), 18 March 1991, 56.

29. Tanjug (21 February 1991), trans. in FBIS, *Daily Report* (Eastern Europe), 25 February 1991, p. 52.

30. Lukić and Lynch, *Europe from the Balkans to the Urals*, p. 178.

31. Silber and Little, *Death of Yugoslavia*, p. 101.

32. Christopher Bennett, *Yugoslavia's Bloody Collapse: Causes, Course and Consequences* (New York: New York University Press, 1995), p. 129.

33. Silber and Little, *Death of Yugoslavia*, pp. 103–104; and Bennett, *Yugoslavia's Bloody Collapse*, p. 127.

34. Tanjug (1 October 1990), trans. in FBIS, *Daily Report* (Eastern Europe), 1 October 1990, p. 63.

35. For details and documentation, see Sabrina P. Ramet, "The Breakup of Yugoslavia," in *Global Affairs*, Vol. 6, No. 2 (Spring 1991).

36. Meier, *Wie Jugoslawien*, pp. 265–266.

37. Ibid., pp. 266, 268.

38. Branka Magaš, *The Destruction of Yugoslavia: Tracking the Break-up, 1980–92* (London: Verso, 1993), p. 311.

39. Ibid., p. 333.

40. Robert J. Donia and John V. A. Fine, Jr., *Bosnia and Hercegovina: A Tradition Betrayed* (New York: Columbia University Press, 1994), p. 216.

41. Ibid., pp. 215–216.

42. Adil Zulfikarpašić, Vlado Gotovac, Miko Tripalo, and Ivo Banac, *Okovana Bosna* (Zürich: Bosnjački Institut, 1995), p. 101.

43. See, for instance, *Oslobodjenje* (Sarajevo), 25 February 1991, p. 3, trans. in FBIS, *Daily Report* (Eastern Europe), 1 March 1991, p. 38.

44. *Daily Telegraph* (London) (18 March 1991), p. 1.

45. *Danas*, no. 459 (4 December 1990), pp. 10–12.

46. *Daily Telegraph* (20 March 1991), p. 15.

47. *Frankfurter Allgemeine* (2 February 1991), p. 2. See also Croatian Democracy Project, news release (7 February 1991).

48. Regarding the Slovenes, see *Frankfurter Allgemeine* (27 December 1990), p. 2; on the Croats, see *Neue Zürcher Zeitung* (22 May 1991), p. 1; on the Albanians, see Belgrade Domestic Service (10 February 1991), trans. in FBIS, *Daily Report* (Eastern Europe), 12 February 1991, p. 59; on the Macedonians, see *Vjesnik* (Zagreb) (13 September 1990), p. 3, and Tanjug (23 February 1991), in FBIS, *Daily Report* (Eastern Europe), 25 February 1991, p. 55.

49. Regarding Serbs in Bosnia, see Radovan Karadžić's interview in *Borba* (12 November 1990), p. 4.

50. See Slobodan Milošević, *Godine raspleta*, 5th ed. (Belgrade: Beogradski izdavačko-grafički zavod, 1989), pp. 264–271, reprinting Milošević's speech to the Seventeenth Session of the CC of LCY, Belgrade, October 1988.

51. Borisav Jović, *Posledni dani SFRJ—izvodi iz dnevnika* (Belgrade: Politika, 1995), pp. 242–243 (entry for 9 January 1991).

52. Ibid., pp. 227–228 (entry for 23 November 1990).

53. Ibid., pp. 256–257 (entry for 21 January 1991).

54. Silber and Little, *Death of Yugoslavia*, p. 124.

55. Ibid., pp. 130–131.

56. Ibid., p. 133. For further discussion of the protests on 9 March 1991, see Robert Thomas, *Serbia under Milošević: Politics in the 1990s* (London: C. Hurst & Co., 1999), pp. 81–91.

57. Full text in *Vjesnik* (12 October 1990), p. 5.

58. The republics' stands on these and other issues are compactly summarized in *Vjesnik* (2 February 1991), p. 4, trans. in FBIS, *Daily Report* (Eastern Europe), 12 February 1991, p. 47.

59. *Neue Zürcher Zeitung* (7/8 April 1991), p. 6.

60. Tanjug (7 April 1991), trans. in FBIS, *Daily Report* (Eastern Europe), 8 April 1991, p. 56.

61. *Delo* (Ljubljana) (21 February 1991), p. 3, trans. in FBIS, *Daily Report* (Eastern Europe), 7 March 1991, p. 33.

62. *The Times* (London) (4 May 1991), p. 10.

63. Belgrade Domestic Service (31 March 1991), trans. in FBIS, *Daily Report* (Eastern Europe), 1 April 1991, pp. 49–50; and *Politika* (Belgrade) (19 March 1991), p. 9.

64. Tanjug (3 April 1991), in FBIS, *Daily Report* (Eastern Europe), 4 April 1991, p. 25.

65. Stipe Mesić, in interview with the author, Zagreb, 30 July 1997.

66. Ibid.

67. Silber and Little, *Death of Yugoslavia*, p. 143; confirmed in Ivan Lovrenović, "Karadjordjevo," in *Tjednik* (Zagreb), (22 August 1997), pp. 12–16.

68. Mesić, in interview with the author (note 65).

69. *Borba* (13 November 1990), p. 3, trans. in FBIS, *Daily Report* (Eastern Europe), 23 November 1990, p. 58.

70. *Borba* (3 August 1990), p. 3; Tanjug (23 February 1991), in FBIS, *Daily Report* (Eastern Europe), 25 February 1991, p. 55. See also *Vjesnik* (13 September 1990), p. 3.

71. *Borba* (6 March 1991), p. 3, trans. in FBIS, *Daily Report* (Eastern Europe), 8 March 1991, p. 56.

72. *Borba* (1 March 1991), p. 9.

73. Croatian Democracy Project, news release (13 May 1991).

74. Stipe Mesić, *Kako je srušena Jugoslavija*, 2nd ed. (Zagreb: Mislav Press, 1994), p. 5.

75. Ibid., pp. 6, 13.

76. See, for example, ibid., p. 26.

77. *The Guardian* (London and Manchester) (16 May 1991), on *Nexis*.

78. *The Independent* (London) (8 May 1991), p. 1.

79. Croatia Democracy Project, news release (13 May 1991).

80. *Neue Zürcher Zeitung* (4 May 1991), p. 2, and (5/6 May 1991), p. 1; *The Times* (4 May 1991), p. 6; and *The Independent* (8 May 1991), p. 1.

81. Quoted in *New York Times* (19 May 1991), p. 8.

82. *Vjesnik* (17 April 1991), p. 4.

83. *Süddeutsche Zeitung* (Munich) (25/26 May 1991), p. 8.

84. *Neue Zürcher Zeitung* (29 May 1991), p. 5.

85. *Neue Zürcher Zeitung* (15 June 1991), p. 2.

86. Tanjug (27 May 1991), trans. in FBIS, *Daily Report* (Eastern Europe), 29 May 1991, p. 41.

87. Tanjug (29 May 1991), in FBIS, *Daily Report* (Eastern Europe), 30 May 1991, p. 25.

88. Stipe Šuvar, in interview with the author, Zagreb, 31 July 1997; and Jović, *Poslednji dani*, pp. 364–365 (entry for 11 July 1991).

89. Janez Drnovšek, *Moja resnica* (Ljubljana: Založba Mladinska Knjiga, 1996), pp. 243–244.

90. Nicole Janigro, *L'Esplosione delle Nazioni: Il caso Jugoslavo* (Milan: Feltrinelli, 1993), p. 21. See also Janez Janša, *Premiki: Nastajanje in obramba slovenske države 1988–1992* (Ljubljana: Založba Mladinska Knjiga, 1992), pp. 174–202.

91. *Daily Telegraph* (8 May 1991), p. 8.

92. *Neue Zürcher Zeitung* (4 June 1991), p. 2; and *Daily Telegraph* (8 April 1991), p. 11.

93. Bennett, *Yugoslavia's Bloody Collapse*, p. 166.

94. It also confirmed the accuracy of both early warnings of the risk of gravitation toward civil war (as in Pedro Ramet, "Yugoslavia and the Threat of Internal and External Discontents," in *Orbis*, Vol. 28, No. 1 [Spring 1984], p. 114) and forecasts on the eve of war itself (as in Sabrina P. Ramet, "The Breakup of Yugoslavia," in *Global Affairs*, Vol. 6, No. 2 [Spring 1991], p. 97).

95. *Neue Zürcher Zeitung* (2 July 1991), p. 1.

96. *Neue Zürcher Zeitung* (5 July 1991), p. 5.

97. Silber and Little, *Death of Yugoslavia*, p. 187.

98. Ibid., p. 189.

99. Miša Milošević, official representative of Serbs in Slavonia, Baranja, and western Srem, as quoted in *Politika* (Belgrade) (9 October 1991), p. 1.

100. Stipe Mesić, in interview with the author (note 65).

101. Slavko Goldstein, in interview with the author, Zagreb, 1 August 1997.

102. Silber and Little, *Death of Yugoslavia*, pp. 191–192.

103. Norman Cigar, "Croatia's War of Independence: The Parameters of War Termination," in *The Journal of Slavic Military Studies*, Vol. 10, No. 2 (June 1997), pp. 54, 55.

104. *Neue Zürcher Zeitung* (10/11 August 1991), p. 7, and (22 August 1991), p. 2.

105. Rada Iveković, *La Balcanizzazione della ragione* (Rome: Manifestolibri, 1995), pp. 40–42.

106. *Danas* (16 July 1991), p. 9.

107. *New York Times* (18 October 1991), p. A4.

108. Quoted in *New York Times* (8 September 1991), p. 6.

109. *New York Times* (16 January 1992), p. 1.

110. Regarding Serbian proposals, see *Neue Zürcher Zeitung* (27 July 1991), p. 3, and (14 August 1991), p. 2.

111. *Politika* (10 August 1991), p. 1.

112. *Politika* (14 August 1991), p. 1.

113. *Politika* (13 August 1991), p. 1.

114. *Politika* (14 August 1991), p. 1.

115. Reprinted in *Politika* (17 August 1991), p. 10.

116. *Süddeutsche Zeitung* (26/27 October 1991), p. 6.

117. Silber and Little, *Death of Yugoslavia*, p. 204.

118. Radio Slovenia Network (Ljubljana) (15 July 1991), trans. in FBIS, *Daily Report* (Eastern Europe), 15 July 1991, p. 35.

119. *Financial Times* (13 September 1991), p. 2; confirmed in *New York Times* (13 October 1991), p. 6.

120. *New York Times* (13 October 1991), p. 6.

121. Quoted in Ibid.

122. *New York Times* (12 September 1991), p. A3.

123. *Neue Zürcher Zeitung* (7 August 1991), p. 17.

124. Jović, *Poslednji dani*, p. 394 (9 October 1991).

125. *Financial Times* (8 November 1991), p. 2.

126. For details, see Sabrina P. Ramet, *Nationalism and Federalism in Yugoslavia, 1962–1991*, 2nd ed. (Bloomington: Indiana University Press, 1992), pp. 262–265; and Ivan Torov, "The Resistance in Serbia," in Jasminka Udovički and James Ridgeway (eds.), *Burn This House: The Making and Unmaking of Yugoslavia* (Durham, N.C.: Duke University Press, 1997), pp. 245–264.

127. Quoted in Michael Dobbs, "Serbian Leader Looks Vulnerable in the Long Term," in *Washington Post*, reprinted in *Manchester Guardian Weekly* (29 September 1991), p. 18.

128. Quoted in ibid.

129. Ibid.

130. On these protests, see Obrad Kesić, "Serbian Roulette," in *Current History*, Vol. 97, No. 617 (March 1998), pp. 97–98.

131. On the incarceration of Albanians who had signed a petition in support of the constitution, see Meier, *Wie Jugoslawien*, p. 219.

132. Jović, *Poslednji dani*, p. 306 (entry for 16 March 1991).

133. On this point, see Tanjug (3 July 1991), in FBIS, *Daily Report* (Eastern Europe), 5 July 1991, p. 53.

134. Meier, *Wie Jugoslawien*, p. 385.

135. William Shakespeare, *Richard III*, Act 1, scene 3.

136. Regarding Germanophobia in connection with a fear that an independent Slovenia and Croatia might come under German influence, see Meier, *Wie Jugoslawien*, p. 389. On Germany's general efforts to conform its policy in Yugoslavia to such consensus as might be obtained among Western European states, see Sabrina P. Ramet and Letty Coffin, "Germany's Policy vis-à-vis the Yugoslav Successor States, 1991–99," manuscript in progress. On other points, see Daniele Conversi, *German-Bashing and the Breakup of Yugoslavia*, The Donald W. Treadgold Papers No. 16 (Seattle: The HMJ School of International Studies of the University of Washington, March 1998); Lukić and Lynch, *Europe from the Balkans to the Urals*, especially chaps. 11, 13, and 15; Thomas Cushman and Stjepan G. Meštrović (eds.), *This Time We Knew: Western Responses to Genocide in Bosnia* (New York and London: New York University Press, 1996), especially the chapters by Daniele Conversi and David Riesman; and Sabrina P. Ramet, "The Yugoslav Crisis and the West: Avoiding 'Vietnam' and Blundering into 'Abyssinia,'" in *East European Politics and Societies*, Vol. 8, No. 1 (Winter 1994), pp. 189–219.

PART II

◆

Religion and Culture

CHAPTER FOUR

◆

The Catholic Church

In his book *The Bridge Betrayed: Religion and Genocide in Bosnia*, published in 1996, Michael Sells confesses to an aspiration "to demonstrate what has so repeatedly been denied concerning the genocide in Bosnia: that it was religiously motivated and religiously justified."[1] As a one-sentence summary of the roots of the war, this will not do, since it would entail a dismissal of economic deterioration, the federal system, the ambitions of Milošević and his coterie, the army leadership's distrust of the post-communist governments in Slovenia and Croatia, and the Serbian media's role as early as 1987–1989 in manufacturing Serbian resentment of non-Serbs on the basis of entirely nonreligious issues. But even if the attempt were assayed to set this claim within a broader context, one is left with the conflation of religion as such and manipulations or political uses of religion. It is true that Sells acknowledges on the same page that "personalities like Milošević merely exploit [religious] fundamentalism for their own political gain," but if this is true, then how was the war "religiously motivated" or "religiously justified"? Moreover, though one can easily cite Serbian bishops who justified the war, is the endorsement of even several bishops tantamount to *religious* justification as such?

It is not my belief that the Serbian Insurrectionary War was about religion. When Serbs blew up mosques and Catholic churches and when Croats destroyed mosques and other religious buildings, they were not, in fact, doing so to spread their own faiths, but rather to destroy the architectural artifacts that established other peoples' history in the area and that helped members of other nationalities remember their past and hold on to their cultural identity. In other words, attacks on religious objects served strictly political purposes; politics was primary, not religion.

But for all that, a review of prior religious history can help one understand the politics of the region, including the recent crisis: first, by showing how interethnic (or, if one prefers, intercommunal) resentments were fed, in part, by setbacks to one or another religious association; second, by showing how the Communist treatment of religion contributed to politicizing religion, to cementing the links between the chief religious associations and "their" peoples, and to associating the religious bodies with opposition; third, by demonstrating how the association of the principal religious bodies with nationalist causes and programs was significantly reinforced and sustained by Communist policy in the sphere of nationalities; fourth, by correcting some glaring misunderstandings about the role played by such religious figures as Catholic Archbishop Alojzije Cardinal Stepinac and Serb Orthodox Bishop Nikolaj Velimirović; and fifth, by enabling the reader to obtain some understanding of why and how the intellectually refined hierarchs of the Serbian Orthodox Church could, in the course of the latter 1980s, accept paranoid mythologies spawned by Vladimir Dedijer and others about a Vatican-Islamic conspiracy against the Serbian people.[2] Noting that refined intellectual achievement is no guarantee against the adoption of paranoid and intolerant attitudes is not an explanation; it is, at best, a footnote. A proper understanding requires the setting forth of a historical context.

In this spirit, I include chapters on the Catholic, Orthodox, and Islamic communities, discussing them in order of size of active membership; although the Serbian Orthodox Church had a larger number of nominal members in the SFRY, the Roman Catholic Church had the largest number of active (or even *actual*) members.

The Symbology of the Church in Yugoslavia

Relations between the Catholic Church in Yugoslavia and the Communist regime were colored by three central symbols: Strossmayer, Stepinac, and Vatican II. For the communist regime, Bishop Josip Juraj Strossmayer of Djakovo (1815–1905) represented the spirit of "Yugoslavism" (promoting the cultural and political unity of Serbs, Croats, Slovenes, and Macedonians) and of cooperation between Church and state, while Alojzije Cardinal Stepinac (1898–1960) symbolized exclusivist Croatian nationalism and the spirit of defiance. For the Church, on the other hand, Strossmayer is remembered also as an active missionary, an ecclesiastical "liberal" who opposed introduction of the principle of papal infallibility, and a champion of Slavic (vernacular) liturgy in Catholic churches in Croatia; Stepinac is associated, in Church eyes, with heroic efforts to protect Serbs and Gypsies from slaughter by the *Ustaše* fascists during World War II, with defiant outspoken criticism of both the *Ustaše* and the Communists, and with unflinching loyalty to the Church. In certain ways, thus—for both regime and Church—twentieth-century Stepinac symbolized the Church's traditional pastoral care for the nation, while nineteenth-century Strossmayer symbolized adaptability, liberality, and hence modernity. It is worth noting, however, that through his progressive social programs and his use of Church funds for charitable programs, Stepinac may be said to have anticipated the "Church of the poor" of the Vatican II period.

The Second Vatican Council (1962–1965) was a watershed for the Church and, more particularly, a time in which modernizing currents within the Church received strong encouragement, in certain aspects, from the Holy See. The results were a new impetus to self-assertion in the Church, a new direction for the Church in its social presence, and a deepening of the division within the Church between traditionalists and modernizers. Interestingly enough, although the Belgrade regime expressed enthusiasm for the "modernizing" Strossmayer, it felt threatened, according to Zlatko Markus, by the reformist wing of the Church, which it viewed as "dangerously" active.[3] Far more to the liking of at least some elements in the regime was the opinion, once expressed by Archbishop Frane Franić of Split (retired in 1988), to the effect that the Church is called upon "to administer the sacraments and to conduct Church services, but political and social revolution should be left to others. That is not our calling."[4] The result is that theological conservatives in the Church (including the mixed conservative Franić and the generally conservative one-time archbishop of Sarajevo Smiljan Čekada) enjoyed better relations than did some of their theologically more liberal colleagues with those elements in the Communist regime who sought to constrict Church activity.

In socialist Yugoslavia, as elsewhere, the traditional–modern dichotomy manifested itself against the backdrop of another, partly reinforcing, partly crosscutting dichotomy between hierarchy and lower clergy. In the early postwar years, tensions between hierarchy and lower clergy centered on the establishment of priests' associations—a move encouraged and supported by the regime. More recently, tensions developed between the episcopal conference and the Christianity Today Theological Society over the latter's unilateral decision, in 1977, to reorganize itself as a self-managing enterprise and thereby obtain certain tax exemptions. The society is responsible for running a formidable publishing house and for issuing the *AKSA* news bulletin.

The Dawn of Communist Rule

Although the Communist regime would later try to portray the Catholic Church's role during World War II monochromatically as the advocacy of Croatian independence and *Ustaše* rule, a rather substantial number of Catholic clergymen actually cooperated with or fought on the side of the Partisans, including Archbishop Kuzma Jedretić, Fr. Franjo Poš from Prezid, Franciscans Bosiljko Ljevar and Viktor Sakić, and the pastor of St. Mark's Church in Zagreb, Msgr. Svetozar Rittig, lauded by one Yugoslav author as "the most important figure in the people's liberation struggle, among Catholic priests."[5] Rittig, who joined the Partisans in 1943 and later became first president of the Croatian Commission for Religious Affairs, remaining active on the political scene until his death in July 1961, is said to have been devoted, in particular, to the ideas of Bishop Strossmayer. By contrast, according to Ciril Petešić, "only a part of the clergy, and a small part at that," actually endorsed the *Ustaša* program, mostly young priests, while most of the older clergy are said to have been pro-Yugoslav.[6]

From the beginning of Partisan warfare, the Partisans had need of priests to cater to the religious needs of their combatants, and this led to the establishment of a Religious Department of the AVNOJ Executive Committee in December 1942. Behind Partisan lines, where religious schools were concerned, the Partisans were eager for religious instructors to teach about Cyril and Methodius (who created the

Glagolitic alphabet), Sava Nemanjić (founder of the autocephalous Serbian Orthodox archdiocese), and Bishop Strossmayer.[7]

After the trying experiences under the Kingdom of Yugoslavia,[8] the Croatian
Catholic hierarchy initially welcomed the establishment of a separate Croatian state.[9]
Some clergy, such as Archbishop Ivan Šarić of Sarajevo, remained sympathetic to the
Ustaše until the very end. Other hierarchs were more critical, on the other hand.
Bishop Alojzije Misić of Mostar, for instance, began condemning Ustaše oppression of
Serbs as early as 1941.[10] Similarly, Zagreb Archbishop Stepinac repeatedly contacted
Minister of the Interior Andrija Artuković (e.g., in letters dated 22 May 1941 and 30
May 1941) to register his objection to the new legislation affecting Catholics of Jew-
ish descent, declared membership in Catholic Action and the Ustaša movement to be
incompatible (in December 1941), worked quietly to obtain the release of Orthodox
believers from prison, and spoke out in his sermons against racism, genocide, and Ustaša policies (for example, in his sermon of 25 October 1943).[11]

But if the local clergy were divided in their attitudes toward the Ustaše, and some
frankly ambivalent about the Croatian state, the Vatican had a clear line where communism was concerned. The difficulties experienced by the Church in the USSR
provided a troubling precedent, and Pope Pius XII adopted a forcefully anticommunist stance. Katolički list (24 April 1937) had put it this way: "Communism is in its
very essence evil. Therefore, the person who values Christian culture will not cooperate with [Communists] in a single thing. If some are seduced into error and on their
part help communism to grow stronger, they will be the first to be punished for that
error."[12] Thus, there was no basis, at that time, for a relationship of trust between the
Vatican and the emerging Communist parties in Eastern Europe.

Meanwhile, as the Partisans captured districts of Croatia, they massacred both
civilians and priests, including more than two dozen unarmed Franciscans at the
monastery of Široki Brijeg.[13] The Independent State of Croatia collapsed in May
1945, and the Communist Party now set up its administration in the remaining
parts of the country.

On 2 June 1945, Communist Party General Secretary Josip Broz Tito, Croatian
President Vladimir Bakarić, and Msgr. Rittig held a meeting with Catholic bishops
Franjo Seper Salis-Seewis and Josip Lach. Tito's statement on that occasion has given rise
to so much subsequent controversy that it is worth quoting at length. Replying to a
statement presented by Bishop Salis, Tito said:

> As I have already explained to Msgr. Rittig, I would like to see a proposal worked out, as
> you see fit, as to how to solve the question of the Church in Croatia, the Catholic Church,
> because we shall be discussing the same thing also with the Orthodox Church. On my
> own part, I would say that our Church needs to be national *[nacionalna]*, that it be more
> responsive to the [Croatian] nation. Perhaps that will seem a bit strange to you when I so
> strongly support nationality. . . . I must say openly that I do not want to undertake the
> right to condemn Rome, your supreme Roman jurisdiction, and I will not. But I must say
> that I look at it critically, because [Church policy] has always been attuned more to Italy
> than to our people. I would like to see that the Catholic Church in Croatia now, when we

have all the preconditions there, would have more independence. I would like that. That is the basic question. That is the question which we want to see resolved, and all other questions are secondary questions which will be easy to work out.[14]

Given the consistency with which Communists in other East European countries were pressing Catholic hierarchs to break with the Vatican,[15] it seems reasonable to interpret this statement along the same lines (though Tito later denied that this was his intention). After all, the so-called Old Catholic Church in Croatia had already provided a precedent. Indeed, this Church, which had formed in reaction to the proclamation of the doctrine of papal infallibility in 1870, was even able to set up additional independent organizations after World War II in Slovenia, Serbia, and Vojvodina.[16]

The following day, Tito and Bakarić received the papal delegate, Abbot Ramiro Marcone, together with his secretary, Don Giuseppe Masucci, who complained that the Communist media were relentlessly attacking the clergy and the Vatican, even claiming that the Vatican had wanted a Nazi victory and that the children were being taught in the schools that there is no God and trained to sing, "We will fight against God! There is no God!"[17]

On 4 June, Tito and Bakarić received Stepinac and, on this occasion, Tito praised Pope Leo XIII for having backed Strossmayer in a dispute with the Court of Vienna about Russia and asked Stepinac to support Belgrade in its dispute with Italy in Istria. Stepinac, in turn, urged Tito to meet with representatives of the Croatian Peasant Party and even those of the *Ustaše* movement and to try to heal the emotional wounds of war.[18] In spite of this meeting, the Communist government continued to arrest Catholic priests and believers, including the bishops of Križevci, Split, and Krk.

Archbishop Stepinac was receiving hundreds of appeals from Croats asking him to intercede with the new authorities on behalf of imprisoned relatives. On 28 June 1945, he took up the matter with the president of the Croatian government and urged the authorities to drop the campaign against "collaborators" because, as Stepinac noted, it would be necessary then to imprison ordinary workers, peasants, and so forth. But part of the reason for the campaign was sheer opportunism on the part of particular individuals in the party, including their desire to seize the opportunity to settle old scores.[19] Stepinac also criticized the secret trials being conducted at the time, calling them inconsistent with the regime's claim to be a "people's" government.

Meanwhile, the regime decided to abolish all private high schools, following completion of the 1945–1946 school year, and moved to eliminate religious instruction from the curriculum of state elementary schools. In late summer 1945, the authorities began bulldozing the cemeteries in which combatants from other sides were buried, stirring protests from believers in the areas affected. Within a month of the war's end, the Communist authorities also began forcible confiscations of Church property in Križevci, Zagreb, Remete, and elsewhere, seized Caritas property and property of the Zagreb archbishopric, and outlined a more extensive program of agrarian land reform that promised to produce further confiscations. When Stepinac complained about these developments in a letter to Tito, the latter replied by alluding to his interest in receiving a reply from the Catholic bishops with respect to "the possibility of coming to an agreement about certain matters between Church and state."[20]

In these circumstances, the first episcopal conference in Yugoslavia in six years was convened by Stepinac on 17–22 September to discuss the new situation in which the Church found itself. Immediately upon convening, the episcopal conference sent a letter to Tito asking for withdrawal of the law on agrarian reform, respect for Christian marriage, respect for continuation of religious instruction in elementary schools, and respect for Catholic cemeteries and offering to consult with the state on a new law on agrarian reform. The following day, after further discussions, the conference sent a second letter to Tito asking for the release from detention of Bishop Janko Simrak, freedom of the press, continuance of the private schools, and the return of confiscated property to the Church.[21] And at the close of the conference the assembled bishops issued a joint pastoral letter recounting the hardships suffered by the Church at the hands of the Communists (243 priests and 4 nuns killed over four years, 169 priests still in prison, and 89 unaccounted for) and demanding complete freedom for Church activities, institutions, and press. This pastoral letter was read in the churches, with copies sent to the Commission for Religious Affairs in each of the federal units.[22]

The letter convinced the Communist authorities that Archbishop Stepinac would be as much a thorn to them as he had been to *Ustaše* leader Ante Pavelić. They therefore reached a decision, shortly after the letter was issued, that a case would be prepared against him and that he would be put away in prison.[23]

The Trial of Archbishop Stepinac

The authorities continued to try to persuade Archbishop Stepinac to break relations with Rome; instead, Stepinac denounced the proposal in yet another pastoral letter.[24] The authorities then tried to persuade the Vatican to remove Stepinac from his seat in Zagreb; the Vatican refused.[25] The archbishop was therefore arrested on 18 September and put on trial together with fifteen other persons who were being tried on criminal charges connected with the excesses of the NDH. On 30 September, the charges against Stepinac were read in court. Specifically, he was accused of collaborating with the *Ustaše* in the calculated hope of enriching the Church and the upper clergy, of allowing the Križari (Crusaders) and Catholic Action to work for fascism, of using traditional religious celebrations as political manifestations in support of the *Ustaše*, of encouraging the coercive conversion of Orthodox Serbs to Catholicism, of serving as a rallying point for enemies of the Communist state after the war, and of concealing *Ustaše* archives and materials of the Croatian Foreign Ministry, under an agreement concluded with Ante Pavelić.[26]

The *official* (edited) record of the trial shows Stepinac refusing to cooperate with his interrogators:

Presiding judge: Nedjelja No. 15 of 27 April 1941 carries a report with the following content: "Archbishop Dr. Alojzije Stepinac, as representative of the Catholic Church and Croatian metropolitan, visited General Slavko Kvaternik as deputy of the Poglavnik in the homeland and conducted a lengthy conversation with him. In that way, as Radio Zagreb reports, the most cordial relations were established between the Catholic Church and the Independent State of Croatia."

Why did you consider it necessary, only two days after the establishment of the Independent State of Croatia and the occupation of our country by the enemy, to hurry to visit the *Ustaše* commander, Slavko Kvaternik?

The accused: I have nothing to say.

Presiding judge: Did you visit Pavelić on 16 April 1941, four days after the occupation of our country but two days before the capitulation of the Yugoslav army, which was at war with the enemy?

The accused: I decline to answer....

Presiding judge: Did you, immediately in the first days of the occupation, i.e., in mid-April or early May, take part in a meeting to which you invited *Ustaše* emigrants, returnees?

The accused: I have nothing to say. If necessary, the defense lawyers appointed for me can answer that.[27]

The prosecution made use of a string of citations from Catholic and *Ustaše* press to try to incriminate the archbishop. But most of the Catholic periodicals cited by the prosecution in substantiation of its charges were published in dioceses lying outside Stepinac's jurisdiction: in particular, the Franciscan publication *Andjeo Čuvar,* the Jesuit publication *Glasnik Srca Isusova,* the Sarajevo weekly *Katolički tjednik,* and the Sarajevo publication *Glasnik sv. Antuna.*[28] The prosecution claimed that Stepinac and other clergy had received decorations from the Croatian government in gratitude for their political support and produced pictures showing the archbishop together with *Ustaše* ministers on official occasions and at official receptions.[29]

Chief prosecutor Jakov Blažević dwelled at length on the Church's cooperation with the *Ustaše* in carrying out forced conversions of Orthodox believers. The archbishop defended himself by insisting that the Church had exerted no pressure on the Orthodox and could not be held responsible for coercion applied by others and by pointing out that a large number of Catholics had converted to Orthodoxy, under pressure, during the period of the Yugoslav kingdom.[30] Against the archbishop's denials, Blažević insisted that between 1943 and 1944 Archbishop Stepinac became involved in vaguely defined "conspiratorial work" with Pavelić and Croatian Peasant Party leader Vlatko Maček, and—in a bizarre turn—"charged" the archbishop with having sent Christmas wishes to Croatian prison laborers in Germany.[31]

L'Osservatore Romano, the Vatican newspaper, scoffed at the charges and held that the real reason for the trial was the pastoral letter of 22 September 1945.[32] By continually returning to the subject of this letter, the authorities seemed to confirm this interpretation:

> *Presiding judge:* In the pastoral letter of last year, 1945, one finds, among other things, the claim that the Franciscans at Široki Brijeg were well-known antifascists. Here is a photograph, taken at Široki Brijeg, showing *Ustaše* colonel Jure Frančetić with Fr. Bonaventura Jelačić, an "'antifascist' from Široki Brijeg." Also in the photograph are [other] Franciscans of Široki Brijeg together with *Ustaše* and Italian officers. Is this the famous antifascist stance of the Franciscans from Široki Brijeg?
>
> *The accused:* I have nothing to say.
>
> *Presiding judge:* You could correct your declaration in the pastoral letter—were they not, maybe, fascists?
>
> *The accused:* I think that we have nothing to correct.[33]

Blažević later returned to this subject in order to assail the idea of freedom of the press:

> *J. Blažević:* Defendant Stepinac, in connection with the facts which have been revealed and established in this trial, I ask you please, for what purpose did you convene the episcopal conference in September 1945 and for what purpose did you write the pastoral letter?
>
> *The accused:* I have nothing to say.
>
> *J. Blažević:* I will cite some passages from the pastoral letter to you and then I will ask you some questions about it. Speaking of the persecutions of priests, etc., ... you say this: "And when we explain all this to you dearest believers, we do not do so in the hope of provoking a battle with the state authorities. We neither desire such battles nor do we seek them." Defendant, you say that you have always sought peace and stable political life and you say, "That peace is so necessary to everyone today, but we are deeply convinced that that peace can only be founded on the pacification of relations between Church and state." What do you say to that, defendant Stepinac?
>
> *The accused:* I have nothing to say.
>
> *J. Blažević:* You have nothing to say, because you are ashamed. In the pastoral letter, in order to realize the principles that you stress, you seek complete freedom for the Catholic press. Is that freedom for the press we have been reading? ...
>
> *The accused:* I have nothing to say.
>
> *J. Blažević:* You have nothing to say. In the pastoral letter you write, "Only under those conditions can circumstances be put in order in our state and can lasting internal peace be achieved." So, you demand freedom for your press, that is, the Catholic press which you commanded and which you converted completely into an instrument of fascism. That press could only return if fascism

would return, if the *Ustaše* were to return.... It's clear that you seek to introduce fascism in our country anew, that you seek [foreign] intervention in the country.[34]

The court rejected most of the witnesses proposed by the defense; on the other hand, most of the fifty-eight witnesses summoned by the prosecution to testify against Stepinac were not from his archdiocese. The trial ended on 11 October, when the court found all but three of the defendants guilty[35] and sentenced Archbishop Stepinac to sixteen years at hard labor, followed by five years' deprivation of civil and political rights. *L'Osservatore Romano* condemned the proceedings as a complete sham whose outcome had been determined in advance and whose script had been drafted to serve political ends and challenged the authenticity of some of the documents produced by the prosecution.[36] (Stepinac was offered his freedom if he agreed to leave the country, but he declined. Despite the sentence, Stepinac did not in fact have to perform hard labor, and the authorities constructed a special double cell for him; a chapel was built into half of this double cell. In 1951, when Tito was trying to improve relations with the Vatican, Stepinac was released from prison but confined to his native village. Elevated to the College of Cardinals shortly thereafter, Stepinac died in 1960.)

Some time after the trial, Milovan Djilas—then still a prominent member of the political establishment—admitted in private conversation that the real problem with Stepinac was not his politics vis-à-vis the *Ustaše*, but his politics vis-à-vis the Communists themselves, and in particular his fidelity to Rome. "If he had only proclaimed [the creation of] a Croatian Church, separate from Rome," said Djilas, "we would have raised him to the clouds!"[37] More recently—in February 1985—Blažević himself admitted this in an interview with the Croatian youth weekly, *Polet*. Admitting that Tito had wanted Stepinac to cut the Croatian Church's ties with Rome, Blažević commented, "That trial of Stepinac was forced on us. If Stepinac had only been more flexible, there would have been no need of a trial."[38]

The Priests' Associations

Since it had proved impossible to coopt the Church hierarchy, the authorities quickly pursued an alternative policy of trying to sow divisions and discord within the Church and to win over *portions* of the clergy into a cooperative relationship. One token of this was the regime's response to the pastoral letter of 22 September 1945. *Borba*, for example, reported that many Catholic priests in Bosnia-Herzegovina refused to read the letter in their churches,[39] while other papers carried a story claiming that Archbishop Nikola Dobrečić of Bar had criticized those bishops who had signed the pastoral letter.[40]

A more tangible symptom of this strategy was the promotion of priests' associations, which would lie outside the authority of the bishops. However, after the controversial trial and imprisonment of Archbishop Stepinac, the clergy, especially in Croatia, were ill disposed to cooperate with the regime. All the same, the first

Catholic priests' association was created in Istria in 1948, under the presidency of Dr. Božo Milanović, and most Istrian priests joined. That same year an attempt was made to set up an association in Slovenia. The first attempt failed, however, and the matter had to be taken up again the following year. These first two associations were more or less spontaneous on the part of the priests, though actively encouraged by the government.

A third priests' association was set up in January 1950 in Bosnia-Herzegovina. The government set up health insurance for members and pressured priests to join, for example, by making permission to give religious instruction contingent on membership (a policy adopted in 1952 but eventually abandoned). By the end of 1952, nearly all the priests in Istria were association members, along with 80 percent of priests in Bosnia-Herzegovina and 60 percent of priests in Slovenia.[41]

The bishops were opposed to these associations and, in a statement dated 26 April 1950, declared them "inexpedient." Two and a half years later, after consulting the Vatican, the bishops issued a decision forbidding the clergy altogether to join the associations. This move provoked a crisis in Church–state relations when the Yugoslav government sent a note of protest to the Holy See on 1 November 1952. The Holy See replied on 15 December detailing the troubles being experienced by the Church, but this note was returned unopened. On 17 December the Yugoslav government terminated diplomatic relations with the Vatican.[42]

By the end of 1953, three more priests' associations for Catholic clergy were created—in Croatia, Serbia, and Montenegro. The associations thus paralleled the federal structure of the political system, with one association per republic. These associations served as conduits for state subsidies—which were welcome given the destruction caused by the war. The Bosnian Franciscan Province, for example, began receiving state subsidies through this source in 1952, and in the period 1952–1964 received a total of 63 million old dinars in subsidies (estimated as equivalent to 315,000 West German marks).[43] Nor were the Franciscans the only ones to receive state aid: Other institutions of the Catholic Church also received aid, such as the Theological Faculty in Ljubljana (which received several state subventions), the diocese of Djakovo (where Strossmayer once presided, which received a subsidy to restore the cathedral), and the diocese of Senj (which received a state subsidy to restore the episcopal palace).

In addition to health insurance, subsidies, and better relations with the bureaucracy, the priests' associations also enjoyed preferential treatment where publications were concerned. Thus, Dobri pastir, the Bosnian association, was able to publish a religious periodical and a calendar beginning in 1950, i.e., even at a time when almost all of the rest of the Church press was suppressed.[44]

The priests' associations were integrated into the structure of the Socialist Alliance of Working People of Yugoslavia (SAWPY) and were officially viewed as a means for clergymen to protect and realize their "professional interests." Despite claims by various observers[45] that the associations benefited the Church, the hierarchy remained deeply suspicious. In 1970, for example, Archbishop Frane Franić of Split wrote that the Franciscans, insofar as they constituted three-quarters of Dobri pastir's member-ship, were "true collaborators with the people's authorities."[46] A meeting of represen-tatives of clergymen's associations in 1978 showed that the antagonism felt by the hi-erarchy toward the associations was working against the latter. Vinko Weber, secretary of the Society of Catholic Priests of Croatia, told that meeting that his once vibrant organization was "now in its last gasp," that it had not been allowed to dis-tribute its publications on Church premises, and that it had subsequently even lost its printing facilities. Weber continued,

> Unfortunately, the days of "non licet non exedi" are still with us. This ban has remained in force right up to the present day. And let me tell you why this is so! Our society has its own statutes, and these statutes include the famous article 3, which, inter alia, states that members of the Society of Catholic Priests shall promote the brotherhood and unity of our peoples, defend the achievements of the national liberation struggle, promote ecu-menism, and so on. And this is the crux of the matter, that is, they cannot forgive us for incorporating this article into our statutes, and this is why they keep trying to foil us in everything we do. Things have finally reached the point where even certain Catholic so-cieties in other republics are starting to refuse to have anything to do with us, thinking that we are some kind of black sheep, and this is only because they have been misin-formed. But the upshot of all this is that nowadays our society is barely managing to keep itself together.[47]

Similarly, the Association of Catholic Priests of Montenegro, which attracted more than twenty of the thirty Catholic priests serving in that republic in 1954, could count only six members as of 1978—and all of them retired priests. Thus, far from being able to serve as an effective mediary between Church and state, the priests' as-sociations turned out to be at the most a useful mechanism for health insurance and other material benefits or, on the other hand, irrelevant vestiges of a failed strategy. In Slovenia, by contrast, the Catholic priests' association was always weak and served, in the 1980s, chiefly as the publication outlet for a quarterly newsletter and for a series of religious books for children.

Phases in Church–State Relations

The years 1945–1953 were the most difficult period for the Church. The Catholic press shriveled, and where there had been about a hundred periodical publications prior to the war, the Church could count only three publications now: *Blagovest* (in Belgrade and Skopje), *Dobri pastir* in Bosnia, and *Oznanilo* in Slovenia, which ap-peared as a two-page (front and back) bulletin from 1945 to 1946 and as a four-page bulletin in the years 1946–1952. (As of 1987, by contrast, the Catholic Church was publishing 134 periodicals in Croatia alone.)[48] Catholic hospitals, orphanages, and homes for the aged were seized and closed, and Catholic secondary schools were na-tionalized. Seminaries were likewise confiscated, for example, in Zagreb, Split, Travnik, Sent Vid, Ljubljana, Maribor, and Sinj.[49] Some 600 Slovenian priests were imprisoned. The faculties of theology of the universities of Ljubljana and Zagreb were separated from the universities by governmental decree in 1952.

The passage of a special Law on the Legal Status of Religious Communities (27 April 1953) stirred hope for change, insofar as it guaranteed freedom of conscience and religious belief. Perhaps as important was Tito's call, in a speech at Ruma that same year, for a "halt to physical assaults on the clergy"[50]—partly in concession to Western public opinion, now that Tito's Yugoslavia had broken with the Soviet bloc. The years 1953–1964 saw some reduction in the pressures against believers, though as Paul Mojzes notes, "excesses—such as torture, imprisonment on false charges, and even murder by the secret police—were still practiced from time to time, more in some parts of the country than in others."[51] Both Church and state were clearly groping toward a *modus vivendi* during this period. Hence, when Yugoslavia's bishops submitted a memorandum in September 1960 detailing their complaints and demands (including the unhindered prerogative to build and repair churches), they also included a calculated invitation to dialogue, noting that "the Constitution guarantees freedom of faith and conscience to all citizens, while the Law on the Legal Status of Religious Communities [gives form to] and defines this constitutional provision more closely. These legal provisions contain the nucleus of all that is necessary for relations between the Church and the State to develop in line with the principle of a free Church in a free State."[52]

By early 1964, there were unmistakable signs of a new atmosphere in Church–state relations. By 1965 Belgrade and the Holy See were engaged in negotiations, and on 25 June 1966 Belgrade and the Vatican signed a protocol and exchanged governmental representatives. In the protocol, Belgrade guaranteed the Roman Catholic Church "free conduct of religious affairs and rites," confirmed the Vatican's authority over Catholic clergy in Yugoslavia in religious matters, and guaranteed the bishops the right to maintain contact with the Vatican. On the other side, the Vatican undertook that priests in the country would respect Yugoslavia's laws and that the clergy "cannot misuse their religious and Church functions for aims which would have a political character."[53]

The hierarchy in Yugoslavia welcomed the protocol. Archbishop Franić saw in it the promise of "a new era for our Church,"[54] while Franjo Cardinal Šeper, then archbishop of Zagreb, commented in 1967, "The Catholic community cannot escape being engaged. But that presumes a greater amount of freedom. We hope that that freedom will steadily increase for the Catholic Church as well as for other social communities. . . . In the Belgrade Protocol, the Catholic Church accepted the existing legislation of Yugoslavia as a starting point. That at least presumes the possibility of legislative development in religious questions, so that [religious policy] would not lag behind the development of reality and become an anachronism."[55] Four years later, Yugoslavia reestablished full diplomatic relations with the Vatican, and in March 1971 Tito paid an official visit to the Vatican.

The general liberalization in Yugoslavia in the late 1960s permitted the launching of a series of Church periodicals, including the fortnightly newspaper (now weekly) *Glas koncila,* which has become an important organ for Church opinion. The

Church also began to revive its social programs for youth, not only in Croatia and Slovenia, but also in Bosnia, where the authorities showed especial misgivings at the Church's new self-confidence.[56] Catholic clergy in Rijeka, Split, Zadar, and Zagreb responded enthusiastically to the Croatian liberal-nationalist groundswell of the years 1967–1971, and in Bosnia-Herzegovina Franciscan priests gathered data on the number of Croats occupying administrative posts in that republic.[57]

It was this renewed self-assertion of the Church, combined with the purge of the liberal faction in the party, in the period 1971–1973, rather than the protocol and exchange of emissaries, that colored Church–state relations at the outset of their fourth postwar phase, 1970–1989. On the Church's part, the tenth anniversary (in 1970) of the death of Cardinal Stepinac was commemorated as demands emerged for his canonization.[58] For the regime, however, the rehabilitation of Stepinac seemed fraught with danger, since his trial had converted him into something of a Croatian mythological hero. Accordingly, Croatian sociologist Srdjan Vrcan warned a seminar at Krapinske Toplice, in January 1973, that "viewpoints, completely political and totally nonreligious in spirit, have again been revived as the widest ideological base, viz., viewpoints that the Croats and Serbs are two completely separate worlds between which no kind of stable and positive form of unity can be established."[59] Stepinac became the focal point for the self-defense of the Croatian Catholic Church (as witnessed in Franjo Cardinal Kuharić's annual sermons in defense of Stepinac) and the foundation of the attempted self-legitimation of the regime.

In the period 1970–1989, there were at least six issue areas that complicated the Church–state relationship.

First, the Church never reconciled itself to the inclusion of courses in atheism and Marxism in the school curricula and repeatedly asked for equal time or, alternatively, the removal of these courses from the schools. The point of view of the LCY was summarized by *Nedjeljna Dalmacija* in 1972: "The LC cannot accept the concept of an ideologically neutral school nor a school pluralism based on the individual right of each parent, because the educational system is the social obligation and affair of a social institution."[60]

The Church, however, complained that it was dissatisfied "with the method [of teaching], with the content, with the textbooks, with the sundry provocations through which believing children … are indoctrinated and atheized."[61] And in late 1987 the Episcopal Conference of Yugoslavia issued a statement calling on the government to respect the right of parents to obtain a religious education for their children.[62]

In autumn 1987, the Episcopal Office set up a theological institute in Mostar, Herzegovina, in cooperation with the Franciscan Province in Mostar. The institute planned to offer a three-year theological program to laypersons and quickly registered forty-five students for the 1987–1988 academic year. Despite the fact that there were precedents for such an institute (in Zagreb, Split, Ljubljana, and Maribor), republic authorities closed it down already in November 1987. The Yugoslav news agency Tanjug explained that the establishment of the institute was "directly opposed to the law on the legal position of religious communities in the Socialist Republic of Bosnia-Herzegovina, which, in article 20, states emphatically that religious communities can form religious schools only for the training of religious officials. Scientific and educational treatment of believers outside the church itself is, therefore, not in conformity with the law."[63] The Catholic paper, *Glas koncila,* issued a strong protest of this action.[64]

Second, the Church from time to time questioned the legitimacy of excluding believers from the ranks of the LCY. In 1971, for instance, the Slovenian Catholic weekly *Družina* published an article urging that the opportunities provided by SAWPY to Christians were inadequate and that their exclusion from the party was a token of political inequality.[65] Again, in 1987, Cardinal Kuharić raised this issue in an interview with the Catholic journal *Veritas,* adding that believers were excluded from high posts in various sectors of public life.[66] The party repeatedly repudiated this interpretation, however, and even urged party members to eschew marriage with believers and to stay away from Church ceremonies.[67] On the other hand, a 1988 article about religious life in Serbia found that only a third of party members in Serbia called themselves atheists, with most giving a positive description of religion.[68]

Third, the Church repeatedly challenged the regime over human rights—whether civil, national, or even the human rights of believers qua believers. In a public statement, Kuharić used his 1987 Easter sermon to plead on behalf of twenty-six-year-old Croatian dissident Dobroslav Paraga. Paraga had been charged with "slandering the state" after he gave an interview to the Slovenian youth magazine *Mladina,* in which he discussed the treatment he had received during a three-year prison sentence for antistate activity.[69] The defenselessness of believers in the face of slander by the secular press also preoccupied the Church, which deplored the lack of objectivity and fairness in the mass media and the inability of those calumniated to reply in the same media.[70] *Glas koncila* figured as probably the Church's single most important vehicle for self-defense against insinuations and distortions in the Communist press.

Fourth, the Church continued to complain that believers were, in other ways, treated as second-class citizens by the Communists, who, the Church claimed, treated religious belief as an *alienable* right. In particular, the Church complained of the fact that military personnel were not allowed to attend Church services in uniform or to receive Church newspapers or religious books in the barracks. The Church also long sought to obtain access to incarcerated believers, regardless of the issue for which they were in prison.[71] The Church also expressed concern about continued discrimination against believers in hiring practices in the public sector: This issue was raised by the Split archdiocesan journal *Crkva u svijetu* in late 1987 and by a special commission of the Provincial Episcopal Conference of Slovenia in 1988.[72]

Fifth, some elements in the Communist political establishment periodically tried to foster and aggravate internal divisions within the Church. For a while, the Christianity Today Publishing House seemed to some to be the ideal beneficiary of official favor in its "liberal defiance" of the hierarchs. Earlier, *Glas koncila* expressed concern that *Nedjeljna Dalmacija* was seeking to drive a wedge between the archbishop of

Zagreb and the archbishop of Split and to set them at odds, manipulating the latter's statements to suggest opposition to or divergence from the policy of the Zagreb archbishopric.[73] This strategy was epitomized by the rival formula which recurrently praised the "vast majority" of the clergy, while condemning the "political extremism" of a "reactionary minority."

And sixth, the legislation governing religious practice was itself an important bone of contention between Church and state, both in the preparatory stage and in discussions about the execution of policy. With the passage of the 1974 constitution, the Religious Law of 1953 was suspended and the republics were entrusted with the task of passing their own legislation in this domain. The new religious laws took effect in Slovenia on 26 May 1976 and in Bosnia-Herzegovina on 4 January 1977. After a vocal debate, Croatia was the last of the eight federal units to pass a new law, which took effect on 17 April 1978. Among the issues in contention were the ban on Church sponsorship of recreational activities, the absence of legal sanction for Church access to radio and television, and an article requiring the consent of the minor before parents could enroll her or him in religious instruction. *Glas koncila* objected, "Many citizens who are believers quite properly observe that neither they nor their minor children are asked for consent to be introduced in the course of their schooling to Marxism in its emphatically atheistic form."[74] The authorities compromised on the last point mentioned, and the final version of the Croatian law required the child's consent from age fourteen on, rather than from age seven, as specified in the draft.

The End of Yugoslavia

As Serb-Croat polemics heated up in the course of the period 1989–1990, the Catholic Church was ineluctably drawn into the fire. Serbian politicians revived the old Communist canard that the Catholic Church had been pro-*Ustaše* in World War II and stirred up fears of partition by talking of the supposedly Orthodox origins of Dalmatia.[75] The Church rebuffed these attacks and replied with a sharp article which suggested that Serbian revanchists might still nurture dreams of including as much as 70 percent of the territory of Yugoslavia within the borders of an enlarged Serbia.[76]

Not surprisingly, it was Slovenia—where both Strossmayer and Stepinac have always been largely irrelevant—that Church–state relations first acquired a somewhat friendlier tone. This was signaled in December 1986, when Ljubljana's Archbishop Alojz Šuštar became the first Yugoslav hierarch in the postwar period to be allowed to wish his flock a Merry Christmas over public radio.[77] The decision sparked a lively national debate, but privately, Slovenian clergy expressed confidence that Christmas would soon be declared a public holiday—if not in 1987, then by 1988—at least in the Republic of Slovenia.[78] Šuštar's Christmas greetings were once again broadcast in December 1987, but only amid massive controversy and discussion in the press. Meanwhile, Mitja Ribičič, a prominent Slovenian politician, suggested that rather than engaging in endless debate about the rectitude of broadcasting the prelate's Christmas greetings, it would be better to discuss how to improve the access of believers to jobs in both local and federal governmental agencies.[79] This was followed by the announcement in 1988 that the Catholic Faculty of Theology in Ljubljana, which had been forced to separate from the university shortly after the war, would shortly be reincorporated into the University of Ljubljana.[80]

Slovenes started to talk openly of the liquidation of priests by Tito in early post-war Slovenia.[81] Slovenian society began opening up. In February 1989, it was announced that Catholic journalists would be allowed to join the Society of Journalists of Slovenia.[82] Four months later, a Society of Catholic Journalists in Yugoslavia was established in Zagreb.[83]

As the Communist monopoly broke down, Catholic prelates joined in the general debate about the country's future. In November 1989, for example, the Iustitia et Pax Commission of the Episcopal Conference of Yugoslavia published a statement urging progress in repluralization, stressing, in particular, the central importance of the establishment of an independent judiciary.[84]

When the first free elections were conducted in Slovenia and Croatia in spring 1990, the Catholic bishops of Ljubljana and Zagreb issued a statement supporting democracy but declining to endorse any particular party. On the contrary, Church elders warned clergy not to become involved in partisan politics.[85] But in other ways the Catholic Church took advantage of the new liberalism to stretch its wings. As early as July 1990, Franciscans in Herzegovina asked for a lifting of the ban on associations based on religious and ethnic affiliation. In Croatia and Slovenia, Catholic prelates began to press for a restoration of (Catholic) religious instruction as a mandatory subject in public schools—succeeding in this endeavor in Croatia, but failing in Slovenia (as will be explained in more detail in Chapter 11). And in both republics, the Catholic Church began to demand that abortion be delegalized. Nor did the Church hold aloof from the most burning questions of the day. Cardinal Kuharić, in particular, took up the subject of confederalization in an article for *Vjesnik* and argued that "the question of confederation does not pass by the religious communities."[86]

The breakup of Yugoslavia and the outbreak of war confronted the Catholic Church in Slovenia, Croatia, and Bosnia with both new challenges and new opportunities. These subjects will be taken up in Chapter 11, in the context of a broader examination of the responses of the religious communities to the war in Bosnia.

Notes

This chapter is a revised and updated version of my earlier chapter, "The Catholic Church in Yugoslavia, 1945–1989," originally published in Pedro Ramet, ed., *Catholicism and Politics in Communist Societies* (Durham, N.C.: Duke University Press, 1990). The author wishes to thank Duke University Press for granting permission to reproduce the chapter here. I am grateful to Stella Alexander, Ivo Banac, and Christine Hassenstab for their helpful comments on earlier drafts of this study.

1. Michael A. Sells, *The Bridge Betrayed: Religion and Genocide in Bosnia* (Berkeley and Los Angeles: University of California Press, 1996), p. 89.

2. For further discussion, see Sabrina P. Ramet, *Nihil Obstat: Religion, Politics, and Social Change in East-Central Europe and Russia* (Durham, N.C.: Duke University Press, 1998), pp. 171–172.

3. Zlatko Markus, "Sadašnji trenutak crkve u Hrvatskoj," *Hrvatska revija* (Buenos Aires), Vol. 25, No. 2 (June 1975), pp. 223–224.

4. Frane Franić, *Putovi dijaloga* (Split: Crkva u svijetu, 1973), quoted in Markus, "Sadašnji trenutak," p. 219.

5. Ćiril Petešić, *Katoličko svećenstvo u NOB-u 1941–1945* (Zagreb: VPA, 1982), p. 130.

6. Ibid., p. 55

7. Petešić, *Katoličko svećenstvo,* pp. 32, 36.

8. See Ivo Banac, *The National Question in Yugoslavia: Origins, History, Politics* (Ithaca, N.Y.: Cornell University Press, 1984).

9. Fikreta Jelić-Butić, *Ustaše i NDH* (Zagreb: S. N. Liber and Školska Knjiga, 1977), p. 214.

10. Petešić, *Katoličko svećenstvo,* p. 95.

11. Richard Pattee, *The Case of Cardinal Aloysius Stepinac* (Milwaukee: Bruce, 1953), pp. 114, 276–281, 300–305. Stepinac's efforts on behalf of the Orthodox are noted in Ivan Cvitković's generally unsympathetic biography, *Ko je bio Alojzije Stepinac,* 2nd ed. (Sarajevo: Oslobodjenje, 1986), p. 209.

12. Quoted in Branko Bošnjak and Štefica Bahtijarević, *Socijalističko društvo, crkva and religija* (Zagreb: Institut za društvena istraživanja Sveučilišta u Zagrebu, 1969), p. 159.

13. O. Aleksa Benigar, *Alojzije Stepinac, Hrvatski Kardinal* (Rome: Žiral, 1974), p. 492.

14. Quoted in ibid., pp. 502–503.

15. See Pedro Ramet, *Cross and Commissar: the Politics of Religion in Eastern Europe and the USSR* (Bloomington: Indiana University Press, 1987), p. 29.

16. Rastko Vidić, *The Position of the Church in Yugoslavia* (Belgrade: Jugoslavija, 1962), pp. 69–70.

17. Giuseppe Masucci, *Misija u Hrvatskoj 1941–1946* [Diary] (Madrid: Drina, 1967), pp. 204–205.

18. Benigar, *Alojzije Stepinac,* p. 508.

19. See article by Dragoljub Petrović, in *Književne novine* (15 October 1985).

20. Quoted in Benigar, *Alojzije Stepinac,* p. 536.

21. Ibid., pp. 540–541.

22. Ibid., pp. 519, 542–543.

23. Ibid., p. 555; confirmed in *New York Times* (20 September 1946), p. 9.

24. *New York Times* (24 September 1946), p. 11.

25. *New York Times* (28 September 1946), p. 5.

26. Benigar, *Alojzije Stepinac,* p. 578; and *New York Times* (26 September 1946), p. 7.

27. Jakov Blažević, *Mać a ne mir. Za pravnu sigurnost gradjana* [Vol. 3 of Memoirs, 4 vols.] (Zagreb/Belgrade/Sarajevo: Mladost/Prosveta/Svjetlost, 1980), pp. 208–209.

28. Benigar, *Alojzije Stepinac,* p. 601.

29. Blažević, *Mać a ne mire,* pp. 211, 234–236.

30. Ibid., pp. 237–238. Pattee (*The Case,* p. 129) estimates that some 200,000 former Catholics who had been pressured into Orthodoxy were among those converting to Catholicism during the war.

31. Blažević, *Mać a ne mir,* pp. 284–285, 360.

32. *L'Osservatore Romano* (30 September 1946), summarized in *New York Times* (1 October 1946), p. 15.

33. Blažević, *Maĉ a ne mir,* pp. 210–211.

34. Ibid., p. 374.

35. Stella Alexander, *The Triple Myth: A Life of Archbishop Alojzije Stepinac* (Boulder: East European Monographs, 1987), p. 178.

36. *L'Osservatore Romano* (12 October 1946), trans. into Croatian in Benigar, *Alojzije Stepinac,* pp. 635–638; and *L'Osservatore Romano* (31 October 1946), excerpted in *New York Times* (1 November 1946), p. 17.

37. Quoted in Benigar, *Alojzije Stepinac,* p. 639.

38. *Polet* (8 and 15 February 1985), as quoted in *Glas koncila* (24 February 1985), p. 3. Regarding Stepinac, see also: Ivan Mužić, *Katolička crkva, Stepinac i Pavelić,* 2nd ed. (Zagreb: Dominović, 1997); J. Batelja and C. Tomić (eds.), *Alojzije Kardinal Stepinac, Nadbiskup Zagrebački: Propovijedi, govori, poruke (1941–1946)* (Zagreb: AGM, 1996); Vjekoslav Ranilović (ed.), *Nevin a osudjen: Dokumenti o Kardinalu Dr. Alojziju Stepincu* (Koprivnica: N.P., 1996); and Marina Stambuk-Skalić, Josip Kolanović, and Stjepan Razum (eds.), *Proces Alojziju Stepincu: Dokumenti* (Zagreb: Kršćanska sadašnjost, 1997).

39. *Borba* (24 October 1945), p. 3

40. This latter story seems to have been a complete fabrication, however, since on 10 December 1945 twenty priests from the Bar archdiocese sent a letter to Stepinac objecting that Archbishop Dobrečić had made no such statements to the press as had been claimed. See Benigar, *Alojzije Stepinac,* p. 546.

41. Stella Alexander, *Church and State in Yugoslavia Since 1945* (Cambridge: Cambridge University Press, 1979), p. 126.

42. Report in *Borba* (18 December 1952), reprinted in Vladimir Dedijer, ed., *Dokumenti 1948,* Vol. 3 (Belgrade: Rad, 1979), pp. 466–468.

43. Fra Ignacije Gavran, *Lucerna Lucens? Odnos vrhbosanskog ordinarijata prema bosanskim Franjevcima (1881–1975)* (Visoko: N.P., 1978), p. 155.

44. Rudolf Grulich, *Kreuz, Halbmond und Roter Stern: Zur Situation der katholischen Kirche in Jugoslawien* (Munich: Aktion West-Ost, 1979), p. 62.

45. E.g., Gavran, *Lucerna Lucens,* pp. 158–159; and Grulich, *Kreuz, Halbmond,* p. 62.

46. Quoted in Gavran, *Lucerna Lucens,* p. 158n.

47. *Vjesnik* (15 July 1978), trans. in Joint Publications Research Service (JPRS), *East Europe Report,* No. 72058 (17 October 1978).

48. *NIN,* No. 1900 (22 March 1987), p. 32.

49. Interview, Ljubljana, July 1982.

50. Quoted in Alexander, *Church and State,* p. 229.

51. Paul Mojzes, "Religious Liberty in Yugoslavia: A Study in Ambiguity," in Leonard Swidler, ed., *Religious Liberty and Human Rights in Nations and in Religions* (Philadelphia: Ecumenical Press, 1986), pp. 25–26.

52. Quoted in Zdenko Roter, "Relations Between the State and the Catholic Church in Yugoslavia," *Socialist Thought and Practice,* Vol. 18, No. 11 (November 1974), p. 69.

53. *New York Times* (26 June 1966), p. 4.

54. Quoted in Zdenko Roter, *Katoliška cerkev in država v Jugoslaviji 1945–1973* (Ljubljana: Cankarjeva založba, 1976), p. 203.

55. Ibid., p. 206.

56. For details, see Pedro Ramet, "Catholicism and Politics in Socialist Yugoslavia," *Religion in Communist Lands,* Vol. 10, No. 3 (winter 1982), pp. 261–262.

57. *Borba* (9 October 1970), p. 6. For further discussion of the Catholic Church's association with Croatian nationalism, see Pedro Ramet, "Religion and Nationalism in Yugoslavia," in Pedro Ramet, ed., *Religion and Nationalism in Soviet and East European Politics,* revised and expanded ed. (Durham, N.C.: Duke University Press, 1989).

58. "Vjernost Alojziju Stepincu—za reviziju sudskog procesa i kanonizaciju!" *Hrvatska revija,* Vol. 20, No. 1 (March 1970), pp. 85–87.

59. *Borba* (14 January 1973), p. 7, trans. in JPRS, *Translations on Eastern Europe,* No. 58221 (13 February 1973).

60. *Nedjeljna Dalmacija* (Varaždin) (9 December 1972), quoted in *Glas koncila* (7 January 1973), p. 12, trans. in JPRS, *Translations on Eastern Europe,* No. 58479 (14 March 1973).

61. *Glas koncila* (25 December 1980).

62. *Frankfurter Allgemeine* (2 November 1987), p. 4.

63. Tanjug (15 November 1987), quoted in *Keston News Service,* No. 290 (17 December 1987), p. 14.

64. *Glas koncila* (6 December 1987), p. 2, and (13 December 1987), p. 2; and *AKSA Bulletin,* Catholic news summary translation service edited by Stella Alexander with Muriel Heppell and Kresimir Sidor (26 January 1988), pp. 5–6.

65. *Družina* (1 August 1971), cited in *Borba* (1 August 1971), p. 5.

66. Interview with Franjo Cardinal Kuharić, in *Veritas* (March 1987), excerpted in *Glas koncila* (8 March 1987), p. 3.

67. Dionisie Ghermani, "Die katholische Kirche in Kroatien/Slowenien," *Kirche in Not,* Vol. 27 (1979), p. 93; *Glas koncila* (19 February 1984), p. 4, and (16 June 1985), p. 3.

68. *Delo* (Ljubljana) (20 February 1988), as reported in *AKSA* (26 February 1988), in *AKSA Bulletin* (14 April 1988), p. 4.

69. *Keston News Service,* No. 274 (30 April 1987), pp. 16–17.

70. *Glas koncila* (25 October 1981), p. 3.

71. Interview with Archbishop of Belgrade Dr. Franc Perko, in *Danas,* No. 260 (10 February 1987), p. 26; and *Keston News Service,* No. 290 (17 December 1987).

72. Drago Simundža, "Ustavni i stvarni položaj vjernika u društvu," *Crkva u svijetu,* No. 4 (1987), reprinted in *Glas koncila* (25 December 1987), p. 5; *Frankfurter Allgemeine* (17 March 1988), p. 1; and *Glas koncila* (3 April 1988), p. 5.

73. *Glas koncila* (7 January 1973), p. 12.

74. *Glas koncila* (22 January 1978), p. 3, trans. in JPRS, *East Europe Report,* No. 70836 (24 March 1978).

75. Bishop Nikodim Milaš, *Pravoslavna Dalmacija* (Belgrade: Sfairos, 1989).

76. This suggestion was made indirectly, by publishing an old Chetnik map of Yugoslavia in the pages of *Glas koncila.* See *Glas koncila* (24 September 1989), p. 3; also ibid. (30 July 1989), p. 5, and (8 October 1989), p. 2.

77. *NIN,* No. 1879 (4 January 1987), pp. 15–16; and *Frankfurter Allgemeine* (2 January 1987), p. 4.

78. Interview, Ljubljana, July 1987.

79. *Borba* (Zagreb ed.) (31 October–1 November 1987), p. 3; *Dnevnik* (Novi Sad) (13 November 1987), summarized in *AKSA* (13 November 1987), as reported in *AKSA Bulletin* (26 January 1988), p. 7; and *Glas koncila* (3 January 1988), p. 3.

80. *Delo* (6 January 1988), reported in *AKSA* (8 January 1988), in *AKSA Bulletin* (9 March 1988), p. 10; and *Ilustrovana politika* (Belgrade) (2 February 1988), reported in *AKSA* (19 February 1988), in *AKSA Bulletin* (14 April 1988), p. 8.

81. *Glas koncila* (8 January 1989), p. 6.

82. *Glas koncila* (26 February 1989), p. 3.

83. *Glas koncila* (18 June 1989), p. 6.

84. *Keston News Service*, No. 342 (25 January 1990), p. 23.

85. *Keston News Service*, No. 348 (20 April 1990), p. 11, and No. 360 (11 October 1990), p. 11.

86. *Vjesnik: Panorama subotom* (6 October 1990), p. 6.

◆

CHAPTER FIVE

The Serbian Orthodox Church

Between 1984 and 1987, there was a dramatic transformation of the status of the Serbian Orthodox Church. Long treated as a despised pariah whose gospel was the dispensation of depraved reactionaries, the Serbian Orthodox Church regained some of its earlier stature and prestige and has more recently been treated—as in the interwar kingdom—as the most constant defender of the Serbian people and their culture.

The Soul of the Church

Prior to 1984, however, the Serbian Orthodox Church became accustomed to vilification. Over time, this affected the psychological state of Orthodox clergy, who came to see themselves as embattled warriors for their Christ, profoundly threatened by a dangerous world. For much of the postwar period, it was more or less routine for the Communist press in Yugoslavia periodically to assail the Serbian Orthodox Church for chauvinism, Greater Serbian nationalism, and reactionary attitudes. The sensitivity with which that Church often reacted to such attacks betrayed a psychological vulnerability fostered by the vicissitudes in the Church's fortunes during the twentieth century and by the erosion of its power on several fronts and expressed in the hierarchy's self-image as a *suffering* Church, even of a Church marked out for *special* suffering. Having lost a fourth of its clergy and many of its churches during World War II, the Serbian Church had to endure the postwar harassment of its priests and the continued obstruction of church construction. Having lived to see the extinction of the artificially created Croatian Orthodox Church, the Belgrade patriarchate had to deal with two further schisms, resulting in the loss of effective jurisdiction over part of the American and Australian congregations as well as the Macedonian dioceses. And although most of the Serbian clergy resisted the Nazis and their allies tenaciously, they found themselves strangely isolated, derided, chastened—until the late 1980s. The Serbian Church remained defiant, but there was a sense of pessimism or perhaps of impotence to that defiance. Accordingly, in the new arcadia of Church–state rapprochement created by Slobodan Milošević, the Serbian priests behave as if they are unsure whether these "freedoms" are here to stay and privately expressed concern in 1989 that everything could be rescinded and retracted overnight. The Church, thus, has retained a sense of insecurity and has not forgotten that, in the greater scheme, it remains impotent.

It was not always this way. In the early part of the century, the Serbian Church took its numerous privileges for granted and identified the purposes of the Serbian kingdom so totally with its own purposes as to be incapable of comprehending differences of interest, except as misinterpretations of their common interest. Yet it should be stressed that the comparatively weak position of the Serbian Church since the war is not the result merely of the decimation of World War II, let alone of Communist rule, but has its roots deep in the past.

The second suppression of the Serbian patriarchate of Peć in 1766 no doubt undermined the institutional power of the Church. Thus, at the opening of the twentieth century, the Serbian Orthodox Church was organized differently in the different political systems in which it had dioceses and lacked a centralized authoritative head. In the Kingdom of Serbia, for instance, the leading Church figure was the metropolitan of Belgrade, assisted by a synod, and the clergy received state salaries. In Montenegro, the Montenegrin government set up a synod, in 1903, as the highest Church authority in that principality, including in its membership all Montenegrin bishops, two archimandrites, three protopriests, and a secretary. In Hungary, Orthodox Church affairs were regulated autonomously by a national Church council over which the metropolitan of Karlovci presided. And in Bosnia-Herzegovina, the Orthodox clergy again regulated the internal life of the Church independently, although the Austrian emperor appointed its bishops.[1]

More significant for the vitiation that began in the late nineteenth century were the ideas of materialism, positivism, and progressive secularism, which infected even some of the clergy (e.g., Jovan Jovanović, rector of the Orthodox Theological Seminary in Belgrade), and the persistent encroachments by the state on ecclesiastical turf. Repeated intellectual attacks on the Serbian Church, combined with the increasingly poorer training given to Serbian clergy, eventually resulted in a sapping of religiosity among the Serbs. Meanwhile, infused with notions of social activism, many of the clergy became involved in Serbian political parties, which encouraged the state to interfere more and more in ecclesiastical affairs. By 1881, with the dismissal of Belgrade Metropolitan Mihailo and the passage of a new law, whereby the government was able to pack the Church synod with its own lay delegates, the state had effectively taken over the Church, reducing it to something akin to a state agency; even the reinstatement of Mihailo in 1889 did not reinvigorate the Church's power.[2] The very organization of the Serbian Orthodox Church was eventually regulated by a law on Church districts passed by the state with the consent of the Church.

Yet there were benefits for the Church in the old Kingdom of Serbia, too. For one thing, under the Serbian constitution of 1903, Orthodoxy was recognized as the official state religion and all state and national holidays were celebrated with Church ritual. Orthodox religious instruction was mandatory throughout Serbia. And all bishops, Serbian Church officials, religious instructors, and army chaplains received state salaries. Moreover, after the establishment of a unified Yugoslavia at the end of 1918 and the revival of the patriarchate, the Serbian patriarch would sit on the Royal Council, while several orthodox clergymen had seats in the National Assembly as deputies of various political parties.

Given the disunity in Church organizations in the first two decades of this century, it was inevitable that the Serbian Church viewed the unification of the South Slavs as *also* a unification of the Serbian Orthodox Church and thus perhaps even as a great turning point. Within six months of the establishment of the interwar Kingdom of Serbs, Croats, and Slovenes (as Yugoslavia was initially called), the Serbian bishops convened in Belgrade and proclaimed the unification of all the Serbian Orthodox provincial churches into a single unified ecclesiastical structure. The following year, on 12 September 1920, the bishops completed the process by solemnly proclaiming the reestablishment of the Serbian patriarchate, in the presence of the highest dignitaries of both Church and state. These moves were fully canonical, undertaken with the concurrence and blessing of the Ecumenical Patriarchate.

The state's interest in this was clear from the outset. Even before the unification conference a governmental delegate, Dr. Vojislav Janić—later to become the Minister of Faiths—revealed that it was "the wish of the government that the reestablishment of the patriarchate be accomplished as soon as the Church is unified."[3] Furthermore, once the patriarch had been elected, the government lost little time in drafting a law that would have imposed greater legislative and judicial unity on the Church and thus made it simpler to regulate and control. Because this draft bill provoked immediate protests from all sides, but especially in the metropolitanate of Karlovac and in Bosnia-Herzegovina, where the local clergy dreaded the diminution of their autonomy, it was withdrawn and a different bill was submitted to the Assembly at the end of 1923. This draft also failed to be passed, and two further drafts were likewise defeated before the government finally succeeded, in 1929, in passing a law drafted by the minister of justice, Milan Srškić. The prolonged controversy over this law revealed the existence of considerable differences of opinion between Church and state regarding state jurisdiction over the Church and also considerable division within the Serbian Church itself.

In the meantime, the Serbian Church and the government signed an agreement in 1926 (between the Episcopal Synod and the Ministry of Faiths) which was the equivalent of a concordat, arranging many questions pertaining to their mutual relations. The state now discovered that instead of simplifying its control over the Church, the reestablishment of the patriarchate had given the Church new resources; and in the course of the 1920s, as a result both of the passage of a new Church constitution (in 1924) and of the fluidity produced by the drawn-out controversy over the Church law—as well as the financial strength derived in part from state subventions to the Church—the Serbian Orthodox Church improved its position vis-à-vis the state and showed itself willing to confront the state over matters of importance. The Church became, at the same time, a unified structure, as differences between provincial Churches disappeared.

Under Yugoslavia's King Alexander (1921–1934), "not only was the dynasty Serbian, but all the important ministries were monopolized by Serbs, the bureaucracy was predominantly Serbian, the police were controlled by Serbs, [and] the high ranks of the military were occupied by Serbs."[4] The monarchy gave the Serbian Orthodox Church generous subsidies. As a result of these, the Serbian Church was able to establish a metropolitanate in Zagreb and to construct three churches in Catholic Slovenia.[5] There was even talk, in the early 1920s, that the Serbian Orthodox Church might open a Theological Faculty in Zagreb.[6] During the 1920s, non-Orthodox believers repeatedly complained that the Serbian Church was manipulating the state to serve its own confessional objectives, and reports that the Royal Dictatorship (established in 1929) was persecuting Catholic schools only deepened the alienation of the Catholic sector of the population.[7]

Although it enjoyed, in some ways, a privileged position in the interwar kingdom, or perhaps precisely *because* it did, the Serbian Church was deeply troubled by the Roman Catholic Church's quest for a concordat, which, it feared, would greatly strengthen the position of the Catholic Church throughout Yugoslavia. Catholic Archbishops Bauer and Stepinac were very much in favor of the concordat, and Vlatko Maček, chair of the Croatian Peasant Party, lent his endorsement to the Holy See's efforts to secure it. The concordat was finally signed on 25 July 1935, shortly after Milan Stojadinović became prime minister, though the state did not publish its contents. The Serbian Orthodox Church, however, published what was purported to be a complete draft of the concordat, together with a point-by-point critique.[8]

The Serbian patriarchate claimed that the concordat was designed to give the Catholic Church exclusive privileges in Yugoslavia. These privileges were said to include: the guarantee that Catholic bishops, clergy, and believers would enjoy complete freedom of direct contact with the Vatican, whereas in the case of the Serbian Church, only the patriarch was guaranteed such access to fellow Orthodox clergy abroad; an extension to Catholic clergy of the same state protection enjoyed by state employees and the protection of the privacy of the confessional; the right to retain buildings and property even in hypothetical cases in which the local congregation should convert en masse to another faith; privileged exemption from the payment of the telegraph tax; the assurance that Catholic bishops would enjoy unlimited rights to inspect religious instruction, whereas the Serbian Church could conduct such inspections only once a year, and the Islamic community only twice a year; the guarantee that Catholic school children not be obliged or even invited to attend religious instruction of any non-Catholic denomination and that the school program be arranged so as not to obstruct Catholic students from carrying out their religious obligations; and the exemption of Catholic priests and monks, but not Orthodox clergy, from military conscription, except in case of general mobilization.[9] The Serbian Church also objected to Article 8 of the proposed concordat, because it would have banned *all* clergymen in *all* Churches from participation in political parties, even though the Serbian Orthodox Church had not been consulted in this regard.[10] Finally, the patriarchate claimed that in the broad sense, the guarantee in Article 1, that the Catholic Church might carry out its "mission," could embrace a right of proselytization, "which is contrary to Article 16 of the state constitution and which can disturb the interconfessional balance."[11]

The Serbian Orthodox Church created a huge uproar over the bill. The Serbian Church even allied itself with opposition Serbian parties in efforts to bring down the proconcordat administration. The government offered to guarantee the Serbian Church the same privileges, but the uproar did not die down. On 23 July 1937, despite violent confrontations between Orthodox believers and police, Stojadinović pushed the bill through the Assembly (the lower house in the bicameral legislature), by a vote of 166 to 128. The same night the patriarch died, and rumors spread that the government had had him poisoned. The Orthodox Synod refused the state funeral which would have been customary for a deceased patriarch and punished the Orthodox parliamentary deputies who had supported the concordat by suspending their rights in the Church.[12] These additional pressures broke the government's will to continue, and Stojadinović decided not to present the document to the senate for approval. On 27 October 1937, Stojadinović informed the Catholic episcopate that the concordat was decidedly dead. The concordat was formally withdrawn on 1 February 1938. This constituted a major victory for the Serbian Orthodox Church, which had been fighting the concordat for more than twelve years.[13] Thus, on the eve of World War II, the Serbian Church could congratulate itself on two major victories—in the controversy over the Church law and in the struggle over the concordat.

The Great Catastrophe

The systematic destruction of hundreds of monasteries and church buildings, the liquidation of hundreds of Serbian Orthodox clergy, and the wartime deaths of at least six of the Church's top hierarchs[14] (three murdered by the *Ustaše*) had a traumatic effect on the Serbian clergy, and even today they live with a complex of bitterness rooted in the wartime debilitation. The Serbian Church had shared in the Serbian nationalist enthusiasm to see Croatia as a zone for Serbian political, economic, cultural, and confessional expansion and viewed Catholicism as a degenerate form of the true faith; this orientation made it all the more painful for the Serbian Church to bear the fruit of wartime Croatia's program of eliminating all traces of Serbdom and Orthodoxy from Croatia. The fact that the program of forced exile and liquidation was supplemented by the coercive conversion to Catholicism of part of the Orthodox population in the fascist Independent State of Croatia (Nezavisna Država Hrvatska, or NDH), in order to "Croatize" them, deepened both the identification of Serbdom and Orthodoxy in the consciousness of the Serbian Church and the sense of threat from the *Ustaša* party of the NDH. Moreover, the Catholic Church by and large seemed to welcome the conversions, even if it sometimes distanced itself from the coercion employed. Mile Budak, NDH *doglavnik* (second-in-command to Ante Pavelić) told an assemblage of representatives of the Catholic Action organization on 8 June 1941: "The Orthodox came to these districts as guests. And they should now leave these parts once and for all. Of course, many will not be able to leave, but in that case they will want to convert to our faith."[15]

In April 1941, there had been 577 Serbian Orthodox clergymen in the territory of the NDH. By the end of 1941, all of them had been removed from the scene: 3 were in prison, 5 had died of natural causes, 217 had been killed by the *Ustaše*, 334 had been deported to Serbia, and 18 had fled to Serbia earlier.[16] Serbian clergy were treated in a similar fashion in parts occupied by other powers. In Vojvodina there was pressure on Orthodox believers. In Bulgarian-occupied Macedonia the Bulgarian Orthodox Church asserted its jurisdiction (in the conviction that Macedonians are Bulgarians rather than Serbs, as the Serbian Church has always insisted), expelled or arrested those clergy who considered themselves Serbs, and sent in about 280 of its own clergy to administer the faith in Macedonia.[17] In the Italian-occupied littoral, Orthodox clergy were imprisoned and executed, and numerous church edifices were destroyed.[18]

The losses suffered by the Serbian Church during the war were colossal both in real terms and in psychological terms. Of the more than 4,200 churches and chapels and 200 monasteries owned by the Serbian Church in Europe prior to the war,[19] almost 25 percent had been completely destroyed and 50 percent of those in Yugoslavia were seriously damaged. As much as a fifth of the clergy in Yugoslavia as a whole had been killed (perhaps as many as 700), and another 300 had died of natural causes during the war.[20] At war's end, without any assured income and with an estimated wartime damage of 2.4 billion dinars, the Serbian Church still had 2,100 parish priests, 537 lay employees, and about 1,000 retired priests (on pension).[21] Under these circumstances, the Serbian Church was faced with a difficult challenge. The Church wanted to rebuild its world as it had been before, but the preconditions for that world no longer existed.

The Communist Assault and the Effort to Rebuild

Understandably, the Serbian clergy had taken an active part in the resistance against the occupation, and some of its clergy, including Patriarch Gavrilo and Bishop Nikolaj Velimirović, had been incarcerated in German concentration camps. But the Serbian Church had naturally viewed the resistance in quite different terms from the Communist Party. For the Church, the resistance was a nationalist cause of the Serbian people against traitorous Croats and imperialist Nazis. For the Communists, on the other hand, the war—which Yugoslav Communists referred to as the national liberation struggle (*narodnooslobodilačka borba*)—was at the same time a social revolution whereby the different peoples of Yugoslavia would subordinate their divisive ethnic interests to joint class interests and through which exploitative "vestiges of the past," such as the Serbian Orthodox Church, would be pushed into an inferior position, in which they could subsequently be snuffed out. Serbian nationalism, which has always been close to the heart of the Serbian Church, was seen by the Communists not merely as an archenemy of the new Yugoslavia, but even as an enemy of the Serbian people itself.

The aims of the Communist Party of Yugoslavia (CPY) diverged from those of the patriarchate in a number of ways. The CPY wanted, first of all, to legitimize its federation and most especially its reconquest of Macedonia in every possible way. Hence, if there were Orthodox clergy in Macedonia eager to set up an autonomous or autocephalous Church, so much the better, as this would reinforce the image of a distinctive Macedonian ethnicity. The patriarchate, which was an expression of union achieved only with some difficulty in 1920, was hostile to any assault on its unity.

Second, the CPY wanted a tame and cooperative Church that would eschew anything smacking of opposition, but be available to support CPY policies when such support was desired. To this end, the government revived the priests' associations (which actually traced a tradition back to 1889), hoping, with some cause, to use these associations to control the Church. The patriarchate was prepared to cooperate with the new regime, but not to be its tame and obedient tool. Thus, although there were those on each side who desired to reach an accommodation, there was much less agreement as to the form that accommodation should take.

Third, the CPY, then still in its Stalinist phase, wanted to uproot religion and to resocialize the population according to the precepts of atheistic dialectical materialism. That is, it was willing to tolerate Churches as institutions, but not as teachers and leaders of the people. The regime therefore initiated a policy of obstructing religious education, confiscating Church buildings, and fining the clergy on various pretexts. Orthodox clergy were, in the early postwar years, harassed, beaten up, and imprisoned on trumped-up charges. In the hope of compromising the prestige of the Church elders, the regime began a practice—which continued until Slobodan Milošević seized the reins of power in Serbia in late 1987—of accusing various Serbian hierarchs of wartime collaboration with the Nazis, such as Bishops Irinej Djordjević and Nikolaj Velimirović, though in fact both of these bishops had been interned by the Axis and were as antifascist as they were anticommunist.[22] But therein lay another problem, for the Communist regime was strongly opposed to an anticommunist clergy. Velimirović was, moreover, an outspoken Serbian nationalist.

There were, at the same time, two respects in which the Serbian Church could be useful to the Communist regime. First, insofar as the patriarch of the Serbs would be seen to be on decent terms with the regime, this would tend to give the lie to accusations that the regime was anti-Serb; this was especially important in the early period, when the regime was preparing to put Chetnik leader Draža Mihailović on trial. Second, the Serbian Church could be useful as a vehicle for maintaining contacts with other Communist countries in which there were prominent Orthodox Churches, i.e., the Soviet Union, Romania, and Bulgaria.

There was thus an ambivalence in the Communist attitude toward the Serbian Church—an ambivalence not shared by the patriarchate, though it must be emphasized that many lower clergy felt disposed to strive for accommodation with the regime, and at least a part of the membership of the priests' associations seems to have felt this way. Reformist lower clergy met as early as November 1942 to revive the Orthodox priests' association, and at war's end priests' associations were set up with government backing along federated lines, corresponding to the federal units erected by the regime. According to Stella Alexander, these Orthodox priests' associations were, in the beginning, "completely under government control."[23] By mid-1952, *Borba* would claim that some 80 percent of the remaining active clergy (approximately 1,700) were members of priests' associations.[24] It was these associations which were now authorized to publish the newspaper *Vesnik,* which began publication on 1 March 1949. *Vesnik,* supposedly a Church paper, immediately published attacks on the Serbian Church synod and on Bishops Irinej of Dalmatia and Nikolaj of Ziba (both in emigration) and in other ways showed itself to be a pliable tool for the regime. Understandably, the synod repeatedly turned down the association's application for official recognition, and the patriarchate remained formally opposed to the associations, though this opposition was, over time, tempered by some forms of accommodation. Indeed, a number of bishops were elected from the ranks of the association.[25]

In May 1953, the Communist regime passed a new Law on Religious Communities. Prior to issuing this bill, Communist authorities consulted with Orthodox and Muslim clergy, though not with either Catholics or Protestants.[26] Despite this limited consultation, the bill represented Communist interests, not Church interests. Among the more controversial stipulations in the law was one guaranteeing that no child could be forced by her or his parents to attend religious instruction. The years 1945 to 1955 were the most difficult of the entire postwar period for the Serbian Church. During these years, Belgrade gave a strict interpretation to clauses of laws curtailing the activity of Churches, imposing heavy penalties on clergymen for any infractions but light punishment, at the most, on those infringing on the rights of religious believers.[27] In a striking illustration of the mood of this period, Bishop Nektarije of Tuzla was roughed up by a mob after he pointed out that the Law on the Legal Status of Religious Communities (1953) expressly permitted the holding of religious services.[28] Under the Law on Agrarian Reform and Colonization (27 May 1945), the state seized 173,367 hectares of land belonging to the religious organizations (85 percent of their total); 70,000 hectares of what was seized had belonged to the Serbian Orthodox Church. The Serbian Church had had considerable investments in apartments, affording it a tangible rental income, but by 1958 the regime completed the nationalization of apartments, depriving the Serbian Church of 1,180 buildings, worth 8 billion dinars.[29] The Church's two printing presses were also expropriated after the war, without compensation,[30] and various difficulties were encountered in the reopening of religious seminaries and in their maintenance, due to bureaucratic pressure.

Despite all this, the Serbian Church was able to rebuild. Between 1945 and 1970, the Church built 181 churches and restored 841, built 115 chapels and restored

126, and built 8 monasteries and restored 48. Even in the Zagreb Eparchy, 20 churches were restored and 2 new chapels built.[31] By 1949, a makeshift seminary was operating in the Rakovica monastery near Belgrade, and shortly thereafter the Church was able to reopen its seminary in Prizren. Subsequently, in 1964, Orthodox seminaries were also opened in Sremski Karlovci and at Krka, in the Dalmatian hinterland. Meanwhile, the Theological Faculty in Belgrade had, by 1966, developed a permanent staff of 8 professors and lecturers and had about 120 students.[32] As of 1982, there were 100–110 students in each of the Church's four seminaries, which came close to the capacity of 120, and there were about 70 students studying at the Theological Faculty in Belgrade. Although the number of male clergy held almost steady at about 2,000 for the next two and a half decades, the number of Orthodox nuns inched upward from 468 in 1965 to 519 in 1966 to about 700 in 1980.[33]

Although the Serbian Church had had a lively and plentiful press in the interwar period, with numerous Church magazines, newspapers, and journals established in the 1920s and 1930s,[34] its publishing activity had to be rebuilt essentially from scratch after World War II. Initially this activity was limited to a single official organ. *Glasnik*, the Serbian Church's oldest journal, was being published in 2,100 copies in 1955 and, beginning in 1965, in 3,000 copies. The Church established the quarterly educational magazine *Pravoslavni misionar* in 1958, and by 1968 it was being printed in 50,000 copies. The patriarchate brought out its first popular newspaper, *Pravoslavlje*, on 15 April 1967, and as of summer 1987 it was being printed in 23,000 copies (of which 1,500 went to foreign subscribers). A monthly children's magazine, *Svetosavsko zvonce*, was added in 1968 and had a circulation of 15,000 in 1982. The wartime deaths of a number of leading theologians complicated the task of the resumption of theological publication, and *Bogoslovlje*, the scholarly journal of the Theological Faculty, which had ceased publication during the war, did not resume until 1957, although three special collections of articles (*Zbornik radova*) were issued in 1950, 1953, and 1954. A decade later, the Archbishopric of Belgrade-Karlovac created its own theological journal, *Teološki pogledi*. In addition to these theological periodicals, there is also *Pravoslavna misao,* a magazine for Church questions, which, in 1970, had a circulation of 2,000.[35] Book publication resumed slowly, after hesitation, in 1951, but by 1982 the patriarchate was literally boasting of its fine editions, scholarly tomes, ample publications, and so forth.

Whittling the Church Down

To understand the Serbian Orthodox Church is to comprehend it as an institution which has repeatedly been whittled down—sometimes unsuccessfully, sometimes successfully. The first twentieth-century challenge to the Serbian patriarchate in this sense was the establishment of the Croatian Orthodox Church in April 1942. Although no Serbian hierarch would accept office in this artificial Church (so that two Russian émigré clergymen had to be contracted to head the dioceses of Zagreb and Sarajevo), a number of Serbian Orthodox clergy did in fact join and cooperate with that structure, in the vain hope of saving themselves and their parishioners. The attempt of the Bulgarian Orthodox Church to "annex" the faithful in Macedonia, like the short-lived Croatian Orthodox Church, likewise met ultimate defeat.

On the other hand, the Serbian patriarchate lost its jurisdiction over its Czechoslovak dioceses between 1945 and 1948, and in 1951 these became the Czechoslovak Orthodox Church. Some Serbian parishes lying within Romania's borders were similarly transferred to the Romanian Orthodox Church in 1969, though the Diocese of Timişoara is still administered by the Serbian Church. The Serbian Church suffered a formal schism in 1963, when Bishop Dionisije Milivojević of the American-Canadian diocese summoned an assembly to declare that diocese an autonomous Church. Only much later, in 1989, would there be a rapprochement between the Serbian patriarchate and the American diocese.[36] Finally, on 17 July 1967, the Macedonian clergy, in open defiance of the Serbian patriarchate to which it had taken oaths of loyalty, unilaterally declared itself an autocephalous Macedonian Orthodox Church, electing a Smederevo native, Dositej, as archbishop of Ohrid. It is natural, then, that the Serbian patriarchate was anxious whenever the Communist regime gave encouragement to ecclesiastical separatism in Montenegro, as it did in the early postwar years,[37] and in this context, Patriarch German's comment in 1970 that Montenegrins are simply Serbs by another name becomes readily intelligible.[38]

Although the Serbian Church remained apprehensive of a regime-backed Montenegrin schism at least into the early 1970s, it is the Macedonian schism which has caused the Church the most grief. Despite its inability to do anything to change the situation, the Serbian Orthodox Church has refused to recognize the schismatic Macedonian Church.

The collaboration of the Macedonian clergy with the Communists stretches back to the war. At the end of 1943, the Partisan high command appointed a Macedonian, Rev. Veljo Mančevski, to take charge of religious affairs in liberated areas. Shortly after the occupation forces were driven out of Belgrade, three Macedonian clergy (Metodije Gogov, Nikola Apostolov, and Kiril Stojanov) presented themselves to the Serbian synod as representatives of the Orthodox Church in Macedonia and members of the Organizing Committee for the Founding of an Independent Church in Macedonia. A premature declaration of autocephaly at this point in time was stymied, but relations between the Serbian patriarchate and the CPY remained tense as long as the patriarchate refused to compromise. The Orthodox priests' association. often inclined to take a stance at odds with the patriarch, supported Macedonian autocephaly all along, despite the misgivings among some Serbian members. Finally, in 1958, after the Macedonian clergy declared themselves an "autonomous" Church on their own initiative, the new Serbian patriarch accepted the fait accompli, though he underlined that it should go no further than autonomy. Directly as a result of the patriarch's acceptance of Macedonian ecclesiastical autonomy, the Serbian Church's relations with the government improved markedly, and by 1961 the regime's encouragement of intraecclesiastical divisions generally seemed to have died down.[39] The interest of the government in the Macedonian Church was shown in its hints of a subvention of 60 million dinars to the Serbian Church if it came to terms with the Macedonian clergy.[40]

The Communist Party was, at this time, seriously divided between advocates of "organic Yugoslavism," led by Slovenian party ideologue Edvard Kardelj, who wanted to knit the country together by making generous allowances to the cultural and national distinctiveness of its component peoples, and advocates of "integral Yugoslavism," led by Vice President Aleksandar Ranković, who wanted to encourage the development of a Yugoslav consciousness in the ethnic sense and who tended to view non-Serbs as "less reliable" than Serbs. The former group thus favored decentralization to the federal units, while the latter favored political and administrative centralism. Ranković, whose Serbian nationalism was never much below the surface, was known for having promoted discriminatory practices against non-Serbs in Croatia, Bosnia, Vojvodina, and Kosovo.[41] The fall of Ranković in July 1966 proved instrumental in fostering a change of regime policy vis-à-vis the Serbian Church, as Ranković had wanted to prevent the erosion of the Serbian position in any sphere, including the ecclesiastical. He dealt with the Church roughly and used threats to obtain ecclesiastical compliance.[42] But as long as he was in office, the Macedonians were unable to obtain full autocephaly.

Ranković was removed from office on 1 July 1966. The Macedonian clergy immediately began preparations for declaring complete autocephaly and were ready in a matter of four months. On 18 November 1966, at a joint meeting of the Serbian and Macedonian synods, the Macedonian clergy demanded full autocephaly. When the Serbian synod demurred, the demand was renewed on 3 December, with the attendant threat of unilateral action if the Belgrade patriarchate did not concur. Since the patriarchate refused to accept this, the Macedonians declared autocephaly on their own authority at an ecclesiastical assembly in Ohrid in summer 1967. Although the Communist government repeatedly encouraged the two Churches, throughout the late 1960s, 1970s, and much of the 1980s, to resolve their differences and advised the Serbian patriarchate that its failure to recognize this latest fait accompli had a negative impact on the political climate, more particularly on Serb-Macedonian relations, as well as in the party's dispute with Communist Bulgaria over the ethnicity of Macedonians, the patriarchate unbudgingly insisted (and insists today) that Macedonians are Serbs and that the Macedonian Orthodox Church has no canonical raison d'être, basing the latter position on the fact that the Macedonian Church was not established on the basis of pan-Orthodox agreement, as prescribed by ecclesiastical tradition.[43]

Church–State Relations, 1970–1986

It is a remarkable fact that Communist regimes, which always talked about wanting the complete separation of Church and state, were consistently the most eager to assert state control or influence over Church policies and appointments. In Yugoslavia, the Communists hoped that their backing of the priests' associations would lead not merely to the cooptation of those associations, but to the cooptation of the Churches themselves, i.e., to the revival of the situation in old Serbia, when the Serbian Orthodox Church functioned in effect as a bureaucratic department of the state.

Instead, however, the Serbian patriarchate's relations with the associations have remained complex, and the continued activity of the latter provided yet another element of internal opposition within the Serbian Church. The Communist regime repeatedly praised the cooperation it received from the Orthodox association[44] and occasionally presented awards to its members,[45] but the patriarchate itself remained cool and distrustful toward the priests' association.[46] Indeed, this distrust occasionally provoked outbursts of frustration from convinced members of the association. In 1978, for example, Archpriest Ratko Jelić, a representative of the Croatian wing of the Orthodox association, told members of a committee of the Socialist Alliance of Working People of Yugoslavia, which was concerned with religious matters, that the patriarchate (presumably through its organ, *Pravoslavlje*) was presenting a distorted picture of the work of the association and proposed to increase the circulation of the association's organ, *Vesnik*, as a foil to *Pravoslavlje*. He continued:

> We have been publishing our *Vesnik* for the past 30 years. True, the number of copies printed per issue is small, a mere 3,000 copies, but I believe that there is no more positive periodical among all of those published by the Church press in this country, especially among those put out by the Serbian Orthodox Church. But this periodical is, unfortunately, not accessible to the public at large. For this reason, I believe that the situation would be entirely different if we were able to inform the members of our faith as to the true nature of our association. As things now stand, it is directly and falsely suggested to them that we are some kind of communist association which wants to destroy the Church and so on and so forth. Thus, people know nothing at all about the work that is being done by our association.[47]

On the same occasion, Archpriest Milutin Petrović, president of the Central Union of Orthodox Priests of Yugoslavia, complained that some clergy had declined to join the association because they feared reprisals from the hierarchy (although 83 percent of all Orthodox priests in Yugoslavia were, in 1978, members of the association), while Veselin Čukvaš, president of the Montenegrin wing of the Orthodox association, accused the hierarchy of frustrating and ignoring the work of the associations.[48]

But even in 1889 the priests' association was conceived in the spirit of opposition to the hierarchy; over the years, the association has felt free to arrive at conclusions that have diverged from the policies of the patriarchate. Hence, it should come as no surprise that the patriarchate has viewed the Orthodox association as an internal opposition, even as a Trojan horse.

Another species of internal opposition was highlighted by *Vesnik* in 1971. *Vesnik* charged that there was no practical ecclesiastical unity in policy matters and painted the patriarchate as a kind of bodyless head "presiding" over a collection of eparchies that operate according to the discretion and wishes of local archpriests. According to

Vesnik, the episcopal council was failing to reconcile these divergent views and functioned as no more than a sounding board for adamantly held positions.[49]

With only half the clergy it had before the war and a tangibly diminished income, the Serbian Church was conscious of its weakness. Despite this, it never allowed itself to be coopted by the Communist regime—at least not until 1987—and assumed an oppositional posture from time to time. In this respect, one could speak of two realms: the assertion of Church interests and the demand for policy change, even if Church interests appear to be in opposition to the regime's; and actual opposition by the Church in matters pertaining to the Serbian nation and its culture. That is to say, the Serbian Church was an opposition force insofar as it was (and is) a nationalist institution.

Although the Catholic Church and the Islamic community experienced little difficulty in the early 1980s obtaining official approval for the construction of places of worship, and although the Macedonian Orthodox Church too did well during this time period in the area of church construction, the Serbian Orthodox Church complained of difficulties in obtaining building permits, especially in the cities.[50] Styling itself as a "patient" Church, it nonetheless spoke out in May 1977 in a petition addressed by the Holy Synod to the presidency of the Republic of Serbia and signed by Patriarch German and two other bishops. The letter asked, inter alia, for (1) routinization of permission to build new churches; (2) extension of state social insurance to the teaching staff and students at theological faculties and seminaries; (3) an end to discrimination against children enrolled in Orthodox religious education; (4) an end to state interference in Church matters; (5) an end to the practice of libeling and slandering clergymen, both living and deceased, in the media; (6) unhindered celebration of funeral rites according to the wishes of the bereaved; and (7) the return of confiscated Church property.[51]

Since then, the Church has chalked up some gains. In 1984, Serbian authorities granted permission for the Church to resume construction of the monumental Church of St. Sava (started in the period 1935–1941, but left unfinished).[52] The following year, the Republic of Croatia returned various icons, books, manuscripts, and sacred objects from the thirteenth to the nineteenth centuries to the Church; they had been confiscated at the end of World War II and kept in state museums for four decades.[53] And in 1986, permission was granted for reconstruction of the historic monastery of Gradac in central Serbia.[54] In an even more striking move, the ideological commission of the Serbian Socialist Youth Federation declared subsequently that young believers could enjoy full equality in the youth organization, even serving in leadership positions, and proposed to support an initiative to create a postgraduate program in religious studies at the University of Belgrade.[55]

Patriarch German had a reputation, both at home and abroad, for being cautious and circumspect in his dealings with the government. That this reputation was both deserved and open to diverse interpretation was suggested by the sending of an impassioned letter to the patriarch, on 26 February 1982, on the part of Orthodox priests from the Raška-Prizren diocese in Kosovo. Their letter touched on matters concerning Kosovo in particular, such as the alleged harassment of Orthodox clergy and believers by local Albanians, and issues affecting the Church's life in other parts, such as their allegation that officials in the Sabac-Valjevo diocese were interrogating and harassing families that attempted to send their children to Orthodox catechism classes. They claimed that the Roman Catholic Church was faring tangibly better in this regard and expressed their dismay that *Pravoslavlje* had ignored these problems and had limited itself to bland announcements that Church representatives and state authorities were conferring about matters of "mutual interest." Their letter was not published in the Orthodox religious press, but appeared in print abroad.[56] Perhaps partly in response to this critical latter, the patriarchate's news organ, *Pravoslavlje*, published a long critique of the regime's policy in Kosovo in its 15 May edition, appealing for the protection of the Serbian population and Orthodox shrines in Kosovo.[57]

The Serbian Church's clashes with the Communist regime over the Macedonian Orthodox Church and over regime policy in Kosovo both stemmed from the Church's self-appointed guardianship over the Serbian people—a guardianship that the Communist regime wanted to deny, but both the Church and the state label as nationalist. The Serbian nationalism of the Serbian Church, expressed in numerous ways over the decades, confronted the Communist regime as a challenge both to its nationality policy and to its claim to be the *exclusive* representative of the political interests of the population. As a nationalist institution, thus, the Serbian Church was, de facto, in opposition, even if in *loyal* opposition.[58]

Rehabilitation

The seizure of power in Serbia by Slobodan Milošević in mid-December 1987 had a direct impact on the fortunes of the Orthodox Church. True, Milošević's predecessor, Ivan Stambolić, was responsible for setting in motion what was, in his day, a limited rapprochement with the Serbian Church. But Milošević extended and deepened this rapprochement. A very explicit token of this rapprochement was Milošević's meeting with a high-ranking Serbian Orthodox delegation in July 1990.[59] Where the pre-Milošević Serbian press had excoriated the Serbian Church for meddling in nationalism, under Milošević, *Politika* praised the Serbian Orthodox Church for its service to the Serbian people and even declared that Orthodoxy was "the spiritual basis for and the most essential component of the national identity [of Serbs]."[60]

The Orthodox Church has benefitted from Milošević's rule in concrete ways. First of all, it has been allowed to undertake a vigorous church construction program, to include the construction of churches in areas from which it had long been barred (e.g., Novi Beograd). Again, in December 1989, permission was granted for *Pravoslavlje* to be sold at public newsstands. Third, in January 1990, Orthodox Christmas was publicly celebrated in downtown Belgrade for the first time in four decades. And again, in June 1990, the Serbian government removed Marxism classes from school curricula and replaced them with religious instruction.[61] In token of the new atmosphere, the Serbian Orthodox Church cooperated with the Milošević government in marking the six-hundredth anniversary of the battle of Kosovo on 28 June 1989. In Orthodox services connected with the commemoration, pictures of Milošević could be seen among religious icons.

Not everyone was happy with this state of affairs, and some Serbian nonbelievers quietly registered concerns that the authorities were becoming too friendly with the hierarchy. Charges of collaboration between Serbian Orthodox Church hierarchy and the Milošević government were more volubly registered by Croatian Catholics, and in November 1990 the Serbian Orthodox Church news organ, *Pravoslavlje*, replied to these accusations by asserting that the Church's contacts with the government's Commission for Relations with Religious Communities were entirely correct and should not be interpreted as active "cooperation," let alone partnership.[62]

As noted in Chapter 4, the disintegration of Serb-Croat relations affected the religious realm as well. Where Orthodoxy is concerned, one may note that the Serbian Church repeatedly polemicized with the Catholic Church after 1989, and only, finally, in May 1991, did the new Orthodox patriarch, Pavle, respond positively to overtures from Catholic Cardinal Kuharić and agree to a meeting.[63]

As in the case of the Catholic Church in Croatia, the Orthodox Church played a visible role in the debate about both the federal constitution (still under discussion in spring 1990) and the proposed draft for a new constitution for Serbia. The Church was not entirely satisfied with either draft document. In the case of the federal draft, the Church indicated that it wanted a constitutional provision to guarantee property and to provide for the return of property confiscated after World War II.[64] In the case of the Serbian draft, *Pravoslavlje* published a tough criticism by Fr. Dragan Terzić in its August 1990 issue expressing concern above all about the proposed retention of a clause barring the "misuse of religious beliefs for political purposes."[65]

Conclusion

What I have tried to produce here is not an exhaustive history of the Serbian Orthodox Church in recent times, but rather an interpretation of the meaning of that history. To understand the Serbian Orthodox Church today is to understand its mindset, its set of working assumptions about the world, which are the product of the problems, privileges, conflicts, advantages, and setbacks experienced by the Church over the years.

The central experience of this century that colors the entire outlook of the Serbian Orthodox Church even today is the savage assault suffered in World War II. This assault, which was experienced as trauma, both stiffened the resolve and defiance of the Church and, reinforced by the Communist takeover, deepened its pessimism. The Serbian Church views itself as identical with the Serbian nation, since it considers that religion is the foundation of nationality. The hierarchs of the Serbian Church deny that Macedonians are anything but "south Serbs." For the Serbian patriarchate, then, the Macedonian Orthodox Church is, in essence, a reincarnation of the spirit of the Croatian Orthodox Church since, in the view of the patriarchate, the one, like the other, represents an endeavor to reduce the Serbian nation by transforming the religious affiliation of a part of its number. The Serbian Church might well repeat the words of the poet Tanasije Mladenović, who, in a controversial poem, asked,

> *Serbia, poor and wretched ...*
> *will you be able,*
> *as in time past,*
> *to renew your strength with a sudden crack?*
> *Or will you,*
> *discouraged and feeble,*
> *disappear among the mountains and nations ...*
> *torn to pieces by apocalyptic forces?* [66]

Notes

This chapter is a revised and updated version of my earlier chapter, "The Serbian Orthodox Church," originally published in Pedro Ramet, ed., *Eastern Christianity and Politics in the Twentieth Century* (Durham, N.C.: Duke University Press, 1988). The author wishes to thank Duke University Press for granting permission to reproduce the chapter here.

1. Blagota Gardašević, "Organizaciono ustrojstvo i zakonodavstvo pravoslavne crkve izmedju dva svetska rata," in *Srpska Pravoslavna Crkva 1920–1970: Spomenica o 50-godišnjici vaspostavljanja Srpske Patrijaršije* (hereafter *SPC 1920–1970*) (Belgrade: Kosmos, 1971), pp. 37–39.

2. Miodrag B. Petrović, "A Retreat from Power: The Serbian Orthodox Church and Its Opponents, 1868–1869," *Serbian Studies*, Vol. 1, No. 2 (spring 1981), pp. 4–12.

3. Quoted in Gardašević, "Organizaciono ustrojstvo," p. 41.

4. James L. Sadkovich, "Il regime di Alessandro in Iugoslavia, 1929–1934: Un'interpretazione," *Storia Contemporanea*, Vol. 15, No. 1 (February 1984), p. 11.

5. Ibid., p. 25.

6. Bertold Spuler, *Gegenwartslage der Ostkirchen*, 2nd ed. (Frankfurt: Metopen Verlag, 1968), p. 122.

7. Viktor Pospischil, *Der Patriarch in der Serbisch-Orthodoxen Kirche* (Vienna: Verlag herder, 1966), p. 55; and Sadkovich, "Il regime," p. 25.

8. *Primedbe i prigovori na projekat Konkordata izmedju naše države i vatikana* (Sremski Karlovci: Patrijaršija štamparija, 1936).

9. Ibid., pp. 9, 22, 34, 35, 41, 43, 50, 52–53, 56.

10. Ibid., p. 36.

11. Ibid., p. 33.

12. Joseph Rothschild, *East Central Europe Between the Two World Wars* (Seattle: University of Washington Press, 1974), p. 254.

13. Ivan Lazić, "Pravni i činjenični položaj konfesionalnih zajednica u Jugoslaviji," in *Vjerske zajednice u Jugoslaviji* (Zagreb: NIP "Binoza," 1970), pp. 50–54; and Viktor Novak, *Velika optužba*, Vol. 2 (Sarajevo: Svjetlost, 1960), pp. 131–136.

14. Bosnia's Metropolitan Petar Zimonjić, Banja Luka's Bishop Platon Jovanović, Gornji Karlovac's Bishop Sava Trlajić, Zagreb's Metropolitan Dositej, Bishop Nikolaj of Herzegovina, and Vicar-Bishop Valerijan Pribićević of Sremski Karlovci.

15. *Katolički tjednik* (Sarajevo) (26 June 1941), as quoted in Dušan Lj. Kasić, "Srpska crkva u tzv. Nezavisnoj Državi Hrvatskoj," in *SPC 1920–1970*, p. 184.

16. Ibid., p. 196.

17. Marko Dimitrijević, "Srpska crkva pod bugarskom okupacijom," in *SPC 1920–1970*, p. 213.

18. See Vaso Ivošević, "Srpska crkva pod italijanskom okupacijom," in *SPC 1920–1970*, pp. 217–220.

19. Milisav D. Protić, "Izgradnja crkava u poratnom periodu," in *SPC 1920–1970*, p. 253.

20. Djoko Slijepčević, *Istorija srpske pravoslavne crkve*, Vol. 2, (Munich: Iskra, 1966), p. 687.

21. Risto Grdjić, "Opšta obnova crkvenog života i ustrojstva," in *SPC 1920–1970*, p. 243; and interview, Belgrade, July 1987.

22. Stella Alexander, *Church and State in Yugoslavia Since 1945* (Cambridge: Cambridge University Press, 1979), pp. 164–173.

23. Ibid., p. 189.

24. *Borba* (3 July 1952), cited in ibid.

25. Trevor Beeson, *Discretion and Valour*, rev. ed. (Philadelphia: Fortress Press, 1982), p. 315; and letter to the author from Stella Alexander, 17 October 1983.

26. Robert Lee Wolff, *The Balkans in Our Time* (Cambridge, Mass.: Harvard University Press, 1956), p. 551.

27. Alexander, *Church and State*, p. 224.

28. *Borba* (22 August 1953), cited in ibid., pp. 200–201.

29. Ibid., pp. 213, 219. Also *Politika* (Belgrade) (1 June 1982), trans. into German as "Die Serbisch-Orthodoxe Kirche und ihre Beziehungen zum jugoslawischen Staat," *Osteuropa*, Vol. 33, No. 1 (January 1983), pp. A53–A54.

30. Radomir Rakić, "Izdavačka delatnost crkve od 1945. do 1970. godine," in *SPC 1920–1970*, p. 291n; and interview, Belgrade, July 1982.

31. Protić, "Izgradnja crkava," pp. 254, 271–272.

32. Stevan K. Pavlowitch, "The Orthodox Church in Yugoslavia: Rebuilding the Fabric," *Eastern Churches Review*, Vol. 2, No. 2 (autumn 1968), p. 171.

33. Rastko Vidić, *The Position of the Church in Yugoslavia* (Belgrade: Jugoslavija, 1962), p. 53; Pavlowitch, "The Orthodox Church," p. 170; *Europa Year Book 1972*, Vol. 1, pp. 1435–1436, cited in Burton Paulu, *Radio and Television Broadcasting in Eastern Europe* (Minneapolis: University of Minnesota Press, 1974), p. 463; Beeson, *Discretion and Valour*, p. 291; and interview, Belgrade, July 1982.

34. For details, see Branko A. Cisarz, "Crkvena štampa izmedju dva svetska rata," in *SPC 1920–1970*, pp. 141–155.

35. Rakić, "Izdavačka delatnost," pp. 291–95; and interviews, Belgrade, July 1982 and July 1987.

36. See *NIN* (Belgrade), No. 2031 (3 December 1989), pp. 26–28.

37. Alexander, *Church and State*, p. 169.

38. Fred Singleton, *Twentieth Century Yugoslavia* (New York: Columbia University Press, 1976), p. 229. Regarding recent developments among the Orthodox of Montenegro, see Sabrina Petra Ramet, "The Serbian Church and the Serbian Nation," in Sabrina Petra Ramet and Ljubiša S. Adamovich (eds.), *Beyond Yugoslavia: Politics, Economics, and Culture in a Shattered Community* (Boulder, Colo.: Westview Press, 1995), p. 116.

39. Alexander, *Church and State,* pp. 270–271.

40. Ibid., p. 265.

41. For a fuller discussion of these political currents and of Ranković's role in the 1960s, see Sabrina P. Ramet, *Nationalism and Federalism in Yugoslavia, 1962–1991,* 2d ed. (Bloomington: Indiana University Press, 1992).

42. Interview, Belgrade, July 1987.

43. *Nova Makedonija, Sabota* supplement (10 October 1981), p. 5, trans. in Joint Publications Research Service (JPRS), *East Europe Report* (29 December 1981); and *Borba* (Belgrade) (6–7 May 1989), p. 6.

44. E.g., *Politika* (6 October 1981), p. 6.

45. E.g., Tanjug (19 June 1981), in *Foreign Broadcast Information Service (FBIS), Daily Report* (Eastern Europe), 22 June 1981.

46. Tanjug (25 February 1982), trans. in *FBIS, Daily Report* (Eastern Europe), 26 February 1982.

47. Quoted in *Vjesnik* (Zagreb) (15 July 1978), trans. in JPRS, *East Europe Report* (17 October 1978).

48. Ibid.

49. *Vesnik* (Belgrade) (1–15 January 1971), p. 1.

50. Interview with Patriarch German, *NIN*, No. 1637 (16 May 1982), p. 18; and *Keston News Service,* No. 232 (22 August 1985), p. 10.

51. "Informationsdienst," *Glaube in der 2. Welt* (February 1978), p. 5, as summarized in "News in Brief," *Religion in Communist Lands,* Vol. 6, No. 4 (winter 1978), pp. 272–273.

52. *Ilustrovana politika* (Belgrade) (20 November 1984), pp. 24–25.

53. *Keston News Service,* No. 229 (11 July 1985), pp. 8–9.

54. Ibid., No. 244 (20 February 1986), p. 11.

55. Ibid., No. 251 (29 May 1986), p. 12.

56. Stella Alexander, "The Serbian Orthodox Church Speaks out in Its Own Defence," *Religion in Communist Lands,* Vol. 10, No. 3 (winter 1982), pp. 331–332.

57. *Pravoslavlje* (Belgrade) (15 May 1982), p. 1.

58. I have examined the nationalism of the Serbian Orthodox Church in more detail in "Religion and Nationalism in Yugoslavia," in Pedro Ramet, ed., *Religion and Nationalism in Soviet and East European Politics,* revised and expanded ed. (Durham, N.C.: Duke University Press, 1989).

59. *Pravoslavlje* (1 July 1990), p. 1.

60. *Politika* (2 September 1990), p. 18.

61. *Süddeutsche Zeitung* (Munich) (23–24 June 1990), p. 8.

62. *Pravoslavlje* (1 November 1990), p. 2.

63. Ibid (15 May 1991), p. 1.

64. *Yugoslav Life* (April 1990), p. 3.

65. *Pravoslavlje* (1–15 August 1990), p. 1.

66. Quoted in *Los Angeles Times* (18 December 1980), Pt. I-B, p. 5.

CHAPTER SIX

◆

Islam

In September 1989 I visited Yugoslavia for the sixth time. As always, there was electricity in the air, and as always, the national question, as Yugoslavs called it, had a great deal to do with that electricity. Serbs feared everyone (so it seemed those days), everyone feared Serbs, Macedonians and Montenegrins feared Albanians, and Montenegrins feared each other. Typical of this atmosphere was a conversation in which I found myself at a Belgrade café, as two local journalists drew and redrew maps of the Balkans, showing a menacingly large arrow projecting northward from Istanbul through Serbia, while they told me of their fears of a Muslim threat to European civilization. "Albanian Muslims and Bosnian Muslims are in this together," they told me, deadly earnest. "They have big families in order to swamp Serbia and Yugoslavia with Muslims and turn Yugoslavia into a Muslim republic. They want to see a Khomeini in charge here. But Belgrade is not their final goal. They will continue to advance until they have taken Vienna, Berlin, Paris, London—all the great cities of Europe. Unless they are stopped."

Psychiatrist Jovan Rašković told *Intervju* magazine in September 1989 that Muslims were fixated in the anal phase of their psychosocial development and were therefore characterized by general aggressiveness and an obsession with precision and cleanliness. (Croats, by contrast, suffer from a castration complex, according to Rašković.)[1]

Non-Muslims in Yugoslavia recalled Libyan dictator Qaddafi's generosity in providing for the Yugoslav Islamic community's mosque-building program, noted Bosnia's long-term interest in building economic and cultural contact with Syria, Iraq, and other Arab states, pointed to the Muslims' efforts to align Yugoslavia with the Arabs during the October 1973 war in the Middle East, and underlined the ongoing contacts between Islamic clerics and believers in Bosnia and their coreligionists in the Middle East, as, for example, in the case of young Yugoslav Muslims who went to the Middle

TABLE 6.1   Proportion of Ethnic Muslims, Serbs, Croats, "Yugoslavs," and Other
Nationalities in Bosnia-Herzegovina, 1948–1991 (percentage)

	1948	1953	1961	1971	1981	1991
Muslims	30.7	31.3	25.7	39.6	39.5	43.8
Serbs	44.3	44.4	42.9	37.2	32.0	31.5
Croats	23.9	23.0	21.7	20.6	18.4	17.3
"Yugoslavs"	n/a	n/a	8.4	1.2	7.9	7.0
Others	1.1	1.3	1.3	1.4	2.2	1.4

SOURCES: Ante Markotic, "Demografski aspekt promjena un nacionalnoj strukturi stanovništva Bosne i Hercegovine," *Sveske,* Nos. 16–17 (1986), p. 292; and Tanjug (30 April 1991), trans. in Foreign Broadcast Information Service, *Daily Report* (Eastern Europe), 1 May 1991, p. 53.

East for Islamic theological training. For some non-Muslims, these were all signs that the Muslim community was in some sense a foreign implant, that Muslims were not fully integrated into Yugoslav society, that they should be feared.

When, after repeated delays, permission was finally granted to Muslims in 1981 to construct a new mosque in Zagreb to replace the one closed down after the war, controversy was inevitable. Like the Serbs, Croats expressed concern that their republic would be Islamicized. Three years later—in June 1984—when much of the construction on the mosque had been all but completed, a fire set by arsonists destroyed much of what had been built up to then. Finally, in September 1987, the mosque was opened, with considerable fanfare.[2]

Needless to say, this fear of the Muslims aggravated intercommunal relations within Bosnia and sharpened the recent debate about Bosnia's place in the federation. Bosnian Muslims repeatedly and unwisely talked of wanting Bosnia declared a "Muslim republic," while Serbs and Croats from time to time hinted that Bosnia might best be divided between Serbia and Croatia. Within Sarajevo, one heard people declare for a united Yugoslavia, on the argument that for inhabitants of Bosnia there was no other realistic option: any attempt at dividing it up—so they argued— would stir up intercommunal violence in this divided republic.

Basic Facts and Resources

Some 44 percent of Bosnia's population registered as "ethnic Muslims" in the 1991 census, as against 31 percent Serbs, 17 percent Croats, and 6–7 percent ethnic "Yugoslavs" (the latter usually the product of mixed marriages).[3] That made Bosnia the only federal unit in Yugoslavia in which no single nationality group constituted a local majority (see Table 6.1). More broadly, however, ethnic Muslims were always a relatively small minority in socialist Yugoslavia—tallying about 9 percent of the total population in 1981.[4] In religious terms, one could speak nominally of about 3.8

million confessional Muslims in Yugoslavia, accounting for about 16 percent of the total population of the country. Religious Muslims included not only the greater portion of ethnic Muslims, but also varying numbers of Albanians, Turks, and Macedonians, as well as some Gypsies, Montenegrins, Croats, Serbs, and even small groups of Pomaks in the region surrounding Pijanac.[5]

The Islamic community in Yugoslavia was organized into four administrative regions: *Sarajevo Region* (Bosnia-Herzegovina, Croatia, and Slovenia, with its Supreme Head Office in Sarajevo); *Priština Region* (Serbia, Kosovo, and Vojvodina, with its Supreme Head Office in Priština); *Skopje Region* (Macedonia, with its Head Office in Skopje); and *Titograd Region* (Montenegro, with its Head Office in Titograd). The Reis-ul-ulema, the head of the entire Yugoslav Islamic community, had his office in Sarajevo.

At the dawn of the post-Tito era, the Islamic community disposed of the following institutional resources and facilities:[6]

Sarajevo Region:

- 1,092 mosques
- 569 mesdžids (smaller places of worship)
- 394 places for religious instruction
- 2 medresas (religious schools)
- 5 tekijas according to usage (cemeteries)

Priština Region:

- 445 mosques
- 125 mesdžids
- 35 places for religious instruction
- ? tekijas
- 1 medresa

Skopje Region:

- 372 mosques
- 19 mesdžids
- 10 places for religious instruction
- ? tekijas
- 1 medresa

Titograd Region:

- 76 mosques
- 2 mesdžids
- 36 other buildings
- 4 turbe (mausoleums)
- ? tekijas

In addition, every Muslim town or village had a separate graveyard for Muslims. The figures for mosques would have been much higher in 1990, having passed the 3,000 mark in 1986 and given the energetic building program that the Yugoslav Islamic community was able to maintain.

As of 1980, some 120,000 children were receiving Islamic religious instruction at the primary school level. This instruction was provided free of charge to believers. Secondary religious instruction was available at two medresas: Gazi Husrefbey's medresa in Sarajevo, and Alaudin medresa in Priština. The former was more than 450 years old. In addition, an Islamic Theological Faculty opened in Sarajevo in 1977, and a women's department was created the following year.

The Gazi Husrefbey Library in Sarajevo was an important repository for Islamic materials, and contained several thousand original manuscripts in Arabic, Turkish, and Persian. Courses in Arabic were offered in Sarajevo, Priština, and Belgrade.

Each of the four regions also had a clerical association, known as an Ilmija. These associations were integrated into the work of the Socialist Alliance of Working People of Yugoslavia and in this way acquired a legitimate role in the public arena.

The Islamic community naturally maintained a number of periodical publications. The chief ones were *Preporod,* a fortnightly newspaper published in Serbo-Croatian, in Sarajevo; *Islamska misao,* a monthly journal devoted to theological reflections and news of the community, likewise published in Sarajevo; *El-Hilal,* a Skopje journal, published in Macedonian, Turkish, and Albanian; the bimonthly journal *Glasnik,* the official bulletin of the Supreme Head Office of the Yugoslav Islamic Community, published in 15,000 copies; *Takvim,* an annual publication; *El-Islam,* which concentrated on religious information; *Edukataiislam,* an Albanian-language publication of the Priština office; and *Zemzem,* a newspaper published by the Gazi Husrefbey medresa that was said to have won credibility among young people. All four regional head offices also had extensive book-publishing programs for religious literature.[7]

Many Bosnian Muslims emigrated, some of them prior to World War I. Today there are Muslims who trace their origins to the lands of what was, until 1991, Yugoslavia living in the United States, Canada, Australia, Turkey, and in smaller numbers in several West European countries, including Austria and Germany. In 1977, Yugoslav Muslims in Canada sent a request to the Islamic community of Yugoslavia to send a delegate to help organize their religious life. A similar request was subsequently submitted also by the Yugoslav Muslim community in Australia.

Yugoslav Muslims also accepted employment at certain times in Libya, Iraq, and Kuwait. This experience must be presumed to have strengthened the affinity of at least some Yugoslav Muslims for the Middle East.

The Social Presence of Islam

Despite this formidable institutional base, the Islamic leadership adopted a much lower profile than either the Roman Catholic Church or the Serbian Orthodox

Church. Although the two Christian Churches were able to celebrate Christmas quite openly for several years, with Christmas Day finally declared a state holiday in Slovenia as of 1989,[8] one could not imagine the Islamic community obtaining the same access to the media in socialist Yugoslavia, let alone seeing its festivals declared state holidays in multiconfessional Bosnia.

A comparison of the leading Muslim newspaper, *Preporod,* with its Croatian Catholic and Serbian Orthodox counterparts—*Glas koncila* and *Pravoslavlje,* respectively—is telling. Whereas *Glas koncila* for years struck a defiant posture, openly polemicizing with the Communist press on a regular basis and publishing highly informative interviews, as well as articles about state atheism, Christian-Marxist dialogue, proposals to change the laws governing religious life in Yugoslavia, and other social issues, with *Pravoslavlje,* for its part, becoming ever more strident (beginning in 1981) in its defense of Serbian interests in Kosovo and its advocacy of Serbian nationalism in general,[9] *Preporod* rarely if ever entered into the social arena, restricting itself by and large to reports on the construction of mosques and the observance of religious holidays, along with information about Islamic teachings.

This same pattern carried over into the behavior of religious leaders. Catholic prelates (such as Zagreb's archbishop Franjo Cardinal Kuharić) delivered sermons defending human rights activists (e.g., Dobroslav Paraga) or demanding an official exoneration of the late Alojzije Cardinal Stepinac, archbishop of Zagreb 1937–1960. Serbian Orthodox prelates were somewhat less bold, but were found celebrating Serbian heroes such as Tsar Lazar,[10] Tsar Dušan, and Vuk Karadžić and taking part in commemorations of Serbian national holidays—most pointedly, the six-hundredth anniversary (in 1989) of the famous Battle of Kosovo Polje. One could not imagine Islamic leaders being allowed to celebrate the anniversary of the Ottoman conquest of Bosnia (or considering such a celebration wise, for that matter) or feeling sufficiently confident to undertake to speak out on human rights issues—at least not in the years prior to 1990.

On the contrary, the Islamic community often found itself on the defensive. For example, in November 1987 the Republican Conference of the Socialist Alliance of Working People of Serbia discussed the activities of the Islamic community and concluded that Islamic fundamentalism "had reached Yugoslavia and ... threatened to spread all over Europe."[11] There were also rumors and charges from time to time, whether in Bosnia, or Macedonia, or Serbia, that Islamic religious education was inspired by nationalist and separatist orientations. (This will be taken up below.)

In fact, the Islamic community adopted a more quiescent and defensive posture—by comparison with the Catholic and Orthodox Churches—from the very beginning and from an early time was able to boast smooth relations with the authorities. In the initial years—roughly 1945 to 1966—religious policy was basically worked out in Belgrade, which meant that religious policy throughout the country was guided, within some limits, by a single vision. The decentralization of the political and administrative system that began in the late 1960s and that was designed to satisfy irresistible pressures on the ethnic level inevitably had consequences for the religious communities. The Catholic Church, with most of its believers living in Slovenia and Croatia, had to worry principally about the orientation of secular authorities in Ljubljana and Zagreb, authorities who, at least in Slovenia, generally showed themselves to be more liberal than their counterparts elsewhere in the country. The Orthodox, living predominantly in Serbia, Macedonia, and Montenegro, had an entirely different set of authorities to deal with. At times, a kind of alliance between Church and party developed at the republic level—as, for example, has occurred in Serbia under Slobodan Milošević.

For the Muslims, with their largest concentrations inhabiting Bosnia and the autonomous province of Kosovo, the authorities in Sarajevo and Priština have been their principal reference points for coexistence. This has made for a more complex situation for Muslims for two reasons. First, the authorities in Bosnia tended toward the dogmatic side through much of the 1970s and 1980s. (This is not the case in postcommunist Bosnia, obviously.) This meant that Bosnian Muslims were more likely to be attacked in the press than were, for example, Slovenian Catholics or Macedonia's Orthodox and more likely to find their news organ subjected to pressure. Second, Bosnia and Kosovo were the two regions in Yugoslavia with the most delicate intercommunal relations. And although these relations were usually defined in terms of ethnic groups, there were also religious dimensions—as was patently clear in 1981 and 1982, for example, after Albanian Muslims allegedly desecrated the Orthodox shrines of Kosovar Serbs, setting fire to the monastery at Peć. An "alliance" between the Muslim community and secular authorities in either Sarajevo or Priština—on the model of Milošević's "alliance" with the Serbian patriarchate or even on the model of the friendly relationship that emerged between the Catholic Church and the Communist authorities in Ljubljana—was obviously ruled out, as Bosnia followed the lead of Slovenia and Croatia and adopted a multiparty system.

Despite the tradition of dogmatic rule in Bosnia and despite the complexities arising from the republic's ethnic fragmentation, Muslims were able to maintain a vigorous mosque-construction program throughout the postwar period. In Bosnia-Herzegovina alone, some 400 new mosques were built between 1945 and 1985, and some 380 mosques were renovated. By 1986, there, as already noted, were some 3,000 mosques in Yugoslavia as a whole.[12]

From time to time, the Communist press would attack the Muslim community for allegedly misusing religious training. For example, in 1973, officials of Tetovo *opština* in Macedonia estimated that some 20 percent of students were receiving religious instruction after regular school hours. The officials claimed, however, that religious instruction was not being used strictly to instruct children in matters of faith and worship. On the contrary, *Nova Makedonija* charged that "in some places, religious education is even used to orient the children in a direction entirely different from our social system, in broadening national intolerance, and in promoting other anti-socialist manifestations." But efforts to reach some understanding with local clergy proved unavailing, according to the Macedonian newspaper. "The measures that we have implemented in this respect have not brought any particular results. We have had discussions on this subject with the Islamic religious community, which has claimed the opposite."13

Aside from questions of the authorities, it was clear that in a multiconfessional society (e.g., Bosnia), individual religions should have to be more circumspect than would be the case in a religiously homogeneous society (such as Slovenia).

For that matter, the Islamic community in Yugoslavia was itself internally divided, insofar as the leaders of the Yugoslav Islamic community gave the cold shoulder to the dervishes (or, as they are more formally known, the Community of the Islamic Alia Dervish Monastic Order). The dervish order was introduced in Yugoslavia in 1974 and by 1986 numbered 50,000 followers, organized in seventy monasteries across southern Yugoslavia (fifty-three in Kosovo, ten in Macedonia, and seven in Bosnia).14 At one point, the Islamic community ordered Sheikh Jemaly Haxhi-Shehu, senior leader of the dervishes, to disband the order. Shehu replied by registering his order as a "self-managing" organization, thus giving himself legal protection—a move paralleled in Croatia, if for different motivations, by the Catholic Christianity Today Publishing House.

Women and Islam

In the course of the 1980s, Muslim women began taking a more independent role in public life. The fact that a large group of Albanian Muslim women organized a large protest, independently, in late 1989 (to protest deteriorating conditions in Kosovo) is a sign of increased self-awareness and self-confidence. Another sign of change came earlier, in 1981, with the graduation of the first woman (Nermina Jasarević) from the Islamic Theological Faculty in Sarajevo.15

By 1986, the first female imams had been educated in Skopje and were delivering sermons (the first being in the Kumanovo mosque). In the course of 1986, Albanian men in Kumanovo went to the authorities to protest the appearance of women at the mosque, since, according to Islamic teaching, women and men should not mix at the mosque. It turned out that the sudden appearance of the women was the result of direct pressure from the Islamic Central Board in Skopje, whose elders were intent on upholding the equality of women and who pointed to the tradition that every mosque has a special, separate room for the women. Why had the women not come earlier? Isa Ismaili, leader of the Islamic community in Kumanovo, blamed space problems:

> For two reasons: first, until now we did not have female imams; now we have them and they are capable of delivering their sermons. Secondly, we in Kumanovo have only a single mosque, which is too small to hold even all the males; this is why we did not insist that the women come.... Long ago we asked the authorities for permission to build a new mosque, but we unfortunately never got an answer. . . . If our women are forbidden to go to the mosque, we will ask the men not to go either. Why should the men [be allowed to] pray and not the women? This is an attack on equality.16

The Twilight of Socialism

In 1989, a small publishing house in Zagreb brought out a *Bibliography of Croatian Writers of Bosnia-Herzegovina Between the Two Wars*. The publication at once stirred controversy because of its inclusion of a number of Muslim literary figures in the ranks of "Croatian writers." The Islamic community was outraged, and its organ, *Preporod*, published a lengthy commentary in which it excoriated the bibliography for the "Croatization" of some thirty-eight Muslim writers. Among this number were such Islamic-sounding names as Salih-beg Bakamović, Enver Čolaković, Abdulatif Dizdarević, Husein Dubravić Djogo, Mustafa H. Grabčanović, Kasim Gujić, Osman Nuri Hadžić, Muhamed Hadžijahić, Mehmed Handžić, and Ahmed Muradbegović. *Preporod* called this a "negation of the cultural independence of a national tradition."[17]

This controversy was symptomatic of a deeper problem that has serious implications for the Islamic community—namely, the tendency of the Croatian and Serbian nations to want to claim the land on which the Muslims have lived for their own nations and to absorb or suppress Islamic culture. Both Croats and Serbs have claimed large parts of Bosnia in the past, and Serbs have viewed Kosovo as their ancestral heartland, depicting the Albanian Muslims as intruders. Whereas Serbs sometimes betray a desire to suppress or eject Islamic culture from Kosovo, where Bosnia is concerned, Serbs and Croats have long registered rival claims to "annex" the Muslim community, claiming alternatively that Muslims are "really" Serbs, or Croats.[18]

It is against this background that periodic Muslim pressures to declare Bosnia a "Muslim republic" must be seen. Serb-Muslim tensions in Bosnia were becoming serious already in 1989, and instead of abating, only grew more intense over the succeeding months. Eventually, as will be explained in Chapter 10, Bosnia disintegrated into open warfare in spring 1992, when Serbs launched a genocidal policy they have called "ethnic cleansing."

The repluralization of Yugoslavia has affected the Islamic community just as it has affected all other areas of public life. From 1946 to 1990, the Reis-ul-ulema (chair of the Islamic Council) was always a political appointee, beholden to the Communist regime. But in March 1991 Jakub Selimoški, a Macedonian Muslim, was elected to that post by a special ninety-six-member electoral body established by the Islamic community itself.[19] The Islamic community simultaneously adopted a new constitution and elected new presiding officers to head its Supreme Assembly.[20] In January 1991, in token of its new independence and new-found courage, the Islamic Supreme Assembly issued a resolution denouncing the Serbian government's policies in Kosovo and demanding the restoration of the natural rights of Kosovo's inhabitants, including a cessation of political interference in the work of the institutions of the Islamic community in Kosovo.[21]

Notes

This chapter is a revised and updated version of an earlier article, "Islam in Yugoslavia Today," originally published in *Religion in Communist Lands* (now called *Religion, State, and Society*),

Vol. 18, No. 3 (autumn 1990). The author wishes to thank the editor of *Religion, State, and Society* and Keston Institute, the journal's publisher, for granting permission to reproduce the chapter here.

1. *Intervju* (Belgrade), No. 216 (15 September 1989), pp. 15–16.

2. *Nedjeljna Borba* (Zagreb ed.) (5–6 September 1987), p. 4; *Vjesnik* (Zagreb) (7 September 1987), p. 3; and *Danas* (Zagreb), No. 290 (8 September 1987), pp. 23–24.

3. Tanjug (30 April 1991), trans. in *Foreign Broadcast Information Service (FBIS), Daily Report* (Eastern Europe), 1 May 1991, p. 53.

4. *Statistički kalendar Jugoslavije 1982* (Belgrade: Savezni zavod za statistiku, February 1982), p. 37.

5. Ahmed Smajlović, "Muslims in Yugoslavia," *Journal Institute of Muslim Minority Affairs,* Vol. 1, No. 2, and Vol. 2, No. 1 (winter 1979–summer 1980), p. 132; and Rudolf Grulich, Der Islam in Jugoslawien," *Glaube in der 2. Welt,* Vol. 7, No. 4, (1979), p. 6. See also Sabrina P. Ramet, "Primordial Ethnicity or Modern Nationalism: The Case of Yugoslavia's Muslims, Reconsidered," *South Slav Journal,* Vol. 13, No. 1–2 (spring–summer 1990).

6. Smajlović, "Muslims in Yugoslavia," pp. 135–136.

7. Ibid., pp. 141–142.

8. *Keston News Service,* No. 336 (19 October 1989), p. 14.

9. See, for example, *Pravoslavlje* (Belgrade) (15 May 1982), p. 1.

10. Regarding Tsar Lazar, see *NIN* (Belgrade), No. 2020 (17 September 1989), pp. 42–43.

11. *Aktuelnosti kršćanske sadasnjosti (AKSA)* (13 November 1987), summarized in *AKSA Bulletin,* No. 8 (26 January 1988), p. 14. See also *Vjesnik* (12 November 1987), p. 4.

12. *Radio Free Europe Research* (30 June 1986), pp. 21–22.

13. *Nova Makedonija* (Skopje) (19 June 1973), p. 2.

14. *Start* (Zagreb) (19 April 1986), as cited in *Radio Free Europe Research* (30 June 1986), p. 21.

15. *Preporod* (Sarajevo) (15 November 1981), p. 10.

16. Quoted in *Radio Free Europe Research* (30 June 1986), p. 23.

17. *Preporod* (1 September 1989), p. 14.

18. For discussion, see Muhamed Hadžijahić, *Od tradicije do identiteta: Geneza nacionalnog pitanja bosanskih muslimana* (Sarajevo: Svjetlost, 1974); and Ramet, "Primordial Ethnicity or Modern Nationalism."

19. *Tehran IRNA* (10 March 1991), in *FBIS, Daily Report* (Eastern Europe), 12 March 1991, p. 60.

20. Tanjug (16 January 1991), trans. in *FBIS, Daily Report* (Eastern Europe), 22 January 1991, pp. 38–39.

21. Tanjug (16 January 1991), trans. in *FBIS, Daily Report* (Eastern Europe), 23 January 1991, p. 43.

CHAPTER SEVEN

◆

Rock Music

Yugoslavia, on your feet and sing!
Whoever doesn't listen to this song,
Will hear a storm!

Goran Bregović and Bijelo dugme
"Pljuni i zapjevaj, moja Jugoslavijo"
1987

When Goran Bregović and his group White Button (Bijelo dugme) began singing their song "Spit and Sign, My Yugoslavia," their fans would rise to their feet, tens of thousands of them, and sing along. The mood of the song was defiant. It was, Bregović maintains, "a song that can frighten the politicians."[1] Later, in spring and summer 1988, when supporters of Serbian leader Slobodan Milošević took to the streets in tens of thousands to protest against the governments of Vojvodina and Montenegro and to show support in Serbia for Milošević, they sang this song. It was, it turned out, a song of insurrection. The governments of Vojvodina and Montenegro fell and were replaced with supporters of Milošević.

This story is unusual only in degree, not in essence. Yugoslav rock music was long deeply colored by political messages and political allusions. In this respect, Yugoslav rock music was more typical of the East than of the West, where rock had reverted, by the 1970s, to its original cast as entertainment and is less likely to engage in political communication. In the Communist world, by contrast, including Yugoslavia, rock was very much attuned to political messages.

Many Yugoslav rock musicians were quite conscious of their role as bards or social critics, and many of their songs were topical, reflecting broader public moods and concerns. As Goran Bregović put it in 1989, "We can't have any alternative parties or any alternative political programs. So there are not too many places where you can gather large groups of people and communicate ideas that are not official. Rock 'n'

126

roll is one of the most important vehicles for helping people in Communist countries to think in a different way."[2]

Rock music in a culturally diverse, politically decentralized environment such as Yugoslavia inevitably develops differently from the way it develops in an ethnically homogeneous, politically centralized system—let alone in a pluralist Western system. To begin with, the composite nationality groups of former Yugoslavia have diverse musical cultures and psychological frameworks, so that musical devices that strike a resonant chord in, let us say, Macedonia, may seem arcane and very foreign in Slovenia or Croatia. Second, in conditions of republic "etatism" (as the Yugoslavs call their version of federalized state ownership), the market is fragmented and divided, with clear barriers. For rock musicians, the absence of a unified market means that there have long been in essence five independent rock networks in the area—in Slovenia, Croatia, Bosnia, Vojvodina, and Serbia—and a star might hit it big in one republic and be ignored elsewhere.[3] There is an "intermittent" rock scene in Macedonia, centered in Skopje, but both because of tighter financial constraints in that republic and because of the language (which restricts the market), there has been no record company in Macedonia. As a result, many Macedonian rock groups have been unable to make albums and therefore, in the absence of publicity, wither away.[4]

The Early Years

The prehistory of rock music in Yugoslavia was not propitious for the free development of the new genre. World War II was scarcely over when Milovan Djilas, then head of propaganda of the CPY, set the tone for the regime's cultural policy in the early years. "America," said Djilas in 1947, "is our sworn enemy, and jazz, likewise, as the product of [the American system]."[5] Tito himself told his biographer, Vladimir Dedijer, at that time, "I like our folk music, but not stylized, as people start to do nowadays. . . . Jazz, in my opinion, is not music. It is racket!"[6] Shortly after the war, therefore, Marshal Tito summoned some of Yugoslavia's top composers to his palace and told them that pop music and jazz cheated people of their money and spoiled young people.

With Tito's expulsion from the Cominform on 28 June 1948, music became potentially dangerous, as many unfortunate Yugoslavs discovered. Singing the wrong song could mean prison or penal labor. Russian songs—in political vogue for the three years immediately prior—were now definitely *out*. American tunes were just as risky, however, as rival groups struggled to prove their Communist "purity." Even Yugoslav folk songs risked accusations of bourgeois nationalism (even if Tito did like that genre). Some music had served several masters—a traditional Croatian football song from earlier in the century had later been adapted, with new words, to serve as a patriotic song for the fascist regime. In the postwar period, the Communists wrote new words. Other songs, innocent in their incarnation, might have become pernicious through later association, and unless the singer was certain, it was better not to sing indigenous music. These factors contributed, thus, to the sudden popularity of

Mexican folk songs among the public, above all because they were ideologically and politically safe.

But 1948 ultimately set Yugoslavia on a different course from the Soviet bloc states. Tito's decision, after his break with Stalin in 1948, to open Yugoslavia to contacts with the West was fateful for the development of rock 'n' roll, because it meant that Western rock would penetrate Yugoslavia more quickly and more easily than it could other countries in Eastern Europe. It meant, in consequence, that Yugoslav rock music would develop much more rapidly than rock music in, let us say, Hungary or Czechoslovakia, let alone Romania or Bulgaria.

As early as 1953, thus, Yugoslav jazz musicians were able—despite the authorities' dislike of the genre—to establish a musicians' association. By 1957, Predrag Ivanović and his Orchestra were at the height of their popularity; their fare—American pop music of the day. By the latter 1950s, rock 'n' roll was making its first inroads in the Balkans.

The early years of rock music in Yugoslavia were very much under the shadow of the West. Indeed, at its inception, the only interesting rock music came from either the United States or Great Britain. Bill Haley and the Comets, Chuck Berry, Buddy Holly, Jerry Lee Lewis, and Little Richard were among the artists whose music was heard in Yugoslavia before the end of the 1950s. Interest among Yugoslav young people in rock music took a leap at the beginning of the 1960s, when they started listening to the British groups Johnny and the Hurricanes and the Shadows. Then the Zagreb record company Jugoton signed a deal with RCA to release some of Elvis Presley's records in Yugoslavia and later brought out a domestic pressing of Chubby Checker's "Let's Twist Again." The Belgrade record company PGP RTB (a spin-off company from Radio-Television Belgrade) released a pressing of Johnny Hallyday's "Twist" also at this time.[7]

One of Yugoslavia's earliest rock stars was Karlo Metikoš, who in 1964 launched his recording career with a PGP RTB record, *Matt Collins Sings R&R*. Singing under a pseudonym, Metikos was the first Yugoslav artist to record covers of some of the original rock classics.[8]

In the years 1960–1961, it was still relatively difficult for Yugoslavs to travel. But local rock musicians, who at that time were largely copying British and American songs, were determined to keep up with the latest releases. They would listen to Radio Luxemburg every night, and at 2 A.M., Radio Luxemburg would play the top ten songs of the day. At that time, the Shadows were the most influential group for Yugoslav rockers; hence, because the Shadows had three guitars and one percussionist, every Yugoslav group at that time had three guitars and one percussionist.[9]

In 1961, Josip Kovač, a composer from Subotica (Vojvodina), came up with the idea of organizing a festival of popular music by young talent. The first festival was so successful that it was repeated a year later; the result was an annual pop festival in which, over time, the rock component became ever more important. Some of Yugoslavia's biggest rock stars have performed at the Subotica Festival at one time or another. The thirtieth annual festival in Subotica was held 24–27 May 1990.[10]

The Beatles were scarcely noticed in Yugoslavia until 1964 or 1965, but then they arrived in force. The Rolling Stones briefly eclipsed the Beatles in popularity in Yugoslavia after the release of their album *Satisfaction*. But the Beatles soon recaptured the limelight. The 25 June 1967 satellite emission of "All You Need Is Love" was seen by an estimated 150 million people around the world, including many young people in Yugoslavia. By October of that year, Jugoton released a domestic pressing of *Sgt. Pepper's Lonely Hearts Club Band*. And by then there were also Yugoslav pressings of *A Collection of Beatles Oldies*, the Beach Boys' *Greatest Hits*, Jimi Hendrix's *Are You Experienced?* and singles by various other artists, including the Walker Brothers, the Spencer Davies Group, and Arthur Brown.[11]

At that time, Yugoslav groups were exclusively oriented toward the American and British repertoire. Groups such as White Arrows (Bijele strijele), Red Corals (Crveni koralji), the Golden Boys (Zlatni dečaci), Indexes (Indeksi), Chameleons (Kameleoni), Silhouettes (Siluete), Robots (Roboti), Elipse, the Boyfriends (Rdečki dečki), the Five Flames (Plamenih pet), and Dreamers (Sanjalice) were characteristic of this trend. Some of these groups, in particular Elipse (from Belgrade), Hurricanes (Uragani, from Rijeka), Robots (from Zagreb), and We (Mi, from Šibenik), became interested in black music, especially the music of Aretha Franklin, Wilson Pickett, and Otis Redding. Later, some of these groups started to write their own soul music, in Croatian, though on the whole without success.[12]

About this time, Drago Mlinarec put together a band he called Group 220. The group played original music modeled on American rock of the time, but showed some versatility, e.g., by doing a rock version of a traditional *Schlager* hit, "Večer na Robleku."

The most important rock groups in Sarajevo in the late 1960s were Čičak and Codex (Kodeksi). While groups in Belgrade and Zagreb were playing soul music, these Sarajevo bands tuned in to progressive rock currents. Codex, in particular—led by Željko Bebek—showed an affinity for the musical styles of Cream and Jimi Hendrix.

One of the most often mentioned groups from the 1960s is Korni Group, named for its leader, Kornell Kovach, a classically trained pianist who would later devote himself to composing and producing records. Korni Group was formed in 1968 in Belgrade and played for six years. The group constantly tested the limits of the market, composing rock "symphonies" and showing a clear preference for longer pieces rather than short commercially oriented songs. Korni Group created a small scandal at a Zagreb concert in 1969 by playing a twenty-minute song; audiences at that time were not accustomed to such things. Korni Group was also the first Yugoslav band to put out an LP on the international market, with an album produced by Carlo Alberto Rossi in Milan.[13]

Rebellion or Conformity

Deliberations about rock 'n' roll took place at the highest level, and Tito and Kardelj are said to have personally decided against the repressive approach favored in

Moscow, Prague, Bucharest, and Tirana, for example. They believed that a policy of toleration within carefully controlled limits could produce better results. The result, according to journalist Dušan Vesić, was that "from the middle of the 1960s until only a few years ago, [Yugoslav] rockers were the greatest servants of the Tito regime!"[14]

Hence, although almost from the beginning the party's cultural commissars were sensitive to rock's potential for stirring rebellious sentiments, they opted for cooptation rather than repression. Astutely, they made it worthwhile for rock musicians to cooperate. The result was a pronounced sycophantic streak in Yugoslav rock, beginning at an early stage.

The group Indeksi, for example—prominent in the mid-1960s—penned a song, "Yugoslavia," which included the lines,

> We knew that the sun was smiling on us,
> because we have Tito for our marshal!

Much later, Indeksi veteran Davorin Popović produced an album, *Mostar Rain: Our Name Is Tito*, which was released shortly after Tito's death in May 1980. It included a song titled "After Tito, Tito" (lyrics by J. Sliška, based on a text by Miša Marić):

> While he lived, he was
> with us and with the world
> While he lived, he was
> the sun above the planet.
> While he lived, he was
> a wild hero in a tale
> While he lived, he was
> such, that we were proud of him.
> And what now, southern land?
> If anyone should ask us,
> we shall say, again Tito:
> After Tito, Tito.
> We shall say, again Tito.
> Tito lives with us
> Tito was just one man,
> but we are also Tito![15]

Kornell Kovach, who retired from performing in 1974 in order to devote himself to composing, has been described, unflatteringly, by *Pop Rock* magazine as having been "the greatest patriot of Yugoslav rock 'n' roll."[16] His early song "People's Government" celebrated Tito's smashing of "the traitorous clique."

Even Bora Djordjević, who donned the mantle of rock rebel in the 1980s, was circumspect in the Tito era. In 1977, for example, he sang a panegyric song, "The

World of Tito," in duet with Gorica Popović, on the album *Brigadier Songs*. Željko Bebek (at one time a close associate of Goran Bregović's) and pop singer Djordje Balašević are other performers who were willing to "carry the torch" for Tito. Not all rock musicians played "panegyric rock," but many did. Their presence and subsequent success provide clues as to the nature of the Tito and post-Tito regimes.

Yugoslav Rock Comes of Age

As Ljuba Trifunović points out, 1974, the year in which Korni Group folded, was also the year in which Goran Bregović created White Button. Bregović's new group drew unabashedly on ethnic melodies and succeeded, in the process, in giving a "Yugoslav" stamp to rock music. White Button quickly established itself as one of the most popular groups in the country—a position it never lost until the war drove Bregović into exile in Paris in 1992. Already in the late 1970s, White Button concerts were rousing young fans (especially of the opposite sex) to paroxysms of "Buttonmania."[17]

By 1976, members of the establishment began to notice that the rock scene was growing. University of Belgrade Professor Sergij Lukač wrote a series of hard-hitting articles for *NIN* which blasted White Button. Similarly, Sladjana Aleksandra Milošević, a soft-rock vocalist from Belgrade, was subjected to regular press attacks at this time; the articles typically criticized her Western-style attire and attacked her for "erotic aggressiveness."[18] Other rock performers were also given rude, even vicious treatment in the press, but for the most part these had no practical significance for the rock scene and no party forum ever undertook to campaign against rock or to obstruct the holding of large rock concerts.[19]

The 1970s were, in fact, the years of the big "Boom" rock festivals in Yugoslavia, drawing thousands of fans to Woodstock-style events in Ljubljana, Novi Sad, and eventually Belgrade. The "Boom" festivals were eventually stopped—for commercial reasons[20]—but smaller festivals continued in Skopje, Zemun, Novi Sad, Avala, and elsewhere.

By the 1970s, Yugoslav rock groups, which at first had felt (like rock groups throughout the world) that rock could only be sung in English, were composing and singing in their own languages—Serbo-Croatian, Slovenian, and, in much smaller numbers, Macedonian.

The major rock groups of the late 1970s were White Button, Azra (now defunct), Index (the first Yugoslav group to play its own material), Bora Djordjević's Fish Soup (Riblja Čorba) from Belgrade, and the Macedonian group Bread and Salt (Leb i sol). The last two bands were established only in 1978.[21]

Belgrade and Sarajevo were the clear centers for rock 'n' roll in the 1970s, with Zagreb and Ljubljana close behind, and for commercial reasons Serbo-Croatian was the language of rock. Bread and Salt aspired to a national audience and therefore sang most of its songs in Serbo-Croatian, not Macedonian. Similarly, the Slovenian group Bulldozer (Buldožer), seeking a national audience, sang in Serbo-Croatian rather than in Slovenian.

Bulldozer became, in fact, one of the legends of the 1970s. A kind of Yugoslav equivalent of the Mothers of Invention, Bulldozer took up political themes at a time when most Yugoslav rock groups still avoided politics. In their song "Good Morning Madame Jovanović," for example, they seemed to satirize both Jovanka Tito and the Yugoslav People's Army at the same time—daring in any era.[22]

Yugoslavia has shared in *all* the major American and world trends in rock music. When punk developed in Britain, for instance, it quickly spread to Yugoslavia, where groups like the Bastards (Pankrti, from Ljubljana), Electric Orgasm (Električni orgazam, from Belgrade), and Dirty Theater (Prljavo kazalište, from Zagreb) got their start playing punk. Ljubljana became a center for punk and even punk-Nazi music, with groups such as Epidemic and the Trash of Civilization. Now, in the post-punk era, Ljubljana is still a haven for underground music, as served up, for example, by the bands Demolition Group and Del Masochistas. Some of these groups—Bastards, Dirty Theater, and Electric Orgasm, in particular—later evolved away from punk.

New wave (*novi talas*) came to Yugoslavia at the end of the 1970s. Rockabilly, heavy metal, trash metal, speed metal, death metal, and assorted other currents have also won adherents in the country. By 1986, heavy metal had built up sufficient presence to make it possible to hold what proved to be only the first in a series of annual heavy metal concerts in Sarajevo. Groups such as Storm Cloud (Storm klaud), Bombarder, Earthquake (Zemljotres), Formula 4, Dr. Steel (from Rijeka), and Legion (Legija, from Zagreb) took part in the first such festival, attended by some 2,000 fans. By 1988, the festival had become a two-day event, and the list of participating bands had grown to include Atomic Shelter (Atomsko sklonište), Kerber, the Eighth Traveler (Osmi putnik, from Split), Heavy Company, and Fiery Kiss (Vatreni poljubac, from Sarajevo).[23]

The most important rock groups in Yugoslavia in 1990 were: the Belgrade groups Fish Soup, Bajaga and the Instructors (formed in 1984), and Yu-Group; Sarajevo's White Button; Ljubljana's Laibach (formed in 1980) and Falcons (formed in summer 1989); and Skopje's Bread and Salt. Other groups that have attracted attention since 1988 include three Zagreb bands—Dee Dee Mellow (formed in 1988 and discussed below), Witches (formed in 1989), and Modesty (formed from the wreckage of two demo bands)—and the Belgrade band Department Store (Robna kuća), formed at the medical faculty of the University of Belgrade in April 1988 and enjoying considerable popularity in Belgrade by 1990. Zagreb's Dirty Theater slowly built its reputation as a solid band and was widely considered Croatia's most popular rock band in 1990 and 1991. Also strong was the band Electric Orgasm from Belgrade, though it did not perform in public for several years beginning around 1988, and the riotous and ever-popular Party Breakers (Partibrejkers), also from Belgrade. Some all-female acts also deserve mention, specifically Cacadou Look (established in the mid-1980s in Opatija and singing largely in English) and Boja (a Vojvodina band). The Rijeka group Flight 3 (Let 3) features females on guitar and bass guitar, while their male lead singer has performed in lingerie.[24]

Yugoslavia's top female solo vocalist in the late 1980s was Snežana Mišković Viktorija, voted top female vocalist by *Pop Rock* readers in a 1988 survey.[25] Other women to make their mark in the late 1980s or early 1990s include Marina Perezić (a member of a duo, Denis and Denis, which made two records before she left the duo and went solo), Neda Ukraden (a pop singer from Sarajevo), Josipa Lisac (who got her start in the early 1970s in Zagreb), Kasandra (a Croatian singer whose album *Ice Cream* was released in 1995), and Baby Doll (alias Dragana Šarić, from Belgrade, who recorded one album and a few singles, spinning exotic songs built on Arabic themes, after spending six months in Cairo).[26] A special mention should also be made of YU-Madonna (alias, Andrea Makoter of Maribor), who performed at a number of festivals in summer 1988, mimicking *the* Madonna in singing style, attire, mannerisms, etc.[27] Among the top male vocalists one may mention Oliver Mandić (a Belgrade singer who created a small storm in the mid-1980s by performing in drag), Rambo Amadeus (whom I like to think of as the PDQ Bach of rock music, because of a piece he once staged for twelve vacuum cleaners),[28] and Tonny Montano (an ever-changing, ever-present entertainer who gradually evolved from punk to rockabilly to parody with a "beat" look). Aside from these, one may make a special mention of Djordje Balašević, a bard singer with wide influence, performing message-songs. In Russia, Balašević would be counted as a "rock" performer because of his lyrics; in Yugoslavia he is considered a pop singer, as he would be in the West, because of his music.

The Ethnic Impulse

When rock first came to Yugoslavia, musical adepts approached it in much the way that one would learn a new language. They studied the existing patterns and techniques and worked to master and replicate them. There was little thought given, at first, to innovation. But as young Yugoslav musicians mastered the new "language" and matured musically, they became increasingly willing to innovate and to look to autochthonous sources of musical inspiration. Inevitably, some of them turned to the folk heritage of Yugoslavia.

The first group to do so was White Button, and the Sarajevo group repeatedly drew upon folk idioms for inspiration. Bregović himself argued that ethnic and folk music was the richest source for material and that it was the most promising future for rock music (and not just in the Balkans).

But White Button was not alone in this. Fiery Kiss, for example, during the ten years of its existence (1977–1987), incorporated many folk elements into its melodies, and some of its songs used a syncopation native to Balkan folk music, not to rock. The group adapted Bosnian folk music, with its blend of Turkish and Arabian elements, and played it on traditional rock instruments. The symbiosis of folk and rock in the performance art of Fiery Kiss was reflected in the fact that a lot of its songs were picked up by the popular folk singer Hanka Paldum and marketed as "folk" songs. In a fitting close to this story, the group's leader, Milić Vukasinović, eventually became dissatisfied with the modest earnings as a rock musician and made the switch to folk.[29]

Another Sarajevo band, Blue Orchestra (Plavi Orkestar), which enjoyed considerable popularity among teenagers, did something similar in its record *Death to Fascism!* (*Smrt fašizmu!*—the old Partisan greeting from World War II). Released in 1987, the album blended folk musical motifs with Partisan themes, singing about the war, the liberation of Belgrade, and Jovanka Tito, the late president's widow. In one song, the group sang the refrain "Fa-fa-fascist! Don't be a fascist!" The album was celebrated as a species of "new patriotism" and inevitably provoked controversy. Some people suggested (ludicrously) that their lyrics had been written by the Central Committee; others attacked them as "state enemy no. 1."[30] They found themselves cast as the "new partisans" of Yugoslav rock music. Saša Losić, the leader of Blue Orchestra, went into deep depression, and when he emerged out of this depression in 1989, with the release of a new album, he was preaching a new musical philosophy: "Rock 'n' roll has reached its limit, the end of its possibilities. We keep going back to the 1950s, the 1960s, the 1970s. Punk was, in reality, a primal energy for rock 'n' roll. Then there were the new romantics of sympho-rock in the 1970s. Now we are returning to the trends of the 1970s."[31]

Ethnic music figured in an entirely different way in the music of the Zagreb group Dee Dee Mellow. Instead of drawing on indigenous sources, the group looked beyond European frontiers for inspiration, and its first album included a rendition of a Peruvian Indian song ("Adios Pueblo de Ayacucho") and an adaptation of an American Indian song, sung in the Sioux language ("Sitting Bull Song").[32] Put together largely by former members of the then dormant group Haustor—specifically, Jura Nolosević, Srdjan "Gul" Gulić, and Igor Pavlitza—Dee Dee Mellow continued Haustor's tradition of social commentary, but with a new twist. Instead of brooding about the gravity of the situation, the new group responded with silliness (the next stage after despair). Hence, in one song, written at a time when newspapers already cost 3,000 dinars and literally everybody had become a "millionaire" in inflated dinars, they sang,

> *What am I going to do*
> *with all of this money?*
> *Wine, yoghurt,*
> *and a half a loaf of bread.*

Other bands also drew upon ethnic music. For example, YU-Group, at the end of the 1970s, did a song ("Kosovo Flower") using traditional Albanian rhythms.

Finally, there were regionally specific trends in Vojvodina and Macedonia which reflected the synthesis of folk elements and rock music. The Hungarian inhabitants of Vojvodina share in a musical phenomenon common also to Hungary and the Hungarian population of Transylvania. Known as *Šogor* rock ("brother-in-law" rock), the genre uses the rhythms of Hungarian folk music and even some of the traditional folk instruments, but plays them in a rock format. The performers themselves are generally attired rather more in the tradition of folk performers than like rock musicians, and their music has no resonance beyond the Hungarian population. Šogor rock started in hotels and bars in the late 1970s, but the first Šogor records were released only in 1987.

Macedonia is far more interesting in this regard, having given birth to a new tendency which, for lack of a better term, one may call "Byzantine rock." To a considerable extent, this is the brainchild of Goran Trajkovski, later the leading musical figure in the independent multimedia cultural group Aporea (Apokrifna realnost, Apocryphal Reality). Trajkovski explained his thinking in these terms: "Everything in Macedonia is connected with Orthodoxy, and Orthodoxy is very much the legacy of Byzantium. The Church was the chief civilizing force here for hundreds of years. So our religion always connects us with our past. As a result, the sense of history is very different here from what it is in Slovenia, for example. Our ideas in Aporea, our work, our music, are all derived from Orthodoxy."[33]

In 1984, Trajkovski created the Fall of Byzantium (Padat na Vizantija) and began to work with Orthodox liturgical music in a rock format. The effect was to preserve the spirit of the traditional music, but to transform it into patterns that are intelligible to the modern listener. The Fall of Byzantium folded in 1985, but its work was continued, in a multimedia format, by Aporea (although it would be hard to call Aporea's music "rock").

Another neo-Byzantine group in the 1980s was the rock group Mizar, which was created in 1981 as a kind of post-punk band. At first it seemed oriented toward something akin to Pink Floyd,[34] but even so, from the very beginning, Mizar drew upon traditional Macedonian music and culture for inspiration.[35] Later Mizar likewise began to look to Orthodox music for material, but with a difference. Whereas Aporea glorified Byzantine culture, Mizar, according to Trajkovski, "rejected Byzantium and Byzantine culture." For almost two years (1985–1987), Mizar was cooperating closely with Aporea, but in 1987 there was a rift and Mizar went its own way. Like the Fall of Byzantium, Mizar sang largely in Macedonian (a point which distinguished it from the better known band Bread and Salt), although Mizar also sang some songs in Old Church Slavonic (the language preferred by Aporea). Mizar has since disappeared from the Macedonian rock scene, but new groups, such as the rather conventional hard rock group Area, have taken its place.

Politicians and Rock

There is something intrinsically "oppositionist" about rock music: that is completely obvious to everyone. Rock is, in its very soul, about freedom, about individual self-determination, about self-expression. That is why any effort to harness rock music to a role supportive of official policy—as was made in the USSR in the case of the official group Happy Guys in the pre-Gorbachev era—is bound to end up looking ridiculous. That is also one reason, though not the only reason, why the first genera- tion of rockers invariably confronted distrust, fear, and even hostility from political authorities—not just in Yugoslavia, but throughout the world, including in the United States, even, to some extent, if they were willing to serve the authorities.[36]

The Sarajevo band Smoking Forbidden (Zabranjeno pušenje) had an experience which may illustrate the point. During a concert in Rijeka in November 1984, one of the loudspeakers (brand name "Marshal") suddenly stopped functioning. Dis- gusted with this unforeseen inconvenience, band leader Nele Karaljić exclaimed, "The marshal has broken down." Everyone at the concert knew that he was talking about the amplifier. But a month later unknown persons hostile to the group de- cided to create trouble, and a series of sharp attacks appeared in *Vjesnik, Politika, Borba,* and elsewhere, asking why Karaljić had not said, instead, "The Marshal *is dead.*" The papers then insinuated that Karaljić had deliberately shown disrespect.[37] The band suffered. Previously scheduled concerts were abruptly canceled, and new bookings could not be obtained. Finally, in early 1985, Karaljić wrote an open letter to *Politika* explaining the situation and making it clear that no disrespect to Marshal Tito had been intended. The letter was published, and in February 1985 the group staged a "comeback" concert in Belgrade, attended by some 10,000 fans. The atmos- phere was nervous, and the first two rows were taken by police.[38]

Fish Soup's Bora Djordjević was taken to court twice—in 1987[39] and in 1989— but was acquitted both times. In both cases, his lyrics got him into trouble. But that did not prevent him from publishing four books of poetry and being elected to the Serbian Association of Writers.

White Button's Goran Bregović was *threatened* with court action after the group performed a song in which the traditional national hymns of the Serbs and Croats were played back to back, but nothing came of it.

On the whole, however, it was rare that the political authorities would take the trouble to discuss the political merits or demerits of a particular ensemble. The Re- public of Slovenia provided a rare exception when the Faculty of Political Science of the University of Ljubljana organized a roundtable discussion about "punk-Nazi- ism," attended by the Slovenian republic Secretary for Internal Affairs and represen- tatives from the Ljubljana City Secretariat for Internal Affairs and the Supreme Court of Slovenia.

The most problematic rock group, from the standpoint of the political authorities in the early 1980s, was the art rock group Laibach, which has, from its beginning, performed in Nazi-style regalia and adopted a proto-fascist demeanor in both its vi- sual presentation and its musical format. Laibach introduced itself as the Musical Division of a totalitarian movement calling itself Neue Slowenische Kunst (New Slovenian Art). German was the preferred language for this movement because it is historically identified with Naziism. A member of Neue Slowenische Kunst told me in 1987, "The very fact that Naziism is always tarred as the blackest evil is a way of not dealing with its social content and meaning." Another NSK member told me in

1989, "We want a great totalitarian leader. God is a totalitarian being. Totalitarianism, for us, is a positive phenomenon. We admire leaders like Alexander the Great, Caesar, Napoleon. As for Hitler, his mistake was to confuse the general with the particular." And yet, Laibach is clearly fixated on Hitler: he is the central inspiration for the group's artistry, in both form and substance. Its record covers feature swastikas, and Laibach's members sing militant, Nazi-sounding "rock" in German; and when the group decided to do a cover of the Beatles' album *Let It Be* in 1988, it pointedly left out the title song and replaced it with a militant rendition of "Auf der Lüneburger Heide." The effect is right out of a Nazi propaganda film.

Earlier, in 1987, the group released an album significantly titled *Opus Dei (The Work of God)*. Taking a song, "Life Is Life," which had originally been performed by a German group, Opus, as an innocent, soft-rock number, Laibach recast it as a militant, eerily totalitarian march. The group sings,

> *When we all give the power*
> *We give our best,*
> *All that we can, our fullest efforts,*
> *With no thought to rest.*
> *And we all get the power*
> *We all get the best*
> *When everyone gives everything*
> *Then everyone will get everything.*
> *Life is life!*
> *Life is life.*
> *When we all feel the power,*
> *Life is life.*
> *When we all feel the pain,*
> *Life is life.*
> *It's the feeling of the people,*
> *Life is life.*
> *It's the feeling of the land.*

Laibach clearly benefitted from the relatively more liberal atmosphere prevailing in Slovenia. In other parts of Yugoslavia, the group might have been banned altogether. But even in Slovenia, authorities would not allow anything to be published in the republic about Laibach until 1983 or 1984, except in the youth magazine, *Mladina*.[40] Elsewhere, Laibach experienced at first hand the significance of decentralization in a federalized system. Laibach was prevented from performing in many cities in Yugoslavia.[41] For example, until 1986, Laibach was banned from appearing in Bosnia-Herzegovina altogether, and the group did not actually play in that republic until 7 April 1989, when it performed at Sarajevo's Center for the Social Activities of Youth. When the manager of that center first scheduled Laibach to perform, there was tremendous pressure on him from the authorities to cancel the concert, including threatening phone calls to his unlisted home phone. He did not sleep for two nights before the concert, but he refused to cave in, and the concert went ahead as planned. Predictably, after the concert, the authorities bragged about what good democrats they were to have authorized the concert.

Created in September 1980, Laibach has released about a dozen albums overseas, although the albums can be purchased, as imports, in Slovenia. That group has succeeded, unlike any other South Slav rock group, in building a worldwide following, and in 1989, for example, the group did an American concert tour, performing in New York, Washington, D.C., Boston, and Los Angeles, and it performed in Seattle in 1993.

Censorship—Now You See It, Now You Don't

Tito did not establish a separate Office of Censorship per se, and there certainly has not been any government office entrusted with the task of listening to rock demos and determining what may and may not be pressed. All the same, the Communist system was set up in such a way that censorship resulted. In any recording company, the responsible editor was always a party member and was required to review all rock songs before a disc would be pressed. Even though they might be sympathetic to the rock musicians, record producers, studio directors, and concert managers frequently feared what *might* happen to them if they allowed certain things to be performed. Hence, rather than take a chance, they tended to play it safe. The result was that rock musicians had to change their costumes, change their record jackets, delete certain songs from certain albums, adjust their repertoire at certain concerts, and even rewrite their lyrics. Talking to rock musicians in Yugoslavia, I heard numerous stories of intervention by nervous record producers and so forth. The intention was sometimes not primarily to suppress anything, but simply to save their own skins. The result was a form of censorship.

For example, Smoking Forbidden made a rock video, "Maniac," about a politician, a family man, who has an illicit romantic adventure, literally going mad in the process. In the video, the mad politician uses "Tops" crackers as bait to lure the girl of his dreams. The video was made in March 1987, a few months before the Agrokomerc corruption scandal broke. But as it turned out, "Tops" crackers were made by Agrokomerc. Nobody would believe that the video had been made *before* Agrokomerc made the headlines. That was a contributing factor to keeping the video off TV.

Goran Bregović's White Button likewise had its share of problems. In 1976, for example, Bregović wanted to title his album *Hey! I Want to Be Stupid.* He had to be happy with the bland *Hey! I Want.* Nor were the authorities happy when Bregović took on religion, and in 1979 he had trouble with the line "and Christ was a bastard and a worry [to his mother]," intended for a song for the album *Batanga and the Princess.* Even in 1986, Bregović ran into trouble when he wanted to engage Vice Vukov to sing a song on his album *Spit and Sing, My Yugoslavia!* Vukov had been viewed as a kind of bard of Croatian nationalism back in 1970–1971 and now, fifteen years later, the chief of police of the Republic of Bosnia took part in discussions about Bregović's desire to involve Vukov in one song.[42] Vukov finally made his comeback in 1989 with a record of Neapolitan songs.

Bora Djordjević had similar problems with his songs and poems. In 1970, for example, he was prevented from singing the line "Yet another scabby day"—lest this pessimism be taken as directed against the system.[43] In 1982, after the release of the latest Fish Soup album, the Veterans Association of Macedonia became upset because some of the old Partisans felt that one of the songs included lines insulting to veterans of the national liberation struggle. Some hotheads in the Veterans Association said the album should be banned; others wanted to ban Fish Soup. A few even talked about getting rock music banned altogether in Yugoslavia—as it was, at the time, in Albania. But Bora had contacts in high places, including a close relative, and eventually an unnamed high official contacted Kosta Nadj (the head of the Veterans Association of Yugoslavia) and told him to call off the hounds.[44]

Again, in 1984, Bora was preparing his album *Tonight, Drunk Musicians Play for You* for release by Jugoton, when the recording company's chief editor, Dubravko Majnarić, rejected Bora's song "Sudba, Udba, Ozna,"[45] with the rhetorical question, "Young man, what do you know about UDBa and OZNA?"[46] The song "Power of the Opposition" could not be included on his 1987 album *The Truth (Istina)* for political reasons, but was released on videocassette a year or two later.[47] Various texts originally intended for his second book (published in spring 1987, while Ivan Stambolić was still the party boss in Serbia),[48] were prohibited at that time, only to be passed for publication in his subsequent book,[49] by which time Slobodan Milošević had replaced Stambolić as the party boss in Serbia. Among the poems originally banned are several nationalist poems about Kosovo, for example:

> *Eenie meenie minie mo,*
> *I'm a little rabbit*
> *I eat little chickens*
> *I have a big stomach*
> *I eat little Serbs.*

No one could mistake the fact that the poem was about Kosovo's Albanians. Or again:

> *I don't buy that pure shit*
> *that they come to šumadija,*
> *but if they come to šumadija,*
> *I prefer to kick the bucket.*
> *I don't need that Balkan city,*
> *I need the Patriarchate of Peć.*
> *I need a little change*
> *in surnames in Prizren.*

And never will there be any peace
between me and the "Illyrian."
Is it possible that some Shiptar
will seize the Serbian crown and scepter?

These poems, out of favor in Stambolić's day, came very much into favor with the political authorities once Milošević took charge in Serbia. Similarly, Bora Djordjević's original criticisms of Tito were courageous when Stambolić was in charge. Later Milošević himself criticized the man he preferred to call "Josip Broz."

But there is more to Bora than just nationalism; he is, above all, quintessentially anti-establishment. In another once banned poem, he writes,

Oh God, give me a black Mercedes,
with a little registration,
so that I can finally view myself
as an official fool.
Oh God, give me a black Mercedes
with at least six doors
so that I can tap my Havana
into a gold ashtray.
Oh God, give me a black Mercedes
because it is a miracle above all miracles.
It is beautiful to drive unpenalized
over flowers and people.[50]

Sometimes, record producers approved an album but pressured the group to make alterations. The Bastards, for example, were compelled to change an album cover in 1982 because the producer was nervous about the original design.[51] Or again, Goran Bregović's White Button had to put up with having sections of their songs literally spliced out, after being recorded, because the words were considered "potentially offensive." Needless to say, this left some telltale signs in their early albums.

It is symptomatic of the nature of a watched society that people fear to get involved in others' troubles. The result, as Vesić dolefully noted in 1990, was a lack of solidarity among Yugoslav rock musicians. When White Button was under fire in 1976, not a single band came to its defense. When the Veterans Association of Macedonia attacked Bora's Fish Soup in 1982, again not a single rock musician or rock band raised a voice in protest, and Bora had to rely on his own resources.[52] Rock musicians who tried to play the gadfly found it impossible, thus, to ignite anything like a protest movement. Or, to put it analogically, in Tito's Yugoslavia the system did not allow enough freedom for anyone to be able to play a role anything like Joan Baez or Bob Dylan did in the late 1960s in the United States.

Editorial interventions of a political nature were thus commonplace, but one should not exaggerate their frequency either. There were many groups who never had any problems with "intervention," especially commercial bands with no social awareness. The problems began when a band became socially aware.

To be socially aware is not necessarily to be politically controversial or critical, however. Rock groups addressed issues of social isolation, growing up, ethnic feuding, and other issues that were not necessarily troubling to the authorities. The late President Tito (elected "without termination of mandate") likewise was long a favorite theme for Yugoslav rock groups. For example, the Elvis J. Kurtović Band of Sarajevo released an album in 1988 with the tongue-in-cheek title *The Wonderful World of Private Business*. It includes a song nominally about Emperor Haile Selassie of Ethiopia:

> *When I was young*
> *the teacher took us to the main street*
> *to see his Majesty Haile Selassie*
> *drive past in a black limousine.*
> *We were all so happy,*
> *and the street was packed with people*
> *all to see our friend from nonaligned Ethiopia.*
> *He was an amazing man,*
> *loved by the masses,*
> *wise like Gandhi,*
> *and as handsome as Nasser.*
> *Of all our friends,*
> *he was the best.*
> *He led his people*
> *to wealth and happiness.*

Set to rock rhythms, the lyrics clearly were not intended to be taken solemnly. Thus, even though the song appeared on the album, the group was not allowed to perform it on television.[53]

Another Sarajevo group, Smoking Forbidden (Zabranjeno pušenje), tried to capture people's mood when Tito died—the sense of loss, the sense of greatness past. The song works allegorically, talking about the great soccer player Hase's last match:

> *The people go into the stadium*
> *and it was hushed.*
> *People said,*
> *Today is Hase's last game ...*
> *They spoke of his past glories,*
> *Of what a great player he had been.*
> *They talked of how he beat the Germans*
> *and the Russians*
> *and the British.*

And then the referee blew the whistle,
With the game tied at 1-to-1.
The people leave in silence,
nobody is talking.
Sunday stops in its tracks,
but May goes on.
Some fans chant,
"Go team, charge.
There is only one Hase." [54]

New Primitivism

When Elvis J. Kurtović, "Dr." Nele Karaljić, and a few other rock musicians in Sarajevo decided to satirize the cultural and political backwardness of some of their fellow citizens, they gave their "movement" a name—"new primitivism." The idea took
shape at a café in the Bašćaršija district of Sarajevo, over a copy of the local newspaper, *Oslobodjenje*. It was 1981, and *Oslobodjenje* was reflecting on a new film,
Quadrophenia, which dealt with teddy boys and mods in Great Britain. *Oslobodjenje*
launched into a long jeremiad about "long-haired punks and hippies" whom "local
good youths" would "devour." Kurtović, Karaljić, and friends knew, of course, that
punks did not have long hair like hippies. But the text inspired them. They decided
to satirize these "local good youth" by dressing and acting like them and singing
about them; they adopted the name "new primitives." "We started to dress without
any taste, quite deliberately," Kurtović recalls. "We looked like those *Gastarbeiter* in
the film *Montenegro.* Our music combined American rock ideologies, Japanese technology, and local domestic primitivism."[55] Their satire was not appreciated by the
"old primitives," however, who understood that they were the butt of "new primitive" humor. But the "new primitives" made a serious point. In Karaljić's words,
"The basic problem in Yugoslavia is not politics, but culture. There is no great culture here—no great classical composers, only a few important writers, a handful of
great sculptors. If you don't have great culture, you can't have great ideas. And if you
are behind in ideas, everything else follows."[56] Or in Kurtović's words, "The problem of this country is primitivism. We can change the whole system and adopt capitalism, but we won't be like West Germany, we'll be like Turkey—primitive."

A classic product of "new primitivism" was the song "Anarchy All Over Bašćaršija," which dealt with the reflections of a typical "old primitive." He feels good
about having beaten up a young hippie, gets nervous when he sees the letter "A"
scrawled on a wall in the Bašćaršija district, and broods about the West, because it is
changing the way young people dress.[57]

New primitivism was, of course, never a movement as such. But this satirical
treatment won the Elvis J. Kurtović Band and Karaljić's Smoking Forbidden a loyal
following among Yugoslav young people and won them the respect of intellectuals in
the country.

The Support System

Rock music is a product that must be managed, promoted, advertised, and sold. The "support system" was, thus, a critical factor in the Yugoslav rock scene.

There were eleven record and cassette companies in Yugoslavia that produced at least some rock (as of 1987). The major companies were Jugoton of Zagreb, which issued about thirty new rock albums each year, and PGP RTB of Belgrade, which issued forty-five to fifty new rock albums each year. Together these two companies thus accounted for 75–80 percent of all new albums marketed in Yugoslavia.[58] The chief recording outlets for Slovenian groups were the Ljubljana companies Helidon and RTV Ljubljana. Relatively few records were reissued after the initial pressings were sold out, and many groups that were popular in their own republics (e.g., the Bastards in Slovenia, and the Niš group Galija in Serbia) received little or no organized promotion outside their own republics. A hundred thousand in sales was widely viewed as the barrier to be broken, but experimental bands generally had to be happy with sales of 2,000–5,000. Several people told me that although the companies put a lot of money into promoting folk music, they made no serious efforts to promote rock music and that there were, for example, practically no commercials for rock records at all. Even so, some rock records sold 500,000 copies or more.

The key person in the life of a rock 'n' roll band is its manager. Some managers work exclusively with one band (e.g., Bajaga's Saša Dragić); others work with two or more groups at once (e.g., Goran "Fox" Lisica, who worked as manager for the Slovenian group Videosex and the Macedonian group Mizar, and more recently has been managing and promoting rock groups in Rijeka and Opatija); still others work within an agency or as the musical director of a Student Cultural Center or House of Youth (such as Skopje's Pande Dimovski); and still others operate as "free-lance managers," working as intermediaries between student cultural centers and the individual groups (such as Belgrade's Ilija Stanković). Managers face various problems in their trade, including the low motivation of directors in subsidized clubs (some clubs, such as Sarajevo's Center for the Social Activities of Youth, were *not* subsidized) and the low prices charged for tickets in economically strapped Kosovo and Macedonia—making it difficult to cover expenses in those regions and hence to schedule concerts by visiting groups there, except as large gala events. In Kosovo, the most successful rock concerts have been produced in Priština's Bora i Ramiz Hall— the largest hall in town—which has a capacity of 10,000.[59] Because the support system is relatively underdeveloped, the group manager sometimes finds himself having to engage in relatively mundane tasks such as chauffeuring, delivering mail, and distributing posters.[60]

The media are also a crucial part of the support system. The "super" channel on television carries a lot of rock videos, from both Yugoslavia and abroad, and this is an important medium for promotion. There are also various television and radio programs that feature individual artists and groups, such as the weekly interview show *U sred srede* ("In the Middle of Wednesday"), featured on Belgrade Television, and a weekly radio rock interview show carried on Belgrade's Radio Studio B. *U sred srede*, directed by Tanja Petrović, had the distinction of being the only long program on Belgrade television (three hours weekly) to play strictly Yugoslav rock.[61]

Finally, the printed media play an important role. In 1989, there were at least five magazines oriented exclusively toward the rock scene. These were Peter Lovšin's now-defunct *Gram* (Ljubljana, in Slovenian), *Heroina* (Zagreb, in Croatian), *Ritam* (Belgrade, in Serbo-Croatian), *Disko selektor* (Skopje, in Macedonian), and *Bao* (Belgrade, Serbo-Croatian, focusing on foreign rock). Petar Popović's *Rock* magazine (later *Pop Rock*) was the most influential rock magazine in the late 1980s, but it folded abruptly in 1990. In its heyday, *Pop Rock* came under fire, from time to time, for favoring Belgrade groups in its coverage, but *Pop Rock* in fact carried articles about all the major groups, including those based in other cities and republics. Aside from these, there are a large number of newspapers and magazines which have regular or semi-regular columns devoted to rock, including *Mladina* (Ljubljana), *Polet* (Zagreb), *Valter* (Sarajevo), *Iskra* (Split), *Mlad Borec* (Skopje), and *Politika ekspres* (Belgrade).

The End of Yugo-Rock

Yugoslav rock made international news in May 1989 when Boardwalk (Riva), a hitherto little-known soft-rock band from Zadar, took first prize at the Thirty-Fourth Eurovision Music Festival, at Lausanne, with its song "Rock Me."[62] The fact that the group came from the small coastal town of Zadar was significant in that it showed that rock 'n' roll in Yugoslavia was by no means the monopoly of the big cities. Later that same year—in September—Novi Sad was host to the Seventh Festival of the European Radio Diffusion Union, a mammoth international event which drew entertainers from such countries as Britain, Ireland, the Soviet Union, Finland, the Netherlands, Hungary, and Sweden.[63] At one time or another, the SFRY hosted many world-class rock performers, including Alice Cooper,[64] Tina Turner,[65] Black Sabbath,[66] David Bowie,[67] Jerry Lee Lewis,[68] and Sisters of Mercy.[69]

The rock scene in Yugoslavia was highly diverse, replicating most, if not all, trends worldwide, including rap music, techno-pop, and—as the Slovenian group Borghesia epitomized—industrial rock containing sadomasochistic overtones.[70] Improvisational rock also had its practitioners, for example, the Zagreb underground band Voodoobuddah. In 1988, Yugoslavia produced its first rock operetta, Vladimir Milačić's *Creators and Creatures* (Kreatori i kreature),[71] and in 1989 its first rock movie, *The Fall of Rock 'n' Roll*, featuring original compositions by Vlada Divljan, Srdjan "Gele" Gojković, and Dušan "Koja" Kojić. In the film, Kojić—otherwise the leader of the Belgrade group, Discipline of the Spine (Disciplina kičme)—played the role of a mini-superhero who wanted to ride on public transport without a ticket and whose big enemy was, thus, the ticket inspector.

Rock music is seen by many of its purveyors as transnational, as a force that can bring people together and create ties of mutual acceptance. Symptomatically, some of the leading figures in the Yugo-rock scene emphasized that they were "Yugoslavs," rather than Serbs or Croats. But as the general political situation in Yugoslavia worsened, bands were increasingly identified with their respective republics. Bands which at one time were able to play in Slovenia, for example (such as White Button and Electric Orgasm), found it impossible, by 1989, to book concerts there. Other bands, like the Serbian group Fish Soup, found that attendance at their concerts in other parts of the country (specifically Croatia, in the case of Fish Soup) dropped in the years after 1987, when nationalism started to rise. Jasenko Houra, lead singer of Dirty Theater (a Zagreb group), told the Croatian weekly *Danas* in 1989 that among Zagreb rock groups only Psychomodo Pop (Psihomodo pop) was still welcome in Belgrade.[72] Like everything else in the SFRY, rock music too was affected by the "national question." This was not hard and fast, of course. At the Avala Rock Festival in Belgrade (in mid-August 1990)—to take an example of interrepublican exchange— groups came from many parts of the country, including Sarajevo (Blue Orchestra), Rijeka (Fit), Split (Devils), and Zagreb (a revived Haustor). Members of the Niš rock group Galija talked of wanting to play all over the country and to serve as a cultural bridge.[73] But already by the end of the 1980s many groups had no ambitions to reach audiences beyond their own republics. Zagreb's Dirty Theater, for example, disclaimed any interest in playing outside Croatia,[74] while the Skopje group Memory, which produced the first Macedonian-language rock LP in Yugoslavia in 1990 (Mizar having produced only cassettes), expressly geared itself to Macedonian national identity and culture.[75]

The partial pluralization of 1988–1991 inevitably had effects on the rock scene. In most republics, rock groups started to enjoy greater freedom (although Slobodan Milošević kept a tight reign on culture in Serbia in those years), but as the economy plummeted in the period 1990–1991, the purchasing power of rock fans declined, contributing to declines in concert attendance throughout the country.[76] The proliferating sense of hopelessness, which made people more vulnerable to nationalist manipulation and chauvinist appeals, could also be detected in the rock scene at that time. For example, the east Slavonian band Satan Panonski (from a village near Vinkovci) played with an equation of *nation* and *punk* in its 1990 album *Nuclear Olympic Games*, capturing some of this sense of hopelessness in the song "Hard Blood Shock" (sung in English):

> *auto-destruction is eruption*
> *it will destroy all my enemies*
> *my victory is toxicant peace*
> *this is not punk*
> *this is not rock*
> *this is this is*
> *hard blood shock.*[77]

As the country slid toward war, as we shall see in more detail in Chapter 11, rock groups took up diverse positions, either identifying themselves with one national cause or another, or associating themselves with the weak antiwar movement, or fleeing into romantic escapism.

Notes

1. Interview with Goran Bregović, leader of Bijelo dugme, Sarajevo, 14 September 1989.

2. Ibid.

3. Conversation with Dražen Vrdoljak, Radio Zagreb music department, Zagreb, 10 September 1989.

4. Interview with Goče Dimovski (director of the House of Youth) and Pande Dimovski (music manager of the House of Youth), Skopje, 26 September 1989.

5. Quoted in Dušan Vesić, "Novi prilozi za istoriju Jugoslovenskog rock'n rolla," Part 1, "Josip Broz i rock'n roll," *Pop Rock* (10 May 1990), p. 2.

6. Quoted in ibid., p. 4.

7. Ljuba Trifunović, *Vibracije* (Belgrade: Kultura, 1986), pp. 99–100.

8. Ibid., p. 100.

9. Interview with Zoran Simjanović, former leader of Elipse, Belgrade (telephone), 28 September 1989.

10. *Pop Rock* (21 February 1990), p. 35.

11. Trifunović, *Vibracije*, p. 102.

12. Interview with Dražen Vrdoljak, Zagreb, 22 June 1987; and interview with Simjanović, 28 September 1989.

13. Interview with Kornell Kovach, former leader of Korni Group, and Bora Djordjević, leader of Riblja Čorba, Belgrade, 18 July 1988.

14. Vesić, "Novi prilozi," Part 1, "Josip Broz i rock 'n roll," p. 4.

15. Quoted in ibid., p. 13.

16. Ibid., p. 12.

17. See Darko Glavan and Dražen Vrdoljak, *Ništa mudro—Bijelo dugme: Autorizirana biografija* (Zagreb: Polet Rock, 1981), pp. 13–18. For a recent interview with Goran Bregović, see *Globus* (Zagreb), 9 June 1995, pp. 28–29.

18. See, for instance, *Sarajevske novine* (22 March 1979). Sladjana Milošević later moved to Los Angeles. See *Vreme International* (Belgrade), 5 June 1995, p. 45, and 7 August 1995, p. 43.

19. This was emphasized and confirmed in interviews with several knowledgeable people, including Vrdoljak, 10 September 1989; Simjanović, 28 September 1989; and Darko Glavan, freelance writer, Zagreb, 28 August 1989.

20. Interview with Vrdoljak, 10 September 1989.

21. Regarding Leb i sol, see *Oko* (7–21 September 1989), p. 27. Regarding a recent concert that this group gave in Belgrade, see *Naša borba* (Belgrade) (22 March 1995), p. 14.

22. Interview with Igor Vidmar, musical coordinator of Radio Student, Ljubljana, 30 June 1987; and interview with Glavan, 28 August 1989. For articles on Buldožer, see *Vjesnik* (16 February 1985), p. 11; and *Pop Rock* (12 July 1989), p. 22.

23. *Pop Rock* (Belgrade) (October 1988), p. 37.

24. *Pop Rock* (21 February 1990), pp. 16–17; and *Vjesnik* (6 October 1990), p. 18. For a recent article about Electric Orgasm, see *NIN* (Belgrade), no. 2307 (17 March 1995), p. 35. For a recent article about Flight 3, see *Arkzin* (Zagreb) (23 December 1994), p. 28. Regarding Witches, see *Narodni list* (Zadar) (3 February 1995), p. 22.

25. *Pop Rock* (3 May 1989), p. 20 (reporting the results of a survey conducted in 1988).

26. Interview with Dragan Todorović, editor of *NON* and staff writer for *Rock* magazine, Belgrade, 10 July 1987; and *Globus* (Zagreb), 30 June 1995, p. 27.

27. See *Vjesnik* (19 July 1988), p. 7, (21 July 1988), p. 7, and (24 August 1988), p. 13.

28. See his interview in *Pop Rock* (24 January 1990), pp. 20–21.

29. Interview with Mimo Hajrić, former member of Vatreni poljubac, Sarajevo, 15 September 1989.

30. Interview with Saša Losić, in *Pop Rock* (March 1989), pp. 16–17.

31. Interview with Saša Losić, in *Pop Rock* (28 June 1989), p. 16.

32. Interview with Jura Nolosević and Srdjan "Gul" Gulić, members of Dee Dee Mellow, Zagreb, 28 August 1989.

33. Interview with the author, Skopje, 25 September 1989. Regarding Trajkovski's ensemble, Anastasia, see *The European Magazine* (London), 16–22 June 1995, p. 19.

34. Interview with Valentino Skenderovski, former member (1985–1986) of Mizar, Sarajevo, 15 September 1989.

35. *Pop Rock* (17 May 1989), p. 22.

36. Regarding the hostility confronted by early rockers in the United States, see John Orman, *The Politics of Rock Music* (Chicago: Nelson-Hall, 1984).

37. See, for instance, Tanjug (26 February 1985), trans. in Foreign Broadcast Information Service (FBIS), *Daily Report* (Eastern Europe), 27 February 1985, p. 18.

38. Interview with Nele Karaljić, leader of Zabranjeno pušenje, Sarajevo, 16 September 1989.

39. See *Večernje novosti* (Belgrade) (30 December 1987), p. 4.

40. Interview with Miha Kovač, former editor-in-chief of *Mladina*, Ljubljana, 3 July 1987.

41. *Pop Rock* (17 May 1989), p. 20. For a recent article about Laibach, see *Permission,* no. 6 (spring 1995), pp. 27–31.

42. *Pop Rock* (13 June 1990), p. 15.

43. Ibid.

44. Ibid.

45. *Sudba* means fate. OZNA and UDBa were successive incarnations of the Yugoslav secret police.

46. Quoted in *Pop Rock* (13 June 1990), p. 15.

47. The song lyrics were also subsequently published in Bora Djordjević's second book, *Hej Sloveni* (Belgrade: Glas, 1987).

48. Ibid.

49. Bora Djordjević, *Neću* (Belgrade: Knjizevna zadruga, 1989).

50. Ibid., p. 123.

51. The story is recounted in Pedro Ramet, "Apocalypse Culture and Social Change in Yugoslavia," in Pedro Ramet, ed., *Yugoslavia in the 1980s* (Boulder, Colo.: Westview Press, 1985), p. 14.

52. Vesić, "Novi prilozi," Part 1, "Josip Broz i rock 'n roll," p. 5.

53. Interview with Elvis J. Kurtović, Sarajevo, 15 September 1989.

54. Interview with Nele Karaljić, Sarajevo, 14 September 1989.

55. Interview with Kurtović, 15 September 1989.

56. Interview with Karaljić, 14 September 1989.

57. There was, in fact, a gang of "old primitives" in Sarajevo who terrorized young people who dressed in Western fashions. After the war reached Bosnia-Herzegovina in 1992, Karaljić

left Sarajevo and took up residence in Belgrade. Kurtović, on the other hand, remained in Sarajevo and has continued to play to local audiences. For a more recent article about Elvis J. Kurtović, see *Nedjeljna Dalmacija* (Split) (30 December 1994), p. 13.

58. These figures all date from 1987. Interview with Siniša Škarica, program director of Jugoton, Zagreb, 24 June 1987; and interview with Aleksandar Pilipenko, editor for Rock and Pop Records, PGP RTB, 20 September 1989.

59. Interview with Ilija Stanković, free-lance manager, Belgrade, 18 September 1989.

60. Interview with Saša Dragić, in *Rock* magazine [original title of *Pop Rock*] (January 1988), p. 50.

61. Interview with Tanja Petrović, director of *U sred srede* show, Belgrade, 23 September 1989.

62. *Borba* (8 May 1989), pp. 1, 14; *NIN*, No. 2002 (14 May 1989), pp. 30–31; and *Danas*, No. 378 (16 May 1989), pp. 71–72.

63. *Oslobodjenje* (Sarajevo), 14 September 1989, p. 6; *Nedjeljna Dalmacija* (Split), 24 September 1989, p. 19; and *Pop Rock* (4 October 1989), p. 30.

64. *Danas,* No. 437 (3 July 1990), pp. 76–77; and *Pop Rock* (8 August 1990), pp. 1–5.

65. *Pop Rock* (11 July 199), p. 12.

66. *Rock* (December 1987), p. 39.

67. *Vjesnik* (6 September 1990), p. 12, and (9 September 1990), p. 14.

68. *Vjesnik* (9 October 1990), p. 8.

69. *Vjesnik* (2 November 1990), insert.

70. For a brief article on Borghesia, see *Danas,* No. 347 (11 October 1988).

71. Vladimir Milačić, *Kreatori i kreature,* RTB 210404 (1988).

72. *Danas,* No. 405 (21 November 1989), p. 75. For a recent article about Jasenko Houra, see *Globus* (Zagreb, 26 May 1995), pp. 20–22. Regarding Srdjan Gojković, see *Vreme International* (7 August 1995), pp. 40–41.

73. *Pop Rock* (11 July 1990), p. 14. The group Galija was included in a cultural delegation sent by Belgrade to Moscow in March 1995 and played to Russian audiences. See *Naša borba* (21 March 1995), p. 13. Regarding Nenad Milosavljević, leader of Galija, see also *Vreme International* (24 July 1995), p. 39.

74. *Pop Rock* (20 September 1989), p. 20.

75. *Pop Rock* (16 May 1990), pp. 20–21.

76. Telephone interview with Peter Lovšin, leader of the Falcons and chief editor of *Gram,* Seattle–Ljubljana, 21 June 1991.

77. Quoted in *Pop Rock* (11 July 1990), p. 20.

PART THREE

War and Transition

CHAPTER EIGHT

◆

Serbia and Croatia
at War Again

It has been said ... that the Brankoviches of Erdely count in
Tzintzar, lie in Walachian, are silent in Greek, sing hymns in
Russian, are cleverest in Turkish, and speak their mother
tongue—Serbian—only when they intend to kill.

Milorad Pavić
Dictionary of the Khazars
1988

It started with the writers. At first, of course, one was struck by the sheer diversity of
themes taken up by Serbian writers. But always the themes of World War II, of victim psychology, of suffering, recurred, played now one way, now another. Among
the novels published in the 1960s and 1970s, some, at least, pulled in the direction
of reconciliation and of transcendence of nationalist concerns. Borislav Pekić's *The
Houses of Belgrade*, for example, first published in 1970, tells the story of Arsenie Negovan, a well-to-do landowner who is consumed by an obsessive, quasi-romantic
love of houses and who, after being accidentally trampled during riots on 27 March
1941, locks himself up in one of his houses for twenty-seven years, finally venturing
out on the very day when, coincidentally, the student riots of summer 1968 were at
their height. In Negovan's view, "*They* [the mob] always demanded the same thing.
They wanted my houses. *They* had wanted them in March 1941 and *They* wanted
them now in June of 1968!"[1] Negovan's obsession with his property even extended
to impelling him to worry about his *hat* at a time when he should have been running
for dear life. Negovan's solicitous concern for even his *former* houses, which took the
shape of an account book in which he maintained an ongoing log of their condition
and occupancy,[2] could be read as an allegorical critique of all forms of avarice, *including irredentism*. The warning went unheeded.

151

And there was also Danilo Kiš, perhaps the greatest Serbian writer of the late twentieth century, whose lyrical novel *Garden, Ashes* (first published in 1975) tells of the mentally unbalanced author of the *Bus, Ship, Rail, and Air Travel Guide*, who, in preparing the third edition of his guide to schedules and transport connections, decided to expand the volume to embrace "an ingenious pantheistic and pandemoniac theory based on scientific achievements, on the principles of modern civilization and the technology of the modern era, ... [a] *summa* of a new religion and new *Weltanschauung*"[3]—all this in the *Bus, Ship, Rail, and Air Travel Guide*. Kiš is clearly critical of the messianic pretensions of the quasi-charismatic author of the *Travel Guide* and his victim complex:

> Impotent before God, obsessed with the idea that he was destined to expiate the sins of his whole family, the sins of all of mankind, he blamed all humanity for his curse and held his sisters and other relatives responsible for all his misfortunes. He considered himself a scapegoat. . . . He wanted everyone to understand that he was a Victim, that he was the one who was sacrificing himself, the one who was fated to be sacrificed, and he wanted everyone to appreciate that and approach him as the Victim.[4]

In a collection of short stories first published in 1983, Kiš draws inspiration from the history of the anti-Semitic *Protocols of the Elders of Zion* to warn against pamphlets and manifestoes that stir up hatred and portray one's own group as the victim of conspiracies and schemes.[5] The recurrence of the theme of victim psychology and Kiš's double warning against such psychology may be taken, at a minimum, as an indication that there were traces of a victim complex in the air as early as the late 1970s and early 1980s. But it was, of course, the ill-famed Memorandum of the Serbian Academy of Sciences and Arts in 1986 which gave effulgent expression to such thinking, painting Serbia as the great "victim" of Titoist Yugoslavia and identifying the "enemies" of the Serbs, namely, the Croats, Albanians, Muslims, Slovenes, and Hungarians, in short, nearly all the non-Serbs of socialist Yugoslavia.

There was a shift in the wind after Tito's death in May 1980, and two new themes emerged: the Tito-Stalin rift of 1948 and the imprisonment of many innocent Yugoslavs in Goli Otok and other prisons; and a reassessment of World War II from the standpoint of *national* suffering. One of the first writers to test these new waters was Gojko Djogo, who, in a collection of satirical poems published in 1981, offered what were widely interpreted as scarcely veiled criticisms of the late Tito.[6] The book provoked a storm of controversy and sent the poet off to prison for a year. Ironically, an earlier collection of poetry by Radovan Karadžić, later leader of the Bosnian Serbs, had been largely ignored until the Bosnian conflict brought its author another kind of fame.[7] Meanwhile, Dušan Jovanović's play *The Karamazovs* opened in Ljubljana in 1980 and in Zagreb in 1982, kindling a reconsideration of the Tito-Stalin split of 1948.[8] Both Jovanović's *Karamazovs* and Antonije Isaković's novel *Tren 2* dealt with the theme of the arbitrariness and injustice of the penal system in early post-1945 Yugoslavia, as did Branko Hofman's stirring novel *Noć do jutra (Night till Morning)*, published in 1981.

More important for our present discussion, however, are those novels and plays which took up the theme of nationalism in the early years after Tito's death.[9] Vuk Drašković, present leader of the Serbian Renaissance Party (at one time the leading opposition party in Milošević's Serbia), wrote *Nož* (*Knife*), a novel that drove home the theme of Serbian suffering during World War II and challenged the LCY (League of Communists of Yugoslavia) thesis that the Bosnian Muslims were a discrete ethnic group, arguing instead that they were merely Serbs whose forefathers had abandoned Orthodoxy out of opportunism.[10] Vojislav Lumbarda's novel *Anatema* was likewise inspired by Serbian nationalism, as was Milić Stanković's historical pamphlet *Sorabi*, which took up the argument that the Serbs are the oldest people in the Balkans.

Nationalism was also the theme of the highly controversial play *Golubnjača (Pigeonhole)*, which opened in Novi Sad in October 1982. Written by thirty-year-old Jovan Radulović, the play was set in the Dalmatian hinterland of the 1960s and showed young Croatian and Serbian children still mired in the prejudices of the internecine struggle of World War II, in which their parents faced each other as foes. The play seemed to indict the LCY for failure to construct a society in which these prejudices could be overcome, yet at the same time complained more particularly that Serbian residents in Croatia were supposedly subjected to constant discrimination even in Tito's time.[11] The play created a sensation.

But more than any other works of fiction, two novels defined the new mood of Serbia in the 1980s, a mood that was increasingly self-absorbed, self-righteous, and self-pitying, indulging in the very kind of portrayal of self as victim against which Kiš had warned. The first of these was the mammoth, epic novel *Vreme smrti (A Time of Death)*, which told the story of Serbia's position in World War I. Written by Dobrica Ćosić, a novelist once expelled from the LCY because of his repeated Serbian nationalist outbursts,[12] the novel shows Serbia betrayed by all its allies and left to withstand, unassisted, the combined attacks of the German, Austro-Hungarian, and Bulgarian armies, as well as, in Ćosić's reinterpretation, the Vatican itself.[13] Where Kiš had once brooded about the danger of conspiratorial thinking, Ćosić has Serbian MP Vukašin Katić tell Prime Minister Pašić, "No political idea in Europe today has as many powerful opponents as our Yugoslav cause."[14] As if the one thing on which all the powers could agree was that Serbia should be thwarted! This leads directly to the thinking captured in the following exchange: " ' … what does our country mean to you?' 'Our country? Suffering, that's my country. People who suffer, who are tormented by pain.'"[15]

In a haunting passage in the final volume of this four-volume work, Ćosić ruminates,

> Brave men will fight for love, but, driven by hatred, all men will fight. In times of storms and tempests which pull up a nation's roots and destroy a man inside his own skin, hatred is the force which gathers and unites all energies, the force which makes survival possible. Hatred is our strongest defense in the face of great evil. . . . With hatred there's nothing a man dare not do, no limit to his endurance.[16]

This, from the pen of the principal author of the 1986 Memorandum, which did more than any other tract or pamphlet written up to then to mobilize Serbian resentment of non-Serbs and legitimate Serbian hatred of all non-Serbs, whether inside or outside Yugoslavia!

Ćosić's novel started a small blaze which gradually spread and, together with other incendiary developments, contributed to inflaming all of Serbia with a desire for a "rectification" of past "injustice." After this, the publication of Danko Popović's short novel (in 1986) about a simple Serbian peasant, Milutin, who tries, in vain, to grapple with the big questions of a nation's destiny and the impact of a nation's history on the individual, comes almost as an afterthought.[17] What Popović's novel contributed was an overt populist dimension, and the incredible popularity of this novel could have provided a clue to observers that Serbia was ready for a populist takeover.

Slobodan Milošević understood what was occurring: a shift in the wind in the cultural sector had contributed, along with other factors, to a shift in the political mood. By 1986, the Serbian public was ripe for change, for big promises, for political messianism. Milošević exploited the new mood and began championing Serbian "rights." By 1988, organized groups supposedly representing the Serbian public were on the streets, clamoring for their messiah to take charge of Kosovo, of Vojvodina, of Montenegro, as he had in Serbia, and there were rumors that Milošević envisioned himself as a "new Tito."

This shift in culture and in the political mood not only sets the context in which the Yugoslav republics became inflamed with nationalism and gravitated toward war, but also provides an explanation for the fierce dialectic of nationalism that has torn even families apart and has set the agenda not only in Serbia, but in a reactive way also in Croatia.

Serbia at War

On 27 March 1941, amid rioting in the streets of Belgrade, Regent Prince Paul was toppled from power and King Peter was declared of age. The coup directly brought about the Nazi invasion of Yugoslavia and the dismemberment of that country. The result was a civil war which set Ustaše, Chetniks, Ballists, and Partisans against each other and cost Yugoslavia more than 1 million casualties. Almost exactly fifty years later, on 9 March 1991, Belgrade's streets were again the scene of riots. Overtly antigovernment (i.e., anti-Milošević in nature), the riots failed under the onslaught of police violence, which left 2 dead and 100 persons injured.[18] Their failure and thus the failure to remove Milošević at that time allowed the country to continue to spiral toward fragmentation and war. The result was an ethnic war which set Serbs, Croats, and Muslims against each other, costing more than 200,000 lives by the end of 1995. In essence, 9 March was the last chance to remove Milošević and—*perhaps*—to avoid interethnic war.

Inevitably, the war contributed to a strong popular identification of the regime with Serbian nationalism itself, thus undermining the already weak position of the opposition. Political figures such as Prince Aleksandar (the heir to the Karadjordjević throne, who had returned from exile in London) and novelist Vuk Drašković, the head of the Serbian Renaissance Party—both of whom had appeared to be at least *conceivable* alternatives to Milošević as of 1990 and early 1991—were, at least temporarily, washed to the margins of Serbian politics. For two years, Milošević was absolutely secure in power, and when at last a challenger appeared, he came from the right: Vojislav Šešelj, the founder and head of the Serbian Radical Party (a party having no organic connection with Nikola Pašić's party of the same name), went so far as to set up a "shadow government" in summer 1993.[19] But when Milošević's grip on the parliament appeared to be shaken, the resourceful Serbian president dissolved parliament, called for new elections, and returned with stronger representation for his own Socialist Party of Serbia than before. Finally, in September 1994, Milošević had Šešelj imprisoned for thirty days on charges that he had physically assaulted Radoman Božović, the speaker of the federal parliament.[20]

The Serb-Croat war, in which Serbian forces took control of at least 30 percent of the territory of the Republic of Croatia, including eastern Slavonia's oil fields, muffled the opposition, indeed made it appear impossible to be both a loyal Serb and an anti-Milošević oppositionist. Milošević, in short, had succeeded in identifying the Serbian national cause with himself. In the days around New Year's, however, the Croatian and Serbian forces signed a truce, and by February 1992 the fighting in Croatia was dramatically receding. The end of the war in Croatia once more emboldened the opposition, and on 9 March 1992, on the anniversary of the 1991 riots, some 30,000 Serbs staged an opposition rally in Belgrade, demanding Milošević's resignation, elections for a constituent assembly, political freedoms (including freedom of the press), and the formation of a transitional government in which Milošević's Socialist Party of Serbia would be permitted to hold no more than 45 percent of the posts (a proportion that accorded with its December 1990 election returns).[21] But the rally failed to generate a more general movement of political upheaval, and Milošević easily rode out the brief storm.

The launching of hostilities against Muslim and Croat communities in Bosnia (to be discussed in Chapter 10) changed perceptions within Serbia, and as of August 1992 Paul Shoup was able to report "a growing reaction in Serbia against the excesses being committed in Bosnia and Herzegovina."[22] Vuk Drašković, leader of the Serbian Renaissance Party, compared Milošević to Iraq's Saddam Hussein,[23] and in a transparent reference declared in May 1992 that "the main enemy of the Serbian people is in Belgrade."[24] Drašković's party joined other opposition parties in boycotting the 31 May elections. About half the members of the prestigious Serbian Academy of Sciences and Arts now declared themselves in favor of Milošević's resignation.[25] The tremors of discontent even reached the general staff, and that same month Milošević forced the resignation of Colonel-General Blagoje Adžić (as JNA commander), Colonel Pavlović (as army chief of staff), Lieutenant-Colonel General Živan Mirčetić (as commandant of the postsecondary military schools of the air force and air defense), Lieutenant-Colonel General Tihomir Grujić (as chief of the

Serbian Republic army staff), Colonel-General Milan Ružinovski (as director of the Center of Military Postsecondary Schools), and other high-ranking generals.[26] The extent of the purge was a sure clue to the depth of opposition to the regime's policies that had appeared in those ranks.

Serbian newspapers and magazines also started to talk openly of the possibility that civil war might break out within Serbia itself. Some imagined that such a war would take the form of a showdown between "Chetniks" and "Partisans," thus replaying the struggle of fifty years earlier.[27] Almost all the political parties of Serbia now expressed themselves on the risk of internal war and outlined their ideas as to how to avert that eventuality.[28] Antiwar demonstrations on 14 June, attended by several thousand people, organized by the Citizens' Alliance of Serbia, the Belgrade Circle, Women in Black, trade unions, and the pacifist Center for Anti-War Actions,[29] and led by Serbian Orthodox Patriarch Pavle, suggested that Serbia might indeed have reached the point of crisis.

In early June, Dragoljub Mićunović's Democratic Party issued a "Platform for the Prevention of Civil War," demanding the creation of new political institutions, the establishment of a coalition government which would include representatives of the opposition, and the formation of a number of "crisis headquarters" which would act as troubleshooters to keep interethnic tensions within Serbia (between Serbs and Albanians, Serbs and Sandžak Muslims, and Serbs and Hungarians in Vojvodina) from escalating.[30] By then a number of opposition parties, including the Serbian Renaissance Party, had formed a coalition known as DEPOS. This coalition also outlined a program designed to remake the system, calling for the immediate resignation of Milošević, the formation of a coalition transitional government, the passage of new laws to regulate elections and the media, and new elections.

About that time, Crown Prince Aleksandar once again presented himself as a candidate for a restored throne, arguing that a monarchy could be a stabilizing and moderating element. But any attempt to restore the Karadjordjević dynasty, even if within a constitutional framework, might well alienate those vestiges of the old Communist left that remain in Serbia and Montenegrins, among whom republican sentiment is strong.

In mid-July, in a move which took Serbia by surprise, Milošević brought in Milan Panić, an émigré Serb who had lived in the United States since 1955 and a self-made millionaire, to serve as prime minister of rump Yugoslavia (the Federal Republic of Yugoslavia, consisting of Serbia and Montenegro, which had been proclaimed on 27 April).[31] Panić promised to bring peace to Bosnia and to set Serbia on the road to capitalism. These were tantalizing promises.

In fact, in the course of 1992, both FRY President Dobrica Ćosić and FRY Prime Minister Panić began to criticize Milošević and to talk openly of removing him from power. Ćosić, for example, told *Politika* in October:

> The existence of three republic presidents in the Federal Republic of Yugoslavia is evidence, in my opinion, that our new state is not consistently a federal state. This is some

kind of 'three-storey,' 'three-phase,' composite state—bureaucratic, too expensive, inefficient. ... I hope that the future constitutional reform will abolish at least two republic presidents and grant more rights to the assemblies and greater responsibility to one president.[32]

The presidents Ćosić wanted to see removed were Serbian President Milošević and Montenegrin President Momir Bulatović.

Meanwhile, Prime Minister Panić decided to challenge Milošević for the presidency in the December 1992 elections, and foreign observers were fascinated as public opinion polls repeatedly showed Panić ahead of Milošević. However, by making use of a number of techniques, including holding up approval of Panić's candidacy until late in the race, using the media to slander Panić, and invalidating the registration of many voters who might be inclined to support the opposition, Milošević assured himself of a victory on election day.[33] In the wake of the elections, Milošević engineered the removal of Panić from the prime ministership.

Meanwhile, Ćosić was making himself all too visible. In early December he visited the command of the First Army at Topčider and addressed the assembled officers as their "supreme commander."[34] Subsequently, in May 1993, Ćosić met with army officers to discuss solutions to the "malfunctioning" of the state.[35] Milošević sensed danger and moved quickly, removing Ćosić, his supposed political superior, as FRY president on 1 June. The next day, when Vuk Drašković, his wife, Danica, and other opposition figures led a large rally protesting the unconstitutional removal of Ćosić, Milošević had the Draškovićes and several dozen other oppositionists arrested. The Draškovićes were handcuffed and then beaten by police, and Vuk Drašković had to be hospitalized. The charges lodged against the Draškovićes were only dropped after the personal intervention of Danielle Mitterrand (wife of the French president) and after an appeal from the Russian government.[36]

No sooner had Milošević disposed of Ćosić, though, than there were renewed signs of trouble within the military. Accordingly, on 26 August, Milošević executed an extensive purge of the army high command, relieving forty-two high-ranking officers of their positions. Among those sent into retirement was Života Panić (no relation to Milan Panić), the chief of the General Staff.[37]

The continued prosecution of the war in Bosnia, which dragged on much longer than either Milošević or Karadžić had expected, had several effects within Serbia. To begin with, the waxing nationalist temper colored the cultural sector, giving birth to bottles of perfume called "Serb" and shaped like hand grenades,[38] revisions of school textbooks (raising Chetnik leader Draža Mihailović to hero status and dwelling at length on Croatian Archbishop Alojzije Stepinac for the purpose of demonizing him),[39] and passionate expressions of alarm on the part of Serbian Minister of Culture Nada Popović-Perišić about the alleged infiltration of Islamic and Turkish elements into Serbian folk music, producing what she has called "a hideous mixture of hip-hop, techno rhythms, antiquated disco music, Arabic yowling, and Bosnian love songs."[40]

Then there has been the economic impact. In 1993 alone, the FRY treasury spent $1.176 billion on arms, materiel, and other supplies for the Serbian militias in Bosnia and Croatia.[41] This large outlay resulted in the general impoverishment of the citizenry[42] (a result that was to some extent reinforced by the economic sanctions). The war also resulted in a proliferation of crime,[43] a veritable explosion of sex-related industries, and a "brain drain" which deprived Serbia of some of its finest artistic, scientific, and political talent.[44] It has also, thanks in no small part to the unremitting chauvinist line adopted by Belgrade Television, resulted in the deepening of ethnic and religious intolerance and in a general poisoning of the political atmosphere. The violence condoned against non-Serbs infected Serbia itself, and there was a dramatic increase in hate crimes within that country.[45] Writing in the pages of the Belgrade newsweekly, *NIN*, Svetlana Djurdjević-Lukić reflected in sorrow:

> We are becoming accustomed to ever more terrible things. Who still remembers the kidnapping of 17 Muslims from Sjeverin, the exodus from Hrtovci, Nikinci, Priboj? ... the machine gunning of houses, the bombs that have been thrown, the firing on the Catholic Church in Novi Slankamen, the demolition of the 230-year-old Catholic church in Banovci, the shops of Muslims set on fire in Pljevlja, the mistreatment of schoolchildren of Slovak nationality in Kisač, the shootings at the mosque in Novi Sad and the detention of activists of the Islamic community there during Ramadan, the Hungarian houses set on fire in Irig, the murder of Omar Omerović and Jasmica Klinger in Belgrade . . . memory is getting too short. By and large there is no information about the attackers.[46]

Research conducted in 1993 by the Social Sciences Institute in Belgrade found that about two-thirds of the citizens of the FRY displayed some form of xenophobia.[47] Not surprisingly, this widespread xenophobia has undermined support for a democratic system, as a telephone poll taken by *NIN* in August 1993 showed. Indeed, according to that poll, a clear majority of respondents were skeptical of the reliability of a parliamentary system and told *NIN* that they did "not believe that it is possible to coordinate differing views without a strong authoritarian leader."[48]

Even so, the economic strains raised questions in many people's minds as to just how long Milošević, and Serbia for that matter, could survive.[49] By August 1993, the quickening inflation had reached an annual rate of 32 million percent,[50] and official unemployment was pegged at 750,000, with another 1 million people holding largely nominal jobs in which they drew salaries, but did little that was productive in nature (often because the lack of raw materials and machine parts had rendered many enterprises inoperative).[51] Serbia was, by then, home to 461,653 refugees, about two-thirds of them from Bosnia-Herzegovina.[52] Industrial production, exports, and labor productivity all fell, and living standards were reportedly falling at a rate of 4 percent per month.[53] By November, the monetary system was said to be near collapse and the Serbian press had published reports documenting the regime's widespread plundering of citizens' bank accounts.[54]

Meanwhile, with the virtual elimination of Ćosić, Panić, and Crown Prince Aleksandar as credible opponents, and with the demonstration of Drašković's vulnerability in the most obvious way, only Vojislav Šešelj, leader of the Serbian Radical Party (SRP), remained as a potential threat to Milošević. In September 1993, Šešelj broke with Milošević and set up a shadow government in Serbia, with Tomislav Nikolić, deputy chair of the SRP, as nominal chief of the shadow cabinet.[55] The following month, the party's Montenegrin branch set up a shadow cabinet in that republic as well, naming Drago Bakrac, an economist from Nikšić, as its head.[56] For a time, Šešelj was ranked by many as the most popular politician in Serbia, even more popular than Željko Raznjatović, better known as "Arkan." Even at this writing, despite Milošević's "disciplining" of Šešelj, Šešelj is by no means out of the game.

With the economy spinning rapidly out of control, Milošević made a bold move in December 1993, appointing Dragoslav Avramović, a hitherto little-known economist, to put together an austerity program. Avramović halted the inflationary hyperactivity of the Belgrade mint, reformed the currency, pegged the new dinar to the German mark, and overnight slashed inflation to minus 0.6 percent.[57] But the stabilization measures did not hold, and by October 1994 the dinar was slipping against the mark, prices were shooting upward once more, and electricity producers were pressing for government approval of a potentially inflationary increase of electricity prices by 50 percent.[58] The proliferation of boutiques[59] and brothels was no substitute for a healthy, productive economy.

With television controlled by the Milošević regime, the Serbian theater has offered Serbs an alternative point of view. Already in 1991, on the eve of war, Lazar Stojanović produced a revised version of Aristophanes' *The Acharnians* at a theater in Subotica, a city with a large Hungarian population. As Stojanović recalled, "In the play a man tries to draw the attention of the Athens assembly to the war with Sparta, but they will not listen. I changed the names of the cities to Belgrade and Zagreb."[60] Two years later, Belgrade audiences were treated to Aleksandar Popović's play *Dark Is the Night*, which explored a young man's reaction to being called up for military duty. Manojlo agonizes about taking flight (as more than 200,000 of his compatriots did, under similar circumstances, in order to avoid military service), but finally decides to go to the front, where he shoots himself in the leg, however. The play became an overnight success.[61]

A 1994 film, *Tito: For the Second Time Among the Serbs*, touched an even more sensitive subject: the officially orchestrated Titophobia among today's Serbs. The brainchild of Zelimir Zilnik, the film is a sort of documentary in which actor Drajoljub Ljubičić, attired as the late Marshal Tito, walked about Belgrade, interacting with whomever he met. Set up, thus, as a kind of Serbian version of *Candid Camera*, the film records that people were all too ready to talk to "Tito" as if he really were Tito.

"I'm a Serb and you are a Croat," said one man, "but I used to admire you." Another said he had been part of an honor guard at Tito's funeral. "Yes, I remember you," responded Tito encouragingly. The man went on: "You were everything for us, you used to warm us like the sun." But another said: "You are guilty, you are a bandit, you hated Serbs."

One man explained to Tito that now "everyone has their own flag, state and coat of arms. For only two hills, 200–300 boys must die." An old man stopped to accuse him of being pro-American and betraying the Soviet Union in 1948.

Slobodan Stupar, deputy director of Radio B-92, which commissioned the film, said that it was a terrible reflection of Serbia in the mid-1990s. "It shows that the common people have lost touch with reality. Everything you tell them through the media they absorb like a sponge."[62]

As a result of the 19 December 1993 elections, Milošević's Socialist Party of Serbia was able to strengthen its hold on parliament, capturing 123 of the 250 seats in the Assembly (as compared with the 101 they controlled in the outgoing Assembly). After those elections, internal challengers were clearly weakened, and the chief challenge to Milošević's authority among Serbs would come from the leaders of the Serbian forces in Croatia and Bosnia: Milan Martić, elected president of the Serbian Krajina (occupied Croatia) in March 1994, and Radovan Karadžić, leader of the Bosnian Serb forces.

Desperate for an easing of the U.N. sanctions, Milošević began advocating a negotiated solution already at the onset of 1994 and took pains to portray himself to Western audiences as a man of peace, a moderate. In particular, Milošević urged Karadžić to settle for control of 49 percent of Bosnia's territory—a suggestion that Karadžić found unacceptable. It is a complicated game that Milošević has been playing, for it is his advocacy of a Greater Serbia that has been his single greatest source of legitimation, and any attenuation of his support for that goal could alienate the very groups upon whose support he is dependent. One indication of this dilemma is that as his conflict with Karadžić (to be discussed more fully in Chapter 10) developed, Patriarch Pavle came out in strong support of Karadžić, while the army high command, albeit twice purged, once again showed signs of disquietude. By October 1994, rumors of the impending resignation of the current chief of staff, General Momčilo Perišić, were spreading, thus providing clear evidence of the tenuous authority that Milošević has enjoyed with his army officers.[63]

Milošević consolidated his power by mobilizing society, by exploiting the wider nationalist potential of a reawakening of civil society in Serbia. But this reawakening of civil society did not lead, as some theoreticians would have had it, to the emergence of a democratic system. The reason, as Tomaz Mastnak has insightfully noted, is that "[although] civil society is a necessary condition of democracy, it is not necessarily democratic itself. If there is no democracy without civil society, it is still not impossible to imagine civil society without, or [even] acting against, democracy."[64] One of Milošević's first acts at the end of 1987 was to assert his control over Radio-Television Belgrade and over the Politika publishing, house, which publishes *NIN*, *Politika*, and *Politika ekspres*. The daily newspaper *Borba* and the weekly magazine *Vreme* remained independent. But in December 1994 Milošević succeeded in placing his information minister, Dragutin Bršin, in charge of *Borba*, thus snuffing out this respected paper's independence.[65] After Milošević came to power, the number of police in Serbia doubled to 110,000,[66] and by late 1994, according to opposition politician Zoran Djindjić, authorities were tapping the telephones of virtually anyone of any importance.[67] Serbia had become a police state.

An Independent Croatia

The seven months of intense fighting that "ended," in a manner of speaking, in February 1992 had taken a bitter toll in Croatia. Between 6,000 and 10,000 persons were dead as a result of the fighting, total material damage was estimated at $18.7 billion, 400,000 were homeless, and one-third of the republic was occupied by hostile forces.[68] Gross industrial production had declined 28.5 percent in 1991 and was to decline another 14.6 percent in 1992. Inflation, which had reached 123 percent in 1991, climbed to 665.5 percent the following year. Net income declined both years, at an accelerating rate, while unemployment rose from 16.4 percent in 1991 to 17.2 percent in 1992. Tourism, the mainstay of the Croatian economy, had crashed by 80.7 percent in 1991 and registered only a meager 5.7 percent revival in 1992.[69] Given all of this, the first priority of the Croatian government in 1992 was to put the economy on a sound footing. Moreover, Croatia confronted this challenge just as the war in Bosnia was raging and as refugees from this new front continued to stream into Croatia. By summer 1994 there were more than 600,000 refugees in Croatia, many of them in Zagreb.

In fact, on most measures Croatia made little headway with its economy in 1993. True enough, Croatia did rebuild its foreign currency reserves and make further progress in reviving its tourist trade, but gross industrial production, exports, and net income all declined that year. As of October 1993, the Croatian economy was on the brink of collapse, and Nikica Valentić, Croatian prime minister since March 1993, now introduced a draconian austerity program which slashed state spending, reformed the currency (pegging it to the German mark), and actually succeeded, by May 1994, in achieving a *negative* inflation rate, as prices started to decline modestly.[70] As the new program began to take effect, Croatia registered its first increase in net income since 1990 and reduced unemployment to the lowest level since 1991.[71]

In late June 1994, Croatia received a significant economic boost from the outside in the form of a World Bank loan for $128 million, to be used to reconstruct buildings and repave roads and streets which had been destroyed in earlier fighting.[72] By August, the monthly inflation rate had been cut to less than 1 percent, and hard currency reserves were pegged at $2 billion and growing. On the other hand, although Croatia had been the first of the Yugoslav successor states to pass legislation concerning privatization,[73] the continuance of the war and efforts on the part of old interest groups to maintain their preexisting privileges, in tandem, contributed to preserving economic-administrative structures virtually intact.[74] Indeed, as of November 1994,

Croatia had succeeded in privatizing only about one-fifth of its social capital.[75] But the tourist sector was expected to bring in $1.3 billion in 1994, which represented a tangible increase over 1993.

It should not be forgotten that the Serbian occupation of one-third of Croatian territory had an enormous impact on the overall economy, even leaving aside the war costs and the burden of refugees.[76] Occupied lands in Slavonia and Baranja include rich agricultural soil, for example, with oil fields at Djeletovci, Privlaka (just south of Vinkovci), and Ilača, which Serbian forces were quick to exploit.[77]

There have been at least five issues that have divided the Croatian political elites since 1991: first, the balance of power between the president and the parliament; second, Croatian nationalism, reflected in sundry issues; third, the prosecution of the war; fourth, freedom of the press; and fifth, the status of ethnic and regional peripheries (to be examined in the following section). I shall take these up in sequence.

Presidential vs. Parliamentary Power

From the beginning, it was clear that Franjo Tudjman, elected president in spring 1990, tended to interpret his role as that of "good shepherd" rather than "leading citizen." Indeed, research conducted among Croatian voters by Ivan Šiber at the time found a high degree of authoritarianism among voters, including both those who voted for left-wing parties and those who voted right-of-center.[78] It soon became apparent that the *Sabor* (the parliament) had little say in matters of the war or of diplomacy, and members of the parliament started to complain about what they called the marginalization of the *Sabor*.[79] This dispute was personified in a clash between President Tudjman and Stipe Mesić, a high-ranking figure in Tudjman's Croatian Democratic Community (CDC) and the president of the *Sabor*. Mesić became increasingly frustrated with what he saw as guileless authoritarianism on Tudjman's part and finally, in spring 1994, broke with Tudjman and, together with several other disgruntled figures in the CDC, set up a new party, the Croatian Independent Democratic Party.[80] Moreover, among the opposition generally there was a widespread belief that the electoral units and electoral laws drawn up by the CDC were designed with an eye to assuring and maximizing its victory.[81] Indeed, a CSCE delegation visiting Croatia 30 July–4 August 1992 concluded that "the [2 August] 1992 elections in Croatia cannot be held as a model for what free and fair elections should be."[82]

Croatian Nationalism

Croatia's new nationalism, which enjoys the wholehearted support of Tudjman's CDC, has been expressed in sundry ways, from the publication of a Croatian orthography, which had been prepared originally in the early 1970s but the publication of which had been held up for political reasons,[83] to the erection of a monument to Croatian fighters killed by Tito's Partisans at Bleiburg in 1945,[84] to the revamping of the Croatian language with idiosyncratic neologisms and restored archaicisms, for the purpose of building up differences from Serbian.[85] The new currency, the kuna, was chosen for nationalist reasons, the name having a resonance with memories of the medieval Croatian state; unfortunately, the kuna was also the currency of fascist Croatia during World War II—a fact which upset Serbs of Croatia. In April 1992, a dispute concerning references to Yugoslavia in school textbooks led to the resignations of the minister of the interior and the minister of education and culture. The following month, the minister of justice and administration, Bosiljko Misetić, resigned to protest the adoption of legislation extending special status to Serbs in those districts where they constituted an absolute majority.

The new nationalism has been controversial from the start. Stipe Mesić, for example, upon joining the CDC, pointedly advocated that policies be based on the spirit of tolerance.[86] Ivo Banac, a Yale professor who has enjoyed a parallel career engaging in polemics in the pages of Croatian newspapers and magazines, sharply criticized the Tudjman government for having suppressed any veneration of Ljudevit Gaj and Bishop Josip Juraj Strossmayer.[87] The latter, in particular, is the historical embodiment of "Yugoslavism," melding Croatian nationalism with an embracive attitude toward other South Slavs.[88] Its critics notwithstanding, the CDC pushed ahead with policies ill suited to winning, let us say, Serbian trust;[89] for example, soon after taking power the CDC restaffed the police forces, relieving many Serbs who had been police officers all their lives, and replaced enterprise managers of Serbian ethnicity with Croats.[90] The CDC soon found itself accused of anti-Semitism, Serbophobia above and beyond what was justified by the war, and misogyny. Indeed, given the atmosphere which has prevailed in Croatia since 1990, thousands of Croatian citizens with "un-Croat"-sounding names changed their names to more Croatian variants; most of those concerned were Serbs, changing names like Jovanka and Jovan into Ivanka and Ivan.[91]

The Prosecution of the War

Franjo Tudjman took office with a reputation as a nationalist. Already on the eve of his election, *Borba* quoted a spokesperson for Tudjman as pledging that Croatia would expand into Bosnia-Herzegovina and annex parts of that republic.[92] Tudjman held firm to this position, telling a press conference on 6 September 1993, "The acceptance of Bosnia-Herzegovina as a unity state would endanger the survival of the Croatian people, as well as the strategic interests of the Republic of Croatia. Therefore, the Croatian people will hold onto those regions in Bosnia-Herzegovina in which Croats constitute a majority."[93]

The Croatian government has held that the pre-July 1991 borders of the Republic of Croatia should be treated as inviolate because they were the administrative borders which had been set down for more than fifty years and because the Serbs constituted a small minority (12.2 percent). On the other hand, Zagreb has wanted to treat the pre-April 1992 borders of the Republic of Bosnia-Herzegovina as open to redefinition, whether by negotiation or by force. This inconsistency was responsible for a significant portion of the bad press that the Republic of Croatia received in the United States and England in the years following the breakup of Yugoslavia. Internal critics realized this. Thus, for example, the independent daily *Novi list* wrote in February 1994: "Due to Tudjman's politics, we have almost been put in the same basket with the aggressor and gambled away our victim status like a dumb gambler playing roulette."[94]

In fact, for all of their other disagreements (as noted above), the decisive issue that was responsible for the rupture between Mesić and Tudjman was the prosecution of the war in Bosnia. Mesić (among others) lamented the establishment of the Republic of Herceg-Bosna in southwestern Herzegovina in July 1992, which he held responsible for the outbreak of hostilities between Croatian and Muslim forces.[95] Banac, again, assembled materials to document his argument that Zagreb had pursued a mistaken policy in Bosnia, publishing the resulting text in book form in October 1994.[96]

Freedom of the Press

A 1993 report of the Council of Europe found the Tudjman government guilty of having tried to muzzle and control the press and electronic media and of silencing independent journalists, highlighting his government's use of the governmental Agency for Reconstruction and Development (later renamed the Privatization Fund) in taking over media enterprises.[97] Although some shares were sold to private investors, it is the government-controlled Privatization Fund that retained most of the shares, giving the government effective control of such "privatized" media concerns.[98] The government takeover of *Vjesnik* and *Večernji list,* suppression of *Start,* suppression and recreation (under new management) of *Danas,* and harassment of *Slobodna Dalmacija* were all symptoms of the Zagreb government's desire to control the information system within the republic. From the beginning, the government used its control of the media to enforce conformity in views. In November 1993, the Croatian Association of Press Reporters took advantage of the continued independence of *Novi list* to publish the following text:

> Lately we have witnessed [a] disturbingly large number of texts and programs in the Croatian media that are crude violations of the laws and fundamental norms of the journalist code.
>
> Certain editorial offices systematically publish writings in which individuals who have different opinions are insulted, labeled, or called to responsibility, and it is not rare that entire peoples are insulted. It all contributes to the atmosphere of persecution, fear, and insecurity, and the frequency with which certain editorial offices publish these text-warrants of arrest gives rise to the suspicion that it is a matter of a calculated editorial policy.[99]

Perhaps more than any other single issue, Tudjman's treatment of the media has contributed to the impression that he is an old-fashioned authoritarian without much tolerance for diversity.[100]

In combination, these four issues have profoundly alienated a large section of the opposition. For all that, Tudjman remained, throughout the 1990s, clearly the most popular politician in Croatia, holding on to 40.5 percent of the votes in a November 1994 opinion poll conducted by *Globus* (up slightly from 38.6 percent in March 1992).[101] This put him comfortably ahead of his closest challenger, Dražen Budiša, chair of the Croatian Social Liberal Party (20.6 percent in October 1994). Aside from Tudjman and Budiša, no one could claim to be the preference of more than 5.6 percent of the electorate (that tally going to the extreme-right politician, Ante Djapić), according to the *Globus* poll. Ivica Račan, chair of the former Communist Party, who had polled 1.5 percent of the vote in an October survey,[102] talked of rebuilding the left, however, and as of July 1994 was said to be working on a comprehensive sociopolitical program for change,[103] but in the November poll, Račan received no votes at all.

Meanwhile, against the backdrop of economic difficulties and political controversies, the war continued, not only in Bosnia but also in Croatia, truce or no truce. In January 1993, Croatian forces launched an offensive across U.N. lines into Serb-held Krajina. In March 1993, there was an escalation in fighting when the Croatian army launched an offensive in northern Dalmatia.[104] Fighting continued in occupied areas of Croatia until early 1994, amid rumors that the Croatian and Serbian sides might agree on a swap of land, perhaps exchanging parts of Bosnia occupied by Croatian forces for sections of western Slavonia occupied by Serbian forces.[105] In March 1994, the two sides signed another truce. Throughout all of this, Croatian officials declared themselves "prepared to discuss anything with the Serbs from the occupied regions of Croatia 'except the integrity and sovereignty of the Republic of Croatia'"[106]—code for the possibility of political autonomy for Croatian Serbs—while Croatian Serbs, for their part, persistently rejected any form of cohabitation with Croats, including even in the form of a confederated Croatia (a solution that in any case, went beyond anything that the Croats were prepared to discuss).[107]

But on 2 November the so-called Zagreb contact group, consisting of the U.S. and Russian ambassadors in Zagreb, together with representatives of the U.N. and the EC, presented a new peace plan for Croatia. The plan called for the restoration of the so-called Krajina to Croatian sovereignty, but with autonomous status, and the full reintegration of eastern and western Slavonia into Croatia.[108] Russian ambassador Leonid Keresteianets, however, proposed an amendment to this plan, under which eastern Slavonia and Baranja would also be granted status as an autonomous region. The Croatian press immediately termed the entire package "unacceptable."[109] But although Croatian authorities insisted on the restoration of Croatian sovereignty within the pre-July 1991 borders and although Western and Russian diplomats expressed their usual optimism that their plan might prove acceptable to both sides, Belgrade pointedly declared its unwillingness to countenance any discussion of what it now called the AVNOJ borders.[110]

ETHNIC PERIPHERIES

The war has mobilized ethnic peripheries in both Serbia and Croatia, thus deepening the divisiveness of both political landscapes. In Serbia, the most important ethnic peripheries are the Albanians of Kosovo (1,686,661 as of 1991), the Hungarians of the Vojvodina (345,376), and the Muslims of the Sandžak (237,358).[111] In Croatia, the "Istrians," a regionally defined group composed of Italians, offspring of Italian-Croatian mixed marriages, and Croats living in Istria, have been politically vocal since the election of Franjo Tudjman in 1990, and their largest political party, the Istrian Democratic Party (IDP) captured 72 percent of votes cast in local elections in February 1993.[112] In 1991, there were 19,041 Italians recorded as living in Croatia.[113]

In practice, these ethnic peripheries have received drastically different treatment. In Serbia, for example, the Albanians of Kosovo were removed from all positions of responsibility; even Albanian physicians were fired and replaced by Serbs. Although 90 percent of the population of Kosovo was ethnic Albanian, the University of Priština was converted to strictly Serbian language in autumn 1990; at the same time, all Albanian-language instruction from elementary through university was terminated. Albanian-language radio service was curtailed, the Albanian-language newspaper *Rilindja* was shut down, even the elected parliament was suppressed. Where Kosovo gave indication of its Albanian heritage, until 1992, in the many towns, streets, and public squares bearing Albanian names, these were all changed, beginning in the latter part of that year. Meanwhile, authorities distributed firearms to local Serbian residents, while conducting periodic house searches of Albanian residents, to make certain that they had no firearms of their own.[114] Serbian police arrested intellectuals and other influential persons in the Albanian community, subjecting them to torture, and beginning in summer 1993 conducted unwarranted searches, beaten Albanians of all ages, and otherwise terrorized Albanian villagers with the aim of driving them from their homes.[115] By 1992, if not before, most of the Albanians of Kosovo had given up on Serbia and were talking in terms of secession and the creation of an independent state not conjoined (at least in the interim) with Albania.[116]

By contrast, none of the other ethnic peripheries have been treated as cruelly, and none of them have deemed it necessary to push for secession. Both the Hungarians of Vojvodina and the Muslims of the Sandžak repeatedly petitioned Belgrade to grant regional autonomy—in the case of the Hungarians, requesting no more than the restoration of the status they had enjoyed, together with local Serbs, prior to 1989. Yet although both groups tried to emphasize their loyalty, both were subjected to active policies of discrimination, harassment, and, according to some sources, "ethnic cleansing."[117] Under these pressures, an estimated 69,000 Muslims had fled the Sandžak by summer 1993, while 60,000 ethnic Hungarians and 40,000 Croats had fled Vojvodina by spring 1994.[118] Meanwhile, Serb authorities had begun settling Serb refugees from Bosnia in Vojvodina, thus changing the ethnic composition of the region and provoking protests on the part of the Federation of Hungarians in Vojvodina.[119]

Finally, there is the case of Istria, a hitherto quiescent region which has become politically aware and which has defined its cultural and political needs as distinct from those of the rest of Croatia. The Istrian Democratic Party has demanded autonomy for Istria, as a protection against "the forcible 'Croatization of Istria' and the imposition of a coarse and fanatical Croatism, as they put it—of the 'Herzegovinan type.' "[120] Furio Radin, an IDP deputy in the Croatian *Sabor*, argued that such autonomy was vital for the cultural protection of the Italian minority in Istria.[121] But popular demands for the grant of regional autonomy run deeper and are also voiced by many Croats living in Istria.[122] Hostile to anything smacking of "disunity," the Tudjman government has rebuffed such demands and even set into motion administrative "reforms" designed to divide Istria among several juridical units.[123]

Conclusion

It is not my purpose here to suggest that the political programs of Croatia and Serbia be equated. To begin with, there is nothing comparable, in Croatia, to the kind of *apartheid* and "ethnic cleansing" to which the Albanians of Kosovo have been subjected. And although there are some striking similarities in the ideologies of Milošević and Tudjman, most particularly when it comes to Bosnia, they have treated both their political rivals and their ethnic peripheries rather differently. I would add that the ostensible stability of Milošević's rule is deceptive. Although repeated predictions that he was about to be removed from power, or would resign, have all proven mistaken, there is some basis for thinking that his rule may depend on the perpetuation of crisis and the constant stoking of hatred.

Setting aside these and other differences, what Serbia and Croatia have in common is that they have become mired in an ethnic war that not only inflames their respective nationalisms and deepens ethnic hatreds, but also creates diverse complications for the twin tasks of economic recovery and economic privatization. The war has allowed the respective ruling parties to engage in seductive oversimplifications of complex issues, to marginalize the representatives of minority interests (whether ethnic or otherwise), and to harness nationalism as a false principle of legitimation.[124] This last process is, by its very nature, ill equipped to provide a basis for the construction of democracy. To the extent that one may judge Serbia to be more fully in the grips of nationalism, one may conclude, in that event, that although Croatia's path to democracy is strewn with obstacles, Serbia does not seem to be on that path at all.

As Vesna Pusić has wisely pointed out,

> Reducing the legitimacy of the government to elections is not a way to restrict democracy, but a way to abolish democracy. . . . General programs that are valuated at the elections are far less important for the citizens than the practice of government, the way policies are implemented, the opportunity to supervise the executive, the degree of protection offered to them by the state, and the efficiency of the instruments of protection against the state at their disposal ... [as well as] "the level of security minorities enjoy."[125]

Failing to measure up to this standard, neither Milošević's Serbia nor Tudjman's Croatia can be said to qualify as democracies, but only, as Pusić puts it, *dictatorships with [the superficial trappings of] democratic legitimacy.*

Notes

1. Borislav Pekić, *The Houses of Belgrade,* trans. from Serbo-Croatian by Bernard Johnson (Evanston, Ill.: Northwestern University Press, 1994), p. 172; emphases as in original.

2. Ibid., p. 111.

3. Danilo Kiš, *Garden, Ashes,* trans. from Serbo-Croatian by William J. Hannaher (Boston: Faber & Faber, 1978), p. 35.

4. Ibid., p. 50.

5. "The Book of Kings and Fools," in Danilo Kiš, *The Encyclopedia of the Dead,* trans. from Serbo-Croatian by Michael Henry Heim (New York: Penguin Books, 1989), pp. 133–174.

6. Gojko Djogo, *Vunena Vremena* (Belgrade: Srpska Književna Zadruga & Beogradski Izdavačko-grafički zavod, reissued 1992).

7. Radovan V. Karadžić, *Pamtivek* (Sarajevo: Svjetlost Izdavačko Preduzeće, 1971).

8. Details in Leonore Scheffler, "Goli otok. Das Jahr 1948 in den jugoslawischen Gegenwartsliteraturen," *Südost Europa,* Vol. 33, No. 6 (June 1984), pp. 355–356.

9. The remainder of this paragraph and the next paragraph are closely paraphrased from Pedro Ramet, "Apocalypse Culture and Social Change in Yugoslavia," in Pedro Ramet, ed., *Yugoslavia in the 1980s* (Boulder, Colo.: Westview Press, 1985), p. 13.

10. Vuk Drašković, *Nož,* 3d ed. (Belgrade: Zapis, 1984).

11. Heinz Klunker, "Die Taubenschlucht öffnet sich," *Theater Heute* (September 1983), p. 20; *Kroatische Berichte,* Vol. 8, No. 1 (1983), p. 7; and *Der Spiegel* (Hamburg) (24 January 1983), pp. 109–110. See also Jovan Radulović, *Braća po materi: savremena proza* (Belgrade: Prosveta, 1987).

12. Details in Sabrina Petra Ramet, *Nationalism and Federalism, 1962–1991,* 2d ed. (Bloomington: Indiana University Press, 1992), pp. 25, 179.

13. Dobrica Ćosić, *South to Destiny,* Vol. 4 of *This Land, This Time* [the English title provided for *Vreme smrti*], trans. from the Serbian by Muriel Heppell (New York: Harcourt Brace Jovanovich, 1981), p. 59.

14. Ibid., p. 41.

15. Ibid., p. 81.

16. Ibid., p. 145. Regarding the role of Ćosić's *Vreme smrti* in mobilizing Serbian nationalism, see Heiko Flottau, "Alle Geschichten, giftige Hetze, verblasene Träume," in *Süddeutsche Zeitung-Wochenende* supplement (Munich), 2–3 September 1995, p. 37. Another important Serbian novel about war is Miodrag Bulatović, *Der Krieg war besser,* trans. from Serbo-Croat into German by Fred Wagner (Munich: Carl Hanser, 1968).

17. Danko Popović, *Knjiga o Milutinu* (Belgrade, 1986).

18. *Daily Telegraph* (London) (14 March 1991), p. 12.

19. *Süddeutsche Zeitung* (Munich) (4–5 September 1993), p. 7.

20. *Seattle Times* (29 September 1994), p. A12. An eight-month jail term was later added on a second assault charge. For details, see Tanjug (28 October 1994), in Foreign Broadcast Information Service (FBIS), *Daily Report* (Eastern Europe), 31 October 1994, p. 58.

21. *Eastern Europe Newsletter,* Vol. 6, No. 6 (16 March 1992), p. 6.

22. Paul Shoup, "Serbia at the Edge of the Abyss," *RFE/RL Research Report,* Vol. 1, No. 36 (11 September 1992), p. 13.

23. *Süddeutsche Zeitung* (20 May 1992), p. 5.

24. Quoted in Tanjug (28 May 1992), trans. in FBIS, *Daily Report* (Eastern Europe), 29 May 1992, p. 57.

25. *Salzburger Nachrichten* (12 June 1992), p. 4.

26. *Borba* (Belgrade) (12 May 1992), p. 13.

27. *Večernje novosti* (Belgrade) (16 June 1992), p. 6.

28. *Vreme* (Belgrade) (15 June 1992), pp. 18–21.

29. Tanjug (14 June 1992), trans. in FBIS, *Daily Report* (Eastern Europe), 15 June 1992, p. 42.

30. Shoup, "Serbia at the Edge of the Abyss," p. 8.

31. Tanjug (28 April 1992), in FBIS, *Daily Report* (Eastern Europe), 29 April 1992, p. 54; *Neue Zürcher Zeitung* (29 April 1992), p. 1; and *International Herald Tribune* (Paris ed.) (15 July 1992), p. 2.

32. Dobrica Ćosić, in interview with Momčilo Pantelić, editor-in-chief of *Politika*, in *Politika* (Belgrade) (16 October 1992), trans. in FBIS, *Daily Report* (Eastern Europe), 5 November 1992, p. 49.

33. Further details in Douglas E. Schoen, "How Milošević Stole the Elections," in *New York Times Magazine* (14 February 1993). See also *Neue Zürcher Zeitung* (19 December 1992), p. 5; and Milan Panić, *So!* (Belgrade: Plato, 1992).

34. RTB Television Network (Belgrade), 8 December 1992, trans. in FBIS, *Daily Report* (Eastern Europe), 9 December 1992, p. 40.

35. *Vjesnik* (Zagreb) (2 June 1993), p. 9; and *Glas Istre* (Pula) (2 June 1993), p. 16.

36. *International Herald Tribune* (Tokyo ed.) (3 June 1993), pp. 1, 4; *Vjesnik* (4 June 1993), p. 9; *Glas Istre* (6 June 1993), p. 5; *The Times* (London) (7 June 1993), p. 12; *Frankfurter Allgemeine* (8 July 1993), p. 2; and *Süddeutsche Zeitung* (16 July 1993), p. 7. For more extensive discussion, see "Belgrade Demonstrations: Excessive Use of Force and Beatings in Detention," *Helsinki Watch*, Vol. 5, No. 13 (August 1993).

37. Tanjug (26 August 1993), trans. in *FBIS, Daily Report* (Eastern Europe), 27 August 1993, p. 41; and *Süddeutsche Zeitung* (1 September 1993), p. 7.

38. See photo and caption in *Japan Times* (18 April 1994), p. 6.

39. The new Serbian school textbooks also pay virtually no attention to the 1903 constitution and the decade of multiparty democracy that followed it. See *The Woodrow Wilson Center, East European Studies*, Meeting report (November–December 1994), p. 9.

40. Quoted in *The Economist* (London) (9 July 1994), p. 88.

41. *Japan Times* (6 March 1994), p. 10.

42. According to a September 1993 Tanjug report, some 90 percent of inhabitants of the FRY were near or below the poverty line. See Tanjug (3 September 1993), in FBIS, *Daily Report* (Eastern Europe), 3 September 1993, p. 25. See also *Ekonomska politika* (Belgrade), No. 2171 (15 November 1993), pp. 6–9.

43. Regarding crime in Serbia, see *Borba* (24 February 1993), p. 7; *Politika* (11 March 1993), p. 1, and (8 August 1993), p. 7; and *Vreme* (23 August 1993), pp. 33–34.

44. Regarding the "brain drain," see *Borba* (22 March 1993), p. 7.

45. See *Dnevnik* (Ljubljana) (5 February 1993), p. 9, trans. in FBIS, *Daily Report* (Eastern Europe), 2 March 1993, pp. 68–69.

46. *NIN* (Belgrade) (12 February 1993), trans. in FBIS, *Daily Report* (Eastern Europe), 4 March 1993, p. 70.

47. Ibid.

48. *NIN* (20 August 1993), p. 15, trans. in FBIS, *Daily Report* (Eastern Europe), 15 September 1993, p. 50.

49. For an excellent treatment of this question, see M. R. Palairet, "How Long Can the Milošević Regime Withstand Sanctions?" *RFE/RL Research Report* (27 August 1993).

50. Radio Belgrade Network (Belgrade), 30 August 1993, trans. in FBIS, *Daily Report* (Eastern Europe), 31 August 1993, p. 68.

51. Jelica Minić, "The Black Economy in Serbia: Transition from Socialism?" *RFE/RL Research Report* (27 August 1993), p. 26.

52. Tanjug (8 March 1993), in FBIS, *Daily Report* (Eastern Europe), 9 March 1993, p. 58.

53. David Dyker and Vesna Bojičić, "The Impact of Sanctions on the Serbian Economy" in *RFE/RL Research Report* (21 May 1993), pp. 51–52.

54. Regarding the monetary system, see Tanjug (9 November 1993), in FBIS, *Daily Report* (Eastern Europe), 10 November 1993, p. 57. Regarding the state's plundering of its citizens, see *Vreme* (9 August 1993), pp. 28–29, trans. in FBIS, *Daily Report* (Eastern Europe), 31 August 1993, pp. 69–71.

55. *Süddeutsche Zeitung* (4–5 September 1993), p. 7.

56. Tanjug (27 October 1993), trans. in FBIS, *Daily Report* (Eastern Europe), 27 October 1993, p. 30.

57. *Japan Times* (6 March 1994), p. 10.

58. *Eastern Europe Newsletter*, Vol. 8, No. 20 (5 October 1994), p. 8.

59. *Ekonomska politika* (Belgrade) (22 February 1993), p. 13.

60. Quoted in *The Economist* (London) (18 December 1993), p. 80.

61. Ibid.

62. *The Economist* (30 April 1994), pp. 96–97.

63. *New York Times* (25 October 1994), p. A7.

64. Tomaz Mastnak, "From the New Social Movements to Political Parties," in James Simmie and Jože Dekleva, eds., *Yugoslavia in Turmoil: After Self-Management* (London and New York: Pinter, 1991), p. 50.

65. *Welt am Sonntag* (25 December 1994), p. 2.

66. *Financial Times* (7 October 1994), p. 3.

67. *Borba* (28 October 1994), p. 1, trans. in FBIS, *Daily Report* (Eastern Europe), 31 October 1994, p. 59.

68. Casualty figures in *New York Times* (28 February 1992), p. A3. Figure for material damage in *Borba* (23 March 1992), p. 11.

69. *Neue Zürcher Zeitung* (13 July 1994), p. 11.

70. *The European* (London) (1–7 July 1994), p. 20.

71. Unemployment was pegged at 16.5 percent in April 1994, by comparison with 16.4 percent in December 1991. *Neue Zürcher Zeitung* (13 July 1994), p. 11.

72. *Slobodna Dalmacija* (Split) (24 June 1994), p. 11; *Večernji list* (Zagreb) (24 June 1994), p. 3; and *Neue Zürcher Zeitung* (30 June 1994), p. 12.

73. Ivo Bićanić, "Privatization in Croatia," *East European Politics and Societies*, Vol. 7, No. 3 (fall 1993), p. 425.

74. *RFE/RL News Briefs* (11 August 1994), p. 16. See also *Neue Zürcher Zeitung* (20 July 1994), pp. 7–8.

75. *Globus* (Zagreb) (11 November 1994), p. 6. See also *Nedjeljna Dalmacija* (Split) (25 November 1994), p. 23.

76. Regarding refugees in Croatia, see *Danas* (Zagreb) (28 April 1992), pp. 7–10.

77. For details, see *Slobodna Dalmacija* (30 September 1992), p. 7, trans. in FBIS, *Daily Report* (Eastern Europe), 7 October 1992, p. 24.

78. Ivan Šiber, "The Impact of Nationalism, Values, and Ideological Orientations on Multi-Party Elections in Croatia," in Jim Seroka and Vukašin Pavlović, eds., *The Tragedy of Yugoslavia: The Failure of Democratic Transformation* (Armonk, N.Y.: M.E. Sharpe, 1992), p. 167.

79. *Vreme* (25 April 1994), p. 12.

80. *Süddeutsche Zeitung* (25–26 June 1994), p. 8.

81. *Vjesnik* (15 June 1992), p. 10.

82. *Parliamentary and Presidential Elections in an Independent Croatia, August 2, 1992* (Washington, D.C.: CSCE, August 1992), p. 30.

83. *Slobodna Dalmacija* (23 June 1994), p. 8.

84. Ibid., p. 32.

85. *Neue Zürcher Zeitung* (28 May 1994), p. 7.

86. *Novi Vjesnik* (Zagreb) (19 June 1992), p. 5A.

87. Ivo Banac, "Hoće li se Predsjednik Franjo Tudjman uskoro ispricati zbog kune?" *Globus* (Zagreb) (27 May 1994), p. 8.

88. For an elaboration of this aspect of Bishop Strossmayer's career, see Pedro Ramet, "From Strossmayer to Stepinac: Croatian National Ideology and Catholicism," *Canadian Review of Studies in Nationalism*, Vol. 12, No. 1 (spring 1985).

89. This is not to say that Tudjman could have won over the majority of Croatian Serbs even if he had tried, only to suggest that it would have been wise for him to have made a far more serious effort than he did. Certainly, the repeated aspersions cast on Tudjman in the Serbian press would have made it difficult for him, under *any* circumstances, to win the trust of the Serbs. See, for example, "Tudjman—odbrana NDH," *Intervju* (Belgrade), No. 217 (29 September 1989), pp. 49–51.

90. *Human Rights and Democratization in Croatia* (Washington, D.C.: CSCE, September 1993), p. 11.

91. *Borba* (20 January 1993), p. 12.

92. *New York Times* (22 April 1990), p. 11.

93. Quoted in *Vjesnik* (7 September 1993), p. 1.

94. *Novi list* (Rijeka) (13 February 1994), p. 2, trans. in FBIS, *Daily Report* (Eastern Europe), 25 February 1994, p. 51.

95. *Süddeutsche Zeitung* (25–26 June 1994), p. 8.

96. Ivo Banac, *Cijena Bosne*, as discussed in *Ljiljan* (Sarajevo/Ljubljana) (26 October 1994), p. 8.

97. As reported in *Danas* (Zagreb), new series (5 March 1993), trans. in *FBIS, Daily Report* (Eastern Europe), 16 March 1993, p. 52.

98. Vesna Kesić, "The Press in War, the War in the Press: The Press in Croatia," *Uncaptive Minds*, Vol. 6, No. 2 (summer 1993), p. 78. Regarding the government's use of "privatization" to effect *nationalization*, see *Feral Tribune* (Split) (24 October 1994), pp. 6–7, trans. in *FBIS, Daily Report* (Eastern Europe), 16 November 1994, pp. 42–44.

99. *Novi list* (3 November 1993), p. 4, trans. in *FBIS, Daily Report* (Eastern Europe), 8 November 1993, pp. 37–38.

100. For further discussion of the media in Croatia, see Jasmina Kuzmanović, "Media: The Extension of Politics by Other Means," in Sabrina Petra Ramet and Ljubiša S. Adamovich, eds., *Beyond Yugoslavia: Politics, Economics, and Culture in a Shattered Community* (Boulder, Colo.: Westview Press, 1995); and Sabrina Petra Ramet, *Social Currents in Eastern Europe: The Sources and Consequences of the Great Transformation*, 2d ed. (Durham, N.C.: Duke University Press, 1995), pp. 427–428.

101. *Globus* (20 March 1992), p. 8, and (25 November 1994), pp. 16, 49.

102. Ibid., (28 October 1994), p. 4.

103. *Feral Tribune* (25 July 1994), p. 9.

104. Radio Belgrade Network (3 March 1993), trans. in FBIS, *Daily Report* (Eastern Europe), 4 March 1993, p. 43; and Tanjug (24 March 1993), trans. in FBIS, *Daily Report* (Eastern Europe), 24 March 1993, p. 47.

105. This is the version repudiated in Radio Belgrade Network (29 October 1993), trans. in FBIS, *Daily Report* (Eastern Europe), 1 November 1993, p. 39.

106. *Vjesnik* (11 October 1993), p. 1.

107. AFP (Paris) (7 September 1993), trans. in FBIS, *Daily Report* (Eastern Europe), 7 September 1993, p. 44; and *Večernje novosti* (Belgrade) (30 January 1994), p. 2, trans. in FBIS, *Daily Report* (Eastern Europe), 2 February 1994, pp. 23–25.

108. *Neue Zürcher Zeitung* (4 November 1994), p. 1.

109. *Nedjeljna Dalmacija* (4 November 1994), p. 3; also *Globus* (11 November 1994), p. 9.

110. See *Die Welt* (Bonn) (5 November 1994), p. 4. But on 2 December Croatian authorities and Croatian Serbs reached an agreement on economic cooperation. See *Süddeutsche Zeitung* (3–4 December 1994), p. 8; also *Evropske novosti* (Belgrade/Frankfurt) (19 November 1994), p. 3.

111. Figures from the 1991 census, as given in "The National Composition of Yugoslavia's Population, 1991," *Yugoslav Survey* (Belgrade), Vol. 33, No. 1, (1992), No. 1, p. 11. In 1991, unlike in previous censuses, separate nationality figures for Kosovo and Vojvodina were not given. It should be kept in mind, therefore, that while most of the Albanians and Hungarians in Serbia live, respectively, in Kosovo and Vojvodina, there may be some living elsewhere in the republic.

112. "Croatia," in *The Europa World Year Book 1994*, Vol. 1 (London: Europa, 1994), p. 886.

113. "National Composition," p. 7.

114. Further details, together with documentation, in Ramet, *Social Currents in Eastern Europe*, 2nd ed., pp. 422–425. See also Elez Biberaj, "Kosova: The Balkan Powder Keg," in *Conflict Studies*, No. 258 (London: Research Institute for the Study of Conflict and Terrorism, February 1993). As of 1990, the Skopje-based *Flaka e Vellazerimit* was the only Albanian-language newspaper being published in Yugoslavia. Later, however, Belgrade allowed the establishment of a new paper in Albanian, *Bujku*, published in Priština.

115. Details and elaboration in Julie Mertus, *Open Wounds: Human Rights Abuses in Kosovo* (New York: Human Rights Watch, 1993). See also Jens Reuter, "Die politische Entwicklung in Kosovo 1992/93," *Südost Europa*, Vol. 43, Nos. 1–2 (January–February 1994), esp. p. 21.

116. *Rilindja* (Zofingen) (4 March 1993), p. 3, trans. in FBIS, *Daily Report* (Eastern Europe), 18 March 1993, p. 45; *ATA* (Tirana) (23 March 1993), in FBIS, *Daily Report* (Eastern Europe), 24 March 1993, p. 59; and *Süddeutsche Zeitung* (11–12 June 1994), p. 9.

117. For details and documentation of discrimination and harassment in the Vojvodina, see Ramet, *Social Currents in Eastern Europe*, 2d ed., pp. 425–426. For details of discrimination and harassment in the Sandžak, see Commission of Security and Cooperation in Europe, *Sandžak and the CSCE* (Washington, D.C.: CSCE, April 1993); and *Borba* (2 August 1993), p. 13. Regarding charges of "ethnic cleansing" in the Vojvodina, see *NRC Handelsblad* (Rotterdam) (1 March 1993), p. 5, trans. in FBIS, *Daily Report* (Eastern Europe), 9 March 1993, p. 73. Regarding charges of "ethnic cleansing" in the Sandžak, see *Oslobodjenje* (Sarajevo–Ljubljana) (11–18 February 1994), p. 24, trans. in FBIS, *Daily Report* (Eastern Europe), 16 February 1994, pp. 54–55.

118. "Abuses Continue in the Former Yugoslavia: Serbia, Montenegro, and Bosnia-Herce-govina," *Human Rights Watch Helsinki*, Vol. 5, No. 11 (July 1993), p. 13; CSCE, *Sandžak and the CSCE*, pp. 1, 6; "Human Rights Abuses of Non-Serbs in Kosovo, Sandžak and Vojvod-ina," *Human Rights Watch Helsinki*, Vol. 6, No. 6 (May 1994), p. 7; and *MTI* (Budapest) (9 September 1993), in FBIS, *Daily Report* (Eastern Europe), 10 September 1993, p. 12.

119. Duna TV (Budapest), 8 November 1994, trans. in FBIS, *Daily Report* (Eastern Eu-rope), 9 November 1994, p. 46.

120. *Vreme* (9 August 1993), p. 30, trans. in FBIS, *Daily Report* (Eastern Europe), 31 Au-gust 1993, p. 54.

121. *Glas Istre* (2 June 1993), p. 3.

122. Ibid., p. 4; *Vjesnik* (26 July 1993), p. 4; and *Danas*, new series (6 August 1993), pp. 12–14.

123. Details in *Borba* (26 January 1993), p. 16, trans. in FBIS, *Daily Report* (Eastern Eu-rope), 19 February 1993, pp. 42–43.

124. Further elaboration of this point, see ibid.

125. Vesna Pusić, "Dictatorships with Democratic Legitimacy: Democracy Versus Na-tion," *East European Politics and Societies*, Vol. 8, No. 3 (fall 1994), pp. 397–398. See also Di-jana Plestina, "Democracy and Nationalism in Croatia: The First Three Years," in Ramet and Adamovich, *Beyond Yugoslavia*.

CHAPTER NINE

◆

On Their Own:
Slovenia and Macedonia
Since 1991

*Fluellen: I think it is in Macedon where Alexander is porn. I tell
you, captain, if you look in the maps of the 'orld, I warrant you sall
find, in the comparisons between Macedon and Monmouth, that the
situations, look you, is both alike. There is a river in Macedonia;
and there is also moreover a river at Monmouth: it is called Wye at
Monmouth; but it is out of my prains what is the name of the other
river; but 'tis all one, 'tis alike as my fingers is to my fingers, and
there is salmons in both.*

Shakespeare
King Henry V

*It regrettably happened that the Yugoslavs, in their joy at turning out
the Turks and becoming masters of Macedonia, pulled down the
beautiful mosque that had stood for three centuries in this commanding
position, and replaced it by an Officers' Club which is one of the most
hideous buildings in the whole of Europe. It is built of turnip-coloured
cement and looks like a cross between a fish-kettle and a mausoleum,
say the tomb of a very large cod. As my husband received the shock of
this building's outline he nearly fell out on the cobbles ...*

Rebecca West
Black Lamb and Grey Falcon
1941

174

During a brief visit to Ljubljana in September 1989, as I was sitting in a café with a group of sociologists from the Institute for Social Research, one of them suddenly turned to me and asked, "Why is it that when fascist states decay, they produce democracy, but when socialist states decay, they produce chaos?" Before I could utter even a syllable in reply, he lunged into an answer of his own: "Fascist states build up the economy first, and decay as a side effect of economic prosperity. But socialists states only decay under the pressure of economic collapse."

He was right, of course, but only partly. The other half of the story is that fascist states usually built up a strong center on principles of linear subordination, minimizing challenges to the structure of authority even as system transformation got under way. Socialist states, including Yugoslavia, on the other hand, frequently divided both authority and administrative responsibility, created complex and overlapping jurisdictions, and founded what, in the Yugoslav case, was a divided and increasingly weak center on the same principle of dual subordination—an organizational principle which, as the socialist system disintegrated, provided a number of openings for administrative rivalry and organizational challenges. It is telling that two of the stronger parties in Slovenia by the mid-1990s—the Liberal Democratic Party and the Associated List of Social Democrats (into which the Socialist Party had merged)—had emerged out of the carcasses of official Communist-sponsored "transmission belts" (specifically, the Youth Organization and, in the case of the Socialist Party, SAWP–Slovenia).

The challenges faced by Slovenia and Macedonia have been remarkably similar up to a point, but there have also been some situational differences related in part to Slovenia's better economic position and to Macedonia's diplomatic difficulties vis-à-vis Greece. In broad terms, one may say that the chief challenges the two new states have faced since June 1991 have been: reprivatizing and reviving the economy; demonopolizing the political system and refashioning it along pluralist lines; reorienting trade flows; developing beneficial relations with foreign powers, especially among neighboring states; and staying out of the Yugoslav war. This list is useful up to a point: it at least sets out clearly the basic processes unfolding in the two Yugoslav successor states that have—at least since July 1991—allowed these states to stay out of the fighting between Serbs and non-Serbs in Croatia and Bosnia. But it also glosses over the considerable differences in the challenges facing these two states at each of these levels. Certainly, Macedonia comes out behind in any comparison with Slovenia at any level. An example may illustrate this: the entire Macedonian Foreign Ministry—so I was told—had only one photocopying machine and only one fax machine even in 1993; needless to say, the Slovenes have not suffered from any comparable lack of equipment.

But at least two other factors not subsumed under any of the challenges listed above further complicate the picture for the Macedonians. The first is that between 21 and 40 percent of the population consists of ethnic Albanians living in compact areas adjoining Albania;[1] their devotion to the new Macedonian state may be open to question. The second complication for Macedonia is that of its four immediate neighbors—Serbia, Bulgaria, Greece, and Albania—only one, Albania, allows that the Macedonian people are entitled to call themselves Macedonians. Most Bulgarians, including political leaders and academics, view the Macedonians as "west Bulgarians" who speak a Bulgarian dialect. The Greek government, on the other hand, has long made a policy of describing Macedonians, at least those living within its borders, but by implication also those living in the Republic of Macedonia, as "Slavophone Greeks"; precisely which Slavic language these "Slavophone Greeks" speak is a matter of indifference to the Greek government, just so long as they do not speak it in public. The Belgrade government has generally kept quiet about the question of Macedonian nationality, except to express its unqualified "understanding" for the Greek position; but virtually the entire Serbian Orthodox Church hierarchy and priesthood, along with many Serbs associated with the most prominent parties (those of Milošević, Šešelj, and Drašković) hold onto the interwar (1918–1941) designation, which held that the Macedonians should be viewed as "south Serbs." Needless to say, the Macedonian government has read irredentist yearnings into these rival "interpretations."

Slovenia's Troubled Path to Prosperity

It was only in 1989 that the question of Slovenia's relation to the Yugoslav federation was first posed, with the drafting of controversial amendments which gave Slovenian authorities more control over the disposition of armed forces within their own republic. The Serbian Republic replied to these purely defensive precautions, which in any event did not go as far as the new Serbian constitution of 1990 would in establishing the priority of republic law over federal law, by sundering economic and commercial ties with the Republic of Slovenia. But in spite of that, through much of 1990 Slovenian politicians clung to the hope of preserving some connection with the other Yugoslav republics, joining Croatia in putting forward a draft treaty of confederation in October of that year.[2] In July, Slovenian Prime Minister Lojze Peterle told an Austrian weekly magazine that confederation, rather than independence, was Slovenia's first choice.[3] And as late as November, Dimitrij Rupel, then Slovenian foreign minister, confirmed that position.[4] But Slovenes were, even then, increasingly convinced, as Slovenian President Milan Kučan put it that same month, "that the interests, and even the survival of the Slovenian people, have been jeopardized [by] the insupportable relations in Yugoslavia."[5] An opinion poll taken that month found that 64.3 percent of Slovenes wanted Slovenia to declare its independence,[6] and beginning in early autumn formal institutional connections between Slovenia and the Yugoslav federation were severed, one by one.[7] The act of "disassociation" was submitted to the Slovenian parliament as early as 20 February 1991, making it all the more preposterous that so many high-ranking U.S. and Western European politicians expressed surprise when the Slovenes in fact seceded four months later. Secession might have been carried out sooner except that, as of early 1991, only part of the military in Slovenia was under Slovenian command, and Ljubljana authorities needed time to try to change this circumstance.[8] Ironically, as the deadline for secession neared, some Slovenes got cold feet, as an opinion poll conducted by the daily newspaper *Delo,* 27–28 March 1991, showed. The *Delo* poll found that only 45.3 percent of respondents were prepared for independence; another 31.2 percent felt that such a move was hasty and that Slovenia was not yet prepared for independence.[9]

As Slovenia approached independence day, strange ideas started to seem plausible to some portions of the Slovenian population. For example, there was the Republican Party of Slovenia, whose founding was announced in July 1990 and which pledged itself to work for annexation to the United States as the fifty-first state.[10] Then there were the various rumors of new political unions, one of the more imaginative suggesting the creation of a new federation that would have included not merely Slovenia and Croatia, but also Furlania, the northern part of Italy.[11] A variant of this xenophilia held that Slovenia's best option was annexation to Austria, and in March 1991 the Serbian daily newspaper *Politika* claimed that 13 percent of Slovenes in fact preferred this outcome.[12] With independence, there were new rumors, such as one in August 1991—after the cease-fire between the Yugoslav army and the Slovenian Territorial Defense forces—which held that the chief of staff of the Yugoslav army had held a secret meeting on 5 August in which it agreed to delay its withdrawal from Slovenia, to infiltrate Slovenian Territorial Defense forces, to blow up the Krško nuclear plant, and to conduct aerial strikes against Maribor and Ljubljana.[13] These rumors were important as indicators of the extreme uncertainty Slovenes felt at the time.

But independence also brought new problems. In the short run, the loss of the Yugoslav market hurt the Slovenian economy and contributed to putting additional people out of work.[14] And there were new problems in foreign relations, as the Slovenes suddenly discovered that they had a border dispute with Croatia.[15] Moreover, the reluctance of the Western Europeans to extend diplomatic recognition to these new republics had economic as well as political consequences, and it was indicative that among the first states to recognize Slovenia were Lithuania, Georgia, and Latvia—themselves newly established states.[16] And finally, there were problems of adjustment, as three successive privatization plans were drawn up and then scuttled for lack of consensus. The last two issues (foreign policy and privatization) became the clubs with which Slovenian Prime Minister Peterle was beaten by his critics, and by February 1992, after the dissolution of the DEMOS coalition, which had brought Christian Democratic Peterle to power, Slovenia was in the grips of a full-blown governmental crisis.[17]

Foreign Relations

As a result of a combination of internal economic pressures, the repercussions of the federal breakup, and ostracism by the West, Slovenia began its independence with an economic nosedive, and by October 1991 its industrial production stood at 17 percent less than the previous October.[18] Already in August, bank representatives from Slovenia issued a plea to Western European banking institutions and politicians to resume normal banking and financing; this call was aimed most especially at Italy, Austria, Switzerland, France, and the United States.[19] But in spite of strong support from Germany, Austria, and Italy, other EC states—most especially Britain, France, and Spain—insisted on a policy of diplomatic and economic isolation of Slovenia and Croatia as long as possible.[20] The Russians stepped in to fill the breach, and on 12 December, even before the EC had finally agreed to recognize Slovenia, Moscow and Ljubljana signed their first trade agreement, under which the Russians promised to deliver 700,000 tons of oil and 450,000 tons of oil derivates and coal to Slovenia in exchange for medicines, footwear, bakery equipment, and other machine equipment.[21] Most of the Western European states extended recognition between December 1991 and January 1992; in fact, among major Western European states, Serbophile France was the last to do so, waiting until 23 April, more than two weeks after the belated U.S. recognition of Slovenia.[22]

With diplomatic recognition, economic contacts quickly rebounded. Economic ties between Slovenia and northern Italy revived,[23] Austrian banks once again invested in Slovenia,[24] and economic relations were soon established with the Benelux countries, Iran, and China[25] alongside Slovenia's traditional trading partners. Slovenian exports increased 8 percent in the period 1991–1992, finding their largest markets in Germany ($1.19 billion), Croatia ($891 million), Italy ($732 million), and Austria ($281 million).[26] Slovenia also signed defense accords with Austria (in November 1992) and with Hungary (in January 1993).[27]

Slovenia's relations with Croatia and Italy remained complicated, however. The Slovene-Croatian dispute over fishing rights was supposedly resolved by an agreement in April 1992,[28] but difficulties in this sphere continued.[29] Other issues remained unresolved even in 1998. Here one may mention the status of the Krško nuclear power plant (Slovenia was demanding full ownership, even though the plant was built using both Slovenian and Croatian resources), Nova Ljubljanska Banka's debts to Croatian depositors, the border at Piran Bay, and Slovene property in Istria.[30] In 1997, an agreement on border traffic between Slovenia and Croatia was signed by both sides and subsequently ratified by the Croatian *Sabor*. However, the Slovenian parliament postponed ratification on three occasions, out of fear that it might prejudice the resolution of the dispute concerning Piran Bay against Slovenian interests.[31] There have also been allegations in the Croatian press that certain Slovenian politicians—among them, People's Party leader Marijan Podobnik, Social Democratic Party leader Janez Janša, and Slovenian National Party leader Zmago Jelinčič—have demanded that portions of Croatian Istria be ceded to Slovenia.[32]

Where Italy is concerned, an unresolved dispute over property rights in the Istrian peninsula sabotaged bilateral talks in October 1994, resulting in an Italian threat to veto Slovenia's application to join the European Union (EU).[33] A change of government in Rome at the end of 1994 contributed to a warming of relations, however, and in 1995, the Italian foreign minister, Susanna Agnelli, signaled that Rome was prepared to abandon its veto of Slovenia's membership in the EU. In June 1996, Slovenia and the EU signed an agreement of association on the strength of the former's commitment to make certain changes to its constitution (which it did in July 1997).[34] Yet another change of government brought Romano Prodi's center-left coalition to power in Rome in May 1996, and with this change came growing recognition in Italian government circles of the importance of mutuality in relations between the two countries and, in particular, of the importance of the Slovenian economy for the Italian border town of Trieste. Prodi's government became an "ardent advocate" of Slovenian membership in both the EU and NATO.[35]

Meanwhile, Slovenia gradually entered a series of international organizations, including the World Bank in February 1993[36] and the Council of Europe, and in October 1994 became a signatory to the General Agreement on Tariffs and Trade (GATT).[37] Slovenia also signed trade agreements with the European Free Trade Association (EFTA) in May 1992 and with the European Community (EC) in April 1993,[38] obtained membership in the World Trade Organization, and began work to prepare for membership in the EU. The last-mentioned undertaking requires, among other things, that about 80,000 pages of EU legislation be translated into Slovenian, so that Slovenian law may be harmonized with EU legislation. For this purpose, some thirty-one working commissions have been established, dealing with areas such as agriculture, science and technology, education, financial services, industrial policy, and transport.[39]

Domestic Affairs

Four issues dominated political discussions in Slovenia in the months following disassociation: the constitutional and legal restructuring of the system; the continued state control of Radio-Television Slovenia (and the advantage the new officeholders suddenly saw in this arrangement); privatization and how to go about it; and the role of Catholic values in the political system. I have described some of these elsewhere[40] and shall restrict myself here to a brief discussion of the fourth issue before taking up an assessment of the challenges faced by the Slovenian government in the economic and political sectors more broadly.

In a word, the Roman Catholic Church, which claims the allegiance of the vast majority of religiously oriented Slovenes, decided to take advantage of the collapse of communism to push for the criminalization of abortion and for the introduction of mandatory (Catholic) religious instruction in elementary and middle schools. The Slovenian parliament's refusal to strike from the constitution a clause guaranteeing a woman's right to an abortion no doubt lay behind the Episcopal Conference's statement, in November 1992, calling for the dissolution of the parliament, "since it has preserved certain characteristics from the nondemocratic times."[41] In fall 1992, the Catholic Church campaigned actively for Christian Democratic candidates and tried to mobilize its members to vote "Christian." In this, the Church failed, however, and the Liberal Democratic Party, a left-of-center secular party, maintained the predominance it had gained in early 1992; and in August 1994 the Liberal Democrats dealt the Church its second setback, ruling against any introduction of religious instruction into the schools.[42] But in 1998, in the wake of parliamentary elections in 1997, in which the proclerical People's Party gained a place in the ruling coalition, the Catholic Church again pressed its interests. In March, noting that in the six years since the passage of the Denationalization Act the Church had not succeeded in regaining all of the properties confiscated by the Communists after 1945, the Ljubljana archdiocese announced its intention to take its case to European courts in Brussels and Strasbourg.[43] Subsequently, in September 1998, in a pastoral letter read in all the churches, Slovenia's bishops called once again for the introduction of Catholic religious education in the public schools.[44]

In the economic sector, 1993 showed the first signs of real economic recovery. In the years 1987–1992, the Slovenian GDP had declined some 23 percent (6.5 percent between 1991 and 1992 alone).[45] Personal consumption declined 24 percent between 1990 and 1992, while gross fixed investment declined 34 percent in the same period.[46] But production staged a robust 4.7 percent rebound in 1993, and by December of that year unemployment was starting to contract, shrinking from a high of 15.5 percent to 15.1 percent.[47] Inflation also slowed in 1993.

Positive economic trends continued in subsequent years, as Slovenia notched GDP growth rates of 5.3 percent in 1994, 4.1 in 1995, 3.1 in 1996, and 3.8 in 1997;[48] government officials predicted a growth rate of between 4 and 5 percent for 1998.[49] Inflation has continued to decline, dipping below 10 percent in 1997,[50] while the unemployment rate sank to 7.1 percent that same year.[51] Tourism has played a role in this recovery, with some 900,000 tourists visiting Slovenia during 1997—an increase of 17 percent over 1996.[52]

Yet the dissolution of Yugoslavia inflicted some hardship on the Slovenian economy all the same. Quite apart from the shift of trade which accompanied the Yugoslav breakup (with 70 percent of Slovenia's commodity trade being oriented to EU countries as of 1997), Slovenia suffered from the nationalization in February 1992 of branches of Slovenian enterprises operating in Serbia,[53] not to mention the unexpected confiscation by the Yugoslav army (at the time of its evacuation from Slovenia in October 1991) of all radar and air-traffic communications equipment.[54] Then there was the impact of the war. By April 1992, Slovenia had given refuge to some 5,000 displaced persons from Croatia, as well as another 11,000 refugees from Bosnia-Herzegovina; the situation was, even then, described as "becoming increasingly serious for our republic."[55] But by June, this figure had risen to somewhere between 50,000 and 60,000,[56] resulting in Slovenia's closing its doors to any additional refugees. But however complicating these developments have been, Slovenia's economic progress has been solid, thanks both to its solid industrial and agricultural infrastructure and to its strong and growing reputation for high-quality manufactures.[57]

In the political sphere, however, challenges have been more subtle. It is one thing to adopt a good constitution and to arrange successfully for the passage of literally hundreds of laws to convert the system from socialism to pluralism; it is another thing to safeguard that pluralism and to make sure that it operates according to its nominal principles. Some people fear that the system has been slow to complete its transformation. For example, in August 1993 writers Drago Jančar and Rudi Šeligo were among fourteen signatories to a protest article alleging that Communist vestiges still dominated Slovenia through cliques and informal groupings said to have been responsible for "a whole series of scandals and deviations."[58] Then there is the case of Rudolf Rizman, an internationally renowned professor of sociology at the University of Ljubljana, who became the victim of a witch hunt. Rizman, an outspoken critic of Janez Janša (the head of the Social Democratic Party, who was dismissed as defense minister in March 1994),[59] warned in newspaper articles that Janša did not respect constitutional principles and was trying to make a bid for (dictatorial) power. Then on 26 March 1994 the state television quoted extensively from two private letters Rizman had written to friends in Germany and the United States in which Rizman had criticized Janša.[60] Rizman and family started to receive death threats and to become victims of other forms of intimidation. In November 1994 Janša used his personal connections to arrange for the public prosecutor to serve Rizman with a summons to appear before the Division of Security Matters in the Ministry of Defense in order to respond to charges that he had betrayed an "official secret." Quite apart from the fact that Rizman's characterization of Janša as megalomaniac was a matter of private opinion based on open materials and expressed in *private* correspondence, by labeling it an official secret the public prosecutor seemed to be admitting the truth of Rizman's description of Janša.[61]

Add to these disquieting signs the continued instability in political parties, as parties continue to split and recombine with other parties,[62] the unresolved question of media freedom, and the marginalization of women's rights,[63] not to mention the likelihood of continued pressure by the Catholic Church in its efforts to sacralize the political sector, and there are grounds enough for concern about the eventual outcome of Slovenia's efforts at democratization. But whereas I believe there are grounds for judging that the principal threats to Slovenian democracy come from the political right, the well-publicized manifesto entitled "The Hour of European Truth for Slovenia," inspired by precisely right-of-center sympathies and signed on 9 July 1997 by various cultural figures and professionals, identifies *the left* (!) as constituting the principal threat to Slovenian democracy. Signed by such figures as Jančar and Šeligo, as well as Niko Grafenauer (the chief editor of *Nova revija*), Jože Pučnik (president of the first coalition of democratic parties in Slovenia, 1989–1991), and Alojz Šuštar, the former archbishop of Ljubljana, the manifesto warned that Slovenian political development "is lagging behind European cultural and democratic standards" and blamed this on "the authoritarian manner of government," which it described as the result of the continued control of government and media by "persons from the previous regime."[64] The signatories complained that the number of extraparliamentary meetings exceeded by far the number of parliamentary sessions[65]—a normal feature in a modern state—and blamed the length of court proceedings on lingering Communist consciousness among judges. Criticizing also the privatization scheme, the conduct of the media, and the alleged failure of the government to cut its "umbilical cord" with the former totalitarian regime, the manifesto makes a classic right-wing appeal in demanding that the Slovenian government champion the interests of Slovenian minorities in other states[66]—a recommendation which would require policies running counter to the very principles of sovereignty upon which the Slovenian state-builders made their bid for independence. Finally, the signatories of the manifesto demanded that the government "acknowledge its own shortcomings, and at the same time tackle the murky practices of the 'continuity' people who, during the privatization process, have succeeded in transforming their former political monopoly into a capital monopoly."[67]

The manifesto created a small sensation, and a number of critics immediately denounced it, some of them spelling out their objections in print. But nothing could disguise the fact that whatever one might make of the manifesto, there was a steady gravitation to the political right taking place in Slovenia. Although opinion polls repeatedly showed an overwhelming support among Slovenes for multiparty democracy and a general admiration for Western European political models,[68] this regard for democracy has not been associated with clear commitment to tolerance, the essential ingredient in *liberal* democracy. For example, in a 1991 poll only 40 percent of respondents thought that equal rights for women were implied and entailed in the democratic project, while in a 1993 poll 20 percent of respondents expressed anti-Semitic sentiments and 93 percent of respondents opposed allowing immigrants to establish political associations to safeguard their interests.[69] Or, to take another example, empirical studies conducted by the Center for Social Psychology of the University of Ljubljana beginning in 1993 found that young people in Slovenia are adopting, in ever greater numbers, attitudes conventionally associated with the political right, including "a retreat into privacy and traditionalism and a concomitant increase in intolerance toward ethnic and social minorities and other socially marginal groups."[70]

This rightward trend has been reflected in election results. Although left-of-center political parties increased their collective strength between 1990 (when they collectively garnered 37.1 percent of the vote) and 1992 (when their share amounted to 39.8 percent), right-wing parties rallied after the setback of 1992 (when their combined tally came to only 26.5 percent) to outpoll the left in local elections in 1994 as well as in republic-wide balloting in 1996. Indeed, in November 1996 polling, a coalition of three right-wing parties (the People's Party, the Christian Democrats, and the Social Democrats) won 45 percent of the popular vote, taking 45 of the 90 seats in the Assembly. Liberal Democratic Prime Minister Janez Drnovšek was able to remain in office only by weaning Marijan Podobnik of the People's Party away from his coalition, offering him a share of power in a left-right coalition as Deputy Prime Minister.[71] Janša, the controversial head of the Social Democratic Party, demanded in spring 1998 that Prime Minister Drnovšek testify before the Constitutional Court concerning a secret agreement between the military intelligence services of Slovenia and Israel concerning arms purchases in 1995, but the Slovenian parliament rejected Janša's proposal.[72] But by October 1998 Janša and other members of his party were demanding that Drnovšek resign altogether, citing the Slovenian-Israeli accord as justification for their demand.[73]

In spite of these controversies, there are grounds for cautious optimism about Slovenia's progress in consolidating liberal democracy. To begin with, the political spectrum has seen the development of a large number of parties and political associations.[74] The repluralization of society has also been manifested in the frondescence of social organizations and societies, whose number rose from 5,306 in 1980 to 9,227 in 1985 to 12,830 in 1993.[75] Moreover, as Danica Fink-Hafner has documented, the role of interest groups in Slovenian politics has been growing steadily, thereby enabling citizens to exert pressure through organized groups.[76]

Macedonia: Reluctantly Independent

The Macedonians were not prepared for independence when Slovenia and Croatia seceded, and for a while Macedonian President Kiro Gligorov continued to think in terms of Macedonia remaining in federal union with Serbia and Montenegro.[77] But as the reality of Yugoslavia's death sank in, Macedonian authorities brought the inevitable question before the public and asked them to vote in a referendum on independence held 9 September. Three-quarters of those voting declared for Macedonian independence. Nine days later, the Macedonian Assembly issued a declaration of independence, but in a new constitution drafted shortly thereafter and adopted on 29 November the Assembly pointedly left open the possibility that Macedonia might join another state.[78]

As Belgrade sent its military juggernaut first against Slovenia, then against Croatia, the Macedonians gave in to deep apprehensions, and Macedonian authorities expressed concern on numerous occasions that the war might spread to their republic. But in January 1992 Macedonia completed its withdrawal from the federation with the removal of all of its representatives and officials from federal organs and bodies.[79] And in the course of the following two months, the Yugoslav People's Army completed its withdrawal from its bases in Macedonia, though not without removing most of the military technical equipment and the main radar system at Petrovec airport and even attempting to dismantle and remove the telephone equipment in the 4 July barracks in Stip—both in contravention of a prior agreement with Macedonian authorities.[80]

Alone at last, Macedonia remained diplomatically isolated until 15 January 1992, when Bulgaria became the first state to accord full recognition to the Republic of Macedonia. Slovenia and Croatia followed in February. But although Macedonia struggled to overcome what amounted to a diplomatic quarantine, its small Serbian minority started to register complaints that sounded all too reminiscent of complaints voiced by Serbs in Croatia and Bosnia before hostilities broke out in those republics. Understandably, Macedonian authorities did not take these complaints lightly.

Foreign Relations

By summer 1992, Macedonia had succeeded in establishing diplomatic ties with only seven countries: Bulgaria, Croatia, Slovenia, Turkey, Bosnia-Herzegovina, Lithuania, and the Philippines. Russia had recognized Macedonian independence in mid-May, but had indicated that it would wait until the EC had granted diplomatic recognition before exchanging ambassadors. But the United States and members of the EC delayed recognition pending resolution of a dispute which had flared up between Greece and Macedonia immediately after Macedonia had declared its independence. In a word, the Greek government declared that Macedonia had no right to its name, flag, or coat of arms, demanded that the Macedonians explicitly forswear any interest in reunion with those parts of southern Macedonia which Greece had annexed in 1913, and soon suggested to the Macedonians that they call their state the Republic of Skopje. The Greeks even started referring to the Macedonians as Skopjans, despite the unnecessary insult given and even though within Macedonia that designation seemed appropriate only to residents of the city of Skopje, and even then not in any sense which might be termed "national." The Greek government also objected to Articles 3 and 49 of the new Macedonian constitution. Article 3 stated that "the borders of the Republic of Macedonia may be changed only in accordance with the Constitution"; Athens claimed that this formulation betrayed irredentist aspirations. Article 49 of the Macedonian constitution stated that the Macedonian government "cares for the status and rights" of Macedonians living in neighboring countries.[81] The Greek government held that, even though no explicit mention was made of Greece in this clause, the wording nonetheless referred to Greece, in spite of the fact that the Greek government held that there were no Macedonians living in Greece. Further, the Greek constitution includes an article (Article 108) providing that the government in Athens "shall care for Greeks residing abroad and for the maintenance of their ties with the Mother Fatherland";[82] the Greek government held that, although it was legitimate for Greece to have such an article in the Greek constitution, it was not legitimate for Macedonia to do likewise.

Declining to throw out Greek objections, EC met on 16 December 1991 and laid down three conditions for recognition to Macedonia: the passage of constitutional amendments guaranteeing respect for existing borders; an explicit declaration that Macedonia harbored no territorial pretensions against its neighbors; and a promise not to interfere in Greece's internal affairs.[83] The EC implied that compliance on the part of Macedonia would make the country eligible for recognition. Obediently, the Macedonian Assembly met on 6 January 1992 and, in unceremonious haste, adopted amendments affecting Articles 3 and 49 of the constitution explicitly declaring Macedonians' commitment to respect existing borders and to abstain from interference in the internal affairs of their neighbors. The Macedonians also declared that they harbored no aspirations toward territorial expansion. These unusual provisions (not normally considered necessary to be given explicit formulation, least of all by a militarily weak and economically endangered country) were passed amid sarcastic comments from the legislators themselves.[84] Subsequently, the Badinter Commission set up by the EC issued a judgment declaring that, among the Yugoslav successor states, Slovenia and Macedonia fulfilled all conditions for diplomatic recognition.

But the EC did not honor its implied promise to the Republic of Macedonia. Instead, the community deferred to the Greeks, who now claimed that the name

TABLE 9.1   Military Strength of Macedonia and Greece (1993)

	Macedonia	Greece
Army troops	11,000–12,000	113,000
Reservists	120,000	34,000
Tanks	4	1,842
Aircraft	0	855
Heavy artillery pieces	0	2,151
Missiles	0	AGM-12 Bullpup, AGM-65 Maverick, AIM-7 Sparrow, AIM-9 Sidewinder, R-550 Magic systems
Navy	0	19,500
Helicopters	0	173

SOURCES: Macedonian figures from Duncan M. Perry, "Crisis in the Making? Macedonia and Its Neighbours," *Südost Europa*, Vol. 43, Nos. 1–2 (January–February 1994), pp. 40, 45. Greek figures from International Institute for Strategic Studies, *The Military Balance 1993–1994* (London: Brassey's, October 1993), pp. 40–50.

"Macedonia" was the historical property of the Greek people and insisted that their northern neighbor omit any derivative or variant of this word in the republic's eventual designation.[85] They also claimed to fear an armed attack by Macedonia, although the figures in Table 9.1 cast considerable doubt on the plausibility of any such scenario. Two factors underlay the Greek response. The first was the calculated fear of the Greek government that the authorities in Skopje, who had long championed the rights of the culturally repressed Macedonian-speaking Macedonian minority in Greece, a group described by the Athens government as "Slavophone Greeks" and denied education in their own language,[86] would continue to act as guardians of Greece's 20,000–50,000 Macedonians.[87] If its independence should be recognized and consolidated, an independent Macedonia could become a magnet for Greece's Macedonians, thus stimulating protests and internal disorder. The second factor was the strong nationalist response that took hold of the Greek public. The Greeks assumed what has never been proven, namely, that no two peoples can ever have any cultural artifacts, history, symbols, historical figures, or images in common. If the Greek assumption is correct, then it is time for France and Germany to go to war over the question of whether Charlemagne was "French" or "German," and for Austria, Albania, and the United States to initiate a three-sided war over who is "really" entitled to use the eagle as a symbol of state.

To the Macedonians' surprise, the EC honored Greek reservations for more than two years, and it was only in December 1993 that the Western European states finally accorded recognition to Macedonia, followed in short order by Japan and by an exchange of ambassadors with Russia. Macedonia was even admitted to the U.N., albeit under the inelegant name the "Former Yugoslav Republic of Macedonia"— though no one seemed concerned as to the precedent set thereby for the treatment of future applicants.

By 1992, the Greeks had blockaded shipments to Macedonia passing through Salonika, stimulating shortages of food, oil, and medicine in that landlocked republic. The Greeks lifted the embargo in the course of 1993, as bilateral talks between Greece and Macedonia began to show some promise. But in October 1993, Andreas Papandreou returned to the prime-ministership, and these bilateral talks were abruptly terminated. Then, a week after the United States declared its intention to extend full diplomatic recognition to the Republic of Macedonia,[88] Papandreou declared the reimposition of a trade embargo against Macedonia, indeed of a tougher embargo than the Macedonians had seen in 1992–1993.[89] Meanwhile, Senator Paul Sarbanes of Maryland, Representative Michael Bilirakis of Florida, and several other prominent Greek Americans with links to the Democratic Party started to turn up the heat at the White House. Exactly a month after the State Department announcement, President Clinton, Vice President Al Gore, and National Security Adviser Anthony Lake met behind closed doors with Sarbanes, Greek Orthodox Archbishop Iakovos, Greek American lobbyist Andrew Manatos, and thirteen other prominent Greek Americans. After the meeting (at which no one from the State Department was present), Clinton announced the abrogation of the earlier statement recognizing Macedonia.[90]

Greece's European partners tried to pressure the Greeks to lift the embargo and even threatened the Greeks with legal action unless the embargo was lifted. When the Greeks ignored a 13 April 1994 deadline to fall into line, the EU took the case to the European Court of Justice. But on 30 June, the court ruled that since the Greek action did not harm the interests of any members of the EU, the Greeks could not be ordered to lift the embargo.[91]

But if the Macedonians could scarcely feel reassured by these developments, they could nonetheless take solace not only in the firm economic support they were getting from Bulgaria and Turkey, but also from the stationing of a U.N. protective force along Macedonia's border with Serbia in July 1993. Given certain troop movements on the Serbian side of the border in 1993 and the repeated Serbian armed provocations along the Macedonian border during 1994, including several armed incursions across the border,[92] the stationing of this force, which consisted of some 1,300 U.N. troops as of October 1994,[93] seemed to offer some reassurance. Moreover, in November, the United States signed an agreement with Macedonia under which Macedonian officers could attend U.S. military academies.[94]

By August 1994, mediation by Germany and France in the Greek-Macedonian dispute was starting to show results, Greek Foreign Minister Papoulias was showing flexibility, and diplomats were expressing optimism that the dispute between Greece and Macedonia might finally be settled by early 1995.[95] In fact, Greece lifted its trade embargo against Macedonia in 1995, and that same year the United States and members of the EC extended diplomatic recognition to the country. Macedonia subsequently joined NATO's "Partnership for Peace" program. The United States provided some $76 million in foreign aid in the years between recognition and spring 1998,[96] and the Greek business community has begun to invest in the Macedonian economy.[97] By 1998, Macedonia's relations with the Western state community could be described as normal.

Domestic Affairs: Nationalities

In March 1991, on the eve of the formal disintegration of Yugoslavia, a census in Macedonia found that nearly 65 percent of the republic's inhabitants were Macedonians and just over 20 percent were Albanians (see figures in Table 9.2). No other group accounted for even 5 percent of the population, and aside from the Turks, all other groups accounted for less than 3 percent of the population each. But there was widespread agreement that the 1991 census was "unreliable," and representatives of at least two nationality groups challenged the census, claiming that the numerical strengths of their respective groups had been underestimated. Xheladin Murati, a member of parliament for the Party for Democratic Prosperity (PDP), told me in 1995 that his party estimated that there were about twice as many Albanians living in Macedonia as were recorded in the 1991 census,[98] while local Serbs claimed that they numbered 300,000, if not 400,000—that is to say, eight to ten times the official estimate.[99] Even the Roma, recorded as numbering 55,575 in the 1991 census, complained that they had been undercounted; Romani leaders held that there were about 220,000 Roma living in Macedonia.[100]

Since these claims held political significance across several policy areas, Macedonian authorities soon began organizing a second census, to be conducted under international supervision. After nearly two years of preparations, the second census was held in June–July 1994. What is interesting about the new figures is that the numbers for all nationality groups, except the Albanians, were smaller now than in 1991, including the number of Macedonians registered, although the growth in the Albanian figure did not nearly approach the claims that continued to be pressed by Albanian spokespersons. Indeed, what was striking about the two censuses was how similar the results were each time—a feature unlikely to please local Albanians or Serbs. In fact, several Albanian political parties had already prepared the ground for continued challenges to the census results by calling, on the eve of the second census, for an Albanian boycott of this census as well.[101] How many did in fact boycott the census is impossible to say.

The most important political force among Macedonia's Albanians is the Democratic Party of Albanians, as the PDP renamed itself in 1996. Electing Abdurahman Aliti as party president in July 1994, the PDP pursued a policy of cooperation and negotiation with ethnic Macedonian parties and leaders and, prior to the elections of October 1994, had twenty-two seats in the Macedonian parliament. In the period 1993–1994, there were five ethnic Albanians among twenty-two cabinet ministers. Other ethnic Albanian parties active in Macedonia have included the Democratic People's Party, the

TABLE 9.2   Population of Macedonia, by Nationality (1991, 1994)

	1991		1994	
Macedonians	1,314,283	64.62%	1,288,333	66.93%
Albanians	427,313	21.01%	434,033	22.55%
Turks	97,416	4.79%	74,267	3.88%
Gypsies (Roma)	55,575	2.73%	43,732	2.27%
Serbs	44,159	2.17%	39,624	2.04%
Others	95,218	4.68%	45,229	2.33%
Total	2,033,964	100%	1,925,011	100%

SOURCES: Figures from the 1991 census as reported in *Broj i struktura na neselenieto vo Republika Makedonija po opštini i nacionalna pripadnost* (Skopje: Republički zavod za statistiku, 1991), p. 6. Percentages for the 1991 distribution as reported in *Vreme* (Belgrade) (9 May 1994), p. 16. Figures and percentages from the 1994 census as reported in *Nova Makedonija* (Skopje) (13 November 1994), p. 3, trans. in *FBIS, Daily Report* (Eastern Europe), 15 November 1994, p. 52.

Democratic Alliance of Albanians/Liberal Party, and the Party of Democratic Action. Far better known in the West than Aliti is Arben Xhaferi, at first head of the radical wing of the PDP and a member of parliament, who was later elected to succeed Aliti as party president. Although Xhaferi has been branded a "militant" and a "saber rattler" by the uncomprehending American press,[102] he is better understood as an articulate champion of liberal values in a state which has proven long on promises, but short on fulfillment of those promises. When I spoke with him in his offices in Tetovo, he told me that there was not a single Albanian in the symphony orchestra of either Skopje or Bitola or in the Macedonian National Opera and that there were only four professors of Albanian nationality teaching at Macedonian universities (all four at the University of Skopje, none at the University of Bitola). Moreover, of the 2.5 million books held in the national library, only 125 were in Albanian as of 1995, according to Xhaferi.[103] Enver Shala, a journalist with *Flaka*, added that of the twenty-two employees at Radio Tetovo (located in a city 80 percent of whose inhabitants are Albanians) there were twenty Macedonians and only two Albanians.[104]

Even before independence, ethnic Albanians in Macedonia were presenting petitions requesting the opening of cultural institutions, schools, and other facilities that would conduct their business in Albanian and the reinstatement of teachers suspended for having allegedly indoctrinated their students with Albanian nationalist ideas.[105] Failing to make any headway in at least some of these areas and drawing inspiration from Titoist practices, which always sought to solve problems by dividing jurisdictions and creating new autonomous zones (whether provinces, republics, or smaller units), Macedonia's Albanians began likewise to think in terms of autonomy.[106]

The Albanian population of Macedonia in fact staged a referendum on ethnic-regional autonomy in early January 1992 in spite of the government's warnings that it considered any such referendum illegal. But the government in fact did little to impede the progress of this referendum, which was conducted publicly at more than 500 polling stations. Some 276,921 Albanians took part in the referendum, of whom 74 percent voted in favor of autonomy.[107] The government declined to take up the question of autonomy, however, fearing that the results could be highly destabilizing. But in reply, ethnic Albanians from all over Macedonia assembled in downtown Skopje on 31 March for a peaceful protest. The meeting was organized by the PDP, whose president at the time, Nevzet Halili, told those assembled that, as "a constituent element in the new Macedonian state," the Albanians of Macedonia were entitled to "territorial, political, and cultural autonomy."[108] The government maintained, however, that autonomy would not in fact serve Albanians' interests, but would, on the contrary, result in the creation of a "ghetto," cutting them off from mainstream Macedonian public life.[109] Frustrated with the government's response, a small group of Albanian nationalists in fact declared the creation of an "Ilirida Republic" in the area around Struga in early 1992, but the declaration was purely demonstrative, without any practical effect.[110]

The government did propose to establish an Albanian quota at the University of Skopje, in effect institutionalizing a form of "positive discrimination," but university officials balked.[111] Later, in November 1994, a session of the Tetovo city assembly gave support to an initiative to establish an Albanian-language university in Macedonia, though not without some of its members noting that such a move lay far outside the nominal jurisdiction of a city Assembly.[112] In February 1995, the Albanian community, losing patience with the Macedonian authorities, unilaterally declared the establishment of a public University of Tetovo, using private funds to jump-start the institution. The authorities refused to accept this move, however, and sent police to bulldoze the facilities and disperse demonstrators on 17 February. In the ensuing disturbances, one Tetovo Albanian was killed.[113]

When I visited Tetovo in March 1995, I saw the wreckage of the university facilities which had been bulldozed by the police. In Skopje, I spoke with Ilinka Mitreva, a member of parliament from the Social Democratic Party, about this question. According to her, there were several problems with the Albanian initiative to set up a university in Tetovo: first, the law prescribes certain procedures for the establishment of a university, and the Albanian community simply ignored these procedures; second, the organizers of the University of Tetovë (to use the Albanian spelling) proposed to conduct instruction in Albanian without first obtaining a change in the constitution, which includes a clause prescribing that all university-level instruction in Macedonia be conducted in Macedonian; and third, the organizers declared that they were setting up the university using private monies, but, in the long run, the university would be unlikely to be able to function without state support.[114] Subsequently, however, authorities in Skopje decided to turn a blind eye to the university, which was reestablished by local Albanians and funded by the Albanian diaspora as well as by contributions by Macedonian Albanians.[115] But the government has also refused to accredit the university "leaving the 300 men and women of its first graduating class without [recognized] credentials for public service."[116]

There were also tensions, including violent clashes between Albanians and Macedonian police in November 1992, fist fights between Albanian and Macedonian young people in June 1994, and the arrest of nine high-ranking Albanian officials in November 1993 on suspicion of smuggling weapons, organizing paramilitary organizations, and preparing for the overthrow of the state.[117] Still, for all that, there was some basis for Duncan Perry's optimistic conclusion that "Macedonia's Albanians, economically better off than their cousins in Albania or Kosovo, seem to recognize that they are a culture apart from other Albanians and that their lot is better cast with Macedonia."[118]

But that recognition has been strained by police brutality against local Albanians and Roma, and by repercussions from the growing tensions and fighting in Kosovo (see Chapter 13). As early as 1997, the mayors of Gostivar and Tetovo, both Albanian nationalists, stirred controversy by ordering that the Albanian flag be flown over their city halls. The country's Constitutional Court declared the order illegal and, when the two mayors refused to take the flags down, American-trained antiterrorist forces were sent to the two cities on 9 July, before dawn, to confiscate the flags. The operation went smoothly in Tetovo, but in Gostivar, several thousand Albanians blocked the police forces. In the ensuing street battle, 3 Albanians were killed and several hundred were injured.[119] Some 312 demonstrators were arrested, though most of them were subsequently released. Among those arrested was Rufi Osmani, Gostivar's mayor. Nine months later, in April 1998, authorities handed down a seven-year prison sentence to Osmani and sentenced Alajdin Demiri, the mayor of Tetovo, to two and a half years in prison.[120] As for police brutality, reports confirming it have been issued by Human Rights Watch and by Amnesty International.[121]

But the massive violence and extensive atrocities in neighboring Kosovo in 1998 sent tremors through Macedonia and have proven highly divisive in relations between local Macedonians and Albanians. There has also been illegal arms smuggling across the Macedonian-Kosovo border; in 1997 Macedonian military and police forces seized 3,000 automatic weapons from Albanians attempting to cross into Macedonia illegally.[122]

The third largest nationality group in Macedonia is the Turks, but despite the existence of several Turkish parties, they have little chance of bringing their concerns to center stage. They are simply too few. Still, despite their sincere protestations of loyalty,[123] there have been expressions of discontent with problems encountered in education, culture, and economic life.[124] Their discontent should not be overestimated, however, according to Meto Jovanovski, President of the Helsinki Committee for Human Rights of the Republic of Macedonia, who cited the establishment of a theological faculty for Turks at the University of Skopje in early 1995.[125]

The Serbs, who number less than 40,000 according to the 1994 census, are the fifth largest nationality group, after the Macedonians, the Albanians, the Turks, and the Roma. Only 2 percent of Macedonia's inhabitants are Serbs. But because of their powerful neighbor to the north, Macedonia's Serbs were in the position to raise a great deal of clamor, demanding many things, including autonomy, to be listed as one of the "state-constituent" peoples of Macedonia in the constitution, education in their own language (they characterize themselves as "socially threatened"),[126] and the erection, by the state and at state expense, of a Serbian National Theater, a cultural association for Macedonia's Serbs, a weekly magazine, a Serbian university, and Serbian broadcasts on state radio—all for a community of 40,000.[127] The fact that they expected the state to provide everything rather than thinking of setting up these institutions themselves is a telling legacy of socialism.

But again, the Macedonian state authorities have made serious efforts to reach negotiated solutions to these questions. For example, in August 1993, Macedonian authorities met with Bora Ristić, a representative of Macedonia's Serbian community, and agreed to guarantee to Serbs the right to primary education in the Serbian language, provided that there are at least fifteen children enrolled in the class, and to secondary education in Serbian, given a minimum class enrollment of twenty-five students.[128]

Domestic Affairs: Economics and Politics

With declines in the social product of 9.5 percent in 1990, 10.0 in 1991, and yet another 14.7 in 1992, and parallel declines in industrial production over those years of 10.6, 17.2, and 11.0 percent, Macedonia's economy got off to a bad start.[129] Moreover, the imposition of the U.N. trade embargo against Serbia had serious negative effects on Macedonia, as did the combined effect of the Greek closure of its border and the obstruction to trade given by the war itself. These three factors cost Macedonia about 60 percent of its trade, according to President Gligorov.[130] The result is that unemployment rose to 17 percent by summer 1994, basic supplies (of oil, food, medicine, etc.) remained scarce, and Macedonia's economy slid downward, coming to resemble that of a Third World country more than anything else.

The rate of deterioration slowed in 1994, when the social product declined by "only" 3.9 percent, and in the subsequent two years the social product grew by an annual rate of 3.0 percent. Inflation stood at 6.0 percent during 1995 and 1996, but as of 1996 unemployment reached a staggering 38 percent.[131] Unemployment still stood at 30 percent in 1998,[132] while inflation has been steadily lowered to 4.7 percent in 1997 and just 3 percent in 1998.[133] And although Macedonia has continued to rack up a trade deficit—7.4 percent of the GDP in 1997—the United States has helpfully bankrolled the deficit.[134] In 1998 the GDP recorded a growth of 5 percent.

The political transition began in 1989, when the local Communist government amended the republic's constitution to permit multiparty elections. The first such elections were held in November–December 1990. Ljupčo Georgievski's IMRO-DPMNU had taken the largest number of votes, winning 37 of the 120 seats in the unicameral parliament, and initially participated in the formation of a coalition government with the LC-Macedonia—Party for Democratic Reform, which had placed second, winning 31 seats in the parliament. But IMRO-DPMNU's strong differences with its coalition partners led to its withdrawal from the coalition, and the Albanian PDP took IMRO-DPMNU's place in the coalition. The result was a new coalition government involving the Social Democratic Union (the former Communists), the Liberal Party, the Socialist Party, and the Party for Democratic Prosperity.[135] Kiro Gligorov, a seventy-three-year-old veteran of the Partisan war known to his comrades as "Lisica" ("the Fox"), who had served as deputy minister of finance in the Yugoslav Communist government from 1947 to 1952, served as an economic adviser to the Belgrade government for most of the next two decades, been elected a member of the Yugoslav presidency in 1972 and president of the parliament in 1974, and retired from politics in 1978, was elected president of the republic.

The parliament approved the country's postcommunist constitution in November 1991. A major controversy had to do with whether the republic would be a "citizens' state," in which equal citizens enjoyed individual rights and rights as citizens, or a "national state," in which case there would also be recognition of the "collective rights" of one or more national groups. Ultimately, a compromise formulation was adopted. The preamble of the constitution defines Macedonia as a "national state," while the remainder of the constitution sets forth rights and duties in accordance with a concept of a "citizens' state."[136] Inevitably the compromise formula has been confusing both to some foreign observers and to locals, who have engaged in controversies which might have been avoided had the republic been defined in purely "citizen" terms.

In preparing for the 1994 elections, the three Macedonian parties of the ruling coalition formed a union called Alliance for Macedonia, which now outpolled Georgievski's party, taking 95 of the 114 parliamentary seats up for election.[137] Gligorov's party won 58 seats; the other 37 seats won by the Alliance were divided between the other two Alliance parties. In the presidential race, Gligorov was reelected president with a thundering avalanche of 78 percent of the vote, easily defeating Ljubiša Georgievski, a theater director, who ran as the standard-bearer for IMRO-DPMNU in place of the party's underage president, Ljupčo Georgievski. Ljubiša Georgievski attracted only 14.4 percent of the vote.[138]

Georgievski and other opposition leaders staged protest meetings on 19 October (after the first round of voting, with about 20,000 persons attending) and again on 26 October (after the second round). Petar Gošev, leader of the opposition Democratic Party, told the second protest meeting that the elections had been rigged and promised to continue to struggle against the system.[139] Opposition supporters lit candles to signify, as they put it, the "burial of democracy" in Macedonia and chanted "Macedonia is ours" and "Death to communism!"[140]

Ljupčo Georgievski received me in March 1995 in his office, under a portrait of Goce Delčev, the Macedonian terrorist leader who was murdered in 1903. He conveyed a general impression of low-key, unassertive nationalism while advocating a welfare state. His image as a family man—I later ran into him in the city park as he was pushing a pram with his wife at his side—was seen as part of his appeal to conservative values. As he related, the system remained—in his view—a totalitarian system and he claimed that the censorship was actually worse under Gligorov than it had been in Communist times.[141] He viewed himself as a champion of "the common man" in a battle against an alliance of political and cultural mafias.

In the wake of this electoral setback, Georgievski explored the possibility of an alliance with Arben Xhaferi's party. But this would have been at best a "marriage of convenience," and any coalition government resulting from this alliance would likely have been extremely unstable. Ultimately, however, Georgievski cast his lot in an alliance with Vasil Tupurkovski, at one time president of the League of Communist Youth of Yugoslavia, who had spent a number of years in Virginia. Georgievski's IMRO party and Tupurkovski's Democratic Alternative fashioned a coalition emphasizing a free-market economy and a program for prosperity. Abandoning its earlier nationalist rhetoric, IMRO strove for a new image in its posters. "One campaign poster showed a ripe tomato, labeled with the party symbol of a lion and a supermarket bar code. Another featured an aluminum drink can with the VMRO [IMRO] lion as brand label."[142] The promarket coalition coasted to victory in elections held on 18 October and 1 November 1998, winning 58–59 seats in the 120-seat Macedonian parliament and ending the eight-year reign of the Social Democratic Party's coalition government. IMRO alone picked up 46 or 47 seats (the remaining 12 went to Tupurkovski's Democratic Alternative), while the Social Democrats trailed far behind with just 29 seats. Xhaferi's Democratic Party of Albanians won 11 seats.[143] Georgievski now became prime minister.

Conclusion

For those postcommunist states of East-Central Europe that have taken the challenge of democratization seriously, there have been both European and non-European models upon whose experience to draw. Among non-European models, the American example looms very large. But the American experience retains, even now, a character of "exceptionalism" for most Europeans, who marvel that many Americans value "liberty" so exclusively that leading spokespersons and dominant political currents bridle at the notion of restricting the alleged right of neo-Nazis to march (a "right" that has been denied and abridged in post-1990 Germany as dangerous), of banning hate speech (in spite of the hurt done to victims), of controlling the access of anti-abortion activists who prevent or obstruct the access of women to medical facilities as if the latter enjoyed no rights of independent judgment and independent action, of prohibiting the proliferation of images of violence on films and television (in spite of the well-documented correlation between exposure to such images and violent behavior), or of introducing effective gun control in a nation languishing with phenomenal rates of urban and suburban violence.

In October 1998, returning to Ljubljana for the eighth time in twenty years, I took part in a conference on "Citizenship and Civic Education in Democracies." One of the other participants, an American professor from a well-known university on the Eastern seaboard, argued impassionedly against incorporating the "harm principle" into any political formula, in spite of the fact that that principle is a well-established component in the liberal project.[144] On his argument, nothing should be adopted which could abridge the "total freedom" once championed by Herbert Spencer; anything less would reveal an underlying distrust of one's fellow citizens, or so libertarians hold. Spencer knew quite well that "total freedom" meant that the rich and the powerful would enjoy unrestricted advantages, with the state not offering any protection to the weak or the poor; indeed, Spencer's understanding of justice recalls the nominalism of Socrates' antagonist Thrasymachus, who defined justice as "what advantages the interest of the ruling class."[145] Against this libertarianism, the Baron de Montesquieu once urged that "political liberty does not [or perhaps ought not] consist in an unlimited freedom. In governments, that is, in societies directed by laws, liberty can consist only in the power of doing what we ought to will."[146] For that matter, the concern for the harm principle may also be found within the American philosophical tradition. No less a figure than James Madison, the fourth president of the United States, argued that "pure democracy" could only give rise to "spectacles of turbulence and contention" and urged, instead, that institutional-legal safeguards be established to safeguard the interests and rights of the weak and the poor.[147] As for "distrust of one's fellow citizens," Madison himself admitted that "if men were angels, no government would be necessary,"[148] thereby underlining that the nonangelic nature of humankind necessitates government controls and protections.

In practice, it has been the right wing which has been the most enthusiastic champion of the "total freedom" of Spencer against the liberalism of Montesquieu and Madison, hoping thereby to open the doors to the unlimited accumulation of wealth, to the insinuation of plutocratic and oligarchic elements into systems with nominally democratic frameworks, and—where the radical right is concerned—to keep open the possibility for unrestrained hate speech. There is, thus, a connection not only between this kind "total freedom" and plutocracy, but also between such "total freedom" and populist and nationalist demagoguery.

In practice, there have been voices calling for rapid transformation, cautious (i.e., slow) transformation, laissez-faire economics, controlled economic transformation, national-state formulas, and citizens' state formulas. For Arben Xhaferi, the problem with Macedonian politics has much to do with the fact that the new state was "created in the spirit of political infantilism, by not accepting the notion that rights should be universal and equal."[149] But the political transition is not complete even now.

Indeed, in spite of the growing sophistication in both systems, the conversion to new ways of doing political business is not yet complete in either country, and among the new laws and procedures which have already been laid down, some will certainly be in need of refinement and adjustment in the coming months and years. The common challenge to both of them, in this time of transition, is to use discretion and judgment in appraising the legacy of communism and not to assume that everything ever done by the Communists was wicked and reprehensible. The challenge, as the quotation from Rebecca West at the outset of this chapter might suggest, is to know when it is better to preserve the artifacts of what is ever an ambiguous past, rather than to bulldoze the national heritage and replace it with a tomb to an unknown cod.

Notes

1. The official government estate prior to 1999 was 21 percent, as given in *Broj i struktura na naselenieto vo Republika Macedonija po opštini i nacionalna pripadnost* (Skopje: Republički zavod za statistika, 1991), p. 6. The figure claimed by Albanian activists in Macedonia was 40 percent.

2. Zagreb Domestic Service (11 October 1990), trans. in Foreign Broadcast Information Service (FBIS), *Daily Report* (Eastern Europe), 12 October 1990, p. 51.

3. *Profil* (Vienna) (30 July 1990), p. 37, trans. in FBIS, *Daily Report* (Eastern Europe), 1 August 1990, p. 58.

4. *Borba* (Belgrade) (10/11 November 1990), p. 5.

5. Tanjug (10 November 1990), in FBIS, *Daily Report* (Eastern Europe), 13 November 1990, p. 71.

6. *Delo* (Ljubljana) (17 November 1990), pp. 1, 3, as summarized in FBIS, *Daily Report* (Eastern Europe), 30 November 1990, p. 72.

7. E.g., in October, the Council of the Federation of the Free Trade Unions of Slovenia severed its connection with its Yugoslav federal counterpart. See Tanjug (29 October 1990), trans. in FBIS, *Daily Report* (Eastern Europe), 30 October 1990, p. 59.

8. *Die Presse* (Vienna) (16 January 1991), p. 4.

9. *Delo* (30 March 1991), pp. 1, 3, summarized in FBIS, *Daily Report* (Eastern Europe), 15 April 1991, p. 55.

10. *Borba* (30 July 1990), p. 14.

11. *Vjesnik* (Zagreb) (6 September 1990), p. 5.

12. *Politika* (Belgrade) (28 March 1991), p. 19.

13. *Neue Kronen-Zeitung* (Vienna) (10 August 1991), pp. 2–3, trans. in FBIS, *Daily Report* (Eastern Europe), 12 August 1991, p. 28.

14. Radio Slovenia Network (Ljubljana) (17 September 1991), trans. in FBIS, *Daily Report* (Eastern Europe), 18 September 1991, p. 30.

15. For details, see Tanjug (22 January 1992), in FBIS, *Daily Report* (Eastern Europe), 22 January 1992, p. 33.

16. Regarding Lithuania, see *Baltfax* (Moscow) (5 July 1991), in FBIS, *Daily Report* (Soviet Union), 9 July 1991, p. 54; and Radio Vilnius Network (Vilnius) (30 July 1991), trans. in FBIS, *Daily Report* (Soviet Union), 31 July 1991, p. 73. Regarding Georgia, see TASS International Service (Moscow) (12 August 1991), trans. in FBIS, *Daily Report* (Soviet Union), 13 August 1991, p. 59; Radio Slovenia Network (12 August 1991), trans. in FBIS, *Daily Report* (Eastern Europe), 13 August 1991, p. 32; and *Neue Zürcher Zeitung* (15 August 1991), p. 2. Regarding Latvia, see Tanjug (3 August 1991), trans. in FBIS, *Daily Report* (Soviet Union), 4 September 1991, p. 73.

17. *Neue Zürcher Zeitung* (1 February 1992), p. 4.

18. *Neodvisnni dnevnik* (Ljubljana), 26 November 1991, p. 5, trans. in FBIS, *Daily Report* (Eastern Europe), 10 December 1991, p. 47.

19. *Financial Times* (2 August 1991), p. 2.

20. Tanjug (12 December 1991), in FBIS, *Daily Report* (Eastern Europe), 13 December 1991, p. 25.

21. Tanjug (12 December 1991), in FBIS, *Daily Report* (Eastern Europe), 13 December 1991, p. 23. See further reports on Russian-Slovenian trade in *Delo* (3 October 1992), p. 2; and *Slovenec* (Ljubljana) (19 February 1993), p. 1.

22. Tanjug (23 April 1992), trans. in FBIS, *Daily Report* (Eastern Europe), 24 April 1992, p. 29.

23. *Il Piccolo* (Trieste) (26 March 1992), p. 8.

24. *Slobodna Dalmacija* (Split) (22 March 1992), p. 7.

25. Regarding the Benelux countries, see *Informacije iz Slovenije* (Ljubljana) (2 March 1992), pp. 2–7, trans. in FBIS, *Daily Report* (Eastern Europe), 1 May 1992, pp. 35–39. Regarding Iran, see Tanjug (10 March 1992), trans. in FBIS, *Daily Report* (Eastern Europe), 11 March 1992, p. 45. Regarding China, see *Delo* (27 February 1992), p. 3, trans. in FBIS, *Daily Report* (Eastern Europe), 6 March 1992, p. 43; and Radio Slovenia Network (11 May 1992); trans. in FBIS, *Daily Report* (Eastern Europe), 12 May 1992, p. 35.

26. Tanjug (12 February 1993), trans. in FBIS, *Daily Report* (Eastern Europe), 16 February 1993, p. 55.

27. Regarding Austria, see Radio Slovenia Network (4 November 1992), trans. in FBIS, *Daily Report* (Eastern Europe), 5 November 1992, p. 43. Regarding Hungary, see MTI (Budapest) (21 January 1993), in FBIS, *Daily Report* (Eastern Europe), 22 January 1993, p. 31.

28. *Dnevnik* (Ljubljana) (15 April 1992), p. 24, trans. in FBIS, *Daily Report* (Eastern Europe), 28 April 1992, p. 36.

29. Tanjug (6 October 1992), trans. in FBIS, *Daily Report* (Eastern Europe), 7 October 1992, p. 25.

30. *Vjesnik* (10 November 1993), p. 11, trans. in FBIS, *Daily Report* (Eastern Europe), 16 November 1993, p. 41; *Croatia Weekly* (Zagreb) (10 July 1998), p. 13, and (24 July 1998), p. 13; and *Slobodna Dalmacija* (Split) (19 October 1998), p. 8.

31. *Croatia Weekly* (5 June 1998), p.13.

32. *Croatia Weekly* (24 July 1998), p. 13. See also *Večernji list* (Zagreb) (18 June 1994), p. 7, reprinted from *Slobodna Dalmacija*; and *Croatia Weekly* (19 June 1998), p. 13.

33. *The European* (London) (28 October–3 November 1994), p. 2.

34. For details on the Slovenian-Italian dispute, see Sabrina P. Ramet, "The Slovenian Success Story," in *Current History*, Vol. 97, No. 617 (March 1998), p. 114.

35. *The Economist* (London) (11 January 1997), p. 41.

36. *Delo* (26 February 1993), p. 1, trans. in FBIS, *Daily Report* (Eastern Europe), 23 March 1993, p. 35.

37. *Neue Zürcher Zeitung* (2 November 1994), p. 11.

38. Regarding EFTA, see Radio Slovenia Network (21 May 1992), trans. in FBIS, *Daily Report* (Eastern Europe), 22 May 1992, p. 26. Regarding the EC trade agreement, see *Neue Zürcher Zeitung* (7 April 1993), p. 13.

39. *Daily Yomiuri* (25 June 1998), p. 5.

40. See Sabrina Petra Ramet, "Slovenia's Road to Democracy," in *Europe-Asia Studies*, Vol. 45, No. 5 (1993), pp. 879–883; and Sabrina P. Ramet, "Democratization in Slovenia—The Second Stage," in Karen Dawisha and Bruce Parrott (eds.), *Politics, Power, and the Struggle for Democracy in South-East Europe* (Cambridge: Cambridge University Press, 1997), pp. 189–225.

41. Tanjug (26 November 1992), in FBIS, *Daily Report* (Eastern Europe), 30 November 1992, p. 48.

42. *Süddeutsche Zeitung* (Munich) (13–15 August 1994), p. 6.

43. *Croatia Weekly* (26 March 1998), p. 10.

44. *Croatia Weekly* (17 September 1998), p. 10.

45. Egon Žižmond, "Slovenia—One Year of Independence," in *Europe-Asia Studies*, Vol. 45, No. 5 (1993), p.887.

46. Ibid., p. 888.

47. Georg Witschel, "Sloweniens Wirtschaftslage im Frühjahr 1994," in *Südost Europa*, Vol. 43, No. 1 (January 1994), pp. 60–61.

48. *Slovenija v številkah* (Ljubljana: Statistični Urad Republike Slovenije, June 1998), p. 61.

49. *Daily Yomiuri* (25 June 1998), p. 5.

50. *Slovenija v številkah*, p. 35.

51. Ibid., p. 26.

52. *Daily Yomiuri* (28 April 1998), p. 5A.

53. Ibid.; and Radio Slovenia Network (27 February 1992), trans. in FBIS, *Daily Report* (Eastern Europe), 3 March 1992, p. 41.

54. Michael Moran, "A Year Later: The State of Slovenia," in *The New Leader* (10–24 August 1992), p. 8.

55. *Delo* (25 April 1992), p. 2, trans. in FBIS, *Daily Report* (Eastern Europe), 8 May 1992, p. 24.

56. *Die Presse* (16 June 1992), p. 3; and *Die Furche* (Vienna) (18 June 1992), p. 1.

57. See *The European—élan* (London) (15–21 April 1994), p. 4.

58. *Delo* (24 August 1993), p. 2, trans. in FBIS, *Daily Report* (Eastern Europe), 17 September 1993, p. 58.

59. *Frankfurter Allgemeine* (30 March 1994), p. 2.

60. *Eastern Europe Newsletter*, Vol. 8, No. 8 (13 April 1994), pp. 7–8. For background, see *Eastern Europe Newsletter*, Vol. 8, No. 7 (29 March 1994), pp. 1–2.

61. For some background, see Rudi Rizman's open letter in *Frankfurter Rundschau* (17 October 1994), p. 20.

62. For example, in March 1993, the Green Party of Dušan Plut split into left and right factions. On this, see *Delo* (18 March 1993), p. 2, trans. in FBIS, *Daily Report* (Eastern Europe), 13 April 1993, p. 27.

63. On women's rights, see Ramet, "Democratization in Slovenia—The Second Stage," passim.

64. *Ura evropske resnice za Slovenijo/The Hour of European Truth for Slovenia* (Ljubljana: Nova revija, 1997), pp. 33, 37.

65. Ibid., p. 38.

66. Ibid., p. 54.

67. Ibid., p. 61.

68. See Danica Fink-Hafner, "Development of a Party System," in Danica Fink-Hafner and John R. Robbins (eds.), *Making a New Nation: The Formation of Slovenia* (Aldershot, England: Dartmouth, 1997).

69. Rudolf M. Rizman, "Radical Right Politics in Slovenia," in Sabrina P. Ramet (ed.), *The Radical Right in Eastern Europe Since 1989* (University Park: Pennsylvania State University Press, forthcoming in 1999).

70. Vlado Miheljak, "Political Culture: Potentials of In/tolerance by Slovene Youth in the 1990s—Empirical Findings," in Mirjana Ule and Tanja Rener (eds.), *Youth in Slovenia: New*

Perspectives from the Nineties (Ljubljana: Youth Department of the Ministry of Education and Sport, 1998), p. 243.

71. Details in Ramet, "The Slovenian Success Story," pp. 116–117. See also *Politika* (Belgrade) (19 October 1998), p. 7; and *Delo* (24 October 1998), pp. 1–2; also *Gorenjski glas* (Kranj) (23 October 1998), p. 7.

72. *Croatia Weekly* (29 May 1998), p. 10.

73. *Politika* (22 October 1998), p. 7; and *Vjesnik* (Zagreb) (24 October 1998), p. 8.

74. Mitja Žagar, "The Republic of Slovenia: Is a Success Story Possible?" (Ljubljana, 1997, manuscript).

75. Danica Fink-Hafner, "Organized interests in the policy-making process in Slovenia," in *Journal of European Public Policy*, Vol. 5, No. 2 (June 1998), p. 290.

76. Ibid.

77. Details in Sabrina Petra Ramet, *Nationalism and Federalism in Yugoslavia, 1962–1991*, 2nd ed. (Bloomington: Indiana University Press, 1992), pp. 256–257.

78. *Eastern Europe Newsletter*, Vol. 8, No. 20 (5 October 1994), p. 5.

79. Radio Belgrade Network (22 January 1992), trans. in FBIS, *Daily Report* (Eastern Europe), 23 January 1992, p. 59.

80. Radio Belgrade Network (5 February 1992), trans. in FBIS, *Daily Report* (Eastern Europe), 6 February 1992, p. 25; Tanjug (13 February 1992), trans. in FBIS, *Daily Report* (Eastern Europe), 14 February 1992, p. 41; Tanjug (21 February 1992), trans. in FBIS, *Daily Report* (Eastern Europe), 24 February 1992, p. 37; Radio Macedonia Network (Skopje) (24 February 1992), trans. in FBIS, *Daily Report* (Eastern Europe), 25 February 1992, p. 47; Tanjug (26 March 1992), trans. in FBIS, *Daily Report* (Eastern Europe), 27 March 1992, pp. 49–50.

81. Loring M. Danforth, *The Macedonian Conflict: Ethnic Transnationalism in a Transnational World* (Princeton: Princeton University Press, 1995), p. 148.

82. As quoted in ibid.

83. *Neue Zürcher Zeitung* (28 April 1992), p. 4.

84. Radio Belgrade Network (6 January 1992), trans. in FBIS, *Daily Report* (Eastern Europe), 6 January 1992, p. 57; and *Politika—International Weekly* (Belgrade) (11–17 January 1992), p. 4.

85. The complaint, if taken literally, would seem to set a precedent for a later Greek complaint about the city of Athens, Georgia.

86. For more details, see Sabrina Petra Ramet, "The Macedonian Enigma," in Sabrina Petra Ramet and Ljubiša S. Adamovich (eds.), *Beyond Yugoslavia: Politics, Economics, and Culture in a Shattered Community* (Boulder: Westview Press, 1995).

87. As estimated by Duncan M. Perry in his article "Crisis in the Making? Macedonia and Its Neighbors," in *Südost Europa*, Vol. 43, Nos. 1–2 (January–February 1994), p. 44. The Macedonian government says there are 230,000 Macedonians in Greece.

88. ET-1 Television Network (Athens) (9 February 1994), trans. in FBIS, *Daily Report* (Eastern Europe), 10 February 1994, p. 38; and *U.S. Department of State Dispatch*, Vol. 5, No. 8 (21 February 1994), p. 98.

89. *Japan Times* (18 February 1994), p. 5.

90. This account is based on Hanna Rosin, "Why We Flip-flopped on Macedonia: Greek Pique," in *The New Republic* (13 June 1994), p. 11.

91. *Mainichi Daily News* (Tokyo) (23 February 1994), p. 3; *Japan Times* (23 February 1994), p. 5, and (9 April 1994), p. 7; *The European* (8–14 April 1994), p. 2, and (1–7 July 1994), p. 2; *Financial Times* (11 April 1994), p. 30; and *New York Times* (1 July 1994), p. A4.

92. *The Times* (London) (13 June 1994), p. 15; and *Neue Zürcher Zeitung* (17 June 1994), p. 5.

93. *The Observer* (London) (16 October 1994), p. 17.

94. *Ljiljan* (Sarajevo-Ljubljana) (23 November 1994), p. 9.

95. *Süddeutsche Zeitung* (13–15 August 1994), p. 6; and *Neue Zürcher Zeitung* (24 September 1994), p. 7, and (27 September 1994), p. 4.

96. *Illyria* (The Bronx) (23–25 May 1998), p. 7.

97. Duncan Perry, "Destiny on Hold: Macedonia and the Dangers of Ethnic Discord," in *Current History*, Vol. 97, No. 617 (March 1998), p. 120.

98. Xheladin Murati, in interview with the author, Tetovo, 20 March 1995. For discussion, see *Süddeutsche Zeitung* (5/6 December 1992), p. 5; for a wide-ranging survey of the historical, demographic, and geographic context of Macedonia's Albanians, see Jovan Trifunoški, *Albansko stanovništvo u Socijalističkoj Republici Makedoniji* (Belgrade: Književne novine, 1988).

99. *Neue Zürcher Zeitung* (27 June 1992), p. 5; also *Dijaspora* [a Serbian publication targeting Serbs outside Serbia], as summarized in *Vjesnik* (1 August 1994), p. 9, trans. in FBIS, *Daily Report* (Eastern Europe), 17 August 1994, p. 38.

100. Zoltan Barany, "The Roma in Macedonia: Ethnic politics and the marginal condition in a Balkan state," in *Ethnic and Racial Studies*, Vol. 18, No. 3 (July 1995), p. 517. For Barany's estimates of the numbers of Roma in seven East-Central European states, see Zoltan Barany, "Ethnic mobilization and the state: the Roma in Eastern Europe," in *Ethnic and Racial Studies*, Vol. 21, No. 2 (March 1998), p. 313.

101. *Neue Zürcher Zeitung* (23 June 1994), p. 3.

102. Branded a "militant" by the *New York Times*; branded a "saber rattler" by the *Christian Science Monitor*. See *New York Times* (11 May 1998), p. A6; and *Christian Science Monitor* (29 May 1998), p. 7.

103. Arben Xhaferi, in interview with the author, Tetovo, 20 March 1995.

104. Enver Shala, in interview with the author, Tetovo, 20 March 1995.

105. Tanjug (28 August 1990), trans. in FBIS, *Daily Report* (Eastern Europe), 29 August 1990, p. 73.

106. Regarding the fallacies associated with claims of a "natural right" to autonomy, see Sabrina P. Ramet, *Whose Democracy? Nationalism, Religion, and the Doctrine of Collective Rights in Post-1989 Eastern Europe* (Lanham, Md.: Rowman & Littlefield, 1997), pp. 94, 159–162, 173–176.

107. Tanjug (11 January 1992), trans. in FBIS, *Daily Report* (Eastern Europe), 13 January 1992, p. 57; *Borba* (13 January 1992), pp. 1–2; Radio Belgrade Network (15 January 1992), trans. in FBIS, *Daily Report* (Eastern Europe), 15 January 1992, pp. 58–59; Tanjug (15 January 1992), trans. in FBIS, *Daily Report* (Eastern Europe), 16 January 1992, p. 59; and Perry, "Crisis in the Making," p. 36.

108. Tanjug (31 March 1992), trans. in FBIS, *Daily Report* (Eastern Europe), 1 April 1992, p. 52.

109. See, for example, *Nova Makedonija* (Skopje) (20 November 1993), p. 4, trans. in FBIS, *Daily Report* (Eastern Europe), 30 November 1993, p. 59.

110. Tanjug (9 April 1992), in FBIS, *Daily Report* (Eastern Europe), 10 April 1992, p. 51.

111. *Borba* (25/26 April 1992), p. 6.

112. *Nova Makedonija* (5 November 1994), p. 4, trans. in FBIS, *Daily Report* (Eastern Europe), 10 November 1994, p. 48.

113. For further discussion, see Sabrina P. Ramet, "All Quiet on the Southern Front? Macedonia Between the Hammer and the Anvil," in *Problems of Post-Communism*, Vol. 42, No. 6 (November–December 1995).

114. Ilinka Mitreva, in interview with the author, Skopje, 24 March 1995.

115. Perry, "Destiny on Hold," p. 123.

116. *Los Angeles Times*, reprinted in *Daily Yomiuri* (31 August 1998), p. 12.

117. MIC (Skopje) (10 November 1993); *Nova Makedonija* (11 November 1993), pp. 1, 4; and Radio Macedonia Network (Skopje) (11 November 1993)—all trans. in FBIS, *Daily Report* (Eastern Europe), 12 November 1993, pp. 62–63, 65–66; *RFE/RL News Briefs* (8–12 November 1993), p. 13; and *The Economist* (London) (20 November 1993), p. 46.

118. Perry, "Crisis in the Making," p. 37. See also Duncan Perry, "The Republic of Macedonia: Finding Its Way," in Dawisha and Parrott (eds.), *Politics, Power, and the Struggle.*

119. *The Economist* (26 July 1997), p. 42.

120. *New York Times* (11 May 1998), p. A6.

121. As reported in *Illyria* (11–13 April 1998), p. 7, (29 April–1 May 1998), p. 5, and (1–3 July 1998), p. 6. See also *Illyria* (5–7 August 1998), p. 7. For further discussion of the situation of Albanians in Macedonia, see Hugh Poulton, *Who Are the Macedonians?* (Bloomington: Indiana University Press, 1995), pp. 182–191; and Ramet, *Whose Democracy*, pp. 77–82.

122. *Washington Post* (16 March 1998), p. A17. Concerning arms smuggling across this border, see also *Los Angeles Times*, reprinted in *Daily Yomiuri* (31 August 1998), pp. 7, 12. Regarding the impact of events in Kosovo on Macedonia, see also *Vjesnik* (24 October 1998), p. 8.

123. See, for example, *Nova Makedonija* (4 January 1992), p. 15, trans. in FBIS, *Daily Report* (Eastern Europe), 29 January 1992, pp. 41–44.

124. Comments by Erdogan Šarac, president of the Democratic Party of Ethnic Turks, as reported in Tanjug (31 October 1992), trans. in FBIS, *Daily Report* (Eastern Europe), 2 November 1992, p. 42.

125. Meto Jovanovski, in interview with the author, Skopje, 16 March 1995.

126. *Politika* (5 October 1992), p. 5.

127. *Nova Makedonija* (23 January 1993), trans. into German as "Die serbische Minderheit in Makedonien," in *Osteuropa*, Vol. 43, No. 9 (September 1993), p. A525. These desiderata are confirmed in Tanjug (20 March 1993), trans. in FBIS, *Daily Report* (Eastern Europe), 22 March 1993, p. 73.

128. *MILS NEWS, Dnevni vesti* (Skopje) (27 August 1993), trans. in FBIS, *Daily Report* (Eastern Europe), 30 August 1993, p. 70.

129. Data from *Neue Zürcher Zeitung* (12 May 1993), p. 19.

130. See his interview with *Die Zeit* (Hamburg) (19 August 1994), p. 9. See also *Slobodna Dalmacija* (Split) (19 October 1994), p. 11.

131. Ramet, *Whose Democracy*, pp. 40–41: the original sources for these statistics are given there.

132. *Financial Times* (3 November 1998), p. 2.

133. *Financial Times* (30 October 1998), p. 3.

134. *The Economist* (7 March 1998), p. 54.

135. Saško Stefkov, Minister without Portfolio from the Liberal Party, in interview with the author, Skopje, 17 March 1995.

136. Danforth, *The Macedonian Conflict*, pp. 144–145.

137. *Nova Makedonija* (15 November 1994), pp. 1, 4, trans. in FBIS, *Daily Report* (Eastern Europe), 19 August 1994, p. 35.

138. *Süddeutsche Zeitung* (22–23 October 1994), p. 9; *Slobodna Dalmacija* (19 October 1994), p. 10; and "Macedonia," in Edward Lawson, *Encyclopedia of Human Rights*, 2nd ed. (Washington D.C.: Taylor & Francis, 1996), p. 977.

139. *Večer* (Skopje) (27 October 1994), p. 4, trans. in FBIS, *Daily Report* (Eastern Europe), 28 October 1994, p. 34.

140. AFP (Paris) (30 October 1994), in FBIS, *Daily Report* (Eastern Europe), 31 October 1994, p. 53.

141. Ljupčo Georgievski, in interview with the author, Skopje, 16 March 1995.

142. *Financial Times* (3 November 1998), p. 2.

143. Ibid. Regarding the elections, see also *Vreme* (Belgrade) (17 October 1998), pp. 48–49; *Politika* (19 October 1998), p. 7; *Die Welt* (Bonn) (20 October 1998), p. 7; *Večernji list* (Zagreb) (21 October 1998), p. 13; *Daily Yomiuri* (21 October 1998), p. 6; *Il Piccolo* (Trieste) (21 October 1998), p. 11; *Vreme* (24 October 1998), pp. 52–53; and *Delo* (Ljubljana) (24 October 1998), p. 4.

144. On this point, see Joseph Raz, "Autonomy, Toleration, and the Harm Principle," in Susan Mendus (ed.), *Justifying Toleration: Conceptual and Historical Perspectives* (Cambridge: Cambridge University Press, 1988), esp. pp. 157, 165.

145. Thrasymachus, as quoted in Plato, *The Republic*, trans. Richard W. Sterling and William C. Scott (New York: W. W. Norton, 1985), Book 1, p. 36.

146. Baron de Montesequieu, *The Spirit of the Laws* (1748), excerpted in Isaac Kramnick (ed.), *The Portable Enlightenment Reader* (London: Penguin Books, 1995), p. 412.

147. James Madison, *Federalist Papers Nos. 10, 51* in Alexander Hamilton, James Madison, and John Jay, *The Federalist Papers* (New York: Mentor Books/New American Library, 1961), pp. 81, 323–324.

148. Madison, *Federalist Paper No. 51*, p. 322.

149. Arben Xhaferi, in interview with the author, Tetovo, 20 March 1995.

CHAPTER TEN

◆

The Struggle for Bosnia

Muslims, Serbs, and Croats had lived in peace for most of the five hundred years they cohabited in Bosnia-Herzegovina.[1] The intercommunal violence which accompanied World War II was an important deviation from this pattern, but even then the situation was complicated. Muslims and Croats, for example, were found in the ranks of both the *Ustaše* and the Communist-led Partisans, while Serbs were found with both Draža Mihailović's Chetniks and Tito's Partisans. The Serbian Insurrectionary War of 1991–1995 was different in that, with the exception of the defenders of Sarajevo, each of the respective sides tended to recruit almost exclusively from the nationality it claimed to represent.

No society slides into fratricidal war until the seeds of intercommunal hatred have been sown. In many historical cases, it was the religious organizations which played the most crucial role in sowing such hatreds; and in the case of Yugoslavia, the Serbian Orthodox Church certainly deserves credit for having done much to embitter Serbs against Albanians, in the first place, and subsequently against Croats. There had been some difficulties in Bosnia throughout the years after World War II, but there were always countervailing tendencies, self-designated "Yugoslavs," threads of Titoism, and a sense and understanding that Bosnia was a community in its own right.

That sense of Bosnianness began to unravel in the latter half of the 1980s, and by 1989 the deterioration of interethnic relations in Bosnia became sufficiently visible to be mentioned in the local press.[2] A well-publicized brawl between Serbs and Muslims in the village of Kožja Luka, near Foča, in August 1990 alerted the Yugoslav public to the growing disintegration of social harmony in that republic,[3] and soon after—in September or October of that year—Bosnian Serbs began setting up illegal military formations in Bosnia, formations that were supplied and trained, on a clandestine basis, by the Serb-controlled JNA.[4] These formations were set up, thus, *before* the elections which would place Muslim leader Alija Izetbegović in the presidency and cannot, therefore, be portrayed as a response to his election. They were, moreover, strikingly discordant with Izetbegović's call for establishing Bosnia as a "free civic union" of all of its citizens and his explicit rejection of any form of Muslim exclusivism.[5]

The census of April 1991 recorded that 43.77 percent of the residents of Bosnia-Herzegovina were "ethnic Muslims," 31.46 percent were Serbs, and 17.34 percent were Croats.[6] There were especially large concentrations of Serbs in western Bosnia—far from the Republic of Serbia—and of Muslims in eastern Bosnia, along the Serbian border. But the picture was rendered even more complex by the fact that in only 32 of Bosnia-Herzegovina's 109 districts did one of the three ethnic groups constitute 70 percent or more of the local population.[7] Muslims constituted the majority group in 11 of these districts, Serbs in another 11, and Croats in 10. Under the circumstances, all three communities had long shared the view that any partition of the republic was entirely out of the question,[8] quite apart from its being injurious to the sense of Bosnian community.

Shortly after the war in Croatia began, the Yugoslav army's high command commissioned a study of likely international responses to the war. The committee entrusted with this assignment studied Western responses to Iraqi threats and to the eventual Iraqi invasion of Kuwait and specifically ruled out any conclusion that a similar Western response might be anticipated in the cases of Croatia or Bosnia. Some of the findings were published in the army journal, *Vojno delo*, in October 1991. In a key contribution to this issue, Milan Radaković summarized the army experts' consensus that there was "little reason to expect international armed intervention in Yugoslavia."[9]

Vojno delo also correctly identified the need for international consensus, especially within the U.N. Security Council, as a critical weakness to be exploited. One of the tactics Belgrade adopted in exploiting this weakness was to play on American tendencies to see trouble spots as potential "Vietnams."[10] Nor was there anything subtle about the Serbian approach, as Bosnian Serb leader Radovan Karadžić, then–Prime Minister Milan Panić, and others explicitly warned that any U.S. involvement would lead to a Vietnam-type situation dragging on for years.[11]

There were isolated calls for a forceful Western response to the Serbian seizure of some 30 percent of Croatia's territory in the months between July 1991 and January 1992. There was also unmistakable evidence of Serbian military preparations for armed action in Bosnia.[12] Slovenian Prime Minister Lojze Peterle told me in March 1992 that he had tried the previous December to persuade the West to press the U.N. to send a peacekeeping mission to Bosnia, to prevent the outbreak of hostilities; he was informed that a peacekeeping mission could not be sent to an area which was still at peace. Indeed, the only Western response during 1991 to the growing tensions within Bosnia was to include Bosnia-Herzegovina in the general arms embargo imposed, at the urgent request of Serbian President Milošević, on all five Yugoslav successor states via the U.N. Security Council on 25 September 1991.[13] During the months between October 1990 and March 1992, as explained in Chapter 3, the illegally established Serbian militias loyal to Bosnian Serb politician Radovan Karadžić benefitted from a steady infusion of armaments, including tanks and heavy artillery, from the Yugoslav army. Bosnia's Croat and Muslim communities were constrained to look elsewhere for arms and, thanks at least in part to the arms embargo, were able to obtain much less in the way of military hardware than the Serbs; this was especially true of the Muslims, whose leading figure made little effort at the time to secure much in the way of weaponry.

In June 1991, Adil Zulfikarpašić, a distinguished Bosnian figure who had been living in exile in Zürich, Switzerland, and Muhamed Filipović met with Radovan Karadžić, Nikola Koljević, and Momčilo Krajišnik, the leaders among Bosnia's Serbs, for the purpose of reaching an agreement on the status of Bosnia-Herzegovina; in so doing, they enjoyed the authorization of the Izetbegović government. An agreement was reached that Bosnia-Herzegovina would remain an integral whole, linked with rump Yugoslavia in a confederative association, and that the Sandžak, which had been conjoined with Bosnia-Herzegovina until 1878, would be granted cultural and administrative autonomy, including complete self-administration in schooling, language, and culture; under the agreement, the local Muslims would enjoy 60 percent representation in the Serbian portion of the Sandžak and a 40 percent representation in the Montenegrin portion.[14] Milošević agreed to the arrangement, as did Izetbegović initially. Subsequently, however, Izetbegović withdrew from the agreement, thereby killing what was perhaps the last chance for peace in Bosnia.

Four Serb autonomous regions were established in Bosnia, and in September 1991 they requested assistance from the FRY army. Well over 5,000 Yugoslav army troops were dispatched in response to this request and had secured the borders of a self-designated "Serb Autonomous Region of Herzegovina" by the end of the month.[15] On 25 September 1991, Yugoslav army units destroyed the Bosnian village of Ravno, inhabited for the most part by Croats.[16] That same week, the independent weekly magazine *Vreme* revealed details of the so-called "Ram" (Frame) plan for the organization of an armed insurrection of Bosnian Serbs.[17] In the course of fall 1991, Serb authorities dismantled some arms production facilities in Bosnia-Herzegovina and transferred them to Serbia.[18] By the beginning of December 1991, moreover, the Yugoslav army had encircled Sarajevo, Mostar, Bihać, and Tuzla with heavy weaponry, thereby signaling Belgrade's intentions with unmistakable clarity.[19]

Between 31 December 1991 and 2 January 1992, the governments of rump Yugoslavia and of Croatia and officials of the Yugoslav army and of the Croatian National Guard agreed to a cease-fire in place and to a plan, brokered by U.N. special envoy Cyrus Vance, which called for the withdrawal of the Yugoslav army from the Republic of Croatia and for the emplacement of some 10,000 (later increased to 13,500) U.N. peacekeeping troops in Croatia. This truce set the stage for the expansion of the war into Bosnia. Also in January, Milošević issued a secret order transferring Bosnian-born army officers back to Bosnia. As a result of this transfer, as Silber and Little point out, "by the time the JNA made its formal withdrawal from Bosnia in May 1992, the vast majority of the officers who remained there were actually Bosnian Serbs. They were not citizens of Yugoslavia, which, by then, was another country."[20]

The Bosnian War to April 1993

On 12 November 1991, Bosnian President Izetbegović had warned of the danger of "total war" breaking out in his republic and had requested the immediate dispatch of U.N. peacekeeping forces to head off the impending conflict (a request seconded, as we have seen, by Slovenian Prime Minister Peterle the following month).[21] On 20 December, three months after Karadžić and Milošević had met to coordinate plans for the Serbian assault on Bosnia-Herzegovina,[22] the Bosnian presidency requested diplomatic recognition from the EC. On the next day, an insurgent Assembly of Bosnian Serbs proclaimed the creation of the Serbian Republic of Bosnia-Herzegovina. This was followed, on 22 December, by Izetbegović's appeal to the U.N. to deploy a peacekeeping force along Bosnia's borders.[23] The U.N. failed to respond, however, and on 9 January 1992, less than a week after the cease-fire in Croatia had taken effect, the Bosnian Serb minority proclaimed the independence of this Bosnian Serb Republic. It was clear to all observers that Bosnia's fragile and tenuous stability was crumbling and that there was a high risk of hostilities. Meanwhile, pressed by the EC's Badinter Commission to let the people of Bosnia vote on their political future, the elected government of Bosnia-Herzegovina held a referendum on independence 29 February–1 March 1992. Karadžić told Bosnian Serbs that it was their duty to boycott the referendum and the Yugoslav air force assisted by dropping leaflets urging Serbs to stay home.[24] The Bosnian Serbs, who had already declared their secession from Bosnia, protested, claiming that by calling for a vote the government of Sarajevo had violated certain unwritten "rules of the game." The Serbs boycotted the referendum, but 63.4 percent of the population nonetheless took part, of which 99.4 percent voted yes. As a result, 62.7 percent of the total number of eligible voters (whether voting or not) declared themselves in favor of the measure.[25]

Zagreb seems to have been confused (or at least divided) as to its goals or strategies at this time. On the one hand, Croatian officials are known to have held secret talks about this time with their Serbian counterparts concerning a possible partition of Bosnia.[26] On the other hand, Josip Manolić, chief of the Secret Service of Croatia, warned the Serbs in mid-March that in the event that the war should spread to Bosnia, Croats would not be able to stand aside,[27] and when the Serbs ignited hostilities in April, the Croats began selling war materiel to the Bosnian army.[28]

The day after the Bosnian referendum on independence was held, the Serbs set up barricades in Sarajevo. Undeterred, the Sarajevo government, under the presidency of Alija Izetbegović, declared Bosnian independence on 3 March. By this point, Bosnian Serb leader Karadžić was talking openly of a war to keep Serbian regions of Bosnia attached to the FRY.

It was now, at the proverbial "last minute," that the EC made an all too feeble attempt at achieving a compromise, proposing a "cantonization" scheme which would have divided Bosnia-Herzegovina into several dozen ethnic-based cantons.[29] (A partition assigning eastern Bosnia to Serbia, southwestern Herzegovina to Croatia, and the rest to the Muslims, if accepted by the three sides and if accompanied by extensive population exchanges, might have had much better prospects of avoiding blood-shed, though that too would have involved hardship.) But all three communities re-jected the cantonization scheme, and as the month progressed, there were ever more serious incidents and confrontations between Serbs and non-Serbs in Bosnia.[30] On 3 April, for instance, there were serious clashes in the towns of Bosanski Brod and Kupres between Serbian irregulars (backed by the Yugoslav army), on the one side, and Bosnian Muslims and Croats, on the other. On 4 April, Serb militia forces, backed up by JNA ground and air forces, launched armed attacks on Croat and Muslim settlements throughout the republic. Finally, on 6 April, Bosnian Serbs opened a military front in the eastern part of the republic and began to push west-ward. Within five weeks, the Serbian insurgents controlled more than 60 percent of Bosnia.[31] In May, responding to international protests, Milošević demonstratively ordered the withdrawal of the Yugoslav army, which had played a central role in the fighting. But the move was largely cosmetic: of the 89,000 Yugoslav army troops that had been fighting alongside Karadžić's irregulars, only about 14,000 were actu-ally withdrawn. The rest were transferred to Karadžić's command and renamed the Army of the Serbian Republic of Bosnia-Herzegovina.[32] By the end of the year, Bosnian Serbs controlled 70 percent of the territory of Bosnia-Herzegovina.

The United States, Western Europe, and the Islamic nations were the powers most directly concerned with debates about the growing Bosnian crisis. The Islamic community realized that any move on its part, even if on a multilateral basis, could actually hurt the Bosnian Muslims by allowing the West to view the conflict as a showdown between the Christian West and "fundamentalist" Islam (as Serbian me-dia portrayed the conflict). In fact, clandestine weapons shipments to the Bosnian Muslims from Iran and other Islamic states began already in 1992, when George Bush was still U.S. president; the shipments were made with Croatian, but not U.S., complicity, however, and the Croats skimmed a percentage off the top, including all heavy weaponry.[33] These shipments remained secret for the time being. Publicly, the Islamic nations deferred to the West and restricted themselves to periodic confer-ences on Bosnia, protests against Western inaction, and demands for a lifting of the arms embargo. The United States, for its part, first under Bush and then (albeit rather inconsistently) under Clinton, chose to leave it to the EC to sort out, on the reasoning that armed conflict in Europe was a "European problem."[34] The European states themselves were divided between traditional friends of the Croats (Germany and Austria), traditional friends of the Serbs (France and Russia), and the tradition-ally apathetic (Great Britain and the Netherlands). Because of these factors, the in-ternational community was slow to react.[35]

Only on 30 May 1992, nearly two months after the opening of full-scale warfare in Bosnia-Herzegovina, did the U.N. Security Council vote to impose trade sanc-tions on Serbia. Thanks to obstruction by Serbia's friend, Russia, the Conference on Security and Cooperation in Europe (CSCE) was even slower to act and voted merely to suspend Serbia (the FRY) from its ranks for three months, taking that vote only on 8 July.

Earlier, in December 1991, the U.N. Security Council had adopted Resolution No. 724, affirming that the conditions for introducing U.N. peacekeeping forces in former Yugoslavia did not yet exist.[36] Later, in April 1992, by which time U.N. peacekeepers had been introduced in Croatia, U.N. Secretary-General Boutros Boutros-Ghali rebuffed calls for an extension of the U.N. mandate in Croatia to include Bosnia. In a report to the U.N. Security Council on 13 May, Marrack Goulding, head of the U.N. Department of Peacekeeping Operations, had warned against any such deployment in war-torn Bosnia.[37] In spite of this warning, the Security Council decided on 8 June to authorize a U.N. Protection Force (UNPROFOR) to take control of Sarajevo airport. The UNPROFOR presence in Bosnia expanded rapidly in the weeks and months thereafter.[38] Boutros-Ghali had, by then, become enamored of the idea of using U.N. forces in this way, and in a policy statement entitled "An Agenda for Peace," Boutros-Ghali claimed to see an opportunity to "achieve the great objectives of the [U.N.] Charter—a United Nations capable of maintaining international peace and security, of securing human rights and justice and of promoting ... social progress and better standards of life in larger freedom."[39]

Meanwhile, the internal division among Bosnian Croats, between figures such as Stjepan Kljuić, who favored cooperation with the Muslims for the purpose of preserving a unified Bosnia-Herzegovina, and figures such as Mate Boban, who favored the annexation of Croat-inhabited parts of the republic by Croatia, was resolved with the replacement of Kljuić by Boban and the assassination, on Zagreb's orders, of Blaž Kraljević, the highly effective commander of the anti-Serbian militia of Croats and Muslims known as the Croatian Defense Forces (HOS, from the Croatian).[40] With Boban at their helm, the Bosnian Croats now adopted a separatist course, concentrating on consolidating their hold on western Herzegovina, where in early July 1992 they proclaimed the creation of Herceg-Bosna (already mentioned in Chapter 8) as a nominally independent Bosnian Croat state whose intended future clearly lay in absorption into Croatia.[41]

Only in August 1992, by which point there were already 50,000 dead (mostly civilians) and more than 2 million homeless as a result of Serbian aggression in both Croatia and Bosnia, did the EC convene the so-called London Conference. The London Conference recognized the territorial integrity of Bosnia-Herzegovina and identified Serbia and Montenegro as aggressors, calling for the introduction of U.N. peacekeeping forces into Bosnia in order to maintain a cease-fire in the area.[42]

The Geneva Peace Conference, which began its work the following month, was tasked to find mechanisms to implement the principles laid down at the London Conference. However, guided by cochairmen David Lord Owen (for the EC) and Cyrus Vance (for the U.N. Secretary-General), the Geneva Conference in effect repudiated its mandate. Instead of honoring the London Conference's recognition of the elected government of Alija Izetbegović as having, by that virtue, a status higher than that of insurgent forces, Vance and Owen introduced the notion of "three warring factions." This placed the government of Sarajevo on the same level with the Croat and Serbian insurgents. This laid the basis for negotiating the partition of

Bosnia, which entailed, in turn, the decision to reward Serbian aggression. The U.N. and EC mediators, along with the Western media, began to treat the Bosnian government as if it represented only Muslims, even though, as of 12 February 1993, the Bosnian cabinet still included six Serbs and five Croats alongside nine Muslims.[43]

Indeed, as already noted, the Croats, who had at first supported the Izetbegović government, had decided to go it alone and seized about 20 percent of Bosnia's territory, including much of southwestern Herzegovina. The war had become a three-cornered conflict, and the Izetbegović government, despite the continued presence of some Croats and Serbs in its ranks and although legitimately elected as the government of all the peoples of Bosnia-Herzegovina, was increasingly seen as the government of Bosnian Muslims only. At the same time, it must be conceded that the Izetbegović government had attracted a heterogeneous and ideologically motley array of supporters, including some Muslims who considered nonbelievers, regardless of their moral convictions, to be—without exception—"satanists."[44]

By this point, the Muslims were scarcely able to feed themselves, and the West undertook to send regular food shipments to the besieged Muslims in several cities, most notably Sarajevo. To protect aid convoys, some 8,000 U.N. soldiers were dispatched to Bosnia in October 1992 and advised that they were allowed to use force only in the event that an aid convoy was actually attacked. The U.N. paid for access to those under siege by permitting Serb forces in Bosnia to skim off about 25 percent of U.N. humanitarian aid supposedly earmarked for besieged Muslims and for refugees; for its part, UNPROFOR felt it lacked the military muscle to refuse the Serbs.[45]

Vance and Owen were appointed to serve as international *mediators*, but they soon found mediation impossible: the warring sides were simply unable to agree on *any* fundamental principles. In particular, while Bosnian President Izetbegović held fast to the principle that the unity of the Bosnian state had to be preserved, Bosnian Serb leader Radovan Karadžić followed Serbian President Milošević in insisting that any area inhabited by Serbs (even if Serbs were only a minority in that area) had the right to be conjoined with the larger Serbian state being created.

Instead of recommending forceful military action on the part of the West to halt the continued aggression being waged against the underarmed Muslims—an option to which Russia had expressed its decided opposition[46]—Vance and Owen proceeded on the premise that parties could engage in meaningful peace negotiations in good faith, in the absence of a cease-fire or any curtailment of genocidal policies euphemistically dubbed "ethnic cleansing." As it proved impossible to stage meaningful peace negotiations, Vance and Owen eventually ignored the warring sides and worked out their own peace plan in October 1992. This was quite appropriately called the Vance-Owen Plan because it represented little besides the optimistic hopes and private notions of Lord Owen and Cyrus Vance.

The Vance-Owen Plan would have divided Bosnia into ten ethnic cantons, but it proposed to do so in such a way as to produce a patchwork quilt in which Muslim cantons would be separated from other Muslim cantons, Serb cantons from other Serb cantons, and so forth.[47] Bosnian Croat leader Mate Boban accepted the plan, which gave the Bosnian Croats much of southwestern Herzegovina, which was the Croats' principal desideratum. Bosnian President Izetbegović resisted at first but under persistent Western pressure eventually caved in and agreed, on behalf of the Bosnian government, to accept it. The Bosnian Serbs, however, explicitly rejected the plan as early as 12 January 1993.

Many observers pointed out that the Vance-Owen Plan had no detectable prospects for long-term stability and would have served only to legitimate the principle that international borders could be redrawn by force (thus repudiating the Helsinki Accords of 1975).[48] But the EC insisted all the same on obtaining the Vance-Owen Plan—first, because it enabled the EC to reject calls for a military response; and second, because the EC did not believe that its interests ultimately extended beyond wanting to dam up the flow of refugees out of the country.

The Vance-Owen Plan in fact made a dramatic break with past diplomatic practice and in one swoop annulled a key principle of international law upon which there had been general agreement in the interest of fostering stability in political transitions. Known as *Uti possidetis, ita possidetis* ("You may keep what you had before"), the principle established that when colonial possessions became independent or when existing states broke up, internal administrative borders should be treated as legitimate. As Rein Mullerson notes:

> The *uti possidetis* emerged in the context of the decolonization of Latin America and was later applied in Africa. The Chamber of the International Court of Justice in its decision on the frontier dispute between Burkina Faso and Mali of December 22, 1986, established that *uti possidetis* constituted a general principle which is logically related to the achievement of independence whenever it occurs. Likewise, the Arbitration Commission on Yugoslavia in its opinion of January 11, 1992, declared that, in the absence of an agreement stating otherwise, previous limitations acquire the character of frontiers protected by international law.[49]

With the Vance-Owen Plan, the EC began its slide away from *uti possidetis* and opened the door to the partial recognition of conquests.

On 6 April 1993, the foreign ministers of the EC states adopted a "Declaration on Former Yugoslavia," indicating that in the event that the Bosnian Serbs failed to sign the Vance-Owen Plan, both they and the Serb-Montenegrin federation would be subjected to long-term international isolation, branded as a pariah state.[50]

On 17 April 1993, the U.N. Security Council approved a resolution (with thirteen votes in favor and only Russia abstaining) calling for a toughening of the hitherto largely ineffectual economic sanctions against Serbia.[51] Lord Owen met with Karadžić on 23 April and offered to press for further concessions to the Serbs, but the following day Karadžić reiterated his earlier rejection of the plan. The West also began, for the first time, to consider a military option against the FRY and the Bosnian Serbs. It was at this point that the United States became actively, albeit only briefly, involved in the efforts to stop the fighting. U.S. President Clinton met with various members of Congress on 27 April to sound them out about air strikes against Bosnian Serbs, and the Pentagon began to collect intelligence on Bosnia, specifically identifying appropriate targets for aerial strikes.[52]

Milošević and Karadžić now conspired to confuse and derail the West. First, Karadžić pretended to cave in and signed the Vance-Owen Plan on 2 May. The West immediately called off further military preparations. The Bosnian Serb parliament was scheduled to convene to ratify the plan at its 6 May session, and in these crucial days the West lost its momentum as Britain and France began to place their hopes once more in "easy" solutions. The Bosnian Serb parliament in due course rejected the plan. But now Milošević and Karadžić played out the second part of their plan—a variation on the familiar "good cop, bad cop" strategy. Karadžić held fast to a rejectionist stance, while Milošević issued a strongly worded condemnation of the Bosnian Serbs and promised to cease supplying them with arms and other equipment (finally conceding what he had denied up to then, i.e., that supplies from Serbia had been and remained crucial to the Bosnian Serb war effort).[53] Meanwhile, Karadžić referred the question to a referendum on which the West appeared to pin some vaguely formulated hopes. On 15 May the referendum was held and the Bosnian Serbs overwhelmingly rejected the Vance-Owen Plan.

The United States now backed off, declaring that it had no vital interests at stake in Bosnia;[54] the EC dropped the Vance-Owen Plan and advised Lord Owen to resume negotiations with the three warring parties.

The Diplomacy of Accommodation: Second Phase

The Croats were astounded at the sudden evanescence of Western resolve. Subsequently, when foreign ministers from the United States, Russia, Britain, France, and Spain (but not Germany)[55] met in Washington, D.C., and timidly proposed to guarantee six "safe havens" to the Bosnian Muslims, *Vjesnik* commentator Nenad Ivanković described the Western response as "the final 'capitulation' of the international community before Serbian aggression."[56] Although Tudjman had signed a pact with Izetbegović on 21 July 1992, placing Croatian Defense Council (HVO) forces in Bosnia-Herzegovina under the command of the Bosnian Territorial Defense forces, there were problems in the Croatian-Bosnian alliance from the beginning; in October 1992, for example, there were Croat-Muslim clashes in Travnik and Prozor, about 50 kilometers due west of Sarajevo.[57] Commentators are generally agreed that the Bosnian Croats felt encouraged by the Vance-Owen Plan to occupy portions of the republic assigned to them under that plan;[58] the result was the outbreak of open hostilities between Croat and Muslim forces in April 1993. In addition, the limpness of Western resolve convinced Croatian hard-liners that it was time to make a deal with the Serbs and facilitated the forging of an anti-Muslim coalition between Bosnian Croats and Serbs in June of that year. The immediate results included the virtual cessation of fighting between Croats and Serbs in Bosnia, the sale of Croatian oil to the Bosnian Serbs,[59] the concentration of Bosnian Croat firepower against the Muslims, a direct meeting between Croatian President Franjo Tudjman and Serbian President

Milošević on 16 June, and the formulation of a joint Serb-Croat plan for the partition of Bosnia-Herzegovina. Lord Owen and Thorvald Stoltenberg, who had replaced Vance as U.N. mediator in May 1993, accommodated themselves to the new reality of a Serb-Croat coalition, and the Owen-Stoltenberg Plan, presented to the warring parties on 20 August, closely followed the Serb-Croat plan: as modified by Owen and Stoltenberg, this second peace plan proposed to assign 52 percent of Bosnian territory to the Bosnian Serbs, 30 percent to the Muslims, and 18 percent (mostly in the southwest) to the Croats.[60] Western mediators at first expressed "optimism" at the prospects for Muslim acceptance of what was, in effect, a Serb-Croat plan and described the ultimate Muslim rejection of the plan as "unexpected."[61]

Throughout 1992 and 1993, the Bosnian government, supported intermittently by the United States and Germany and steadfastly by the Islamic states, tried to persuade the U.N. Security Council to lift the arms embargo. Britain and France obstinately insisted on keeping the arms embargo in place, leading U.S. State Department officials to speculate that despite their protestations to the contrary the British and French actually hoped for a *Serbian* victory.[62] Douglas Hogg, State Minister at the Foreign Office, declared his full agreement with Romanian Foreign Minister Theodor Melescanu in December 1992 that "there are too many weapons in the area" already,[63] omitting to mention that most of these weapons were, at the time, in Serbian hands. For his part, British Foreign Secretary Douglas Hurd observed, rather transparently, that giving the Muslims access to weaponry would "only prolong the fighting"[64]—a rather obvious point which did not, in and of itself, explain why Secretary Hurd preferred the "quicker" result obtainable via total Serbian victory. In June 1993, the United States, with the active support of several Islamic states, introduced a resolution in the U.N. Security Council to lift the arms embargo. Eight votes were required for adoption, but with Britain, France, Russia, and six other members abstaining, the resolution obtained only six votes and died on the table. Later, in December, the U.N. General Assembly passed a resolution calling on the Security Council to lift the arms embargo against the Muslims. Britain and France brandished their veto powers within the Security Council and effectively scuttled the initiative.

Thanks to the Western arms embargo, it took months before the Muslims were able to arm themselves (though not impressively). A key breakthrough came in May 1993, when Muslim forces daringly attacked a Serbian column and captured some 15,000 weapons. These were mostly small arms, but also included some anti-armor rockets and a number of mortars.[65] In addition, despite the loss to Bosnian Serbs of a vital arms factory in Banja Luka, the Muslims continued to hold on to Travnik, where the Bratstvo ("Brotherhood") ammunition factory produced much needed ammunition. (This factory was the target of a Croatian rocket attack on 13 January 1994, however.)[66] With these modest resources, the Bosnian Muslims managed to defend their remaining positions (amounting in 1993 to less than 10 percent of the republic's territory) and to score some successes against both Croatian and Serbian forces.

The Serbian side had the supreme advantage of being able to manufacture much of what it needed and, indeed, exported a tangible portion of that to certain states in

Africa, even while the war in Bosnia was continuing. Noel Malcolm claims, further, that the Yugoslav army was manufacturing sarin (an ingredient in chemical weaponry) during the Bosnian war.[67] According to General Anton Tus, the Croatian Chief of Staff, Belgrade also benefited from a steady supply of Russian weaponry and was repeatedly able to introduce new, high-tech weapons on the battlefield.[68] Later, in March 1995, by which time the Bosnian Serb side was suffering from growing problems of sinking morale, shortages of spare parts, and lack of coordination in the field, Karadžić would dispatch a delegation of Bosnian Serb officers to Moscow with a suitcase of American dollars to try to purchase "a special nuclear device" on the military black market. The officers did, in fact, purchase what they took for a nuclear device, but once back in Pale, they discovered that they had been sold a dud and that, instead of plutonium, the "weapon" was filled with a nonradioactive gelatine-like substance.[69]

As of June 1993, the military balance was as follows. The Bosnian (Muslim) army had 120,000 active troops and an additional 80,000 reserves, 40 tanks, and 1 aircraft. The Bosnian Serb army, by contrast, had only 60,000 troops, supplemented by up to 20,000 Yugoslav army troops, 350 tanks, and 35 aircraft.[70] That the striking imbalance in military hardware owed at least something to the Western arms embargo is indisputable.

Given their vast inferiority in arms, the Bosnian Muslims had initially agreed "in principle" to the Owen-Stoltenberg Plan on 30 July 1993, but efforts to flush out the details soon bogged down. In the meantime, Bosnian Serb militias tightened their stranglehold on Sarajevo and continued the bombardment of the city. Once more the West discussed the possibility of aerial strikes against selected Bosnian Serb targets, and Clinton administration officials announced that plans for such strikes were being developed. On 2 August, U.S. officials tried, during lengthy negotiations with other NATO ministers, to obtain agreement to launch aerial strikes against the Bosnian Serbs; objections by the Canadian delegate held up any consensus for the time being. A week later, after further discussions and ensuing compromises, NATO officials agreed on an elaborate and complex set of procedures for conducting aerial strikes against the Serbs, requiring approval from Lieutenant General Jean Cot of France (then-commander of the U.N. "peacekeeping" forces in the Balkans), U.N. Secretary-General Boutros Boutros-Ghali, and all sixteen members of NATO.

There ensued a series of disagreements between General Cot and Boutros-Ghali in which the latter reportedly rebuffed requests by General Cot for authorization for aerial strikes. U.N. Secretary-General Boutros Boutros-Ghali increasingly found himself at the center of controversy and (in December 1993), in an effort to extricate himself, appointed Yasushi Akashi, a Japanese national with U.N. experience in Cambodia, to take the position of chief of the U.N. "peacekeeping" mission.[71] Akashi now inherited Boutros-Ghali's authority to approve requests for NATO air strikes against Bosnian Serbs and put it to use by repeatedly (although not consistently) vetoing NATO requests to conduct punitive strikes against the Serbs.[72]

In these circumstances, it is not surprising that a group of Muslims controlling the Bihać enclave in northwestern Bosnia decided, in October 1993, to break with the

Izetbegović government and establish a working relationship with Karadžić instead. Their understanding was formalized on 7 November, and Bihać leader Fikret Abdić subsequently received artillery and other weaponry from Bosnian Serb arsenals. The Izetbegović government was, in turn, compelled to divert part of its war effort to fighting the Bihać secessionists. By early August 1994, however, Bosnian government loyalists turned the tide in their struggle against Abdić, and at least 5,100 civilians and 1,600 soldiers loyal to Abdić fled to Serbian-held parts of Croatia.[73]

U.S., Russian, and Other Foreign Responses

During 1993, Britain and France began lodging recriminations against the United States for not sending U.S. troops to join the so-called peacekeeping force in the war zone. Ironically, at the same time that Britain and France were demanding that the United States send in troops, they started talking about pulling out their own troops, regardless what the United States might do.[74] The United States consistently resisted British and French pressure to commit U.S. ground forces to a Bosnian operation. Instead of involving itself with the Anglo-French concept of "peacekeeping" in a war zone, the Clinton administration preferred to press for lifting the arms embargo and, aside from that, to emphasize containment. Repeated visits by congressmen and other high-level officials to Kosovo, Albania, Bulgaria, and Macedonia are one reflection of this policy. As early as July 1993, the United States dispatched a small contingent of peacekeeping troops to Macedonia to help monitor activity along that republic's border with Serbia—a contingent which grew to more than 500 by April 1994. Then, on 8 October 1993, the United States signed an agreement with Albania providing for military assistance, including U.S. training for Albanian officers and high-level meetings to discuss international security.[75] In early 1994, the CIA began flying unmanned surveillance missions over Serbia and Bosnia from Gjader air base in Albania. Albanian President Sali Berisha publicly offered to make available "airport facilities that NATO may need to accomplish its missions within the U.N. framework,"[76] although the Pentagon denied harboring any intention of building a military base in Albania.[77]

Russia experienced deep ambivalence in connection with the war in Bosnia. During autumn 1991, the Russian government repeatedly and consistently criticized Serbian military operations in Croatia[78] and, in May 1992, lent its support to the imposition of U.N. economic sanctions against Serbia. Now, in the context of the Bosnian war, Moscow found itself torn between its desire to reinforce its financially rewarding relationship with the West and its confessionally rooted affinity for the Serbs. By April 1993, the Russian parliament had adopted a resolution calling on the government to use its Security Council veto to block any proposed U.N. military action against Bosnian Serbs—a move only partly mitigated by Deputy Foreign Minister Vitaly Churkin's reassurance that the government intended to ignore the vote.[79]

In spite of these reassurances, Russia provided assistance at a variety of levels, both diplomatic and military. In May 1994, the Russian Writers' Union even bestowed the Mikhail Shokolov prize on Radovan Karadžić, in recognition of "the aesthetic value of his work and of his high moral principles."[80] The previous year, Karadžić had been awarded the most prestigious Montenegrin prize for literature for his collection of poetry *The Slavic Guest*.[81] In bestowing these prizes on Karadžić, the prize-givers were engaging in the diplomacy of cultural symbology, using the prestige of literary prizes to try to build up an alternative image for the Bosnian Serb leader.

In the military sphere, high-ranking Russian officials signed a secret deal on 22 January 1993 agreeing to supply Serbian forces in Croatia and Bosnia with T-55 tanks and antiaircraft missiles, according to British defense analysts. The deal was said to have been worked out between Russian army and intelligence service officials and Serbian military authorities.[82] A senior Russian Trade Ministry official later acknowledged sales of Russian missiles and other weaponry to Bosnian Serbs, but denied that the Russian government was involved.[83] Bosnian Radio also reported on the flow of Russian arms to the Bosnian Serbs, noting in particular a large convoy of eight trailers, stocked with arms, which was said to have reached Karadžić's forces in January 1994.[84] Later, there were signs of growing Russian impatience with Bosnian Serb refusal to accept a compromise, but throughout the entire war in Bosnia, the Russians remained opposed to the use of aerial strikes to combat Bosnian Serb aggression.[85] Impatient or not, the Russians continued to make available to the Bosnian Serb forces sophisticated weaponry, including eighty-three 122 mm. caliber howitzers, mobile SA-6 surface-to-air missiles, and ultrahigh-tech S-300b antiaircraft missiles. Indeed, in the latter months of 1994, more than 4,000 Russian freight cars loaded with war materiel were sent to the Balkans.[86]

Ironically, 1993 also saw continued calls in the international community for a lifting of the U.N. economic embargo against *Serbia*—at the very point when it appeared to be *slowly* shaking the Milošević regime's will to continue the war. Romania, Bulgaria, and Greece had been bridling at the reins all along, pointed out the costs of the embargo to their own economies, and in November 1993 joined ranks to make a joint appeal to have the U.N. economic embargo against Serbia lifted as soon as possible.[87] About the same time, France and Germany proposed to lift international sanctions against Serbia if the latter conceded some additional territory to the Muslims at the negotiating table in Geneva.[88] The Bosnian Muslim government of Alija Izetbegović took umbrage at this proposal, but in any case, two days later, at a meeting of NATO ambassadors, the U.S. publicly rebuked France and Germany for this initiative.[89] Meanwhile, some Church circles in the West started to become nervous about the effects of the embargo on Serbia's population. In mid-October 1993, for example, the Central Conference of Methodist Churches from Central and Southern Europe criticized the U.N. sanctions, blaming them for contributing to additional injustice in the region.[90] At the end of the same month, the Ecumenical Council of Churches and the Conference of European Churches issued a statement criticizing U.N. sanctions against Serbia and Montenegro as "unfair" and "one-sided."[91]

Islamic states, by contrast, overwhelmingly opposed the continuation of the arms embargo against the Bosnian Muslims and used international conferences and forums to express their outrage at both Serb aggression against Muslim communities and Western inaction. As early as May 1992, King Fahd of Saudi Arabia authorized emergency aid amounting to $5 million for the Bosnian government, increasing that figure to $8 million the following month. In July, Saudi Arabia began relief shipments to Sarajevo.[92] Iran also began sending food, medicine, and other staples to the Bosnian state about this time and assumed a role coordinating assistance from the Islamic world.[93] In September of that year, Islamic countries used the nonaligned meeting in Djakarta, Indonesia, to obtain a collective condemnation of the Bosnian Serbs. That same month, Iran staged a nationwide rally to protest Serbian atrocities. Later, in May 1993, members of the Organization of the Islamic Conference pledged some $85 million in additional aid for Bosnia and reiterated their earlier demand for a repeal of the arms embargo against the Muslims.[94]

The Islamic countries lobbied hard at the U.N. for a lifting of the arms embargo against Bosnia. Their efforts culminated in the aforementioned abortive Security Council vote in June 1993. As Islamic hopes for a Western reassessment faded, Iran authorized an additional $1.7 million in aid to the Bosnian Muslims and Teheran Radio began broadcasting to Bosnia in Serbo-Croatian.[95]

Turkey, with ambitions to expand its influence in the Balkans, was especially concerned about the war in Bosnia and became one of the first states to extend diplomatic recognition to Bosnia-Herzegovina. Shortly thereafter, the Turkish government signed an economic and technological assistance pact with Bosnia. In August 1992, just four months after the outbreak of open warfare in Bosnia, the Ankara government outlined a plan for solving the crisis which included limited aerial bombardment of Bosnian Serb military positions.[96]

There were repeated popular demonstrations in Turkey on behalf of the Bosnian Muslims in the years 1992–1995, alongside repeated efforts by the Ankara government to contribute to a solution. An important Turkish initiative came on 12 November 1993, when Ankara endeavored (evidently with some success) to mediate the temporary conflict between the Muslims and the Croats.[97] Later, in February 1994, Pakistan's Prime Minister Benazir Bhutto joined Turkish Prime Minister Tansu Ciller in paying a demonstrative visit to Sarajevo that culminated in a tripartite Agreement of Mutual Friendship and Cooperation.[98] But when the first Turkish contingents arrived in Bosnia in May and June 1994, as part of the UNPROFOR,[99] Serbs were quick to draw parallels with the bygone Ottoman Empire.

A major complication for Croatian and Muslim resistance was the fact that Bosnian Croats and Muslims remained at loggerheads through the end of 1993. A precondition both for bringing effective supplies to the Bosnian government forces and for stabilizing the lines was to achieve a reconciliation between Croats and Muslims in Bosnia-Herzegovina. The United States played a key role in bringing the Croats and Muslims together, adding muscle to the mediation effort in the first week of January 1994, when the U.S. threatened Croatian President Tudjman with sanctions unless he began to collaborate with the Bosnian government. In spite of this threat, Tudjman temporarily continued to escalate the military conflict with the Muslims.

However, a string of Bosnian battle victories compelled Tudjman to rethink his stance.[100] On 2 March 1994 the so-called Washington Agreement was announced, creating a Muslim-Croat federation in Bosnia-Herzegovina, thus restoring the original (though at the time stillborn) anti-Serbian alliance. This agreement facilitated the shipment of arms from the Islamic world and, in the wake of the agreement, the Bosnian army received arms and war materiel from Iran, Pakistan, and Sudan as well as from nongovernmental sources in Tunisia and Afghanistan—all or most of it paid for by Islamic foundations in Saudi Arabia.[101] The United States had intervened at least once with the Croats previously in order to halt the shipment of arms from Iran—in deference to the ill-advised U.N. arms embargo.[102] But on 27 April 1994, U.S. President Clinton approved a policy of turning a blind eye to Iranian arms shipments to Croatia and Bosnia, keeping the decision quiet at the time.[103]

The European Union Plan of June 1994

The Bosnian war had moved into a new phase with the conclusion of the Washington Agreement in February 1994, and the infusion of arms from Iran quickly proved its value. In late May 1994, Bosnian government troops, backed up by tanks and heavy artillery, launched a major offensive to retake ground from Serbian forces west of Tesanj in northern Bosnia. In early July, after some initial successes, the Bosnian government army staged a massive assault against Serb positions around Mount Ozren in central Bosnia, but the Bosnian Serbs eventually repulsed the attack, inflicting 2,500 casualties on Bosnian government forces.[104] This setback ended the first Bosnian offensive of 1994.

Meanwhile, U.N. and EU mediators devised a third partition plan, which they presented in June with the support of the United States and Russia. The plan proposed to assign 51 percent of Bosnian territory to the Croat-Muslim federation and 49 percent to the Bosnian Serbs.[105] The Western powers now signaled that if the Bosnian Serbs accepted the plan, the economic sanctions against Serbia and Montenegro would be lifted. On the other hand, the Western powers threatened to lift the arms embargo against the Muslims and Croats if the Serbs rejected the plan.[106] The threat was not sincere, however, and the Bosnian Serbs called the bluff by rejecting the plan.[107] While the "contact group" met to decide what to do next, the Bosnian Serbs stepped up the sniping of civilians in Sarajevo, in effect thumbing their noses at the West. In response, U.N. officials quickly ruled out aerial strikes of any significant scope because the U.N.'s ineffectual "peacekeeping" troops on the ground would be exposed to Serbian retaliatory strikes. Others advised inaction on the grounds that "the time for the West to fight a just war was two years ago, not now."[108]

The scenario of April 1993 was then reenacted. Karadžić referred the question to the Bosnian Serb Assembly, which in turn rejected the plan altogether (on 3 August). But the Assembly in turn called for a general referendum among Bosnian Serbs on 27–28 August, although this one was no more likely than the referendum of 15 May 1993 to reverse the decision of the Bosnian Serb leadership. Finally, as before, rumors were quickly circulated about a fresh rift between Milošević and Karadžić, as Milošević ostentatiously declared his borders closed to arms traffic to Bosnia.[109] Western observers were tantalized by the launching, in the Serbian media, of a defamatory campaign against Karadžić and other Bosnian Serb leaders, portraying them as drunkards, gamblers, and womanizers. This disinformation campaign notwithstanding, arms, ammunition, and fuel continued to flow across the Drina from Serbia to Bosnian Serb territory; indeed, the fact that Russia considered it necessary to use its Security Council veto (for the first time in the Yugoslav war) to kill a proposal to block fuel from crossing Serbia to the Bosnian Serbs[110] showed how porous this self-declared "embargo" was.

War Crimes

As early as 16 December 1992, Acting Secretary of State Lawrence Eagleburger called for the establishment of a war crimes tribunal to try war criminals in the Bosnian war, specifying, among others, Serbian President Milošević, Bosnian Serb President Karadžić, Bosnian Serb commander General Ratko Mladić, Serbian Radical leader Vojislav Šešelj, and paramilitary leader Željko Raznjatović ("Arkan").[111] Like other supporters of this proposal in the United States, Germany, and elsewhere, Eagleburger thought chiefly in terms of *Serbian* offenders.

The first, albeit hesitant, step in this direction had come earlier, on 13 July 1992, when the U.N. Security Council had affirmed that all parties to the Serbian Insurrectionary War were bound by the provisions of international humanitarian law. Subsequently, on 13 August, the U.N. Security Council passed a resolution (No. 771) expressing alarm at reports of atrocities in Bosnia, which clearly contravened these conventions.[112] Among other things, Resolution No. 771 underlined the "mass forcible expulsion and deportation of civilians, imprisonment and abuse of civilians in detention population, and wanton devastation and destruction of property."[113] Finally, on 22 February 1993, the Security Council adopted a resolution establishing an international tribunal "for the prosecution of persons responsible for serious violations of international humanitarian law committed in the territory of the former Yugoslavia since 1991."[114] All three sides set up detention camps at which torture and substandard conditions were commonplace. At the Celebići camp run by the Bosnian government, for example, there were reports of murder and torture.[115] Among the best-known camps were the Serb-run camps of Keraterm, Trnopolje, and Omarska (all three in the vicinity of Prijedor) and Luka (in Brčko).

A specific feature of the Bosnian war has been the incidence of organized systematic rape—or rather, forced impregnation, since pregnancy was a conscious goal of the Serbs. An EC investigative mission produced a report in January 1993 estimating that some 20,000 Bosnian Muslim women had been raped by Bosnian Serb men in what could be called "rape camps."[116] In a cogently argued piece about the use of rape in the Bosnian war, Dorothy Thomas and Regan Ralph noted that, in warfare, "rape is neither incidental nor private. [On the contrary,] it routinely serves a strategic function in war and acts as an integral tool for achieving particular military objectives. In the former Yugoslavia, rape and other grave abuses committed by Serbian forces are intended to drive the non-Serbian population into flight."[117] Serbian sources have, predictably, routinely denied allegations of any campaign of systematic rape.[118]

In June 1994, a U.N. commission on war crimes completed a study of the Prijedor district in northwest Bosnia, concluding that Serbian forces had killed or deported 52,811 persons *from that district alone*.[119] Despite considerable interest in the tribunal,[120] preparations for judicial procedures unfolded slowly, and it was only in October 1994 that the U.N.-sponsored tribunal in The Hague was finally ready to take up its first case: a former Bosnian Serb prison guard, Dušan Tadić, arrested in Germany and later charged with genocide.[121] In a transparently political gesture, the Serbian side staged its own "war crimes" trial in Šabac in the second half of November; the accused, Dušan Vučković, a Serb paramilitary, was charged with having shot several Muslim prisoners to death in 1992. But observers confidently predicted that the defense, which sought to portray Vučković as a psychopath, would have its way—meaning that the accused would be confined to a mental institution for the rest of his life.[122]

Belgrade's Friends in the West

From the beginning, Serbia has had its supporters in the West. In the case of the French, Serbophilia is "traditional," reflecting, in part, a French desire to counter German friendship for Croatia. Moreover, French businessmen were eager to resume economic cooperation with Serbia and maintained contact with their Serbian counterparts throughout the war.[123] The British advocacy of "not so benign neglect" during the Serbian Insurrectionary War seems at first harder to explain, but is probably the result of a combination of English Islamophobia,[124] English loathing of secessionist movements insofar as they mirror certain currents in Scotland and Northern Ireland, and a more general antipathy toward fragmentation regardless of the human rights issues that may be at stake. The repeated assertions by British Prime Minister John Major and Foreign Secretary Hurd that there were enough weapons in the area (even though the overwhelming majority of heavy weaponry was in the hands of the aggressors) and to the effect that any further infusion of arms could only prolong the war can only be seen as veiled revelations of a covert British government sympathy for the Serbs, albeit set against a history of British diplomatic apathy sometimes carried to the point of bungling.[125] For that matter, Peter Lord Carrington himself, the man appointed to serve as chief negotiator at the London Peace Conference in 1991–1992, had close links with Serbian elites and marked pro-Serbian sympathies and adopted a practice of treating "the odd Croat sniper and a Serb artillery barrage" as equivalents, even if both occurred on Croatian territory within the context of a Serbian campaign to annex large portions of Croatia.[126] The promotion of groundless Germanophobia and the promulgation of fanciful "Fourth Reich" conspiracy theories also served to

confuse the picture and to distract the more naïve from the actual atrocities being perpetrated by Bosnian Serb forces above all by focusing their attention on the atrocities
committed half a century earlier by the Nazis and their allies.[127]

The Serbs have had their advocates in the United States as well. A key role was
played by U.S. Congresswoman Helen Bentley (a member of the House until 1994),
who traveled to Yugoslavia in 1989 in order to attend ceremonies to commemorate
the six hundredth anniversary of the Battle of Kosovo and who allegedly used the resources of her congressional office to disseminate Milošević's political agenda to Serb
Americans and to lobby on behalf of the Serbian expansionist program.[128] According to Brad Blitz, for as long as she had a seat in the Congress, "she repeatedly fought
against the imposition of sanctions on Serbia-Montenegro and the creation of resolute policies aimed to ensure the delivery of humanitarian aid to those most in need
in Bosnia."[129] Again, Congressman Lee Hamilton, chairman of the House Committee on Foreign Affairs, blocked diplomatic recognition of Macedonia and worked
hard to retain the arms embargo against the Sarajevo government; he is said to have
received nearly $50,000 in itemized contributions from leading figures in the Serb
American and Greek American communities in the years 1993–1995.[130]

For many of the post-Watergate, post-Vietnam generation, it is no longer believ-
able that there are any "pure aggressors" or "pure victims." Moral thinking is rela-
tivized to the point where everyone becomes equally guilty. In consequence, the only
"rational" response seems, to relativists, to be total indifference or studied "even-
handedness." Carl Jacobsen is a good example of this trend. In an article for *Mediterranean Quarterly* published in 1994, Jacobsen mysteriously claimed that "foreigners"
had invaded Serbia (where and when he does not say),[131] called for including Bosnian President Izetbegović in a future "war crimes" trial,[132] and even offered the dubious assertion that "Bosnia was historically Serb"[133] (a proposition which, even if
true, would not entitle twentieth-century Serbs to expel non-Serbs from their land).
Jacobsen's recipe called for a nonpunitive attitude toward Serbia and Bosnian Serbs,
regardless of their behavior.

Other writers[134] accused the U.S. media of bias and one-sided reporting because
the media devoted more time to reporting Serbian atrocities against non-Serbs than
vice versa. No doubt there were those who, in World War II, considered it "biased"
that the American media devoted so little attention to discussing the "atrocities" perpetrated by the Polish resistance against Nazi occupation forces.

Still others, offering themselves as "steeled realists"—thereby advertising their ec-
static abandonment of long-range interests in favor of short-run "payoffs"—argued
for a full rehabilitation of Serbia. In a bold statement of this position, Marten van
Heuven, a retired U.S. Foreign Service officer, argued, in the fall 1994 issue of *Foreign Policy*, for a gradual lifting of U.N. sanctions, a restoration of Serbian membership in international organizations, and the extension of IMF and other financial assistance to Serbia as incentives to obtain some limited concessions from Serbia:
respect for negotiated borders with Croatia and Bosnia, respect for the independence
of Macedonia, and adequate guarantees for human rights for the Albanian popula-

tion of Kosovo.[135] Van Heuven's specific recipe, like those of self-declared "realists" in general, failed to acknowledge the fundamental difference between illegitimate governments and legitimate governments, allowing him to fancy that mere coddling could cause an illegitimate government to behave as legitimate governments do. Another "realist," Charles Boyd, offered this revisionist interpretation in support of his moral equivocation: "The Serbs are not trying to conquer new territory, but merely [want to] hold onto what was theirs."[136]

I have suggested elsewhere[137] that so-called foreign-policy realism is twin to conventionalism and moral relativism and, of necessity, entails the suffocation of Natural Law (and the consequent relativization, if not extirpation altogether, of natural rights). It is, then, not surprising that among those "realists" who have stepped forward with offers to guide the West out of its confusion were some so consistent as to embrace moral relativism wholeheartedly and openly. These "kamikaze scholars" want nothing so much as to strike a death blow to foreign-policy idealism and to the demands of idealists that political tyranny be recognized as distinct from other forms of government, showing that they inhabit a dark world in which, to use Hegel's apt phrase, "all cows are black." Plato, still one of the best champions of the idealist position, noted the obvious two thousand years ago when he underlined the fundamental difference between tyrannies and other forms of government, warning,

> The longer [the tyrant] rules, the more oppressive his tyranny.... [And] power makes him grow steadily worse. It magnifies everything we have said about his person and his public role and thrusts him still further into the realm of envy, faithlessness, and unjust behavior. He becomes ever more friendless and sacrilegious. He is the very source and contagion of wickedness; this supremely wretched man goes about making everyone else as wretched as he is.[138]

By contrast with Plato's lucidity, these "kamikaze scholars" cannot state their arguments baldly; indeed, the vulnerability of their arguments is indicated in the very fact that they can only be insinuated. But this very strategy of presentation constitutes the source of their self-destruction, so that, unlike their airborne forebears who gave up their lives for the sake of making an effective strike, these new earthbound "pilots" risk all only to crash so far from their targets as to leave their targets not only undamaged but, indeed, entirely unaffected by their overheated vapors.[139]

Still others, likewise thinking of themselves as "realists," took to asserting that it was "too late" for aerial strikes against Bosnian Serb positions (even though non-Serb communities were still being subjected to bombardment by Serb forces and even though Croats and Muslims still fielded armies), "too late" to do anything for Bihać (even before Bihać had fallen), "too late" to do anything except pull out.[140] This orientation lent itself to a view of the Serbs as "invincible."

Finally, there are those such as Fareed Zakariah and Karen Elliott House who seemed to be motivated by a deeply ingrained distrust of U.S. government rhetoric and purposes. For these writers, calls for action to bring an end to mass murder, mass rape, and mass expulsions only reflect a grand megalomania born of naïvete and crystallized in an arrogation to self of the role of "masters of the universe."[141] In their view, advocates of countermeasures are deluded idealists who dream of a new world order of democracy and harmony and view the war in Bosnia as an obstacle to their aspirations.[142] In their view, such advocates are guilty of the arrogance of power.

But there is also the argument that power brings certain responsibilities and hence that the United States is morally bound to take the lead in combating genocide and other crimes against humanity. In an articulate statement of this position, syndicated columnist Hodding Carter wrote:

> Former Senator William Fulbright, Clinton's fellow Arkansan and occasional mentor, once spoke wisely of the "arrogance of power" as applied most notably to U.S. policy in Vietnam. But there are two possible kinds of arrogance. One is to have power and influence and [to] abuse them. The other is to have both and, in a situation that cries out for their application, fail to use them.[143]

The End of the Embargo

On 11 August 1994, President Clinton announced that he was setting a deadline of late October for the Bosnian Serbs to accept the new peace plan. If the Serbs still refused to cooperate, Clinton promised to "seek" to have the arms embargo against the Muslims lifted.[144] The Bosnian Serbs, in fact, did not take so qualified a threat at all seriously. Indeed, the Bosnian Serbs repeatedly showed their utter disrespect for the U.N. and the West. They repeatedly disarmed and humiliated U.N. troops, took potshots at them, and stole heavy weapons held under U.N. guard when they so pleased. In April 1994, they even placed some forty U.N. military observers under "virtual house arrest" for several days, posting sentries outside their doors—a tactic they repeated in November 1994, when they detained a number of U.N. "peace-keepers." The Bosnian Serb forces repeatedly violated the U.N.-proclaimed "no-fly zone" in Bosnia, as well as the heavy weapons' exclusion zones around Sarajevo and Goražde. They dragged their feet in meeting supposedly strict U.N. deadlines (an approach replicated by Slobodan Milošević in the context of Kosovo in October 1998), violated cease-fires, and treated promises as tools of deception, not as words of honor. And yet, for all that, the West continued to show infinite patience, continued to pursue a diplomacy of accommodation. Indeed, by late August 1994 there were ever more voluble rumors that the West was preparing to pull out of Bosnia-Herzegovina altogether, lift the arms embargo, and simply wash its hands of the entire affair.

On 11 November, the United States belatedly declared that it would no longer enforce the arms embargo and withdrew its two ships from embargo enforcement in the Adriatic. But NATO continued to operate sixteen other ships in the Adriatic for purposes of enforcing the embargo.[145] Britain and France howled in protest, but in fact the embargo had increasingly become a chimera, as Serbs found it relatively easy to obtain weapons from Russia (shipped through Romania) and even from sources in Germany,[146] and as Islamic states, fed up with the West's pusillanimity and lack of resolve, stepped up arms aid to the Croat-Muslim alliance.[147] That alliance, as Croatian Defense Minister Gojko Šušak conceded, was enjoying increasing success in purchasing arms in Pakistan, Iran, Germany, Poland, Bulgaria, even Russia. Some of these arms, including antitank weapons and ammunition for mortars, cannons, and machine guns, were passed on to the Muslims.[148] In addition, the Croats had succeeded, by 1994, in building up a formidable arms industry and were manufacturing their own tanks, fighter aircraft (the MiG-21), and other weaponry.[149] Among those plants the Croats were able to restore to operation, thanks to purchases of military components in the former Soviet bloc, was the Djuro Djaković tank factory in Slavonski Brod which, by 1994, was once more producing M-84 battle tanks. Plant executives said at the time that the factory would be able, within a short time, to match prewar production levels of 100–150 tanks per year.[150]

After the Bosnian Serb rejection of the third EC plan in August, the Geneva process lost momentum. At the same time, there was an escalation of fighting both in the northwestern corner of Bosnia and in central Bosnia. In the northwest, Bosnian government troops succeeded in overcoming the forces loyal to Fikret Abdić in the Bihać enclave, and by late August the number of civilians to have taken flight from Bihać had increased to 20,000.[151] But although strengthened by a recent infusion of light arms, the Bosnian army had neither the equipment nor the technical support for strategic operations. Thus, most of the Bosnian army's battlefield gains were in the countryside; at this point in time, the Bosnian army did not attempt to retake occupied towns and cities.[152]

Having rejected the EC-brokered peace plan, which the Croats and Muslims had accepted, Bosnian Serbs defied international negotiators and the entire Geneva peace process by proclaiming, on 18 August, their intention to seek to link their territories with the FRY and Serb-occupied territories of Croatia,[153] an announcement that should not have come as a surprise to anyone aware of Karadžić's earlier programmatic statements.[154] Consistent with previous French actions, French Foreign Minister Alain Juppe declared, shortly thereafter, that the Bosnian Serbs had every right to link their conquests with the FRY.[155] Yet, even as Juppe offered his support to the Bosnian Serbs, the latter continued to expel Gypsies, Muslims, and Croats from Banja Luka, Bijeljina, Janja, and other areas long secured by Serbian forces. These expulsions of noncombatants began in May 1994. Between mid-July and mid-September alone, more than 6,000 Muslims living in these Serb-held towns were driven from their homes by Serb forces. A Bosnian government official said that the Serbs had promised to expel another 6,000 before the end of the year.[156] Bosnian Serbs raped non-Serb women and girls in Banja Luka on a wide scale, used force to evict non-Serbs from their homes, orchestrated the mass dismissal of non-Serbs from their jobs, and even recruited non-Serbian men into slave labor brigades.[157] The resultant changes in the ethnic composition of Serb-held territory in Bosnia are shown in Table 10.1.

Yet at the very moment when Bosnian Muslim forces were showing a new strength, Western diplomats signed an agreement with Slobodan Milošević offering

TABLE 10.1   Ethnic Composition of Bosanska Krajina (1991, 1994)

	1991	1994
Serbs	625,000	875,000
Croats and Muslims	550,000	50,000

SOURCE: "War Crimes in Bosnia-Hercegovina: U.N. Cease-Fire Won't Help Banja Luka," *Human Rights Watch Helsinki*, Vol. 6, No. 8 (June 1994), p. 5.

to reward Milošević for his supposed break with Karadžić and agreeing to ease international trade sanctions in exchange for his agreement to the stationing of 135 civilian observers to monitor the FRY-Bosnian border.[158] On 8 September, however, Serbian forces in Croatia and Bosnia launched a joint campaign against Bosnian government forces in Bihać. More than 1,000 Croatian Serb forces were deployed in the action, backed by tanks and heavy artillery.[159] Croat and Bosnian government forces replied by launching a counteroffensive, driving the Serbs back on three fronts. By the end of October, Bosnian government forces had retaken 100–150 square kilometers of territory to the east and southeast of Bihać, setting Bosnian Serb soldiers and civilians to flight and capturing four tanks and dozens of mortars abandoned by the Serbs.[160] But when units of the Bosnian army succeeded in crushing a Serbian battalion (killing 20 Serb troops) in battle action around Sarajevo, U.N. troops intervened (on 7 October) to expel more than 500 Bosnian troops. That same day, Yasushi Akashi, Boutros-Ghali's special envoy to Bosnia, visited Bosnian President Izetbegović and issued an acidic protest, threatening the Bosnian government with serious countermeasures in the event of a recurrence.[161]

The United States was, by now, lobbying hard for more resolute military action against the Bosnian Serbs. U.S. Defense Secretary William Perry, for example, said on 28 September that he wanted NATO to use "compelling force" against Bosnian Serb forces.[162] But the British and French remained opposed. Lieutenant General Sir Michael Rose, UNPROFOR commander in Bosnia, responded to U.S. pressures by emphasizing his concept of "peacekeeping" as self-limiting in the means employed.[163] Rose demonstrated what he meant by authorizing pin-prick strikes against a Bosnian Serb tank near Sarajevo (on 22 September) and against a runway at Udbina (in occupied Croatia, on 21 November), the latter coming as a response to an attack by two Serbian Orao fighter aircraft from Udbina air base on civilians at Bihać and Cazin.[164] The Bosnian Serb military command issued a cocky riposte: "This means that UNPROFOR and NATO forces are [now] legitimate targets. We reserve the right to retaliate how and when we see fit."[165] Unintimidated by the U.N.-NATO approach, the Bosnian Serbs even attacked a U.N. aid convoy on 18 October.[166] As for the Bosnian Muslims, they called on the U.N. to remove Sir Michael Rose as commander of the U.N. forces in Bosnia, accusing him of favoring the Serbs and of executing British, rather than U.N., policy.[167]

TABLE 10.2   Troop Strengths of the Rival Forces (November 1994)

Estimate Source	Bosnian Serbs	Bosnian Muslims	Bosnian Croats
McNeil-Lehrer	80,000	100,000	50,000
Die Welt	60,000	210,000	n/a
Jane's Defence Weekly	102,000	164,000	50,000*
Nedjeljna Dalmacija	80,000	120,000	n/a

*1993, from The Military Balance.

SOURCES: McNeil-Lehrer News Hour, 4 November 1994; Die Welt (Bonn) (4 November 1994), p. 4; Jane's Defence Weekly, as cited in The Sun (Baltimore) (6 November 1994), p. 11A; International Institute for Strategic Studies, The Military Balance 1993–1994 (London: Brassey's, October 1993), p. 74; and Nedjeljna Dalmacija (Split) (4 November 1994), p. 21.

The U.N. commitment was, by then, flagging. The British and French, in particular, were increasingly impatient to terminate their participation in the ill-conceived "peacekeeping" forces, although they remained steadfastly opposed to any arming of the Muslims—betraying all too clearly the pro-Serbian attitude which underlay British and French policy statements. In late July, U.N. Secretary-General Boutros Boutros-Ghali recommended to the U.N. Security Council that the U.N. "peacekeepers" in Croatia and Bosnia be withdrawn.[168]

The Croat-Bosnian offensive pressed forward until mid-November, capturing the town of Kupres on 3 November, dislodging Bosnian Serbs from several locations in the mountains overlooking Sarajevo, and tightening a noose around Trnovo, a key town whose capture could relieve Bosnian Serb pressure on several Muslim-held towns.[169] In a misdirected retaliation that hit civilians only, Bosnian Serb forces fired seven missiles into Bihać on 3–4 November. One of these hit a school, wounding a woman and six children.[170] Bosnian Serb forces also continued to shell suburban Sarajevo, provoking a strange comment by French Lieutenant General Bertrand de Lapresle, commander of U.N. troops in the Balkans, to the effect that the United States and the West in general should give more "support" to and show more "understanding" for Bosnian Serb forces.[171] The military strengths of the Muslim, Bosnian Croat, and Bosnian Serb forces are shown in Tables 10.2 and 10.3.

But the Bosnian Serbs rallied, as rebel Serb forces from neighboring Croatia crossed the border to join in the fighting. The Serbs began to regain the upper hand in the first half of November, recaptured about 80 percent of the territory lost earlier to the Muslims, and by the end of the month were encircling the town of Bihać and pushing toward its center.[172]

NATO ambassadors met on 24 November to consider the possibility of further aerial strikes against Bosnian Serbs, but failed to reach an agreement.[173] Three days later, a morose U.S. Defense Secretary Perry declared the Serbs "unstoppable" and opined that further NATO air strikes could not make any difference.[174] A despondent Boutros-Ghali, conscious of his utter lack of credibility with any of the parties

TABLE 10.3   Armaments Possessed by the Combatants in Bosnia (November 1994)

	Tanks	Artillery Pieces	Armored Personnel Carriers	Aircraft*
Bosnian Serbs	330	800	400	37
Bosnian Muslims	40	a few*	30	0
Bosnian Croats	75	200	n/a	0

*1993.

SOURCES: McNeil-Lehrer News Hour, 4 November 1994; and International Institute for Strategic Studies, *The Military Balance 1993–1994* (London: Brassey's, October 1993), pp. 74–75.

to the conflict, announced at the end of the month that it might be time to pull U.N. "peacekeepers" out.[175] The following day, perhaps more to show contempt for the U.N. and NATO than anything else, Bosnian Serbs crossed into Croatia and seized seven Ukrainian soldiers assigned to U.N. "peacekeeping" duty. Taking stock of NATO's miserable performance in Bosnia, a *New York Times* editorial writer pronounced NATO dead, pointing to Anglo-French obstructionism as the source of NATO's seeming impotence.[176]

Meanwhile, the United States began taking the first steps toward belatedly arming the Croats and Muslims. In mid-October, officials announced that a U.S. military mission consisting of fifteen officers and headed by retired General John Galvin would soon arrive in Sarajevo to help integrate the joint Muslim-Croat forces and train them for combat.[177] The Pentagon drew up a plan to provide military training and as much as $5 billion in weapons to Bosnian government forces.[178] Meanwhile, CIA operatives were dispatched to Bosnia to begin training Bosnian government troops.[179] Americans were also said to be involved in the construction of a secret airfield in an isolated valley in central Bosnia, between Visoko and Kakanj; the airstrip was said to be designed to receive air shipments of weaponry.[180] Finally, on 29 November, U.S. Defense Secretary Perry received his Croatian counterpart and signed a "Memorandum of Cooperation on Defense and Military Relations" between the United States and Croatia. The text did not mention arms supplies, but called for an expansion of defense contacts and bilateral cooperation, to include periodic meetings of officials, exchanges of delegations, and military training for Croatian forces, to be provided by the U.S. International Military and Training Program.[181]

As late as the first week of December 1994, France and Britain held to their plan to pull their troops out of Bosnia.[182] Since British and French forces accounted for about a third of UNPROFOR's total strength in Bosnia (see Table 10.4), their withdrawal would have compelled the U.N. to terminate its mission in Bosnia. Russian Foreign Minister Kozyrev quickly announced that his country might maintain its military presence in Bosnia even after the termination of the UNPROFOR man-

TABLE 10.4   Composition of UNPROFOR Troops Stationed in Bosnia
(December 1994)

Country of Origin	Number of Troops
France	3,646
Britain	3,390
Pakistan	3,016
Netherlands	1,650
Malaysia	1,544
Turkey	1,462
Spain	1,259
Bangladesh	1,235
Sweden	1,051
Canada	863
Norway	663
Ukraine	581
Russia	506
Egypt	426
Denmark	286
Belgium	276
New Zealand	249
Jordan	100
United States*	5
Total	22,208

*Part of U.N. headquarters in Sarajevo; fifteen more were attached to relief agencies and other units.

SOURCE: *USA Today* (9–11 December 1994), p. 5A.

date—an announcement that had no visible effect on either the British or the French. But on 6 December, Bosnian President Izetbegović announced that a number of Islamic countries had pledged to send "replacement" forces in the event that UNPROFOR troops were withdrawn.[183] Within a few days of this announcement, the French performed an about-face and not only announced their intention to keep their troops in Bosnia after all, but even called for an expansion of the UNPROFOR mission.[184] In fact, the French clearly took a great interest in the conflict, taking part in meetings of NATO defense ministers in 1994 for the first time in twenty-eight years[185] and repeatedly demanding concessions for the Serbs.[186] For that matter, the Bosnian Serbs were not too pleased about talk of the removal of U.N. troops, since UNPROFOR had been allowing Bosnian Serb forces to skim off nearly 50 percent of all food brought in for "humanitarian" purposes and nearly 40 percent of all UNPROFOR fuel, according to *The Christian Science Monitor*.[187] As that paper put it, "The Karadžić war machine is literally fueled by U.N. aid."[188]

The relationship between the Anglo-French use of the UNPROFOR as a supplier of the Bosnian Serbs and their insistence on maintaining the arms embargo against the Muslims and Croats, not to mention their earlier efforts to suffocate Slovenian and Croatian efforts to escape from Serbian tyranny, was not generally understood in the United States. Yet this background sets the context for understanding the Anglo-French initiative of 3 December 1994, which scrapped the supposedly sacrosanct principle of the integrity of Bosnia's borders (even if compromised with formulas of cantonization and ethnic sectors) and offered Bosnian Serbs the prospect of international recognition of their political union with Serbia proper.[189]

Impotent NATO

Despite continued Serbian rejection of any and all peace plans, continued Serbian policies of murder of civilians and expulsion of non-Serbs not only in war zones but also in Serb-held towns such as Banja Luka, Bijeljina, Rogatica, and Bosanska Gradiška[190] as well as in several regions of the Republic of Serbia (specifically Kosovo, Vojvodina, and the Sandžak), transparent Serbian intentions of annexing large portions of Croatian and Bosnian territory,[191] and even repeated Serb confinement or chaining up of U.N. soldiers,[192] the U.N. and NATO declined to translate repeated threats of significant military action into the real thing. In a typical expression of the thinking underlying the mild posture adopted by the U.N. and NATO in response to repeated Serbian aggression, one North American scholar (Lenard Cohen of Simon Fraser University) argued (without either offering evidence or confronting countervailing evidence) that

> air strikes would likely have only a very limited and futile impact [on the Serbs].... For example, air strikes could not effectively and permanently roll back Serbian victories or the results of "ethnic cleansing," could not punish those responsible for atrocities, and thus would not be much of an object lesson deterring others from committing similar acts in other localities outside the Balkan region. Moreover, only delicate political negotiations, not air strikes, would potentially establish a viable system of governance in Bosnia-Herzegovina or its constituent parts.[193]

Leaving aside Cohen's suggestion that aerial strikes against Bosnian Serb positions might be intended, in part, to deter tyrants "outside the Balkan region"—say, in the southern tip of Latin America or in West Africa—there are some obvious (I believe) problems with his argument that the Serbian side would have been unimpressed by any and all aerial strikes (i.e., regardless of the payload delivered or the amount of destruction inflicted), with his assumption that the wholesale destruction of Bosnian Serb military and economic resources would not punish the perpetrators of atrocities and could not "roll back Serbian victories," and with his supposition that political negotiations are best advanced by swearing off the use of force to enforce adherence to internationally mediated agreements. If military force is so useless to achieve political change, how does Professor Cohen suppose the Bosnian Serbs came into possession of 70 percent of Bosnia's land in the first place? And does he really suppose that the aerial bombing of certain Bosnian Serb targets at the end of summer 1995 and the immediate expression on the Serbian side of willingness to negotiate were unrelated events having no connection with each other?

But Cohen was not expressing an isolated opinion here. On the contrary, his (mis)understanding of the situation represented, at least, the standard ideological justification for inaction and perpetual mollification of Serbs offered by the hesitant governments of Britain, France, and the United States, some of their military commanders, and at least some U.N. and NATO spokespersons—all under the banner of so-called "realism." An example is Lieutenant General Sir Michael Rose, commander of the U.N. forces in Bosnia until January 1995, who, in an interview with *Oslobodjenje* the preceding September, "warned against the dangers of [NATO's] using excessive force [in Bosnia], which he said could plunge the U.N. operation here into a Somalia-type debacle."[194] And although no one is going to advocate or defend the use of "excessive" force, Rose's intention was not to state a tautology, but to criticize advocates of a hard line against Serbian aggression.

Misha Glenny, the distinguished *Times* correspondent lent his support to this counsel of perpetual patience:

> If the world accepted the advice of Senator Bob Dole and former Prime Minister Margaret Thatcher [advocates of aerial strikes against Serbs], [dire] consequences would be likely to close in on us like a garrote. To offer large-scale military support to the Bosnian Government would trigger a ferocious response from Belgrade, bringing the unbridled might of the Serbian and Bosnian Serb armies into play.[195]

In this brief, translucent paragraph, Glenny stated explicitly the governing assumption of those who abjured counterforce in the face of genocide and preferred to rely on rational discourse alone.[196] But, as Herbert Okun, Cyrus Vance's deputy during his engagement as Bosnian peace negotiator, once quipped, "Diplomacy without the threat of force is like baseball without a bat."[197] Needless to say, none of those advancing the myth of Serbian invincibility pointed to the fact that the Bosnian Serb machine was, as already noted, dependent upon UNPROFOR for supplies of fuel and food and, hence, that the situation was actually *worse* in some ways as a result of UNPROFOR's involvement than it would have been without UNPROFOR.

Yet even as some Western commentators were declaring the Serbs for all practical purposes "invincible" and more than a few even declaring that the war was "over" and that the Serbs had "won," a rather different picture of Serb and Bosnian Serb military strength began to emerge in news reports and military analyses. A detailed analysis of Bosnian Serb strength published in *Ljiljan* in November 1994 revealed that the Bosnian Serb military budget was exhausted and that salaries to Mladić's soldiers were, depending on the area, anywhere from three to eighteen months in arrears; in attempting to cope with the situation, the demoralized Bosnian Serb soldiers resorted to thefts from each other or to going AWOL and looking for more remunerative jobs.[198] The internal command system was also said to have broken down to the extent that, in Mladić's own words, Serbian soldiers had become "incapable of acting and performing combat activities on their own."[199] The Bosnian Serb army was also said to be plagued by poor intelligence, widespread apathy, and bad discipline, and Mladić's soldiers, like soldiers in the Krajina Serb army, were said to be spending much of their time drunk.[200]

A report in *Slobodna Dalmacija*, published in February 1995, indicated that the Krajina Serbs were seriously outmanned and outgunned by the Croatian armed forces, and that, although possessing large stocks of heavy artillery, they were relying on missiles and tanks technologically inferior to what the Croats had succeeded in obtaining.[201] And in July 1995, the London daily newspaper *The Independent* indicated that the same analysis might well be extended to the Yugoslav army (of the FRY) itself. Sapped of its earlier strength by a steadily tightening budget, by Milošević's frequent political purges of qualified generals, and by the wholesale flight of qualified physicians, engineers, and other persons with university degrees from the army and indeed from the country, seeking to take up new residences abroad, the army was said to be spending part of its time courting the small private sector in Serbia in search of private firms willing to "sponsor" army bases.[202] Yugoslav army General Borivoje Jovanović even admitted, in a 1995 article for *Vojska* (the Yugoslav army official journal), that "the army's inability to pay its bills has caused the state electrical company to threaten to cut electricity supplies to bases and installations."[203] Added to that were the prospects for rising unemployment in the munitions industry (resulting in a significant decline in Serbian arms and ammunitions production) and further cuts in the FRY/Serbian military budget.[204]

While Serbian military strength declined, Croatian and Bosnian Muslim military strength increased. By February 1995, the Croatian army was reported to have at its disposal some 100,000 troops on active duty with another 180,000 troops in reserve, 36 fighter aircraft, 320 battle tanks, 2,000 artillery batteries, and 3,000 anti-tank weapons. This high-morale army (which had benefited from training by qualified Western officers)[205] enjoyed, thus, a clear advantage over the Krajina Serbs, who possessed at that time 28 fighter aircraft, 250 battle tanks, something over 1,000 artillery batteries, and 62 missile batteries, with only 50,000 men under arms.[206]

As for the Bosnian army loyal to the government headed by Alija Izetbegović and Haris Silajdžić, *Jane's Defence Weekly* had reported already in November 1994 that it had doubled in size within the previous twelve months and now stood at 164,000 troops, "all in uniform and equipped."[207] Moreover, thanks to more or less clandestine supply flights, the Bosnian army had, by March 1995, a growing arsenal of heavy weaponry, including mortars and middle-range artillery. General Rasim Delić, chief of the General Staff of the Bosnian army, admitted, however, that thanks to the arms embargo, his army remained short of long-range artillery, tanks, and aircraft.[208]

The Croatian Campaigns of May–August 1995

By January, rumors were afloat that Croatia would soon put its new military strength to the test.[209] As spring arrived and the weather warmed, tensions began to mount along the frontier between the Republic of Croatia and Serb-occupied parts of Croatia. The Serbs expected an attack, but were unsure which enclave the Croats would target first—the so-called Krajina ("Frontier"), western Slavonia, or eastern Slavonia. Then, on 1 May, the Croatian army struck with force against western Slavonia, crossing effortlessly through U.N. cease-fire lines. More than 2,500 Croatian troops participated in the initial attack backed by tanks and heavy artillery; altogether, some 7,200 Croatian troops were involved in the thirty-one-hour action against 4,500 Serbian troops. Serbs attempted to retaliate by shelling Zagreb and, in the process, killed 6 people and wounded another 185.[210] Among combatants, between 350 and 450 Serbian soldiers and 33 Croatian soldiers and 9 Croatian police lost their lives in this operation.[211] By the end of 2 May, Croatian leaders were able to claim victory in western Slavonia, announcing the liberation of about 1,000 square kilometers of Croatian territory. Between 8,000 and 13,000 Serbs fled the area in the following days, leaving only, at most, 1,500 Serbs behind in western Slavonia as of late June.[212] While Croatia celebrated the reconquest of one of the three areas seized by rebel Serbs, dissension and recrimination ripped through Serbian ranks. One high-ranking general in the so-called Krajina army (Milan Celeketić) resigned his commission, blaming the reversal on the failure of Milošević and Karadžić to render assistance.[213]

Some Western observers interpreted such recriminations rather literally. The prestigious London daily newspaper *Financial Times*, for example, reported that "Belgrade has so far remained on the sidelines" and offered as evidence the observation that "Milošević has been restrained in his comments on the latest fighting in Croatia."[214] The facts tell a different story. According to evidence assembled by Croatian authorities, Belgrade had participated directly in the occupation of Croatia all along: by assigning one of its own officers, Lieutenant General Mile Mrkšić, hitherto Assistant Chief of the General Staff of the Yugoslav (i.e., Serbian) army, to assume command of the Serb paramilitary forces in Croatia; by assigning other Yugoslav army officers to direct occupation forces in the three sectors; by paying the salaries of these officers as well as of other Croatian Serb military and governmental personnel (albeit, behind schedule); and by sending military supplies and other materiel to Serb occupation forces in occupied Croatia.[215] The Croatian government offered some telling details:

> On June 13, 1995, two Yugoslav army tank units totaling 26 M-84 MBTs operated by the Yugoslav Army's 211th Armored Brigade were sent from Niš, Serbia, across the border with Bosnia and Herzegovina, and deployed in Slunj, in the occupied territories of Croatia in sector Glina. In addition, on June 12, 1995, one unit of armored personnel carriers (APCs) consisting of 10 vehicles operated by the Yugoslav Army Second Motorized Brigade was sent from Valjevo, Serbia, across the border with Bosnia and Herzegovina, and deployed in the same region in Croatia, at Banovina. Furthermore, on June 19, 1995, the Yugoslav army supplied equipment for two MI-8 rotary-wing aircraft located at the Udbina airport in the occupied territories, sector Knin, through the territory of Bosnia and Herzegovina.[216]

The U.N. did not have to rely on the Croatian authorities, however, for evidence of FRY involvement in the occupation of the Krajina and parts of Slavonia. The

London weekly newspaper *The European* had already created a stir in early April by reporting that Major General Aleksandr Perelyakin, commander of the Russian and Belgian U.N. troops in the so-called Krajina region, had ordered the troops under his command to allow a Serbian convoy of six M-36 tanks, six howitzers, six 100-mm. guns, and a busload of Serb soldiers to cross into Krajina to reinforce Serbian occupation forces there.[217] The Belgian soldiers complained bitterly, and the senior-ranking Belgian officer, Colonel François Thonon, protested that these orders were contrary to U.N. guidelines. The convoy went through, but shortly thereafter, Perelyakin was dismissed by the U.N. for "severe shortcomings."[218]

In the weeks following the Croatian reconquest of western Slavonia, Serbian occupation authorities in the so-called Krajina forcibly recruited as many able-bodied Serbs as they could, including recent refugees from western Slavonia.[219] On 28 July, Croatian forces overran the towns of Glamoč and Bosansko Grahovo, thereby choking off the Serbs' supply route to Knin. Then, on 4 August, the Croatian army, its morale enormously boosted after its recent victory in western Slavonia, trained its guns on the Krajina. The Croatian Serb capital at Knin was bombarded by Croatian heavy artillery, and about 120,000 Croatian troops moved into the Krajina in a massive, multipronged attack. Within thirty-six hours the Croats had retaken Knin, and within another twelve hours the Croatian army had liberated about 80 percent of the so-called Serbian Krajina.[220] Some 4,000 Serb fighters south of Zagreb surrendered to the Croats, while 150,000 other "Krajina" Serbs fled to Serb-occupied western Bosnia, abandoning their homes, their belongings, and their heavy weapons.[221] The operation also relieved the long Serbian siege of the Bihać enclave, where some 180,000 people (mainly Muslims) had endured hunger and privation for months. General Ivan Tolj, a Croatian Defense Ministry spokesperson, triumphantly proclaimed, "Nothing is going to be the same again after this. Any dreams about a 'greater Serbia' are past." As for the Croatian Serb forces in the "Krajina," their fighting capacity had now been "totally destroyed."[222]

The British,[223] French, and Russian governments—all unsympathetic to the Croatian and Bosnian governments—condemned the Croatian offensive. The United States and Germany restricted themselves to expressing the opinion that a peaceful solution would have been preferable—in effect applauding the successful and virtually bloodless Croatian offensive. By the end of the week, the Croatian army had established its control throughout what the Serbs had called the "Krajina" after the old "Vojna Krajina" ("Military Frontier") of Habsburg times, but what, in this century, has generally been known either as central Dalmatia or as the Dalmatian hinterland.[224] Moreover, as a result of this campaign, the Serbian presence in Croatia, which had accounted for about 12 percent of the republic's population in 1991, was reduced to a mere 3 percent.[225]

Serbian refugees from the Krajina streamed into Bosnian Serb territory and into Serbia proper, some reduced to begging on the streets of Belgrade. The Holy Synod of the Serbian Orthodox Church now spoke out against Milošević, on 8 August, in its sharpest criticism since June 1992. "The short-sighted policy of the Yugoslav, Serbian, and Montenegrin leadership," the statement said, "has brought the Serbian people into a dead-end, from which there is no escape."[226] Asserting that the Milošević regime had shown itself "incapable of continuing to lead this people," the synod demanded Milošević's resignation and the establishment of a "government of trust."[227]

Hamlet in Bosnia

To strike or not to strike, that is the question. In the years of the Serbian Insurrectionary War, that was always the question. But like Shakespeare's Hamlet, the U.N. seemed to require almost indefinite time to reflect on the essential question, and even then did not come up with a clear answer. For the U.N.—and here, in particular its Secretary-General and Security Council—it seemed easier to postpone the point of decision, and so the decision was postponed and postponed and postponed again.

In fact, the U.N.'s endless dithering about "what to do" may well lead one to conclude, as David Rieff suggested at one point, that "U.N. peacekeeping was an entirely unsuitable instrument for dealing with an ongoing conflict of the kind taking place in Bosnia."[228] Indeed, as Rieff conceded, there are sufficient grounds to speculate "that the great powers did not in fact want anything to be done [about the genocide in Bosnia], but rather wanted to give the appearance of doing something as a way of mollifying domestic public opinion in their respective countries."[229] And insofar as that may have been their chief motivation, cheap and easy measures were infinitely preferable to the more ambitious measures which would have been required to restore regional stability and establish justice and safeguards for human rights in the Balkans, *even though "cheap and easy measures" always prove costlier in the long run in terms of time expended discussing the problems, commitments of manpower by the Great Powers, local casualties, or financial outlays by the Great Powers.* But in line with such thinking, the U.N. and NATO were generous with threats, proclamations, and statements of intent and stingy when it came to backing up their threats with action or enforcing their own proclamations (e.g., of the famous "no-fly zones"). Former U.S. Secretary of State George P. Schulz spoke to precisely this issue in testimony before Congress in October 1994, when he told those present, "You can't just snap your fingers. We don't need more statements, because we have got statements. The Universal Declaration on Human Rights says it all. What we need is operational capability. And I think the U.N. should try to do that."[230]

Aerial strikes are employed to serve three distinct purposes—punitive, tactical, and strategic. *Punitive air strikes* are designed as purely retaliatory measures and have the objective of changing the targeted party's attitude and behavior. Punitive air strikes do not, by definition, change the balance of power either locally or throughout the theater of operations. NATO aerial strikes conducted against Bosnian Serbs between 1993 and July 1995 were strictly punitive in nature (although by no means without military and diplomatic significance). *Tactical air strikes*, by contrast, are designed to weaken the targeted party's capabilities locally and usually only temporarily. They are, therefore, useful in connection with specific battles or campaigns or in support of the realization of limited objectives. They usually involve targets such as weapons emplacements, radar sites, and communications facilities. The NATO air strikes against the Bosnian Serbs which began on 30 August 1995 included some targets of a tactical nature and therefore had the potential to make a tactical difference, but Western governments chose to limit the strikes to achieving largely "punitive" aims, aspiring to change the Bosnian Serbs' attitudes and behavior rather than their capabilities.[231] *Strategic air strikes*, finally, are designed to weaken the targeted party's capabilities throughout the theater of operations, preparatory to imposing a dictated peace. Only strategic air strikes could have played any role in ending the political role of nationalists in the region's politics and, more specifically, in removing the illegitimate government of Slobodan Milošević from power and enabling antiwar liberals in Serbia to establish a legitimate government, respectful of human rights, in its place.

Advocates of aerial strikes against Serbian and Bosnian Serb positions generally had in mind *strategic* air strikes, on the supposition that practitioners of genocide and mass rape should be considered "unreasonable" men, not readily restored to rational thinking. Yet, as Richard Holbrooke concedes in his memoirs, it remains a matter of contention as to whether the West would have achieved a more just settlement by continuing the strikes for a longer period.[232] More generally, advocates of aerial strikes deeply resented claims during 1993, 1994, and much of 1995 that aerial strikes had been tried and shown to be ineffective against the Serbs, because such claims missed the point—strategic air strikes were never tried by NATO at any point during the years 1991–1995.

But the point was not lost on the Bosnian government, which, by 1995, treated the U.N. and NATO with increasing disdain and prepared its forces for counteroffensives against Bosnian Serb positions. Former U.S. President Jimmy Carter visited the region in December 1994 and negotiated a four-month cease-fire amid unrealistic expressions of optimism that the cease-fire might lead directly to peace in Bosnia.[233] The cease-fire was a convenience for both sides, given the inconveniences associated with Bosnia's winter. The most concrete result of the cease-fire was an exchange of prisoners, on which the Bosnian government and Bosnian Serbs agreed in mid-January.[234] The Bosnian government used the cease-fire to prepare its military for a spring offensive. During these months, there were repeated flights of C-130 transport aircraft into Bosnia, landing on a Bosnian government-controlled airstrip outside Tuzla. Among the weaponry delivered were Stinger antiaircraft missiles. The identity of the supplier remained undisclosed, although it was speculated that Turkey, Iran, and perhaps the United States might have been responsible for the flights.[235] The Serbian side took advantage of the lull to complete the construction of a new detour road for use in Belgrade's continued supply of Karadžić's forces, bypassing international observers monitoring the main highway.[236] Serbs also denied U.N. monitors access to their radar equipment for a period of four days in early February 1995, during which time "unexplained helicopter flights" were reported by U.N. ground troops.[237] In August 1995, the *Wall Street Journal* reported that, over the course of the preceding months (i.e., since Milošević's promise to terminate all military supplies to and support for the Bosnian Serbs—a promise for which Milošević had been rewarded with an easing of U.N. sanctions), Milošević had "rotated something like 108,000 troops in and out of Bosnia and supplied Bosnian Serbs with 512 tanks, 506 armored personnel carriers, some 250 mortars, howitzers and other types of artillery, 10 high-performance military jets, 18 transport helicopters, and 8,700 tons of fuel."[238]

On 2 March 1995, in flagrant disregard of the terms of the still valid cease-fire accord, Bosnian Serbs revoked permission for food shipments to continue to be sent into besieged Bihać in northwest Bosnia, even though international aid workers "warned that civilians could starve to death."[239] Within three weeks, heavy fighting resumed in central and northeastern Bosnia, with battles around Tuzla and Travnik. Just north of Tuzla lay the strategic Posavina Corridor, a narrow strip of land that served Bosnian Serbs as a vital lifeline for supplies from Serbia.[240] Bosnian Serbs now raided the U.N.-supervised heavy weapons depot at Lukavica, southeast of Sarajevo, ignoring the fact that a Security Council resolution had threatened to unleash air strikes in such an eventuality.[241] The ensuing confrontations between government forces and Bosnian Serb forces were described as the bloodiest battles since the beginning of the Bosnian phase of the war three years earlier, prompting German journalist Carl Gustav Ströhm to speculate that the Bosnian government's struggle to overcome Serbian aggression may have reached a turning point.[242]

Thrown on the defensive, Bosnian Serb leader Karadžić responded by ordering artillery bombardment of Sarajevo, Tuzla, Bihać, and Goražde (all of them U.N.-declared "safe havens"), by announcing a general mobilization, and by calling for immediate peace talks and the return to the battle lines of 23 December.[243] In early April, Bosnian government forces captured Mount Vlasić from the Serbs; overlooking the town of Travnik, Mount Vlasić represented an important strategic stronghold.[244] Bosnian government forces also fought their way into the Majevica mountain range north of Tuzla. Representatives of the international "contact group" held talks in Belgrade and Zagreb, although they had nothing new to offer. These discussions took place amid renewed Serbian shelling of U.N. "safe havens" at Sarajevo, Bihać, and Tuzla. But although fighting in Bosnia intensified, NATO commanders talked not of enforcement of the "safe havens," but of withdrawal.[245]

The Bosnian Serbs launched a counteroffensive in early May, supported by massive artillery fire and tank forces. Unable to make any headway against the Bosnian government forces, the Bosnian Serbs took out their frustration on populations already under their jurisdiction, by blowing up at least six Catholic churches in Banja Luka and its immediate vicinity in the course of May alone, killing a Catholic priest and a nun, placing the Catholic bishop of Banja Luka under house arrest, and driving other Catholic priests, monks, nuns, and laypersons from the area.[246] The Serbs had blown up all sixteen of Banja Luka's mosques two years earlier.[247]

Belatedly responding to the Bosnian Serb seizure of heavy weapons from Lukavica, the U.N. demanded that the weapons be returned by noon on 25 May, threatening air strikes if the Serbs failed to comply. Bosnian Serbs rebuffed the U.N., issuing counterthreats of their own. The U.N. therefore authorized NATO warplanes to bomb a Bosnian Serb munitions depot outside Pale.[248] Bosnian Serbs, in turn, shelled all six U.N. "safe havens," killing more than 70 persons in Tuzla alone. NATO aircraft once again attacked Serb positions, bombarding the munitions depot a second time and destroying six bunkers. The same day, Bosnian Serbs rounded up more than 370 U.N. troops and chained them up in front of an ammunition depot and at other sites, using them as human shields.[249] On 29 May, Bosnian Serb leader Radovan Karadžić and the Supreme Command of the Bosnian Serb army announced that they were unilaterally canceling "all U.N. resolutions to which they had been a party because the United Nations 'interfered in the war and allied with our enemies.'"[250] Interestingly enough, this Serbian claim to be exempt from international law and from the decisions of international bodies came within two weeks of a decision by the U.N. War Crimes Tribunal in The Hague to name Karadžić, Bosnian Serb General Ratko Mladić, and Karadžić's secret-police chief, Mico Stanišić, as war criminals.[251]

Although the U.N. shortly negotiated the release of its peacekeepers, albeit amid rumors that in exchange for their release local U.N. commanders had pledged never to use NATO airpower in Bosnia again,[252] the humiliation was an object lesson to advocates of the "soft touch." The immediate impact was to prompt policy-makers in Britain, France, and other countries to agree to establish a mobile "rapid reaction" force consisting of 4,000 troops and to move more military equipment into the area. In connection with this new force, U.S. Defense Secretary William J. Perry announced on 4 June that the United States would establish a secret intelligence-gathering unit to assist in monitoring Bosnian Serb movements of troops and military hardware.[253] The United States also agreed to provide close air support for operations of the rapid reaction force, including AC-130 gunships.[254]

In mid-June, the Bosnian government massed between 15,000 and 30,000 troops north and northwest of Sarajevo around the towns of Breza and Visoko in what was described as an unprecedented concentration of forces. In the ensuing offensive, government troops made territorial gains at the Serbs' expense. In the course of the June offensive, Bosnian government forces captured Mount Treškavica, south of Sarajevo, and temporarily cut off a key access road to Pale. The Serbs replied by shelling Sarajevo's main hospital and other civilian targets in the Bosnian capital.[255] As civilian casualties in Sarajevo continued to mount and responding, more specifically, to a violation of the "no-fly" zone by two Serb warplanes, NATO requested authorization to destroy the main Bosnian Serb air base. But as had happened several times previously, the request was denied.[256] In a potentially portentous development, the U.N. "withdrew all of its peacekeepers who were manning weapons collections points around Sarajevo, in effect acknowledging [its] inability to stop the Serbs from shelling the city," and simultaneously denied a request from Lieutenant-General Rupert Smith, U.N. commander in Bosnia, for permission to use force to secure a corridor for food supplies to be brought into Sarajevo.[257]

General Smith's request was indicative. Indeed, since assuming command of U.N. forces in Bosnia in January 1995, the general had repeatedly demanded that the U.N. and NATO get tough with the Serbs.[258] But even as Britain, France, and Russia continued to prevent the U.N. and NATO from even providing an effective defense of Bosnian civilians, British Prime Minister John Major told the G-7 leaders at a June meeting in Halifax, Nova Scotia, that all of them collectively were "at a loss [as to] how to end the bloodshed" in Bosnia[259]—ignoring the fact that President Clinton and German Chancellor Kohl, not to mention former British Prime Minister Margaret Thatcher, did not consider themselves "at a loss," but merely road-blocked—by Major, among others. As General John Shalikashvili, Chairman of the U.S. Joint Chiefs of Staff, admitted, "The problem has not been with my colleagues in this Administration. The problem has been in the inability to convince our international partners."[260]

Ironically, it was the Bosnian Serbs themselves who would soon help to convince Britain of the necessity of military action. Having lost land in central Bosnia, the Bosnian Serbs decided to seek compensation in the east, specifically by overrunning the government-held towns of Srebrenica and Žepa, both U.N.-declared "safe havens." The first "safe haven" to fall to the Serbs was Srebrenica (where 42,000 persons were housed), which fell to a 1,500-man force on 11 July. Bosnian Serb forces immediately began rounding up women and children and putting them on buses; the men were taken away, allegedly to be "screened for war crimes." Eventually, some 30,000 refugees from Srebrenica made it to Tuzla, another "safe haven." But according to Red Cross figures, some 6,546 persons were missing and presumed dead, most of them men.[261] The U.N. was soon able to document that the Serb forces had liquidated them *en masse* and buried them in a mass grave. Refugees tearfully described scenes of intense cruelty and brutality, including rapes, physical degradation, and outright slaughter of unarmed civilians.[262] The U.N. made no response, however. A U.N. official explained: "To reclaim Srebrenica, you'd have to be prepared to fight … and there is no political will to do that."[263]

Disgusted with the U.N.'s evident weakness, Bosnian government troops surrounded U.N. bases and observation posts in Žepa and Goražde and confiscated the U.N. forces' weapons. In Žepa, the 70 Ukrainian soldiers who comprised the U.N. "peacekeeping" force there at first refused to surrender their arms. But after Bosnian government troops surrounded their base and mined the entrance, the Ukrainians reconsidered and turned over their weapons. The Bosnian government troops then took the Ukrainians into custody and moved them to the front lines to serve as human shields against the expected Serb attack.[264] The Serbs overran Žepa a few days later, all the same, allegedly using poison gas to subdue resistance.[265] The Bosnian commander of Žepa, Colonel Avdo Palić, attempted to negotiate a surrender, but the Serbs ignored the tradition of safe passage and executed Palić on the spot.[266] The ill-fated Ukrainians now fell into Bosnian Serb hands and were once again put to use as "human shields"—this time to ward off NATO air strikes. Some of Žepa's 16,000 inhabitants were shot by the Serbs, though at least 3,000 escaped into the hills around Žepa. After taking the town, the Serbs looted Žepa, then torched it, firing shots into the woods in hopes of killing any civilians who might be hiding there.[267]

As the Powers took stock of these developments, Radovan Karadžić defiantly warned that Bosnian Serb gunners would shoot down any NATO warplanes that might attempt to salvage either of these two fallen "safe havens." The White House now drew up a proposal for intensive NATO bombing of Bosnian Serb positions and began lobbying with the British and French. The French readily agreed, and on 20 July the British likewise gave their assent. The result was a rather unbelievable warning to the Serbs that any assault on the Bosnian-government enclave of Goražde would meet with a "substantial and decisive response" by the international community.[268] Russian Defense Minister Pavel Grachev registered Moscow's opposition to the resolution, but U.S. Secretary of State Warren Christopher dismissed Russia's objections, observing, "The Russians do not have a veto" over NATO decisions.[269] On 1 August, ignoring Russian objections, the NATO allies extended their guarantee of air strike retaliation to the other three remaining "safe havens," Sarajevo included.

The Uses of Military Power

Over the preceding two and a half years, the presence of U.N. "peacekeepers" had repeatedly been cited by U.N. and EC spokespersons as a reason for not bombing the Serbs; on their argument, any such bombardment would risk retaliation against the "peacekeepers." Gradually, however, a consensus emerged in NATO and EC councils that if the presence of "peacekeepers" obstructed actions necessary to impose peace, then they were not peacekeepers at all, but *peace obstructers*. It was with this realization that the U.N. began moving its so-called peacekeepers out of Goražde in mid-August.[270] Even so, it took two further incidents to bring NATO to the moment of decision. The first was a fatal attack on three high-ranking diplomats, who were driving along the Mount Igman road into Sarajevo.[271] After initial hesitations, the Western states eventually blamed the Bosnian Serbs for the attack. The second incident occurred on 28 August when Bosnian Serbs fired a 120-mm. mortar into downtown Sarajevo, killing at least 39 persons and wounding more than 80.[272] The Bosnian Serb attack was probably inspired by military reverses that the significantly better-armed Bosnian Serb forces had experienced in the field since the latest Croat-Muslim joint offensive.[273] Western leaders expressed outrage, and the United States now pressed its NATO partners to agree to a strong response.

NATO's response came two days later when more than sixty NATO aircraft began bombing Bosnian Serb missile sites, radar sites, communications facilities, artillery positions, ammunition dumps, and other military objects. After several hours of bombing, NATO spokespersons claimed that the air strikes had already achieved their "preliminary objectives" and that "a substantial number of targets were damaged or destroyed" as a result of the first day's strikes.[274]

NATO's air strikes continued over the next two days, hitting army barracks, weapons depots, artillery batteries, and other military targets. The Bosnian Serbs fired back at NATO aircraft, but in three days of aerial strikes succeeded in downing only one French jet.

NATO called a temporary halt to air strikes on 1 September in order to give the Serbs the opportunity to signal their willingness to cooperate. When such signals failed to materialize, NATO resumed bombing on 5 September.[275] As NATO continued to destroy radar sites, barracks, communication centers, and ammunition dumps, not only around Sarajevo and Pale, but also at other locations throughout Bosnia, Bosnian Serb General Mladić struck a bizarre note, accusing NATO of having been "more brutal than … Hitler."[276] But despite the ostensible toughness, NATO was in fact carefully circumscribing its attacks. As the *Washington Post* noted, "Few air strikes have been directed against front-line units … including the artillery ringing Sarajevo. NATO has specifically placed those targets off-limits so as not to be seen as trying to strategically affect the outcome of the war."[277]

But as the strikes continued, Russian President Boris Yeltsin protested and warned that Moscow would reassess its relationship with the West unless the air strikes ended quickly.[278] Equally unsurprising was the Greek government's expressions of "strong reservations" about the strikes, even though Athens had been required to render its assent before the strikes had begun.[279]

The air strikes continued for more than a week; the Serbs remained defiant at first and even fired two missiles on a NATO reconnaissance jet near Goražde on 15 September.[280] But eventually the Serbs gave in to U.N. and NATO pressure and began to pull their heavy guns out of the U.N. weapons exclusion zone. By nightfall, 16 September, the Bosnian Serbs had moved some 43 heavy weapons away from Sarajevo.[281] But as the Serbs gradually complied with an extended U.N. deadline, Bosnian and Croatian troops rolled back the Serbs in western Bosnia, mopping up Jajce and moving, by 17 September, to within striking distance of Banja Luka, the Serbs' biggest prize in western Bosnia.[282]

Even as the NATO allies threatened to continue aerial strikes until the Serbian threat to "safe havens" had been removed and the Serbs showed signs of abiding by U.N. decisions, U.S. Assistant Secretary of State Richard Holbrooke continued to press the Serbs to agree to negotiate. On 13 September, Holbrooke presented a draft agreement to Milošević, Karadžić, and Mladić, calling for an immediate cessation of all offensive operations in the Sarajevo area within a week, the opening of two land routes to Sarajevo (one of them to be the Kiseljak road) to "unimpeded humanitarian road traffic," and the reopening of the Sarajevo airport within twenty-four hours. In return, NATO would call off bombing for seventy-two hours.[283] Holbrooke and U.S. Ambassador Peter Galbraith met with Croatian President Tudjman on 14 September and again on 17 September. On the latter occasion, Holbrooke encouraged Tudjman to seize Sanski Most, Prijedor, and Bosanski Novi, pointing out that capture of these towns would strengthen Croatia's hand at the negotiating table, but warned Tudjman against laying siege to Banja Luka, as its capture would generate more than 200,000 additional refugees.[284] On 19 September, Tudjman and Izetbegović met in Zagreb. In the two days it had taken Holbrooke and his associates to arrange this meeting, the Croatian army had been dealt a reverse by strong Serbian resistance at the Una River on the Croatian-Bosnian border. The Croatian side suffered twenty-five dead, with fifty soldiers still trapped.[285] This setback contributed to caution on the Croatian part; moreover, Mladić had taken the heavy artillery withdrawn from Sarajevo (in accord with the Holbrooke-brokered agreement) and had deployed it just east of Banja Luka. But gradually the three sides were brought around to the idea of negotiating and, after certain conditions were set down, peace talks got underway in Dayton, Ohio, on 1 November 1995.

Conclusion

Casualties in the Serb-Croat war, as of 1 September 1993, amounted to 6,651 killed, 12,706 persons missing and presumed dead, and 24,028 wounded, according to Croatian government statistics.[286] By contrast, casualties in the Bosnian war were vastly higher. Vladimir Žerjavić, the distinguished Zagreb demographer, has estimated that in the years 1992–1995 some 215,000 persons died in Bosnia-Herzegovina and that among the dead were about 160,000 Muslims, 30,000 Croats, and 25,000 Serbs. Moreover, although the bitterness of Croat-Muslim battles cannot be denied, Žerjavić's calculations show that only about 2,000 Muslims were killed by Croatian forces; the remaining 158,000 died at the hands of Serbian forces. Of the 30,000 Croats who lost their lives in Bosnia, 2,000 were killed by Muslims and about 28,000 were killed by Serbian forces, according to Žerjavić. And of the 25,000 Serbs who lost their lives in Bosnia, Žerjavić estimates that about half of them were killed by Muslims and half by Croats.[287] In addition to the dead, at least 2.7 million persons had been reduced to refugees.[288] An estimated 20,000–50,000 Bosnian Muslim women had been raped by Bosnian Serb soldiers in a systematic campaign of humiliation and psychological terror.[289]

Beyond the sheer human suffering, the war had an impact far greater than skeptics were prepared to believe back in 1991 or even in 1992. To begin with, the West declined to defend either the Helsinki Accords, the Geneva Conventions, or the Genocide Convention of 1948,[290] suggesting that the West either considers it impossible to defend these accords or no longer values them. Second, the established principle of international law known as *uti possidetis*, mentioned earlier, under which new states that emerged from the fracturing of larger states were recognized within their preexisting administrative boundaries, however they might have been drawn, has now been scuttled in favor of the principle that aggression should be rewarded.[291] Third, given NATO's timidity and the eagerness of the West to place it under U.N. authority, questions have now been raised as to whether NATO has any practical military utility at all (these questions were being raised again in the context of NATO's slow and ambiguous response to the crisis in Kosovo in 1998). Fourth, as David Rieff has suggested, with the obvious failure of the U.N. in Bosnia, it may be that only unilateral action by the Great Powers can effectively impose stability in unstable societies.[292] And finally, as many observers have pointed out, if, despite so much clamor and so many threats, neither the U.N. nor the West proved capable of defending either moral principles or political order, then it is not clear why either the U.N. or the West should be regarded with respect.

One of the problems afflicting the West in regard to Bosnia had to do with the notion of democracy. In the West, democracy is taken to be operative when fair elections and referenda are held and when duly elected officials take office and policies endorsed by the majority are put into effect. In the case of Bosnia, however, many Westerners accepted the principle that an ethnic numerical minority, even if not inhabiting a compact area, need not feel bound by the will of even two-thirds of the citizens and might, on the contrary, resort to force, embracing even "ethnic cleansing" as an instrument, in order to resist and combat the will of the majority.[293] If some persons in the West have such a poor grasp of the concept of democracy—the very core of which is majority rule[294]—then no one need be surprised when fundamental social and political changes that subvert democracy *in the West* are not even recognized by most of those directly affected.

Notes

1. See, for example, Mariana Jovevska, "Tolerance in Serbian Church Life in Bosnia at the End of the 19th Century (Specific Bosnian Features or a Balkan Syndrome)," in *Etudes balkaniques* (Sofia), No. 2 (1995). Regarding the weak and muted national consciousness among South Slavs until the mid-nineteenth century, see Ivo J. Lederer, "Nationalism and the Yugoslavs," in Peter F. Sugar and Ivo John Lederer (eds.), *Nationalism in Eastern Europe* (Seattle and London: University of Washington Press, 1969; reissued 1994), pp. 396–399, 411–413.

2. See Chapter 3 of this book.

3. See *Večernji list* (Zagreb) (30 August 1990), p. 4.

4. *Vjesnik* (Zagreb) (15 October 1990), p. 14.

5. Laura Silber and Allan Little, *The Death of Yugoslavia* (London: Penguin Books and BBC Books, 1995), p. 230.

6. *Popis stanovništva domačinstva, stanova i poljoprivrednih gazdinstava 1991. Prvi rezultati za republiku i po opštinama*, S. R. Bosna i Hercegovina, Statistički bilten No. 219 (Sarajevo: Republički Zavod za Statistiku, May 1991), p. 11.

7. According to figures from the 1981 census, as reported in Ante Markotić, "Demografski aspekt promjena u nacionalnoj strukturi stanovništva Bosne i Hercegovine," in *Sveske* (Sarajevo), Vol. 16–17 (1986), p. 299 and fold-out facing p. 302.

8. Some close observers even suggested that the sheer heterogeneity of Bosnia's population was a guarantee against interethnic war. For one example, see interview (February 1991) with Svetozar Stojanović, "Optimistic About Yugoslavia: Interview with Svetozar Stojanović," in *East European Reporter*, Vol. 4, No. 4 (Spring-Summer 1991), p. 14.

9. James Gow, "One Year of War in Bosnia and Herzegovina," in *RFE/RL Research Report* (4 June 1993), p. 6, summarizing Milan Radaković, "The European Community: The Possibility of Military Integration" [title as given in Gow], *Vojno delo*, Nos. 4–5 (July–October 1991), pp. 188–203.

10. Gow, "One Year of War," p. 6.

11. For further discussion of this point, see Sabrina Petra Ramet, "The Yugoslav Crisis and the West: Avoiding 'Vietnam' and Blundering into 'Abyssinia,'" in *East European Politics and Societies*, Vol. 8, No. 1 (Winter 1994).

12. See Chapter 3 of this book; and Branka Magaš, *The Destruction of Yugoslavia: Tracking Yugoslavia's Break-up, 1980–92* (London: Verso, 1993), pp. 261, 311, 333.

13. *New York Times* (26 September 1991), p. A3. The five successor states are Slovenia, Croatia, Bosnia-Herzegovina, Macedonia, and the Federal Republic of Yugoslavia (the last-mentioned consisting of Serbia and Montenegro).

14. Adil Zulfikarpašić, Vlado Gotovac, Miko Tripalo, and Ivo Banac, *Okovana Bosnia— Razgovor*, ed. by Vlado Pavlinić (Zürich: Bosnjački Institut, 1995), 103–108.

15. Noel Malcolm, *Bosnia: A Short History* (New York: New York University Press, 1994), pp. 227–228.

16. Reneo Lukić and Allen Lynch, *Europe from the Balkans to the Urals: The Disintegration of Yugoslavia and the Soviet Union* (Oxford: Oxford University Press, 1996), p. 203.

17. Tim Judah, *The Serbs: History, Myth and the Destruction of Yugoslavia* (New Haven: Yale University Press, 1997), p. 170.

18. Robert J. Donia and John V. A. Fine, Jr., *Bosnia and Hercegovina: A Tradition Betrayed* (New York: Columbia University Press, 1994), p. 228.

19. Viktor Meier, *Wie Jugoslawien verspielt wurde*, 2nd ed. (Munich: C. H. Beck, 1996), p. 368.

20. Silber and Little, *Death of Yugoslavia*, p. 240.

21. Tanjug (12 November 1991), trans. in Foreign Broadcast Information Service (FBIS), *Daily Report* (Eastern Europe), 13 November 1991, p. 41.

22. *Vreme* (Belgrade) (30 September 1991), p. 5.

23. *New York Times* (28 December 1991), p. 4.

24. Donia and Fine, *Bosnia and Hercegovina*, p. 238.

25. Francis A. Boyle, *The Bosnian People Charge Genocide: Proceedings at the International Court of Justice Concerning Bosnia v. Serbia on the Prevention and Punishment of the Crime of Genocide* (Amherst, Mass.: Aletheia Press, 1996), p. 8.

26. See *Daily Telegraph* (London) (29 February 1992), p. 8.

27. *Der Standard* (Vienna) (17 March 1992), p. 2.

28. *New York Times* (6 November 1992), p. A4.

29. *Večernji list* (19 March 1992), p. 9, and (26 March 1992), p. 7.

30. See, for example, *Salzburger Nachrichten* (28 March 1992), p. 4; and *Die Presse* (Vienna) (28/29 March 1992), p. 1.

31. *Neue Zürcher Zeitung* (15 May 1992), p. 1.

32. Donia and Fine, *Bosnia and Hercegovina*, pp. 243–244; confirmed in *L'Orient-Le Jour* (Beirut, Lebanon) (9 May 1992), p. 1; reconfirmed in Silber and Little, *Death of Yugoslavia*, p. 240.

33. Richard Holbrooke, *To End a War* (New York: Random House, 1998), pp. 50–51.

34. See *The Times* (London) (21 June 1993), p. 9.

35. For further details, see Viktor Meier's brilliant expostulation in chapter 7 of his *Wie Jugoslawien verspielt wurde*, due to be published in English translation by Routledge Press in summer 1999.

36. Amy Lou King, "Bosnia-Herzegovina—Vance-Owen Agenda for a Peaceful Settlement: Did the U.N. Do Too Little, Too Late, to Support This Endeavor?" in *Georgia Journal of International and Comparative Law*, Vol. 23, No. 2 (1993), p. 354.

37. David Rieff, "The Illusions of Peacekeeping," in *World Policy Journal*, Vol. 11, No. 3 (Fall 1994), p. 1.

38. Ibid., p. 2.

39. Quoted in ibid., p. 4.

40. Lukić and Lynch, *Europe from the Balkans*, pp. 209, 212, 215.

41. *Financial Times* (6 July 1992), p. 12. See also *Nedjeljna Dalmacija* (Split) (22 June 1994), p. 7.

42. Kasim Trnka, "The Degradation of the Bosnian Peace Negotiations," in Rabia Alia and Lawrence Lifschultz (eds.), *Why Bosnia? Writings on the Balkan War* (Stony Creek, Conn.: Pamphleteer's Press, 1993), pp. 203, 203n.

43. Donia and Fine, *Bosnia and Hercegovina*, p. 6, also pp. 261–263.

44. I am indebted to an anonymous source for sharing this information with me in the course of a conversation in Bergen in spring 1997.

45. Lukić and Lynch, *Europe from the Balkans*, p. 294.

46. Itar-TASS World Service (Moscow) (26 June 1992), trans. in FBIS, *Daily Report* (Central Eurasia), 1 July 1992, pp. 15–16.

47. For details of the plan, see David Owen, *Balkan Odyssey* (London: Victor Gollancz, 1995), pp. 89–93; for the context and discussions concerning the plan, see Tom Gjelten, *Sarajevo Daily: A City and Its Newspaper Under Siege* (New York: HarperCollins, 1995), pp. 179–182; for a general discussion of the plan, see Silber and Little, *Death of Yugoslavia*, pp. 306–322.

48. E.g., letter to the editor from Flora Lewis, in *Foreign Affairs*, Vol. 72, No. 3 (Summer 1993), p. 221.

49. Rein Mullerson, "New Developments in the Former USSR and Yugoslavia," in *Virginia Journal of International Law*, Vol. 33, No. 2 (Winter 1993), p. 313.

50. *Borba* (Belgrade) (7 April 1993), p. 4.

51. *New York Times* (18 April 1993), p. 1; *Politika* (Belgrade) (19 April 1993), pp. 1–2; and *Washington Post* (27 April 1993), p. A1.

52. *Los Angeles Times* (10 May 1993), p. A18.

53. *Süddeutsche Zeitung* (Munich) (8/9 May 1993), p. 2.

54. *Glas Istre* (Pula) (4 June 1993), p. 6.

55. Germany subsequently protested its exclusion from this meeting.

56. *Vjesnik* (23 May 1993), p. 5.

57. Attila Hoare, "The Croatian Project to Partition Bosnia-Hercegovina, 1990–1994," in *East European Quarterly*, Vol. 31, No. 1 (March 1997), pp. 129, 131.

58. Ibid., pp. 132–133; and Letty Coffin, "Tudjman and Bosnian-Croat Relations," in *South Slav Journal*, Vol. 18, No. 3/4 (Autumn/Winter 1997), pp. 29–30.

59. Judah, *The Serbs*, p. 247.

60. *Danas* (Zagreb), new series (24 August 1993), p. 33.

61. *New York Times* (2 September 1993), pp. A1, A8.

62. These speculations are reported in *The Times* (12 May 1993), p. 1.

63. *Rompres* (20 December 1992), in *BBC Summary of World Broadcasts* (24 December 1992).

64. Quoted in Malcolm, *Bosnia: A Short History*, p. 244.

65. Gow, "One Year of War," p. 9.

66. *International Herald Tribune* (Tokyo ed.) (15/16 January 1994), p. 2.

67. Noel Malcolm, *Kosovo: A Short History* (London: Macmillan, 1998), p. 345.

68. As cited in Meier, *Wie Jugoslawien*, p. 300.

69. *Scotland on Sunday* (11 January 1998), p. 17.

70. Gow, "One Year of War," p. 2; and *Frankfurter Allgemeine* (28 August 1993), p. 5.

71. *Japan Times* (4 December 1993), p. 1.

72. See, for example, *Kyodo* (Tokyo) (11 February 1994), trans. in FBIS, *Daily Report* (Eastern Europe), 14 February 1994, p. 34; and again, *The Globe and Mail* (Toronto) (1 June 1994), p. A7.

73. Tanjug (8 November 1993), in FBIS, *Daily Report* (Eastern Europe), 9 November 1993, p. 36; and *The Globe and Mail* (10 August 1994), p. 1.

74. Regarding British demands that the United States commit ground troops to Bosnia, see *Sunday Telegraph* (London) (9 May 1993), p. 2; editorial comment in *New York Times* (12 May 1993), p. A10; *Washington Post* (14 November 1993), p. A25; and *Japan Times* (2 February 1994), p. 5. Regarding French demands to the same effect, see *New York Times* (6 January 1994), p. A8; and *Japan Times* (27 January 1994), p. 5. Regarding British and French discussions about withdrawing their forces (and parallel declarations on the part of Canada and Spain), see *The Times* (28 December 1993), p. 8; and *Mainichi Daily News* (Tokyo) (23 January 1994), p. 1.

75. *International Herald Tribune* (Tokyo ed.) (21 October 1993), p. 2.

76. TVSH Television Network (10 February 1994), trans. in FBIS, *Daily Report* (Eastern Europe), 14 February 1994, p. 10.

77. *Philadelphia Inquirer* (15 May 1994), p. A17.

78. Lukić and Lynch, *Europe from the Balkans*, p. 338.

79. *The Times* (1 May 1993), p. 10.

80. Quoted in *Frankfurter Allgemeine* (2 June 1994), p. 2.

81. *Süddeutsche Zeitung* (21–22 August 1993), p. 7.

82. *The Times* (2 March 1993), p. 14.

83. *Kyodo* (1 October 1993), in FBIS, *Daily Report* (Eastern Europe), 5 October 1993, p. 42.

84. Radio Bosnia-Herzegovina (Sarajevo) (23 February 1994), trans. in FBIS, *Daily Report* (Eastern Europe), 23 February 1994, p. 34.

85. See, for example, *Boston Sunday Globe* (31 July 1994), p. 2; and *Die Welt* (Bonn) (4 November 1994), p. 4.

86. DDP/ADN (Berlin) (12 November 1994), trans. in FBIS, *Daily Report* (Eastern Europe), 14 November 1994, p. 37; and *Manchester Guardian Weekly* (18 December 1994), p. 4.

87. *Frankfurter Allgemeine* (18 November 1993), p. 9. Regarding Bulgaria's response to the Yugoslav conflict, see Ekaterina Nikova, "Bulgaria in the Balkans," in John D. Bell (ed.), *Bulgaria in Transition: Politics, Economics, Society, and Culture After Communism* (Boulder: Westview Press, 1998), pp. 294–298.

88. *International Herald Tribune* (Tokyo ed.) (9 November 1993), p. 2.

89. *International Herald Tribune* (Tokyo ed.) (15 November 1993), p. 5.

90. *Süddeutsche Zeitung* (15 October 1993), p. 8.

91. *Süddeutsche Zeitung* (30–31 October–1 November 1993), p. 8.

92. Tetsuya Sahara, "The Islamic World and the Bosnian Crisis," in *Current History*, Vol. 93, No. 586 (November 1994), p. 387.

93. *Ljiljan* (Sarajevo-Ljubljana) (23 November 1994), p. 25.

94. Sahara, "The Islamic World," pp. 387–388. See also *Malaysian Digest* (Kuala Lumpur) (October 1992), p. 1.

95. *The Times* (2 June 1994), p. 12.

96. Sahara, "The Islamic World," p. 389.

97. *Süddeutsche Zeitung* (13–14 November 1993), p. 2.

98. *Oslobodjenje—European edition* (18 February 1994), trans. into English in *Oslobodjenje*, 1st English ed. (Sarajevo-Washington, D.C.), April 1994, p. 15.

99. *Neue Zürcher Zeitung* (22–23 May 1994), p. 1; and *The European* (London) (17–23 June 1994), p. 1.

100. Norman Cigar, *Genocide in Bosnia: The Policy of "Ethnic Cleansing"* (College Station: Texas A & M University Press, 1995), passim.

101. *Daily Telegraph* (16 November 1994), p. 13.

102. *Federal News Service* (12 March 1997), on *Nexis*.

103. *Chicago Tribune* (28 January 1997), p. 7.

104. As reported later in *Washington Post* (3 November 1994), p. A31.

105. *Boston Sunday Globe* (19 June 1994), p. 6; *Večernji list* (21–22 June 1994), p. 8; and *La Repubblica* (Rome) (1 July 1994), p. 13.

106. *Financial Times* (8 July 1994), p. 13.

107. On 21 July 1994, by attaching so many conditions as to render it null and void.

108. A senior Western military official in Bosnia, as quoted in *Independent on Sunday* (London) (31 July 1994), p. 11.

109. "Das Duell der Kriegsverbrecher," in *Stern* (Hamburg) (11 August 1994), pp. 102–105.

110. *New York Times* (4 December 1994), p. 11.

111. "The Relentless Agony of Former Yugoslavia: 1. Naming War Criminals in Bosnia-Herzegovina," in *Foreign Policy Bulletin* [The Documentary Record of United States Foreign Policy], Vol. 3, Nos. 4–5 (January-April 1993), p. 57.

112. "United Nations: Secretary-General's Report on Aspects of Establishing an International Tribunal for the Prosecution of Persons Responsible for Serious Violations of International Humanitarian Law Committed in the Territory of the Former Yugoslavia" [3 May 1993], *International Legal Materials*, Vol. 32, No. 4 (July 1993), p. 1165.

113. Quoted in "War Crimes and the Menace of Winter in Former Yugoslavia," in *Foreign Policy Bulletin*, Vol. 3, No. 3 (November-December 1992), p. 49.

114. Quoted in "United Nations: Secretary-General's Report," p. 1164.

115. See the later judgment by the War Crimes Tribunal in The Hague, as reported in *The Daily Yomiuri* (17 November 1998), p. 4, and (18 November 1998), p. 4.

116. Dorothy Q. Thomas and Regan E. Ralph, "Rape in War: The Case of Bosnia," in Sabrina P. Ramet (ed.), *Gender Politics in the Western Balkans: Women and Society in Yugoslavia and the Yugoslav Successor States* (University Park: The Pennsylvania State University Press, 1999), pp. 213–214.

117. Ibid., p. 206. For further discussion, see Alexandra Stiglmayer (ed.), *Mass Rape: The War Against Women in Bosnia-Herzegovina*, including translations by Marion Faber (Lincoln: University of Nebraska Press, 1993).

118. See, for example, *Politika* (10 February 1993), p. 22, and (23 February 1993), p. 6; and *NIN* (Belgrade) (19 February 1993), pp. 26–28. Also interview with Dobrica Ćosić in *Adevarul* (Bucharest) (24 February 1993), pp. 1, 8, trans. in FBIS, *Daily Report* (Eastern Europe), 1 March 1993, p. 43.

119. *The Times* (2 June 1994), p. 12.

120. See, for example, Jeri Laber and Ivana Nizich, "The War Crimes Tribunal for the Former Yugoslavia: Problems and Prospects," in *The Fletcher Forum of World Affairs*, Vol. 18, No. 2 (Summer/Fall 1994).

121. *Frankfurter Allgemeine* (15 October 1994), p. 1; *Slobodna Dalmacija* (Split) (20 October 1994), p. 10; *The European* (21–27 October 1994), p. 13; and *Philadelphia Inquirer* (9 November 1994), p. A4.

122. *Boston Sunday Globe* (20 November 1994), p. 10.

123. *Ekonomska politika* (Belgrade) (1 March 1993), p. 14.

124. See comments by Bosnian Vice President Ejup Ganić in *International Herald Tribune* (Tokyo ed.) (26–27 June 1993), p. 2; also *Ljiljan* (23 November 1994), p. 9.

125. For specifics, see Ramet, "The Yugoslav Crisis and the West."

126. Mark Almond, *Europe's Backyard War: The War in the Balkans* (London: Heinemann, 1994), p. 243, as quoted in Daniele Conversi, *German-Bashing and the Breakup of Yugoslavia*, The Donald W. Treadgold Papers in Russian, East European, and Central Asian Studies No. 16 (Seattle: The HMJ School of International Studies of the University of Washington, March 1998), p. 15.

127. Among whom one would have to include, among others, also Serbian quislings and fascists. On this point, see Philip J. Cohen, *Serbia's Secret War: Propaganda and the Deceit of History* (College Station: Texas A & M University Press, 1996).

128. Brad K. Blitz, "Serbia's War Lobby: Diaspora Groups and Western Elites," in Thomas Cushman and Stjepan G. Mestrovic (eds.), *This Time We Knew: Western Responses to Genocide in Bosnia* (New York and London: New York University Press, 1996), pp. 197–198.

129. Ibid., p. 199.

130. Ibid., p. 214.

131. Carl G. Jacobsen, "Yugoslavia's Wars of Secession and Succession: Media Manipulation, Historical Amnesia, and Subjective Morality," in *Mediterranean Quarterly*, Vol. 5, No. 3 (Summer 1994), p. 35.

132. Ibid., p. 39.

133. Ibid., p. 26. For a corrective, see Malcolm, *Bosnia: A Short History.* For an example of extreme Germanophobia from the same author, see Carl J. Jacobsen, "Washington's Balkan Strategy: Aberration or Herald?" in *South Slav Journal*, Vol. 17, No. 1/2 (Spring/Summer 1996), pp. 67–70.

134. See Peter Brock, "Dateline Yugoslavia: The Partisan Press," in *Foreign Policy*, No. 93 (Winter 1993/94).

135. Martin van Heuven, "Rehabilitating Serbia," in *Foreign Policy*, No. 96 (Fall 1994), p. 40.

136. Charles Boyd, "Making Peace with the Guilty: The Truth about Bosnia," in *Foreign Affairs*, Vol. 74, No. 5 (September 1995), p. 25, as quoted in Thomas Cushman, *Critical Theory and the War in Croatia and Bosnia*, The Donald W. Treadgold Papers in Russian, East European, and Central Asian Studies No. 13 (Seattle: The HMJ School of International Studies of the University of Washington, July 1997), p. 31.

137. Sabrina P. Ramet, *Whose Democracy? Nationalism, Religion, and the Doctrine of Collective Rights in Post-1989 Eastern Europe* (Lanham, Md.: Rowman & Littlefield, 1997), pp. 64–65.

138. Plato, *The Republic*, trans. Richard W. Sterling and William C. Scott (New York: Norton, 1985), Book 9, pp. 267, 270.

139. For an effective rebuttal of the claims of moral relativism and a coherent defense of universalism, see John J. Tilley, "Cultural Relativism, Universalism, and the Burden of Proof," in *Millennium: Journal of International Studies*, Vol. 27, No.2 (1998).

140. For example, in August 1993, John Lampe, director of East European Studies at the Wilson Center, Washington, D.C., asserted that "it may be too late to reverse the majority of Serb gains in Bosnia," as reported in *Digest of the Helsinki Commission*, Vol. 16, No. 4 (August 1993), p. 3.

141. Karen Elliott House, "The New Masters of the Universe," in *Wall Street Journal* (4 May 1993), p. A18.

142. Fareed Zakariah, "Bosnia Explodes 3 Myths," in *New York Times, Weekly Review* (international ed.) (26 September 1993), p. 7.

143. Hodding Carter, "Punishing Serbia," in *Foreign Policy*, No. 96 (Fall 1994), p. 55.

144. *New York Times* (12 August 1994), p. A3.

145. *Süddeutsche Zeitung* (12/13 November 1994), p. 1. Regarding continued U.S. efforts to lift the arms embargo, see *Ljiljan* (2 November 1994), p. 9; and *Evropske novosti* (Belgrade-Frankfurt) (19 November 1994), p. 9.

146. Regarding Serbia's ability to obtain Russian weapons from what had been the GDR, see *Der Spiegel* (Hamburg) (14 November 1994), pp. 65, 68, 70.

147. See ibid., p. 154.

148. *The Sun* (Baltimore), 6 November 1994, pp. 1A, 11A.

149. Ibid., p. 1A.

150. *New York Times* (5 November 1994), on *Nexis*.

151. *Neue Zürcher Zeitung* (23 August 1994), p. 2.

152. See comments by Brigadier General Mustafa Hajrulahović of the Bosnian General Staff in *Daily Telegraph* (20 August 1994), p. 13.

153. *New York Times* (19 August 1994), p. A2.

154. See, for example, Karadžić's indication, on 18 October 1993, that his goal was to adjoin Serb-conquered areas in Bosnia-Herzegovina to a "Greater Serbia," in *Süddeutsche Zeitung* (19 October 1993), p. 6.

155. *Neue Zürcher Zeitung* (7 September 1994), p. 1.

156. These figures are reported in *Boston Sunday Globe* (18 September 1994), p. 15. See also *New York Times* (5 September 1994), p. 5; and *The Globe and Mail* (20 September 1994), p. A8. Regarding the use of police to expel non-Serbs, see AFP (Paris) (28 October 1994), in FBIS, *Daily Report* (Eastern Europe), 1 November 1994, p. 33.

157. "War Crimes in Bosnia-Hercegovina: U.N. Cease-Fire Won't Help Banja Luka," *Human Rights Watch Helsinki*, Vol. 6, No. 8 (June 1994), pp. 1–3, 13–21, 30–31.

158. *New York Times* (9 September 1994), p. A1; *Boston Sunday Globe* (25 September 1994), p. 23; *Neue Zürcher Zeitung* (16 September 1994), p. 2; *Daily Telegraph* (17 September 1994), p. 14; and *Welt am Sonntag* (25 September 1994), p. 6.

159. *New York Times* (9 September 1994), p. A7; and *Globus* (Zagreb) (23 September 1994), pp. 2–3.

160. The 100-square-kilometer estimate comes from *The Globe and Mail* (28 October 1994), p. A7; the 150-square-kilometer estimate comes from *Süddeutsche Zeitung* (29–30 October 1994), p. 1; other facts from *New York Times* (28 October 1994), p. A1.

161. *Bosna Press* (Frankfurt), in Croatian (13–20 October 1994), p. 3; and *The Globe and Mail* (8 October 1994), p. A12.

162. *The Globe and Mail* (29 September 1994), p. A8.

163. *New York Times* (29 September 1994), p. A4.

164. *Ljiljan* (23 November 1994), p. 5. Regarding demands by several commentators that NATO forces bomb the Bosnian Serb capital of Pale, see *Ljiljan* (30 November 1994), p. 9.

165. Quoted in *Sunday Telegraph* (25 September 1994), p. 31.

166. See details in *Neue Zürcher Zeitung* (20 October 1994), p. 2.

167. *The Times* (26 October 1994), p. 15.

168. *Neue Zürcher Zeitung* (27 July 1994), pp. 1, 3; and *Ljiljan* (27 July 1994), p. 16.

169. *Neue Zürcher Zeitung* (2 November 1994), p. 2; *Philadelphia Inquirer* (4 November 1994), p. A2; and *The European* (4–10 November 1994), p. 2.

170. *Washington Post* (5 November 1994), p. A17.

171. U.S. Defense Secretary William J. Perry rebutted de Lapresle's comments, declaring, "I don't think myself that understanding is the appropriate response to aggressive military actions," both quoted in *Philadelphia Inquirer* (2 November 1994), p. A4.

172. AFP (Paris) (14 November 1994), trans. in FBIS, *Daily Report* (Eastern Europe), 14 November 1994, p. 36; *Philadelphia Inquirer* (15 November 1994), p. A4, (16 November 1994), p. A8, and (18 November 1994), p. A32; *La Stampa* (Torino) (22 November 1994), pp. 1, 9; *La Repubblica* (22 November 1994), pp. 1, 14–15; *Nedjeljna Dalmacija* (25 November 1994), pp. 15–16; and *Chicago Tribune* (25 November 1994), p. 3.

173. *Pittsburgh Tribune-Review* (25 November 1994), p. A1.

174. *Los Angeles Times* (28 November 1994), p. A1.

175. *The Globe and Mail* (1 December 1994), p. A1.

176. *New York Times* (28 November 1994), p. A15.

177. *New York Times* (21 October 1994), p. A4.

178. *Daily Telegraph* (London) (19 November 1994), p. 14.

179. *The European* (18–24 November 1994), p. 1; confirmed in *The European* (25 November–1 December 1994), p. 4.

180. *The European* (18–24 November 1994), p. 1.

181. From the authentic English text, courtesy of the Embassy of the Republic of Croatia.

182. *The European* (2–8 December 1994), p. 1.

183. *RFE/RL Daily Report* (7 December 1994).

184. *New York Times* (13 December 1994), p. A1.

185. *Neue Zürcher Zeitung* (1 October 1994), p. 1.

186. *Neue Zürcher Zeitung* (1 December 1994), p. 5.

187. *Christian Science Monitor* (20 December 1994), p. 5.

188. Ibid.

189. *Sunday Telegraph* (London) (4 December 1994), p. 2.

190. For documentation of Serb "ethnic cleansing" in these areas 1994–1995, see *New York Times* (30 August 1994), pp. A1, A5; *Vreme* (Belgrade) (12 September 1994), pp. 18–19, trans. in FBIS, *Daily Report* (Eastern Europe), 5 October 1994, pp. 35–37; Radio Croatia (Zagreb) (6 February 1995), trans. in FBIS, *Daily Report* (Eastern Europe), 7 February 1995, p. 45; *Welt am Sonntag* (26 February 1995), p. 2; AFP (Paris) (1 March 1995), in FBIS, *Daily Report* (Eastern Europe), 2 March 1995, pp. 30–31; and *Reuters World Service* (2 June 1995), on *Nexis*.

191. Manifested, for example, in the announcement in February 1994 that the Bosnian Serb "Republic" was joining the FRY monetary and financial system. See Srpski Radio-Televizija Studio (Pale) (28 February 1994), trans. in FBIS, *Daily Report* (Eastern Europe), 1 March 1994, p. 32.

192. For some examples of confinement and chaining, see AFP (Paris) (19 September 1994), in FBIS, *Daily Report* (Eastern Europe), 19 September 1994, p. 25; *Neue Zürcher*

Zeitung (5 April 1995), p. 2; *Frankfurter Allgemeine* (8 April 1995), p. 6; *New York Times* (30 May 1995), p. A1; and *Focus* (Munich) (3 June 1995), p. 228.

193. Lenard J. Cohen, *Broken Bonds: Yugoslavia's Disintegration and Balkan Politics in Transition*, 2nd ed. (Boulder: Westview Press, 1995), p. 293.

194. AFP (Paris) (29 September 1994), in FBIS, *Daily Report* (Eastern Europe), 30 September 1994, p. 19.

195. Misha Glenny, "Counsel of Despair," in *New York Times* (6 December 1994), p. A15.

196. Cf. Lt.-Gen. Sir Michael Rose: "We are pro-reason. And I don't think anyone can criticize us for that," quoted in *New York Times* (29 January 1995), p. 6.

197. Quoted in David Rieff, "The Lessons of Bosnia: Morality and Power," in *World Policy Journal*, Vol. 12, No.1 (Spring 1995), p. 84.

198. *Ljiljan* (9 November 1994), p. 15, trans. in FBIS, *Daily Report* (Eastern Europe), 23 November 1994, p. 36.

199. Quoted in ibid., p. 36.

200. Ibid., p. 37.

201. *Slobodna Dalmacija* (25 February 1995), p. 8, trans. in FBIS, *Daily Report* (Eastern Europe), 7 March 1995, pp. 40–41.

202. *The Independent* (London) (10 July 1995), p. 8.

203. Ibid.

204. *Globus* (Zagreb) (17 February 1995), pp. 12–13, trans. in FBIS, *Daily Report* (Eastern Europe), 23 February 1995, p. 62.

205. Reports as to who actually provided the training have differed. *Evropske novosti* (29 July 1995), p. 4, claimed that U.S. officers and instructors provided training at the Petar Zrinski military school in Zagreb.

206. The figure for the number of troops in the Krajina Serb army comes from *Slobodna Dalmacija* (25 February 1995), p. 8, trans. in FBIS, *Daily Report* (Eastern Europe), 7 March 1995, p. 40. All other figures reported here come from *Die Welt* (28 February 1995), p. 4. Regarding Croatia's new military strength, see also *Balkan News International & East European Report* (4–10 June 1995), p. 15.

207. Quoted in *The Sun* (Baltimore), 6 November 1994, p. 11A.

208. *Večernji list* (8 March 1995), p. 7, trans. in FBIS, *Daily Report* (Eastern Europe), 10 March 1995, p. 18. For further discussion, see *Ljiljan* (19 July 1995), pp. 5–6.

209. See reports in *Welt am Sonntag* (29 January 1995), p. 2; *New York Times* (10 February 1995), p. 4; and *Naša borba* (20 March 1995), p. 2.

210. *Financial Times* (5 May 1995), p. 3.

211. Croatian Radio (Zagreb) (4 May 1995), trans. in *BBC Summary of World Broadcasts* (5 May 1995); and cro- news@well.ox.ac.uk (5 May 1995).

212. *Neue Zürcher Zeitung* (22 June 1995), p. 5. See also *Stern* (Hamburg) (11 May 1995), pp. 200–202.

213. *The Economist* (London) (20 May 1995), p. 51.

214. *Financial Times* (5 May 1995), p. 3.

215. Ambassador Šarčević's "Memorandum to the Members of Congress," in *Croatia Today: Newsletter of the Embassy of the Republic of Croatia*, No. 7 (July 1995), p. 2. Milošević's personal responsibility for placing General Mrkšić in command in the so-called Krajina is confirmed in *Christian Science Monitor* (5 July 1995), p. 6.

216. "Memorandum to the Members" (note 215).

217. *The European* (London) (7–13 April 1995), p. 1.

218. *Daily Telegraph* (12 April 1995), p. 13. See also *The European* (14–20 April 1995), pp. 1–2.

219. *Neue Zürcher Zeitung* (20 June 1995), p. 1.

220. *Süddeutsche Zeitung* (5/6 August 1995), p. 1; *Salt Lake Tribune* (6 August 1995), pp. A1, A10; and *Der Spiegel* (Hamburg), 7 August 1995, pp. 112–113.

221. *The Globe and Mail* (9 August 1995), p. A1; and *The Economist* (12 August 1995), p. 13.

222. Quoted in *Salt Lake Tribune* (6 August 1995), p. A1.

223. The ruling Conservative Party led by Prime Minister John Major pursued a pro-Serb policy in the Serbian Insurrectionary War. However, the opposition Labour Party showed itself to be not only critical of this policy orientation, but favorably disposed toward the Bosnian and Croatian governments.

224. *Neue Zürcher Zeitung* (12/13 August 1995), p. 1; also *Evropske novosti* (26 August 1995), p. 4. For details of subsequent fighting between the Croatian Army and Serbian forces in western Bosnia (in mid-August), see *Globus* (25 August 1995), pp. 5–6.

225. This figure was reported in *New York Times* (10 August 1995), p. A4.

226. Quoted in *Neue Zürcher Zeitung* (9 August 1995), p. 1.

227. Ibid.

228. Rieff, "Lessons of Bosnia," p. 80.

229. Ibid., p. 81.

230. *Hearing before the Subcommittee on International Security, International Organizations and Human Rights of the Committee on Foreign Affairs, House of Representatives*, 103rd Congress, 2nd Session, October 24, 1994 (Washington, D.C.: U.S. Government Printing Office, 1994), p. 11.

231. *CNN World News* (29 August 1995), evening. It was already 30 August in Sarajevo at the time of the broadcast.

232. Holbrooke, *To End a War*, pp. 145–146.

233. For the text of the cease-fire, see *Neue Zürcher Zeitung* (4 January 1995), p. 5.

234. *The Weekend Australian* (Sydney) (14/15 January 1995), p. 19.

235. *Der Spiegel* (6 March 1995), p. 158. See also *New York Times* (1 March 1995), p. A6; *The European* (3–9 March 1995), p. 2; and *The Sunday Times* (5 March 1995), p. 16.

236. Radio Bosnia-Herzegovina (Sarajevo) (9 February 1995), trans. in FBIS, *Daily Report* (Eastern Europe), 10 February 1995, p. 26.

237. *New York Times* (9 February 1995), p. A6. See also *Slobodna Dalmacija* (14 February 1995), p. 32.

238. *Wall Street Journal* (31 August 1995), p. A10.

239. *New York Times* (3 March 1995), p. A5.

240. *The Times* (London) (21 March 1995), p. 9; and *Neue Zürcher Zeitung* (21 March 1995), p. 1.

241. *The Times* (22 March 1995), p. 9; and *Süddeutsche Zeitung* (22 March 1995), p. 9.

242. *Die Welt* (Bonn) (25/26 March 1995), pp. 1, 3, and 27 March 1995, p. 6. See also *Slobodna Dalmacija* (23 March 1995), p. 32.

243. *Boston Sunday Globe* (26 March 1995), p. 26; and *Die Welt* (27 March 1995), p. 4; (28 March 1995), p. 4; and (29 March 1995), p. 3.

244. *The Times* (5 April 1995), p. 10.

245. *Neue Zürcher Zeitung* (6 April 1995), p. 2; *Frankfurter Allgemeine* (12 April 1995), p. 6; *Neue Zürcher Zeitung* (26 April 1995), p. 2; and *The Times* (26 April 1995), p. 11.

246. *Süddeutsche Zeitung* (15 May 1995), p. 2, and (16 May 1995), p. 9; *National Catholic Reporter* (19 May 1995), p. 11; *Reuter—German language service* (19 May 1995), on *Nexis*; *The Toronto Star* (20 May 1995), p. A26; and *Slobodna Dalmacija* (23 May 1995), p. 3, and (24 May 1995), p. 2. For further discussion of the repression of non-Serbs in Banja Luka, see *Neue Zürcher Zeitung* (15 August 1995), p. 2; *Oslobodjenje* (European ed.) (24–31 August 1995), p. 21; "Abuses Continue in the Former Yugoslavia: Serbia, Montenegro, and Bosnia-Hercegovina," *Human Rights Watch Helsinki*, Vol. 5, Issue 11 (July 1993); and David Rieff, *Slaughterhouse: Bosnia and the Failure of the West* (New York: Simon & Schuster, 1995), chap. 4.

247. As reported in *New York Times* (16 August 1995), p. A4. The Serbs expelled about 30,000 Croats and Muslims from Banja Luka between 1992 and summer 1995. Regarding Serb expulsions of yet another 5,000 Croats and Muslims from Banja Luka in the first half of August 1995, see *Christian Science Monitor* (14 August 1995), p. 5.

248. *Lloyds List* (26 May 1995) and AFP (26 May 1995), both on *Nexis.*

249. *Los Angeles Times* (26 May 1995), p. A1; *Süddeutsche Zeitung* (27/28 May 1995), p. 1; and *New York Times* (27 May 1995), p. 1.

250. *Los Angeles Times* (30 May 1995), p. A8.

251. *Die Welt* (16 May 1995), p. 4.

252. Holbrooke, *To End a War*, pp. 64–65.

253. *Los Angeles Times* (5 June 1995), p. A1.

254. *Los Angeles Times* (4 June 1995), p. A1.

255. *The European* (16–22 June 1995), p. 1; *Irish Times* (Dublin) (17 June 1995), p. 1; and *Neue Zürcher Zeitung* (19 June 1995), p. 1.

256. It was denied by the U.N. commander of U.N. forces in the Former Yugoslavia, Gen. Bernard Janvier. See *Washington Post* (22 June 1995), p. A25.

257. *Washington Post* (22 June 1995), p. A25.

258. *Christian Science Monitor* (8 June 1995), p. 7.

259. *Reuters World Service* (18 June 1995), on *Nexis* .

260. Quoted in *New York Times* (29 June 1995), p. 4.

261. Red Cross figure as cited in Jan Willem Honig and Norbert Both, *Srebrenica: Record of a War Crime* (London: Penguin Books, 1996), p. 65.

262. *Christian Science Monitor* (10 July 1995), p. 2; *New York Times* (13 July 1995), p. A1, and (14 July 1995), pp. A1, A4, A10; *The Economist* (15 July 1995), p. 31; "Pad Srebrenice", in *Vreme* (Belgrade) (17 July 1995), pp. 8–10; *Neue Zürcher Zeitung* (26 July 1995), p. 2; *New York Times* (10 August 1995), pp. A1, A4; and *Christian Science Monitor* (25 August 1995), pp. 1, 7. See also the moving report *Bosnia-Hercegovina: The Fall of Srebrenica and the Failure of U.N. Peacekeeping* (New York: Human Rights Watch/Helsinki, October 1995).

263. Quoted in *Christian Science Monitor* (14 July 1995), p. 18.

264. *Christian Science Monitor* (17 July 1995), p. 6; and *Neue Zürcher Zeitung* (19 July 1995), p. 1.

265. *Los Angeles Times* (18 July 1995), p. A1; and *Evening Standard* (28 July 1995), p. 22.

266. *Boston Sunday Globe* (30 July 1995), p. 1.

267. Ibid. See also *Balkan News & East European Report* (30 July—5 August 1995), p. 3; *Ljiljan* (23 August 1995), pp. 12–13; and *Osobodjenje* (European ed.) (24–31 August 1995), p. 23.

268. *New York Times* (21 July 1995), p. A1; and *The Guardian—International* (22 July 1995), p. 1.

269. Quoted in *The Guardian—International* (22 July 1995), p. 1.

270. *New York Times* (19 August 1995), p. 4; *Neue Zürcher Zeitung* (26/27 August 1995), p. 2; and *Welt am Sonntag* (27 August 1995), p. 1. Regarding Bosnian government concerns

about the withdrawal of U.N. forces from Goražde, see *New Zealand Herald* (Auckland) (26 August 1995), p. 9.

271. Details in *Christian Science Monitor* (21 August 1995), pp. 1, 18.

272. *New York Times* (29 August 1995), p. A1.

273. On this, see *Welt am Sonntag* (13 August 1995), pp. 1, 6–7.

274. *CNN Headline News*, 30 August 1995 (11:00 A.M.); and *Financial Times* (31 August 1995), p. 1. The time of broadcast for CNN Headline News in this and all subsequent notes is the time of reception in Seattle.

275. *Süddeutsche Zeitung* (2/3 September 1995), p. 1; and *Neue Zürcher Zeitung* (6 September 1995), p. 1.

276. Mladić's own words, in a letter to Lt.-Gen. Bernard Janvier, commander of U.N. forces in the Former Yugoslavia, as quoted in *New York Times* (8 September 1995), p. A1.

277. *Washington Post*, as reprinted in *Seattle Times* (13 September 1995), Morning ed., p. A3. (The evening edition of that day did not carry the story.)

278. *Reuters World Service* (6 September 1995), *TASS* (7 September 1995), and *Deutsche Presse-Agentur* (7 September 1995), all on *Nexis*.

279. *Xinhau News Agency* (6 September 1995), on *Nexis*.

280. The Serbs missed. *CNN Headline News,* 15 September 1995 (10:36 P.M.) and 16 September 1995 (9:39 A.M.).

281. *CNN Headline News*, 16 September 1995 (10:41 P.M.).

282. *CNN Headline News*, 17 September 1995 (11:00 P.M.).

283. Holbrooke, *To End a War*, p. 151.

284. Ibid., p. 160.

285. Ibid., p. 164.

286. *Slobodna Dalmacija* (1 September 1993), p. 2, as cited in Lukić and Lynch, *Europe from the Urals*, p. 193.

287. *Globus* (Zagreb) (9 January 1998), p. 24.

288. Stockholm International Peace Research Institute estimate as of autumn 1992, as reported in *SIPRI Yearbook 1993: World Armaments and Disarmament* (Stockholm, 1993), p. 5.

289. Slavenka Drakulić, "Women Hide Behind a Wall of Silence," in Ali and Lifschultz (eds.), *Why Bosnia?* p. 118. The Sarajevo State Commission for the Investigation of War Crimes estimated that some 50,000 Muslim women had been raped by Serbs between April 1992 and October 1992 alone.

290. Regarding the Convention on the Prevention and Punishment of the Crime of Genocide, adopted by the U.N. General Assembly on 9 December 1948, see John Webb, "Genocide Treaty, Ethnic Cleansing, Substantive and Procedural Hurdles in the Application of the Genocide Convention to Alleged Crimes in the Former Yugoslavia," in *Georgia Journal of International and Comparative Law*, Vol. 23, No. 2 (1993).

291. See Mullerson, "New Developments," pp. 313–315, 320–322; and Rein Mullerson, "The Continuity and Succession of States, by Reference to the Former USSR and Yugoslavia," in *International and Comparative Law Quarterly*, Vol. 42, Pt. 3 (July 1993).

292. Rieff, "Illusions," p. 18.

293. See, for example, Robert M. Hayden's mockery of majority rule as a so-called superior right in his article, "The Constitution of the Federation of Bosnia and Herzegovina: An Imaginary Constitution for an Illusory 'Federation,'" in *Balkan Forum*, Vol. 2, No. 3 (September 1994), p. 79.

294. Norberto Bobbio, *The Future of Democracy*, trans. from Italian by Roger Griffin (Cambridge: Polity Press, 1987), p. 63.

CHAPTER ELEVEN

◆

Repercussions of the War in Religion, Gender Relations, and Culture

The three rivers of the ancient world of the dead—the Acheron, the Phlegethon, and the Cocytus—today belong to the underworlds of Islam, Judaism, and Christianity; their flow divides the three hells— Gehenna, Hades, and the icy hell of the Mohammedans—beneath the one-time Khazar lands. And there, at the junction of these three borders, are confronted the three worlds of the dead: Satan's fiery state, with the nine circles of the Christian Hades, with Lucifer's throne, and with the flags of the Prince of Darkness; the Moslem underworld, with the kingdom of icy torment; and Gebhurah's territory, to the left of the Temple, where the Hebrew gods of evil, greed, and hunger sit, in Gehenna, under Asmodeus' rule.... In the Jewish hell, in the state of Belial, the angel of darkness and sin, it is not Jews who burn, as you think. Those like yourself, all Arabs or Christians, burn there. Similarly, there are no Christians in the Christian hell—those who reach the fires are Mohammedans or of David's faith, whereas in Iblis' Moslem torture chamber they are all Christians or Jews, not a single Turk or Arab.

Milorad Pavić
Dictionary of the Khazars
1988

Serbian novelist Milorad Pavić probably was not thinking about a future Yugoslav ethnic war when he wrote the lines quoted above, but what he understood all too clearly is that religion has often functioned historically as a mechanism for consigning enemies of the ethnoconfessional group to hell—whether a supernatural hell, a natural-secular hell, or both. He understood, too, that religion has the capacity to sacralize violence, deception, land grabs, and even genocide.[1]

In fact, not only have religious organizations contributed to preparing the ground for war, but so too has the cultural sector. By the same virtue, the war has had repercussions for the religious sphere, as well as for gender relations and the cultural sector. This chapter will examine these sectors and show how the war has affected them, noting, where appropriate, how prominent figures in these sectors have responded to the tide of hate which has overcome a country which once boasted of its "brotherhood and unity."

In the Name of God

The Serbian Orthodox Church played a significant role in weaving the tapestry of hate that eventually covered all of Serbia. The Church's strong response to the Albanian riots of 1981 (discussed in Chapter 5) and one-sided manipulation of the distorted memories of World War II[2] only foreshadowed the explicit irredentism that, dressed up as cultural history, had crept into the pages of the patriarchal organ, *Pravoslavlje*, by 1991.[3]

As interethnic relations in Yugoslavia soured, interconfessional relations did likewise. In early 1990, Serbs scrawled anti-Muslim graffiti (such as "Death to Muslims!") on Islamic buildings.[4] Catholic-Orthodox dialogue broke down, even at the highest levels, while anti-Catholic propaganda continued unabated in Orthodox Serbia. The publication of Vladimir Dedijer's anti-Catholic diatribe *Vatikan i Jasenovac*[5] set the tone for a proliferation of theories about alleged Vatican conspiracies, in league with Croats and Germans, directed against the always blameless Serbs.

While the Serbs prepared for war in the period 1990–1991, the Croats were focused on their own internal programs, as the election of the first noncommunist government in spring 1990 led immediately to a need to draft new legislation across a wide array of policy spheres. The Catholic Church exerted pressure on the government to strike from the constitution a provision prohibiting the formation of associations based on religious affiliation.[6] The Catholic Church also pushed for the reintroduction of Catholic religious instruction into state schools in the face of resistance from non-Catholic parents. But Catholic religion was quickly becoming a badge of Croatian national identity; hence, the restoration of religious instruction took on some of the character of a nationalist cause.

During the final year before the breakup of Yugoslavia, interconfessional relations soured monumentally across the country, as already mentioned. In Croatia, Orthodox (Serb) bystanders pelted buses carrying Catholic (Croatian) pilgrims with stones. While the Serbian Orthodox Church engaged in a campaign to defame the Catholic Church's role in World War II, the Catholic weekly newspaper *Glas koncila* started a series in March 1990, based on newly available archival material, revealing the Serbian Orthodox Church's collaboration with the Nazi-installed Nedić regime in Belgrade during that same war.[7] As the country veered toward the brink, the hierarchy of the Serbian Orthodox Church in Croatia, meeting in Pakrac, issued a statement encouraging Serbs "to secure for themselves the right to life on their age-old hearths in Croatia by [setting up] armed sentinels [and] barricades."[8] The Serbian Orthodox patriarchate in Belgrade endorsed this statement and in March 1992 offered that "in this new independent state of Croatia, as in the earlier one, there is no life for Orthodox Serbs."[9] The previous month in Banja Luka, in an ominous anticipation of impending events, unknown persons had vandalized a mosque and an Islamic burial chamber.[10]

Even when, in response to the expansion of the war into Bosnia, the Synod of Bishops of the Serbian Orthodox Church began demanding that Milošević resign, it nonetheless continued to purvey a self-righteously sketched portrait of Serbia as the great victim of history.[11] When, after Pavle succeeded German as patriarch of the Serbian Church, ecumenical contacts between the Orthodox and Catholic Churches resumed, it was effectively too late for the Churches to dampen the hatreds stirred up most especially from 1987 on. Nor was Pavle himself able to rise above the situation: on meeting with Roman Catholic Franjo Cardinal Kuharić and Islamic Reis-ul-ulema Jakub Selimoški in November 1992, he made a point of telling his Islamic counterpart that Bosnian Serb massacres and expulsions of the Muslims from their lands were "justified" because, as he put it, Serbs were themselves endangered in Bosnia-Herzegovina.[12]

Serbian polemicists and publicists have repeatedly construed the war as religious in character in an effort to use confessional difference to concentrate Serbian prejudice and hatred. Catholic prelates, however, have repeatedly denied that the conflict can legitimately be construed as a "religious war."[13] In fact, the war was ignited by rising tempers of ethnic hatreds and did not at first have the character of a "religious" war, but as time passed, the war took on ever more religious characteristics. Imams and Christian clergy followed their troops into battle, blessing them and praying for their success in battle. (Some forty-eight imams had died in battle by September 1994, according to official figures of the Islamic community.)[14] Catholic religious instruction was introduced in Croatia in 1991[15]—a policy move which provoked complaints that such instruction was being used to Catholicize Serb children of the Orthodox faith.[16] Later, after the war spread to Bosnia, Islamic religious instruction was introduced in schools run by the Bosnian government.[17] In areas controlled by the Bosnian Serbs, the Serbian Orthodox Church was allowed likewise to introduce religious instruction into the secular schools.[18] Although such religious instruction was at least formally nonobligatory in Croatia, for example,[19] the Serbian Orthodox Church made a big push in 1992 and again in 1994 to have *mandatory* Orthodox religious instruction introduced in state schools in the FRY, only to be rebuffed by the Federal Assembly.[20]

Even before the open hostilities broke out in Bosnia-Herzegovina, Serb Orthodox Metropolitan Amfilohije from Montenegro had already offered his endorsement of

Serb fears in Bosnia by describing the Bosnian Serb community, in January 1992, as "the last redoubt of unsullied holiness, of untroubled and unpolluted truth."[21] Then, as the war escalated, the Serb Orthodox Church allowed itself to become ever more politicized. In April 1993, for instance, Patriarch Pavle and Metropolitan Amfilohije publicly supported the Bosnian Serbs' rejection of the Western-backed Vance-Owen Plan.[22] The two Church elders opposed the plan for the same reasons that Karadžić did, in spite of Pavle's calls for peace in June 1992! The irony does not end there. In a further irony, recapitulating in Serb-held lands a practice associated with the *Ustaše* fascists of World War II, Orthodox clergymen were reported to have sold baptism certificates to Muslims hoping to avoid persecution or expulsion; the going rate for a baptismal certificate was DM 50.[23]

As religion became politicized, imams were found telling Bosnian Muslims, by autumn 1994, that they should try to avoid marrying non-Muslims, and there were increasing incentives to Muslim women to cover their heads in public. In Mostar, in-struction in Arabic was introduced in Muslim-run schools as a token of the Bosnian Muslims' growing tendency to look East for friends, rather than West.[24] Ironically, by driving more conservative rural Muslims into the cities, Bosnian Serbs gave the towns a more conservative cast, underpinning and reinforcing Islamic consciousness in the cities.[25]

Inexorably, waxing Serb hatred of Catholics and Muslims came to be expressed in efforts to extirpate all traces of multiconfessionality in areas occupied by Bosnian Serb forces. By June 1994, Bosnian Serbs had succeeded in destroying 45 percent of Catholic churches in the Vrhbosanska-Sarajevo archbishopric, 50 percent of Catholic churches in the bishopric of Banja Luka, and more than forty Catholic churches and church edifices in the bishopric of Mostar; in addition, they had caused serious damage to an additional 30 percent of Catholic churches in Vrh-bosanska and an additional 45 percent in Banja Luka.[26] In Serb-occupied areas of Croatia, Serb forces destroyed an additional 115 Catholic parish churches.[27] That this destruction was premeditated and calculated is evident both from subsequent Serb claims, in many regions, that no non-Serbs had ever existed there and from the fact that many of these edifices were dynamited after the Serbs had taken control of the towns in question. In Serb-held Banja Luka, for example, Bosnian Serbs de-stroyed all 212 mosques by September 1993, dynamiting two mosques of consider-able aesthetic and historical importance in May 1993—the ornate Ferhad Pasha mosque (built in 1583) and the Arnaudija mosque (built in 1587).[28] By August 1994, Bosnian Serb forces had destroyed or ruined some 650 mosques across Bosnia-Herzegovina.[29] In addition, Catholics (all of Slovenian, Croatian, or Hun-garian extraction) living in the archbishopric of Belgrade were repeatedly harassed by local Serbs beginning in about 1989, and between 1990 and 1993 the number of Catholics remaining there dropped from 34,000 to fewer than 9,000.[30]

To some extent, Croatian forces replied in kind, targeting both Serbian Orthodox churches and Islamic mosques[31]—in the process providing grist for Serbian propa-ganda.[32] But in Bosnian government–controlled Sarajevo, by contrast, Serb Orthodox churches were treated with respect by the multiconfessional force defending the city.[33] Far from being the hotbed of Islamic fundamentalism painted by Serbian propaganda, thus, Sarajevo continued to display a unique degree of religious tolerance. In one token of this, a new Catholic school center opened in Sarajevo in autumn 1994.[34]

Not surprisingly in these circumstances, religious figures assumed an unusual prominence in their respective societies. For example, a poll conducted by the weekly newspaper *Globus* in September 1994 found that the most respected person in Croatia was Franjo Cardinal Kuharić, with a 30.7 percent approval rating—well ahead of second-place Franjo Tudjman (21.6 percent) and third place Nikica Valentić (the prime minister, 14.6 percent), let alone opposition leader Dražen Budiša (with a 2.0 percent rating).[35] Similarly, when asked whom they hated, 68.4 percent of Croats named Patriarch Pavle (but 96.1 percent also named Serbian President Milošević).[36]

The Politics of Serbian Orthodoxy

When socialist Yugoslavia disintegrated, Serbian Orthodox hierarchs were quick to sketch out programs for a restoration of the privileges they had enjoyed in the interwar Kingdom of Yugoslavia (1918–1941). Despite some setbacks, such as the government's refusal to introduce obligatory religious education in the schools and, for that matter, the federal government's refusal to establish Christmas, Easter, and St. Vitus' Day as state holidays,[37] the Orthodox Church has, in fact, prospered under Milošević. Quite apart from the revival of its publishing activity, the Church also obtained permission to restore the historic Gradac monastery in central Serbia and was able to continue construction of the gargantuan Church of St. Sava (resumed only in 1984, after having been suspended forty-three years earlier). Beyond that, the Serbian Orthodox Church embarked on an ambitious church construction program, erecting monasteries on the territory of the Bosnian Serb republic[38] and giving especial stress to the architectural "reconquest" of Kosovo. Thus, as the Slovenian daily newspaper *Delo* reported in 1993, "There is almost not a village in Kosovo where some church facility (church, monastery, parish) is not being built."[39] When, however, the Serbian Church took possession of a hitherto state cultural facility in Priština, the presidency of the Kosovë Democratic Alliance issued a statement of protest.[40] In another equally hazardous move, the Serbian Orthodox patriarchate continued to press its claims to ecclesiastical jurisdiction in Macedonia, even after the Republic of Macedonia had declared its independence. In a sharply worded statement issued on 17 December 1992, Metropolitan Jovan of Zagreb-Ljubljana reiterated the Serbian Church's traditional position that it retained legitimate "title" to all ecclesiastical structures in Macedonia, but added a new point by claiming the right of the Serbian Church to organize parallel structures in Macedonia to cater to the small Serbian minority in that republic. "We are obliged to protect our believers and the numerous Serbian shrines in that republic," Metropolitan Jovan said,[41] without specifying against what threat such protection was thought to be necessary.

Within rump Serbia, Serbian Orthodox clerics sounded the alarm, claiming that because of the drastic impoverishment of their Church, there was a growing danger that the Croatian state might simply "nationalize" Serbian Orthodox churches and monasteries on Croatian territory.[42] This, in turn, contributed to an appeal from the Holy Synod to its believers to rally to the Church and to raise funds for its use, not just in Croatia but throughout the post-Yugoslav region.[43]

The Serbian Orthodox Church would like very much to play a greater role in Serbian society, but a 1994 survey found that only 48 percent of women and 37 percent of men in Serbia considered themselves religious. Among supporters of Milošević's ruling Socialist Party, only 42 percent were believers at that time.[44] This is not a sufficiently broad base upon which to establish some of the policies and programs the Church would like to see.

Nonetheless, the Church continued to build a presence through its political engagement, receiving foreign visitors such as Greek Prime Minister Konstantin Mitsotakis[45] and Vladimir Zhirinovsky, leader of the Russian radical-right Liberal Democratic Party,[46] denying that there were any rape camps operated by Serbs,[47] and speaking out against Milošević when he announced the supposed imposition of a blockade against the Bosnian Serbs in August 1994.[48] By contrast with the Roman pontiff, who aspired to address himself to all nations, including all three parties to the Yugoslav conflict, Patriarch Pavle did not once presume to look beyond his Serbian flock. This attitude provoked the Bosnian newspaper *Oslobodjenje* to complain:

> Patriarch Pavle last year came to Pale to bless the Serbian barbarians and devout criminals. He did not come to Sarajevo, where even today there are five times as many Serbs as there are in Pale. Never once did he condemn the monstrous Serbian crimes against the Bosnian Muslims. He made no mention of the destruction of their oldest and most beautiful mosques, he remained mute about the wiping out of all traces of Islamic culture and civilization in these areas.[49]

On the contrary, in an interview with *Evropske novosti* in December 1994, Patriarch Pavle waxed rapturous about those individuals who had allegedly earned for Serbs the epithet "heavenly Serbia."[50]

A Papal Visit

From the very beginning of the conflict, Pope John Paul II spoke out—calling for tolerance, peace, and a setting aside of nationalist passions. Although the Vatican was one of the first to accord diplomatic recognition to the newly independent republics of Slovenia and Croatia, Pope John Paul II directed his pastoral concern to all peoples of Serbia, Croatia, and Bosnia alike. Thus, when in 1994 the Pope began to plan his "pilgrimage for peace" to the region, he requested permission from Serbian authorities to include Belgrade in his itinerary and indicated an especial interest in having talks with Serbian Patriarch Pavle.[51] Pavle, however, deemed a papal visit "inopportune," and Belgrade refused permission.[52]

Despite this setback, the pontiff proceeded with plans to visit the capitals of the two other combatants, Sarajevo and Zagreb. Both Bosnian President Izetbegović and Croatian President Tudjman expressed considerable enthusiasm at the prospect of a papal visit, the former seeing in it the potential for awakening the international community's slumbering conscience.

Then the problems began. The Bosnian Serbs refused to guarantee the pope's security and even made vague threats, implying that they were prepared to blame the Muslims for any mishap.[53] With the visit to Sarajevo scheduled for 10 September, the pope held fast to his plans until Yasushi Akashi, evidently prodded by Britain and France, sent the pope a letter on 7 September indicating that the U.N. could not guarantee the pontiff's security and advising that he cancel his projected visit.[54] This letter culminated several weeks of pressures by U.N. officials on the pope to cancel his visit[55] and now, at the last minute, Pope John Paul II bowed to what was starting to seem like fate and canceled his visit to Sarajevo. The cancellation provoked despondency in Sarajevo among both Catholics and Muslims.

But plans proceeded for a papal visit to Zagreb, scheduled for 10–11 September, a visit which culminated Vatican efforts over more than twenty years to obtain permission for a trip to Croatia.[56] As with his earlier visits to Poland, Pope John Paul II's visit to Croatia was transparently political in nature. On his arrival in Zagreb, the pope praised the late Alojzije Cardinal Stepinac, whom Serbs have falsely sought to portray as a Nazi collaborator and whom he would later beatify in October 1998,[57] and spoke of the tragedy inflicted on the towns of Vukovar, Dubrovnik, and Zadar by besieging Serbian forces. He also talked of Sarajevo, calling it "a martyred town, which I as a pilgrim of peace and hope wanted fervently to visit."[58] The next day, more than a million people gathered to hear the pope speak. Setting himself squarely against Croatian President Tudjman's efforts to harness Catholicism as an element in official nationalism, the pope warned (in fluent Croatian) about "the risk of idolizing a nation, a race, [or] a party and justifying in their name hatred, discrimination, and violence."[59] Urging his listeners to put aside notions of vengeance and hatred, he called on Croatian Catholics to "become apostles of [a] new concord between peoples."[60] Although condemning the "inhuman practice of so-called ethnic cleansing," he offered a "kiss of peace" to leaders of the Serbian Orthodox Church.[61]

Among Muslims there was praise for the pope, both for his criticism of some of Tudjman's policies in Bosnia-Herzegovina and for his commitment to end the suffering of the peoples of all three republics.[62] The pope's visit, if anything, confirmed the confidence expressed by Sefko Omerbašić, president of the Mesihat (council of Islamic elders) for Croatia and Slovenia, in February 1993, when, acknowledging the Catholic Church's role in providing humanitarian assistance to all victims of Serbian aggression, he told *Delo*, "I am convinced that with this war the Catholic Church has gained lasting [esteem], which we Muslims will know how to foster and develop. That quality is actually also the biggest guarantee that it will be possible to resolve the Croatian-Muslim dispute considerably more easily than it appears at this moment."[63]

Two months after his visit, Pope John Paul II elevated thirty bishops to the College of Cardinals—among them, Vinko Puljić, the archbishop of Sarajevo. The forty-nine-year-old Puljić became the youngest member of the College of Cardinals.[64] The pope took advantage of Puljić's elevation to draw attention once again to the suffering in Bosnia and to bemoan the elusiveness of peace in the region.

The New Patriarchy

In early 1990, members of the lesbian and gay community in Belgrade formed a lesbian and gay lobby, Arkadia, which began holding public discussions and writing articles for the press. In September 1990, Arkadia issued an open letter responding to one of the leaders of the Serbian Renaissance Party who had urged Serbian women to concentrate their energies on "reproduc[ing] the greater Serbian nation."[65] The Arkadia letter showed a keen awareness of the dangerous waters into which the Serbian ship of state was sailing: "One supposes," the letter stated, "that young Serbian foetuses will be immediately baptized, conditioned to hate, and lead the war against the many Enemies of the Serbian nation."[66]

Two months later, on the eve of Serbian national elections, a group of Belgrade women, among them Žarana Papić and Lina Vušković, formed a Women's Party. The party favored a nonauthoritarian system based on a mixed economy, with free medical care and emphasis on education and environmental protection. The party campaigned against Milošević in the December elections and urged voters to avoid candidates who appealed to nationalist or chauvinist sentiments. By January 1991, the party had 500 members, but they labored under the difficulty that the regime had already succeeded in stigmatizing the appellation "feminist," with the result that they felt constrained to define themselves more elliptically.[67] In any event, they had little, if any, impact on the outcome of the elections, and the Serbian parliament elected in December 1990 consisted of only 1.6 percent women, the lowest representation of women in any European parliament. In response to this low representation, Serbian feminist activists formed an opposition "Women's Parliament" on 8 March 1991 (8 March being the traditional day designated for honoring women and women's equality in many European countries). They also took up the pacifist banner and on 9 October 1991 protested on the streets of Belgrade against the war against Croatia.

In August 1990, Belgrade's feminists had appealed for the "demilitarization" of Yugoslavia, and in December of that year they issued a protest against new textbooks that emphasized "nationalist, patriarchal, and sexist values."[68] They subsequently protested against discrimination against lesbians and gay men, against sexist behavior on the part of Serbian MPs, and against sexist language in Serbia's independent media.

A small group of activists called Women in Black has operated independently of the Women's Party and the Arkadia lobby, but for similar goals. Women in Black drew attention, most especially, to the patriarchal character of nationalism and war, protesting, among other things, against the killing of civilians, "ethnic cleansing," and compulsory mobilization.[69]

But in Serbia, as in Croatia, feminists found it hard to function, and by 1993 the (Serbian) Women's Party was dead. Meanwhile, in Croatia, the small feminist community was fragmented, as several members left for foreign soil (the United States, France, or elsewhere) and as those who remained in Croatia began to attack both each other and those who had left.[70] In essence, the war has so transformed politics in both Serbia and Croatia that antifeminist sentiments have been inflamed and feminists demonized—a result which has only been accentuated by feminists' embrace of pacifism as an integral element in their programs. The infamous "five witches" article is only the best-known manifestation of this tendency.[71]

Even while they demonized feminist advocates of gender equality, conservative voices urged that women accept, as their divinely ordained fate, that the roles of wife, mother, cook, and housekeeper should take precedence over all other roles. Alongside the domestication of women, conservatives also promoted what Tatjana Pavlović has called "hypermasculinity" as the ideal type for men; men "should" be muscular, domineering, and capable of unleashing fierce violence against antagonists, on the model of Rambo or Conan the Barbarian.[72] In this respect, there were markedly similar tendencies in Serbia and Croatia. One finds, thus, Stojan Adašević, a Serbian academic, urging (in April 1993), "In order for the [Serbian] people to survive, every woman must give birth to at least three children.... No one is master of his own body, whether male or female. Women must give birth to replacements, while men must go to war when the state calls them."[73] In Croatia, Don Anto Baković, a retired cleric, established the Croatian Population Movement (CPM) in order, in his words, "to save the Croatian nation from extinction." Baković says, "It is the fundamental goal of the CPM to create a pro-life disposition among the Croatian population, who will decide on a third child in the city, and on a fourth child in the village."[74] In such a universe, where there is a sharp and unambiguous sexual division of labor and women are expected, as a matter of national duty, to bring forth children, there is no room for gays and lesbians, no room for tolerance of any kind, indeed. As Pavlović notes, "Both Serbs and homosexuals 'betray' the Nation" in Croatia; in symbolic terms, "the homosexual/Serb exemplifies the creation, reification, and expulsion of the Other."[75] The family, then, must be heterosexual and, for the nationalist, it is ideally also authoritarian. Hence, it comes as no surprise that in May 1992 a law was drafted in Croatia which exempted violence within the family from prosecution.[76] Indeed, among the five Yugoslav successor states, only Slovenia recognizes that a woman might be raped by her husband.[77]

In spite of the intensification of chauvinist rhetoric and the creation of a climate hostile to feminism, feminist groups have continued to be active. Some women's groups, such as Women of Bosnia-Herzegovina and Pearl, have taken an interest specifically in Muslim women refugees, while others, such as Bulwark of Love and Cherry Tree, have devoted themselves to working with Croatian women. But there have also been a number of women's groups in the region that have worked for women's rights without regard for the nationality of the women concerned, such as the Autonomous Women's House in Zagreb, the Center for Women Victims of the War, and the Women's Lobby in Belgrade.[78] In Belgrade, a phone-in organization called SOS Telephone for Women and Children Victims of Violence was established in 1991 and provided assistance to some 770 persons in the first three years of its existence.[79] Similar organizations began operating in Kraljevo in June 1990, in Kruševac in November 1993, and in Priština.[80]

Another gender issue is rape as a weapon of war. What is so staggering about all the accounts of rape to come out of the Serbian Insurrectionary War, whether well documented or not, is that the act of rape, an act of violence and power by the male against the female, is given a specifically *national* content: it is the rape of a *Muslim* woman by a *Serbian* man, or of a *Serbian* woman by a *Muslim* man. Rape is thus used to act out in symbolic terms the subjugation of one nation by another, transmuted to the level of sexual *conquest*. At the same time, rape affirms the subordination of gender issues (such as respect for the equality of the other sex) to nationalist concerns.[81]

Even in Slovenia, which escaped with comparatively less damage from the brief hostilities of June–July 1991, the subordination of gender issues to nationalist concerns makes itself manifest. Take, for example, the Slovenian Alliance, organized by Ales Žužek in early 1993. Modeling itself on the French National Front of the 1970s, this radical-right party quickly drew up a program placing "ethnic purity" at the center of its concerns. But how to assure "ethnic purity"? The Slovenian Alliance proposed to expel all residents not of Slovene descent and offered the following guidelines to determine who is and is not a bona fide Slovene:

> A mixed marriage is considered to be Slovene only in the case of a marriage between a Slovene man and a non-Slovene woman, and the descendants of that marriage are also considered to be Slovene. Such families are exempt from being [expelled]. A marriage between a non-Slovene man and a Slovene woman is considered to be a non-Slovene marriage, and the descendants of such a marriage are non-Slovenes, and those families must also be returned to the homeland of the non-Slovene spouse.[82]

Thus, although sociological studies of interethnic marriage have shown that children of such marriages are far more apt to identify with the national identity of the mother,[83] Žužek's party prefers to make the father's nationality determinative of the nationality of the offspring.

In Communist times, women filled 22 percent of elective posts in Slovenia (in 1986). But after the multiparty elections of 1990, only 10 percent of those elected to the Slovenian Assembly were women.[84] After the 1996 elections, women made up only 8 percent of deputies in the Assembly.[85] Moreover, as Mežnarić and Ule comment, "as a result of financial difficulties and the media's loss of interest in independent women's movements [in Slovenia] since the mid-1980s, women's initiatives in almost all fields lack support and have difficulty attracting public recognition."[86]

It should be clear, thus, that it is not just the war that is reviving patriarchy in the western Balkans. Otherwise, how is one to explain the fact that all across East-

Central Europe people have witnessed a deepening of patriarchal values and forms, a shelving of women's issues and women's concerns, and a widespread removal of women from positions of prominence? Obviously, other factors are at work. Among these one might note the profound reaction against everything associated with socialism (hence, all talk of women's equality) that set in as soon as people realized that communism was finished. Perhaps even more important here was the dedication with which the Christian Churches, now freed of the constraints imposed by the Communist parties, set about dismantling some of the prerogatives enjoyed by women (most especially access to abortion) and affirming the "naturalness" of what is rather self-servingly called the traditional role of women. Yet another factor contributing to this result is that men already enjoyed an advantaged position under socialism, and with the relaxation of the strictures imposed by socialism and the expansion of possibilities for free enterprise, men have been better situated than women and have thus quickly widened the gap in their incomes. Finally, given the economic duress under which not just the Yugoslav successor states, but almost all of the East-Central European states have labored, all too many women were driven to take jobs as prostitutes and topless dancers, taking "advantage" of the new positions opened up by "free enterprise." This phenomenon has been especially striking in Serbia,[87] Macedonia,[88] and Albania.[89]

The problem, as Rada Iveković has pointed out, is how to transform women from being *objects* of history into being *subjects* of history, on an equal basis with men. "Just how precarious women's rights are," Iveković writes,

is now shown by the development[s] in ex-socialist countries: [such rights] are historically never safe, they can be threatened and done away with by the arbitrary decision of men (males). The law is, after all, not divine or neutral. There is, behind it, a human subject and author: historically, he is masculine. Women and minorities appear only as the objects of law, *in* the framework construed by the historically dominant subject. Unless we develop and put into action a concept of plural co-subjectivity, that is, unless we dismantle and reconstruct the framework of the law itself (with all the practical, political, social, and other implications), women (or others in an analogous situation) will remain subordinated to men.[90]

The Cultural Sector

Culture has most transparently figured in this war as an arena in which political ambitions have been projected. To conquer a territory in the fullest sense entails also the conquest of its history, an "annexation" of the history of the region to one's own national history. This is also why the victors in wars for territorial gain typically rewrite the history books upon the conclusion of their wars, in order to justify their conquests. It is also why, in the Serbian Insurrectionary War of 1991–1995, the Bosnian Serbs took such care to destroy not only the mosques and Catholic churches in areas of which they took possession, but also other buildings of historical, aesthetic, and cultural importance.

A correspondent for the *Boston Globe* captured this thinking all too well in recollections published in July 1994:

> In September 1992, a reporter covering the Bosnian conflict for the BBC asked a Serb artillery commander why his men were shelling a Holiday Inn in Sarajevo that housed foreign journalists. The commander apologized. It was only the National Museum behind the hotel that his men were trying to blow up, he said. The error was promptly corrected, and the shells reached their intended target.[91]

In Croatia, Serbs damaged or destroyed more than 500 monuments and historical buildings and more than 370 museums, libraries, and archives in the short period between July 1991 and January 1992. Among the targets damaged or destroyed were the eleventh-century Church of the Trinity in Split; a newly excavated fourth-century Roman palace (also in Split); the fifteenth-century Church of St. John Capistran (in Ilok), along with its richly furnished monastery; and historical sections of Dubrovnik and of Vukovar, including some beautiful and ornate buildings dating from the sixteenth century. These buildings had survived the Turkish conquest and occupation, the Napoleonic Wars, the turmoil of 1875–1878, and World Wars I and II, including Nazi occupation. That they were shelled now was the result of a deliberate Serbian policy of targeting other peoples' cultural treasures, on the formula "the more precious the site, the more vulnerable it is to attack."[92] Self-styled "Chetniks" even entered Catholic churches in Dubrovnik in order to destroy valuable works of art hanging inside.[93]

Both Serbian and Croatian forces targeted mosques in Bosnia-Herzegovina. On 9 November 1993, Croatian forces blew up the famous arched bridge in Mostar, which had spanned the Neretva River for more than four hundred years and which, for many Westerners, had come to symbolize the Islamic heritage of Bosnia-Herzegovina. Croatian forces also demolished the sixteenth-century Serb Orthodox Zitomislic monastery in Herzegovina. Serbian forces reduced the National Library in Sarajevo to rubble, sending many irreplaceable manuscripts and books up in flames, and destroyed Sarajevo's Oriental Institute, along with its 22,000 manuscripts. Bosnian Serb forces also targeted the National Museum in Sarajevo, the archives in Herzegovina, music schools, local museums, clockyards, and even graveyards, so that even the dead were not allowed to "rest in peace." The Muslims, in retaliation, destroyed or damaged a number of Serbian Orthodox churches, particularly in the Tuzla region.[94] In the case of Zvornik, a town in northeastern Bosnia, long renowned for its Muslim poets, saints, mystics, and cultural life in general, Serb forces massacred or expelled the entire Muslim population between April and July 1992 and dynamited and ploughed over all the mosques that had formerly dominated the Zvornik skyline. When this systematic demolition was over, the new Serbian mayor of Zvornik declared, "There never were any mosques in Zvornik."[95]

In a moving gesture of solidarity with the people of Sarajevo, internationally renowned conductor Zubin Mehta, a former conductor of the Los Angeles Philharmonic and New York Philharmonic orchestras, journeyed to Sarajevo in June 1994 to lead the Sarajevo Symphony Orchestra and chorus in a televised performance of Mozart's *Requiem*.[96] Held in the charred ruins of the National Library, the concert was a poignant recognition of the intense suffering that the people of Sarajevo and all of Bosnia had endured.

Efforts to erase all signs of the culture of the "enemy" extended even to pop music. Thus, in September 1994 the host of a Sarajevo radio show, Mimo Sahinpašić, who had been playing *antiwar* songs by Djordje Balašević and other Serbian singers, was ordered by Bosnian Minister of Culture Enes Karić to stop playing "aggressor music." Sahinpašić, however, promised to defy the proscription.[97]

Thus it is when culture is an *object* of attack. Culture has also figured as a *subject*, refracting political messages, reflecting on the war, and sometimes serving simply to raise spirits.

In fact, culture is one of the mediums in which politics may manifest itself, and it is often (especially in times of social stress) permeated with political meanings, influences, and symbols. Just as politics is culturally grounded and reflects the assumptions and values of a society, so too is culture grounded in politics. It is for these reasons that changes in politics tend to be accompanied by and even adumbrated in changes in the cultural sector. Hence too—to borrow a line from von Clausewitz—cultural products may figure at times as "a continuation of politics by other means." Susan Sontag, the American novelist, was most certainly conscious of this use for culture when she staged Samuel Beckett's play *Waiting for Godot* in Sarajevo in August 1993.[98]

The Artists

Artists have told the story of the war in paintings, graphics, and sculptures which have been displayed worldwide. New York's Kunsthalle, for example, hosted an exhibit of works in sundry mediums by a group of Sarajevo artists in March 1994. The setting was apt: the Kunsthalle had been devastated by a fire two years earlier, which had left a hole in the ceiling and the floors scuffed.[99] The art on exhibit in New York was composed from such materials as the artists found in the ruins of Sarajevo. The works on display showed images of the cramped conditions of Sarajevans, of graves, of people changed, even physically distorted, by war. A sculpture by Mustafa Skopljak showed small heads peaking out from a grave. Another sculpture, the work of forty-three-year-old Nusret Pašić, placed distended, twisted figurines on bricks lined up in a row. With one figurine to a brick, the fantasy evoked a scene of the claustrophobia and isolation experienced by Sarajevans under siege. Multimedia artist Sanjin Jukić used his artistry to indict Western diplomats and politicians for their failure to respond effectively, putting together a collage of CNN and European television video clips to bring home the message that, for the West, Sarajevo often seemed to be little more than a "media sound bite."[100]

A similar exhibition was organized by Dunja Stjepanović and Robert Ness and staged in the Seattle Convention Center, April–July 1994. Bringing together paintings and sketches by seventeen artists created between June and September 1992 during the siege of Sarajevo, the exhibit also featured documentary photographs by Milena Sorée-Džamonja.[101] The artists, all professors or graduates from the School of Fine Arts at the University of Sarajevo or local professional artists, rendered their impressions of the war.

Playwrights and Poets

Macedonian playwright Goran Stefanovski's play about the siege of Sarajevo, *Sara's Story*, represented one effort to make the tragedy concrete. Written in 1992, it opened at the International Theater Festival in Antwerp, Belgium, in 1993.[102] In Sarajevo itself, two Bosnian rock musicians—Srdjan "Gino" Jevdjević and Amir "Lazy" Beso—staged the legendary musical *Hair* in Sarajevo's Kameni Theater in November 1992. *Hair*'s pacifist message provided powerful commentary both on the Serbian siege of Sarajevo and on the slowness of the West to react. Admission was free, and the show, which played at least three days a week for weeks on end, was publicized by word of mouth only.[103]

Poets likewise responded to the destruction and carnage. In Serbia, Croatia, and Bosnia, newspapers printed poems that appealed to nationalist sentiments and talked of homeland, defense, hope, even revenge. Other poets, whether in the former Yugoslavia or abroad (such as Judi Benson or P. H. Liotta), aspired to be sounding boards for the world's conscience. Still others retraced paths of history and tried to take stock of the uses that politicians have made of myth or record the images and emotions associated with the war.

The Musicians

Vadran Smailović, a cellist in the Sarajevo Symphony, outraged by the massacre of innocent civilians in front of a bakery, went out to the site of the battle every day for twenty-four days to play Albinoni. It was an inspiring demonstration of the power of music to console, to inspire, to commemorate. Others have found other means, such as British composer Nigel Osborne, who composed a chamber-opera, *Sarajevo*, to express his empathy with the people of that city and his anger at a world that seemed to remain impassive in the face of Bosnia's ongoing agony.[104]

Among the rock musicians of Serbia and Croatia, there were both pacifists (such as Zagreb's Steamroller and Belgrade's Rambo Amadeus), who performed concerts for peace, and bards of bellicose nationalism (such as Zagreb's Psihomodo pop[105] and Montaž stroj—the latter known for its 1992 hit "Fight, fight, resist!"—and Belgrade's Oliver Mandić and Simonida Stanković), who recorded songs about victory and serenaded the troops in the field.[106] Rijeka's popular band, Let 3 (Flight No. 3), which had made its name with its apolitical 1989 album *Two Dogs Fuckin* (original title in English), turned political in 1994 with an album bearing the simple title "Peace."[107] Inspired by Psihomodo pop's example, an all-girl quartet began performing under the name Napalm Girl.[108]

War politicized rock in other ways. In Croatia, for example, radio stations observed a quiet embargo against rock albums by Serbian musicians,[109] while in Bosnia, some Muslim imams condemned *all* rock music as the work of "Satan."[110] Some rock musicians reacted by taking flight from politics. Jasenko Houra and his band, Dirty Theater, are a good example. At a time when politicians talked of national causes and national survival and called on their respective nations to concentrate on the "great tasks" at hand, Dirty Theater took to emphasizing romantic songs. Said Houra in 1993, "I think that a time of romanticism is coming, when small things become important."[111]

Other rock musicians redefined their "opposition." Bora Djordjević, who provided a *nationalist* alternative when Ivan Stambolić was Serbian party boss, was starting to sound more and more like the official rock bard of the Republic of Serbia once Milošević came to power. But by 1992, Bora was once again striking out on his own. Later, in *Zbogom Srbijo*, a rock album released in summer 1994, Bora sang against the war and its savagery, even while asserting his own brand of pacifist nationalism.[112] The title song evoked both the ultimate pointlessness of violence and the sadness it instilled:

> *I'm going to die,*
> *To take the head of a stranger,*
> *Go with God, Serbia.*[113]

Elsewhere on that same album, Bora makes a play on the ruling party's slogan ("That's the way it should be") to offer the following suggestion:

> *Today there's no milk,*
> *Today there's no bread,*
> *Because of that, eat shit.*
> *That's the way it should be.*[114]

The enduring Slovenian classic rock group Bulldozer tried to capture the atmosphere of the war with its 1995 song "Wild Hordes":

> *Wild hordes bashed their way in,*
> *Took everything, took everything.*
> *Wild hordes rushed in,*
> *Destroyed, destroyed.*
>
> *Wild hordes attacked,*
> *Killed, killed.*
> *They saved us from ourselves,*
> *Made us savages,*
> *Almost like them.*[115]

Then there is the mournful song "O, my Belgrade friend," which played in Croatia during the war years and served to remind Croats of a time when Serbs and Croats walked literally arm in arm even while admitting that that time was irrevocably lost:

> *Beautiful Belgrade girls, you really knew how to kiss.*
> *I still remember my little blond darling from Novi Sad.*
> *Her villages, too, I came to love, riding along the*
> *   Danube and Sava.*
> *O, I was so happy then.*
>
> *O, my Belgrade friend,*
> *We will meet again near Sava.*
> *And you will know me and you will shoot.*
>
> *I will not even aim and will pray to God that I will*
> *   miss you.*
> *But in the end, I will not miss.*
> *I will mourn you and close your eyes,*
> *Oh, I was so sad because I lost my friend.*[116]

Still others have been sucked into the very tidepools of war. Here was Simonida Stanković, decked out in miniskirt and black leather jacket, singing to troops in the field about their "glory":

> *They're protecting Serb glory,*
> *They're defending Serb lands,*
> *Arkan's Tigers,*
> *They're heroes without a flaw.*[117]

Although Stanković's rock panegyrics propelled her to fame, another would-be rock warrior, Sonja Karadžić (Radovan's daughter), had less success in this medium. Described by friends as "a good Serbian woman, complete with moustache,"[118] thirtyish Sonja Karadžić released her first rock video in 1992, singing, not too tactfully, about the "degenerate, materialistic, obsessive Serbs in Belgrade who owe everything to the real Serbs in Bosnia."[119] As a result, Belgrade Television circumspectly decided not to broadcast her video. Her first rock album, *Warrior from Paradise*, did not fare much better, and by August 1994 she had taken the post of chief of the press office in Pale, the Bosnian Serbs' political headquarters.

But it is the Slovenian rock group Laibach which has perhaps best captured the sheer senselessness and irrationality of the war. In the group's 1994 album *NATO*,[120] the title number is a wordless, hard-driving piece that starts out with the sound of bombs dropping and then shifts into a rock beat overlay on "Mars" from Gustav

Holst's *The Planets*. "In the Army Now" includes the mournful but ambiguous comment,

> *Vacation in the far-off land*
> *Uncle Sam does the best he can.*

The album also includes covers on the Pink Floyd song "Dogs of War" and the cult classic "In the year 2525," albeit with an adapted text viewing the world through the prism of Yugoslav developments. Later, in 1995, on the eve of the Dayton peace talks, Laibach performed in Sarajevo, where the group proclaimed the establishment of an "anarchist state" and passed out Laibach "passports."[121]

Belgrade's imaginative rocker Rambo Amadeus offered his own comment on the Yugoslav ship-of-state with his album *Titanic*, which included the sardonic song "Ripe for a Pension."[122] But the final word in this chapter belongs to a Slovenian rock soloist who performs under the name Magnifico. In a song sung in English, Magnifico summed up the conclusion he had drawn from the Wars of Yugoslav Succession:

> *I think and I got an idea*
> *That there is too much nation,*
> *Too much nation for liberation,*
> *And too much nation for one railway station.*[123]

Notes

1. See also Mark Juergensmeyer, *The New Cold War? Religious Nationalism Confronts the Secular State* (Berkeley and Los Angeles: University of California Press, 1993), pp. 33–34.

2. For details, see Sabrina Petra Ramet, "The Serbian Church and the Serbian Nation," in Sabrina Petra Ramet and Donald W. Treadgold (eds.), *Render unto Caesar: The Religious Sphere in World Politics* (Washington, D.C.: American University Press, 1995), esp. pp. 311–312.

3. Details in ibid., pp. 313–315.

4. Tanjug (28 March 1990), trans. in Foreign Broadcast Information Service (FBIS), *Daily Report* (Eastern Europe), 29 March 1990, p. 56.

5. Vladimir Dedijer, *Vatikan i Jasenovac: Dokumenti* (Belgrade: Izdavačka Radna Organizacija, 1987). The English edition is Vladimir Dedijer, *The Yugoslav Auschwitz and the Vatican: The Croatian Massacre of the Serbs during World War II*, trans. from the German translation by Harvey L. Kendall (Buffalo, N.Y.: Prometheus Books, 1992).

6. Jure Kristo, "The Catholic Church in a Time of Crisis," in Sabrina Petra Ramet and Ljubiša S. Adamovich (eds.), *Beyond Yugoslavia: Politics, Economics, and Culture in a Shattered Community* (Boulder: Westview Press, 1995), p. 441.

7. Ibid., p. 442. For further discussion and documentation concerning this point, see Philip J. Cohen, *Serbia's Secret War: Propaganda and the Deceit of History* (College Station, Tex.: Texas A & M Press, 1996), pp. 15–16, 32–33, 45, 81–84.

8. Quoted in Kristo, "The Catholic Church," p. 443.

9. Quoted in *Danas* (Zagreb) (17 March 1992), p. 27.

10. *Glas koncila* (Zagreb) (8 March 1992), p. 3.

11. See the official Church translation of the Memorandum of the Holy Synod of the Bishops of the Serbian Orthodox Church, 28 May 1992.

12. Recounted in David A. Steele, "Former Yugoslavia: Religion as a Fount of Ethnic Hostility or an Agent of Reconciliation?" in *Religion in Eastern Europe*, Vol. 14, No. 2 (October 1994), p. 5.

13. E.g., Catholic Archbishop France Perko of Belgrade, in interview with *NIN* (Belgrade), No. 2235 (29 October 1993), p. 31.

14. Interview with Hadzi Hafiz Halil efendi Mehtić, mufti of Zenica, in *Globus* (Zagreb) (2 September 1994), p. 42.

15. *Kana* (Zagreb) (March 1992), p. 37; *Novi vjesnik* (Zagreb) (28 September 1992), p. 4A; and *Slobodna Dalmacija* (Split) (29 September 1994), p. 6.

16. *Borba* (Belgrade) (17 February 1993), p. 8; confirmed in *Nedjeljna Dalmacija* (Split) (25 November 1994), p. 7. For discussion, see Sabrina P. Ramet, "The Croatian Catholic Church since 1990," in *Religion, State and Society: The Keston Journal*, Vol. 24, No. 4 (December 1996), pp. 346–347.

17. *Ljiljan* (Sarajevo-Ljubljana) (5 October 1994), p. 8.

18. *Süddeutsche Zeitung* (Munich) (13–15 August 1994), p. 6.

19. *Glas Slavonije* (Osijek) (8 June 1994), pp. 26–27.

20. *Vreme* (Belgrade) (13 June 1994), p. 22.

21. Quoted in Norman Cigar, *Genocide in Bosnia: The Policy of "Ethnic Cleansing"* (College Station, Tex.: Texas A & M Press, 1995), p. 78.

22. Ibid., pp. 66–67.

23. Ibid., p. 111.

24. *Süddeutsche Zeitung* (29–30 October 1994), p. 4. See also *Globus* (11 November 1994), pp. 44–45.

25. *Philadelphia Inquirer* (18 November 1994), p. A39.

26. *Glas Istre* (Pula) (11 June 1994), p. 14.

27. Ibid. See also *Večernji list* (Zagreb) (21 March 1992), p. 4.

28. *New York Times* (8 May 1993), p. 1; AFP (Paris) (9 September 1993), in FBIS, *Daily Report* (Eastern Europe), 14 September 1993, p. 35; and Sabrina P. Ramet, *Nihil Obstat: Religion, Politics, and Social Change in East-Central Europe and Russia* (Durham, N.C.: Duke University Press, 1998), p. 177.

29. *National Catholic Reporter* (26 August 1994), p. 11.

30. *NIN*, no. 2235 (29 October 1993), p. 30.

31. On the destruction of Serb Orthodox churches by Croatian forces, see *War Damage Sustained by Orthodox Churches in Serbian Areas of Croatia in 1991* (Belgrade: Ministry of Information of the Republic of Serbia, 1992); on the destruction of mosques, see, for example, *Globus* (29 April 1994), p. 3; and Tanjug (18 September 1994), in FBIS, *Daily Report* (Eastern Europe), 19 September 1994, p. 31.

32. See, for example, *NIN* (9 October 1992), pp. 26–28; and *Politika* (29 October 1992), p. 14.

33. Trudy Rubin, "Bosnian Serbs Have Helped Create a Muslim State Right Next Door," in *Philadelphia Inquirer* (18 November 1994), p. A39.

34. *Ljiljan* (21 December 1994), p. 23.

35. *Globus* (23 September 1994), p. 11.

36. In an earlier *Globus* poll, reported on 10 December 1993, as cited in Wolf Oschlies, "Zur politischen Rolle orthodoxen Kirchen auf dem Balkan," in *Südost Europa*, Vol. 42, No. 10 (October 1993), p. 587.

37. Details in *Evropske novosti* (Belgrade-Frankfurt) (26 November 1994), p. 6.

38. Oral presentation by Obrad Kesić, American Association for the Advancement of Slavic Studies, Philadelphia, 18 November 1994.

39. *Delo* (Ljubljana) (27 February 1993), p. 27, trans. in FBIS, *Daily Report* (Eastern Europe), 17 March 1993, p. 56.

40. Radio Tirana Network (Tirana) (8 December 1992), trans. in FBIS, *Daily Report* (Eastern Europe), 10 December 1992, pp. 57–58.

41. Quoted in *Politika* (Belgrade) (18 December 1992), p. 9, trans. in FBIS, *Daily Report* (Eastern Europe), 15 January 1993, p. 67.

42. *Evropske novosti* (19 November 1994), p. 6.

43. *Evropske novosti* (10 December 1994), p. 5.

44. *Politika* (7 June 1994), p. 14.

45. *Borba* (7 April 1993), p. 1.

46. Tanjug (2 February 1994), trans. in FBIS, *Daily Report* (Eastern Europe), 3 February 1994, p. 36.

47. Karadžić denied that there were any concentration camps of any kind at all. See Laura Silber and Allan Little, *The Death of Yugoslavia* (London: Penguin Books and BBC Books, 1995), p. 275.

48. Tanjug (10 August 1994), trans. in FBIS, *Daily Report* (Eastern Europe), 11 August 1994, p. 44; *The European* (London) (19–25 August 1994), p. 2; and *The Sunday Times* (London) (21 August 1994), p. 19. Regarding the waxing amity between Karadžić and Patriarch Pavle, see *Ljiljan* (30 November 1994), p. 9.

49. *Oslobodjenje*, European ed. (21 January 1994), trans. into English in *Oslobodjenje*, English ed. (Sarajevo-Washington, D.C.) (April 1994), p. 12.

50. *Evropske novosti* (24–26 December 1994), p. 10.

51. *Globus* (19 August 1994), p. 6.

52. *Neue Zürcher Zeitung* (9 September 1994), p. 3; and *La Repubblica* (Rome) (18 August 1994), p. 3.

53. *The Sunday Times* (4 September 1994), p. 14. See also *The Sunday Telegraph* (London) (4 September 1994), p. 20.

54. *New York Times* (8 September 1994), p. A8.

55. *Neue Zürcher Zeitung* (26 August 1994), p. 3.

56. *Danas* (Zagreb), new series (20 September 1994), p. 4. See also *Neue Zürcher Zeitung* (5 August 1994), p. 3; and *Vreme* (12 September 1994), p. 8.

57. *Slobodna Dalmacija* (Split) (2 October 1998), pp. 1–3; and *Večernji list* (Zagreb) (2 October 1998), pp. 1–3. The decision to beatify Stepinac was not made by the pope personally, but by the Congregation for the Causes of Saints. See *Croatia Weekly* (Zagreb) (10 July 1998), p. 2.

58. Quoted in *Boston Sunday Globe* (11 September 1994), p. 11.

59. Quoted in *National Catholic Reporter* (23 September 1994), p. 7.

60. Quoted in ibid. See also *The European* (16–22 September 1994), p. 7.

61. Quoted in *New York Times* (9 September 1994), p. A7.

62. *Bosnjački avaz* (Sarajevo) (1–15 October 1994), p. 3. For the interpretation of the papal visit offered by a Serbian journalist, see Ramet, *Nihil Obstat*, p. 177.

63. Sefko Omerbašić, in interview with *Delo* (6 February 1993), p. 22, trans. in FBIS, *Daily Report* (Eastern Europe), 4 March 1993, p. 55.

64. *Boston Sunday Globe* (27 November 1994), p. 14; and *Neue Zürcher Zeitung* (29 November 1994), p. 3. See also the cover story about Puljić's elevation to the College of Cardinals in *Arena* (Zagreb) (19 November 1994).

65. Quoted in Lepa Mladjenović and Vera Litricin, transcribed by Tanya Renne, in "Belgrade Feminists 1992: Separation, Guilt and Identity Crisis," in *Feminist Review*, No. 45 (Autumn 1993), p. 115. See also "Protest Arkadije i Beogradskog Ženskog lobija: žene, homoseksualci i lezbejke," in *Žene za Žene* (Belgrade: Žene u crnom, 1994), p. 60.

66. Quoted in Mladjenović and Litricin, "Belgrade Feminists 1992," p. 115.

67. Cynthia Cockburn, "A Women's Political Party for Yugoslavia: Introduction to the Serbian Feminist Manifesto," in *Feminist Review*, No. 39 (Winter 1991), pp. 155, 157.

68. Mladjenović and Litricin, "Belgrade Feminists 1992," p. 166. See also Ružica Rosandić, "Patriotic Education," in Ružica Rosandić and Vesna Pesić (eds.), *Warfare, Patriotism, Patriarchy: The Analysis of Elementary School Textbooks* (Belgrade: Centre for Anti-War Action Association MOST, 1994), pp. 41–57.

69. "Reakcije prolaznica/prolaznika na protest Žena u crnom," in *Žene za Žene*, p. 15. See also Bojan Aleksov and Staša Zajović, "O mobilizaciji i antimobilizaciji" (pp. 36–40) and "Protest protiv opšte mobilizacije u republici Srpskoj i protiv formiranja Ženskih jedinica" (pp. 46–47) in the same volume; and Žarana Papić, "Women in Serbia: Post-Communism, War, and Nationalist Mutations," in Sabrina P. Ramet (ed.), *Gender Politics in the Western Balkans: Women and Society in Yugoslavia and the Yugoslav Successor States* (University Park: Pennsylvania State University Press, 1999), pp. 158–161, 163–164, 167, 169.

70. For one reflection of this, see Asja Armanda and Natalie Nenadić, "Activists Warn Do Not Be Fooled by Genocide/Rape Revisionists," in *Northwest Ethnic News* (Seattle), November 1994, pp. 2, 7.

71. "Hrvatske feministice siluju Hrvatsku," in *Globus* (11 December 1992), p. 33.

72. Tatjana Pavlović, "Women in Croatia: Feminists, Nationalists, and Homosexuals," in Ramet (ed.), *Gender Politics in the Western Balkans*, pp. 133–134.

73. Quoted in Cigar, *Genocide in Bosnia*, p. 79.

74. *Vjesnik* (Zagreb) (15 June 1993), p. 3.

75. Pavlović, "Women in Croatia," p. 134.

76. Rada Iveković, "The New Democracy—With Women or Without Them?" in Ramet and Adamovich (eds.), *Beyond Yugoslavia*, p. 406.

77. Ibid., p. 403. For further discussion of post-1990 Slovenia, see Vlasta Jalušić, "Women in Post-Socialist Slovenia: Socially Adapted, Politically Marginalized," in Ramet (ed.), *Gender Politics in the Western Balkans*, pp. 109–129.

78. Lepa Mladjenović, "Ženska prava i rat u Bosni," in *SOS bilten* (Belgrade), Nos. 6–7 (December 1993), p. 44.

79. Zorica Mršević, "Istraživanje 'tri godine rada SOS telefona za žene i decu žrtve nasilja," in *Feminističke sveske* (Belgrade), No.2 (1994), p. 43. See also *Žene za žene: Protesti, apeli, izjave, informacije autonomnih ženskih inicijativa* (Belgrade: Žene i društvo, November 1993), pp. 7–10.

80. Svetlana Stanić, "Iskustva SOS-a," p. 63, and "Izveštaj o radu SOS-a u Kruševcu," p. 55—both in *Feminističke sveske*, No. 2 (1994); and Julie Mertus, "Women in Kosovo: Contested Terrains," in Ramet (ed.), *Gender Politics in the Western Balkans*, p. 173.

81. Regarding the role of rape in "ethnic cleansing," see Nadežda Cetković, "Feministička alternativa nacionalizmu i ratu," in *SOS bilten* , Nos. 6–7 (December 1993), p. 71. See also Zorica Mrsević, *Ženska prava su ljudska prava* (Belgrade: STEP, 1994), pp. 125–148.

82. Quoted in *Dnevnik* (Ljubljana) (9 February 1993), p. 3, trans. in FBIS, *Daily Report* (Eastern Europe), 4 March 1993, p. 52.

83. See, for example, Brian Silver, "Social Mobilization and the Russification of Soviet Nationalities," in *American Political Science Review*, Vol. 68, No. 1 (March 1974).

84. Silva Mežnarić and Mirjana Ule, "Women in Croatia and Slovenia: A Case of Delayed Modernization," in Marilyn Rueschemeyer (ed.), *Women in the Politics of Postcommunist Eastern Europe* (Armonk, N.Y.: M. E. Sharpe, 1994), p. 161.

85. Jalušić, "Women in Post-Socialist Slovenia," p. 125.

86. Mežnarić and Ule, "Women in Croatia and Slovenia," pp. 161–162.

87. *Vjesnik* (8 June 1993), p. 25.

88. *The Sunday Times* (29 May 1994), p. 17.

89. *Welt am Sonntag* (Hamburg) (4 December 1994), p. 3.

90. Iveković, "The New Democracy," p. 398.

91. *Boston Sunday Globe* (31 July 1994), p. 7.

92. Alexandra Tuttle, "Croatia's Art and Architecture Buried in Rubble," in *Wall Street Journal* (16 January 1992), p. A8.

93. Details in *Novi vjesnik* (Zagreb) (16 June 1992), p. 24A.

94. *RFE/RL News Briefs* (8–12 November 1993), p. 13; *RFE/RL News Briefs* (22–26 November 1993), p. 15; *New York Times, Weekly review* (International ed.) (27 February 1994), p. 4; and Michael A. Sells, *The Bridge Betrayed: Religion and Genocide in Bosnia* (Berkeley and Los Angeles: University of California Press, 1996), p. 149.

95. Quoted in Sells, *Bridge Betrayed*, p. 4.

96. *New York Times* (20 June 1994), p. A7.

97. *New York Times* (10 October 1994), p. A3.

98. The people of Sarajevo had been waiting for NATO to come to their rescue by conducting aerial strikes against Bosnian Serb positions.

99. Jamey Gambrell, "Sarajevo: Art in Extremis," in *Art in America* (May 1994), p. 102.

100. Ibid.

101. Dunja Stjepanović, in interview with the author, Seattle, 8 December 1994.

102. *MILS NEWS, Dnevni vesti* (18 March 1993).

103. "Bosnian Blues," in *The Stranger* (Seattle) (22–28 November 1994).

104. *The European—élan* (London) (19–25 August 1994), p. 10; and *Globus* (30 September 1994), pp. 23, 25.

105. See the group's song, "Hrvatska mora pobijediti" [Croatia must win] on Psihomodo pop's album, *Maxi Single za Gardiste*, Croatia Records MS-D 2 03553 3 (1991); and article in *Večernji list* (24 June 1994), p. 15.

106. For an elaboration regarding these and other performers since the war began, see Sabrina Petra Ramet, "Shake, Rattle, and Self-Management: Making the Scene in Yugoslavia," in Sabrina Petra Ramet (ed.), *Rocking the State: Rock Music and Politics in Eastern Europe and Russia* (Boulder: Westview Press, 1994), pp. 125–126; and Sabrina Petra Ramet, *Social Currents in Eastern Europe: The Sources and Consequences of the Great Transformation*, 2nd ed. (Durham, N.C.: Duke University Press, 1995), p. 261. See also "B92: Struggling for Air," in *Uncaptive Minds*, Vol. 6, No. 3 (Fall 1993), pp. 101–102; and *Nedjeljna Dalmacija* (6 January 1995), p. 36.

107. See *Nedjeljna Dalmacija* (23 December 1994), pp. 36–37.

108. *Nedjeljna Dalmacija* (24 May 1996), p. 25.

109. *Vreme* (Belgrade) (5 September 1994), p. 37.

110. *Der Spiegel* (Hamburg) (24 October 1994), p.160.

111. Quoted in *Vjesnik* (15 April 1993), p. 14. See also interview with Houra: Nina Oze-gović, "Jasenko Houra: Ostao sam dečko s ceste," in *Tjednik* (Zagreb) (31 October 1997), pp. 50–53.

112. For three recent short articles about him, see *Vreme* (30 May 1994), p. 34; *Vreme* (22 May 1995), p. 42; and *New York Times* (17 January 1997), p. A4.

113. I am grateful to Obrad Kesić for providing me with the English translation of the song. I have neither seen nor heard the album myself.

114. Ibid.

115. "Divje horde" [Wild Horses], on Buldožer's album, *Noć,* Helidon Records 6751750 (1995). Translated for me by Mitja Žagar.

116. Quoted in Pavlović, "Women in Croatia," p. 144.

117. Quoted in *The European* (4–10 July 1993). See also *Vreme* (13 June 1994), p. 34.

118. As quoted in *Daily Telegraph* (London) (12 August 1994), p. 15.

119. Quoted in ibid.

120. Laibach, *NATO* , Mute Records, 61714–2 (1994). For two articles about this album, see *Globus* (7 October 1994), pp. 30–31, and (21 October 1994), p. 33.

121. Telephone conversation with a member of the Laibach collective, Kyoto-Ljubljana, 25 November 1998.

122. Rambo Amadeus, *Titanic*, Komuna Records, CD–147 (N.D.).

123. Quoted in Oto Luthar, "The Night in Sarajevo: Production of sources for civic educa-tion," paper presented at a conference on "Citizenship and Education in Slovenia," Ljubljana, 22–24 October 1998.

PART FOUR

◆

Peace Without Rights?

CHAPTER TWELVE

———————— ◆ ————————

A Peace of Dayton

They're not people, they're targets.

Silent Trigger
1996

The Dayton Peace Accords were the product of compromise—both in the sense that the leaders of the three national groups at war engaged in give and take in order to manufacture an agreement and in the sense that the process and substance of the accords were designed to find a middle ground between the West's intermittent feeling that it was under some obligation, whether moral or material, to do something to stop the violence in Bosnia and its fundamental unwillingness to make a major commitment, whether military or financial, to doing so. Therein lies the underlying flaw of the Dayton Peace Accords. Rather than representing the product of a soundly researched collective effort to engineer stability and lasting peace in the area, it represented, on the West's part, merely another in a continuing series of efforts to find not the most efficacious instrument to achieve the stated goals of policy, but the "cheapest." But, as political writers from Machiavelli to Brinton have recognized, the "cheap" solutions usually end up costing more over the long haul.

Reason would have dictated, for example, that in a region torn by intolerant nationalisms, but in which there were some nonnationalist (even antinationalist) moderates endeavoring to change the political landscape, peace could have best been assured by barring nationalist parties and politicians from all three sides from holding office in the area for the duration of the IFOR (Implementation Force) presence, if not longer. In fact, no effort was made in this direction, and nationalists dominated the political spectrum in the first two years of transition, especially among the Serbs and Croats of Bosnia-Herzegovina.

Second, given the potent role played by the media in fomenting the hatreds among the three groups (beginning as early as 1986/1987), a strong argument could have been made for the centrality of banning all media expressing nationalist or chauvinist views and of supporting and fostering the development and success of nonnationalist media. In fact, the very opposite was done, and nationalist thugs were allowed to beat up staff members of nonnationalist media with impunity. The success of Allied forces in recasting German and Austrian news media after World War II and in overhauling the educational systems in those countries provides a clear model of what is necessary if one aspires to the replacement of a dialogue of hatred and revenge with a dialogue of liberalism and human rights.

Third, it would seem self-evident that rushing with elections could be counterproductive and that, on the contrary, the first priority should have been to place moderates (i.e., nonnationalists) in power and to arrest those persons indicted for war crimes. But again, the very opposite was done. Rather than concentrating on placing moderates in power, elections were speeded along, with the not surprising result that nationalists won in the first post-Dayton elections on 14 September 1996. Taking the second and third points in combination, we may say that the West has chosen to emphasize democratic form over liberal substance, though, as Fareed Zakaria has wisely warned, "Democracy without constitutional liberalism is not simply inadequate, but dangerous, bringing with it the erosion of liberty, the abuse of power, ethnic divisions, and even war."[1]

Fourth, given Dayton's nominal commitment to the free movement of persons and given, further, the essential role that this would need to play in any peace, one might have hoped that IFOR would have provided the military muscle to guarantee free movement. In fact, IFOR did nothing of the sort, and Bosnian Serb police soon took to charging unauthorized tolls (in German marks) of persons wishing to cross their lines.

Fifth, given the inflammatory nature of hate speech and the legal precedent established by other European states for banning hate speech, it might have been thought appropriate that some such ban be passed and enforced. Nothing of the sort was done.

And sixth, given both the geostrategic impracticality of a divided Bosnia (unless its parts were to be partitioned between Croatia and Serbia) and the fact that, by according Bosnia a seat in its General Assembly, the U.N. had recognized Bosnia as a territorially integral republic, one might have expected that the West would have insisted on the establishment of institutions that would guarantee the unity and cohesiveness of Bosnia-Herzegovina. But again, the opposite path was taken, that of endorsing autonomism and de facto partition, so that the so-called Serbian Republic (*Srpska Republika,* as it is often called in texts which are otherwise written in English) was allowed to sign a defense pact with the FRY on 15 March 1997. This challenge to the spirit of the Dayton Accords was only compounded when, in December of that year, the Bosnian Serbs' Serbian Republic signed an agreement on dual citizenship with the FRY.[2] Moreover, although a common Bosnian currency was accepted in April 1997, problems quickly developed when Momčilo Krajišnik, the Serbian member of the collective presidency, proposed that one of the new notes show a Serbian Orthodox monastery which is not located in Bosnia-Herzegovina at all, rejecting Izetbegović's suggestion that local flora and fauna be depicted on the bills.[3] And that is just the beginning.

It is not my argument that the Dayton Peace Accords were wholly bad. The mere fact that some people (though not all wishing to do so) have been able to return to their homes and that the economy (especially in the Croatian-Muslim federation) has gradually been rebuilt is positive. Moreover, a string of alleged war criminals have been brought to trial, even if not the best known among those indicted. And in spite of a very rocky start during 1996–1997,[4] there were increasing signs, by 1998, of progress toward the stabilization of multiethnic institutions capable of handling administrative tasks, of an improvement in public security, in the possibility for some of the refugees to return to their homes, and where the confiscation and destruction of heavy weaponry is concerned.[5] In a statement before the House National Security Committee on 18 March 1998, U.S. Secretary of State Madeleine Albright urged the interpretation that "the psychology of cooperation, as well as the ethos of democracy, are beginning to replace the psychology of confrontation and the ethos of corruption which flourished for so long."[6] But it seems clear enough that by ending the bombing when it did, the West did not exert as much pressure on the Serbian side as it might have, therefore setting the stage for settling for considerably less than the best that could have been obtained, as Richard Holbrooke, the U.S. special envoy to the Balkans, has suggested[7]—indeed, that the "Dayton path" has not been the most direct route to a just and stable peace, let alone to interethnic harmony. "Realists" will be quick to proclaim that "second best" (or perhaps even "fourth best") is "the best" that could have been achieved in Bosnia. How do they know, one might ask, since the West readily settled for so much less than an optimal solution?

The Modesty of Dayton

Whatever else may or may not be said of the Dayton peace talks, no one will ever accuse their architects of hubris; on the contrary, modesty was the byword of the Dayton peace talks, though a modesty backed up with a set of tough procedural rules upon which the three key participants—Izetbegović, Milošević, and Tudjman—agreed before the talks were launched:

1. That they each come to the United States with full power to sign agreements without further recourse to parliaments back home;
2. That they stay as long as necessary to reach agreement, without threatening to walk out; and
3. That they not talk to the press or other outsiders.[8]

The peace talks began on 1 November 1995, and on 8 November the U.S. mediators brought out the map in order to discuss territory; this move resulted in six hours of utterly fruitless exchanges on 8 November. The first breakthrough came during the evening of 10 November, when then–Secretary of State Warren Christopher came up with a compromise formula on the return of eastern Slavonia to Croatia. But there were further frustratingly fruitless exchanges concerning maps on 11 and 12 November, leading to a conclusion among the Americans that they would have to present an American map. The talks dragged on. Then on 16 November, Haris Silajdžić and Slobodan Milošević negotiated an agreement on a land corridor to Goražde; it was the first territorial agreement and prepared the way for subsequent delineation of the so-called Clark corridor to Goražde.[9] Two days later, responding to American pressure, Milošević agreed to negotiate the return of Serb-held parts of Sarajevo to Bosnian government control. At one point, U.S. mediators had obtained 55 percent of Bosnia-Herzegovina for the Croat-Muslim federation, but the Izetbegović delegation, instead of agreeing to that, held out for more; Milošević, who had not realized just how much he had given away, then saw a chart alluding to this percentage, which had been inadvertently left in easy view, and retrenched. Milošević now insisted on the 51–49 ratio established by the 1994 Contact Group Plan, which had been endorsed by the U.N. Security Council, but rejected by the Bosnian Serbs. But this percentage now became "inevitable," and a solution was found in ceding to the Bosnian Serbs an egg-shaped region south of Highway 5 in western Bosnia. By the morning of 21 November, all three sides had agreed to the territorial apportionment and subsequently signed the document. In the course of the ceremonies, which began at the Hope Center that same day at 3 P.M., Bosnian President Izetbegović made his pitch for the plan, addressing his countrymen:

> And to my people, I say, this may not be a just peace, but it is more just than a continuation of war. In the situation as it is and in the world as it is, a better peace could not have been achieved. God is our witness that we have done everything in our power so that the extent of injustice for our people and our country would be decreased.[10]

Dreams of California

According to the World Bank, about one-third of Bosnia's health facilities, half of its schools, and about two-thirds of its housing were destroyed in the course of the three-and-a-half years of open warfare in the republic.[11] Much of the transportation and telecommunications systems had also been destroyed. Even a year later, industrial production stood at about 10 percent of prewar levels in both sectors, with unemployment pegged at 60 percent in the Muslim-Croat federation (as of October 1996) and at 90 percent in the (Bosnian) Serbian Republic (as of March 1997).[12] Once vigorous factories, such as the Famos truck and bus factory in Lukavica and the VW automotive factory at Vogošća, operated at far below their prewar levels, with only 200 of the VW factory's 9,000 workers back at their jobs as of October 1996, for example. The United States and other donors pledged some $1.8 billion in early 1996 to rebuild Bosnia as part of a projected five-year reconstruction program costing $5.1 billion.[13] But the donors punished the Serbian Republic for its alleged lack of cooperation in implementing key points of the accords by directing most of its aid to the federation.

Organized crime flourished in this context, as gangs with foreign connections moved into Bosnia-Herzegovina, bribing local officials and police and setting up schemes ranging from loan sharking to extortion to smuggling.[14] In Mostar, local Croatian leaders were said to have links with organized crime dealing in illegal drugs and prostitution.[15] And yet, as bleak as the situation was, some locals permitted themselves to dream of a better future. One such dreamer, General Mehmed Alagić, told a *New York Times* reporter in April 1996, "We're going to make this place into California. Why not?"[16] An associate of Alagić's, former Mayor of Sanski Most Mirzet Karabeg even had a plan: "The first step," he explained, "is to start cutting back on all this free food those humanitarian aid agencies are sending in here. As long as people can eat for nothing, they won't work."[17] Waxing rapturous at the thought of his cinematic role models, Glenn Ford and John Wayne, Karabeg continued, "We will have large ranches, like in California, not small farms where families just produce for themselves."[18]

A Modicum of Stability

The Dayton Peace Accords established that there would be limits negotiated among the sides on their holdings of heavy weapons, confirmed the territorial integrity and unified sovereignty of Bosnia-Herzegovina even while assigning half of it to administration by local Serbian authorities and half of the land to administration by Croat-Muslim federal authorities, called for OSCE-supervised elections within nine months of the signing of the accords, barred indicted war criminals from holding public office, guaranteed the right of refugees to return to their homes, guaranteed free movement, called for the disarming of all armed civilian (paramilitary) groups, provided for the arrest of indicted war criminals, and set forth guidelines for the structure and jurisdiction of the central government in which the two sector governments were expected to cooperate.[19] The accords also set up the IFOR, led by NATO, which was entrusted with the task of separating the sides and guaranteeing that the agreement be honored. IFOR consisted of about 60,000 troops operating on a one-year mandate. When the mandate expired, IFOR was "replaced" by the Stabilization Force (SFOR), likewise led by NATO but involving only 35,000 troops. As of October 1998, the Bosnian peacekeeping mission was said to be costing about $7 billion per year.[20] Western diplomats did not consider the dividing line between sectors to be capable of translation into an international border, because they considered the two sectors to be economically unviable except as parts of a unified whole.[21]

But problems soon developed. Refugees were prevented from returning to their homes, ethnic cleansing continued (about 90,000 persons were evicted from their homes between January and August 1996[22]), Bosnian Serb television stations continued to churn out hate propaganda until NATO took control of four transmitters in September 1997,[23] and private citizens were subjected to beatings, confiscation of goods, unauthorized tolls, and so forth.[24] A report issued by Human Rights Watch in June 1996 held that "the parties, especially the Serbs, have not cooperated with the tribunal, failing to turn over Karadžić and Mladić or to enforce arrest warrants for others indicted by the tribunal. Only the Bosnian government in Sarajevo has turned over indicted persons to the tribunal."[25]

The "peace of Dayton" got off to a bad start when Bosnian Serb families streamed out of the Ilidža suburb of Sarajevo on the eve of its transfer to Bosnian government control. Numbering as many as 70,000, these Serbs said that they feared for their lives and would only feel safe in an area controlled by Serbian authorities. In a distinctive reflection of Serbian thinking, some families were said to have disinterred the last remains of their deceased kin, in order to take them across the frontier for re-burial in "Serbian soil."[26] Other Serbs fled the town of Vogošća north of Sarajevo and other municipalities being transferred; they were said to have been goaded on by Bosnian Serb radio and television, which warned Serbs of untold dangers if they stayed behind. But some Serbs, such as seventy-year-year-old Vlado Koprivica, remained unruffled by the warnings from radio and television and decided to stay in their homes.[27]

Fear and hatred are often mixed, producing a dangerous compound that expresses itself in violent outbursts. In the months following the Dayton accords, such outbursts included the stoning of a busload of Muslim women trying to return to the Prijedor area in May 1996, armed resistance by local Serbs to the return of Muslim refugees to the village of Koraj in northeastern Bosnia in November 1996, and shootings and beatings between Croats and Muslims in Mostar in late 1996 and early 1997.[28] Most of these incidents involved clashes between Muslims and non-Muslims. Human Rights Watch also reported that some 200 Bosniaks (Muslims) who had been living in the vicinity of Teslić in central Bosnia were forced by Serbs to leave the area between May and August 1996.[29] Mostar was particularly sensitive, with the city effectively divided into two separate sectors—one Croat, one Muslim. Only in August 1996 did the two sides reach an agreement on the formation of a common government for the city of Mostar, but even that did not end the problems. In October 1997, for example, there were tensions between Croats and Muslims in Mostar when the former refused to recognize the electoral victory by the latter in local elections (in which the Muslim SDA coalition won fourteen out of twenty-four seats in the city council).[30] Nor were Muslim-Croat frictions restricted to Mostar. The parish church in the village of Donje Putićevo (near Travnik) and another Catholic church, St. Mary's Heart, in the village of Humac (in Bugojno municipality), were destroyed by explosives in March 1997; insofar as these churches had stood in an area controlled by Muslim authorities, the destruction was interpreted as reflective of continued Croat-Muslim frictions.[31]

But Serb-Croat relations have also been marred by tensions. Specifically, in what is perhaps the most spectacular series of incidents to date, local Serbs attacked Sarajevo Cardinal Puljić's entourage in Derventa on 23 April 1998, trapping Puljić and several hundred other Croats in Derventa's parish church. In ostensible retaliation the next day but also, notably, on the eve of the imminent return of Serbian refugees to the city, several hundred Croat civilians attacked an installation of the U.N. police force (IPTF) in Croat-controlled Drvar, also wounding the Serbian mayor, Milan Marčeta.[32] Seven buses of Croats were halted by roadblocks on the road to Plehane on 25 April. The Serbian returnees made an attempt to return to their homes in Drvar, but during the night of 25/26 April fled the city after their homes had been set on fire by rioting Croats.[33] The next day, 26 April, Bosnian Serbs smashed the windows of Croat parishioners who were driving to the local church to hear Mass.[34] Commenting on the violence, Major Chris Kinsville-Heyne, a British spokesperson, declared, "These incidents will not be tolerated by SFOR. Violent protests are totally unacceptable."[35] Ultimately, Norwegian peacekeepers from the NATO-led SFOR evacuated Puljić and about 650 worshipers from the church, ending the standoff on its third day.

Resignations, Elections, and Reconciliations

Under the Dayton Peace Accords, as already noted, no indicted war criminal was to be allowed to hold office in either sector of Bosnia-Herzegovina. This provision was aimed, in the first place, at Radovan Karadžić, who reluctantly agreed in July 1996 to step down as president of the Serbian Republic, relinquishing that office to Biljana Plavšić, a professor of biology in her late fifties who was once described by magazine columnist Mirjana Marković (wife of Slobodan Milošević) as the Serbian "Dr. Mengele."[36] Karadžić also stepped down as president of the Serbian Democratic Party (SDS)—which was a precondition for that party's being allowed to contest elections scheduled for mid-September of that year. Four months later, Plavšić dismissed General Ratko Mladić, a man described by Richard Holbrooke as a "charismatic murderer" with a tendency to engage in staring contests with his colloquitors,[37] from his post as commander of the Bosnian Serb army, indicating her intention to replace the entire, compromised general staff.[38]

In July 1996, more or less at the same time that Karadžić was stepping down, disquieting reports emerged alleging that Bosnian Serb officials had been preventing Serb refugees from returning to their homes in Croat-controlled or Muslim-controlled territory and compelling them to sign written pledges to vote for Karadžić's SDS before allowing them access to local soup kitchens.[39] But for all that, some 30 percent of Serbs voted against the SDS's candidate for the collective presidency, Momčilo Krajišnik.[40] The leading nationalist parties of the three national groups were the big winners in the elections held 13–14 September, a result not entirely welcome in the West. There were also some signs of trouble during the election campaign. For example, campaigning in Grebak, about 40 miles south of Sarajevo, Alija Izetbegović addressed a crowd of 10,000 supporters at a rally featuring Islamic religious music and verses from the Qur'an, making it clear that he was appealing, in the first place, to the Muslim vote.[41] Moreover, having calculated that some 2.3 million persons were eligible to vote, OSCE officials were dismayed when final tallies showed that more than 2.6 million persons actually voted.[42] Still, in the wake of these elections, there were bilateral talks between Bosnian Serb Prime Minister Gojko Kličković and Federation Prime Minister Edhem Bičakčić on the functioning of joint institutions.[43]

Follow-up elections at the municipal level were conducted on 13–14 September 1997, once again organized under the auspices of the OSCE. Intent on averting widespread fraud, "[OSCE] supervisors played a more intrusive role in the election process, not only monitoring what was going on but working with the polling committees and making recommendations to them as well."[44] The campaign itself was largely uneventful, except for a clash on 8 September (in Banja Luka) between the two rival SDS factions—one more opportunistic, associated with the increasingly pro-Western Plavšić, and the other more ideological in coloration, associated with the nationalist Krajišnik. To nobody's surprise, the ruling parties—the Muslim SDA, the Serb SDS, and the Croatian HDZ—garnered a majority of seats on municipal councils, with other parties or coalitions achieving majorities only in a few municipalities.[45]

Parliamentary elections in the Bosnian Serb rump state were held two months later, on 23 November, with the SDS taking twenty-four out of eighty-three seats, a decline for this party, and with the Radićal Party, an SDS ally, winning fifteen seats (up from six); Biljana Plavšić's party won fifteen seats, tying with the Radićals.[46] In the wake of these elections, Milorad Dodik, a pro-Western moderate who had criticized the war and who had been one of the first Bosnian Serb politicians to speak out against Karadžić,[47] became Bosnian Serb Prime Minister, at the head of a five-party coalition, promising that refugees would be welcomed back to their homes and that he would effect Church–state separation and assure freedom of the press.[48] But if this election seemed to mark a break with radical nationalism among Bosnian Serbs, Bosnia-wide elections on 12–13 September 1998 admitted of less sanguine interpretations. In these elections, the West's favorite, Biljana Plavšić, was voted out of office and replaced by Nikola Poplašen, leader of the Serbian Radical Party, the Bosnian branch of Vojislav Šešelj's fascistic party of the same name.[49] The increasingly moderate former HDZ member Krešimir Zubak also lost his race for reelection as the Croatian member of the collective presidency to hard-liner Ante Jelavić, the candidate favored by Croatian President Tudjman, while Serb hard-liner Krajišnik was defeated by Živko Radišić, a candidate seen as being more favorably inclined toward cooperation with the West.[50]

Although the U.S. State Department tried to put a good face on the election results, the truth is that the election of Jelavić was as much a setback as that of Poplašen. Indeed, the elections, mixed as they were, accurately reflected the mixed reality of Bosnia today. On the one hand, there remain considerable hatred and resentment, as one would expect in an area so recently torn by war. In Banja Luka, to take one example, the mufti has been seeking permission to rebuild the Ferhadija mosque, originally built in 1579 but completely demolished during the war. Carlos

Westendorp, the international community's highest representative in Bosnia, backed the mufti's request, only to see the mayor of Banja Luka, Djordje Umičević, turn the request down, with the explanation, "The international community has to stop insulting the Serbs and asking them to rebuild the monuments from the darkest days of slavery."[51] Then there is the town of Vlasenica in eastern Bosnia where some local people seriously blame the Serbian Insurrectionary War on "the Jews," while others take the approach articulated by thirty-year-old Ranka Kraljević: "It's not that I hate Muslims. It's just that I'll never trust them again."[52]

On the other hand, there are also signs of reconciliation and of "*ćuprija* building" ("bridge building"), to coin a phrase. Some of this is a matter of individuals willing to defy nationalist rhetoric and pressure tactics. One striking example is Father Stipan Radić, a Franciscan priest in Zenica, who has worked hard both during the war and after to reconcile people of different religious and cultural traditions.[53] Sadik Pažarac, a Muslim journalist who continues to make his home in Serb-controlled Bijeljina, is another example; he has found the courage to write explicit exposés about human rights violations and corruption within the Bosnian Serb republic, publishing them in the Sarajevo-based daily newspaper *Oslobodjenje*.[54] The Serbian mayor of Drvar, Mile Marčeta, is yet another example; Marčeta, seriously wounded in riots in April 1998, remains committed to a multiethnic and multicultural Bosnia and has found himself at odds, thus, with both Bosnian Croat nationalists who want to keep Drvar homogeneously Croat and Bosnian Serb nationalists who do not want to allow Serb refugees to return to Drvar and become reconciled with Croats.[55] Nongovernmental organization activity has been of especial importance here, though it is rarely discussed in print. But it is at this level where there has been some real intercommunal *ćuprija*-building, sometimes at an individual level, sometimes at the level of small groups or institutions. One example, disclosed to me by Professor Robin Remington, has involved ethnically mixed groups of Bosnian journalists who have been coming to the University of Missouri for workshops in journalism and, along the way, have found themselves learning something about toleration too.[56]

Part of the calculus of reconciliation is coping with trauma. In Croatia, the media talk of a "Vietnam syndrome" among soldiers and civilians.[57] In postwar Bosnia, where women comprise 70 percent of the adult population, the need for therapeutic care for women and men, whether for posttraumatic stress disorder or for other psychiatric problems brought on or worsened by the war, is severe. And yet, although the United States has provided $400 million toward rearming the Muslim-Croat federation and $45 million in loans to small businesses, the U.N. and the U.S. Agency for International Development (USAID) decided that psychological counseling was not sufficiently important and cut funding for services of this nature.[58] Interestingly enough, Radovan Karadžić, a trained psychiatrist, has nurtured some thoughts of returning to his profession and of setting up a private mental hospital that might deal with some of the disorders spawned by the war in which he played so prominent a role.[59]

Exhumations

No sooner had the accords been signed than the search began for evidence of war crimes. U.N. workers played a central role in the search for and exhumation of mass graves, discovering them at Srebrenica (at the Glogova site, involving perhaps 2,000–5,000 Muslims killed by Serbs),[60] Sanski Most (involving Croats killed by Serbs),[61] Lušći Palanka (involving up to 120 Croats and Muslims killed by Serbs),[62] Nova Kasaba (involving up to 2,700 Muslims killed by Serbs),[63] and Glumina (involving 274 Muslims killed by Serbs).[64] Human rights activists pleaded with IFOR to post guards at the sites of these mass graves, but NATO determined that aerial surveillance would suffice to monitor the sites. Heavy cloud cover was a problem during the months following the identification of the sites around Srebrenica, however, and in early April it was revealed that someone or some persons had tampered with two key mass graves and that important evidence had been dug up and removed, thus weakening the International War Crimes Tribunal's case in regard to the massacre at Srebrenica.[65] But human rights officials said that the tribunal probably had enough evidence to prosecute those involved, and forensics experts were still unearthing fresh evidence of the slaughter at that site as recently as April 1998.[66] Bosnian Serbs began unearthing a suspected mass grave in Sarajevo in late November 1998—in their first action of this kind—having uncovered evidence suggesting that Serbian civilian victims of the war were buried there. Alexandra Štiglmayer, a spokesperson for the Office of the High Representative in Bosnia-Herzegovina, said that the Serb victims had been murdered by Bosnian Muslim paramilitary forces.[67]

War Crimes

For many, the fundamental test of the Dayton Peace Accords has lain in the ability of their would-be enforcers to bring indicted war criminals to justice. Yet it was precisely this aspect of the accords which seemed to get off to the slowest start. To be sure, Canadian authorities in Toronto put a Canadian army commander on trial in July 1996 on charges that Canadian soldiers under his command had committed various offenses while stationed at the Bakovci mental hospital between October 1993 and April 1994.[68] But it was only on 29 November 1996 that the International War Crimes Tribunal handed down its first sentence of ten years' imprisonment for Dražen Erdemović, a twenty-five-year-old Croat in the Bosnian Serb army who had taken part in the murders at Srebrenica.[69] The first sentence of 1997 came in May, when Dušan Tadić, a forty-one-year-old Serb, was convicted of having slit the throats of two Muslim policemen. Tadić was the first indicted war criminal to be tried, however, since Erdemović had pled guilty.[70] But even before Tadić's trial had ended, a group consisting of three Muslims and one Croat was put on trial in The Hague on charges of murder and rape at the Bosnian government–run prison camp at Celebići, 30 miles southwest of Sarajevo.[71] Failing to obtain Milošević's cooperation in the surrender of suspects,[72] NATO forces decided to use their muscle to arrest two indicted war criminals, killing one of them—Simo Drjlaća, a key figure at the three concentration camps in and around Prijedor—and taking his associate, Milan Kovačević, into custody.[73] About this time, Bosnian police began arresting several dozen persons suspected of attacks on the Croatian community—among them, Islamic fighters from outside the country.[74] And by the end of September, yet another suspect—Tihomir Blaškić, a Croatian general accused of failing to stop his men from committing acts of mayhem and murder against Muslims in 1993—was on trial in The Hague.[75]

But some observers worried that in handing down its verdict in the Tadić case in May 1997, the tribunal had ruled that the prosecution had failed to show that the Belgrade regime had exercised complete control over Bosnian Serb forces or that the Geneva Conventions applied in the case. In effect, the tribunal agreed with the defense that Tadić's actions did not constitute genocide.[76]

Whatever one might make of the legal precedent set by the Tadić trial, it was clear that the pace of arrests and trials quickened in the course of 1998. Yet it is interesting that in May 1998, the International War Crimes Tribunal in The Hague dropped charges against fourteen Bosnian Serbs, at least some of whom had been accused of perpetrating atrocities against Muslim civilians in the Keraterm and Omarska camps.[77] The principal reason for the quickened pace of arrests was the establishment in summer 1997 of a U.S. special operations task force to gather intelligence and arrest indictees. In September 1997, more than 100 persons involved in the task force met at Fort Bragg, North Carolina, to draw up plans for the arrest of Karadžić and others; when Karadžić went underground about that time, U.S. operatives suspected that their Italian collaborators were leaking information to Karadžić, but were unable to find anything incriminating.[78] American officials later learned that a French army major (Herve Gourmelon) had passed key details of the plan to arrest Karadžić to the plan's intended target.[79]

But other arrests were made, all the same. These included Dragoljub Kunarac, a former Bosnian Serb paramilitary commander who entered a plea of "guilty" to rape as a war crime in March 1998;[80] Milorad Krnojelac, a school principal said to have commanded a Serbian prison camp during the Bosnian war and to have overseen the execution of at least 29 Muslims during 1992 and 1993 and the torture of many more;[81] a group of 6 Bosnian Croats accused of having participated in the massacre of more than 100 Muslims in the village of Ahmići on 16 April 1993 and brought to trial in the sixth case tried by the tribunal;[82] Dario Kordić, a Bosnian Croat accused of having led a campaign which nearly succeeded in extirpating all traces of a number of Muslim communities in the Lasva Valley between 1991 and 1994;[83] Mario Čerkez, a Bosnian Croat military commander accused of 22 counts and named in the same indictment with Kordić;[84] and Goran Jelišić, a thirty-year-old Bosnian Serb who once boasted that he was a "second Hitler," who is thought to be personally responsible for the deaths of more than 100 persons, and whose trial for genocide began on 30 November 1998.[85] As senior as some of these figures were, their importance paled in comparison with that of General Radislav Krstić, arrested in northern Bosnia by NATO troops on 3 December. Krstić, commander of the Drina Corps, which began shelling Srebrenica on 6 July 1995 and whose troops were said, in the indictment, to have executed thousands of unarmed Bosnian men at that town, was indicted on charges of genocide, complicity to commit genocide, extermination, and murder.[86] Krstić pled "not guilty" to the charges.

Not all the litigative action has been in The Hague, however. In early May 1998, for example, a Serb accused of the murder of nineteen civilians selected for death because of their Muslim names, went on trial in Bijelo Polje, Montenegro.[87] Or again, in August 1998, Kemal Mehinović, a Muslim who owned two restaurants and a bakery in Bosanski Šamac when he was taken into custody by Bosnian Serb forces in May 1992 and who now lives in the United States, brought a lawsuit against Nikola Vučković, a Serb now living near Atlanta, accusing the latter of torture and acts of violence during the Bosnian war.[88]

For many observers, however, Karadžić looms large among those figures yet to be brought to justice. In April 1998, as Westendorp clamored for Karadžić's arrest, rumors circulated that the former president of the Bosnian Serb Republic was about to turn himself in and was negotiating the details of his surrender. These rumors were, however, flatly and energetically denied by Ljiljana Karadžić, Radovan's wife, who asserted defiantly that "this tribunal ... has enough evidence of his innocence, and not a single piece of evidence of his guilt."[89]

Much of the credibility of the Dayton Accords is bound up with the question of war crimes. The more indictees are brought before the court, the greater the likelihood that aggrieved parties will feel that there has been at least some justice done, and the greater the overall legitimacy of the Dayton peace. For a flawed peace may, all the same, legitimate itself over time and those flaws, however serious at the inception, may, with sufficient time, seem perhaps less weighty. This is less a matter of speculation, however, than an insistence that observers keep an open mind as the tribunal and Dayton put themselves to the test.

Increasingly one hears calls for the arrest and trial of Milošević himself. As early as 6 April 1995, in testimony before the House Commission on Security and Cooperation in Europe, Ambassador Richard C. Holbrooke testified that

> during our hearing a couple of days ago, Cherif Bassiouni made a very, very compelling assertion that, as they were compiling information leading towards pointing the finger at higher-ups in Serbia, all of a sudden his mandate came to a grinding halt. Funding was not to be found, and it is the belief of many that our government has information—the CIA perhaps has it, maybe others—that would directly implicate or at least show that very high officials in Serbia are responsible for this genocide.[90]

Subsequently, Paul Williams and Norman Cigar prepared a forty-six-page report, assessing whether there existed a *prima facie* case for the indictment of Slobodan Milošević. They concluded that "there is a compelling legal and factual case that Slobodan Milošević, through forces and agencies under his control, is responsible for directing and aiding and abetting war crimes on an extensive scale."[91] By the end of

1998, the U.S. State Department seemed to be coming around to this view. The department's spokesperson stated: "Milošević has been at the center of every crisis in the former Yugoslavia over the past decade. He is not simply part of the problem. He *is* the problem."[92] As Hegel once wrote, the owl of Minerva flies at dusk.

Building a Deterrent

Among the lessons learned from the war—though it was a surprise to many that this lesson had not been learned from previous experience, if not from sheer logic—was that leaving one side in a conflict at a severe military disadvantage could be expected to encourage the side at a military advantage to push forward with its war aims, even perhaps to extend them. Based on this "lesson," the United States undertook, after Dayton, to provide arms and training to the Bosnian Federation Army, also allowing the federation to contract with Military Professional Resources, Inc., a private firm in Alexandria, Virginia, to manage the program.[93] The U.S. "Train and Equip" Program for the Bosnian Federation followed, to some extent, the lines proposed in a 200-page classified study produced by the Institute for Defense Analyses for the Pentagon, with the supply of uniforms and small arms getting under way as early as mid-March 1996. Shipments of tanks, artillery, and other heavy weaponry began after June 1996.[94]

Critics sympathetic to the Serbian side quickly found fault in the "Train and Equip" program. Lee H. Hamilton, the ranking Democrat on the House International Relations Committee who, as was noted in Chapter 10, had received a small level of contributions from Serbian Americans and who had insisted on keeping the arms embargo in place against the Bosnian government of Alija Izetbegović, wrote an editorial for *The Christian Science Monitor* in September 1997 urging that "the U.S. should terminate the train and equip program" because, in his view, American "assistance to the Bosnian Army is working at cross-purposes with our goal of stability ... [by] shifting the military balance of power in favor of the Bosnian Muslims." Hamilton expressed the fear that "Muslims see an opportunity to reclaim all of Bosnia by force."[95] Another critic, Charles G. Boyd, urged in *Foreign Affairs* in early 1998, in similar fashion, that "the coalition partners should halt the Train and Equip program, which has led to a growing military superiority for the Federation that is deeply destabilizing."[96] Not only did Boyd fear that the Muslims might be encouraged to act precipitously, but he did not take into account the possibility that the FRY might come to the assistance of the so-called Serbian Republic in a future war (or, perhaps, assumed that this eventuality was too remote to be worth probing).

Yet, although a June 1996 agreement on arms control signed in Florence set strict (nominal) limits on five types of weapons, under which the Bosnian Federation would be allowed 274 tanks, 1,000 artillery pieces over 75 mm. caliber, no armored combat vehicles, no combat aircraft, and no attack helicopters, against the 137 tanks, 50 heavy artillery pieces, no armored combat vehicles, no combat aircraft, and no attack helicopters allowed to the (Bosnian) Serbian Republic,[97] this is not the whole story. To begin with, as of October 1996, the Bosnian Serbs were thought to have 450 battle tanks, more than three times the number they are permitted under the Florence agreement, and some 3,000 artillery pieces, six times the level allowed under the agreement. The Croat-Muslim federation was thought to have had about 4,000 artillery pieces at that time, rather than the 1,000 allowed under the agreement, while the federation was, at the time, awaiting a shipment of M-60 tanks and UH-1D helicopters from the United States.[98] By the end of 1996, as Mark Clark points out, the federation "had received $98.4 million worth of American-produced automatic weapons, M-60 tanks, M-113 armored vehicles, and UH-1D helicopters from the United States alone. Additional weapons and training facilities have been provided by other states."[99]

And further, there is the question of FRY and Croatian military strength, also regulated by the Florence agreement. Indeed, under this agreement, the FRY was granted sufficient military wherewithal to cancel out the combined military strength of the Republic of Croatia and the federation, at least judging on strictly numerical grounds, which is all that the Florence agreement regulates. The agreement allows the FRY 1,025 tanks against 410 for Croatia, 3,750 heavy artillery pieces against 1,500 for Croatia, 850 armored combat vehicles against 340 for Croatia, 155 combat aircraft against 62 for Croatia, and 53 attack helicopters against 21 for Croatia.[100] Third, military analysts are well acquainted with the general rule that there is a strong psychological and logistical advantage with the defender, so that an aggressor would need overwhelming superiority in order to crush an intended victim (as the Serbian Insurrectionary War amply bore out). In consequence, strict parity is not needed in order to deter a would-be aggressor from launching a conventional attack. And fourth, the FRY is known to have developed an extensive chemical weapons arsenal, while an internal NATO report suggested that the Yugoslav army may have some biological-weapons capability as well.[101] All of these considerations suggest that it was highly unlikely that the Bosnian Federation would enjoy an offensive capability against Serbian forces, at least prior to NATO's bombardment of the FRY which began in late March 1998, and thus, that the arguments offered by Hamilton and Boyd are specious and misguided.

Quite to the contrary, the training and equipping of the Bosnian Federation Army is likely to help to maintain the peace in the short term, giving locals time to overcome hatreds and resentments, and to set aside the manufactured nationalisms which drove them to war in the first half of the 1990s.[102]

Post-Dayton Croatia

Where Croatia is concerned, the Dayton Accords promised a return to Croatian sovereignty of Serb-held eastern Slavonia and the Montenegrin-held Prevlaka peninsula, the possibility for Croatian refugees to return to their homes in eastern Slavonia, and the possibility for Serbian refugees to return to their homes in the Krajina or elsewhere in Croatia. In addition, the Republic of Croatia has demanded that the FRY return works of art confiscated from museums lying within territories under temporary Serbian control, including from the Benkovac museum (from which some

4,000 pieces of art were said to have been removed) and from the Vukovar museum (from which some 30,000 pieces of art were said to have been removed),[103] and that the FRY pay reparations to Croatia for damages caused during the war.[104] At this writing, neither issue has been resolved.

The territorial issues have been, in some ways, the simplest, at least where the transfer of jurisdiction as such is concerned. Eastern Slavonia reverted to Croatian control in January 1998, after a two-year "transition,"[105] but despite efforts by Croatian authorities to signal their determination to guarantee human rights to all residents of Croatia, nearly half of the 120,000 Serbs who were living around Vukovar as of 1996 had fled the area by March 1998, with many more said to be preparing to leave.[106] Repeated assaults and beatings by local Croats and evictions from housing, together with the firing of many Serbs under the newly restored Croatian administration, contributed to this outcome. Moreover, of the 1,500 houses whose owners have received state reconstruction funds, only 6 belong to Serbs.[107]

The Republic of Croatia had expected that the Prevlaka peninsula would be restored to Croatian control likewise in 1998, but in July 1998, the U.N. monitors' mission on the peninsula was extended for another six months. Croatian sources speculated that the destabilization in Kosovo had contributed to nervousness at the U.N. about any immediate change in the status of Prevlaka.[108]

By contrast, the return of refugees has been riddled with complexities and problems, some of them bureaucratic and logistical in nature, some of them due to the fact that the homes to which the refugees lay claim may have become homes for other displaced persons in the meantime, and some of them due to the deep rancor which still pervades the region. Even as Germany indicated its intention to return some 80,000 Croatian refugees to their native country,[109] adding to the pressure for scarce housing, the Croatian government issued mixed signals concerning the welcome Croatian Serbs could expect to receive in the republic. Whatever his subordinates might say, however, Croatian President Tudjman has been quintessentially blunt, telling representatives of the United States, the EU, Germany, Britain, the Netherlands, and France in May 1997, "No reasonable person in the international community can expect the Croats to accept the Serbs back."[110] That same month, the *International Herald Tribune* reported that the Croatian government had been confiscating tens of thousands of homes which had belonged to local Serbs in eastern Slavonia, in order to settle Croatian refugees from Bosnia and from parts of Serbia in the seized property.[111] Although the press was full of protests from the international community about the Croatian government's actions on this score, there was little, if any, evidence in the press of any such protest against Belgrade for actions which were driving Croats from their homes in Vojvodina, Serbia proper, and Kosovo. For its part, the Croatian government had, by July 1998, enabled some 13,000 Croatian Serbs, who had temporarily fled to eastern Slavonia from other parts of Croatia, to return to their homes.[112] In June, in a significant signal, *Večernji list* announced that Serbian Orthodox priests would soon be able to return to their churches in Croatia, in the process giving further proof of the vast differences between Croatia and Serbia.[113]

A Banana Republic with No Bananas

Corruption is endemic in the postcommunist Balkans. I have written elsewhere of elements of corruption in Croatia[114] and have alluded to problems of this nature in post-Dayton Bosnia earlier in this chapter, while the problems of corruption in Macedonia, Bulgaria, and Albania are well known. In Serbia, corruption has had its own character, consisting more of cronyism than nepotism. *U.S. News & World Report* spent two months investigating corruption in Serbia in 1997 and concluded that graft was widespread in Milošević's government. Mirko Marjanović, then–prime minister of Serbia was said to be worth about $50 million; he and other ministers got rich thanks to "special access to information on monetary measures, such as devaluation, extremely favorable credits, and hard-to-get import licenses."[115] According to that magazine, many Serbian ministers were heading private firms into which state funds were being illegally pumped, in essence using public money to bankroll private capital investment. As early as December 1990, the Milošević government effectively made off with $1.8 billion in dinars from the federal treasury, which it spent in Serbia; later, in 1993, "Milošević and his ministers seized all foreign-currency accounts, ... [thereby confiscating] about $3.8 billion in foreign exchange."[116] These funds were taken out of the country and deposited in bank accounts in Moscow and Cyprus. A Belgrade attorney characterized the Milošević government as "some strange mixture of mafia and profiteering and police," adding, "We are like a banana republic, but we don't even have the bananas."[117]

Conclusion

The U.N. lifted its arms embargo against the FRY in June 1996, formally suspending other sanctions against that country on 1 October that same year.[118] Within two weeks, *The European* was warning that the suspension of sanctions had been premature and that it had removed an important means of exerting pressure on the Serbian side.[119] Compliance of the three sides on the return of refugees and on the surrender of indicted war criminals had not been assured. Moderate (i.e., nonnationalist) media were still being harassed and intimidated in Bosnia. And, perhaps most important, there continued to be serious human-rights violations within the FRY itself, including the virtual absence of alternative, independent media in Serbia, the aforementioned use of government channels and funds to enrich the government's ministers at the expense of ordinary Serbs, the sundry violations of human and civic rights in Kosovo (to be discussed in the next chapter), and violations of human and civic rights in the Sandžak and Vojvodina.[120] There was, thus, every reason to keep the sanctions in place, and no reason at all to lift them. But the U.N. lifted them all the same, revealing once more the powerful pro-Serbian tilt in Paris, Moscow, and— under the Tories—Whitehall.

None of the parties to the Dayton Accords are committed to the preservation of the unworkable Dayton system over the long haul. The Dayton system was, in fact, not designed with local interests in mind at all, despite its having been worked out by Izetbegović, Milošević, and Tudjman, with heavy American involvement. The design of the Dayton system can, at best, serve the short-term interests of those three men, the short-term interests of local capitalists, and the short-term interests of the Great Powers. As Warren Bass has noted, "Dayton represented not the vindication of the liberal ideals with which Bill Clinton excoriated George Bush on the 1992 campaign trail ... but rather a version of the chilly realpolitik that kept the Bush administration out of Bosnia."[121] If—and this is a big "if"—peace nonetheless becomes stable in the area, something along the lines of multiethnic tolerance returns, and something like a Bosnian unity is restored—all of which remains rather hard to imagine at this writing—it will be *in spite of* the "realism" of Dayton, rather than because of it.

Notes

1. Fareed Zakaria, "The Rise of Illiberal Democracy," in *Foreign Affairs*, Vol. 76, No. 6 (November/December 1997), pp. 42–43.

2. *Der Tagesspiegel* (Berlin) (15 December 1997), p. 2.

3. *Christian Science Monitor* (31 March 1997), p. 19; *New York Times* (16 April 1997), p. A4; and *The Economist* (London), 6 September 1997, p. 42.

4. For a pessimistic appraisal written at this time, see Susan L. Woodward, "Bosnia after Dayton: Year Two," in *Current History*, Vol. 96, No. 608 (March 1997), p. 102.

5. Madeleine Albright, "Making Progress Toward a Lasting Peace in Bosnia," in *U.S. Department of State Dispatch* (April 1998), p. 7.

6. Ibid., p. 8.

7. Richard Holbrooke, *To End a War* (New York: Random House, 1998), passim.

8. Ibid., pp. 199–200.

9. Details in ibid., pp. 280–285.

10. Quoted in ibid., pp. 311–312.

11. As cited in *Christian Science Monitor* (20 December 1995), p. 18.

12. *New York Times* (27 October 1996), p. 6, and (11 March 1997), p. A4. Unemployment rates for the Croat-Muslim federation in March 1997 or for the Serbian Republic in October 1996 were not provided in these articles.

13. *New York Times* (6 January 1997), p. A6.

14. *New York Times* (7 October 1996), p. A4.

15. *New York Times* (28 February 1997), on *Nexis*.

16. Quoted in *New York Times* (26 April 1996), p. A4.

17. Quoted in ibid.

18. Quoted in ibid.

19. From "Overview of the Dayton Peace Agreement," in *Bosnia Report* (London), Issue 13 (January 1996), pp. 1–4.

20. *International Herald Tribune* (Tokyo ed.) (16 October 1998), p. 8.

21. *Christian Science Monitor* (19 September 1996), p. 5.

22. *The Economist* (24 August 1996), p. 31.

23. *Briefing on Bosnia by Region* (Washington, D.C.: Commission on Security and Cooperation in Europe, 5 February 1998), p. 17.

24. *Bosnia-Hercegovina—A Failure in the Making: Human Rights and the Dayton Agreement* (New York: Human Rights Watch/Helsinki, June 1996), pp. 9–24.

25. Ibid., p. 7.

26. *New York Times* (12 January 1996), p. A3.

27. *New York Times* (23 February 1996), p. A3.

28. *New York Times* (28 May 1996), p. A6; SRNA (11 November 1996), trans. in *BBC Summary of World Broadcasts* (13 November 1996); AFP (11 November 1996), on *Nexis*; *New York Times* (14 November 1996), p. A7; and AFP (18 March 1997), on *Nexis*.

29. *Bosnia-Hercegovina—Update: Non-compliance with the Dayton Accords* (New York: Human Rights Watch/Helsinki, August 1996), p. 5; also *Christian Science Monitor* (30 May 1996), p. 2.

30. *New Europe* (Athens), 11–17 August 1996, p. 25; and *Der Tagesspiegel* (12 October 1997), p. 6.

31. Habena news agency (Mostar) (21 March 1997), trans. in *BBC Summary of World Broadcasts* (24 March 1997).

32. *Der Tagesspiegel* (25 April 1998), p. 2.

33. *Der Tagesspiegel* (27 April 1998), p. 2; and *The Daily Yomiuri* (27 April 1998), p. 4.

34. *Daily Yomiuri* (27 April 1998), p. 4.

35. Quoted in *Daily Yomiuri* (26 April 1998), p. 3.

36. *The Economist* (5 July 1997), p. 42. See also *The Times* (20 May 1996), on *AmeriCast*.

37. Holbrooke, *To End a War*, p. 149.

38. *New York Times* (9 November 1996), p. 6.

39. *Washington Post* (28 July 1996), on *AmeriCast*.

40. *New York Times* (21 September 1996), p. 4.

41. *New York Times* (2 September 1996), p. 5.

42. *Christian Science Monitor* (23 September 1996), p. 6.

43. Bosnian Serb television (Pale) (18 March 1997), trans. in *BBC Summary of World Broadcasts* (20 March 1997).

44. *The 1997 Municipal Elections in Bosnia-Herzegovina* (Washington, D.C.: Commission on Security and Cooperation in Europe, October 1997), p. 4.

45. Ibid., p. 10.

46. *Der Tagesspiegel* (8 December 1997), p. 1.

47. *Christian Science Monitor* (3 March 1998), p. 6.

48. *The Economist* (24 January 1998), p. 43.

49. *International Herald Tribune* (Tokyo ed.) (17 September 1998), p. 4. For a discussion of the fascistic nature of Šešelj's party, see Ognjen Pribićević, "Changing Fortunes of the Serbian Radical Right," in Sabrina P. Ramet (ed.), *The Radical Right in Central and Eastern Europe Since 1989* (University Park: Penn State Press, in press). See also *Der Tagesspiegel* (4 February 1998), p. 7.

50. *Daily Yomiuri* (27 September 1998), p. 3.

51. *Washington Post,* reprinted in the *Daily Yomiuri* (15 May 1998), p. 10.

52. *The Independent* (London), reprinted in the *Daily Yomiuri* (27 September 1998), p. 9.

53. *Los Angeles Times,* reprinted in the *Daily Yomiuri* (19 October 1998), p. 8.

54. Ibid., p. 12.

55. Ibid., p. 7.

56. Telephone conversation with Robin Alison Remington, Kyoto—Columbia, 2 December 1998.

57. See "Vijetnamski sindrom," in *Globus* (Zagreb) (23 January 1998), pp. 28–32; and "Vijetnamski sindrom na Hrvatski način," in *Globus* (20 February 1998), pp. 34–37.

58. Jan Goodwin, "A Nation of Widows," in *On The Issues* (Spring 1997), pp. 28–29.

59. AFP (5 April 1996), on *Nexis*.

60. *Christian Science Monitor* (19 January 1996), pp. 1, 9.

61. Radio Bosnia-Herzegovina (Sarajevo) (8 March 1996), trans. in Foreign Broadcast Information Service (FBIS), 12 March 1996, p. 22.

62. *New York Times* (17 March 1996), p. 10.

63. *Times* (17 July 1996), on *AmeriCast*.

64. *Illyria* (The Bronx), 14–16 October 1998, p. 6.

65. *Christian Science Monitor* (3 April 1996), pp. 1, 9.

66. Ibid., p. 9; and *Daily Yomiuri* (22 April 1998), p. 5.

67. *Japan Times* (27 November 1998), p. 6.

68. *New York Times* (18 July 1996), p. A7.

69. *Neue Zürcher Zeitung* (30 November/1 December 1996), pp. 1–2.

70. *New York Times* (8 May 1997), pp. A1, A13.

71. *New York Times* (3 April 1997), p. A3.

72. *New York Times* (27 May 1997), p. A7.

73. *Christian Science Monitor* (18 July 1997), p. 18.

74. *New York Times* (5 December 1997), p. A5.

75. *Christian Science Monitor* (1 October 1997), p. 6.

76. *New York Times* (18 May 1997), p. E4.

77. *Der Tagesspiegel* (9 May 1998), p. 2.

78. *U.S. News & World Report* (6 July 1998), pp. 45–47.

79. Ibid., p. 47; confirmed in *Der Tagesspiegel* (24 April 1998), p. 2.

80. *New York Times* (10 March 1998), p. A10.

81. *International Herald Tribune* (Tokyo ed.) (16 June 1998), p. 4; and *Daily Yomiuri* (16 June 1998), p. 4.

82. *Mainichi Daily News* (20 August 1998), p. 4.

83. *Daily Yomiuri* (15 October 1998), p. 4.

84. Ibid.

85. *International Herald Tribune* (Tokyo) (1 December 1998), p. 5; *Daily Yomiuri* (2 December 1998), p. 5; and *Independent*, reprinted in *Daily Yomiuri* (6 December 1998), p. 9.

86. *Daily Yomiuri* (4 December 1998), p. 6, and (5 December 1998), p. 4; and *The Weekend Australian* (5/6 December 1998), p. 19.

87. *Illyria* (6–8 May 1998), p. 3.

88. *Daily Yomiuri* (29 August 1998), p. 4.

89. Quoted in *Daily Yomiuri* (12 April 1998), p. 3.

90. *The United Nations, NATO and the Former Yugoslavia*, Hearing before the Commission on Security and Cooperation in Europe, One Hundred Fourth Congress, First Session, April 6, 1995 (Washington, D.C.: U.S. Government Printing Office, 1995), p. 10.

91. Paul Williams and Norman Cigar, *War Crimes and Individual Responsibility: A Prima Facie Case for the Indictment of Slobodan Milošević* (Washington, D.C.: Balkan Institute, N.D.), p. iii.

92. Quoted in *The Economist* (5 December 1998), p. 65.

93. Mark Edmond Clark, "No Military Action is the Best Action for the Bosnian Federation to Take," in *The Brown Journal of World Affairs*, Vol. 5, Issue 1 (Winter/Spring 1998), p. 297.

94. Ibid., pp. 297–298.

95. Lee H. Hamilton, "Tipping the Bosnian Balance," in *Christian Science Monitor* (26 September 1997), p. 19.

96. Charles G. Boyd, "Making Bosnia Work," in *Foreign Affairs*, Vol. 77, No. 1 (January–February 1998), p. 53.

97. Clark, "No Military Action," p. 298.

98. *International Herald Tribune* (Paris ed.) (11 October 1996), p. 5.

99. Clark, "No Military Action," p. 298.

100. Ibid., p. 298.

101. *New York Times* (28 March 1997), p. A5. See also *Former Yugoslavia—Clouds of War: Chemical Weapons in the Former Yugoslavia* (New York: Human Rights Watch/Helsinki, March 1997), pp. 6–12.

102. For an argument that nationalism is an artificial construct, see Seth G. Jones and Nikhilesh M. Korgaonkar, "Bosnian Lessons: The Myths of Nationalism," in *Christian Science Monitor* (19 April 1996), p. 18. See also Miroslav Hroch, "Real and Constructed: The Nature of the Nation," in John A. Hall (ed.), *The State of the Nation: Ernest Gellner and the Theory of Nationalism* (Cambridge: Cambridge University Press, 1998), pp. 91–106.

103. *Croatia Weekly* (17 July 1998), p. 3.

104. *Croatia Weekly* (17 July 1998), p. 13.

105. Miomir Žužul, "A Just Settlement: The Return of Eastern Slavonia to Croatia," in *Harvard International Review*, Vol. 20, No. 2 (Spring 1998), pp. 16–20.

106. *International Herald Tribune* (Tokyo ed.) (20 March 1998), p. 4. See also *Croatia Weekly* (12 February 1998), p. 3.

107. *International Herald Tribune* (Tokyo ed.) (20 March 1998), p. 4.

108. *Croatia Weekly* (24 July 1998), p. 13.

109. *Croatia Weekly* (22 May 1998), p. 13.

110. Quoted in *New York Times* (28 May 1997), p. A9.

111. *International Herald Tribune* (Paris ed.) (15 May 1997), p. 7.

112. *Croatia Weekly* (10 July 1998), p. 3.

113. *Večernji list* (Zagreb), reprinted in *Croatia Weekly* (5 June 1998), p. 5.

114. See Sabrina P. Ramet, "Liberalizam, moral i društveni poredak: Slučaj korumpiranog populističkog pluralizma u Hrvatskoj," in *Erasmus*, no. 24 (May 1998).

115. *U.S. News & World Report* (21 July 1997), pp. 38–39.

116. Ibid., p. 41.

117. Quoted in ibid., p. 38.

118. *Neue Zürcher Zeitung* (20 June 1996), p. 2; and *New York Times* (2 October 1996), p. A4.

119. *The European* (London) (10–16 October 1996), p. 2.

120. The term "human rights" corresponds to *natural rights*. The term "civic rights" corresponds to *positive rights*.

121. Warren Bass, "The Triage of Dayton," in *Foreign Affairs*, Vol. 77, No. 5 (September–October 1998), p. 96.

◆

CHAPTER THIRTEEN

Milošević, Kosovo, and the Principle of Legitimacy

In a work published in 1968, Samuel P. Huntington suggested that the most essential distinction among systems was between those capable of assuring public order and those not capable of performing this function.[1] Placing himself, thus, in the tradition of Hobbes and Machiavelli, Huntington's suggestion was simultaneously prescriptive and empirical. It was *prescriptive* in the sense that his preference for order underlay his entire book, which indeed presumed order as the fundamental principle of state; and it was *empirical* insofar as the value of political order was tied not to an overarching normative theory, but to an empirical theory of political participation, state development, and stability.

In contrast to Huntington, I would suggest that the most essential distinction among political systems in terms of both short-term performance and long-term prospects is between legitimate systems and illegitimate systems; although this distinction is grounded in normative theory, it has clear empirical consequences, and the distinction between legitimate and illegitimate systems may be subjected to empirical hypotheses and tests. In taking an expressly normative frame of reference as my incunabulum, I am associating myself with a different branch of the liberal tradition, namely, that of John Locke, Immanuel Kant, and John Stuart Mill. Unlike Hobbes and Machiavelli, these thinkers never presumed to disassociate political theory from the metaphysic of morals; indeed, such a disassociation would have been, in their view, both unhealthy and unsound.

Hobbes and Machiavelli might be called the *Urväter* of "liberal realism," understanding by "realism" that branch of political prescription which dismisses ideals as largely irrelevant to the interests of state and which bases itself on protecting the status quo and fostering stability. In negotiating scenarios, "confidence building" and "compelling national security interest" figure as the bywords of the so-called realists. Hence when, in June 1998, top officials at the Pentagon expressed their opposition to any military involvement in containing or combatting Milošević's attacks on the Albanian population of Kosovo, they argued that "Washington has no compelling national security interest in Kosovo"[2]—a proposition self-declared idealists would consider at best trivially true, insofar as it assumes, first, that an escalation of hostilities in the vicinity of Greece, Macedonia, Albania, and Turkey is of no great moment where national security is concerned (an assumption which even some "realists" consider out of touch with reality) and, second, that Washington should base its policies *only* on the assessment of "compelling national security interest" (an assumption which idealists challenge). "Justice" and "legitimate government," and even "human rights," are terms abhorred by true "realists." To the extent that "realists" speak the language of morality, they seek to base it on empirical factors and considerations—a point to which I shall return shortly—even on interest itself.

Kant, Locke, and Mill may be credited as the fathers of "liberal idealism," in contrast. By "idealism" I mean political thinking which takes moral considerations as its starting point, founding concepts of legitimacy on a metaphysic of morals and arguing that policies fashioned without reference to justice, rights, and morality—understood within the liberal framework of a secular concept of Natural Law or Universal Reason[3]—are bound to fall short of their goals, if not to fail altogether in the long run. For "idealists" there is no disjunction between the "interests of state" properly understood and the moral law, and only the moral law—and not mere mundane, empirical values—may properly serve as the ground for action. As Kant wrote in his *Groundwork for a Metaphysic of Morals*:

> Everything that is empirical is, as a contribution to the principle of morality, not only wholly unsuitable for the purpose, but ... even highly injurious to the purity of morals. ... Against the slack, or indeed ignoble, attitude which seeks for the moral principle among empirical motives and laws we cannot give a warning too strongly or too often; for human reason in its weariness is fain to rest upon this pillow and in a dream of sweet illusions (which lead it to embrace a cloud in mistake for Juno) to foist into the place of morality some misbegotten mongrel patched up from limbs of very varied ancestry and looking like anything you please, only not like virtue, to him who has once beheld her in her true shape.[4]

When I say that the principle of legitimacy defines the most essential distinction among political systems, I mean to suggest (1) that some of the expectations which we have of legitimate systems (e.g., respect for human rights, behavior in accordance with the rule of law) are not apt to be fulfilled under illegitimate systems, (2) that legitimate systems are apt to be more stable and better equipped to weather economic travails and political storms than illegitimate ones, as well as to generate constitutional systems which pass the test of time, and (3) that illegitimate systems are apt to remain chronically in a state of crisis, generating crisis almost as a source of nutrition and being, at the same time, incapable of moving beyond crisis. The reason both the Kingdom of Yugoslavia and Communist-era Yugoslavia were perennially in a state of crisis was that they were, at base, illegitimate. This is not to say that every last institution in either incarnation of Yugoslavia was illegitimate or without merit, but, rather, to suggest that the fundamentals of state (the mode of selection of leaders, the division of power, political succession, and the very justification of the state itself) were in dispute.[5]

In the Yugoslav case, the evolution from a system deficient in sound legitimating principles to a situation in which one republic began to push the entire system in the direction of chauvinistic nationalism and centralized control, much against the wishes of large numbers of people, was tied not merely to the psychological receptivity of Serbs under the spell of their *traumatic nationalism*,[6] or even to the actions of willing collaborators, but, in a central way, to the role of Milošević and his coterie as "enablers." This was already discussed in Chapters 1–3. What should be emphasized here is that in choosing to jettison the Titoist approach (together with its sundry shibboleths, such as "Every nationalism is dangerous" and "Religion is the private affair of the individual"), Milošević and his coterie set Serbia on a course from which it would be difficult to veer. Milošević built his power on a foundation of hatred and xenophobia; in the process, hatred of non-Serbs was inflamed, fanned, and justified, proliferating throughout Serbian society with damaging effects. It should be emphasized that Milošević and his collaborators did not invent or create the hatreds in the region, most of which could be traced as far back as 1918 (some Serb-Albanian hatreds can be traced back at least to the late nineteenth century), but they aggravated those hatreds and, in the course of providing new "reasons" for hatred, made it immeasurably more difficult to restore the *modus vivendi* which had been tenuously achieved in the late Tito era.

The Psychology of Slobodan Milošević

Slobodan Milošević was born in 1941 in Požarevac, Serbia. World War II continued to rage during the critical first four years of his life when, as psychologists agree, a child is most in need of domestic stability and parental attention.[7] He was reared with tales of Serbian warrior mythology and exposed to the staunch religiosity of his father,[8] which he rejected, becoming involved in Communist party activities in 1959 (at age eighteen, thus), while he was still in high school. Family life in his childhood has been described as troubled and intermittently stormy,[9] and, as a youngster, Slobodan was withdrawn and showed no interest in sports and other pursuits which engaged other youngsters, though in the course of rejecting these activities, he may have come to feel rejected himself.[10] As John Bowlsby notes, such withdrawal most commonly reflects deprivation of adequate parental love and attention; Bowlsby adds, however, that in a later stage of this syndrome such children and adolescents are apt to be "quiet, obedient, easy to manage, well-mannered and orderly, and physically healthy."[11] This description is confirmed in regard to Milošević's adulthood by a long-time neighbor of his, who reports that Milošević was "very polite to everyone, very quiet, and introverted," always trimly and conservatively dressed and, by all accounts, certainly *orderly*; "he made an excellent impression."[12]

Indeed, Milošević has always been concerned about the impression he makes on others. Obrad Kesić recounts an incident in the mid-1980s, in which the strictly monogamous Milošević, having listened to the repeated boasts of his peers about having mistresses, asked to borrow the key to his friend Stambolić's private apartment (not having such an apartment himself), pretending to need the privacy for a romantic liaison. Unfortunately for Milošević, Stambolić and Pavlović were so curious that they spied on him and discovered that he had no other business at the apartment than to read the day's *Politika*; the entire "affair" was a ruse. The next day, pretending not to have seen anything, they asked him how it was; he is said to have replied, "It was great. I was crazy with lust."[13] Milošević, conservative in his personal life, was concerned nonetheless to look "hip" in the eyes of his peers.

Milošević's biography shares some points in common with the biographies of other dictators and extreme nationalists. Like fellow dictators Hitler, Stalin, Napoleon, Franco, and Tito and like fellow nationalists Josua Frank and Corneliu Zelea Codreanu, Milošević was a man from the borderland—his parents having migrated to Serbia from Montenegro.[14] Like Hitler and Stalin, he had to endure the premature death of his father; indeed, both of Milošević's parents committed suicide (his father in 1962, when Slobodan turned twenty-one; his mother a decade later). Although Milošević was already a young adult when he lost his father, Alan Sugarman reports that "fatherless boys ... have been reported initially to be less aggressive and more feminine after the loss of the father and then to overcompensate for this initial passivity during latency."[15] Milošević also shares with Hitler and Stalin an early exposure to historical mythology or sharply defined religious orthodoxy (indeed, both in Milošević's case, his father, Svetozar, having studied theology.)[16]

Slavoljub Djukić recounts that Milošević's childhood was unhappy,[17] and without question the suicides of both of his parents can only have been deeply unnerving and distressing for Milošević. Anthony Storr confirms that there is an organic connection between depression and aggression,[18] and the tendency toward aggression would only have been amplified if Milošević also nurtured some vague and indefinable guilt after these suicides. According to various observers, Milošević had developed a number of unresolved complexes in the course of his difficult childhood, adolescence, and young adulthood. Belgrade psychiatrist Stevan Petrović has said that Milošević is "narcissistic [and] has no capacity to feel guilt,"[19] which is to say that Milošević is clinically psychopathic. According to Kesić, Milošević suffers from an "inferiority complex" and is a "pathological liar."[20] Or again, although Branka Magaš describes Milošević (as of December 1987) as "the country's leading neo-Stalinist," crediting him (in October 1989) with having resurrected "the cult of [the] personality,"[21] David Lord Owen, who had considerable occasion to meet with Milošević during the four years of the war in Bosnia, comments tellingly that Milošević "gives vent to a paranoia about the international community in public almost as an obligatory jibe, but even so not to an excessive degree."[22] Lord Owen's supposition that a certain degree of paranoia might be "obligatory" in Serbia may be interpreted as a Freudian slip, revealing his contemptuous attitude about the Serbian public; if one discounts the notion that paranoia is "obligatory" there or anywhere else, but on the contrary is highly irresponsible, we are left with the question as to why an unparanoid person would expostulate paranoid theses. The answer would seem to be that appeals to paranoia are more likely to be issued by persons with at least some inclination toward paranoia; that Milošević may have developed some paranoid proclivities after such turbulent years would, indeed, not be surprising.

In the context of explicating "paranoid hostility," Storr writes that "aggression turns to hatred when it comes to contain an admixture of revenge; and the tendency to persecute those who are already defeated [e.g., the Albanians of Kosovo throughout the 1990s], or who are obviously weaker than the aggressor, can only be explained by the latter's need to revenge himself for past humiliations."[23] Milošević's propaganda machine began as early as the end of the 1980s (i.e., well before the outbreak of the Serbian Insurrectionary War in the first half of 1991) to portray the Vatican, Germany, Croats, Muslims, Hungarians, Albanians, and miscellaneous other foreign powers as bent on the destruction of Serbia, vowing, at the six-hundredth-anniversary commemoration of the 1389 Battle of Kosovo, "We shall win despite the fact that Serbia's enemies outside the country are plotting against it, along with those in the country."[24] For the leader of one of the constituent republics of a country supposedly at peace to make so belligerent a statement and to amplify it by warning that it might soon be necessary to take up arms again is suspiciously suggestive of paranoid schizophrenia with aggressive overtones. Indeed, as Storr reports,

> Paranoid schizophrenia is not infrequently ushered in by phantasies or dreams that the whole world is about to be destroyed, an illusion which reflects the subject's own intense hostility to a world which he feels has rejected him.... Paranoid schizophrenics ... conceive themselves to be extremely important.[25]

But Storr, noting that psychopathic personality disorders may usually be traced to lack of parental affection,[26] describes psychopaths as "not insane, ... but ... inclined, to a far greater extent than is customary ... to confuse their own imaginations with reality" and as "egotistical, selfish and impulsive" and often characterized by "an incredible lack of foresight."[27]

My purpose here is not to prove or even to argue that Milošević suffers from psychopathic paranoia, but rather to present the evidence that the Serbian leader is suffering from an acute personality disorder and to suggest that, both in the history of his early years and in his statements and actions in mature adulthood, Milošević displays symptoms characteristic of paranoid schizophrenia and psychopathic hostility. It is worth remembering that paranoid personalities, even when fomenting violence themselves, tend to ascribe hostile intentions to others, to identify aggressive plans where there are none, to interpret all incoming data as "proof" of the irrational "hostile" intentions of outsiders and domestic traitors alike, and to dream forever of resistance and revenge.[28]

That a politician suffering from acute personality disorders may not be the ideal person to manage a state's transition from the illegitimate politics of "self-managing socialism" to the legitimate politics of a liberal state should be clear enough.

Kosovo Under Serbian Rule, 1918–1945

After the defeat of the Turkish army at the gates of Vienna in 1683, Austria carried the war into Ottoman territory, pushing deep into the Balkans in 1689; with the encouragement of the Orthodox Patriarch of Peć, Arsenije III Čarnojević, many Serbs joined Austrian ranks. But Turkish forces rallied and, the following year, drove the Austrian army back. Many Serbs fled with the Austrians, led by Arsenije III himself, obtaining safe refuge in Austrian-controlled Bačka (today's Vojvodina). Temperley claims that more than 30,000 Serbian families took part in this great northward migration.[29] The Serbian migration emptied entire villages in Kosovo, opening them up to Albanian immigration. Thus began a fresh series of Albanian migrations into Kosovo that would continue into the 1840s,[30] although some Albanians had come earlier.[31] As Bohumil Hrabak has noted, tensions between Kosovo's Albanian and Serbian residents remained high in the latter half of the nineteenth century and early years of the twentieth century. Local Serbs complained of violent confiscations of their land and of the plundering of their churches. Between 1877 and 1912, about 150,000 Serbs fled the area, 55,000 of them from Peć alone.[32] M. Vuić, Minister of Foreign Affairs of the Kingdom of Serbia, complained in a demarché to the Sublime Porte in 1903 that

> respect for the authorities is diminishing all the time, while the unruliness of Albanians is constantly increasing.... Because of this, the situation of Serbs in old Serbia [Kosovo] has become intolerable to the point of being unbearable. Their properties, honour and life are not protected any longer: properties are seized and plundered, honour is stained, women and girls are raped and people lose their lives not only to satisfy the whim of a bully or ruffian, but according to plan ... [33]

When the First Balkan War broke out in 1912, the Serbian army encountered essentially no resistance, reaching the outskirts of Prizren on 31 October. By the end of the month, the Serbian conquest of Kosovo was complete. The Great Powers (Britain, France, Germany, Austria-Hungary, Italy, and Russia) convened a conference in London in December 1912 to discuss the territorial changes in the Balkans. Austria-Hungary pressed for the inclusion of all Albanian-inhabited lands in the emergent Albanian state—which would have entailed the withdrawal of Serbian forces from Kosovo, where Albanians already outnumbered Serbs—but Britain, France, and Russia were more favorably disposed toward Serbia. Kosovo and part of Metohija were, accordingly, recognized as parts of Serbia, while Montenegro (toward whom Russia felt favorably disposed) received Peć, Djakovica, and Istok.[34]

At the end of World War I, Belgrade sent troops to Kosovo, which was in turmoil. The anti-Yugoslav resistance of local Albanians failed, and in January-February 1919 alone the Serbian army killed some 6,040 persons in Kosovo and destroyed 3,873 homes, according to statistics originally published in Italy.[35] Altogether, more than 12,000 Kosovar Albanians were killed by Serbian forces between 1918 and 1921, when pacification was more or less completed.[36] The Albanians of Kosovo remained unreconciled to their fate. As early as 1919, a Kosovo Committee was set up in Albania to work for the annexation of the province by Albania. According to Branko Petranović, the Kosovo Committee reached an agreement in 1920 with the Bulgarian terrorist organization IMRO (which the contemporary Macedonian political party IMRO-DPMNU claims as its symbolic predecessor and progenitor) on joint "anti-Yugoslav" activities, and in January 1924 Aleksandar Protogerov (on behalf of IMRO) and Albanian representatives agreed to launch a coordinated uprising in March 1924 in Kosovo and Macedonia, both regions having been incorporated into the Kingdom of Serbs, Croats, and Slovenes.[37] Meanwhile, the Belgrade government set a course of "denationalization" of the region, forbidding schools and publications using the Albanian language.[38] In fact, Yugoslav authorities had pledged to provide primary education in the local language in minority areas and to permit communities to establish private schools, at their own expense, with language of instruction as they chose; this pledge had been incorporated into the Treaty for the Protection of Minorities (signed in 1919).[39] As of 1930, however, there were no Albanian-language schools in all of Kosovo, except for a few operating on an underground basis, even though there may have been some 800,000 Albanians in the Yugoslav kingdom, most of them in Kosovo, according to the 1931 estimate of a Romanian demographer.[40]

The interwar Yugoslav authorities undertook a colonization program, seizing land from local Albanians and turning it over to Serbian colonists. Von Kohl and Libal claim that some 45,000 Albanians left Kosovo during the years 1918–1941 as a result of Serbian pressure, estimating the Albanian population in Kosovo as 700,000 as of 1940. They claim that the colonization program brought about 60,000 Serb colonists to Kosovo.[41] Altogether, Belgrade authorities confiscated at least 47,044 hectares of arable land from Kosovar Albanians, that being the lowest estimate I have found.[42] There were also serious discussions between 1933 and 1938 between the Yugoslav and Turkish governments concerning the possible deportation of large numbers of Albanians to Turkey. An agreement was signed finally on 11 July 1938 involving the forced transfer of 40,000 Albanian families to Turkey during the years 1939–1944, but the outbreak of World War II prevented this plan from being put into action.[43]

The legacy of the interwar era was, thus, bitter, as was its harvest. During World War II, Kosovo was divided into three occupation zones, but the largest of these was the Italian zone, conjoined with Italian-occupied Albania. The Albanians of Kosovo were gratified by the transfer of jurisdiction and found Italian occupation less harsh, in terms of culture, education, and language use, than rule by Belgrade. Now the "colonization" program was reversed, as Albanians let out their fury against Serbs, setting houses on fire and killing local Serbs. During the years 1941–1944, about 100,000 persons are said to have fled Kosovo, most of them Serbs, including from Kosovska Mitrovica, Vučitrn, and Podujevo.[44] Some of these refugees joined the Communist Partisans; others enlisted in Mihailović's Serb-nationalist Chetnik movement. As the tide turned against the Axis, the Yugoslav and Albanian Partisans discussed postwar territorial arrangements. The CC of the Communist Party of Albania exerted pressure on the CPY, beginning in autumn 1943, to agree to the post-war assignment of Kosovo and Metohija to Albania; the CPY leaders, however, were firmly opposed to any changes in the Yugoslav-Albanian border and were, at most, willing to concede Kosovo to Albania on the condition that Albania join Yugoslavia as its seventh constituent republic.[45] Then, in December 1944, "an armed uprising of massive proportions broke out in Kosovo ..., which led ... to difficult struggles and to military excesses on the part of the 'Ballist' [Albanian anticommunist] forces in mid-February 1945," according to Petranović.[46] Units of the Yugoslav (Partisan) army smashed the main body of the Balli Kombëtar resistance during January–February 1945, but smaller Ballist units held out for a while in the highlands of Montenegro, around Drenica, in Žegarac, and in Ćećevica. The last remnants of Ballist resistance were not liquidated until 1951–1952.[47]

The Communist Era, 1945–1987

By comparison with the interwar regime, Yugoslav *cultural* policy after World War II was relatively generous toward ethnic minorities (Albanians, Bulgarians, Hungarians, Romanians, Ruthenes, Slovaks, and Turks), for whom 1,012 elementary schools and 124 middle schools in minority languages were provided as early as the 1947–1948 academic year.[48] Kosovo was given autonomous status as a "region" *(oblast)* within the Republic of Serbia and was elevated to an "autonomous *province*" *(autonomna pokrajina)* in 1963, though still within the Republic of Serbia. But demands registered by loyal Albanian Communists in the province for elevation of Kosovo's status to republic level, on a par with Serbia, Croatia, Slovenia, and the others, were turned down with the nominalist and self-serving argument that only "peoples" could have republics, while mere "nationalities" were not entitled to republics.[49] Why this should have been so was never adequately explained.

Since the incorporation of Kosovo was not recognized as legitimate by the majority of its population, the CPY decided on an "iron glove" approach. On the orders of Aleksandar Ranković, Yugoslav Minister of the Interior from 1945 to 1966, security police conducted house searches looking for weaponry during the 1950s and terrorized the local Albanian population. Shkëlzen Maliqi reports that Yugoslav police tortured some 60,000 Albanians during house searches during 1956, for example.[50] Since the Albanians had not been met "halfway" (which would have entailed a grant of republic status), it was deemed necessary to entrust its administration to a largely Serbian cadre. Some of those Albanians who did try to work within the system were put on trial in July 1956, in Prizren, on charges of collaboration with the Sigurimi, the secret police of the Republic of Albania, and of espionage for Albania. Although heavy sentences were handed down at the Prizren Trial, twelve years later, on the basis of conclusions of the provincial Assembly, the provincial Executive Council of Kosovo and Metohija reported, on 9 February 1968, that the Prizren Trial had been "orchestrated and counterfeit."[51] Meanwhile, Albanians were organizing resistance. Here one may mention the Revolutionary Movement for Union with Albania, established by Adem Demaqi, which armed itself, distributed irredentist pamphlets among the local population, and is said to have engaged in acts of sabotage. The movement was uncovered by police in 1964, at which time it was said to have about 300 members.[52]

By the early 1960s, there was increasing opposition to the hard-line policies being carried out in Tito's name by Ranković, not only within Kosovo itself but also within Slovenia and Croatia. Vladimir Bakarić, the Croatian party secretary at the time, wanted a general reform of the political system to include a reorganization of the party, and by late April 1966 Tito seems to have been persuaded by Bakarić—as signaled by Tito's announcement that the next plenary session of the CC would devote its attention to "cadres policy" (which lay within Ranković's domain).[53] Just over two months later, Ranković was forced to resign and, on a motion by Veljko Vlahović, the party appointed Mijalko Todorović, the incoming secretary of the CC, to head up a large, new commission charged with making recommendations for radical changes in the LCY's organization.

With change in the air, the Albanians of Kosovo pressed their case, lodging once again their demand for an improved status. Dobrica Ćosić and Jovan Marjanović, prominent Serbian Communists, raised their voices against what they called "autonomist tendencies." But the wind had shifted and such criticism was no longer welcome: at the Fourteenth Session of the CC of the LC-Serbia, Ćosić and Marjanović were expelled from the party. With Kosovo's rate of economic development lagging behind rates in other parts of Yugoslavia and the continued denial of republic status, and in spite of certain small concessions (including the expulsions of Ćosić and Marjanović and the exoneration of those convicted in the Prizren Trial), Albanians crossed the threshold of tolerance in late 1968. Specifically, on 27 November 1968, demonstrations broke out across Kosovo, as demonstrators shouted slogans in praise of Enver Hoxha and the People's Republic of Albania. Significantly, they also shouted against "Serbian oppressors." Some demonstrators again raised the demand for republic status within the Yugoslav federation.[54] The demonstrations continued the next day, by which time columns of tanks and army units were moving into Priština.

In the wake of these demonstrations, various concessions were made to the Albanians. Some of them, such as redesignating the autonomous province a *socialist* autonomous province and allowing locals to fly the Albanian flag beneath the Yugoslav flag, were purely symbolic. Others involved real substance, such as the decision to allow Albanians to take control of the party apparatus in Kosovo and the establishment of a University of Priština, with Albanian as the language of instruction. Steps were also taken to upgrade the effective political clout of the two autonomous provinces within federal bodies.[55] Meanwhile, even as Albanians made gains in official organs, there were confirmed reports that underground irredentist organizations were being set up in Priština, Podujevo, Titova Mitrovica, Peć, Djakovica, Prizren, and Gnjilane. One of the key figures in these underground activities was Adem Demaqi, who spent many years in prison as a result of these activities and who, in summer 1998, would become the political representative of the Kosovo Liberation Army (KLA).[56]

Meanwhile, the migration of Serbs and Montenegrins from Kosovo had resumed after the dismissal of Ranković. Between 1968 and 1971 alone, some 15,000 Serbs left Kosovo according to Branka Magaš; another 30,000 left between 1971 and 1981.[57] In late February 1969, authorities in Priština took up the question, highlighting that there had been "numerous chauvinistic and hostile attacks" on local Serbs.[58] Moreover, increasingly statistics were cited to support a case that "reverse discrimination" was now being practiced—against Serbs and Montenegrins. For example, whereas Serbs and Montenegrins accounted for 19.9 percent of newly hired workers in 1976, they accounted for only 1.3 percent of the newly hired in 1982, according to Miloš Mišović.[59] There were also reports of the vandalization of Serbian and Montenegrin graves in Kosovo at the time.

The irony was that the sharp increase in hostile underground activity on the part of local Albanians coincided with significant gains for the Albanians in the fields of political administration, cadres policy in the security forces, employment in the social sector, education, and media. But few in Belgrade noticed the rising anger of Kosovo's Serbs at the time.

In fact, neither the Albanians nor the Serbs were content with the situation in the province in the late Tito era. On the Albanian side, there was deep resentment of the fact that, in spite of a steady flow of party rhetoric in favor of bringing the province's standard of living and economic indicators closer to the Yugoslav average, economic data revealed that the province was steadily sinking lower and lower by comparison with the overall Yugoslav average.[60] Nor had the legacy of interethnic bitterness been erased. On 11 March 1981, there were riots at the student cafeteria of the University of Priština. After these riots, local authorities decided to detain potential "troublemakers" until celebrations of Tito's official birthday (23 March) were behind them. This action provoked protests on Priština's streets on 23 March, which set the stage for province-wide unrest by 2 April. On 3 April, martial law was proclaimed in the province; it was lifted two months later, but the security reinforcements remained.

By July 1983, some 55 illegal groups had been uncovered by the authorities.[61] The Albanians were once more on the defensive, and in the ensuing dragnet some 700 persons were arrested between April 1981 and September 1982. Of this number, some 320 were tried in district courts.[62] Prominent Albanians were now dismissed from positions in the provincial party apparatus, the university, and the media. Even Mahmut Bakalli was forced to resign his post as provincial party secretary. But the out-migration of Serbs and Montenegrins continued, amid complaints that "hostile activity" on the part of local Albanians was continuing.[63] There were repeated protests and petitions from Kosovar Serbs and those sympathetic to their complaints. One such protest came in January 1986 when a petition was presented to the Yugoslav and Serbian assemblies signed by 200 prominent Belgrade intellectuals including Ljubomir Tadić, Zagorka Golubović-Pešić, and Mihailo Marković. The petition charged no less than that the Albanians of Kosovo, through actions ranging from physical attacks to rape, were perpetrating "genocide" against the Serbian population of Kosovo. The petition charged, in part,

> Everyone in this country who is not indifferent has long ago realized that the genocide in Kosovo cannot be combated without deep social changes in the whole country. These changes are unimaginable without changes likewise in the relationship between the Autonomous Province and the Republic of Serbia ... Genocide cannot be prevented by the ... gradual surrender of Kosovo and Metohija to Albania [—] the unsigned capitulation which leads to a politics of national treason.[64]

Demands for a dissolution of Kosovo's limited autonomy had been raised by Serbs ever since the concessions of 1968. But they were now pressed with increasing urgency and force.

Meanwhile, there were recurrent charges that local Albanians were raping Serbian women—charges which inflamed the Serbian public, though they were steadfastly denied by Albanians. In 1987, a weeping Serbian woman appeared on Belgrade television and was barely able to tell her story through the tears and sobs. Her appearance on television electrified Serbian society, leaving Serbs stunned and outraged that such a thing could have happened. In 1990, nonetheless, an independent committee of Serbian lawyers and human-rights activists undertook a serious study of the incidence of rape, reviewing the statistics for the 1980s, and found that while the incidence of rape in inner Serbia was 2.43 cases per year for every 10,000 men, in Kosovo it was only 0.96, and of these, 71 percent involved assailant and victim of the same nationality.[65] But in politics, as is well known, it is beliefs, rather than facts, which often determine the course of events.

The sexual edge was sharpened as Serbs compared Albanian birthrates with their own birthrates. In 1994, the birthrate in central Serbia was, for example, −2.94, while the overall birthrate in Kosovo was +17.38. Žarana Papić cites an article in *Politika*, according to which "the causes of the lower birthrate among Serbs and the higher birthrate among Albanians are not social, economic, or historical but ideological, political, and naturalistic. Thus, according to this interpretation, Albanians have many children not because of the strong rural/patriarchal system and economic underdevelopment (97 percent of Albanian women are unemployed), but because it is the long-term political strategy of Albanians to outgrow the Serbian nation."[66] Although it would be unprecedented in the history of humankind for couples in a given community to adjust their sexual habits to fit some overarching politically inspired conspiracy, shouldering the burden of large numbers of children as part of an irredentist scheme, the image of the fast-growing Albanian community took hold in the Serbian collective consciousness.

Meanwhile, the migration of Serbs and Montenegrins from the province continued, with migrants reciting a litany of abuse to which they said they had been subjected by Kosovo's Albanians. Increasingly, the idea took hold among Serbs that things in Kosovo had to be "set right."[67] But during the years 1981–1987, federal authorities tried to hold the line against any constitutional change in Kosovo, branding every nationalism as "dangerous," characterizing all autonomist strivings as de facto "irredentist," and accusing Albanian activists in Kosovo of seeking to create an ethnically "pure" Kosovo.[68]

A Decade of Grief, 1988–1997

The suppression of the autonomy of the autonomous provinces was a high priority in Milošević's program and was closely connected with his bid to become champion and leader of the Serbian *nation*, as opposed to just the Serbian *republic*. In 1988, Milošević orchestrated the resignation of the province's two top leaders, Azem Vllasi and Kaqusha Jashari; in 1989, he compelled the provincial Assembly to approve amendments severely reducing the province's autonomy; in 1990, he ordered the suppression of the provincial Assembly and the province's Executive Council and obtained passage, by the Serbian Assembly, of a new constitution for the Republic of Serbia, which effectively snuffed out the last vestiges of the province's once considerable autonomy; and that same year, Albanian-language instruction from elementary school to university level was terminated, inaugurating a crisis in education that has not been resolved even at this writing. In 1991, on 16 October, the Serbian parliament declared the abolition of the Academy of Sciences of Kosovo in response to an underground referendum conducted by the Albanians two weeks earlier. In 1992, Albanian street names in Priština were changed to Serbian ones, and when, in May of that year, Albanians of Kosovo organized province-wide elections and elected Ibrahim Rugova, a Shakespeare scholar and president of the Democratic League of Kosovë, president of "the Republic of Kosovo," Milošević declared the elections illegal and refused to recognize Rugova's standing.

During these years, Albanians were fired from their jobs and replaced by Serbs sometimes brought to the province from outside (under the regime's "resettlement" program). The student body at the University of Priština was "trimmed" and Serbian students were encouraged to enroll there; many faculty members were fired and their places given to Serbs. Human-rights monitors reported beatings and police interrogation under torture.[69] During the first half of the 1990s, thousands of Kosovar Albanians fled abroad; according to *Delo*, the Slovenian newspaper, about 25,000 Albanians fled to Italy from Kosovo between November 1994 and mid-January 1995 alone.[70] Even though some Serbian and Montenegrin "settlers" who came to Kosovo on the strength of promises of good living conditions and high pay were dissatisfied with what they encountered in the province, local political activist Kosta Bulatović and other Kosovar Serbs demanded that the Serbian "resettlement" program be accelerated.[71] In response, the Belgrade government, having confiscated land from local Albanians, reiterated the offer of free land to Serbs willing to move to Kosovo. Local police of Albanian nationality were dismissed and brought to trial on trumped-up charges, with confessions extracted under torture.[72] Meanwhile, the political parties of Kosovo, which had formed in connection with the breakdown of the Communist system in Yugoslavia, held to a fixed policy of boycotting Serbian elections. The result was that in the federal elections of 1996, the ruling Socialist Party won twelve of Kosovo's thirteen mandates in the Chamber of Citizens; the remaining seat was won by Vojislav Šešelj's Serbian Radical Party.[73]

The Albanian Uprising of 1998

Through all of this, the Albanians of Kosovo declined to take to arms, despite their growing outrage both at the Belgrade government and at an international community, which ignored their plight. But for the time being, they preferred to follow Rugova's Gandhian counsel to follow passive resistance, supporting his government with voluntary tax payments. In late 1995, Rugova pleaded with Western states to keep sanctions against Belgrade in place until the problems in Kosovo could be resolved; the West ignored Rugova's pleas and lifted the sanctions even as Milošević continued his brutal policies against the Albanians. In this context, divisions were growing within the Albanian community during 1996 and 1997; there was disappointment over the failure of the Dayton Peace Accords to make any provision for Kosovo, driving some Albanians into the ranks of those leaders favoring a more militant strategy. By mid-1997, reports were circulating about the existence of a Kosovo Liberation Army, said to have numbered about 100 fighters at the time.[74] Although negotiations between Belgrade authorities and representatives of Kosovo's Albanian community concerning the return of Albanian schoolchildren to the public schools continued, distrust between the two communities remained high.

On 4 December 1997, the KLA perpetrated a series of terrorist actions, attacking Serbian police and police stations, and were said to have killed two police, according to the Belgrade news agency Beta.[75] Throughout the latter half of 1997, small arms smuggling across the border with Albania changed Albanians' estimation of their relative strength,[76] and in early 1998, the KLA, whose very existence had been in doubt only a few months before, declared an insurrection. By this point, according to the BBC, KLA rebels were obtaining antitank weapons from China and sophisticated missile launchers from sources in Germany.[77] As late as March 1998, there were probably only a few hundred Albanian KLA guerrillas in the hills of Kosovo, but by July the KLA's ranks had swollen to several thousand.[78] Security forces were initially unable to cope with the resistance, which, by the latter half of July 1998, controlled about 40 percent of the province's countryside including some key towns.[79] As of mid-June, the Serbian authorities had lost control of the province's main east-west artery (connecting Priština to Peć) as well as a northern route between Kosovska Mitrovica and Peć.

The uprising threatened to undermine Ibrahim Rugova, who continued to insist on pacifism and negotiation. But a meeting between Rugova and FRY President Milošević on 15 May failed to produce any concrete results.[80] In the meantime, in spite of the reimposition by the international community of a weapons embargo against Belgrade in early March, Belgrade sent military reinforcements to Kosovo in mid-April.[81] The imposition of new economic sanctions by the EU and the United States on 9 June only enraged Belgrade officials, who denounced the declaration of sanctions as a "strange and unreasonable decision."[82]

The first week of June 1998 saw a significant escalation of violence in Kosovo, as columns of Serbian tanks entered the province and helicopter gunships were used to attack Albanian villages. By then, according to the British newspaper *The Guardian*, there were already 100,000 Albanian refugees.[83] About this time, the Albanian government claimed that there had been several incursions into sovereign territory of the Republic of Albania by Serb commando teams scouting the area, though there was no independent confirmation.[84] But Tirana's accusations contributed to sharpening the mood in Western capitals. As the fighting escalated, British Foreign Secretary Robin Cook (of the new Labour Government), speaking on behalf of the European Council of Ministers, issued a threat on 8 June: "I hope Milošević is listening this time—this is his last warning. He should back off now."[85] Javier Solana Madariaga, NATO's Secretary-General, issued a similar warning in Rome: "On Kosovo, let me be quite clear that NATO will not stand idly by. We will not allow a repeat of the situation in Bosnia in 1991."[86] In fact, NATO strategists were tasked, about this time, to prepare plans for a joint air-land operation in Kosovo that would force Serbian security and army forces to withdraw and impose an autonomous government, desired neither by the Serbian side nor by the Albanian side, on Kosovo.[87] At this point, however, Moscow entered its own views, insisting that any NATO operation in Kosovo would have to be approved by both the U.N. Security Council and the Belgrade government itself. Russian President Boris Yeltsin met with German Chancellor Helmut Kohl in Bonn on 9 June, on which occasion the Russian president offered to meet with President Milošević. Yeltsin did, in fact, meet with Milošević on 16 June, but Milošević refused to withdraw his forces from Kosovo, offering only to negotiate further with Rugova, to allow diplomats and representatives of international organizations (but not journalists) access to the province, and to allow refugees to return to their homes.[88] But by 11 June, NATO officials were backing away from earlier threats, distancing themselves from the tough "last warning" rhetoric of Robin Cook, and emphasizing the need to find a diplomatic solution.

But as of the end of June, Belgrade had deployed some 50,000 special police and army troops in Kosovo and was said to be spending U.S. $2 million per day to keep its forces at this strength.[89] On 29 June, Serbian forces in Kosovo launched a series of attacks on insurgent positions, thereby initiating a counteroffensive that quickly showed just how underarmed and overconfident the KLA had been. The Albanian resistance lost battle after battle, and by mid-September 1998 there were more than 700 dead and more than 265,000 homeless.[90]

Although there were no large-scale demonstrations on Belgrade's streets to match those of late 1996 and early 1997 (in protest of Milošević's effort to deny electoral victories in various municipal elections to opposition parties), there were signs that some Serbs were becoming critical of their government. In May 1998, for example, Belgrade authorities withdrew radio frequency authorization from thirty private Serbian radio and television stations that had been critical of the government; this move was tantamount to the closure of twenty independent radio stations and ten independent television stations, though Nenad Čekić, the director of Radio Index, a Belgrade ratio station critical of the Milošević government, announced that his station planned to continue to broadcast without a license.[91] At the beginning of June, some

100 Serbian police were dismissed for refusing to be transferred to Kosovo, and there were reports of desertions by young Yugoslav army recruits in Kosovo as well.[92] In fact, according to a German newspaper, by mid-June 1998 more than 600 Serbian police had refused to be transferred to Kosovo, mostly police from Belgrade; in the first half of June, moreover, more than 100 officials in the government were fired, while others had resigned earlier of their own accord.[93]

But most Serbs, far from becoming outraged at the atrocities being carried out in their name, were, on the contrary, enraged at the casualties that Serbs were suffering in this uprising. Quite apart from the targeting of Serbian police and security forces, Albanian rebels were, in fact, responsible for a "wave" of kidnappings and terror against local Serbs, according to the *New York Times*, and by the end of August 1998 more than eighty Serbian civilians were reported missing and presumed dead.[94] This, in turn, drove some Kosovar Serbs to take flight from the province. Albanians were also said to have begun abducting Serbs from rural villages, rural roads, and isolated farms as early as April and to have demolished Serbian homes, for example, in the village of Leucina.[95] In August, the Serbian press ran reports of KLA atrocities said to have been committed against Serbian civilians.[96] On 31 August, Serbian women staged a protest outside the U.S. Information Center in Priština, hurling stones at the facility. Some 200 women took part in the protest, demanding that the United States take steps to help locate certain Serbs who they believed had been kidnapped by the KLA separatists.[97] Then, in September, FRY authorities discovered the bodies of thirty-four Serbs in a canal in central Kosovo and reported that they had been tortured and shot by the KLA.[98]

The Serbian media disputed Albanian claims as to the number of refugees (Western press estimates stood at 250,000–265,000 as of mid-September, while Albanian sources estimated 400,000 refugees). The Belgrade weekly magazine *NIN* rejected these figures, however, suggesting that about 140,000 persons had been displaced from their homes and that, as of early September, "only" about 20,000 Albanians were camped in the woods under the open sky.[99] The Serbian media "accused Western journalists of fabricating stories about massacres of Albanians and looting in Kosovo by Serbian security forces"[100] and emphasized what the KLA openly declared, that it was fighting for an independent Kosovo, which might conjoin itself to Albania.

In this context, it is perhaps not surprising that the bulk of the forces deployed by the government in Kosovo remained both loyal and effective and, wielding overwhelming firepower, continued to score one victory after another against KLA rebels, taking the key KLA stronghold of Junik in mid-August. With their scorch-and-burn policy, Serbian forces threatened to create as many as twenty-five ghost towns in Kosovo's southwest alone, according to Fernando del Mundo, a U.N. refugee official.[101] As of late August 1998, the KLA, with Adem Demaqi now serving as its political representative, was changing its tactics, abandoning its earlier endeavor to seize and hold fixed territory and opting for hit-and-run tactics. Until mid-September, most of the fighting had been confined to the southwestern portion of Kosovo. But on 16 September, Serbian forces bombarded twelve villages in the north of Kosovo, driving hundreds of locals to take flight.[102]

In early September, John Shattuck, U.S. Assistant Secretary of State for Democracy and Human Rights, visited Kosovo together with former Senator Robert Dole and reported afterward, "We have see horrendous human rights violations, violations of humanitarian law and acts of punitive destruction on a massive scale."[103] Kosovo was in a paroxysm of agony, weeping, and grieving, trying to avoid sliding into hopelessness. One may recall the words Aeschylus put into Clytaemestra's mouth in his immortal play *Agamemnon* twenty-five hundred years ago:

> *They are kneeling by the bodies of the dead,*
> *embracing men and brothers, infants over*
> *the aged loins that gave them life, and sobbing,*
> *as the yoke constricts their last free breath,*
> *for every dear one lost ...* [104]

By this point, American and European governments were becoming aware that those refugees who had fled to the woods and who were living in tents, without secure water sources, electricity, heating, or reliable food supplies, were at serious risk of contracting pneumonia and other illnesses in the course of the approaching winter.[105]

Milošević offered on 1 September to extend a "degree of self-rule" to Albanians in Kosovo,[106] but Albanians saw little reason to embrace this vague and limited offer. Meanwhile, Amnesty International published a report, *Kosovo: The Evidence*, noting that more Albanians than Serbs had died in Kosovo in the course of 1998 and, while accusing the KLA of "serious breaches of humanitarian law and the Geneva conventions"[107] in the execution of Serbian hostages, reported "Serb massacres in February and March ... left 80 Albanians dead in the Drenica area,"[108] with "executions" of 8 Albanians in nearby villages in May and some 200 Albanian casualties in the course of the Orahovac offensive. In mid-September, even as Serbian security forces attacked twelve villages between Kosovska Mitrovica and Podujevo, north of Priština, the NATO allies renewed their warning to Yugoslav President Milošević that they remained prepared to resort to military intervention unless Belgrade called a halt to its operations in Kosovo.[109] As more evidence of Serbian atrocities reached the media, the U.N. Security Council issued an ultimatum to President Milošević on 23 September. Speaking for the Western alliance, Foreign Secretary Cook declared, "There must now be a cease-fire and rapid progress on a political dialogue, which is the only route to a lasting solution to the humanitarian problem."[110]

Less than a week later, Prime Minister Mirko Marjanović announced that the Belgrade government's "anti-terrorist activities" in Kosovo had ended, asserting that they would be resumed only in the event of a resumption of "terrorist" actions in the province.[111] A day later, however, Western diplomats at the village of Gornje Obrinje saw the remains of fifteen Albanian civilians shot in the head. As the *International Herald Tribune* reported, "Two of the bodies had been decapitated. One woman was missing her foot. One elderly man had his throat cut, apparently with a kitchen knife that lay on his chest. A boy of less than 10 also had his throat slit."[112] Another fourteen Albanian civilians were found slaughtered in cold blood in another village.[113] Serbian police immediately issued a denial, but even if one believed their denial, there could be no doubt but that the murders had been committed by Serbs infected by the xenophobic nationalism being churned out by Belgrade's press and television.[114] These murders, which included young children (ten of the sixteen corpses at Gornje Obrinje were those of women, children, or old people), touched a nerve. Quite abruptly, NATO, which had been fulminating and issuing "last warnings" for months, readied its forces for a possible aerial attack against Serbian forces and installations.

Sensing correctly that, this time, the Western alliance meant business, Milošević ordered most of the army units deployed in Kosovo, though not the special security forces, to return to their barracks. At the same time, the Serbian Assembly appointed Zoran Andjeljković to head an eighteen-member Executive Council as a kind of surrogate Kosovo government. Local Albanians were unimpressed, and Edita Tahiri, a leading figure in Kosovo's Albanian community, dismissed the new council as an entirely illegitimate body.[115] As the United States, Britain, Australia, Japan, and other countries advised their citizens to leave or avoid traveling to the FRY, Russia and China continued to register their objection to the use of force against Serbia, though Russian Foreign Minister Igor Ivanov indicated on 12 October that a military response by Russia was "out of the question," but underlined that NATO air strikes would cause "international chaos."[116] Veteran negotiator Richard Holbrooke hurried to Belgrade for eleventh-hour negotiations with Milošević, describing his protracted discussions with the Serbian leader through the night of 11–12 October as "intense, indeed, and at times very heated."[117]

Then, on 13 October, Holbrooke emerged from yet another lengthy session with Milošević, having ignored the KLA altogether in his effort to bring the two sides "together," while engaging in only brief talks with Rugova,[118] to announce that the FRY president had agreed to commit to the cessation of military actions in the province, to grant Kosovo some form of autonomy, to hold "free and fair elections ... for the organs of authority of Kosovo," and to grant freedom of movement to some 2,000 "compliance verifiers" with diplomatic status. NATO set a ninety-six-hour deadline within which observable progress was supposed to be made.[119] Albanians in the region expressed deep bitterness that NATO had backed away from the moment of decision, and condemned the agreement as inadequate. Albanians camped in the woods of Kosovo vowed that they would stay in the woods rather than return to the villages where Serbian security forces could butcher them.[120] "The Americans have sold us out," said one refugee. "We don't get independence, air strikes, or NATO troops. All we get is more Serb brutality."[121] Elez Biberaj, a distinguished specialist in Albanian affairs based in Washington, D.C., described the fruit of Holbrooke's talks with Milošević as "a very bad agreement," noting that it gave the Albanians less than the Contact Group had been demanding for them in late 1997, before the uprising had begun. Biberaj also pointed out, on 13 October, that the KLA had not been crushed and predicted that a new uprising would be underway by spring 1999.[122]

The concept of autonomy under a repressive and illegitimate government—and, at that, not within the FRY, but within Serbia—suffers from a fundamental flaw. As I wrote in 1997:

> The right to resist tyranny is … grounded in a (Lockean) concept of individual rights.… [But] what autonomists seek is to negotiate a recognition of their aggregated individual rights from a state that does not recognize such rights at all. Or, to bring the argument down to practice, it requires that an outlaw state behave in a law-abiding (or right-abiding) manner vis-à-vis the autonomous zone.[123]

But the absurdity does not end there. On the contrary, U.S. mediation on behalf of *autonomy* for Kosovo's Albanians entailed, at some level, the postulate that Albanians enjoy a "right" to live within an autonomous zone within a tyrannical state. But note that the Albanians are to be denied the exercise of the right affirmed in the U.S. Declaration of Independence, that "when a long train of abuses and usurpations pursuing invariably the same Object evinces a design to reduce them under absolute Despotism, it is their right, it is their duty, to throw off such Government, and to provide new Guards for their future security." This is not, in the understanding of the British and American Enlightenment, a question of some sort of "right of national self-determination,"[124] but a question of certain "inalienable [human] rights." For the U.S. mediation team, it would appear that the Albanians of Kosovo not only do not enjoy a right to escape from despotism, but also do not have any such duty either. If, then, the rights and duties declared in one of the founding documents of the United States to be "universal" are held not to be valid in the case of Kosovo, one may fairly ask, is this because these "universal" human rights only apply to *some* people, or because the United States has forgotten or even repudiated its liberal principles altogether, or because the members of the negotiating team failed to see in the Albanians of Kosovo agents enjoying full human rights?

A Missed Opportunity

We may never know for sure whether the West backed down in 1998 because of Russian pressure,[125] because of uncertainties connected with Serbian stockpiles of chemical weapons and possibly also biological weapons,[126] because of confused thinking on matters of principle, or for some other reason. What is known is that a French army officer, Major Pierre Bunel, was arrested on 3 November 1998 on charges of having shared a twenty-five-page plan pertaining to possible NATO air strikes against the FRY with Belgrade.[127] Hence, when state-controlled Belgrade television broadcast patriotic messages in the first part of October, pledging that Serbia would resist an imminent NATO attack, it was not pure bravado. Milošević knew what NATO's contingency plans entailed.

The agreement negotiated by Holbrooke on 12 October called for Milošević to pull most of his forces out of Kosovo by 16 October (reducing their strength to the level prior to 28 February) or face aerial strikes. Remarkably, Milošević did not display any particular sense of urgency after the agreement, however, and on the next day (i.e., 13 October) Serbian tanks and artillery continued to fire on the village of Drenica, destroying dozens of Albanian-owned homes and shops.[128] Although NATO had assembled between 400 and 650 aircraft, mainly at bases in Italy, for possible use against Milošević and in spite of Milošević's dilatory tactics and continued attacks on Albanian villages, NATO decided on 16 October to extend Milošević's deadline until 27 October.[129] At least 144 Yugoslav tanks and other military vehicles were driving toward the provincial border with Serbia (i.e., ostensibly leaving the province) as of 16 October, signaling a degree of compliance on Belgrade's part.[130]

The KLA ordered its cadres to restrict themselves to purely defensive actions.[131] But although international observers reported that Serbian forces were continuing to launch attacks on KLA positions,[132] the Belgrade daily *Politika* wrote that "the Albanian fanatics do not want peace."[133] But reports differed and the situation on the ground was sometimes confused. As an example of this, a Croatian newspaper reported on 21 October that KLA forces had launched an attack against Serbian police in the province.[134] The British daily *The Independent* gave a different account, reporting that Serbian police and army had *reinforced* their positions around the village of Terpeza on 18 October and were firing on Terpeza and surrounding villages on 19 October.[135]

As the deadline drew near, NATO chiefs repeatedly tried to impress upon Milošević the seriousness with which they viewed the situation and the seriousness of their resolve.[136] On the eve of the deadline, General Wesley Clark, the American supreme commander of NATO, and General Klaus Naumann of Germany, the alliance's highest European military chief, flew to Belgrade for consultations with Milošević.[137] The Belgrade press claimed that the Yugoslav government was doing everything possible to "normalize" the situation.[138] But as of 26 October, there were still 14,000 Serbian police in Kosovo, according to NATO sources, which is to say more than twice the 6,500 who had been stationed, according to NATO estimates, in the province prior to 28 February 1998.[139] Then, within the final twenty-four hours before the NATO deadline, Belgrade pulled out thousands more special Interior Ministry troops, and NATO decided to accept this as "in good faith" compliance, even while warning that NATO forces remained available if need arose.[140]

The 12 October agreement had called for the stationing of some 2,000 unarmed OSCE observers in the province—a stipulation about which NATO ministers were now said to be "growing increasingly concerned."[141] NATO addressed this issue by arranging for an increase in surveillance flights over Kosovo.[142] Meanwhile, the number of Albanians camped in the woods fell from a peak of 50,000 to an estimated 10,000 by the end of October, as they gradually trickled back to their homes, even if, in many cases, their homes lay in ruins.[143]

Leaders of the Albanian community, who had at first peremptorily rejected the Holbrooke-Milošević agreement, were by late November signaling a willingness to negotiate on the basis of that agreement and, in what they described as a "goodwill gesture," freed two Serbian reporters as well as two Albanians with sympathies for the Belgrade regime, whom they had held in custody.[144] But there were, in fact, three "plans" on the table. There was, of course, the Serbian plan for limited self-administration within the Republic of Serbia, which Serbian President Milan Milutinović continued to champion in spite of the refusal of Albanian leaders to meet with him.[145] Then there was the Albanian plan, which called for a transition period ending in the grant of full independence for Kosovo.[146] And finally, there was the "American plan," as drafted and redrafted by Christopher Hill, which tried to find a compromise formula between the Serbian and Albanian models. But on 8 December, the Serbs and Albanians joined in rejecting Hill's latest plan, and Demaqi, as chief spokesperson for the KLA, suggested that Hill was too "biased" and needed to be replaced.[147]

In the meantime, the Belgrade government, which had barred U.N. war crimes prosecutor Louise Arbour (a Canadian judge) from investigating alleged atrocities in Kosovo,[148] prevented a Finnish forensics team from exhuming the remains of massacre victims in Kosovo,[149] issued a "veiled threat" against the unarmed U.N. "verifiers" in Kosovo,[150] arranged for the assassination of an Albanian guerrilla commander, and authorized mass arrests of Albanian men, who were typically tortured into signing prepared confessions. Such "trials" usually achieve their goal—of terrorizing both their immediate victims and the broader population as well. But the case of Ismet Gashi presented a striking deviation from the established pattern. As Mike O'Connor reported:

> Police guards brought Ismet Gashi, a 36-year-old farmer, to stand before a three-judge panel Dec. 4 in the western city of Peć. He stood in an attitude of submission, shoulders down, eyes fixed on the dirty orange carpeting.... A judge read his signed confession. He had admitted joining the rebels and being with them in three villages. The confession was similar to hundreds of others in which defendants say they fought for the rebels or fed them or in some way were a party to what the government calls terrorism.
>
> But when the chief judge asked Mr. Gashi to affirm his confession, the defendant did something that made the police officers present begin to fidget.
>
> "They beat me and made me sign that," Mr. Gashi said, mumbling at first. As he continued, his voice gained strength. "They beat me so much that I could not walk afterward. I needed 10 minutes just to put my signature on the paper."
>
> Then he indicated why disclosures like his were rare. "Just before court, the police told me they would be waiting for me afterward, and if I did not agree with the confession, I would see what happened to me," he said.
>
> Ariana Zherka, a field worker for the Humanitarian Law Center who attended the hearing, said, "I've never heard anything like it before. He will have big problems now." Ms. Zherka said she thought that the presence of a reporter for an American newspaper in the courtroom had emboldened the defendant.[151]

As 1998 drew to a close, there were no optimists in evidence in any country; regardless of interests and perspectives, all observers seemed gloomy about the future, and most predicted a fresh outbreak of violence in spring 1999, if not before.

From Rambouillet to NATO Strikes

On 23 November 1998, Belgrade issued its proposal for a political framework for "Kosovo and Metohija."[152] On paper, the proposal promised much, though not autonomy of course, but Albanians were not prepared to rely on Belgrade's good faith alone, noting the Serbs' failure to comply with the terms of the October 1998 accord. Under that accord, Milošević had been obliged to reduce Yugoslav army strength from 18,000 troops as of October to 12,500. Instead, Yugoslav army strength was beefed up to 23,500 as of 23 December and to 29,000 by 24 March 1999.[153] The numbers of tanks, armored personnel carriers, and artillery pieces deployed in Kosovo also exceeded agreed levels as of February 1999.

The buildup was part of a top-secret Serbian plan code-named "Operation Horseshoe," which included the confiscation of documents from local Albanians, the arming of local Serb civilians,[154] the spreading of terror through a campaign of executions and murders of innocent civilians, and the deployment of paramilitary units under Željko Raznjatović and Franko "Frenki" Simatović, whose *modus operandi* could be compared to that of the Ku Klux Klan in the early decades of the twentieth century.[155] The campaign got under way on 24 December, a holy day for those Albanians who are of Roman Catholic faith—making a mockery of the Serbs' later demand that NATO observe a cease-fire on Orthodox Easter.

In the course of January 1999, some 20,000 Albanians were driven from their homes by Serb forces, under the pretext of suppressing the lightly armed KLA; this brought the total number of displaced persons to about 200,000 by the end of January.[156] The massacre of 45 Albanian civilians in the town of Raçak on 15 January left no doubt of Belgrade's commitment to a strategy of confrontation and war. Altogether some 151 Albanians were killed in Kosovo during January 1999, according to the Priština-based Council for the Defense of Human Rights and Freedoms.[157] At least 19 Albanians were killed in the course of February, while at least a dozen were wounded in sundry incidents that month, though these figures represent incomplete compilations from fragmentary data.[158]

In these inauspicious circumstances, the Balkan "contact group" convened a last-ditch peace conference at Rambouillet, France, on 6 February, to which the Belgrade government and the Kosovar Albanians sent delegations. The Western compromise was, at first, unacceptable to both sides. It offended the Albanians by offering only autonomy, rather than independence,[159] and alienated the Serbs by proposing to introduce 30,000 NATO ground troops in Kosovo to guarantee the agreement.[160] But even as the Rambouillet peace talks got under way, Serbian tanks and artillery continued to pound Albanian villages in the areas surrounding Podujevo, Decan, Vushtrri, Mitrovica, Suhareka, and Orahovac, as well as the villages of Llapashtia and Burica.[161] By 10 March, as the Rambouillet process was still under way, the Yugoslav army had reinforced its contingent in the province, sending M-84 tanks into Kosovo and stockpiling fuel and ammunition in secret caches in the province. Between the end of December and mid-March 1999, some 80,000 Albanians were driven from their homes by Serbian forces, while the death toll for the period March 1998 through mid-March 1999 stood at more than 2,000.[162]

As of mid-February, Rambouillet seemed to have reached a dead-end. But then the Albanians realized that unless they agreed to the accord, the Western states might simply disengage, whereas if they agreed to the terms proposed at Rambouillet, NATO would be prepared to act on their behalf. Accordingly, on 23 February, the Kosovar Albanian delegation at the peace talks agreed in principle to the terms offered by the West. The talks were then adjourned for three weeks, even as Serbian forces continued their assault against Albanian villages. When the talks resumed in mid-March, the Albanians confirmed their willingness to sign, while the Serbs continued to reject the accord, citing the "unacceptability" of stationing NATO troops on FRY territory.

The staffs of the U.S. and other Western embassies had already begun to pack up and leave Belgrade.[163] Then, on 20 March, the international human-rights monitors headed by U.S. diplomat William Walker, who had been on site since the October 1998 agreement, also departed Kosovo, removing the last obstacle to a full-scale attack on the Albanians. The same day, in the words of a NATO intelligence official, "all hell broke loose," as Serbs brought the full measure of their military muscle to bear on the Albanians.[164] In the week ending 20 March, some 20,000 Albanians were driven from their homes by Serb forces.[165]

The NATO powers were acutely aware that Serbian actions constituted genocide, as defined by the Geneva Conventions. On 19 March, U.S. President Clinton drew the obvious conclusion (belatedly living up to his campaign promises of 1992): "Make no mistake," Clinton said at an afternoon news conference. "If we and our allies do not have the will to act, there will be more massacres. In dealing with aggressors in the Balkans, hesitation is a license to kill. But action and resolve can stop armies and save lives."[166] After a last-minute diplomatic effort by Richard Holbrooke to persuade FRY President Milošević to agree to the Rambouillet compromise, NATO finalized its war plans and, at 2 P.M. EST, 24 March, struck at targets in Serbia, Kosovo, and Montenegro. Though hampered by cloud cover, NATO attacks proceeded according to plan, striking at Yugoslav air-defense installations, command and control centers, supply routes, oil refineries, factories manufacturing war materiel, Serbian forces in Kosovo, and Belgrade television.[167]

Instead of halting their assault against Albanian civilians, however, Serb forces escalated the ground war, while seeming to ignore the destruction being inflicted on them from the air. On 27 March, British Defense Secretary George Robertson gave this report: "The Serbs have been torching villages," he said, "and, in a grisly echo of the savagery of the Bosnian war, separating the men from their families and shooting them.... The Serbs are bombarding villages to the point of obliteration. We have heard that some villages do not exist [any longer]."[168] Subsequently, satellite photographs provided evidence of mass graves in Kosovo.

Meanwhile, the U.S. resolve was tested by some Americans' expectation of instantaneous gratification or, in this case, overnight victory. When Milošević did not immediately cave in, cynics began to suggest that NATO had already "lost" the war, even though, as of 23 April, NATO losses amounted to three servicemen captured and one downed aircraft—rather slight losses for the presumed "loser." Others worried that NATO's attacks somehow provided "cover [for Belgrade] to drive a million of them [of Albanians] into foreign exile or [force them to] become displaced persons at home..."[169] For A. M. Rosenthal, author of the foregoing passage, it is inexplicable that the North Atlantic Treaty Organization should be focusing its efforts in the region of the North Atlantic, rather than attending to the problems of the South Atlantic (West Africa) or the Pacific (East Africa or South Asia). In search for some answer as to why NATO restricts its attention to the North Atlantic region, Rosenthal cites (evidently with approval) a comment by former Secretary of State Lawrence Eagleburger: "At the back of my head I have to ask whether some of this isn't racist."[170] Presumably, in Rosenthal's view, NATO should undertake missions in all parts of the world, and presumably, for him, the notion of European and North American powers stepping in to solve problems in Africa and Asia would be less "racist" than allowing the countries in those continents to resolve their own problems through their own regional organizations.

Isolationism also reared its head in the United States, as right-wing critics absolved themselves of any duties in the world arena under the slogan, "We are not the world's policeman." In the latter half of April 1999, Representative Tom Campbell (R-California), a five-term congressman from San Jose, introduced two measures in Congress designed to stop what he characterized as an "illegal war" on Clinton's part.[171] Of course, if the United States should prove unwilling to shoulder its NATO responsibilities, the question arises as to whether the United States should withdraw from the alliance, thereby signing the alliance's death notice. To this, Stephen M. Walt, a professor of political science at the University of Chicago, responded that "the North Atlantic alliance is an idea whose time has passed...[;] it is increasingly irrelevant to contemporary security problems. The conflict in Kosovo demonstrates this fact daily."[172] The solution, Walt implied, is to shut down NATO. Would Europe be safer without NATO around? Unfortunately, Walt maintained his silence on this crucial point.

Rather strangely, it was only more than three weeks into the aerial campaign that NATO ministers took up the question of imposing a ban on oil shipments to Yugoslavia. France, Italy, and Greece initially opposed such a ban, in spite of the compromise to NATO's military campaign which continued oil shipments represented.[173] Indeed, there were unconfirmed reports that supplies of oil from Russia, the Ukraine, and Greece were still reaching Serbia through the Montenegrin port of Bar as of 23 April,[174] though experts suggested that most of Yugoslavia's oil imports arrived by land, via Romania, rather than by sea.[175]

As of mid-April, the U.N. High Commissioner for Refugees estimated that some 671,000 Albanians had been driven out of the province since March 1998 and that possibly no more than 400,000 Albanians were still inside Kosovo. Of those who had fled, the largest number (357,000) were in Albania.[176] Meanwhile, having initially ruled out the introduction of ground troops until the military capabilities of the FRY had been "degraded" and "destroyed," NATO ministers began gingerly to consider the possibility of introducing ground troops with a more active combat mission, as public support for ground troops grew in both the United States and Europe. As Zeb Bradford, a former NATO strategic planner, told CNN, a purely aerial campaign amounted to a war of attrition—in effect, a modern counterpart to the medieval siege—which, while offering the prospect of eventual success, could perhaps do so only over a protracted period of time.[177]

Conclusion

Between 24 March and 3 June, NATO conducted 12,575 strike sorties against the FRY, destroying more than one third of the Yugoslav Air Force, 314 artillery pieces, 120 tanks, 203 APCs, 40 bridges, 29 percent of ammunition storage, and 57 percent of petroleum reserves.[178] As a result of repeated aerial strikes against hydroelectric installations, some 80 percent of serbia was without electricity and most of the country's oil refining capability had been destroyed by early June, while strikes against water pumps had left Belgrade with only 10 percent of its pre-strike water reserves by late May 1999.[179] On the other side of the ledger, by the first week of June, more than 4,500 Albanians had been killed since March 1998,[180] while the number of Albanian refugees to have fled Kosovo stood at 855,000.[181]

On 27 May 1999, the U.N. War Crimes Tribunal announced the indictment of FRY president Slobodon Milošević, Serbian President Milan Milutinović, Serbian Interior Minister Vlajko Stojiljković, and two other high-ranking Yugoslav officials on three counts of crimes against Humanity and one count of violation of the laws or customs of war.[182] On the following day the FRY government announced its acceptance of the principles for a peaceful resolution as spelled out by the Group of 8, confirming a more qualified announcement made on 18 May.[183]

Russian envoy Viktor Chernomyrdin and Finnish President Martti Ahtisaari now hurried to Belgrade for discussions with Milošević, and on 3 June, Milošević's government announced its acceptance of the brokered peace plan, though the details still needed to be ironed out.[184] But as of 6 June, as peace talks hit a snag, Yugoslav forces shelled several locations across the border in Albania, including the town of Kruma.[185] NATO ministers, in reply, vowed to continue the bombing of Serbia until full compliance with NATO demands was assured.

While the NATO mission was clearly successful, it would be a mistake to search for a durable solution in mere compacts with unreformed nationalists. On the contrary, if the problem is illegitimate government, then the solution is legitimate government, and, where the Albanians are concerned, the solution could lie either in achieving independence and legitimate government for Kosovo as such, or in achieving legitimate government for the entire FRY. At this writing, both tasks appear difficult. But in the long term, as Kant argued and as Frank Fukuyama (who is, in some ways, more Kantian than Hegelian, in spite of himself) understood, it is more difficult to maintain illegitimate government than to maintain legitimate government, once you have it. The point is to get to legitimate government.

Nationalism, however, in all of its guises, is a false solution which promises much, but delivers mainly hardship, prejudice, injury, pain, and constant dangers. Often the product of deliberate stoking by politicians seeking to build a popular power base in support of territorial revisionism or internal repression, "all nationalism is reactionary in its nature," as Rudolf Rocker has written, "for it strives to enforce on the separate parts of the great human family a definite character according to a preconceived idea ... [and] creates artificial separations and partitions within that organic unity" which comprises humankind.[186] I find myself in agreement with Brian Barry that the state community is capable of generating moral obligations (and concomitant rights), but that "there is nothing about common nationality *as such* that can make contact with any morally compelling basis for ascribing special obligations."[187] To the extent that there are rights and duties within a nationality group or among its members, these rights and duties derive from some source other than the group itself. To set against this the thesis that the nation—or rather, The Nation—itself generates obligations and rights for itself as a collectivity as well as for its members qua members of the collectivity is to break with liberalism and to embrace an anti-universalist morality in which equality has no place. It is, at best, to embrace a certain version of Rousseau, in which the General Will is apotheosized and divinized and made the very foundation for morality. But once morality is derived from Will, even if from the General Will of The Nation, it has lost its absolute quality, has lost its claim to serve as a reference point for anything. The "morality" approved by nationalists has little claim to be what it purports to be, thus, and in consequence, nationalism cannot serve as the basis for legitimate politics.

Notes

1. Samuel P. Huntington, *Political Order in Changing Societies* (New Haven: Yale University Press, 1968).

2. *Washington Post* (6 June 1998), p. A18.

3. See Sabrina P. Ramet, *Whose Democracy? Nationalism, Religion, and the Doctrine of Collective Rights in Post-1989 Eastern Europe* (Lanham, Md.: Rowman & Littlefield, 1997), introduction, chap. 3, and conclusion.

4. Immanuel Kant, *Groundwork of the Metaphysic of Morals*, trans. H. J. Paton (London and New York: Routledge, 1948), pp. 88–89.

5. See also Vesna Pusić, "A Country by Any Other Name: Transition and Stability in Croatia and Yugoslavia," in *East European Politics and Societies*, Vol. 6, No. 3 (Fall 1992).

6. See Sabrina Petra Ramet, "The Serbian Church and the Serbian Nation," in Sabrina Petra Ramet and Donald W. Treadgold (eds.), *Render Unto Caesar: The Religious Sphere in World Politics* (Washington, D.C.: American University Press, 1995), esp. pp. 301–310, 312–316.

7. John Bowlby, *Child Care and the Growth of Love* (London: Penguin, 1990; reprint of 2nd ed., 1965), chap. 2.

8. Branka Magaš, in telephone interview with the author, Kyoto-London (11 June 1998).

9. Viktor Meier, *Wie Jugoslawien verspielt wurde*, 2nd ed. (Munich: C. H. Beck, 1996), p. 73.

10. Slavoljub Djukić, *Izmedju slave i anateme: Politička biografija Slobodana Miloševića* (Belgrade: Filip Višnjić, 1994), p. 14; and Laura Silber and Allan Little, *The Death of Yugoslavia* (London: Penguin Books & BBC Books, 1995), p. 41.

11. Bowlby, *Child Care*, pp. 27, 31.

12. Ljubiša S. Adamovich, in telephone interview with the author, Kyoto-Tallahassee (29 June 1998).

13. Obrad Kesić, in telephone interview with the author, Kyoto-Washington, D.C. (29 June 1998).

14. Hitler was born in Austria, Stalin in Georgia, Napoleon in Corsica, Franco in Galicia, and Tito, of mixed Slovenian-Croatian parentage, in rural Croatia. Josua Frank, of German-Jewish stock, became a Croatian nationalist; Corneliu Zelea Codreanu, of Jewish stock, became an anti-Semitic Romanian nationalist.

15. Alan Sugar, "Dynamic Underpinnings of Father Hunger as Illuminated in the Analysis of an Adolescent Boy," in Albert J. Solnit, Peter B. Neubauer, Samuel Abrams, and A. Scott Dowling (eds.), *The Psychoanalytic Study of the Child*, Vol. 52 (New Haven: Yale University Press, 1997), p. 238.

16. Djukić, *Izmedju slave i anateme*, p. 14.

17. Ibid.

18. Anthony Storr, *Human Aggression* (Harmondsworth, Middlesex: Penguin, 1992; reprint of 1968 ed.), pp. 111–112.

19. Quoted in *Novi Vjesnik* (Zagreb) (12 October 1992).

20. Obrad Kesić, in telephone interview with the author, Kyoto-Washington, D.C. (29 June 1998).

21. Branka Magaš, *The Destruction of Yugoslavia: Tracking the Break-up 1980–92* (London: Verso, 1993), pp. 110, 235.

22. David Owen, *Balkan Odyssey* (London: Victor Gollancz, 1995), p. 127.

23. Storr, *Human Aggression*, p. 126.

24. Belgrade Domestic Service (19 November 1988), trans. in Foreign Broadcast Information Service (FBIS), *Daily Report* (Eastern Europe), 21 November 1988, pp. 72–73.

25. Storr, *Human Aggression*, p. 130.

26. Ibid., p. 143.

27. Ibid., pp. 139, 141.

28. Ibid., pp. 131, 137.

29. Harold W. V. Temperley, *History of Serbia* (London: G. Bell & Sons, 1917; reissued, New York: Howard Fertig, 1969), pp. 128–129.

30. Atanasije Urošević, "Ethnic Processes in Kosovo During the Turkish Rule," in *Kosovo: Past and Present* (Belgrade: Review of International Affairs, 1989), p. 43.

31. Noel Malcolm, *Kosovo: A Short History* (London: Macmillan, 1998), pp. 41–43.

32. Bohumil Hrabak, "Albanians of Kosovo and Metohija from the League of Prizren to 1918," in *Kosovo: Past and Present*, pp. 57, 61–62.

33. Quoted in Milija Šćepanović, "The Exodus of Serbs and Montenegrins 1878–1988," in *Kosovo: Past and Present*, p. 146.

34. Malcolm, *Kosovo: A Short History* , pp. 254–257; L. S. Stavrianos, *The Balkans Since 1453* (New York: Holt, Rinehart & Winston, 1958), p. 511; Jens Reuter, *Die Albaner in Jugoslawien* (Munich: R. Oldenbourg, 1982), p. 21; and Dušan Janjić, "National Identities,

Movements, and Nationalisms of Serbs and Albanians," in *Balkan Forum* (Skopje), Vol. 3, No. 1 (March 1995), p. 28.

35. Cited in Malcolm, *Kosovo: A Short History*, p. 273.

36. Ibid., p. 278.

37. Branko Petranović, *Istorija Jugoslavije 1918–1988, Vol. 1: Kraljevina Jugoslavija 1914–1941* (Belgrade: Nolit, 1988), pp. 34, 89.

38. Magaš, *The Destruction of Yugoslavia*, p. 30.

39. Malcolm, *Kosovo: A Short History*, p. 267.

40. Ibid, p. 268.

41. Christine von Kohl and Wolfgang Libal, *Kosovo: gordischer Knoten des Balkan* (Vienna and Zürich: Europaverlag, 1992), pp. 42–43, 44.

42. Nikola Gačesa, "Settlement of Kosovo and Metohija After World War I and the Agrarian Reform," in *Kosovo: Past and Present*, p. 102.

43. Malcolm, *Kosovo: A Short History*, pp. 285–286.

44. Branko Petranović, *Srbija u drugom svetskom ratu 1939–1945* (Belgrade: Vojnoizdavački i novinski centar, 1992), pp. 251–252.

45. Ibid., pp. 556–557.

46. Ibid., p. 691.

47. Branko Petranović, *Istorija Jugoslavije 1918–1988, Vol. 3: Socijalistička Jugoslavija 1945–1988* (Belgrade: Nolit, 1988), pp. 65–66.

48. Ibid., p. 158.

49. See Miloš Mišović, *Ko je tražio republiku: Kosovo 1945–1985* (Belgrade: Narodna knjiga, 1987).

50. Shkëlzen Maliqi, "Kosovo kao katalizator jugoslovenske krize," in Slavko Gaber and Tonči Kuzmanič (eds.), *Kosovo—Srbija—Jugoslavija* (Ljubljana: Krt, 1989), pp. 71–72.

51. Quoted in Petranović, *Istorija Jugoslavije*, Vol. 3, p. 388.

52. Nikola Milovanović, *Kroz tajni arhiv UDBe*, Vol. 2 (Belgrade: Sloboda, 1986), p. 248.

53. Duncan Wilson, *Tito's Yugoslavia* (Cambridge: Cambridge University Press, 1979), p. 160.

54. Petranović, *Istorija Jugoslavije*, Vol. 3, p. 389.

55. See discussion in Sami Repishti, "The Evolution of Kosova's Autonomy within the Yugoslav Constitutional Framework," in Arshi Pipa and Sami Repishti (eds.), *Studies on Kosova* (Boulder: East European Monographs, 1984).

56. Sinan Hasani, "Chauvinist and Separatist Organizations in Kosovo and Their Links with Foreign Centres," in *Kosovo: Past and Present*, pp. 222–223.

57. Magaš, *The Destruction of Yugoslavia*, p. 47, n. 59.

58. Mišović, *Ko je traž io republiku*, p. 255.

59. Ibid., p. 265.

60. Details in Sabrina P. Ramet, *Nationalism and Federalism in Yugoslavia, 1962–1991*, 2nd ed. (Bloomington: Indiana University Press, 1992), chaps. 8–9.

61. Magaš, *The Destruction of Yugoslavia*, pp. 15–16.

62. Anton Logoreci, "A Clash between Two Nationalisms in Kosova," in Pipa and Repishti (eds.), *Studies on Kosova*, p. 185.

63. Milovanović, *Kroz tajni arhiv UDBe*, Vol. 2, p. 267.

64. Quoted in Magaš, *The Destruction of Yugoslavia*, p. 49.

65. As reported by Noel Malcolm in his *Kosovo: A Short History*, p. 339.

66. Žarana Papić, "Women in Serbia: Post-Communism, War, and Nationalist Mutations," in Sabrina P. Ramet (ed.), *Gender Politics in the Western Balkans: Women and Society in*

Yugoslavia and the Yugoslav Successor States (University Park: Pennsylvania State University Press, 1999), p. 162.

67. For more details concerning the 1980s, see Sabrina P. Ramet, *Social Currents in Eastern Europe: The Sources and Consequences of the Great Transformation*, 2nd ed. (Durham, N.C.: Duke University Press, 1995), pp. 205–206. For a Serbian point of view from this era, see Dimitrije Bogdanović, *Knjiga o Kosovu* (Belgrade: Srpska Akademija Nauka i Umetnosti, 1985). For a source sympathetic to the Albanian point of view, from this era, see Branko Horvat, *Kosovsko pitanje* (Zagreb: Globus, 1988).

68. Ramet, *Social Currents*, p. 210.

69. See Julie Mertus, *Open Wounds: Human Rights Abuses in Kosovo* (New York: Human Rights Watch/Helsinki, March 1993); and "Human Rights Abuses of Non-Serbs in Kosovo, Sandžak, and Vojvodina," in *Human Rights Watch Helsinki*, Vol. 6, No. 6 (May 1994).

70. *Delo* (Ljubljana), 13 January 1995, p. 16, trans. in FBIS, *Daily Report* (Eastern Europe), 13 February 1995, p. 43.

71. *Borba* (Belgrade), 21 October 1994, 12, trans. in FBIS, *Daily Report* (Eastern Europe), 2 November 1994, pp. 40–41.

72. Oesterreich 1 Radio (Vienna) (24 July 1995), in *BBC Summary of World Broadcasts* (25 July 1995).

73. Zoran Lutovac, "Političko angažovanje kosovskih Albanaca," in Vladimir Goati (ed.), *Partijski mozaik Srbije 1990–1996* (Belgrade: Beogradski krug i AKAPIT, 1997), p. 153.

74. *International Herald Tribune* (Tokyo ed.) (2 July 1998), p. 5.

75. *Der Tagesspiegel* (Berlin) (6 December 1997), p. 2.

76. *International Herald Tribune* (Tokyo ed.) (4 June 1998), p. 1.

77. *BBC News* (10 June 1998).

78. Regarding the number in March, *International Herald Tribune* (Tokyo ed.) (26 March 1998), p. 4; regarding the number in July, *Croatia Weekly* (Zagreb) (17 July 1998), p. 10.

79. *The Australian* (22 July 1998), p. 9.

80. *Financial Times* (16/17 May 1998), p. 2.

81. *Der Tagesspiegel* (10 March 1998), p. 1; and *Der Tagesspiegel* (22 April 1998), p. 2.

82. Quoted in *USA Today* (10 June 1998), p. 4A.

83. *The Guardian* (London and Manchester) (9 June 1998), p. 11. Regarding the use of helicopter gunships and the entry of tanks, see *The Times* (London) (8 June 1998), p. 11.

84. *New York Times* (4 June 1998), p. A12.

85. Quoted in *The Guardian* (9 June 1998), p. 2.

86. Quoted in *International Herald Tribune* (Tokyo ed.) (15 June 1998), p. 8.

87. *The Guardian* (9 June 1998), p. 11.

88. *Illyria* (The Bronx) (6–8 June 1998), p. 3; *Asahi Evening News* (Tokyo) (10 June 1998), p. 2; and *The Guardian* (17 June 1998), p. 14.

89. *International Herald Tribune* (Tokyo ed.) (27/28 June 1998), pp. 1, 4.

90. *International Herald Tribune* (Tokyo ed.) (30 June 1998), p. 1; and *The Daily Yomiuri* (13 September 1998), p. 3.

91. *Frankfurter Rundschau* (18 May 1998), p. 1.

92. *The Times* (8 June 1998), p. 11; and *Der Tagesspiegel* (13 June 1998), p. 2.

93. *Der Tagesspiegel* (12 June 1998), p. 5.

94. *New York Times* (31 August 1998), p. A3.

95. Ibid.

96. See, for example, *Glas javnosti* (Belgrade) (31 August 1998), pp. 1, 9.

97. *Washington Post* (1 September 1998), p. A14.

98. *Glas javnosti* (10 September 1998), pp. 1, 9. The discovery is also discussed in *International Herald Tribune* (Tokyo ed.) (5 October 1998), p. 6.

99. *NIN* (Belgrade) (17 September 1998), p. 10.

100. *International Herald Tribune* (Tokyo ed.) (3/4 October 1998), p. 4.

101. *Daily Yomiuri* (11 September 1998), p. 4.

102. *Illyria* (22–24 August 1998), p. 3; *Illyria* (26–28 August 1998), p. 3; and *USA Today* (17 September 1998), p. 4A.

103. Quoted in *New York Times* (7 September 1998), p. A8.

104. Aeschylus, *Agamemnon*, lines 328–332, trans. Robert Fages (Harmondsworth, Middlesex: Penguin Books, 1977; revised 1979), p. 115.

105. *New York Times* (16 September 1998), p. A8.

106. *Washington Post* (2 September 1998), p. A26.

107. Quoted in *The Times* (18 September 1998), p. 18.

108. Paraphrased by *The Times* (18 September 1998), p. 18.

109. *Washington Post* (17 September 1998), p. A24.

110. Quoted in *The Independent* (London), reprinted in *Daily Yomiuri* (27 September 1998), p. 9.

111. *International Herald Tribune* (Tokyo ed.) (29 September 1998), p. 6.

112. *International Herald Tribune* (Tokyo ed.) (30 September 1998), p. 5.

113. *USA Today* (1 October 1998), p. 1A. See also *Washington Post* (30 September 1998), pp. A1, A21.

114. *USA Today* (1 October 1998), p. 4A; and *International Herald Tribune* (Tokyo ed.) (1 October 1998), pp. 1, 12.

115. *International Herald Tribune* (Tokyo ed.) (5 October 1998), pp. 1, 6; and *Mainichi Daily News* (5 October 1998), p. 3.

116. Quotes derived from *Daily Yomiuri* (13 October 1998), p. 1; and *The Australian* (13 October 1998), p. 9.

117. Quoted in *Daily Yomiuri* (13 October 1998), p. 1.

118. *Daily Yomiuri* (16 October 1998), p. 4.

119. *International Herald Tribune* (Tokyo ed.) (14 October 1998), p. 1; and Tanjug (Belgrade), quoted in *Daily Yomiuri* (15 October 1998), p. 1.

120. *BBC News* (14 October 1998).

121. Quoted in *USA Today* (14 October 1998), p. 1A.

122. Elez Biberaj, in telephone interview with the author, Kyoto-Washington, D.C. (13 October 1998).

123. Ramet, *Whose Democracy*, p. 160.

124. On this point, see my essay "The So-Called Right of National Self-Determination and Other Myths," in *Human Rights Review* (forthcoming).

125. See *Nedeljni Telegraf* (Belgrade) (14 October 1998), pp. 2–3; and *The Australian* (13 October 1998), p. 9.

126. See *New York Times* (28 March 1997), p. A5.

127. *Asahi Evening News* (4 November 1998), p. 2; confirmed in *New York Times* (5 November 1998), p. A14; reconfirmed in *US News & World Report* (16 November 1998), p. 52.

128. *USA Today* (14 October 1998), p. 1A.

129. *International Herald Tribune* (Tokyo ed.) (12 October 1998), p. 1, and 17/18 October 1998, p. 1.

130. *Daily Yomiuri* (18 October 1998), p. 3.

131. *Die Welt* (Bonn) (20 October 1998), p. 7.

132. *The Times* (London) (20 October 1998), p. 12; confirmed in *Daily Yomiuri* (20 October 1998), p. 4.

133. *Politika* (Belgrade) (19 October 1998), p. 14.

134. *Večernji list* (Zagreb) (21 October 1998), p. 13.

135. *The Independent* (London) (20 October 1998), p. 12.

136. See *Daily Yomiuri* (22 October 1998), p. 4; *Vjesnik* (Zagreb) (24 October 1998), pp. 1–2; *Die Welt* (24 October 1998), p. 7; and *Welt am Sonntag* (25 October 1998), p. 4.

137. *International Herald Tribune* (Bologna ed.) (24/25 October 1998), pp. 1, 5.

138. *Politika* (22 October 1998), p. 17.

139. *USA Today* (27 October 1998), p. 4A.

140. *Japan Times* (28 October 1998), p. 1; *Der Tagesspiegel* (29 October 1998), p. 8; and *Daily Yomiuri* (29 October 1998), p. 1.

141. *USA Today* (29 October 1998), p. 4A.

142. *International Herald Tribune* (Tokyo ed.) (29 October 1998), p. 6.

143. *Illyria* (The Bronx) (21–23 October 1998), p. 6; *The Independent*, reprinted in *Daily Yomiuri* (25 October 1998), p. 9; *The Australian* (28 October 1998), p. 9; and *Daily Yomiuri* (31 October 1998), p. 4.

144. *Financial Times* (15 October 1998), p. 2; *Daily Yomiuri* (26 November 1998), p. 4; and *Financial Times* (28/29 November 1998), p. 2.

145. *USA Today* (18 November 1998), p. 4A; and *Japan Times* (27 November 1998), p. 6.

146. *Daily Yomiuri* (2 December 1998), p. 4.

147. *Mainichi Daily News* (10 December 1998), p. 3.

148. *Washington Post* (5 November 1998), p. A58.

149. *Daily Yomiuri* (11 December 1998), p. 16.

150. *International Herald Tribune* (Tokyo ed.) (8 December 1998), p. 7.

151. Mike O'Connor, "Serbs Try Mass Arrests in Kosovo," New York Times Service, in *International Herald Tribune* (Tokyo ed.) (12/13 December 1998), p. 2.

152. For the full text, see "Joint Proposal of the Agreement on the Political Framework of Self-governance in Kosovo and Metohija" (23 November 1998), at www.serbia-info. com/news.

153. Regarding the accord's provisions, *New York Times* (26 February 1999), p. A7; regarding the actual troop levels, *New York Times* (14 April 1999), p. A12.

154. *Kosova Daily Report* #1697 (19 February 1999), at www.kosova.com.

155. *Washington Post* (11 April 1999), p. A26.

156. *Illyria* (Bronx), 27 January–3 February 1999, p. 1.

157. *Kosova Daily Report* #1689 (10 February 1999), at www.kosova.com.

158. See news items in *Kosova Daily Report* #1680-A (1 February 1999), #1863 [1683] (4 February 1999), #1687 (8 February 1999), #1688 (9 February 1999), #1690 (11 February 1999), #1692-B (13 February 1999), #1699 (21 February 1999), #1705-B (27 February 1999), and #1706-B (28 February 1999)—all at www.kosova.com.

159. See *Kosova Daily Report* #1691 (12 February 1999), at www.kosova.com.

160. *Boston Sunday Globe* (21 February 1999), p. A1.

161. See news items in *Kosova Daily Report* #1681 (2 February 1999), #1698 (20 February 1999), #1700 (22 February 1999), #1702 (24 February 1999), #1703 (25 February 1999), #1704 (26 February 1999), and #1707 (1 March 1999)—all at www.kosova.com.

162. Regarding reinforcements and stockpiling, *Washington Post* (11 April 1999), p. A26, and also *Sunday Oregonian* (Portland), 18 April 1999, p. A13; regarding numbers driven from their homes and number killed, *Frankfurter Allgemeine* (16 March 1999), p. 1.

163. *Süddeutsche Zeitung* (Munich) (20/21 February 1999), p. 1.

164. As quoted in *Washington Post* (11 April 1999), p. A26.

165. *Boston Sunday Globe* (21 March 1999), p. A3.

166. Quoted in *New York Times* (20 March 1999), p. A1.

167. See *Wall Street Journal* (24 March 1999), p. A3; *Boston Sunday Globe* (11 April 1999), pp. A24–A25; and *New York Times* (14 April 1999), p. A12.

168. Quoted in *Sunday Post* (Glasgow) (28 March 1999), p. 1. See also *Die Welt* (Bonn) (27 March 1999), p. 1.

169. A. M. Rosenthal, "Lessons of Kosovo," in *New York Times* (16 April 1999), p. A25.

170. Quoted in Ibid.

171. *USA Today* (23 April 1999), p. 5A.

172. *USA Today* (23 April 1999), p. 14A.

173. *USA Today* (21 April 1999), p. 8A; and *Wall Street Journal* (22 April 1999), p. A16.

174. *CNN News* (23 April 1999).

175. *Wall Street Journal* (22 April 1999), p. A16.

176. *New York Times* (17 April 1999), pp. A6–A7; and "Kosovo Crisis Update" (UNHCR), at www.unhcr.ch/news/media/kosovo.htm.

177. *CNN News* (23 April 1999).

178. *Wall Street Journal* (4 June 1999), p. A7.

179. *CNN Headline News* (6 June 1999); and *USA Today* (25 May 1999), p. 6A.

180. *Washington Post* (28 May 1999), A1, at www.washingtonpost.com.

181. *Miami Herald* (3 June 1999), at www.herald.com.

182. Press release from the International War Crimes Tribunal for the Former Yugoslavia (27 May 1999), at www.latimes.com.

183. *Washington Post* (18 May 1999), at www.washingtonpost.com.

184. *USA Today* (3 June 1999), p. 1A; and *Wall Street Journal* (4 June 1999), pp. A1, A12.

185. *CNN Headline News* (6 June 1999).

186. Rudolf Rocker, *Nationalism and Culture*, trans. from German by Ray E. Chase (Montreal and New York: Black Rose Books, 1998), p. 213.

187. Brian Barry, "Nationalism versus liberalism?" in *Nations and Nationalism*, Vol. 2, Part 3 (November 1996), p. 431.

Epilogue

Socialist Yugoslavia was always a Tower of Babel whose builders not only spoke different languages, but talked past each other. In many ways, the diverse peoples of socialist Yugoslavia failed to comprehend each other's cultures. Disintegration seemed to be sewn into the very fabric of the state.

There were, of course, signs of trouble even before the socialists took power, indeed, from the very beginning. When Serbian armies entered Dubrovnik at the end of World War I, for example, they hoisted Cyrillic banners to celebrate the event—even though local Croats could not read them and viewed that alphabet as completely foreign. The Belgrade government followed this up by mandating that Croats and Bosnians learn to use Cyrillic. This was a sign of things to come. During the interwar period, Croats experienced exploitation and discrimination at the hands of Serb politicians and lost the leader of their Peasant Party (Stjepan Radić) to a Serb assassin's bullet. But the Serbs had their resentments as well. They were convinced that the Croats were trying to have it both ways (benefiting in military terms and in foreign policy from political association with the Serbs while enjoying de facto independence), and often viewed Radić as little more than a "loose cannon." The other peoples of the Yugoslav kingdom had their own complaints. World War II only drove the sundry peoples further apart, insofar as many people preferred to view the combat as Croat versus Serb versus Muslim, rather than see the war as a struggle between fascism and communism in which the advocates of peasant democracy were marginalized.

In the post–World War II period, the real troubles began around 1980, when the economy started to fall apart. Coincidentally, 1980 was also the year in which Tito died. By the early 1980s, the gathering economic, ethnic, political, and moral crisis was already pushing the country toward disintegration. Historian Milovan Dželebdžić had a foreboding of this as early as January 1982 when he fretted "lest we experience some new trauma, some new civil war, some new massacre."[1] In October the following year, Slovenian historian Dušan Biber told a group of historians in Zagreb that if the trends then prevailing should continue, "we will turn into a second Lebanon."[2] I echoed these warnings about a month later, writing that, as a result of the mishandling of liberal currents in 1971 and the ensuing political line, "it is probably only a matter of time before another bloodbath occurs between Serbs and Croats."[3] It was not that bloodletting was already inevitable; on the contrary, at that point in time there was much that could have been done to change direction. The point was rather that the danger already existed. It was as if gunpowder had already been laid in place. But it would still take someone to light the fuse; that someone, to the extent that one person did more than anyone else to push the country over the brink, was Slobodan Milošević.

It would be a tricky business and, in part, no doubt artificial, to try to pinpoint any single event as a turning point in the disintegration of Yugoslavia. But to the extent that we may speak of a turning point, we should look to Milošević's coup in the Serbian party in late 1987. Although Milošević did not create the resentments in Yugoslavia, at least not all of them, he amplified them and manipulated them. Still, as Viktor Meier has emphasized in his classic study of Yugoslavia's last years, there were other major players whose responsibility in the unfolding drama ought not be underestimated—above all Borisav Jović (a Serb), Stipe Šuvar (a Croat), Lazar Mojsov (a Macedonian), and the army leadership.[4] Other players who "strutted their hour upon the stage"[5] and played their role in pushing the country toward catastrophe included Radovan Karadžić (a major player from 1991 onward), Raif Dizdarević (a Bosnian Serb), Milan Pančevski (a Macedonian), Kosta Bulatović (a Kosovar Serb), Momir Bulatović (a Montenegrin), and even, during a moment of confusion when he seemed to absolve the Serbian party of procedural irregularities, Stane Dolanc (a Slovene). (I would count Vojislav Šešelj, Mate Boban, Ratko Mladić, and even Željko Raznjatović as tertiary players in fostering disintegration and fomenting the war. On the other hand, it is quite obvious that once the war was in process, these figures played important roles.)

But it is quite another matter to assert, as Nicholas Miller does, that "it is difficult to accept the proposal that Serbia is *fully* responsible for the wars; it is even more difficult to agree that Croats have suffered genocide."[6] The problem with asserting that "Serbia" is guilty is that it seems to implicate *all* Serbs, even though, as I pointed out in Chapter 11, Serbian women organized pacifist groups such as Women in Black precisely in order to combat the war and its associated complexes. Even reducing this to the proposition that "the Serbian government" was or was not guilty strikes me as not without its problems. The basic one is what political scientists call the level-of-analysis problem. The starting point is to distinguish between guilt of complicity and guilt of passivity, of failure to oppose evil, and again between the guilt of those who played pivotal roles and the guilt of those who played "in the orchestra," as it were. In the "Serbian orchestra," for example, Jović was at best the "concertmaster." Milošević, however, was the conductor in that "orchestra," and his symphony of orchestrated hatred resounded throughout the country in the years 1987–1990.

Nor does it make any sense to try to include Tudjman and Izetbegović as equally responsible for the outbreak of the war. Although they made key mistakes (Tudjman sitting on his hands while the army charged into Slovenia, Izetbegović sitting on his hands while the army provided backing for Serbian insurgents in Croatia), the war was planned by Milošević, Jović, and the army leadership, and the hatreds had been stoked to fever pitch long before the elections which brought DEMOS to power in Slovenia or Tudjman to power in Croatia. Tudjman stands indicted by many Croats (including Žarko Puhovski, Ivo Banac, and Stjepan Kljuić) of pushing the Bosnian Croats toward a war against Bosnian Muslims. But the war in Bosnia would have broken out even if Tudjman had been intent on honoring his nominal alliance with the Muslims, whereas there would have been no war in Bosnia had it not been for Milošević, Karadžić, Jović, and their adherents and collaborators.

But Milošević and his collaborators worked within a context which was particularly favorable for stoking hatreds and propelling the country toward war. The key ingredients conducive to this result were: (1) the aforementioned economic deterioration, creating rising tides of discontent; (2) the decentralized, ethnic-based federal system that Tito had created, which channeled discontent along ethnic lines and guaranteed that programs to remedy the situation would be addressed to the ethnic audience associated with each given republic (with Bosnia-Herzegovina, as is generally known, being a special case); (3) the failure to resolve the legitimacy problem in socialist Yugoslavia; and (4) the appearance of Milošević, a politician willing to set a match to this tinderbox by endeavoring to stoke and exploit ethnic hatreds for his own purposes.

The Legitimacy Problem

I have alluded above to the "legitimacy problem." In a word, I would advance the following proposition: legitimation is the central problem of politics, the single most essential task of any system. To this proposition I shall attach three corollaries. If a state cannot solve this problem, or if its administrators choose not to make an endeavor to do so, the strengths, vulnerabilities, and behaviors (both internally and externally) of that state will be profoundly different from the strengths, vulnerabilities, and behaviors of a legitimate state: that is the first corollary. The second corollary is this: the processes of delegitimation and relegitimation can have momentous implications for the borders of any state, and most poignantly a multiethnic state—with potential implications for questions of international security. And the third corollary: the processes of delegitimation (which, in the Yugoslav case moved the system from at best "quasi-legitimate" to fully illegitimate) which lead to the collapse of systems begin far in advance of actual system breakdown, so that perceptive observers may be aware of the dangers implied in certain processes of delegitimation long before they reach the actual moment of truth.

Legitimacy may be viewed triadically, as consisting of *moral legitimacy* (the extent to which a state's laws, policies, and practices are in accord with Universal Reason, which philosophers also call Natural Law), *political legitimacy* (the extent to which political succession and change in office follow fixed, predictable procedures which have been accepted within a given society), and *economic legitimacy* (the extent to which a system is structured so as to ensure general economic sufficiency for all and

to prevent the accumulation of vast private wealth).[7] I have quite deliberately specified "the extent to which" in each case, because I believe that legitimacy is a matter of
degree, not of absolutes, though, of course, the difference between extremes even
along a continuum will also be one of an "absolute" character. Translating these concepts into terms of discourse, a system which is fully legitimate in moral terms is
called a "liberal" state (in so saying, I betray the fact that, like Kant, Locke, Hobbes,
Jefferson, Madison, and J. S. Mill, I view liberalism as a moral category, rather than a
purely political one). A system which is fully legitimate in economic terms is called a
"solidarist" state (meaning, one that is in harmony with the Natural Law requirements already specified by liberalism). As for political legitimacy, history has generated two stable systems which have been characterized by accepted procedures of political succession, namely, hereditary monarchy and democracy.[8]

   In order for a political elite to make its claim to legitimacy stick, it must be able to
make a case that it came to power by generally accepted means. Insofar as Tito and his
Partisans openly admitted that they held power because of the military might they had
built up in the course of the antifascist struggle—even if they did not put it in quite
these terms—they hoped to be validated by what Marxists might have called "the sanction of history." But, in practice, Yugoslavia's Communists were never able to make
this claim stick. Symptomatic of this failure was the gradual emergence, in the course
of the 1950s, of ostensibly derivative appeals to the principles of self-management,
brotherhood and unity, and nonalignment, covering the realms of economic management, ethnic politics, and foreign policy. But these were principles of a different order,
whose claim to validity was not self-evident and which provided no roadmap for political succession. Indeed, Tito changed his mind about succession several times during
his lifetime, thinking at first of Aleksandar Ranković as his heir presumptive and later
of Edvard Kardelj for this role, and finally deciding to set up an elaborate system of
collective leadership operating according to rules of regular rotation.

   Tito was able to make a certain appeal to his people, but largely on a charismatic
level. He was not successful in his effort to establish historical sanction as a principle
capable of legitimating his successors, let alone of providing procedural guidelines.
Hence, Tito's death in 1980 inflicted a serious blow on the *perceived* (political) legitimacy of the system, albeit a blow not immediately apparent to the Yugoslavs themselves. The system of rotating leaders *might* perhaps have acquired some legitimation
if the Yugoslavs had been convinced that the system made sense, that it was appropriate, and that the party forums appointing deputies to sit in these political carousels
were in fact entitled to make such appointments. But this was a big "if," too big for
the system to bear. Moreover, most Yugoslavs quickly became convinced that the system was at least cumbersome, if not unwieldy and ultimately unworkable.

   It was quite natural, therefore, that Milošević, in looking for ways to win a following outside his native Serbia, should have promised a "bureaucratic revolution." But
Milošević too was bedeviled by the legitimacy problem. Insofar as he took power
through a palace coup, could he hope that palace coups would be construed as the
normal and accepted way of changing leaders in Serbia? No one can answer this

question in the affirmative, which is why he could not solve the prime legitimacy problem of his rule. Nor would fixed elections and an arranged transfer from the Serbian presidency to the FRY presidency square the circle. Milošević therefore registered his claim to legitimacy not on the basis of being legitimately elevated, but on his representation of himself as "Protector of the Serbian People."[9] The appeal to nationalism, which of necessity entailed the scuttling of Natural Law and the subordination of individual rights (both of non-Serbs and of Serbs) to the collective rights of the Nation,[10] was manifested in the indiscriminate rehabilitation of "fallen" Serbs from Ranković[11] to Draža Mihailović[12] to King Aleksandar Karadjordjević.[13] But even if one sets aside the question of nationalism's problematic relationship to human rights, nationalism could not serve as a source of *political* legitimation in any event, because it does not provide a guide as to political succession. Nationalism is not in the same category with elections and primogeniture; it is of an entirely different order. At base, nationalism is moral—or more exactly, amoral—in nature. But, as already noted, insofar as nationalism repudiates the moral universalism of Universal Reason, it results in delegitimation, not the reverse.

Variations on a Triadic Theme

Some writers try to refer the question of legitimacy to such things as the mere holding of elections (regardless of the choice of candidates offered), economic performance, stability, or even some fuzzy notions about "legality" divorced from the moral law. Analyses of this nature lead their practitioners into confusion, inducing in them—if they are policy-makers—misguided policies founded on false assumptions. Rather than tying legitimacy to performance—which would entail absurd conclusions such as that the U.S. government was "less legitimate" after the stock market crash of 1929 than it had been before the crash, or that the Somoza government in Nicaragua was "more legitimate" when the country's economy was relatively strong than in less prosperous times—I shall, instead, link legitimacy to the triad of principles outlined in the foregoing section.

Following this line of approach, then, we may start by operationalizing the concept of *moral legitimacy*. I have already indicated that, under this expression, I understand that a system should be in accord with moral universalism. In practice, this means (1) that the government should permit the functioning of a free press, (2) that the government should foster tolerance in ethnic, interconfessional, and gender relations, and (3) that the government should follow its own laws, which in turn must be published and available to inspection by members of the public. Reviewing the performance of Slovenia, Croatia, Serbia, and Macedonia—I set aside Montenegro and Bosnia-Herzegovina for purposes of this discussion—Slovenia obtains the highest marks for establishing and maintaining a free press and also gets high marks for compliance with its own laws. Although the U.N. Human Rights Committee, in a resolution adopted at its session of 20–22 July 1994, expressed "concern about remaining areas of discrimination against women, particularly regarding the extent of

TABLE 14.1   Measures of System Legitimacy for Post-1990 Slovenia, Croatia, Serbia, and Macedonia

	Moral legitimacy	*Political legitimacy*	*Economic legitimacy*
Slovenia	Legitimate	Legitimate	(Quasi-)legitimate
Macedonia	Partially legitimate	Legitimate	Largely Illegitimate
Croatia	Partially legitimate	Legitimate	Largely Illegitimate
Serbia	Illegitimate	Illegitimate	Illegitimate

their participation in the conduct of public affairs,"[14] the Slovenian system has, on the whole, done well to combat intolerance. I therefore record the post-1990 Slovenian system as "morally legitimate" (see Table 14.1). Insofar as office-holders owe their positions to elections or appointments as provided under law, there can be little doubt of the political legitimacy of the system. Finally, the conversion to a free-market economy has been accomplished without either notable corruption or scandal, and, in consequence, the system may be judged also *economically* legitimate (though in judging it so, I admit that I am relaxing somewhat my demand for a strictly "solidarist" approach).

The other three systems rank somewhat lower. Among these, I would rank Croatia in second place overall, chiefly on the strength of the system's rather self-evident *political legitimacy.* There have been no scandals concerning elections, which all observers agree have been free and fair, or concerning the government's compliance with its own laws, broadly speaking. Even the well-known nepotism and cronyism under the Tudjman government[15] have been overlooked by citizens who are still celebrating their victory in the Serbian Insurrectionary War. On the other hand, the economic corruption is at least as extensive as in the Macedonian case, and President Tudjman's *purchase* of the presidential palace has outraged some Croats, who point out that it would be out of the question, in the United States, for one or another president to *purchase* the White House! Moreover, by November 1998 it was being openly admitted that some members of the Croatian cabinet had used their offices to enrich themselves illegally, while there was growing controversy about certain semisecret bank accounts of President Tudjman.[16] I would therefore rate the Croatian economic system and practice as *largely illegitimate* (the same ranking as I assign to Macedonian economic practice).[17]

It is in the realm of *moral legitimacy* where most of the controversy about the Croatian case has been concentrated. With regard to rhetoric, President Tudjman revised his controversial book, changing some of his statistical estimates and generally qualifying some of his statements, he has apologized to the Jewish community for certain past statements of his, retracting them, and in May 1998 his government unanimously adopted an instruction to enable Croatian citizens who had fled the republic during the war to return to Croatia, promising financial assistance; the instruction was understood to refer, in the first place, to Serbs.[18] And yet Tudjman has not been given credit for this actions. As Stjepan Meštrović points out in a brilliant paper, President Tudjman has repeatedly come across as awkward and ineffective "due to his non-reliance on public relations experts. His jokes, remarks, and writings have been manipulated by ... experts in the West in order to depict him as a racist and anti-Semite."[19] But to the extent that we may speak of Tudjman's ideological bearings, it makes more sense to refer to his commitment to neotraditional values (and hence his preference for the patriarchal, heterosexual family) and to a notion of a Greater Croatia. Racism is not part of Tudjman's *Weltanschauung*, certain ill-considered and infelicitous remarks of his notwithstanding.

Croatia's record on the treatment of minorities is mixed. On 4 December 1991, the Croatian *Sabor* adopted a new law on minorities, which it later amended on 8 May 1992. The Badinter Commission reviewed Croatia's legislation on minorities at that stage, and on 3 June of that year concluded that "even if the Constitutional Law in question does sometimes fall short of the obligation assumed by Croatia when it accepted the draft Convention of 4 November 1991, it nonetheless satisfies the requirements of general international law regarding the protection of minorities."[20] In Article 9 of the law, as published in its final form on 17 June 1992, it is guaranteed that "possession and use of national or ethnic emblems and symbols of national and ethnic communities or minorities shall be free."[21] Moreover, Croatian authorities have repeatedly stressed their commitment to reintegrate those Serbs seeking to return to Croatia.[22]

On the other hand, the OSCE issued a report in May 1998 alleging that Croatian authorities were continuing with discriminatory practices at the expense of Croatian Serbs, in the school system, in scientific and education associations, and in the textbooks themselves. Croatian authorities denied the allegations.[23] Yet it is clear that, up to now, the Croatian educational system has failed (as have educational authorities in almost all postcommunist societies in East-Central Europe) to inculcate values of moral universalism, such as concepts of human equality, tolerance, fair play, and love for the moral law. One observer, commenting on Croatian life in late 1998, described the society as "worse than I had expected, politically, economically, and psychologically, and it affects [the] morality and manners of the whole place. It has become a very corrupt and lawless place, where the rights of a person are not much."[24] Insofar as rights can only be grounded in morality[25]—so that one may even affirm that "natural law is a philosophy of rights"[26]—it is not surprising that where moral universalism is eroded, respect for rights is also eroded. The failure of authorities to campaign for notions of equality, tolerance, and fair play seemed aptly symbolized in the scandal surrounding the deposing of "Miss Croatia" in 1998. Two weeks after Lejla Šehović had been elected Miss Croatia, she was stripped of the title and the erstwhile runner-up, Ivana Petković, was elected in her stead. Although the contest jury claimed that there had been voting "irregularities," most Croats and foreign observers believed that the real reason was that the jury, and perhaps other persons too, had discovered, in the meantime, that Šehović was a Muslim.[27]

Where women's equality is concerned, although the Croatian constitution specifically forbids discrimination on the basis of gender, it does not, according to Vesna

Kesić, provide any mechanisms for guarding against discrimination.[28] Moreover, the semiofficial campaign for the retraditionalization of gender roles must be seen as incompatible with the principles of moral universalism.

And yet Croatia's ranking in terms of *moral legitimacy* is partially redeemed by its relatively free press, in spite of the scandal surrounding the ruling party's moves to bring the key papers, *Vjesnik* and *Večernji list*, under its indirect control (through cronyism). But it should not be forgotten that among independent print media in contemporary Croatia one may number the weekly magazines *Tjednik* and *Globus*, the biweekly newspapers *Istarski glas* and *Brodski list*, the monthly magazines *Zaposlena* (which focuses on feminist themes broadly conceived), *Arkzin* (earlier a weekly newspaper), and *Start: nove generacije*, the weekly newspapers *Feral Tribune* (Split), *Nacional* (a tabloid published in Zagreb), and *Bumerang* (Osijek), daily newspapers *Novi list* (in Rijeka, and currently highly respected), *Karlovački list* (which consists in part of pages from *Novi list* and in part of local material), *Glas Istre* (published in Pula and sympathetic to Istrian autonomism), *Otok Ivanić* (run by a reputedly rebellious priest fighting for moral values), *Samoborski list*, and the Zagreb weekly newspaper *Vijenac*. In addition, the monthly magazine *Nova Hrvatska ljevica*, run by Stipe Šuvar, caters to the old socialist left, while *Hrvatsko Slovo* and *Narod* cater to persons with sympathies markedly right of the political mainstream. In addition, there is *Ultra*, a biweekly magazine launched at the end of 1997 by Denis Kuljiš with the declared purpose of working toward the "deprovincialization" of Croatian society, and *Erasmus*, a scholarly publication inspired by a strong moral commitment to liberal ideals.[29] Hence, although the Zagreb government falls short in terms of fostering ethnic, interconfessional, and sexual tolerance, it scores much better in terms of freedom of the press, and hence the "partially legitimate" rating I assigned Croatia under the rubric of "moral legitimacy."

Macedonia comes in third place in my ranking, due among other things to continuing controversies as regards the large Albanian minority in the western (especially northwestern) parts of the republic. In the sphere of *political legitimacy*, Macedonia deserves to be rated at least *partially* legitimate. The system has been characterized by procedural regularity in at least some spheres, and the change of leadership effected in the autumn 1998 elections is proof that fair and free elections have been held in the republic. On the other hand, allegations of corruption bear directly on the *economic legitimacy* of Macedonia and impinge on political legitimacy insofar as they undermine people's faith in the *system*. As Duncan Perry noted in a March 1998 publication, thus before the elections that year, "scandals, cronyism, and favoritism have become a staple in the newspapers and on television," while "the gray or informal economy is estimated to account for as much as 35 percent of the GDP."[30] As for *moral* legitimacy, the mere fact that reports of scandals and cronyism have become widespread in the local press constitutes a fair measure of the relative freedom the Macedonian press has come to enjoy. On the other hand, the coalition government headed by the Alliance for Macedonia approached the concerns of the Albanian minority in what could be generously described as, at the very minimum, a clumsy and insensitive manner. In consequence, the Macedonian system ranks as only *partially* legitimate, based on its performance, 1990–1998.

The Serbian regime of Slobodan Milošević, on the other hand, ranks as illegitimate in moral, political, and economic terms. That his regime's program of fostering intolerance and hatred of Croats, Muslims, and Albanians through the media and through public rallies is incompatible with notions of moral universalism would not seem to require specific argument. Further, the regime's repressive policies against its own citizens, especially though not exclusively against non-Serbs, mark this regime as one founded on chauvinistic intolerance and hatred, not as one in accord with the moral law, as reflected, for example, in the Universal Declaration on Human Rights and the Geneva Conventions. In terms of its policy toward women and the family, as I have already argued in Chapter 11, the Milošević regime scarcely differs from that of President Tudjman in Croatia, while in terms of media policy, the Milošević regime is, among the Yugoslav successor states, in a class by itself.

As early as 1992, the prestigious monthly journal *Index on Censorship* reported that independent journalists in Serbia were under intense psychological pressure from the political establishment, while the official media (*Politika, NIN, Politika ekspres*, and Radio-Television Belgrade) were kept on a short leash.[31] Later, Milošević established his control also over the daily newspapers *Borba* and *Večernje novosti* and briefly took the independent radio station B-92, off the air, until the United States stepped in to broadcast B-92 programs over American-owned stations. In March 1997, the Serbian government passed a new, more restrictive broadcasting law, providing that "no private radio or television station would be allowed to broadcast to an audience of more than 25 percent of the 10.5 million population."[32] Then, in October 1998, the regime temporarily shut down Serbia's three remaining independent daily newspapers—*Dnevni Telegraf, Danas*, and *Naša borba*—prompting the editorial staffs to prepare to move their headquarters to Montenegro.[33] The Ministry of Information of the Belgrade government based its actions on a governmental decree making it illegal to spread "anxiety, panic, and defeatism" among the public in the context of the ostensible showdown with NATO.[34] A new law on the media was published on 22 October,[35] prompting the Association of Independent Electronic Media in Serbia to issue a statement, declaring, "It [the new law] destroys what little freedom there was and leads the country into dictatorship and darkness."[36]

About the same time, the regime suspended thirty opposition-minded professors at the University of Belgrade and imposed strict controls on the research of those faculty remaining at their jobs.[37] Vice Premier Šešelj, known for his right-wing extremist views, took a seat in the university council, vowing to carry out an additional "political purge" in university ranks.[38]

On all measures, thus, the Milošević regime must be seen as utterly devoid of any shred of moral legitimacy.

In terms of *political* legitimacy, I have already alluded to the problem presented in the fact that Milošević obtained power through a palace coup. The extensive "irregularities" during the 1992 Serbian presidential elections[39] are a matter of public record, as is Milošević's ultimately unsuccessful attempt to deny opposition parties victories in local elections in 1996.[40] To this one must add Serbia's failure to undertake serious privatization, the creation of a wealthy class consisting of a combination of Milošević's cronies and local mafiosi, and the local brand of corruption. The record adds up to illegitimacy also in the political and economic spheres.

The Serbian public is not homogeneous, by any means, and Milošević counts on the countryside for his firmest support. In the capital city, by contrast, the mood has been apocalyptic for years. Bora Djordjević, the lead singer of the Serbian rock group Fish Soup, captured the mood of the city in January 1997, belting out his song of despair and helpless protest:

> *On to chaos and disintegration,*
> *We are led by Grandma Jula,*
> *Who uses us all.*
> *We dance in a vampire ball,*
> *run by our decrepit Grandma Jula.*[41]

Reflections

This book has argued that it makes a difference for political practice whether a given system is legitimate (in the sense in which I have defined the concept of legitimacy), that nationalism is a form of illegitimate politics from root to branch, that political dynamics are reflected in, and even adumbrated by, changes in the cultural sphere, and that the religious sphere underpins and legitimizes actions and decisions taken in the political sphere. The political, cultural, and religious spheres do not exist apart from each other; they are, rather, organic parts of a religio-political-cultural system in which activity in one part has intentions, reflections, and consequences in other parts. Hence, the Serbian Orthodox Church's endorsement of the Serbian military campaign in 1991[42] heightened the political profile of that Church, deepened and cemented its growing alliance with the Serbian government of Slobodan Milošević, and distorted the Church's gospel itself. Yet so involved did the Serbian Church become in the Serbian nationalist revival and in support for the military campaign that the Vatican, which was overtly sympathetic to Croatian aspirations for independence, sent its Secretary for Foreign Relations, Jean-Louis Toran, to Belgrade on 7 August 1991 to confer with Patriarch Pavle about the crisis.[43]

More broadly, the disintegration of the political fabric in Yugoslavia was presaged by an unremitting fixation, on the part of Serbian writers, with war and war-induced suffering[44] and by a deterioration of interethnic relations in various spheres, including in ecumenical contacts, the media, and even, as outlined earlier in this book, rock music. Later, the rise of nationalist movements in Serbia, Croatia, and Slovenia was reflected in sundry spheres, including in rock music, where the strident tones of Laibach in particular served as a warning, and in the sphere of gender relations, where the new chauvinists expressed disdain for feminists and impatience with demands that women be treated with dignity. More recently, the psychological scarring that the war has produced in Serbian society was reflected in the names of some of the newest rock bands. These include bands such as Acroholia, Bloodbath, Bomba za system ("A Bomb for the System"), Boneblast, Corpus Delicti, Dead Ideas, Ekstremisti, Hands in Ashes, Malfunctions, Mortuary, Napred u Prošlost ("Forward into the Past"), Pogibja ("Catastrophe"), Purgatory, and Scaffold. One of Serbia's new breed of "turbo-rock" bands offered this bleak alternative: "We are going to Mars. Life is better there."[45]

Some cultural figures sought to assail the very cultural underpinnings of each other's nations. For example, *Politika* reported claims made by certain Serbian figures at Croats' expense. Milan Paroški, a deputy in the Serbian parliament, told that body that "Croats did not have any literature except for Serbian literature"; and Serbian writer Antonije Isaković declared, "Seeing that they could not constitute a nation on the čakavian and kajkavian dialects [spoken in parts of Croatia], Croats got the idea to take our language [Serbian]."[46] The denigration of the culture of the "enemy" nation even extended to disparagement of specific songs. For example, the Serbian daily *Politika* claimed, in August 1991, that Croats were singing patriotic songs honoring wartime fascist leader Ante Pavelić.[47] The denigration of the other's culture is, thus, one side of the political-cultural coin.

The other side of the coin is that political atavism invariably entails cultural atavism. Hence, just as Croatia restored its medieval coat of arms and its medieval currency, the kuna, there were calls in Serbia for the restoration of the old Serbian coat of arms and anthem.[48] In fact, intercommunal political conflict necessarily has a cultural dimension. And victory or defeat in the political sphere may entail as well corresponding victory or defeat in the cultural and religious spheres.

The Titoists had some sense of this, and this is why they argued back and forth in the 1950s and early 1960s as to whether they should aspire to create a new culture, a Yugoslav culture, which would melt down and assimilate the "partial" cultures of the component peoples of the country, or whether they should rather extend toleration to all component cultures, while promoting a thin overlay of "Yugoslav culture" based ultimately on Partisan mythology from World War II and notions of self-management. In 1964, at its Eighth Party Congress, the LCY opted for the second strategy: toleration while promoting a thin overlay of "Yugoslavism." The internal contradiction here, not noticed at the time, was that in tying this Yugoslavism to the Partisan mythology, this strategy entailed constant reminders of the intercommunal internecine strife of that war. Hence, even while trying to build a concept of "Yugoslavism," Yugoslavia's Communists constantly stirred up reminders of the old fires of intergroup hatred.

Could the alternative approach—energetic homogenization—have produced a happier result? Successful instances of this approach in Europe tend to involve cases where unification and adoption of this policy occurred much earlier (e.g., England, France, Spain). Twentieth-century European attempts to pursue such a policy (the USSR, interwar Czechoslovakia, early postwar Yugoslavia, and Romania in regard to Transylvania) have all run up against serious difficulties.

A 1991 article by Andrei Simić sheds additional light on the dynamics of these processes. Describing the concept of a "moral field" (defined as "an interactional sphere where those engaged typically behave towards each other with reference to ethically perceived imperatives, that is, rules which are accepted as being 'good,' 'God-given,' 'natural,' 'proper,' and so forth"),[49] Simić argues that the membership of a moral field depends on criteria of recruitment which generally are functions of kinship, tribe, or nation. "Within a moral field," Simić points out, "members are expected to act towards each other with reference to a common set of shared ideas by which behavior is structured and evaluated. In contrast, behavior outside the moral field can be said to be *amoral* in that it is primarily idiosyncratic and as such may be purely instrumental or exploitative without being subject to sanctions. Thus, for the individual, those belonging to other moral fields can be said to form part of his or her *amoral* sphere."[50] And hence, actions which might be deemed morally reprehensible when committed against a fellow member of the moral field (such as murder, torture, rape, confiscation of goods) may be seen as morally commendable when committed against persons not included in the group's moral field.

Viewing the issue in this way, it is apparent that the Titoists did not manage to create a common moral field in which all Yugoslavs would be included, much less to inculcate notions of moral universalism. Instead, moral fields remained coincident with ethnic communities, heightening the risks and dangers of political disintegration. Morality, molded and manipulated by politics, culture, and religion alike, ultimately lay at the heart of the breakdown of the Yugoslav system and of Yugoslavia itself and has lain also at the heart of the continuing problems in the Yugoslav successor states.

As long as the politicians and citizens in these states remain "realists," each society content to defend its Nation, the fundamental task will remain unattained. That task, the serious assaying of which will bring in tow the movement toward the positive resolution of a society's social, political, and even economic problems, is no less than the quest for moral excellence.[51] And for this purpose, as Plato urged in *The Laws*, states should ideally be founded on the following principles:

A.   That certain absolute moral standards exist.
B.   That such standards can be, however imperfectly, embodied in a code of law.
C.   That most of the inhabitants of the [morally refined] state, being innocent of philosophy, must never presume to act on their own initiative in modifying *either* their moral ideal *or* the code of laws which expresses it.[52]

Notes

1. Quoted in Ivo Banac, "The Dissolution of Yugoslav Historiography," in Sabrina Petra Ramet and Ljubiša S. Adamovich (eds.), *Beyond Yugoslavia: Politics, Economics, and Culture in a Shattered Community* (Boulder: Westview Press, 1995), p. 60n.
   2. Quoted in *Radio Free Europe Research* (25 November 1983), p. 2.

3. Pedro Ramet [Sabrina P. Ramet], "Yugoslavia and the Threat of Internal and External Discontents," in *Orbis*, Vol. 28, No. 1 (Spring 1984), p. 114. (The article was written in November 1983.)

4. See Viktor Meier, *Wie Jugoslawien verspielt wurde*, 2nd ed. (Munich: C. H. Beck, 1996), passim.

5. Adapted from Shakespeare, *Macbeth*, act 5, sc. 4.

6. Nicholas J. Miller, review of Stjepan G. Meštrović's *Genocide after Emotion: The Postemotional Balkan War* (1996), in *Slavic Review*, Vol. 57, No. 2 (Summer 1998), p. 441.

7. This scheme is based on my book, *Whose Democracy? Nationalism, Religion, and the Doctrine of Collective Rights in Post-1989 Eastern Europe* (Lanham, Md.: Rowman & Littlefield, 1997).

8. I am indebted, for this understanding of political legitimacy, to Guglielmo Ferrero, *The Principles of Power*, trans. from Italian by Theodore R. Jaeckel (New York: Putnam, 1942).

9. See Slobodan Milošević, *Godine raspleta*, 2nd ed. (Belgrade: Beogradski izdavačkigrafički zavod, 1989); and Slavoljub Djukić, *Izmedju slave i anateme: Politička biografija Slobodana Miloševića* (Belgrade: Filip Višnjić, 1994), pp. 49–55, 103–116. See also Ognjen Pribićević, *Vlast i opozicija u Srbiji* (Belgrade: B-92 Press, 1997), pp. 15–16 and *passim*.

10. I have presented the arguments in support of this contention in my *Whose Democracy* (especially the introduction, chapter 3, and the conclusion) and shall not repeat them here.

11. *Borba* (Belgrade) (9 May 1989), p. 3; (14 June 1989), p. 13.

12. *Politika* (Belgrade) (15 May 1992), p. 9.

13. *Politika* (23 March 1992), p. 13.

14. Quoted in "Slovenia," in Edward Lawson, *Encyclopedia of Human Rights*, 2nd ed. (Washington, D.C.: Taylor & Francis, 1996), p. 1378.

15. See examples and discussion in Sabrina P. Ramet, "Liberalizam, moral i društveni poredak: Slučaj korumpiranog populističkog pluralizma u Hrvatskoj," in *Erasmus: Časopis za kulturu demokracije*, No. 24 (May 1998), pp. 6–7.

16. See *Focus* (Munich) (9 November 1998), p. 357.

17. For a recent discussion of Croatian economic trends, see the interview with Branko Horvat: "Idemo u susret dužničkoj krizi," in *Večernji list* (Zagreb) (21 October 1998), p. 25.

18. *Croatia Weekly* (Zagreb) (22 May 1998), p. 1.

19. Stjepan G. Meštrović, "Between Postmodernism and Postcommunism: New Meanings of Citizenship, Education and Democracy," presented at a conference on "Citizenship and Education in Democracies," Ljubljana, 22–24 October 1998.

20. Conference for Peace in Yugoslavia, Arbitration Commission, "Comments on the Republic of Croatia Constitutional Law of 4 December 1991, as amended on 8 May 1992," as quoted in Reneo Lukič and Allen Lynch, *Europe from the Balkans to the Urals: The Disintegration of Yugoslavia and the Soviet Union* (Oxford: Oxford University Press, 1996), p. 280.

21. *The Constitutional Law on Human Rights and Freedoms and the Rights of National and Ethnic Communities or Minorities in the Republic of Croatia*, first published on 17 June 1992 (Zagreb: Narodne novine, 1993), Article 9, p. 151.

22. See, for example, *Croatia Weekly* (19 June 1998), p. 2.

23. *Croatia Weekly* (8 May 1998), p. 13; (22 May 1998), p. 3.

24. Letter to the author from a friend in Croatia, 20 October 1998.

25. On this point, see L. W. Sumner, *The Moral Foundation of Rights* (Oxford: Clarendon Press, 1987); Robert P. George (ed.), *Natural Law, Liberalism, and Morality: Contemporary Essays* (Oxford: Clarendon Press, 1996); and Norberto Bobbio, *Thomas Hobbes and the Natural Law Tradition*, trans. from Italian by Daniela Gobetti (Chicago: University of Chicago Press, 1993).

26. Lloyd L. Weinreb, "Natural Law and Rights," in Robert P. George (ed.), *Natural Law Theory: Contemporary Essays* (Oxford: Clarendon Press, 1992), p. 298.

27. See "Nezapamćen skandal u izboru Miss Hrvatske 1998", in *Mila* (Zagreb) (21 October 1998), pp. 40–41; "Hrvatska ove godine neće imati svoju predstavnicu na izboru Miss svijeta!" in *Globus* (Zagreb) (23 October 1998), pp. 74–75.

28. Vesna Kesić, "Državotvorne suknje," in *Tjednik* (Zagreb) (27 February 1998), p. 27.

29. Most of this paragraph is drawn from the English original of my "Liberalizam, moral i drustveni poredak," p. 7.

30. Duncan Perry, "Destiny on Hold: Macedonia and the Dangers of Ethnic Discord," in *Current History*, Vol. 97, No. 617 (March 1998), pp. 121, 123.

31. See *Index on Censorship*, Vol. 21, No. 9 (September 1992), p. 9.

32. *New Europe* (Athens) (16–22 March 1997), p. 32.

33. *Financial Times* (15 October 1998), p. 2; *International Herald Tribune* (Tokyo ed.) (22 October 1998), p. 5.

34. As quoted in *Frankfurter Rundschau* (15 October 1998), p. 5.

35. "Zakon o javnom informisanju Republike Srbije," in *Politika* (Belgrade) (22 October 1998), pp. 21–22.

36. Quoted in *International Herald Tribune* (Tokyo ed.) (22 October 1998), p. 5. See also *Vreme* (Belgrade) (17 October 1998), pp. 28–29, concerning Radio Indeks.

37. *Duga* (Belgrade), no. 1702 (10–23 October 1998), pp. 14–15.

38. *Frankfurter Rundschau* (15 October 1998), p. 5.

39. For details and documentation, see Sabrina Petra Ramet, *Social Currents in Eastern Europe: The Sources and Consequences of the Great Transformation*, 2nd ed. (Durham, N.C.: Duke University Press, 1995), pp. 421–422.

40. For a general discussion, see Obrad Kesić, "Serbian Roulette," in *Current History*, Vol. 97, No. 617 (March 1998). On local reactions, see *Vreme* (28 December 1996), pp. 6–31.

41. Quoted in *New York Times* (17 January 1997), p. A4.

42. See any issue of *Pravoslavlje* in 1991 for documentation and confirmation; also *Politika—International Weekly* (Belgrade) (22–28 June 1991), p. 6.

43. *Politika* (8 August 1991), p. 5.

44. See especially Vasa D. Mihailovich, "War in the Works of Dobrica Ćosić," in *Serbian Studies*, Vol. 3, Nos. 1/2 (Fall/Spring 1984/85); Heiko Flottau, "Alle Geschichten, giftige Hetze, verblasene Hetze," in *Süddeutsche Zeitung, Wochenende* supplement (Munich) (2/3 September 1995), p. 37.

45. Quoted in *Wall Street Journal* (27 June 1995), p. A1. See also *The Sunday Times* (London) (2 July 1995), on *Nexis*.

46. Both quoted in *Politika—International Weekly* (3–16 August 1991), p. 7.

47. *Politika* (17 August 1991), p. 3.

48. *Politika—International Weekly* (3–16 August 1991), p. 7.

49. Andrei Simić, "Obstacles to the Development of a Yugoslav National Consciousness: Ethnic Identity and Folk Culture in the Balkans," in *Journal of Mediterranean Studies*, Vol. 1, No. 1 (1991), p. 31.

50. Ibid. Along the same lines, see the comments by Dušan Kecmanović, as cited in "Grupni portret nacionalizma," in *Vreme International* (22 May 1995), especially p. 28.

51. I am leaning here on Plato, *The Laws*, trans. Trevor J. Saunders (London: Penguin Books, 1970), bk. 4, p. 179.

52. As paraphrased by Trevor J. Saunders, in his introduction to ibid., p. 29.

Anti-bibliography:
Reviewing the Reviews

In preparing this discussion of recent book reviews, three considerations have guided me: first, with the exception of a highly influential review coauthored by Gale Stokes, John Lampe, and Dennison Rusinow, with the assistance of Julie Mostov, in which a few generally innocuous comments about two of my books were made more or less in passing, I have omitted from this discussion not only reviews I have written, but also reviews in which my own work is discussed; second, I have concentrated for the most part on reviews published between 1994 and 1998 dealing with books concerned with the Yugoslav crisis and/or war or having a connection with that subject; and third, insofar as I am sitting down to write this essay while finishing a nine-month sojourn at Ritsumeikan University in Kyoto, Japan, I have perforce been limited to such materials as are either in the Ritsumeikan library or in my own files. Omissions from this review essay reflect the foregoing considerations and limitations.

I

In approaching reviews, one generally expects much the same (in some regards, at least) as one expects from a book. One expects a review, certainly, to stick to the subject, to address the salient issues, to raise the right questions, to document its assertions in a responsible fashion, to cover its subject coherently, to be balanced, and, saving the most important for last, to display a commitment to integrity and honesty, discussing its subject faithfully and without malicious distortion. Although the foregoing are the most obvious substantive requirements of a review, there are others, both of form and of substance. Of form, I would offer two: that the reviewer observe good etiquette, refraining from ad hominem attacks on his or her subject, and that the reviewer use correct English grammar and syntax. Although the latter may seem an obvious point, I note that in 1998 *Ethnic and Racial Studies* published a book review in which a disagreement of number was allowed to slip by.[1] Of substance, I would offer two further expectations: that the reviewer comment on the adequacy of the language, organization, and documentation of the work under review, and that the reviewer indicate whether the book under review, if it is on a topic likely to have a more general interest, seems to her or him to be appropriate for classroom adoption and at which level. On the former point, I note with some disappointment that none of the reviews I have reviewed noted the problems with English grammar and usage in prominent books by Christopher Bennett and David Lord Owen.[2] Indeed, the occasional lapses in Bennett, although not frequent, are particularly regrettable to me personally, since the substance of the book is admirable. Could Bennett's British publisher not afford a competent copy editor?

Of the requirements I proposed above, the most controversial is probably the question of *balance*, even if the controversy is not, for the most part, out in the open. But just what is "balance" anyway? Is it equivocation? Is it vagueness? Is it a studied avoidance of any terminology which might suggest that one has any idea as to who started a given conflict or who committed the largest number of atrocities? Does "balance" require that one merely identify the warring parties and then share the "blame" equally, as if "balance" were a mathematical formula? Does "balance" impose any responsibility in use of sources and in attribution of potentially controversial views, at least where the author suspects that a certain view may be considered controversial by some readers? Does "balance" require that one make a clear and sharp distinction between the leadership of a given state and its people or that one highlight differences of opinion within the population and, where relevant, within the given leadership? Does "balance" require—and I may tip my hand here and affirm that I believe that it does so require—that one critically reassess the inherited conventions and shibboleths in order to purge any possible myths which might otherwise creep into one's writing? And finally, does "balance" entail a "balancing act" in which one needs to set the atrocities of one side always against atrocities by others, to set the errors of one side or group of persons always against either the errors of some other side or other groups of persons or against the alleged wisdom of the original side or group of persons?

II

With regard to balance, the reviews written by Christopher Cviić, Charles King, and Martin van Heuven impress me particularly favorably. Cviić's 1995 comparative review of five books dealing with the Yugoslav crisis both summarizes the main points of the books under review and conveys something of their spirit, adding lengthy prefatory remarks placing the discussion of the literature in context.[3] Cviić's subsequent (1997) review of works by Tanner and Judah upheld the same high standard of scholarship as his previous review article.[4] Charles King's review of a book coauthored by Reneo Lukić and Allen Lynch, although it does not capture the split personality of their collaborative effort—in which Lynch was more interested in the theoretical questions raised by the dissolution of Communist federations, while Lukić was more interested in the dynamics of the Yugoslav war as such—nonetheless successfully highlights both the theoretical arguments and the analytical conclusions of the book, concluding that the authors "have performed an inestimable service by providing a lucid, well-argued and empirically rich" study.[5] For his part, Marten van Heuven serves his readers particularly well in a comparative review of books by Susan Woodward, David Owen, and Silber and Little by highlighting the radically different theories being advanced by these authors. He shows that Woodward highlights economic decline and the declining strategic importance of Yugoslavia in the post–Cold War world, though his brief summary of why Woodward considers the latter to have contributed to Yugoslavia's breakup leaves me unconvinced. Laura Silber and Allan Little, as van Heuven notes, trace the war to Milošević and his collaborators; indeed, their account does not, in this regard, have any important differences from my own interpretation, as far as I am aware. Lord Owen, by contrast, blames the EC for not holding Yugoslavia together—by force?—and Western institutions for their quite evident failure.[6] Owen seems blissfully unaware of his own contribution to that failure, however, though van Heuven does not go into this.

"Balance" may, of course, become an issue within a review as such. For example, in review-ing *This Time We Knew*, edited by Thomas Cushman and Stjepan Meštrović, and *The Bridge Betrayed*, by Michael Sells, Robert Hayden charges that the former work not only lacks bal-ance, but has as its purpose "the pursuit of Serbian evil." Although the reviewer does not sum-marize the book as such, he accuses Cushman and Meštrović of using "the classic propaganda ploy of labeling those with whom they agree virtuous and truthful and those with whom they disagree either Serb propagandists or dupes of the Serbs."[7] I confess that I am unable to locate the passage or passages in the Cushman and Meštrović book on which Professor Hayden based this assessment. Central to Hayden's allegation that *This Time We Knew* is engaged in anti-Serbian propaganda is his belief that "Cushman and Meštrović ... engage in *nothing greater* than advancing the Croatian cause."[8] If this is so, however, Hayden must have a theory about how the following passage in the editors' introduction advances the Croatian cause:

Croatian offensives against Bosnian Muslims in 1993, particularly in the city of Mostar, were contemptible and indefensible.... The International War Crimes Tribunal has in-dicted seven Croats, including individuals directly and closely linked to Franjo Tudj-man. Indictments of Bosnian Croats for war crimes are one indication that no side is without blemish in this conflict. In the late summer of 1995, Croatian troops recap-tured the rebel-held Krajina area.... The European Commission on Human Rights, U.N. observers, Amnesty International, Helsinki Watch, and the Red Cross all reported that atrocities such as burning, looting, and the murder of a number of Serbs who re-mained in the region were committed by these Croatian troops.[9]

It is a pity that Professor Hayden did not discuss this passage in the light of his charges.

Also of relevance to the issue of "balance" is an exchange of reviews between Reneo Lukić and Aleksandar Pavković. Lukić fired the "first shot" in this exchange, if I may be excused for referring to his nuanced review in this way. Lukić allowed that Pavković "excels in detailing the intellectual output of the various nationalist ideologues which can be traced back long be-fore the 1918 Kingdom,"[10] but tasked Pavković for the uncritical acceptance of certain theses articulated by Serb nationalists (e.g., that Tito's Communists collaborated with the Vatican to subjugate the Serbs), for treating all nationalist ideologies as "equally dangerous," and for characterizing "the three wars launched by the JNA" as civil wars.[11]

By contrast, Pavković, in his review of *Europe from the Balkans*, charges that the book re-vealed "nothing about the nationalist movements in the Baltics or in the Ukraine ... and little about Russia's nationalist movements," complaining further that, in his view, the book equated Milošević and his coterie with "fascists and Nazis." Pavković ends his review on a dis-missive note: "The book appears to have been written primarily on the basis of secondary ma-terial. Possibly because of this, it does not contain many novel insights. In its systematic con-demnation of Serb (but no other!) evildoers and their alleged helpers (the French and the United Kingdom, and, at times, the Russian government) as well in its advocacy of the United States' military intervention, it appears to be more a work of polemics than of scholarship."[12] Readers may compare the documentation of *Fragmentation* with that of *Europe from the Balkans* and come to their own assessment as to which book relies more heavily on secondary sources and which book offers the more extensive documentation. Here I shall observe only that Pavković mentions U.S. assistance to Croatia and Bosnia, but does not note the signifi-cance of Russian military assistance to Serbia both before and during the war,[13] avows that in film footage taken at Serb-run camps "not all prisoners pictured were starving" (p. 171), estimates that there were but 2,300 rapes (including Croat and Serb women) as of February 1993 (p. 171), characterizes the Bosnian Serb rejection of the Contact Group Plan in 1994 as "not surprising" (implying his agreement with this rejection, p. 175), writes of Croatian "mobs" and Serb "families" (e.g., pp. 179, 186), and seems to be unaware that research in Yugoslavia, Germany, the United States, and elsewhere has found that persons with *less* interaction with foreigners are *more* likely to have hostile attitudes toward foreigners (p. 188).[14]

III

Many of the reviewers find fault with the explanations offered for the war. Anita Singh, for example, worries that Christopher Bennett's *Yugoslavia's Bloody Collapse* "does not adequately discuss whether the seeds of economic catastrophe lay in the political system itself" and questions whether Bennett's assignment of culpability for the breakup to Milošević, the JNA, and the media in Serbia and Croatia is sufficient to account for the breakup.[15] That same reviewer, in turning to John Lampe's history of Yugoslavia, complains that the notion of "'ethnic conflict' does not explain why war has only involved Serbia, Croatia, and Bosnia, and not Macedonia, or Serbia and its Hungarian and Albanian minorities," forgetting about the Muslims of the Sandžak and closing with her suggestion for what sort of book Lampe *should* have written (in her view).[16] Stevan Pavlowitch, turning to the recent study of Bosnian history by Donia and Fine,[17] claims that, in their effort to debunk the absurd thesis of "ancient hatreds" as the ultimate source of the recent Yugoslav war, the authors offer the opposite extreme, carrying the story forward amid "errors" of fact and "plain inventions."[18] The seven pages allotted to Pavlowitch were not sufficient to enable him to make a convincing case for his rejection of the Donia and Fine thesis about a Bosnian tradition of tolerance and cooperation, at least in my view, and I, for one, would be interested in seeing an alternative history of Bosnia from Pavlowitch's pen.

And Ivo Banac, although conceding the spit and polish of Misha Glenny's literary style, believes that Glenny devotes so much of his space to recounting his own escapades that he never quite manages to provide much insight into what was going on around him. Banac finds Glenny's bibliographic cupboard to be bare and notes that Glenny's account is built largely on conversations he had had with locals.[19]

Some reviewers are clearly guided in their reviews by special interests of their own. To some extent, this is unavoidable. But, to take just one example, Ian Williams, in a review of three rather different works, asserts that all three—by Radha Kumar, Jasminka Udovički and James Ridgeway, and Kemal Kurspahić—"deal with that modern aberration we accept uncritically: the nation-state," noting that many states are multicultural.[20] This comment may appeal to those who are unaware that in the field of history the term "nation-state" is restricted to nationally *homogeneous* states, so that, in fact, *none* of these books deal with that "aberration" at all, and to those who fancy that the growing strength of multinational corporations is rendering the traditional state apparatus obsolete, but it does not provide much of a clue as to the contents of the Udovički and Ridgeway book, at least, and even the reviewer's further comments about the "Procrustean approach to nation-building" may not undo the confusion which might be sown by his review.

A recurrent theme throughout both the reviews and the books they review is that the endeavor to trace the origins of the Serbian Insurrectionary War to allegedly "ancient hatreds" is not merely misguided, but actually dangerous. Noel Malcolm denounces the "ancient hatreds" thesis[21] and is seconded here by reviewer Robert Donia,[22] who, in his own book with John V. A. Fine, Jr., does likewise. Christopher Bennett in turn has no more use for the thesis of "ancient hatreds" than does *his* reviewer.[23] Charles King, in his review of the Lukić and Lynch volume, likewise takes time to condemn the "ancient hatreds" thesis,[24] as do Jasminka Udovički and Ejub Štitkovac in their sophisticated contribution to *Burn This House* (1997).[25] This theme takes on some interesting variations in David Fromkin's review of Michael Ignatieff's latest book. Ignatieff is, like almost everyone else who takes up a pen, dismayed by the persistence and popularity of the "ancient hatreds" thesis in the media, but, as Fromkin points out, Ignatieff sees a related, if more sophisticated and hence more dangerous, interpretation at work in Samuel P. Huntington's "clash of civilizations" theory, which, says Fromkin, likewise "trace[s] today's civil wars to the distant past."[26] Where the Serbian Insurrectionary War is concerned, Ignatieff, in his *The Warrior's Honor: Ethnic War and the Modern Conscience* (1998), would have us trace it not to the distant past of primordial feuds whose specifics are, at best, remembered "through a glass darkly," as the phrase has it, but to the more proximate past of World War II. But Fromkin does not like this solution and counters:

> Like so many answers in history, however, the one above provides no resting point. Let's say that the Serbs, Croats, Bosnians, and other Yugoslavs betrayed, tortured, mutilated, raped, and slaughtered in the 1990s because they did so in the 1940s, but why did they do so in the 1940s? Ignatieff does not confront that question, and indeed takes a wrong turn here in his discussion.[27]

The wrong turn, Fromkin says, is that Ignatieff locates the "ultimate" source of the problem in the cultural *similarity* of Serbs and Croats, basing this assessment on a notion Ignatieff attributes to Sigmund Freud. This "explanation" may satisfy some, but it has more of the character of an article of faith than of a perspicuous scientific explication.

Be that as it may, this obsessive pursuit of so threadbare a thesis is, of course, the result of the unfortunate influence that Robert D. Kaplan's best-selling *Balkan Ghosts* (1993) has had among some Western policy-makers and journalists. Henry Cooper's insightful review for *Slavic Review* says all that needs to be said on the subject of Kaplan's book. Noting Kaplan's ignorance of local languages and history, Cooper characterizes *Balkan Ghosts* as "a dreadful mix of unfounded generalizations, misinformation, outdated sources, personal prejudices and bad writing." Cooper further observes that, in Kaplan's view, the Romanians have "the Latin bent for melodrama," Greek politics is "erotic," Bulgarians are "mongrel products," and somewhere in the Balkans "men had their arms around the oily backsides of women." Moreover, "his Danube flows through Serbia but not Croatia," there is (for Kaplan) "little room for moral choices" in the Balkans, and bigotry is—again in Kaplan's representation—ubiquitous in that part of the world. Cooper calls Kaplan's *Ghosts* "a distasteful mix of tired clichés, undigested or incorrect historical fact, and personal bias,"[28] leaving it, however, to the review's readers to speculate as to the continuing legacy of Kaplan's commercially promoted misinformation.

IV

In examining alternative reviews of the same work, one hopes to be able to factor out (or in) the given reviewer's known biases and to obtain a sense of how the book is being received not just in one or another camp in our polarized field, but in the field as a whole.

The most ambitious review article to date—coauthored by Gale Stokes, John Lampe, and Dennison Rusinow, with the collaboration of Julie Mostov—is the only review article of which I am aware which seems to aspire to define the consensus of the field *for* the field. That, at any rate, I would guess was at least one motivation for three of the most senior figures in the field to decide to collaborate in this enterprise. And hence too, when Stokes, Lampe, and Rusinow crown Christopher Bennett, Lenard Cohen, Susan Woodward, and the team of Laura Silber and Allan Little as the authors of "the short list of required reading on the Yugoslav crisis,"[29] they assume responsibility for shaping, or at least for contributing to shaping, scholarly opinion about the literature on the Yugoslav war. So too, when they suggest that "[Noel] Malcolm's distress at the devastation he witnessed personally at times gets the better of the balanced approach to which the book aspires,"[30] one is expected to conclude that "scholarly balance" is somehow incompatible with moral outrage. Immanuel Kant would not have agreed. Nor would Mark Almond, who cites, with approval, Aristotle's acknowledgment that there are "occasions when indignation is the only appropriate response."[31]

Susan Woodward's *Balkan Tragedy* (1995) has generally fared well with reviewers, though the picture is not unmixed. Several reviewers have noted Woodward's tendency to blame the Slovenes and Germans for the breakup of Yugoslavia. Although I consider this assignment of culpability to be bizarre and at extreme variance with the facts, Alex Dragnich, reviewing her book for *Journal of Politics*, endorses Woodward's interpretation here, which, Dragnich says, "shows, on the one hand, how Western European actions, notably those of Germany and Austria, gave aid and comfort to Slovenia and Croatia prior to the secessions in the determination of those republics to undermine Yugoslavia, and on the other hand, how Slovene and Croat officials, while still part of Yugoslavia's governing system, conspired with officials in Bonn and Vienna to destroy the state."[32] It boggles the mind that some eighty years after the Triple Entente's dismantlement of the seven-hundred-year-old Habsburg Empire, reducing Austria to minuscule proportions, some observers can still see Metternich's ghost in the vicissitudes of European politics.

In fact, as Letty Coffin and I have demonstrated elsewhere, (1) the notion of a German-Austrian conspiracy to break up Yugoslavia originated with Milošević's mouthpieces, *Politika* and *Politika ekspres*, and was first energetically promoted only after Serbian machinations had driven the Slovenes and Croats to rush for the exit doors; (2) the German government's hard pressure on its EU partners to agree to recognize Slovenian and Croatian independence came only after the JNA had begun its bombardment of the resort town of Dubrovnik, a city having essentially no strategic value; (3) the other EU states had leaders capable of thinking for themselves and agreed with German leaders in December 1991 that continuing to withhold recognition six months after the formal declarations of independence and more than two months after the expiration of the moratorium on independence imposed on Slovenia and Croatia by the EU made no sense and could serve no useful purpose; (4) the demonization of Germany which had begun with Belgrade was soon picked up by Lord Carrington, who was eager to cover up his own failings; and (5) the myth became the semiofficial "doctrine" of the British Conservative government of John Major only later, after the failure of the Anglo-French policies in Bosnia became apparent, at which time Whitehall was eager to pin blame on a scapegoat.[33] Thus was born the myth of Germany's "premature" recognition of Slovenia and Croatia, a myth which has seen widespread uncritical acceptance.[34] Dragnich's three criticisms of Woodward's book are that "it is too long," that it should have discussed Alija Izetbegović's "Islamic Declaration" (a document typically cited by persons sympathetic to Belgrade and/or Pale), and that Woodward's discussion of the so-called safe havens is "inadequate."[35]

Chris Cviić agrees that Woodward "rejects out of hand what she calls 'conventional wisdom' which blames the war on Slobodan Milošević's effort, in alliance with the Yugoslav Army, to carve out a Greater Serbia," but Cviić says that Woodward traces the crisis and conflict to "the disintegration of government authority amid the breakdown of a political and civil order which occurred while Yugoslavia was trying, at the behest of its international capitalist creditors, to transform itself into a functioning market economy and a pluralist democracy."[36] Just how pusillanimous Yugoslavia's efforts to move toward a market economy were has been amply described and documented by Viktor Meier.[37] As for its supposed interest in "pluralist democracy," this was not an interest shared by Milošević or Kadijević or Mikulić or Planinc or Jović or Šuvar or Mojsov or Dizdarević or any of a number of other political figures occupying prominent positions in the years 1986–1991. But, Cviić points out, Woodward also highlights the pivotal role of economic decline of Yugoslavia's decentralized system, suggesting that, in Woodward's view, the ultimate collapse of the SFRY may have been "overdetermined."

Stokes, Lampe, Rusinow, and Mostov, while clearly marveling at what they called her "tightly packed narrative,"[38] question some of her economic analysis.[39] Noting, moreover, Woodward's tendency to see the *Slovenes* as the "real" culprits in the story, they point out that "She hardly discusses the Kosovo crisis [at all] and finds a number of ways to defend the policies of Slobodan Milošević. Some of these defenses are hard to accept."[40] One reviewer accused Woodward of spinning her story without regard to chronology, suggesting that the tale would have read rather differently had she followed a strict chronological scheme.[41] Yet another reviewer finds nothing to criticize and calls the book "the first major scholarly book in English on the dissolution of Yugoslavia and the partitioning of the south Slav lands and peoples"[42]—a phraseology which may or may not have been intended to dismiss as less than "major" previous tomes by Cohen (1993),[43] Almond (1994),[44] and Jopp (1994).[45]

And van Heuven, in his review article of 1996, notes that Woodward portrays Croatian President Tudjman as "a manipulative, right-wing nationalist";[46] he appears to have been convinced by Woodward that the conflict did not have an "ethnic" nature[47] and that Yugoslavia was worth saving.[48] But were not the hatreds which were provoked first by the Serbian media and somewhat later also by the Croatian media "ethnic" in content, or do Woodward and van Heuven believe that the hatreds were targeted along "nonethnic" lines—for example, along class lines? If they do not believe this, then along what alternative lines do they suggest such hatreds were mobilized? But if, on the contrary, the hatreds stirred up did indeed have an "ethnic" content— Serbs hating Muslims *qua* Muslims, Croats hating Serbs *qua* Serbs, and so forth—then how and why should we not see an "ethnic" character also in the war fueled by these hatreds? And further, if Yugoslavia was worth saving, was *any sort* of Yugoslavia worth saving, for example, a tyrannical Yugoslavia dominated by a leader lacking respect for human rights, and if so, why?

Lenard Cohen's *Broken Bonds* has been possibly the most commercially successful scholarly book on the Yugoslav war to date. Adopted by the History Book Club as a selection, Cohen's book was also cited favorably by Richard Holbrooke in testimony before a committee of the U.S. Congress. *Broken Bonds* was recently published in its third edition, making it a "moving target" as it were. And as with any book which has gone through three editions, there is room for uncertainty concerning the extent to which points made in reviews based on the first or second edition may still be applicable to the third edition. My own comments on Cohen's durable account are based on a reading of his *second* edition.[49]

Cohen wins high praise from the collaborative team of Stokes, Lampe, Rusinow, and Mostov, who characterize Cohen's criticism of Germany as "cautious."[50] I would describe it as "unnecessary" and "misleading." But in virtually sequential passages which appear to have been written by different members of that team, they write that "for Cohen, Slobodan Milošević was the initiator of the nationalist fever" that engulfed Yugoslavia and, just two paragraphs later, that "Cohen ascribes the eruption of violence in 1991–92 to three long-term causes: persistent ethnic and religious animosities, the stirring up of memories from the bloodlettings of World War II, and the post–World War II failure of political modernization and of the communist nationalities policy."[51] Of these three factors, the first brings Cohen perilously close to articulating a new reductionism. At the outset of his book, Cohen refers to "the [Yugoslav] population's predilection for political extremism."[52] The choice of the word "predilection," rather than the equally reductionist "tradition" or "legacy," tells us that Cohen does not subscribe to the historical reductionism of Kaplan, but to a *psychological* reductionism reminiscent of passages in Ignatieff's aforementioned book. The wording implies that Yugoslavs are somehow "more extreme" than other peoples—for example, than Americans or Canadians or English. The second factor—"the stirring up of memories" of World War II—is, of course, part of the equation, but how much prominence should this be given, and should it be represented as more important than, let us say, the country's growing economic problems in the 1980s or the fact that these memories were being manipulated rather specifically by nationalists with specific agendas? As for the third factor, if the problem lay somehow in Communist nationalities policy, then what were the factors which resulted in *that* failure? That would seem to be a critical question, and one to which a review of Cohen's book should have addressed itself. On this point, Bennett, by contrast, has been described by Cviić as "an extremely fair critic of the Tito regime's nationality policy *which he considers to have been a partial success.*"[53]

Jasna Dragović, a reviewer for the British journal *Millennium*, judges Cohen's book to be "analytical and balanced" and declares that it is "required reading," following the style of academic reviewers who imagine that, with their reviews, they are making class assignments to the profession.[54] She also writes that "Cohen shows how the hasty decision to recognize Bosnia-Hercegovina before agreement was reached between its three constitutive nations (the Croats, the Moslems, and the Serbs) contributed to the explosion in the republic,"[55] even though, of course, as Donia and Fine have shown, the fragile peace in Bosnia had been unraveling since 1989,[56] and even though Milošević and Karadžić had sat down in August 1991 to plan the launching of open hostilities in Bosnia the following spring,[57] so that the albeit naïve international recognition at the most provided a pretext for Serbian violence. (Moreover, although the international community may have been naïve about the South Slavs, one fault of which the international community *cannot* be accused in any step along the way, save for the pro-Serbian decision to impose an arms embargo on all the Yugoslav successor states, is *haste!* Quite to the contrary, the international community displayed a penchant to respond with quasi-glacial lethargy, regardless of the situation at hand.)

One of Cohen's stiffer reviews comes from Professor Ivo Banac, of Yale University, who charges that Cohen ignores almost all the important literature, producing "a tedious and lazy book … [with] a cornucopia of historical howlers," in which no interpretation is advanced, except to advocate the opinion "that everybody is equally guilty in the Yugoslav meltdown." Banac adds that for the more contemporary chapters, Cohen depends almost exclusively on the Foreign Broadcast Information Service (FBIS) translation service, ignoring other useful material.[58] Although Professor Cohen seems to be less inclined to make use of the secondary literature—even of the so-called required reading—than other authors, even in his second edition, my own quarrel with his use of the FBIS is rather different from that of Professor Banac. I have long considered the FBIS service to be invaluable, *provided* that one clearly indicates the original source and notes that one is citing from the FBIS translation of said source; I consider the completeness of the citation important, since it makes a difference for the significance of a report on, for example, Bosnian Croat atrocities against Muslims whether the report originated with a Bosnian Muslim source, a Croatian (opposition) source, a Serbian source, or a German source. Yet in his documentation for the second edition, Cohen lists only the FBIS reports in his notes, depriving the reader of the ability to trace the ultimate sources of statements with any ease. This, to my mind, is a serious failing, but perhaps one he may have been able to remedy in his third edition (which I do not, regrettably, have on hand).

Branka Magaš's *The Destruction of Yugoslavia,*[59] published in 1993, was one of the first books in what has become a deluge on the subject of Yugoslavia's breakup and descent into war. Bringing together her journalistic writings from a period of over twelve years, the book shows both her prescience and her courage over the years. Needless to say, her firm criticism of Milošević and Serbian nationalists in general has not won her applause from those quarters sympathetic to the Serbian cause. Stokes, Lampe, Rusinow, and Mostov praise her for being "an astute observer and an intelligent analyst" and then go on to say that "she understood better than most the subversive effect that *Slovenian* aspirations were having on the rest of Yugoslavia."[60] This description is scarcely in the spirit of the book, but perhaps the text in *Slavic Review* incorporates a misprint—"Slovenian" for "Serbian" (?).

Strangely, Michael Ignatieff, in the *New York Review of Books*, accused Magaš of failing to note the "objective causes" of tumescent Serbian nationalism[61]—a claim promptly rebutted by Banac, who documents in detail Magaš's contribution to understanding the entire context in which the Serbian national movement gathered steam in the course of the 1980s. Along related lines, in his bibliographic essay at the close of his own book, Christopher Bennett commends Magaš for having provided the most comprehensive discussion, in English, of the waxing problems in Kosovo, which contributed so much to the growth of the Serb national movement. By contrast with the foregoing discussion, Jonathan Stoneman's brief review of *The Destruction of Yugoslavia* for *International Affairs* adds little except to note that, in his view, the inclusion of certain polemical exchanges with a group of *Praxis* philosophers–turned–Serbian nationalists, in the early 1980s, will be too abstruse and "too arcane" to be intelligible to nonspecialists. For all that, Stoneman judges her book to be "well worth reading," while highlighting the advantages and disadvantages of the book's organizational scheme.[62]

Few books in the field of Yugoslav studies have excited so much attention, or so much disappointment, as John Lampe's *Yugoslavia as History* (1996).[63] The book certainly has its strengths. As a blow-by-blow historical narrative of the political and economic life of this ill-fated country from gestation and birth through its final fractious fissure and fragmentation in the course of 1988–1991, Lampe's contribution will surely remain useful in the years ahead. Lampe is especially strong on economic and diplomatic history and his familiarity with the literature, as reflected in his notes, is nothing short of dazzling.

But from the beginning critics have raised tough questions, repeatedly complaining of certain omissions from the 421-page volume. Among the first reviews was one written by Attila Hoare for *International Affairs*, which complains that Lampe's "Hobbesian model [of the SFRY] obscures more than it explains" and complains further that the text "omits several key historical episodes, among them the union of Montenegro with Serbia in 1918, the Partisan movement in Macedonia during the Second World War, and the Kosovo uprising and its suppression by the Yugoslav security forces in 1981. The final outbreak of war between the Yugoslav People's Army and first Slovenia and then Croatia is confined to two short sentences."[64] More ominously, Hoare charges that although Lampe discusses Serbs' tribulations at the hands of both Croatian authorities and the Albanians of Kosovo, he omits any discussion of the army's role in the suppression of Kosovo's autonomy in 1989 or the arming of Serbian civilians in Croatia in 1990 or even the army's assault on the Slovene republic in June 1991.[65] Ivo Banac writes in a similar vein, lamenting the exclusion of certain issues from Bosnian, Macedonian, Montenegrin, and Slovenian history. Banac also lists a series of questions not addressed by Lampe, from the nature of King Aleksandar's political program to the reasons for the monopolization of the Croatian national cause in the interwar period by a peasant party to the relationship between religion and nationality in that same era to the impact of the occupation regime during World War II. Banac also notes the virtually complete absence of cultural history from Lampe's treatment.[66] Professor Singh of the London School of Economics and Political Science also complains of an omission: "His account tells us more about the nationalisms that ultimately overturned Yugoslavia than about the appeal of the idea of Yugoslavia. Indeed, he leaves the reader somewhat confused about what it meant to its advocates, and with the impression that ethnic conflict *was* somehow inevitable."[67]

More laudatory, though not uncritically so, is John Allcock's review for *Europe-Asia Studies*. Allcock praises Lampe for striking an analytical balance as well as for his skill in destroying certain myths which have gained some currency. Among these myths, Allcock mentions the notion that the student unrest in Belgrade in 1968 and the work of the *Praxis* group "should be seen as somehow 'progressive.'"[68] Allcock's criticism of Lampe is so minor that it can be safely left aside.

Both Banac and Hoare charge Lampe with the commission of factual errors,[69] while Banac bemoans Lampe's decision to write his history through the lenses of the present—a strategy also employed by Tim Judah, with occasionally distracting effects, in his otherwise admirable history of the Serbs.[70]

The last case I shall take up is not a book as such, but rather a pair of books, written by James Gow, a British specialist in military and security affairs. *Legitimacy and the Military: The Yugoslav Crisis*, which Gow finished in July 1991 and which Pinter Publishers managed to bring out before the end of the year (much to their credit!), received high accolades from James Pettifer in a succinct review for *International Affairs*. Pettifer notes that Gow recounts the role of the Yugoslav army leadership in destroying the SFRY system, organizing his material around the thesis that "the army had other choices in the late 1980s and early 1990 which it could have exercised."[71] Stokes, Lampe, Rusinow, and Mostov provide a slightly longer summation of the book, stressing three key pressures the army faced in the post-Tito era.[72]

James Gow's *Triumph of the Lack of Will*, published two years after the Dayton Accords and thus benefiting from the relative closure those accords brought to the Bosnia story, has, if anything, confirmed his standing in the field. Writing for *Europe-Asia Studies*, Cathie Carmichael called Gow's book "one of the best" on its subject and claimed that it "surpasses much of the literature in this boggy field."[73] Along similar lines, Michael Stewart, writing for the *London Review of Books*, notes that Gow "provides a good account of the bad timing, bad judgment, disunity, and, crucially, lack of political will which weakened international diplomacy and allowed the crisis to turn into a war."[74]

V

In compiling this review of reviews, I was struck by several things. First, books of which I had expected to find reviews sometimes left no trace in scholarly journals otherwise interested in offering reviews of the literature. Whatever the reason, this is regrettable. Second, reviews in English-language journals of impressive works on this subject in German are so few and far between as to render a comparative review of English-language reviews of literature in German impractical. Third, even allowing for the sundry lines of polarization in the field of Yugoslav studies and the unfortunate tendency of some reviewers to lose their critical faculties when reading wildly distorted passages which support their own notions, I found *more* consensus in the field than I had expected. The works of Woodward, Cohen, Magaš, Lampe, and Gow—selected both because of their influence and because of the number of available reviews of these books—have a more or less clear profile in the field; indeed, among the five, only Woodward's thesis is given multiple interpretations by reviewers, suggesting that her thesis may have gotten lost along the way. And fourth, with one or two exceptions, reviewers seem to have maintained an appropriate level of decorum, though I remain troubled by what I fear may be a rising tide of nastiness and general rudeness in the field, manifesting itself in the first place in reviews and letters, with offenders often proving to be "repeat offenders." The subject of genocide, in particular, is bound to excite deeply felt passions; but that is all the more reason to maintain a level of dignity and decorum in scholarly discourse.

Notes

1. Review of Bogdan Denitch's *Ethnic Nationalism: The Tragic Death of Yugoslavia* (1996) and of Michael A. Sells's *The Bridge Betrayed: Religion and Genocide in Bosnia* (1996), by John B. Allcock, in *Ethnic and Racial Studies*, Vol. 21, No. 1 (January 1998), p. 168: "If anybody is … they should read …"

2. Christopher Bennett, *Yugoslavia's Bloody Collapse: Causes, Course and Consequences* (New York: New York University Press, 1995); and David Owen, *Balkan Odyssey* (London: Victor Gollancz, 1995).

3. Christopher Cviić, "Review article: Perceptions of former Yugoslavia: an interpretative reflection," in *International Affairs*, Vol. 71, No. 4 (October 1995), pp. 819–826.

4. Review of Marcus Tanner's *Croatia: A Nation Forged in War* and of Tim Judah's *The Serbs: History, Myth, and the Destruction of Yugoslavia*, by Christopher Cviić, in *International Affairs*, Vol. 73, No. 4 (October 1997), pp. 811–812.

5. Review of Reneo Lukić and Allen Lynch's *Europe from the Balkans to the Urals: The Disintegration of Yugoslavia and the Soviet Union* (1996), by Charles King, in *Europe-Asia Studies*, Vol. 49, No. 7 (November 1997), p. 1339, hereafter "King on Lukić and Lynch."

6. Marten van Heuven, "Understanding the Balkan Breakup," in *Foreign Policy*, No. 103 (Summer 1996), pp. 176–178.

7. Robert M. Hayden, "The Tactical Uses of Passion," in *Current Anthropology*, Vol. 38, No. 5 (December 1997), the first quotation from p. 924, the second quotation from p. 925.

8. Ibid., p. 924, my emphasis.

9. Thomas Cushman and Stjepan G. Meštrović, "Introduction," in T. Cushman and S. G. Meštrović (eds.), *This Time We Knew: Western Responses to Genocide* (New York: New York University Press, 1996), p. 16.

10. Review of Aleksandar Pavković's *The Fragmentation of Yugoslavia: Nationalism in a Multinational State* (1997), by Reneo Lukić, in *Europe-Asia Studies*, Vol. 49, No. 8 (December 1997), p. 1545.

11. Ibid.

12. Review of Reneo Lukić and Allen Lynch's *Europe from the Balkans to the Urals: The Disintegration of Yugoslavia and the Soviet Union* (1996), by Aleksandar Pavković, in *Slavic Review*, Vol. 57, No. 3 (Fall 1998), pp. 627–628.

13. Documented in Viktor Meier, *Wie Jugoslawien verspielt wurde*, 2nd ed. (Munich: C. H. Beck, 1996).

14. Aleksandar Pavković, *The Fragmentation of Yugoslavia: Nationalism in a Multinational State* (New York: St. Martin's Press, 1997).

15. Review of Christopher Bennett's *Yugoslavia's Bloody Collapse: Causes, Course and Consequences* (1995), by Anita Inder Singh, in *Nations and Nationalism*, Vol. 2 (1996), Pt. 2, p. 341, hereafter "Singh on Bennett."

16. Review of John R. Lampe's *Yugoslavia as History: Twice There was a Country* (1996), by Anita Inder Singh, in *Nations and Nationalism*, Vol. 19, No. 1 (January 1996), pp. 187–189.

17. Robert J. Donia and John V. A. Fine, Jr., *Bosnia and Hercegovina: A Tradition Betrayed* (New York: Columbia University Press, 1994).

18. Stevan K. Pavlowitch, "Review article: The History of Bosnia and Herzegovina," in *Ethnic and Racial Studies*, Vol. 19, No.1 (January 1996), pp. 187–189.

19. Ivo Banac, "Misreading the Balkans," in *Foreign Policy*, No. 93 (Winter 1993/94), p. 178.

20. Ian Williams, "The Butcher Shop," in *The Nation* (12/19 January 1998), p. 28.

21. Noel Malcolm, *Bosnia: A Short History* (New York: New York University Press, 1994).

22. Review of Noel Malcolm's *Bosnia: A Short History* (1994), by Robert J. Donia, in *Slavic Review*, Vol. 54, No. 2 (Summer 1995), pp. 505–506.

23. Singh on Bennett, p. 341.

24. King on Lukić and Lynch, p. 1339.

25. Jasminka Udovički and Ejub Štitkovac, "Bosnia and Hercegovina: The Second War," in Jasminka Udovički and James Ridgeway (eds.), *Burn This House: The Making and Unmaking of Yugoslavia* (Durham, N.C.: Duke University Press, 1997), pp. 176, 202.

26. David Fromkin, "Retrogressive Little Wars: Honor Forgotten," in *Foreign Affairs*, Vol. 77, No. 1 (January/February 1998), p. 145.

27. Ibid., pp. 146–147.

28. Review of Robert D. Kaplan's *Balkan Ghosts: A Journey through History* (1993), by Henry R. Cooper, in *Slavic Review*, Vol. 52, No. 3 (Fall 1993), pp. 592–593.

29. Gale Stokes, John Lampe, and Dennison Rusinow, with Julie Mostov, "Instant History: Understanding the Wars of Yugoslav Succession," in *Slavic Review*, Vol. 55, No. 1 (Spring 1996), p. 148.

30. Ibid., p. 151.

31. Quoted from Mark Almond's *Europe's Backyard War* (1994), by Branka Magaš, in her review of Almond's book for *International Affairs*, Vol. 71, No. 2 (April 1995), p. 409.

32. Review of Susan L. Woodward's *Balkan Tragedy: Chaos and Dissolution After the Cold War* (1995), by Alex N. Dragnich, in *Journal of Politics*, Vol. 58, No. 3 (August 1996), p. 930, hereafter "Dragnich on Woodward."

33. Sabrina P. Ramet and Letty Coffin, "Germany's Policy vis-à-vis the Yugoslav Successor States, 1991–98," scheduled to be published in a book edited by Eric Shiraev and Richard Sobel, and, in Slovenian translation, in *Teorija in praksa*. See also Daniele Conversi, *German-Bashing and the Breakup of Yugoslavia*, Donald W. Treadgold Papers in Russian, East European, and Central Asian Studies, No. 16 (Seattle: The HMJ School of International Studies of the University of Washington, 1997).

34. For example, by A. Mark Weisburd, in his "The Emptiness of the Concept of *Jus Cogens*, as Illustrated by the War in Bosnia-Herzegovina," in *Michigan Journal of International Law*, Vol. 17, No. 1 (Fall 1995), pp. 4–5.

35. Dragnich on Woodward, p. 931.

36. Cviić, "Perceptions of former Yugoslavia," p. 824.

37. See Meier, *Wie Jugoslawien verspielt wurde*, chaps. 1–3.

38. Stokes et al., "Instant History," p. 145.

39. Ibid., p. 140.

40. Ibid., p. 146.

41. Review of Susan Woodward's *Balkan Tragedy: Chaos and Dissolution After the Cold War* (1995) by Michael Libal, in *Harvard International Review*, Vol. 18, No. 2 (Spring 1966), p. 67.

42. Review of Susan Woodward's *Balkan Tragedy: Chaos and Dissolution after the Cold War* (1995), by Robert M. Hayden, in *Slavic Review*, Vol. 54, No. 4 (Winter 1995), p. 1114.

43. Lenard J. Cohen, *Broken Bonds: The Disintegration of Yugoslavia* (Boulder: Westview Press, 1993).

44. Mark Almond, *Europe's Backyard War: The War in the Balkans* (London: Heinemann Press, 1994).

45. M. Jopp (ed.), *The Implications of the Yugoslav Crisis for Western Europe's Foreign Relations* (Paris: Institute for Security Studies of the WEU, 1994).

46. van Heuven, "Understanding," p. 180.

47. Ibid., p. 185.

48. Ibid., p. 188.

49. Lenard J. Cohen, *Broken Bonds: Yugoslavia's Disintegration and Balkan Politics in Transition*, 2nd ed. (Boulder: Westview Press, 1995).

50. Stokes et al., "Instant History," p. 144.

51. Ibid.

52. Cohen, *Broken Bonds*, 2nd ed., p. 21.

53. Cviić, "Perceptions of former Yugoslavia," p. 825, my emphasis.

54. Review of Lenard J. Cohen, *Broken Bonds: The Disintegration of Yugoslavia*, 1st ed. (Boulder: Westview Press, 1993), by Jasna Dragović, in *Millennium*, Vol. 23, No. 3 (Winter 1994), p. 741.

55. Ibid., p. 742.

56. Robert J. Donia and John V. A. Fine, Jr., *Bosnia and Hercegovina: A Tradition Betrayed* (New York: Columbia University Press, 1994), passim.

57. *Vreme* (Belgrade) (30 September 1991), p. 5. Moreover, as Cviić notes, Norman Cigar, in his *Genocide in Bosnia: The Policy of "Ethnic Cleansing"* (College Station, Tex.: Texas A & M University Press, 1995), "demonstrates, from a wealth of original material, that there was nothing spontaneous about this policy [ethnic cleansing]. It was developed from above by politicians in Serbia who knew what they were doing." Cviić, "Perceptions of former Yugoslavia," p. 826.

58. Review of Lenard J. Cohen, *Broken Bonds: The Disintegration of Yugoslavia*, 1st ed. (Boulder: Westview Press, 1993) by Ivo Banac in *Political Science Quarterly*, Vol. 109, No. 4 (Fall 1994), p. 728.

59. Branka Magaš, *The Destruction of Yugoslavia: Tracking the Break-up* (London: Verso, 1993).

60. Stokes et al., "Instant History," p. 137, my emphasis.

61. As cited in Banac, "Misreading," p. 180.

62. Review of Branka Magaš's *The Destruction of Yugoslavia: Tracking the Break-up 1980–92* (1993), by Jonathan Stoneman, in *International Affairs*, Vol. 70, No. 2 (April 1994), p. 369.

63. John R. Lampe, *Yugoslavia as History: Twice There Was a Country* (Cambridge: Cambridge University Press, 1996).

64. Review of John Lampe's *Yugoslavia as History* (1996), by Attila Hoare, in *International Affairs*, Vol. 73, No. 3 (July 1997), p. 590.

65. Ibid.

66. Review of John Lampe's *Yugoslavia as History* (1996), by Ivo Banac, in *Slavic Review*, Vol. 57, No. 2 (Summer 1998), pp. 438–439.

67. Review of John Lampe's *Yugoslavia as History* (1996), by Anita Inder Singh, in *Nations and Nationalism*, Vol. 4, Pt. 2 (April 1998), p. 290, Singh's emphasis.

68. Review of John Lampe's *Yugoslavia as History* (1996), by John B. Allcock, in *Europe-Asia Studies*, Vol. 49, No. 6 (September 1997), p. 1121.

69. See especially Attila Hoare's review for examples.

70. Tim Judah, *The Serbs: History, Myth and the Destruction of Yugoslavia* (New Haven: Yale University Press, 1997). See also Christopher Cviić's laudatory review of Judah's book in *International Affairs*, Vol. 73, No. 4 (Octoober 1997), pp. 811–813.

71. Pettifer's paraphrase, in review of James Gow's *Legitimacy and the Military* (1991), by James Pettifer, in *International Affairs*, Vol. 69, No. 1 (January 1993), p. 161.

72. Stokes et al., "Instant History," pp. 138–139.

73. Review of James Gow's *Triumph of the Lack of Will: International Diplomacy and the Yugoslav War* (1997), by Cathie Carmichael, in *Europe-Asia Studies*, Vol. 50, No. 3 (May 1998), pp. 560, 561.

74. Michael Stewart, "Atone and Move Forward," in *London Review of Books* (11 December 1997), p. 15.

About the Book and the Author

The third edition of this critically acclaimed work includes two new chapters and a new epilogue, as well as revisions throughout the book. Sabrina Ramet, a veteran observer of the Yugoslav scene, traces the steady deterioration of Yugoslavia's social and political fabric in the years since 1980, arguing that, whatever the complications entailed in the national question, the final crisis was triggered by economic deterioration, shaped by the federal system itself, and pushed forward toward war by Serbian politicians bent on power—either within a centralized Yugoslavia or within an "ethnically cleansed" Greater Serbia. The book sheds light on the contributions made by Croatian naïvete and Western diplomatic bungling to the tragedy in Bosnia, discusses the course of the Serbian Insurrectionary War in both Croatia and Bosnia, and devotes a chapter to examining the separate paths of Slovenia and Macedonia, before turning to an assessment of the record in post-Dayton Bosnia and Serb-Albanian frictions in Kosovo during 1989–1998. Chapters on the primary religious associations and on the rock scene help to set the political developments in perspective. With her detailed knowledge of the organic connections between politics, culture, and religion, Ramet paints a strikingly original picture of Yugoslavia's demise and the emergence and politics of the Yugoslav successor states.

Sabrina P. Ramet is a Professor of International Studies at the University of Washington in Seattle. She is the author of six other books, among them *Whose Democracy? Nationalism, Religion, and the Doctrine of Collective Rights in Post-1989 Eastern Europe* (1997) and *Nihil Obstat: Religion, Politics, and Social Change in East-Central Europe and Russia* (1998). She has also edited a dozen books, mostly about Eastern Europe and Russia.

Index

Manatos, Andrew, 186
Mančevski, Veljo, 108
Mandić, Oliver, 133, 265
Manolić, Josip, 205
Marčeta, Milan, 283, 285
Marcone, Ramiro, 83
Marinc, Andrej, 15
Marjanović, Jovan, 305
Marjanović, Mirko, 292, 312
Marković, Ante, 26, 50
Marković, Draža, 15
Marković, Dragoslav, 14, 15
Marković, Mihailo, 19, 306
Marković, Mirjana, 58, 283
Markus, Zlatko, 81
Martić, Milan, 66, 160
Mastnak, Tomaz, 160
Masucci, Don Giuseppe, 83
Materialism, 100
May Declaration, 32
Media
    dissolution of Yugoslavia and, 38–40
    rock music, 143–144
    role in fomenting hatred, 277–278
Mediterranean Quarterly, 219
Mehinović, Kemal, 288
Mehta, Zubin, 263–264
Meier, Viktor, 51, 70, 330
Melescanu, Theodor, 211
The Memorandum 19–20, 152, 154
Memory, 145
Mesić, Stipe, 59, 61–64, 66, 162–164
Meštrović, Stjepan, 334
Metikoš, Karlo, 128
Metropolie Trans, 37
Mićunovi c, Dragoljub, 156
Mihailović, Draža, 26, 35, 36, 105, 157, 202, 333
Mihailović, Kosta, 19
Mikulić, Branko, 5
Milačić, Vladimir, 144
Milanović, Božo, 88
Military balance, Bosnians vs. Bosnian Serbs, 212
Military budget, 55, 58, 68
Military Professional Resources, Inc., 289
Military strength
    Bosnia, 289–290
    Macedonia and Greece, 185
Military training, Bosnia, 289
Militias, formation of Serbian, 57–58
Milivojević, Dionisije, 108
Mill, John Stuart, 297–298, 332
Miller, Nicholas, 330
Milošević, Sladjana Aleksandra, 131
Milošević, Slobodan, 59, 62, 67–68, 210–211, 330–331
    Bosnian war and, 205–206, 210–211, 222–223, 238
    censorship and, 139–140
    consolidation of power, 40, 42–43
    Dayton peace talks and, 279–280
    elections 190, 54–55
    legitimacy and, 299, 332–333, 337–338

Muslim community and, 122
    opposition to, 60–61, 69, 154–161
    psychology of, 299–301
    rise to power, 6, 15, 17, 25–30
    role in Croatian occupation, 230–232
    Serbian opposition, 36, 310–311
    Serbian Orthodox Church and, 99–100, 112
    Serb nationalism and, 19, 34–38, 154
    Slovenian opposition, 31–32
    suppression of Kosovo, 308, 309
    unconstitutional acts, 69–71
    as war criminal, 288–289
Milošević, Vladimir, 64
Milutinović, Milan, 316
Mirčetić, Živan, 155
Mirić, Jovan, 15
Misetić, Bosiljko, 163
Misić, Alojzije, 82
Mišović, Miloš, 306
Mitreva, Ilinka, 189
Mitsotakis, Konstantin, 257
Mitterand, Danielle, 157
Mizar, 135, 143
Mlad Borec, 144
Mladenović, Tanasije, 114
Mladić, Ratko, 66, 217, 228, 235, 238, 282, 283, 330
Mladina, 31, 39, 92, 137, 144
Mlinarec, Drago, 129
Modestry, 132
Moizes, Paul, 90
Mojsov, Lazar, 6, 30, 65, 330
Monarchy, 156, 332
    interest in revival of, 38
Montano, Tonny, 133
Montaž stroj, 306
Montenegrin Party Congress, 17
Montenegrins, as Serbs, 35
Montenegro, 27, 40, 42
    economy, 49
    Milosevic and, 29
    pressure for annexation, 62
    priests' associations, 88–89
    Serbian Orthodox Church in, 100
Montesquieu, Baron de, 194
Moral field, 340
Moral law, 298
Moral legitimacy, 331, 333–336, 340
    Macedonia, 336
    Serbia, 337
    See also Legitimacy
Morina, Rahman, 29, 69
Mortuary, 339
Mosques
    construction, 122
    destruction, 255
    effects of war, 263
Movement for All-Macedonian Action, 62
Movement for the Unification of Serbia and Montenegro, 62
Mrkšić, Mile, 230
Mullerson, Rein, 209